D1610984

A Nuclear Winter's Tale

Transformations: Studies in the History of Science and Technology
Jed Z. Buchwald, general editor

For a list of the series, see page 405.

A Nuclear Winter's Tale

Science and Politics in the 1980s

Lawrence Badash

WITHDRAWN

The MIT Press
Cambridge, Massachusetts
London, England

For information on quantity discounts, email special_sales@mitpress.mit.edu.

Set in Stone Sans and Stone Serif by SNP Best-set Typesetter Ltd., Hong Kong. Printed and bound in the United States of America.

Library of Congress Cataloging-in-Publication Data

Badash, Lawrence.
A nuclear winter's tale : science and politics in the 1980s / Lawrence Badash.
    p.   cm.—(Transformations, studies in the history of science and technology)
Includes bibliographical references and index.
ISBN 978-0-262-01272-0 (hardcover : alk. paper)
1. Radioactivity—History—20th century. 2. Climatic changes—History—20th century. 3. Science—History—20th century. 4. Science and state—History—20th century. I. Title.
QC794.98.B325   2009
509.73'09048—dc22

                                                                        2008039040

10 9 8 7 6 5 4 3 2 1

And the heavens swallowed the smoke.
—*Beowulf*

And the icy earth swung blind and blackening in the moonless air.
—Lord Byron, "Darkness"

The world will end—not with a bang, but with a winter.
—Jack Geiger, quoted from a 1983 radio show titled *Prescription for Survival* (Pacifica Radio Archive)

Contents

Preface

Highly speculative theories of worldwide destruction—even the end of life on Earth—used as a call for a particular kind of political action serve neither the good reputation of science nor dispassionate political thought.

—Edward Teller, "Widespread after-effects of nuclear war," *Nature* 310 (23 Aug. 1984), 621–624, quote on 624

For myself, I would far rather have a world in which the climatic catastrophe cannot happen, independent of the vicissitudes of leaders, institutions and machines. This seems to me elementary planetary hygiene, as well as elementary patriotism.

—Carl Sagan, "Nuclear war and climatic catastrophe: Some policy implications," *Foreign Affairs* 62 (winter 1983–84), 257–292, quote on 286

The concept of nuclear winter (NW) burst upon the consciousness of the American public toward the end of 1983. The idea was all the more alarming because until then a nuclear winter had not been among the anticipated effects of nuclear war.

The story did not begin there, of course. Many research specialties, pursued over many years, provided the background of personnel, information, techniques, and ideas that coalesced in the shocking concept that fires from nuclear explosions could produce enough smoke to block sunlight for extended periods of time. Added now to the horror of the immediate effects of nuclear war was the threat of long-term reductions in continental temperatures, extending to noncombatant nations, such that the living would have additional cause to envy the dead.

NW was (and remains) a controversial concept. All scientists did not agree on the technical assumptions or on the value of the computer programs needed to simulate the effect. But the validity of the NW prediction is not the central issue in this book. As a historian of science, it is not my task to solve scientific controversies but to report and analyze them. Thus, I trace the story of the several scientific specialties that came together to suggest the concept of NW, and then the subject's development as a specialty of its own. Basic sciences such as physics and chemistry led to interdisciplinary subjects, including meteorology, ecology, and the effects of nuclear weapons.

Further, some scientists, and others, objected to the "marketing" of NW in the media. They questioned the behavior of scientists, the standards of the scientific community, and the manner in which science policy was formed.

Because the consequences of nuclear war were of concern to the government and the general public, suggestions for avoiding NW meshed tightly with the ongoing national security debate and were often regarded as politically motivated. The Reagan administration's hard-line military stance and its budgetary realities dictated some aspects of the scientific program. In the historical trade this influence by society on science is now called "social construction of science."

In this book I seek to describe three lines of NW activity: science, popularization, and politics. If ever they were uncomplicated pursuits, they certainly were not by the second half of the twentieth century. No longer largely self-contained, they interacted continually. And there were nuances, such as the different international and national styles of politics and the scientific community's concern about its self-image.

I am conscious of my inability to tell the "entire" story. The science would require a technical text, which is not my intention. Another constraint is that today so much business is conducted by telephone, in face-to-face discussions, and by means of unpreserved correspondence that much of the story cannot be documented. For the politics, I can rely upon printed sources and some unpublished materials, but I can only guess at the motivations of many individuals. In short, this is a normal historical work. In it I strive for accuracy, fairness, and a balanced presentation of the subject while nonetheless expressing my point of view. But I do not pretend to cover the topic in encyclopedic fashion; rather, I use the materials available to me, and I recognize that my picture inevitably is incomplete. It is, moreover, biased in the sense that I focus primarily on the issue of smoke in the atmosphere and its effects on the climate. Other serious consequences of nuclear warfare, such as the downwind distribution of radioactive fallout and pyrotoxic materials and increased ultra-violet radiation reaching the Earth's surface once the skies have cleared somewhat, are mentioned only in passing.

Careful readers will note that I use the abbreviation NW in a variety of ways. It may refer only to the climatic consequences of urban fires or also to the effects upon agriculture and Earth's population. In other cases, it may refer to people (such as "NW supporters") who accepted as valid the dire predictions of global cooling and the need for political action to prevent such a tragedy. I believe that the meaning is obvious in each instance and that the shorthand is useful.

In writing the book, I consciously rejected "structural" arguments that give dominant weight to economic considerations, technological imperatives, ideological forces, geopolitical hegemonic struggles, domestic politics, or bureaucratic inertia, recognizing that each of these things played a part but none predominated in framing attitudes or determining events. My "thesis," if such a commonplace explanation of events is worthy of the term, is that normal human behavior set the stage and gave the actors their lines. Scientists investigated subjects that interested them and then debated the results; politicians sought to take advantage of new events and at the same time defend their long-time interests.

After World War II, when science and technology were recognized as extremely important to society (not just to national security), agencies and structures were created to encourage and manage the flow of technical advice to government. In this story about NW, the bureaucratic process worked, but the picture is a messy one nonetheless. Some agencies had to be prodded to action, while others worked at cross-purposes. Guidance from outside the government and its usual circle of advisors was both welcomed and rejected. Perhaps because the US is so large, with so many government and private entities, the process could not have been more rational. It is logically frustrating to observe the chaos that ensued as scientific ideas attempted to influence policy positions; at the same time, it is democratically exhilarating that there were so many pathways for such attempts.

Just as I noted above that I did not intend to write a science textbook, it is useful to note that I did not intend to write a political science manual. While I recognize that there are flow charts describing the relationships among various government agencies, and that analyses of lobbying efforts exist, I see no deterministic picture of NW information flowing in prescribed ways from source to receptacle. It is a muddled, chaotic, controversial, and very human story of a scientific idea moving through the scientific community and the government bureaucracy.

As I just intimated, beyond the main story about the development of this scientific specialty I see NW as an exemplar of twentieth-century interaction between science and society. In many cases, if not most, the lone scientist, working with small apparatus and on a small budget, has given way to Big Science, with its team research, large machines, generous funding, high visibility, and frequent political-military-economic impacts. This has been an enormous change in the workings of science and in science's dealings with the rest of society.

For most of recorded history, scientists interacted with government far less than did the clergy, the military, lawyers, and merchants. Among the ancient and medieval exceptions were Archimedes, Hero of Alexandria, Galen, astrologers, and alchemists. Courtly patronage of natural philosophers (scientists) grew during the Renaissance. In early modern times, Galileo and Lavoisier were prominent for their connections to the ruling elite. In the nineteenth century, some governments supported geology, mapping, public health, and other "useful" activities. But the total number of examples of such interactions was relatively small. By the twentieth century, however, science was far more integrated into daily life. It not only provided intellectual value (in the form of ideas about nature that added to a nation's prestige); it also offered concepts and devices that were important to a nation's economy and security.

With the increased prominence of science, the public came to the unsettling realization that scientists often disagreed, and that the vaunted "scientific method" was not an infallible tool for reaching the "truth"—whatever "truth" meant. Experiments were challenged for the validity of the data they produced, and the meanings of the results were disputed even more. And when the results affected public policy, politics entered the discussion. Scientists became still more polarized, and the public could wonder whether their personal views on war, peace, social welfare, and economics influenced the way they read the consequences of their experiments and their analyses.

Of course, NW was not the only area of science to have an enormous potential impact on society; molecular biology, weather modification, medical research, and agricultural research are other examples. But I find the story of NW intrinsically interesting and important, and I see it as a useful illustration of my view of the current complex relationship between science and society.

More particularly, NW serves as an example of the problems faced by scientific Cassandras. Scientific prophets of disaster must first make themselves heard; then they must convince fellow scientists, the public, and government that they are correct. But doing so is enormously difficult. New interpretations of scientific data step on the toes of people with established careers. Proposed policies or innovations may introduce new dangers (for example, ozone depletion caused by supersonic aircraft, the spraying of malathion—a carcinogen—to combat Medfly infestation). Onerous changes in the operation of businesses or in daily life may be required (for example, industrial pollution controls, bans on DDT and on barbeque lighter fluid). Large sums of money may be needed, and may have to be redirected from existing appropriations (as in the case of a Superfund cleanup). And a call to action may be a call to topple a long-held political conviction (military superiority, freedom to make and sell products, freedom to dump wastes). Those who accepted the validity of NW and then sought to effect changes in national policy found, like Chicken Little, that some leaders might be solicitous but few were disposed to respond with action to the cry that the sky was falling.

The chapters in part I provide background information about the arms race and the state of the several scientific specialties that led to the point at which NW could emerge from computer printouts. The chapters in part II describe the birth of the concept, the initial efforts to popularize it, concerns within the scientific community about its own standards and procedures, and various political maneuvers and policy proposals, all before the end of 1983. Part III (the heart of the book) explores developments in 1984 and 1985, the years that saw the greatest amount of NW activity. Chapters in this part treat such topics as public relations; congressional hearings; administrative meanderings; debates between critics and supporters of NW; new research on computer models, on fire phenomena, and on ecology; several reports by prestigious committees; the diminishing role played by Soviet scientists; and policy proposals of many kinds. The chapters in part IV finish the historical story, including the uncertain lessons learned from the 1991 oil well fires in Kuwait; in these chapters I attempt to place NW in the larger context of providing scientific advice to a government that does not always want it.

This book is not only for the relatively few historians, sociologists, and philosophers of science interested in contemporary issues; it is aimed also at scientists and the general public. Thus, I avoid the in-house "science culture war" debates about theoretical and methodological approaches to the study of the scientific enterprise.

I was fortunate in my efforts to gather information for the book. Many of the most prominent scientists investigating NW gave generously of their time for interviews, provided correspondence and documents, and in other ways responded graciously to my inquiries. I warmly thank them collectively for their assistance, while accepting responsibility for any errors. These "actors" and others who gave support include Thomas Ackerman, Margot Alexander, Steven Van Beek, Hans Bethe, George Bing, Linton Brooks, George Carrier, Curt Covey, Paul Crutzen, Sylvia Curtis, Freeman Dyson, Paul Ehrlich, Joann Eisberg, J. J. Gertler, Christopher Griffith, Jacob Hamblin, John Harte, Tsuyoshi Hasegawa, Frank von Hippel, John Holdren, Marcel LaFollette, Barbara Levi, Bruce Lewenstein, Harold Lewis, Fredrik Logevall, Michael MacCracken, Robert Malone, Patrick McCray, Roger Meade, Eugene Miya, Jeannie Peterson, James Pollack, George Rathjens, Alan Robock, Carl Sagan, Jacob Scherr, Stephen Schneider, David Simonett, Tina Skandalis, Jeffrey Stine, Starley Thompson, O. Brian Toon, and Richard Turco.

I wish also to express my appreciation for a grant from the University of California's Institute on Global Conflict and Cooperation under its founding director, Herbert York; for grant number DIR-9012305 from the Ethics and Values Studies program of the National Science Foundation, and program director Rachelle Hollander; for a grant from the Interdisciplinary Humanities Center of the University of California at Santa Barbara; to a series of research assistants, including Adolph Tiddens, Peter Neushul, Zuoyue Wang, Peter Nolan, Matthew Aberman, and Greg Whitesides; and to the superb staffs of the UCSB Library, the National Archives, and the Ronald Reagan Presidential Library. I am most grateful to the editor of the distinguished series in which this book appears, Jed Buchwald, and to acquisitions assistant Erin Mooney, acquisitions editor Marguerite Avery, and senior editor and word wizard Paul Bethge at the MIT Press. Finally, very special thanks are due to my colleague Bernard Kirtman, of UCSB's Department of Chemistry, whose assistance early in this project was invaluable.

A Nuclear Winter's Tale

I Background

1   Nuclear Peril

On Sunday, 30 October 1983, more than 20 million American families encountered an unfamiliar but ominous phrase in *Parade*, a magazine offered by many newspapers as a Sunday supplement. The phrase—"nuclear winter"—appeared in a story credited to Carl Sagan, a planetary astronomer and a renowned science popularizer.

Research on normal atmospheric phenomena had led Sagan and his colleagues to investigate the effects on Earth's climate of the explosion of numerous nuclear weapons. Computer simulations of various nuclear war scenarios suggested to Sagan and colleagues that so much dust, smoke, and soot would be lofted into the atmosphere by city fires that the midday sun would be almost entirely obscured across much of the Northern Hemisphere. Except along the coastlines, continental temperatures would fall to –25°C (–13°F), a decrease of about 38°C, and would remain below 0°C for months. (For comparison, the difference in average temperature between the last ice age and the present is estimated at somewhere between 5°C and 15°C.[1]) In this cold and dark environment, Sagan said, many biologists anticipated the extinction of numerous species of plants and animals. Human civilization—its social order, its economy, its intellectual achievements—would be destroyed. The human population would stabilize at prehistoric levels . . . or *Homo sapiens* might become extinct.

In the past, scientists, especially those who worked for various government agencies examining the consequences of nuclear explosions, had underestimated the seriousness of radioactive fallout. They also had not foreseen the crippling of electronic apparatus by the electromagnetic pulses that nuclear explosions caused. And they had failed to predict depletion of the ozone layer by fireballs caused by high-yield explosions. Now it seemed they also had failed to notice the potential of striking climatic effects from dust and smoke. "What else," Sagan asked, "have we overlooked?"

Sagan, a man with strong political feelings, nonetheless restricted the *Parade* article to the popularization of a scientific discovery, albeit one with tremendous implications. The antiwar position was not controversial; no one was *for* a nuclear war. Sagan proposed no solutions here; he merely noted the danger of the superpowers' arsenals and argued that by "concentrating always on the near future" we had "ignored the long-term consequences of our actions" and "placed our civilization and our species in jeopardy."[2]

The Reagan Context

The announcement that a nuclear winter might occur came as a shock to the public. Many felt frustrated by the Reagan administration's apparent hostility toward the arms-control process and appalled by the ongoing arms buildup and the increasingly frigid Cold War. With respect to radioactivity, these critics were weary of US government inaction, indifference, and even misbehavior under the cloak of national security. "Atomic veterans," the American GIs who were commanded to sit in trenches near ground zero at the Nevada Test Site in the days before atmospheric testing was banned in 1963, sought compensation in federal court for the cancers they associated with that experience. "Downwind people"—civilian residents of communities such as St. George, Utah, who were deliberately told by the Atomic Energy Commission (AEC) that hazardous levels of radioactivity from the tests were "safe" and who, like the atomic veterans, experienced uncommon rates of cancer—also fought an unsympathetic government.[3]

Arms-control measures—particularly the Strategic Arms Limitation Treaty (SALT II), signed in 1979 by Presidents Jimmy Carter and Leonid Brezhnev, were derided as "fatally flawed" by the American political right.[4] With little chance of ratification in the Senate, Carter used the pretext of the USSR's invasion of Afghanistan to withdraw SALT II from consideration.[5] Not that the American left thought highly of a treaty that merely enshrined existing arsenals instead of reducing them. (There were roughly 10,000 strategic weapons in each superpower, plus perhaps 30,000 tactical weapons in both countries; the numbers held by the United Kingdom, France, China, Israel, and India were relatively insignificant.) But negotiations, it was broadly felt on the left, were preferable to escalating tensions. Now, for the first time in years, the US and the USSR had no discussions under way on controlling strategic nuclear weapons.

Thirty-eight years into the arms race, it seemed that problems were compounding instead of being solved. Many people clearly were frightened by the program for arms expansion and harsh rhetoric of President Ronald Reagan's administration. Half of the American public believed that Reagan was playing nuclear "chicken" with the USSR.[6] The *Bulletin of the Atomic Scientists* moved the hands of the "doomsday clock" on its cover closer to midnight. Liberals, who normally had nothing good to say about Richard Nixon, recalled favorably the détente he maintained with the USSR. Under Nixon, "sufficiency" in nuclear weapons replaced unattainable "superiority"—if indeed superiority had any real meaning.

But whether a valid concept or not, superiority seemed to be the goal of the Reagan administration. Secretary of State Alexander Haig spoke approvingly of firing a nuclear warning shot across the bow if the Soviet Union were to misbehave in Europe.[7] Secretary of Defense Caspar Weinberger sought to improve the nuclear-war-fighting capability of the United States in order to "prevail" in an encounter that, he felt, could be limited.[8] And the president, in word and deed, gave many people reason to debate whether he really sub-scribed to the inevitability of the Book of Revelation's "Armageddon prophecy."[9]

Just as the environmental movement was galvanized to action by the perceived determi-nation of Secretary of the Interior James Watt to remove protection from natural resources, Reagan's view of national security energized the "Nuclear Freeze" movement and drove up the membership and contributor lists of numerous "peace" organizations. Not only general membership groups (e.g., the Committee for a Sane Nuclear Policy) but also associations with special expertise (among them the Union of Concerned Scientists, Physicians for Social Responsibility, and the Center for Defense Information) flourished.[10] Indeed, half of the American organizations that focused on peace, disarmament, defense, nuclear war, and weapons were founded during Reagan's first term.[11]

Jonathan Schell's enormously popular book *The Fate of the Earth* (1982) reflected public disenchantment with the casual attitude toward nuclear weapons displayed by government officials.[12] And such books and organizations fed and were fed by a growing popular recog-nition that nuclear war must not be fought, and that a limited nuclear conflict almost inevitably would escalate.[13] On television, the ABC network aired *The Day After*, a fictional account of a nuclear attack on Kansas. Hollywood produced the film *Testament*, a vision of the consequences of the destruction of San Francisco. It was during this turmoil that the concept of nuclear winter emerged.

Controversial nuclear issues abounded. These ranged from the US government's inability to find a transportation mode for the MX mobile intercontinental missile to the USSR's admittedly foolish and provocative placement of SS-20 mobile intermediate-range missiles in position to threaten Western Europe.[14] NATO's response was for the US to plant Pershing II ballistic missiles and ground-launched cruise missiles on European soil, where parts of the USSR were within their range. The Pershing IIs were regarded as especially destabilizing, since their flight times—and therefore the USSR's reaction times—were much less than those for intercontinental ballistic missiles. Hundreds of thousands of people rallied in European and American cities to oppose this escalation of the arms race.[15]

In 1981, when the retired American diplomat George F. Kennan suggested a 50 percent reduction in the strategic arsenals, his proposal was ridiculed as fanciful, but within a few years this idea became the basis of Strategic Arms Reduction Treaty negotiations, and START II achieved a two-thirds reduction.[16] In 1983, with the best of intentions and the worst of intelligence, Reagan advanced his concept of a Strategic Defense Initiative (SDI).[17] His desire to render nuclear weapons impotent and obsolete was commendable, but unfortunately it was impossible to achieve: ballistic-missile defense cannot be 100 percent effective, and the warheads that "leak" through will suffice to destroy the country.

Moreover, SDI (or "Star Wars," as it was popularly and derisively called) was not without its own problems. For example, it would be enormously expensive; the Soviets would respond to it by increasing the number of their ICBM warheads and/or building their own inadequate space shield, thus ratcheting up the arms race another notch; testing SDI components threatened to violate the agreement signed along with the 1972 SALT I Treaty, which limited anti-missile experimentation; and construction of SDI could be interpreted as provocative, for if the Soviet Union believed that the United States felt it was now safe from attack—and thus liable to be more belligerent in a crisis—it might attempt a preemptive strike.

In the early 1980s, political events and defense-policy controversies such as those recounted above set the stage for the whirl of science, military stonewalling, and public discourse that followed the announcement of the NW phenomenon to an American public that was rather sophisticated concerning nuclear weapons. Newspapers, newsmagazines, journals of opinion, radio, television, books of fiction and nonfiction, and films, in addition to the numerous "peace" organizations, had provided an enormous range of information about the arsenals, politics, and effects of these weapons of mass destruction. Since President Harry Truman's announcement of the atomic bombing of Hiroshima on 6 August 1945, few subjects had received as much media attention.[18] The high level of public "nuclear awareness" at the time of NW's debut did not, however, translate into a broad, vigorous, and sustained effort to change the superpowers' nuclear policies. The public did, nonetheless, observe a generally cordial and intelligent debate and a fine example of both the normal progress of science and the normal, though terribly haphazard, process of providing scientific advice to the government.

A Nuclear Winter's Tale focuses upon one of the effects of nuclear explosions: lowered temperature and illumination due to reduced sunlight. The development of nuclear arsenals and the history of nuclear weapons policies and politics are not major parts of this story and will be mentioned only in passing.[19] Among the effects of nuclear explosions, the best-known consequences are the immediate and relatively short-range ones (blast, heat, ionizing radiation)—but they are not central to the story. Nor are the societal factors of population loss and economic, industrial, political, social, and cultural devastation examined carefully in this study. Instead, attention is directed to long-range physical consequences to the environment.

Global Incineration

During the summer of 1942, J. Robert Oppenheimer, a theoretical physicist with appointments at both the University of California at Berkeley and the California Institute of Technology, headed a study group whose task was to investigate the construction of nuclear weapons (also termed fission weapons and, less accurately, atomic bombs). The United States was at war and feared that Germany would build such weapons first. The US government's commitment to build this novel explosive was not formalized until the Manhattan Project cranked up its operations in the fall of 1942, but many scientists had been studying the possibility of such a bomb since early 1939, when the discovery of nuclear fission was announced. The US government had been apprised of the prospect in a famous letter from Albert Einstein to President Franklin D. Roosevelt in that same year.[20]

Oppenheimer and his colleagues were most concerned with a bomb made of fissionable uranium, yet the alternative concept of energy released from the fusion of hydrogen isotopes was raised by Edward Teller, who had left Europe in 1935 for a post at George Washington University. Teller wondered if the atmosphere could be set afire by the high temperatures reached in such fusion reactions. In alarm, Oppenheimer traveled east to consult with Arthur Compton, the director of experimental and theoretical work on the bomb. Before Oppenheimer returned to Berkeley, Hans Bethe, another mid-1930s refugee from Europe, checked Teller's calculations and concluded that the atmosphere could not be ignited. Teller was reasonably well convinced.[21]

By late 1944, however, when the major design questions about the first fission bombs had been settled at the Los Alamos Laboratory, some theorists had broached the concept that the atmosphere might be ignited even by a fission detonation. A variety of nuclear reactions, mostly by nitrogen but also by hydrogen, oxygen, and carbon in the atmosphere, might be triggered by the explosion and propagate throughout the atmosphere. Or would the large amounts of energy be dissipated too fast for this to occur? The physicists Emil Konopinski, Cloyd Marvin, and Edward Teller examined the problem, using "worst-case" choices when precise values were not available, and concluded that "no ignition point exists," though they were deferential enough to the uncertainties of the calculation to recommend further investigation.[22]

A question as monumental as global incineration was bound to arise again, as indeed it did before the 1946 Crossroads series of bomb tests at Bikini Atoll, which included an underwater test. Concern was expressed that hydrogen in the sea would join in a global fusion reaction. And before the first fusion detonation (in 1952), additional studies were made, once more concluding that no self-propagating nuclear reaction in the atmosphere was possible.[23]

Radioactive Fallout

Decades after World War II, accidents at the civilian nuclear power plants at Three Mile Island in Pennsylvania (1979) and Chernobyl in the Ukraine (1986) drew renewed attention to the danger of radioactive fallout. None of the residents downwind of Three Mile Island died as a result of the incident there.[24] The Chernobyl accident was far more serious, with 31 immediate radiation fatalities, unofficial reports of 300 deaths, and an ultimate cost of $416 billion.[25] Furthermore, there was a much greater likelihood of future radiation-induced illness for the population ranging from the vicinity of Kiev northwest across the former Soviet Union and other European countries, and especially for the people of Poland and Scandinavia, where the radioactive clouds released significant amounts of their deadly cargo.[26]

Radioactive fallout was well known before these events, however. It was, indeed, a predicted consequence of a nuclear explosion. In March 1940, two physicists who had recently fled Nazism, Otto Frisch and Rudolf Peierls, presented to the British government calculations which suggested that an atomic bomb could be made within a few years.[27] It also was certainly on the minds of those who organized the test of the very first atomic bomb, at Alamogordo, New Mexico, on 16 July 1945. Plans were made to monitor the cloud of radioactive debris and to evacuate the few ranchers who lived downwind. The evacuation proved unnecessary, although a number of range cattle in the vicinity suffered skin burns.[28] More pertinent to our concern about long-distance effects, radioactivity from the test was washed out of the air by a rainstorm 1,000 miles away in Illinois. This was detected, and its origin was deduced, when Eastman Kodak found that its x-ray film was fogged by cardboard packing material produced in the midwest.[29] Detection at an even greater distance—2,700 miles—occurred in April 1953, when radioactive debris from an air burst at the Nevada test site was propelled across the continent by the jet stream. A rainstorm washed it out of the air above Troy, New York, where it set Geiger counters at the Rensselaer Polytechnic Institute clicking rapidly.[30]

In the early postwar years, all US nuclear explosions were conducted in the atmosphere (atop a tower or dropped from an airplane), either in Nevada or at the Pacific proving grounds. Little attention was given to radioactive particles transported long distances, because their effect was considered too small to be harmful. This does not mean too small to be usefully measured and analyzed, however; the detonation of the first Soviet atomic bomb, in August 1949, was detected from the radioactivity of high-altitude dust samples collected by specially equipped US aircraft.[31]

The American reaction to this Soviet accomplishment was to consider a "crash" program to develop a hydrogen fusion "superbomb." In a report dated 30 October 1949, the General Advisory Committee of the Atomic Energy Commission urged the commissioners *not* to grant fusion research extraordinary priority. Indeed, a majority of the GAC recommended that the United States unilaterally renounce such weapons. Of course, we know that President Truman listened to other counsel, but the interest for us in this long-secret report lies in one of the reasons advanced by James B. Conant, Hartley Rowe, Cyril Stanley Smith, Lee A. DuBridge, Oliver E. Buckley, and GAC chairman J. Robert Oppenheimer: "We are alarmed as to the possible global effects of the radioactivity generated by the explosion of a few super bombs of conceivable magnitude."[32] The potential for global phenomena was recognized.

Soviet scientists too developed hydrogen bombs, and they too were concerned about their potential effects. In March 1954, the scientific leader of the USSR's work on nuclear weapons from its inception, Igor Kurchatov, and three senior colleagues sent a classified report to V. A. Malyshev, Minister of Medium Machine Building (the nuclear weapons ministry). Malyshev forwarded it to Nikita Khrushchev, first secretary of the Central Committee of the Communist Party. The scientists argued that fusion weapons created a new and perilous situation. Not only would the combatants be destroyed, but radioactive materials, carried by the wind, would contaminate Earth's surface. Whereas life on Earth might be extinguished by the explosion of thousands of fission bombs, they wrote, it would take only about 100 fusion explosions to produce the same result.[33]

As these examples show, a few scientists and government officials were occasionally prodded to consider the possibility that nuclear weapons might have both long-range and long-term effects. Yet the public remained ignorant of such dangers until the mid 1950s. They were not warned by the 1950 Department of Defense and Atomic Energy Commission volume *The Effects of Atomic Weapons*, which surveyed the global circulation of Krakatoa's (1883) volcanic debris and the continental transport of both dust from storms and radioactive matter from the Alamogordo test. That report concluded that "in most circumstances the fall-out from an air burst will not be a serious radiological hazard," that fallout from a low air burst "might be an inconvenience, but it would not in general represent a real danger," and that, although contamination from a surface blast might be harmful, it would be localized. Worldwide, long-term effects were not predicted, because explosive yields were as yet too small to pump large amounts of radioactive particles high into the atmosphere.[34]

Samuel Glasstone's *The Effects of Nuclear Weapons*, successor to the above book and immediately (and to the present time) recognized as the "bible" on the subject, was published in 1957 with a separate chapter titled "World-Wide Fallout and Long-Term Residual Radiation." By then, thermonuclear weapons had been developed and tested. As before, larger pieces of debris would fall in the vicinity of the explosion. But now fine particles could be carried far by the wind. Their radioactivity would have the potential to cause long-term bodily harm, such as cancer, and also genetic effects, such as deformities, in succeeding generations. Nuclear explosions in the kiloton range (a kiloton, abbreviated KT, being equivalent to 1,000 tons of TNT) produce the characteristic mushroom-shaped cloud, which usually stays within the troposphere. This lower portion of the atmosphere, whose ceiling ranges from 30,000 to 50,000 feet, contains the weather. Rain and snow frequently are the means by which radioactive particles are carried to the surface. Hydrogen fusion explosions, which generally are in the megaton (MT, meaning equivalent to 1 million tons of TNT) range, pump nearly all the bomb debris into the stratosphere. There strong winds circulate the fine particles globally, and gravity is the primary cause of their slow descent. The longer these particles stay aloft, the less radioactive they are. But the long half-lives of the most biologically dangerous isotopes—cesium-137 (30 years) and strontium-90 (28.5 years)—mean that they will be harmful even after a delayed return to the surface.[35]

In the United States, in Japan, in Western Europe, and even in the developing nations, this information became the subject of heated debate after the "Bravo" test at Bikini Atoll on 1 March 1954. This was the detonation of a 15-MT fusion device (not yet a deliverable weapon), the largest man-made explosion yet. Unanticipated winds caused lethal doses of radioactive ash to fall on Rongelap Atoll, 100 miles away, and forced the unscheduled evacuation of the islanders. Ash also fell on the open sea, where a Japanese fishing boat, the *Lucky Dragon*, lay outside the published danger zone. Crew members experienced varying degrees of radiation sickness, one death occurred, and the boat's catch was found to be radioactive upon its return to Japan.[36]

The global reach of fallout became more apparent over the next few years as both the US and the USSR built and tested hydrogen bombs. During the 1950s, the two superpowers conducted 222 announced nuclear explosions (both fission and fusion), only 18 of them underground or underwater.[37] More and more often, newspapers reported that scientists in one community or another had detected unusual levels of radioactivity in surface water, or milk, or children's teeth.[38]

In the 1956 presidential campaign, Democratic candidate Adlai Stevenson spoke out against atmospheric testing. Around the same time, the chemist Linus Pauling became a leading advocate for an end to nuclear explosions; he was both accused of Communist support by the Senate Internal Security Subcommittee and awarded the Nobel Peace Prize.[39] Groups were formed to oppose radioactive "contamination without representation." These included the Committee for a Sane Nuclear Policy in the United States and the Campaign for Nuclear Disarmament in Great Britain.[40] This public protest led first to a moratorium on testing (in 1958), then (in 1963) to the Limited Test Ban Treaty, which prohibited nuclear explosions in the atmosphere, under water, and in space, but allowed them underground.[41] Out of sight meant out of mind. Although the pace of nuclear weapon testing actually increased when the superpowers took it underground,[42] and the arms race was not hampered, global levels of fallout decreased, and the dangers of radioactivity ceased to be a prominent public issue.

Electromagnetic Pulse

In Hawaii, on the evening of 8 July 1962, many street lights and power lines suddenly failed, and burglar alarms began to ring. The atmospheric testing moratorium of 1958 had ended, and the subsequent "gentleman's agreement" not to test had been violated by the USSR in 1961, followed by resumption of the US program. Hawaiians had grounds to suspect a connection between their curious experience and the detonation of a 1.4-MT hydrogen bomb that had been fired 248 miles into space atop a Thor rocket, but the mechanism baffled scientists. More than a year later, they had an answer. The rocket had been launched from Johnston Island, about 800 miles southwest of Honolulu. Gamma rays from the explosion had stripped electrons from air molecules in the upper atmosphere, and these electrons had moved in conformity with Earth's magnetic field, creating an electromagnetic pulse (EMP) with a range of hundreds or even thousands of miles.[43]

EMP may be compared roughly with the electromagnetic fields generated in the vicinity of a lightning stroke. But while lightning may merely cause static in radio receivers, EMP would likely burn out radios connected to long antennas. The potential of a high-altitude nuclear explosion to destroy electronic equipment operating on AM, short-wave, VHF, and UHF frequencies came as a shock. If these communication links were impaired, battle management would be impossible.[44]

In addition to the disruption of coast-to-coast communications, EMP would, as one writer put it, perform "an electromagnetic lobotomy on computer memories."[45] Unfortunately, this could be accomplished easily. A single warhead exploded 200 miles over Nebraska would bathe all of the contiguous United States in a powerful and disabling EMP. The reason this phenomenon had not been detected earlier was that most of the electronic equipment used during the 1950s contained vacuum tubes. By the early 1960s, the semiconductor revolution was well under way, leading to miniaturized electronics, microscopic circuitry, and tiny chips in both military and civilian equipment. Unhappily, this new solid-state technology was 10 million times as vulnerable to EMP as vacuum-tube devices.[46]

When the Safeguard anti-ballistic-missile site at Grand Forks, North Dakota, went operational in April 1975, there were fears that detonation of one of its Spartan interceptors about 150 miles above the United States would destroy not only the hostile incoming reentry vehicle but also communication and power equipment across the country. In another scenario, defense planners contemplated a president unable to issue emergency messages, regardless of the 43 or more different ways available to the commander-in-chief to communicate. Not only war-fighting, but war-termination orders could be casualties of an EMP-induced loss of electronic command, control, communications, and intelligence (C^3I) functions. Since then, millions if not billions of dollars have been spent on hardening electronic equipment. An EMP simulator, with a B-52 bomber sitting atop a twelve-story-high wooden scaffold, has been built at Kirtland Air Force Base in Albuquerque to test the shielding of aircraft electronics. And EMP-resistant fiber optics are increasingly employed for communications. Still, one cannot be confident that catastrophic failure of computers and communication due to EMP can be avoided. Though EMP occurs only at the time of a high-altitude nuclear explosion and thus is not long-term, it does qualify as long-range, and its unanticipated occurrence justifies its inclusion in this focused survey of nuclear weapons' effects.[47]

Ozone Depletion

Ozone, a molecule consisting of three oxygen atoms (O_3), was a novelty at the end of the nineteenth century. People went to the seashore to "take in the ozone." In 1894, to entice enthusiasts of this "health" craze, a "penny-in-the-slot galvanic battery" was installed on the new pier in Brighton, England.[48] Scientifically, ozone has been known since 1930 or earlier to engage in chemical reactions in the upper atmosphere, where it is formed by the action of sunlight on ordinary molecules of oxygen (O_2).[49] Although it is only a trace gas—no more than 10 parts by volume per million parts of air—its existence in the stratosphere is crucial because it acts as a natural sunscreen, blocking most of the solar ultraviolet (UV) radiation heading for Earth's surface. (In the troposphere, where it contributes to smog, ozone is harmful.)[50]

If all the stratospheric ozone were brought to Earth's surface, atmospheric pressure would squeeze it into a film only 3 millimeters thick.[51] Yet without ozone's filtering action in the stratosphere, humans would experience an increase in skin cancer and agriculture would be seriously affected. Indeed, it is believed that life on Earth's surface had to await the buildup of ozone that occurred during the Pre-Cambrian period. Ozone decomposes when it interacts with UV radiation and with various trace chemicals in the atmosphere. In addition, ozone's formation and removal involve heat changes in the stratosphere, and these variations affect atmospheric circulation. More will be said in chapter 3 about other hazards to the ozone layer; here it is appropriate to discuss the threat caused by nuclear explosions.[52]

For each megaton of explosive yield, the fireball of an air burst creates about 10^{32} molecules of nitrogen oxides. The fireball of a megaton-size warhead rises into the stratosphere, where about 90 percent of atmospheric ozone resides.[53] Thus, these nitrogen compounds, which are prodigious catalysts for the consumption of ozone, are placed where they can do the most damage.[54]

In 1970, attention was called to the connection between nitrogen oxides and ozone photochemistry by Paul Crutzen, a Dutch atmospheric chemist. Crutzen was a European Space Research Organization postdoctoral fellow at Oxford University's famous Clarendon Physics Laboratory.[55] He found that nitrogen oxide combined with ozone to form nitrogen dioxide and ordinary molecular oxygen ($NO + O_3 \rightarrow NO_2 + O_2$). The nitrogen dioxide then combined with monatomic oxygen to re-create the ozone-destroying nitrogen oxide and more molecular oxygen ($NO_2 + O \rightarrow NO + O_2$). In these reactions, the NO was recycled.

Where did the monatomic oxygen come from? It was produced in the ordinary photochemical reaction of light energy with ozone ($O_3 + energy \rightarrow O + O_2$). The ozone layer apparently was far more vulnerable to chemical attack than anyone had believed. However, it was not nuclear explosions but the effect of exhaust from supersonic transport (SST) aircraft on the ozone that lay behind this interest in the "chemosphere" in the early 1970s. In 1971, also with the SST as a stimulus, Harold Johnston, a chemist at the University of California's Berkeley campus, showed that nitrogen oxides were indeed a threat to stratospheric ozone, far more so in fact than the widely feared water in SST exhaust.[56] Two years later, Henry Foley and Malvin Ruderman, both of Columbia University's physics department, made the connection between nuclear explosions and ozone depletion by nitrogen oxides. Yet their imaginative examination of surface ozone measurements, recorded at a global network of meteorological stations, showed no rapid changes during the hectic period of atmospheric testing just before the 1963 Limited Test Ban Treaty.[57] Only 2 months after this paper was published, however, Harold Johnston described his longer-time-span study, which extracted a real effect from the background noise. There was, he claimed, a 5 percent increase in ozone over the period 1963–1970, which could be attributed to the atmosphere's recovery following the test ban.[58] The rapidity with which work on this "hot" topic was published was repeated with the NW phenomenon. Also similar were several of the personnel involved, for the subject remained atmospheric chemistry to them. Johnston shared the authorship of his paper with two other scientists, one of whom (John W. Birks) would join with Paul Crutzen a decade later to set the problem that resulted in the conceptualization of NW.

To John Hampson, nuclear explosions were a potential "photochemical war on the atmosphere." Hampson, at Laval University in Quebec, speculated in 1974 that the amount of explosive energy needed to degrade the atmosphere might be much less than already existed in the arsenals maintained for purposes of deterrence. If this was true, he suggested, the knowledge "could be used as a lever to cajole the nuclear powers to move towards a more positive view of the need for arms control."[59]

As if in response to Hampson's call, investigations did occur. At the Lawrence Livermore Laboratory in California (now the Lawrence Livermore National Laboratory, or LLNL; it and Los Alamos are the nation's only nuclear weapons design facilities), Michael MacCracken and Julius Chang used a one-dimensional computer model of the stratosphere to examine chemical and photochemical reactions and the movement of matter vertically. They concluded in 1975 that past atmospheric nuclear testing could have caused an ozone reduction of no more than a few percent, an amount almost indiscernible against normal variations. But a large war might deplete 25–50 percent of the global ozone, and even incomplete recovery would take several years.[60]

Throughout their report, MacCracken and Chang emphasized the tentative nature of their findings, for their model was only an approximation of three-dimensional reality. Models of two and three dimensions would involve an enormous increase in complexity, and would still rarely match the richness of nature's intricacies and feedback mechanisms. Models, further, are constructed to describe "normal" processes of nature. The sudden injection into the stratosphere of nitrogen oxides from a 10,000-MT war, MacCracken and Chang observed, pushed their model to the limit of credibility. Although the chemistry would be reasonably represented, the validity of vertical transport was not clear. Such reservations are characteristic of an advancing science, and uncertainty is not cause for embarrassment. The research front is a place of constant change, as scientists build on the work of their colleagues and competitors, sometimes incorporating previous concepts and sometimes rejecting them. Similar concerns about models would be expressed when NW was studied.

While these Livermore scientists were occupied with the ozone problem, the director of the US Arms Control and Disarmament Agency (ACDA), Fred Iklé, grew concerned enough to commission a study by the National Academy of Sciences (NAS) published as *Long-Term Worldwide Effects of Multiple Nuclear-Weapons Detonations* (1975).[61] As is true of most NAS investigations, the procedure was not to undertake new experiments but to review the existing literature. The panel examined the consequences of a 10,000-MT exchange of nuclear weapons and concentrated on long-term worldwide effects.

Ozone depletion was the new actor in this drama. While admitting the uncertainties of the simplified model, the panel concluded that the concentration of stratospheric ozone might be reduced in the Northern Hemisphere by 30–70 percent. Natural processes would restore about 60 percent of this within 2–4 years, and most of the rest within 10–20 years. Ultraviolet damage to crops, micro-organisms, animals, and humans in the interim would likely be severe, but extinction—particularly in the nations not involved in the fighting—was unlikely.[62] Still, ozone depletion added a dimension of self-deterrence to nuclear strategy. Here was a phenomenon that could kick back at the aggressor. Within 10 years, the same concept would appear in the form of NW.

Climate Change

In the first edition of *The Effects of Nuclear Weapons* (1957), the physicist Samuel Glasstone examined speculation about weather changes caused by huge fusion reactions and concluded that they were not likely. The energy released, the quantity of debris injected into the atmosphere, and the intensity of the ionizing particles all were, he felt, not enough to affect the weather, let alone its more persistent manifestation, climate.[63] The question did not die, however, and in succeeding years a number of people returned to it.

In a popular book titled *Nuclear Disaster* (1964), Tom Stonier, a plant physiologist at Manhattan College, argued that, although radioactive fallout could inflict a great ecological catastrophe, it could not change the climate. Other debris injected into the atmosphere from explosions, however, did have the potential to do this. Indeed, in the extreme, Stonier forecast another ice age. Dust particles would serve as nuclei for water droplets, wringing more rain and snow from the sky, and cooling would come about as atmospheric dust prevented sunlight from reaching Earth. Stonier provided calculations of the amount of soil lofted by a 20-MT surface burst, and gathered data about temperature reductions due to both volcanic dust and forest fire smoke. Yet Stonier's circumstantial case was at bottom "hand-waving" (gesturing rather than proving).[64] He lacked much scientific information that would become available in the next two decades, such as the relationship between volcanic dust and solar radiation. In this period before the widespread use of computers, Stonier understandably could not even conceive of an interactive global circulation model.

Increasingly during the early 1970s, fear was expressed that a major nuclear war could alter the climate. "Major" meant somewhere around 10,000 MT of explosive yield, an amount about half the size of the superpowers' strategic arsenals. The novelty of the heightened concern lay in the emphasis on chemistry, physics, and computer modeling. Research was expanded. Current understanding was recognized as inadequate for many photochemical reactions, the circulation of particles, and the effects of large energy changes in the stratosphere. So-called defense intellectuals had calculated war scenarios on the basis of population, cities, or industry destroyed. Should the prime consideration now be chemical reactions initiated by sunlight?[65]

Research is not accomplished overnight, and informed conjecture continued to fill the information vacuum. The Stanford University biologists Paul and Anne Ehrlich maintained the tradition of speculation in their popular textbook *Population, Resources, Environment: Issues in Human Ecology* (1970). They pointed to explosive dust injections and smoke from huge fires as potential engines of regional and global climate change.[66] For the third edition, they added the UC Berkeley physicist John Holdren as a co-author, changed the title to *Ecoscience: Population, Resources, Environment* (1977), and adopted the then-novel phenomenon of ozone depletion as another important agent of change.[67] Increased photochemical activity involving the ozone molecule would store in the stratosphere solar energy that otherwise would heat the troposphere and the ground. Although the authors contributed nothing new to the scientific understanding of climate alteration (had they done so in a textbook, it would have been surprising), they certainly popularized the concept. In 1983, the Ehrlichs would be among the several authors of a paper on biological effects that was a companion to the sensational new report on the possible physical effects of nuclear war.

Another scientist who speculated about climate changes in this early period, and later was a prominent participant in the research and debate about NW, was Stephen Schneider, a climatologist at the National Center for Atmospheric Research in Boulder. While explicit that the data were still soft, in a book titled *The Genesis Strategy: Climate and Global Survival* (1976) he suggested that ozone depletion and dust injections into the stratosphere might cause Earth's surface to cool from a fraction of a degree to a few degrees Celsius. He thus echoed the now widespread recognition that this was a topic in need of greater attention. Schneider largely discounted the possibility of a new ice age, arguing that "the estimated changes in stratospheric composition were not anticipated to persist more than a decade or so."

One of the most interesting features of Schneider's commentary was his discussion of the climatic effects of industrialization, farming, deforestation, and other human activities. For example, it could well be assumed that after a nuclear war agriculture in the Northern Hemisphere would be severely disrupted. Fields that once were plowed would lie fallow, and the new, wild vegetation would have a different surface albedo (the fraction of sunlight that is reflected) and changed moisture-holding characteristics. Similarly, decreased deforestation and industrial activity would presumably lower the amount of dust in the atmosphere. Schneider's point was that changes in human social patterns could have climatic consequences just as real as those from the physical and chemical effects of nuclear explosions.[68] These "social assumptions" were excised from Schneider's contribution to the 1975 NAS study mentioned above. Hewing more closely to "fact," that report acknowledged that global temperatures might decline as much as several degrees, with disastrous consequences for agriculture. On the other hand, only negligible cooling or even a slight warming was also possible. The temperature decrease could result from the absorption, reflection, and scattering by dust of direct sunlight or light reflected from Earth. Ozone depletion could lead to a more significant effect, due to an altered pattern of stratospheric heating. This, in turn, would affect the tropospheric thermal structure, with a noticeable change in climate. But current understanding of climatological phenomena simply was inadequate to predict such effects with confidence. "They would probably lie within normal global climatic variability," the chair of the NAS panel, Alfred Nier, wrote, "but the possibility of climatic changes of a more dramatic nature cannot be ruled out."[69]

A final example of the assertion of widespread climate change appeared in a 1979 article by Kevin Lewis, a graduate student in political science at the Massachusetts Institute of Technology. It was published in *Scientific American*, a periodical known for its frequent stories on technical aspects of the arms race. In an excellent review titled "The prompt and delayed effects of nuclear war," Lewis, who had gained his expertise as a member of the congressional Office of Technology Assessment staff that composed *The Effects of Nuclear War* (1979), discussed urban firestorms, but only as a local phenomenon. Continental weather changes, however, appeared in his survey in connection with the burning of huge forests and grasslands in the US and the USSR. The resulting transfiguration in ground cover would alter the albedo of Earth's surface, a point also made by Stonier and Schneider. Additionally, Lewis said, the pall of smoke would obscure sunlight, while moisture would condense around particulate matter to increase cloud cover and precipitation.[70]

We see in these examples attempts to predict certain climatic consequences of nuclear war. They look to the obscuration of sunlight as the main mechanism, with ozone depletion and the altered reflection of sunlight, be it by abandoned farm land or scorched earth, as additional paths. That they failed to make many converts was not because they were unreasonable, but because they were more metaphor than science. The technical data and the comprehension of atmospheric processes were yet too unsophisticated. But this process by which new knowledge is generated is not by any means a true-or-false activity. The construction of experiments, the interpretation of data, and especially the forecast of complex phenomena carry with them a large dash of personal art, which is the spice of science. What is it, then, that determines when information convincingly supports predictions?

Summary

In this chapter I have surveyed a number of the effects of nuclear weapons. They were unanticipated before being detected (EMP, ozone depletion), initially known only in the local manifestation (fallout), postulated and then discounted (global incineration), and forecast but only in insufficiently quantitative terms (climate change). Seemingly a disparate assortment, they are nonetheless linked by the geographical extent of their consequences.

In a speech to the Chicago Council on Foreign Relations in 1975, Richard Nixon's ACDA director, Fred Iklé, expressed his awe about the discovery of ozone depletion in nuclear fireballs: "The more we know, the more we know how little we know." Surveying the other past surprises, he added: "Each of these discoveries tore a hole in the facile assumptions that screened the reality of nuclear war. Each brought a new glimpse into the cauldron of horrors. What unexpected discovery will be next?"[71]

Department of Defense spokesmen regarded this uncertainty as not necessarily bad, for it would deter a rational adversary from potential suicide. Secretary of Defense James Schlesinger, for example, when asked by the Senate Committee on Foreign Relations about Iklé's "cauldron of horrors," was sanguine about the predictability and controllability of nuclear war. He admitted that future discoveries might change attitudes, and hoped that merely one nuclear device would deter even the most irrational opponent. In the meanwhile, however, the United States must maintain great strength and flexibility.[72]

Schlesinger's remarks were condemned by the physicist J. Carson Mark, the long-time head of the Los Alamos Laboratory's Theoretical Division, as an example of the "stultifying effects of nuclear weapons on official thought." If currently known explosion effects are not awesome enough to stop plans for nuclear warfare, the experienced bomb designer asked, can we expect our leaders to possess any sensitivity to additional effects?[73] Several years earlier, the Soviet Union's most famous bomb designer, Andrei Sakharov, came to similar conclusions about the madness of believing that a nuclear war could be fought and "won."[74] Such concern in both superpowers was appropriate. In the United States, for example, the Department of Defense continued to believe that a full range of nuclear war options in the hands of the president was essential to deterrence.

Nearly a decade later, when the NW concept was postulated, Reagan administration officials would seek to employ it as justification for an arms buildup. Politicians and bureaucrats had learned little in the interim. But science progressed inexorably, and a new phenomenon was on the horizon. Much work had still to be accomplished, and the fortunate interaction of several scientific fields had to occur. Then NW would rise from the computer printout, and another powerful voice against nuclear warfare would emerge.

2   Scientific Disciplines in Isolation, 1: Those with Obvious Connections to Nuclear War

General Leslie Groves, the Manhattan Project's military leader, had a mania for the compartmentalization of information. It was, he thought, better to limit what one knew. The scientists disagreed strongly with this emphasis on secrecy; their careers had been built in the tradition of free exchange of information. Though mindful of the need to keep secrets from the enemy, they felt that it was counterproductive to be kept ignorant of the topics and progress of their colleagues in offices down the hall. Leo Szilard, the Hungarian-born physicist who foresaw a neutron-induced chain reaction half a decade before it was discovered, claimed that the atomic bomb was delayed by a year and a half because scientists could not bounce ideas off their co-workers (except at the Los Alamos Laboratory).[1]

Not all compartmentalization is deliberate. Much compartmentalization occurs simply because scientists in one field have no inkling that those in another field are doing work of potential relevance. It is widely accepted that some of the most exciting science comes from the cross-fertilization of disciplines, the offspring of which eventually may evolve into disciplines themselves. Thermodynamics, geophysics, electromagnetism, biophysics, biochemistry, astrophysics, and molecular biology are examples of such a process; their very names underscore that they are mergers of fields. But distance to the research front and the social structure of science militate against breadth of knowledge. While there are popular journals such as *Scientific American*, and professional organizations such as the American Association for the Advancement of Science, designed to keep both scientist and layman abreast of progress across the spectrum of activity, the professional journals and meetings, scholarly societies, and university departments are almost invariably (and probably necessarily) organized by specialty.

Scientists think of themselves as physicists, chemists, geologists, astronomers, and so on. Indeed, specialization has progressed much further, to the point where subdisciplines claim both the allegiance of scientists and the right to run their own conferences. This process, for example, led the American Physical Society to split itself into divisions representing such subjects as condensed-matter physics, nuclear physics, high-energy physics, plasma physics, fluid dynamics, and astrophysics, among others. It is little wonder, then, that work may proceed in different sciences for some time before a serendipitous event or a person with unusual breadth of interest recognizes some connections, and a "hybrid science" develops. Research conducted on the nuclear winter phenomenon (if not a hybrid science certainly a hybrid subject) fits this pattern. In contrast with the others, however, not two but more than half a dozen fields contributed to it: particle microphysics and atmospheric chemistry, fire and smoke research, volcanic eruptions, ozone depletion, planetary studies, dinosaur extinction, and of course research specifically on the effects of nuclear weapons. All these fields involved meteorological or climatic considerations, but the connections among disciplines were not always obvious and the central importance of urban fires was not yet considered quantitatively. We turn now to these ingredients of NW. The intent in this chapter and the next is merely to sketch some relevant aspects of these specialties, not to provide exhaustive descriptions of them.

Research on the Effects of Nuclear Weapons

The wide range of consequences of nuclear war has spawned a large literature. Much has come from the pens of those who seek peace through arms control; far more has been issued by those who seek peace through strength of arms. Government sponsorship has dominated the latter publications, emanating from such bodies as the Rand Corporation, the Hudson Institute, the Stanford Research Institute, the Institute for Defense Analyses, the National Academy of Sciences, the Federal Emergency Management Agency and its predecessors, the Central Intelligence Agency, Congress, and of course, the Atomic Energy Commission, the Department of Energy, and the Department of Defense. While many of these books, articles, and reports deal with such interesting and important topics as the scenarios and controllability of nuclear war, civil defense, and economic, administrative, social, and psychological factors, we survey in this section only those types of investigations that were relevant to the discovery of NW.[2] Note also that not all research related to nuclear explosions is compressed into this section; for convenience, atmospheric dust injections and fire research are treated elsewhere in this chapter. Moreover, it is impossible to avoid a bit of overlap, and thus some topics, such as fallout and weather/climate effects, appear in more than one place.

It had been known since 1900 or 1901, when F. O. Walkhoff in Germany and Henri Becquerel in France suffered accidental burns from radium, that the emitted radiation could cause injury.[3] Indeed, the popular use of dilute radioactive materials in nostrums early in the twentieth century was based on recognition of a physiological effect, and the widespread treatment of cancer and other diseases by radium took advantage of the circumstance that rapidly growing cells are more readily affected by radiation than normal cells.[4] That radium could kill as well as cure was brought home to the public in the 1920s in a notable case involving workers in New Jersey whose job it was to apply radium-laced luminous paint to watch dials. They rolled the fine brushes on their lips to get a good point, and eventually they ingested enough radium to cause sickness and death.[5]

The scientists and physicians of the Manhattan Project were aware of the dangers of radioactivity. Aside from the normal precautions taken during research, provisions were made to monitor the radioactive cloud produced by the bomb test at Alamogordo on 16 July 1945. In the postwar period, the Atomic Energy Commission maintained a relatively low level of interest in the biological effects of fallout, which were seen as the only real long-term consequences of nuclear explosions.[6] The Department of Defense (DoD), the successive civil defense agencies, and other government offices likewise studied fallout patterns, but more in connection with various war scenarios, in order to determine the likely number of casualties or the area of land contaminated.

During World War II, the Manhattan Project site at Oak Ridge, Tennessee, was the place where bomb-usable uranium-235 was separated from its more abundant isotope, uranium-238. After the war, both the production facilities and the research laboratory at Oak Ridge continued to function as part of the AEC empire. In 1949, the Oak Ridge physicist Nicholas Smith calculated that 3,000 Hiroshima-size weapons would have to be detonated, in a single growing season, before the crops in a downwind area of 350,000 square miles (more than twice the size of California) would cause serious harm to people who ate them. This study was called Project Gabriel. When a portion of US nuclear testing was moved from the South Pacific to the newly prepared site in Nevada in 1951, bringing radioactive fallout much closer to Americans, Smith repeated his study, making use of data from two recent series of tests. This time he estimated that 10,000 weapons could be detonated before the long-term hazards would become serious. A review committee cautioned that fallout also could be dangerous in the short term, near ground zero and even hundreds of miles away, if radioactivity was washed out of the cloud by rain. Genetic effects seem not to have been contemplated.[7]

While Project Gabriel was classified, a similar and probably simpler calculation appeared in the 1950 DoD-AEC publication *The Effects of Atomic Weapons*. Uniform worldwide contamination to dangerous levels by fission fragments, the book's authors claimed, would require about 755,000 bombs of "nominal" size (20 KT, approximately the yields at Hiroshima and Nagasaki), and that 70 million such explosions would have to occur before plutonium became a hazard.[8] The magnitude of the US nuclear arsenal was secret then, but the public could well assume that far fewer bombs than these numbers had been made. Only decades later was it revealed that in 1950 the United States had only 700 nuclear weapons.[9]

Soon, however, the arsenals of both superpowers increased in size, and fusion or thermonuclear bombs were developed. Their total yield was still well below the presumed danger levels, but these levels were based on incomplete knowledge of fission-product formation and decay and of their biological effects. Thus, in 1953 the Atomic Energy Commission and the Air Force commissioned a new study of long-range fallout by the Rand Corporation. This effort, called Project Sunshine, reaffirmed Project Gabriel's conclusion that strontium-90 was the most dangerous radioisotope in fallout, as it is readily formed in fission, has a relatively long half-life (believed to be 20 years then but now established as 28.5 years), and is easily incorporated into bones, where it is a carcinogen. Project Sunshine also called for further investigation of a number of variables, particularly the amount of strontium from previous tests deposited in the soil around the world. Using a then-current standard for the maximum permissible concentration of radioactivity, the Rand authors concluded that 25,000 MT, or about a million nominal bombs, would be needed to reach that level.[10]

In the second half of the 1950s, spurred by the worldwide fear of invisible, tasteless, and odorless radioactive contamination, more research, more committee reviews, and numerous hearings were conducted.[11] By the time of the 1963 Limited Test Ban Treaty, which permitted testing underground only (and which was ignored by France and China for some years), there was fairly widespread agreement among radiation biologists (with some notable and vocal dissenters) about the hazard. Along with strontium-90, cesium-137, with its half-life of 30 years and its easy incorporation in soft tissue, was of concern, as was iodine-131, which concentrates in the thyroid. But cesium-137 leaves the body fairly rapidly, and iodine-131's half-life of eight days likewise presents only a short-term somatic problem. Carbon-14, not a fission fragment but formed by the reaction of neutrons with atoms of nitrogen in the air, and with a half-life of 5,730 years, is of potential genetic danger, as is cesium-137.[12]

The superpowers agreed to a testing moratorium in 1958; this held until 1961, when first the Soviet Union and then the United States resumed testing in the atmosphere. This in turn brought pressure on them to negotiate the treaty that eventually was signed in 1963. By 1958, about 100 megaton equivalents of fission products had been injected into the atmosphere. The increase in radiation exposure over the background from the naturally occurring distribution of radioactive materials in water, earth, building materials, and so forth was estimated to be only 5 percent. Without question there would be more cases of bone cancer, leukemia, and other assaults on the body, and more instances of birth defects due to genetic effects. (That radiation can cause mutations had been well known since Herman Muller's experiments on fruit flies in the 1930s.) But—and this was a value judgment, not a scientific conclusion—it was felt by many that the military and political benefits were worth perhaps 75 additional leukemia cases a year and 2,500–100,000 further genetic defects. The 40,000 automobile fatalities annually on American highways were often cited as a biological hazard we accept.[13]

The studies of fallout were not limited to the identity and proportions of the radioactive contaminants. Fallout patterns created locally, regionally, and globally by winds were obviously of related interest. Nor did the studies focus only on human irradiation; trees, crops, and animals were examined for their ability to tolerate radiation and their potential to concentrate radioactivity.[14]

The study of fallout patterns is, to a great degree, the science of meteorology. The fireball produced by a nuclear explosion cools rapidly as it expands and mixes with large volumes of air. When its temperature reaches that of the surrounding atmosphere, in several minutes, it ceases to rise. At that point it behaves like other large air masses, and in a temperate zone it participates in the general west-to-east circulation. The heavier debris is drawn to the surface by gravity. Lighter material stays aloft, moving with the radioactive cloud; a portion may enter the stratosphere. Within the troposphere, smaller and larger weather systems distort the cloud and move it somewhat north or south. But the major movement in the mid latitudes is easterly, with the top of the cloud, pushed along by strong winds at 30,000–40,000 feet, extending about 200 miles ahead of the base after a day. Turbulent eddies, such as convection currents (which sometimes result in thunderstorms), further deform the air mass. Rainfall, mass transport, and gravity bring particulate matter to the surface, but the variability of the forces acting on the cloud ensures that the fallout is not spread uniformly. Nonetheless, calculation of fallout patterns and intensity of radioactivity under different conditions was a continuing activity of the Atomic Energy Commission.[15]

Everyone talks about the weather, so the adage goes, but no one does anything about it. The first part of this axiom remained true after 1945, with the added twist that many people blamed bad weather on nuclear testing. The cliché's latter half, however, was upset, as others urged the AEC to use atomic bombs to scatter violent storms. By the mid 1950s, US Weather Bureau scientists felt obliged to examine the possible effects of explosions on weather. Rainfall was known to occur in the vicinity of a detonation, as heat from the fireball and from fires ignited by the thermal pulse rose into moist air; this happened at Hiroshima. But at distances from ground zero, no unusual weather had been reported by pilots monitoring the radioactive clouds or by meteorological ground stations. Still, was it possible that "the atmosphere is so unstable that some small impulse . . . could produce a weather change that might otherwise never take place"?[16]

Lester Machta and D. L. Harris, Weather Bureau meteorologists in Washington, DC, examined the evidence for cloud seeding by the nuclear debris or by dust propelled into the atmosphere and found it to be an improbable event. Likewise, the only potential effect of ionized particles on the electrical conductivity of the air was a decrease in the amount of lightning, but this had not been detected. A reduction in the amount of sunlight reaching Earth's surface due to dust in the atmosphere, such as occurred in everyone's favorite example—the 1883 eruption of Krakatoa—was unlikely, since the quantity of material lofted by a bomb was orders of magnitude smaller than the several cubic kilometers of debris thrown out by the volcano. In fact, atomic bombs are puny relative to normal weather phenomena. A day's thermal energy in the springtime sunlight falling on one square mile of the Nevada test site was equivalent to the thermal and kinetic energy of two nominal bombs, while the condensation of water vapor in an average thunderstorm released energy comparable to that in thirteen Hiroshima-size bombs. In short, no changes in temperature, precipitation, or any other variable could be attributed to weapons testing. Even the dramatic increase in reported tornadoes in the United States was due to improved reporting procedures, not to nuclear detonations. Thermonuclear explosions, though not as well studied since they were of recent vintage, also showed no effects on the weather.[17]

In 1966, E. S. Batten of the Rand Corporation reexamined weather effects for the Atomic Energy Commission. Whereas Machta and Harris had focused on single explosions, Batten considered a 10,000-MT war. He looked at the influence of the bombs' energy, debris, and radioactivity on atmospheric processes involving movement, moisture, and solar radiation. Debris (essentially dust) had by far the largest effect on both precipitation and the heat balance. Debris could act as condensation nuclei and as ice nuclei, influencing cloud formation and rain patterns. High cirrus clouds, and above them fine dust particles in the stratosphere, could interfere with the inbound and outbound radiation in the atmosphere. Batten concluded that weather *might* be affected by a nuclear war, but it was not yet possible to quantify the change. A deeper understanding of atmospheric processes and their interactions was required.[18]

Several months earlier, the DoD's Office of Civil Defense sponsored a somewhat similar study by Robert U. Ayres of the Hudson Institute. The motivation seems to have derived from interest in fallout and blast shelters, about which there had been intense debate at the time of the Cuban Missile Crisis in 1962, and in the question of post-attack recuperation. Ayres looked at a wide range of environmental problems that might result from the radiological, thermal, and atmospheric effects of a large-scale nuclear war. He also examined many secondary damage mechanisms, including human, animal, and plant diseases; infestations of rodents, insects, and bird and plant pests; ecological succession; erosion, flood, and silting; and glaciation.

In agreement with Batten, Ayres felt that changes in the weather were possible. The kinetic energy of a large hurricane at any moment (not the summation) was estimated to be equivalent to about 170 MT. A large nuclear war (several thousand megatons) was significant on this scale; it would loft many cubic miles of air and would affect the precipitation mechanism, and thus the weather. The upper troposphere would be warmer and cloudier, while the surface would be cooler and drier (despite initial rainfall). Effects longer than several weeks were not expected, since most debris would settle or be washed out of the troposphere in that period. Dust raised to the stratosphere, however, might initiate a cooling cycle, and, although it was believed to be far-fetched, a new ice age could not be excluded. Smoke too was known to produce cooling under it, but Ayres admitted that "little is known about the details."[19] Neither Batten nor Ayres paid much attention to the effects on the atmosphere of large-scale fires.

Through the 1970s and into the 1980s, a range of nuclear explosion effects continued to be studied, supported by such government agencies as the DoD's Defense Nuclear Agency. Far more prominent in the public's eye, however, was a series of articles and reports that summarized what was already known. These were attributable to the Nixon administration's desire in the early 1970s to develop greater ability to conduct a limited nuclear war, then to the Senate's failure, as the decade ended, to ratify the SALT II Treaty. Also contributing were the resumption of rigid Cold War rhetoric in an increasingly conservative America and the arms buildup during Reagan's first term.[20] These commentaries offered little new technical information or insight, but were symbolic of the widespread interest in, and fear of, the consequences of nuclear war, which seemed closer then than during the earlier period of détente.

Particle Microphysics and Atmospheric Chemistry

Studies conducted during the Manhattan Project on the effects of nuclear weapons included observation of the sizes of the particulate matter produced and attention to fireball temperatures. The latter determined the chemical reactions among air atoms and molecules, fission fragments, un-fissioned uranium and plutonium, and bomb casing materials. The goal was to learn more about the stages of the explosion, the chemistry and physics of the radioactive cloud, and the characteristics of the fallout. These investigations continued at the 1946 Crossroads tests in the Pacific and through subsequent test series in the 1940s, the 1950s, and the early 1960s. Their data were analyzed and summarized in several of the documents mentioned above, such as the report of Project Gabriel (1949), *The Effects of Atomic Weapons* (1950), the report of Project Sunshine (1953), and *The Effects of Nuclear Weapons* (1957). From such work came the understanding, for example, that most of the airborne material from an air burst is 1 or 2 micrometers (millionths of a meter) in radius, which means that this is the approximate size of the radioactive fallout and rainout from such explosions. Another result was that about 80 percent of the radioactive material is found in the more volatile elements, those that form chemical compounds and/or solidify when the volume has cooled to its greatest extent. This means, for example, that volatile strontium-90 has less time to grow as solid particles and will be more thoroughly mixed throughout a large volume of air. For ground bursts, in which huge amounts of surface materials are lofted, it was learned that bombs exploded on the coral atolls of the Pacific yielded different results than those detonated on the silicate sands of Nevada. Molten silica acts as an unusually good solvent for metallic oxides and collects small particles efficiently, in contrast to the coral's calcium carbonate, on whose surface radioactive particles tend to plate.[21]

In his wide-ranging 1965 report, Robert Ayres pointed to some processes that were not so well understood. Data accumulated from years of artificial rain-making attempts suggested that *too many* condensation nuclei inhibited the growth of ice crystals, since they competed with each other for the available moisture. Large explosions that entrained much debris could, therefore, saturate an air volume, so that raindrops would be less likely to fall than under optimum conditions. The apparent ability of droplets to coalesce suddenly and fall was another poorly comprehended process. If the phenomenon was electrical in origin, then the ionization due to beta-particle emitters in the debris could be significant.[22]

By the early 1970s, with Rachel Carson's *Silent Spring* a best seller and with the oil spill in the Santa Barbara Channel, hazardous smog in many urban areas, and photographs from space of our beautiful blue planet all suggesting the fragility and interdependency of our ecological systems, the "Environmental Movement" was a recognized social force.[23] Scientific research benefited from this public concern. Atmospheric aerosols, for instance, were of interest not only for their practical connection to human respiratory problems, but also for their possible effect on the climate. Carbon dust particles are a case in point. They are commonly found in polluted air over cities, and they are capable of absorbing sunlight. Consequently, data were gathered on the radiative properties of graphite, soot, and coal particles of different sizes.[24]

The length of time particulate elemental carbon remains in the atmosphere is obviously related to this problem. Studies showed that its "atmospheric lifetime" is similar to that of sulfate aerosols, which suggested that both were mixed within the same grains, or at least that both were removed from the atmosphere by similar processes of scavenging by rainfall and precipitation by gravity.[25] Carbon dioxide has long been known for its effect on the climate, humankind's contribution from burning fossil fuels being a major factor in current "greenhouse effect" concern. Hydrocarbons, further, are well-recognized sources of local and regional air pollution. In contrast, the properties of elemental carbon have only recently been established as important. It plays several roles, but its greatest impact is seen in heating of the atmosphere, as the carbon absorbs sunlight. This is the major insight of the NW proponents, so it is no coincidence that three of the five authors of a 1983 survey of elemental carbon's global cycle were already members of the as-yet-unpublished team that pioneered NW research: Richard Turco (of R&D Associates in Marina del Rey, California) and Owen Brian Toon and James Pollack (of the National Aeronautics and Space Administration's Ames Research Center at Moffett Field, California).[26] This team, which also included Thomas Ackerman and Carl Sagan, became widely known as TTAPS, an amalgam of the first letters of their surnames.

Other scientists approached carbon from a different perspective, examining it not as a pollutant or hazard, but for its potential benefits. If a 100–300-km cloud of carbon black particles about 0.1 micrometer in size were to be formed in the upper troposphere (for example, by the afterburners of modified jet aircraft), it might absorb as much as 15 percent of the incoming solar radiation. This artificial heat source might then enhance cloud formation and thus increase precipitation along dry coastlines, reduce the intensity of hurricanes, moderate high tropical temperatures by the formation of a layer of cirrus clouds, and accomplish other economically desirable modifications of the weather. In this and in other investigations, one-dimensional, two-dimensional, and even primitive three-dimensional circulation models were employed on large-capacity computers.[27]

Digital computers, generally available for scientific research by the 1960s, were initially regarded as no more than fast number-crunching machines. They were clearly useful in large theoretical calculations. But in that decade it became apparent that computation was more than simply a tool; computer simulation developed as a third research method, in addition to experiment and theory. It was not conceptually different, for simulation was in the tradition of using an equation to calculate a result. Various data were entered into old-fashioned equations and a velocity, or an energy value, or a planetary position was generated. Computers do the same thing, but with incredibly greater power, flexibility, and speed, making possible the testing of slight variations of the input conditions. It was the ability of the machine to compute the consequences of phenomena through complex calculations, even incorporating feedback from previous cycles, that was awesome. The Livermore scientists Michael MacCracken and Julius Chang expressed the problem simply: "The basic structure of the atmosphere is due to the interaction between its radiation balance and chemical composition, with atmospheric transport providing the dynamic mechanism to balance the total system."[28] The solution of the problem, because of its complexity, was by no means simple. But science was approaching the point of making great strides with this new technology. By the late 1970s, the degree of computer sophistication (for our purposes applied to atmospheric research) was considerable, even in one-dimensional models.[29]

A good example is the study published in 1979 by the Ames Research Center. It was a model for stratospheric aerosols, fashioned especially for the layer of sulfuric acid and water droplets known since 1961 to reside at altitudes of between 15 and 30 kilometers. The discovery of this layer excited atmospheric scientists, all the more so when it was suggested that it might be the cause of remarkable sunsets and other optical phenomena, and might even have a significant effect on Earth's climate. Interest was heightened further by concern that human activity was adding to the stratosphere's burden of sulfur and other particulates, which could, among other things, lead to a reduction of ozone.

Particles of this sulfate layer were captured by high-flying aircraft and balloon-borne instruments. The layer was also probed by lasers, and its ability to scatter sunlight observed from satellites. From the mass of experimental evidence and its theoretical interpretations the authors constructed a one-dimensional model that fit the data closely and which then could be used for predictive purposes. It simulated the atmosphere from the ground up to 58 kilometers, incorporated a range of particle sizes, embraced photochemical reactions that convert sulfur gases into sulfuric acid vapor, described the formation of droplets on condensation nuclei and their development, diffusion, and settling, and did a number of other things. In short, this was a state-of-the-art physical-chemical aerosol model that simulated quite well phenomena that occur in the stratosphere. To repeat a caveat, such computer models only approach reality, for the true atmosphere is far more complex than even the most sophisticated three-dimensional models of a decade later. But scientists are accustomed to glean facts of nature by judicious approximations; it is a proven approach. Again, not coincidentally, the two lead authors of this study, Turco and Toon, would shepherd the investigation of NW a few years later.[30]

Turco and Toon, and their Ames Research Center colleague R. C. Whitten, followed construction and analysis of this stratospheric aerosol model with a broad review in 1982 of stratospheric aerosol research. They concluded that a wide array of chemical, photochemical, and microphysical data was available, as were computer models with which it was possible to simulate the many reactions to a significant degree. Better data in certain areas and multi-dimensional models were desired, but these were being collected and developed. In a prophetic line, they asserted that "man can affect the stratospheric aerosols (and possibly the climate) through high-altitude emissions of particles." And those particles included soot. Their focus then was on emissions from jet and rocket engines and from industry, but soon the source of soot under scrutiny would be fires ignited by nuclear explosions.[31]

In 1979, adding to the personal expertise of the TTAPS team, Toon and Pollack joined their former professor, Carl Sagan, in a review of human activity that altered Earth's surface. Deforestation in the tropical and temperate zones encouraged desertification and salinization. Urbanization, occurring over millennia, also caused regional and global climatic changes. In the former case the increased albedo suggested a corresponding cooling of the planet, as more sunlight was reflected back to space.[32] Toon and the fifth TTAPS member, Thomas Ackerman, also of the Ames Research Center, collaborated on the design of computer mathematical programs to represent the light scattered by particles and on a study that suggested the importance of tropospheric graphitic carbon (soot) in absorbing radiation.[33] Radiative transfer models that ask how much light an aerosol allows to be transmitted, reflected, and absorbed were crucial to NW calculations, for the unburned carbon found in smoke absorbs visible solar radiation quite well while being relatively transparent to infrared light. Soot, therefore, produces an effect opposite to that of greenhouse gases.

In 1981, consolidating the basis for their NW expertise further, Turco and Toon, along with P. Hamill of the Systems and Applied Sciences Corporation and R. C. Whitten, studied the interaction of meteoric debris with the gases and aerosols of the stratosphere. Meteors enter Earth's atmosphere regularly, depositing about 1.6×10^4 tonnes (1 tonne = 1 metric ton = 10^6 grams, or about 2,200 pounds) of material annually. While this is only a few percent of the volcanic input in a quiet year, meteoric sodium has an important role in the chemistry of the stratosphere, especially its reaction with sulfuric acid vapor. But the technique concerns us more than the conclusions. This was a pioneering investigation by computer model of the effects on stratospheric aerosols of the debris from meteors. Turco et al. matched observational data of many sorts with computer predictions and found good agreement. Then, with confidence in their model, they began to explore other particle-gas interactions. They found that particle size was an important determinant in the formation of condensation nuclei.[34]

Fire and Smoke Research

Large forest fires are more common than large city fires, and more is known about them. Yet in 1965 even what was known about forest fires was not very much when Robert Ayres made a stab at quantifying the subject. On the basis of a very crude calculation, Ayres listed the energy released in several of the biggest fires in the United States, topped by 300 MT in an 1871 blaze in Wisconsin and Michigan. Smoke, Ayres noted, was considered only in regard to the detection of forest fires, despite its obvious ability to produce widespread haze and its being somewhat analogous to fallout.[35] The smoke cloud, in fact, was known to obscure solar radiation, sometimes to a remarkable degree. A 1950 forest fire in Alberta was believed to have blocked 54 percent of the sunlight over Washington, DC, lowering the capital's temperature by 10°F. Further, the heated air above such blazes often provokes thunderstorms, and combustion products serve as condensation nuclei for rainfall.[36]

World War II provided an opportunity to learn more about urban fires, in which the fuel concentration is greater than in forests and inflammability is less seasonal. Yet, despite the notable mass fires caused by bombing in Dresden, Hamburg, and Tokyo, and the even more pertinent fire storm in Hiroshima, those who first studied the effects of nuclear weapons clearly were far more impressed with the destruction caused by the blast wave. The existence of smoke columns was noted on occasion, but no attempts were made to quantify them. For most people, smoke brought colorful sunsets but was scientifically unimportant.[37] Though in subsequent years some investigators of nuclear effects promoted fire research, maintaining that heat effects extended to greater distances and could produce more casualties than the pressure surge, attention was diverted from fires by interest in radiological effects. By 1960, however, congressional, scientific, and public concern focused for a brief time on the consequences of the thermal pulse and the secondary blast effects. The thermal pulse ignites fires by the visible and infrared light from the fireball. The secondary blast effects include fires kindled by overturned stoves, as at Hiroshima, broken gas mains, and short-circuited wires. Many small blazes may coalesce to form the mass fire.[38]

Two types of mass fires were recognized: the fire storm, in which a stationary chimney of rising hot gases pulls in air from the perimeter, and the conflagration, in which a great fire is pushed along by prevailing winds. A fire storm is capable of generating winds of hurricane velocity. In both cases, the intense fires consume all combustibles within several hours, whereas the burning of San Francisco (in 1906), Moscow (in 1812), and Hamburg (in 1842) took days.[39]

Critical to the ignition of a mass fire by a nuclear explosion are a number of variables, including the amount and type of kindling, the air's relative humidity (which affects the moisture content of the fuel), the clarity of the atmosphere, the height of the burst, and the duration of the thermal pulse (which varies directly with the weapon's size). Under the optimum conditions of a dry and clear day, a 10-MT air burst could ignite fires more than 35 miles from ground zero, a distance at which blast damage would be minor. Once ignited, the most important factor in the development of an urban mass fire is the amount and distribution of fuel. Originally measured by "building density" (the ratio of projected roof area to total ground area), the standard now is "fuel loading" (mass of fuel per unit surface area), which better accounts for the contents of multi-level buildings.[40]

The Hiroshima ruins showed evidence of charring, which suggested that the fires ignited by the thermal pulse were almost immediately extinguished by the pressure wave that followed. This interpretation was first accepted and then rejected. The weight of scientific opinion then returned to its original position in 1970, when the Office of Civil Defense (which became the Defense Civil Preparedness Agency in 1972, then the Federal Emergency Management Agency in 1979) constructed a blast simulator in which tests showed that flames were indeed extinguished by winds in all cases except when there were very low overpressures.[41]

A related, controversial subject was (and is) the conditions necessary for a mass fire. The Defense Civil Preparedness Agency contracted for a number of analyses of World War II fires. Severity was measured by average heat output in millions of British Thermal Units (1 BTU = the amount of heat needed to raise a pound of water one degree Fahrenheit) per square mile per second. Fires in Hiroshima and Nagasaki emitted up to 300 million BTU per square mile per second, killed up to 5 percent of the endangered population, and, at Hiroshima, caused inrushing winds of 35 miles per hour. By the definitions adopted, they were called group fires. True firestorms generate 600–700 million BTU per square mile per second, kill 12–20 percent of the threatened population, and provoke inrushing winds of 50 miles per hour or more.

Regardless of name, however, the likelihood of large fires remained uncertain. To explore this problem, the Office of Civil Defense joined with the US Forest Service and the Defense Nuclear Agency to conduct a series of tests from 1963 to 1967. In Operation Flambeau they stacked timber in large piles representing houses, and burned as much as 40 acres of such arrays. A firestorm, they concluded, required more than 8 pounds of fuel per square foot of fire area, more than 50 percent of the structures alight initially, no more than gentle winds at the start, and a fire area larger than half a square mile. Since it was estimated that a nuclear explosion would ignite only 10 percent of the structures exposed to it, mass fires would not result from a nuclear attack.[42] This conclusion was controversial, in view of the experience at Hiroshima and a feeling that the Flambeau data were barely analyzed. Even Flambeau's first director complained that hardly anything was done with the voluminous film records and mountains of data. Indeed, at least as late as the mid 1970s, "due to the high degree of uncertainty as to the validity [of] extrapolating from these limited experiences" of World War II—and it would not be unreasonable to add Project Flambeau—the Office of the Secretary of Defense reported to the Senate Foreign Relations Committee that "no attempt has been made in DoD analyses to mathematically model fire storm generation."[43]

In addition to the issue of whether mass fires would occur, the extent to which rain would extinguish fires was (and remains) unclear. Information about the concentration and size distribution of cloud condensation nuclei and water droplets was needed to quantify this problem. In the early 1970s, atmospheric scientists from the University of Washington flew an aircraft into the plumes of both planned and wild forest fires. Measurements of the size of the nuclei of water droplets were not obtained, but their concentrations were much higher in the plumes than outside, with the conclusion that rainfall was enhanced.[44]

Data on the weight of particulates per ton of various types of fuel burned in wildland fires were accumulated from many sources during the 1970s, as were data which showed that most particles were about 0.1 micrometer in radius. Still, a review written for a US Forest Service workshop near the end of the decade bemoaned that "the effects of fire have been studied since the beginning of organized Forest Service research, but the results are scattered over a wide range of outlets. In addition, research is conducted on the effects of fire under several appropriation line items, and in some instances lacks the interdisciplinary approach needed to make the results as useful as possible to land managers."[45] Substitute "scientists" for "land managers" and the lament was equally true.

The situation, however, was changing, with government agencies initiating the first con- centrated attempt to evaluate damage from fires of nuclear origin. Of particular importance was the insistence by Harold Brode (of the Pacific-Sierra Research Corporation) that nuclear fire damage was just as predictable as blast destruction.[46]

On the eve of the revelation that a NW scenario was a likely consequence of a nuclear war, the Federal Emergency Management Agency commissioned an "analysis of the large urban fire environment" by the Pacific-Sierra Research Corporation. In late 1982, staff scientists D. A. Larson and R. D. Small presented a mathematical model of fires ignited by nuclear weapons. Assuming 1-megaton warheads, a reasonable fire radius of 12 kilometers, and heat release of the magnitude and rate measured in the 1943 Hamburg firestorm, they tested three different city models and varied several parameters in each case. Hurricane-force winds were a consistent product of these circumstances. As expected, temperatures and winds increased as fire size, fuel loading, and burning rate increased. A novel feature of the study was the suppression of fire in the center, which left an annular ring ablaze. This simu- lation, in which a later warhead's blast wave partially extinguished the flames of an earlier explosion, provided surprising results, for the final damage was relatively unchanged from the single-explosion case.[47] Irrespective of the specific conclusions, the analysis by Larson and Small was notable, for it marked a more quantitative and mathematics-driven approach to the study of fires. It also showed that the Federal Emergency Management Agency was not as insensitive to its mission as its critics claimed.

As these examples clearly suggest, the focus of pre- (as well as post-) NW research was on urban fires, which produce the most smoke and soot—far more than forest or grassland blazes. Some might argue that such quantitative investigations of fires were beside the point, since it was US policy from the early 1970s onward not to target population centers specifi- cally.[48] Despite this policy, however, there were industrial and military targets in or near the USSR's 200 largest urban areas. The defense analysts William Arkin and Richard Field- house, both of the Institute for Policy Studies, calculated that these cities had "an average of 19.1 warheads with 6.33 equivalent megatons" aimed at them.[49] Cities *would* burn.

3 Scientific Disciplines in Isolation, 2: Those with Less Obvious Connections to Nuclear War

Volcanic Eruptions

Despite an inexact match, nuclear war analysts traditionally compared nuclear detonations to volcanic eruptions, the latter being among the largest explosions experienced on Earth. A 10,000-megaton war, for example, with half the weapons set to burst at ground level, would send about 25 cubic kilometers of rock and soil into the air. This was estimated to be about twice the volume of debris lofted by Krakatoa in 1883.[1] But volcanoes were of interest for other reasons too.

In 1975, Stephen Schneider and Clifford Mass authored a paper in *Science* that attempted to connect global temperature trends to various phenomena. Schneider has already been mentioned as a climate specialist at the National Center for Atmospheric Research and one of the principal actors in the NW drama. This research is another good example of the personal expertise the participants developed, such that NW could be predicted and analyzed. Schneider and Mass's proposed grounds for climatic change fell into two categories. Internal causes included the energy exchanges among the large reservoirs of the "climatic system": the oceans, the atmosphere, and ice masses. External causes (that is, sources of change not themselves affected by the climate) included variations in the solar constant (the amount of energy received per square centimeter per minute at the mean distance of Earth from the Sun), anthropogenic changes in the makeup of the atmosphere and in the surface features of Earth, and volcanic eruptions that spewed dust into the stratosphere.[2]

Specifically, Schneider and Mass conducted a quantitative analysis of surface temperature versus variations in volcanic dust and the solar constant, insofar as these variations could be correlated to sunspot activity. Since thermometers and telescopes (to observe sunspots) were not invented until the seventeenth century, Schneider and Mass's time line began then, although the early data were sparse and of questionable accuracy. Despite this uncertain record, and despite inadequacies in their climate model and a lack of climatic feedback channels, their reconstruction from eruption and sunspot data of annual surface temperatures since 1600 bore impressive similarities to historical records of winter severity in Europe. Temperatures also correlated well with analyses of ice cores from Greenland and with ring samples from bristlecone pine trees from California. Schneider and Mass declined to draw strong conclusions from their work, pointing out that their historical samples were drawn from limited regions. But their study pointed out once again the necessity for more and better quantitative information and the strong likelihood that surface temperatures are directly linked in some measure to external climatic events.[3]

By no means did Schneider and Mass prove that volcanic eruptions caused climatic changes, yet the connection seemed reasonable. The relationship, suggested long ago by Benjamin Franklin and others, was not examined seriously until the early twentieth century. Notable eruptions then studied included those of Mount Tambora, on the Indonesian (then Dutch East Indian) island of Sumbawa, in 1815; Krakatoa (also called Krakatau), off the western coast of Java, in 1883; Katmai, in Alaska, in 1912; and Bali's Mount Agung, in 1963. In the case of Tambora, the largest volcanic explosion in history, the sky was black for a day or two in many places within a radius of 600 kilometers, and ash fell on land and sea more than 1,000 kilometers away. The mountain's height was lowered from 4,000 meters to 2,800 meters, and according to one of the smaller estimates 40–90 cubic kilometers of debris (dense rock equivalent) was ejected. Fine dust and sulfur gases (which slowly turn to sulfuric acid upon contact with water vapor) reached the stratosphere, where they circulated around the world, causing striking sunsets for the next year.[4]

The year 1816 was notorious in New England as "the year without a summer" or "eighteen hundred and froze to death." Snow and frost in June, July, and August, and failed crops, made the year memorable. Western Europe experienced similar low temperatures. To early-twentieth-century scientists the explanation was straightforward: atmospheric dust from Tambora absorbed or reflected incident sunlight, with a consequent cooling of Earth's surface by about 0.5°C. Later investigations, however, cast doubt on this conclusion. Whereas the intensity of direct solar radiation is attenuated, the total energy reaching the surface remains the same, as the reflected beam is still scattered forward. Moreover, the cold summer of 1816 occurred more than a year after the volcanic eruption, by which time stratospheric aerosols should have been fairly evenly distributed. Yet weather stations in Eastern Europe reported much milder temperatures. Such differences are part of the *normal* record, expected as features of the persistent long-wave circulation patterns. Indeed, a statistical analysis of temperatures at a number of North American and European stations showed little correlation with volcanic eruptions and, even more, that minima, such as 1816 in New England, were not extremes but reasonable departures from the norm.[5] However, a still later study of the data (using different groupings of the reporting stations, weightings, and analytical techniques) suggested that the Tambora dust veil was after all responsible for a reduction of the Northern Hemisphere's mean temperature by 0.4–0.7°C in 1816.[6]

Apparent inability to reach a firm conclusion is actually a normal stage in the development of many scientific topics. In this case, sparse records were reworked and reinterpreted from more recent insights in volcanology, oceanography, glaciology, meteorology, climatology, and astronomy. With new information came new conclusions, but the level of confidence still could be debated. Precisely the same situation obtained in the case of NW, with the different sciences described in this chapter and the previous one contributing to a conclusion, yet this inference was by no means universally accepted.

Scientific uncertainties are usually explored by the acquisition of more and better data. Recognition that quantification was extremely important dates from the late sixteenth century, when the Danish astronomer Tycho Brahe took observations nightly and not just on special occasions, as had been the norm. Such data gathering continued with the development of actuarial statistics in the early seventeenth century and the understanding of the importance of chemical formulas in the eighteenth century. By the end of the nineteenth century, the quantifying spirit in the physical sciences was almost a mania.

In this numerical tradition, volcanic emissions were examined with care by atmospheric scientists from the mid 1970s onward. To determine more accurate size and quantity distributions of ejecta than could be acquired on the ground (because particles remained aloft a long time), aircraft equipped with quantitative sampling instruments flew through the eruption clouds of three active Guatemalan volcanoes.[7] Other studies looked at grain size and distribution data, which suggested particle aggregation and, thus, faster settling times. The 1980 eruption of Mount St. Helens, in Washington State, provided a particularly accessible subject.[8]

Most of the members of the TTAPS group were active in this field, for volcanoes were but another source of aerosols that bore on their consuming interest in atmospheric phenomena that cause climatic change. Looking at visible and infrared light wavelengths, a team that included Pollack, Toon, and Sagan calculated the effect of various amounts of volcanic dust and sulfur gases on the global albedo, taking into consideration the often vexing problems of multiple scattering of the radiation and the atmosphere's vertical inhomogeneity. Unlike most earlier investigators, who focused on the silicate dust, they also paid particular attention to sulfuric acid aerosols created by photochemical action on the sulfur gases. Indeed, they came to the striking conclusion that "sulfuric acid is the dominant aerosol species during most of the time that the particles from a volcanic eruption affect the global heat budget."[9] Volcanic explosions, which ultimately cool the Earth, do so in proportion to the quantity of sulfuric acid aerosols produced.

The same team also surveyed the historical data linking volcanic eruptions and surface temperatures, using evidence such as the dust, ash, and sulfate content of ice cores from Greenland and Antarctica and from ocean sediments. From this they concluded that volcanic debris very likely was responsible in part for the decrease of about 5°C during the last major ice age (between 75,000 and 12,000 years ago), and for the 0.5°C depression during the "little ice age" (ca. 1450–1915). Looking at a related question, they found that stratospheric aerosols from supersonic jet aircraft and from space shuttles, projected over the next few decades, would have a barely measurable climatic effect.[10]

A fourth member of the already formed but still unpublished TTAPS group, Richard Turco, also plied the volcanic subject, as he, Toon, and colleagues used their computer model,

mentioned above, to explore the physical and chemical processes generated in the stratosphere by the Mount St. Helens eruption. This model was especially applicable, as it
accounted for gas phase and sulfuric acid phase chemistry, the nucleation and growth of
aerosols, and expansion of the aerosol cloud. It then generated results showing the concentration of gases over time, the size distribution of aerosols, and the quantity of ash in the
volcanic clouds. In keeping with previous work, they found that the most important stratospheric burdens were sulfur dioxide, water vapor, and dust, yet the amounts in this eruption
were insufficient to affect the climate appreciably. At most, surface temperature in the
northern hemisphere decreased by 0.05°C.[11]

Volcano studies, such as those described above, were extremely useful in providing certain
data and tests of analytical tools. But it was now recognized that a direct comparison to
nuclear war was inappropriate, since sulfuric acid and silica dust have quite different absorption properties than dark smoke. Additionally, the distributions of particle sizes are different,
and warfare would produce fine particles from a great number of sources instead of from a
single location.[12] Only from some gigantic prehistoric eruptions was it possible to theorize
atmospheric opacities of the same order as those expected from NW.[13]

Ozone Depletion

Half a century ago, few would have thought that there was a connection between vehicles
propelled through the stratosphere and liquids propelled from pressurized spray cans. Nor
would anyone have been eccentric enough to add styrofoam coffee cups and home refrigerators to the list. But around 1970 the relationships began to appear.

One part of the story concerns a high-speed, high-flying aircraft called the supersonic
transport (SST). On 23 September 1969, President Richard Nixon announced his decision
to build the SST (already under prototype development for a few years) to continue "American leadership in air transport." But Nixon's approval was controversial, for the United
States already led in this technology with the Mach-3 military reconnaissance plane known
as the SR-71, and domestic airlines could buy the British-French Concorde to compete with
foreign carriers. Moreover, the United States' balance-of-payments problem could equally
well be addressed by selling subsonic aircraft abroad. These arguments were important, for
a panel of experts that advised the president's Office of Science and Technology had recommended termination of the development contracts. They felt that the American SST, the
already airborne Concorde, and the Soviet TU-144 would generate sonic booms far greater
than an unacceptable surface level of one pound per square foot, and should therefore be
prohibited from flying over the United States.[14]

The panel further noted dire economic predictions. Private financing for further
development and production of the airframe by Boeing and the engines by General Electric
seemed remote, and the US government was likely to lose its own substantial investment.
The SST also suffered from an exceedingly small (possibly unprofitable) payload coupled to

uncertainty in the number of passengers willing to pay the fare surcharge demanded for their swift flights. Economic and technological arguments of this sort dominated the committee's thoughts. Some environmental problems were mentioned frequently, as in the case of sonic booms, and others but briefly, as in the case of the effect on climate of moisture in the exhaust of a fleet of SSTs traveling at 60,000–70,000 feet. In the latter case, it was feared, ice crystals formed by the water vapor might reflect a significant amount of sunlight.[15]

Congress killed the American SST project in 1971, largely on economic grounds but also out of fear of a future filled with sonic booms.[16] But the connection of nitrogen oxides in SST exhaust to ozone depletion had already been made by Paul Crutzen and by Harold Johnston. And this recognition of ozone's importance was not diminished by a 1974 Department of Transportation report which concluded that fears of the SST's environmental impact were overdrawn.[17] Indeed, interest in ozone increased as the general public became aware of this trace gas' utility in filtering solar ultraviolet radiation. Without it, UV radiation, by damaging the surface cells of plants and animals, would harm crops, livestock, and other flora and fauna, and would increase the incidence of skin cancer in humans.[18]

By 1974, Mario Molina and F. Sherwood Rowland of the University of California at Irvine had detected the destruction of ozone by chlorofluorocarbons (CFCs). CFCs are placed in the atmosphere by a number of sources, including the coolant freon escaping from discarded or leaky refrigerators and air conditioners, the gases used to propel the contents of spray cans, and the gases used to make the bubbles in styrofoam products. CFCs are inexpensive, non-toxic, and non-flammable, and they remain gaseous over a wide range of suitable temperatures. Most significantly, they are remarkably stable, with a residence time in the atmosphere of perhaps 40–150 years. However, the portion that rises to the stratosphere will be photodissociated, yielding chlorine atoms that serve as recyclable catalysts for the removal of ozone.[19]

This potential for harm struck a resonant chord. The "war on cancer" and other medical concerns, including mercury in swordfish and tainted cranberries, were almost continually in the news at that time. Also, the environmental movement was in its vigorous infancy. Further, much public attention was accorded to Club of Rome's projections about the non-sustainable consumption rate of the world's resources and to E. F. Schumacher's economic concept that "small is beautiful."[20] Technological growth and the resultant change had numerous, familiar benefits. Now, however, their negative side was becoming increasingly apparent.[21]

Ozone depletion became a major environmental issue in the mid 1970s. This was odd in a way, as the harmful consequences were not yet measurable. It took much longer for legislatures to act on the well-documented effects of acid rain from smokestack emissions and of lead in gasoline. Though the universality of the havoc caused by diminished ozone might explain the relatively quick reaction, this is by no means certain. More likely, the science was clear-cut and the eventual dire consequences recognized as unavoidable. An interesting nuance is that a major use of fluorocarbons was regarded as a luxury that could be abandoned in the interest of environmental safety, especially when the industry could then claim to be environmentally sensitive.

By 1975, the "spray can war" was on.[22] This "war" pitted environmentalists against the giant chemical manufacturers DuPont and Allied-Signal, the producers of aerosol spray valves (invented by Richard Nixon's friend Robert Abplanalp), and the companies that filled the cans with paint, deodorant, whipped cream, shaving soap, hair spray, insecticide, disinfectant, polish, and numerous other consumer products. Though it might be necessary to disperse some of these liquids in a mist of tiny droplets, in most cases spraying them was widely regarded as little more than a convenience. Convenience in modern, industrial society, however, is big business. In 1973, for example, about 2.9 billion spray cans were filled in North America (half the world total), half of them using CFCs as propellants.[23]

There followed the usual statements by industry that more study was needed, and the expected scientific committee reports that warned of a danger, but declined to recommend immediate action. Nonetheless, in the face of legislation introduced in Congress and in several state legislatures, the "spray can war" was short-lived. Bowing to the threat of being labeled a foe of the environment, the spray-can industry cut its losses. It introduced other gases suitable as propellants or merely replaced the spray valve with a finger-operated pump, and the chemical companies continued to manufacture CFCs for their other applications. These other uses continued to expand, in the Third World as much as in the developed countries. Newer applications, including their use in solvents to clean electronic parts, kept global production on a positive growth curve. Then, discovery of the ozone "hole" above Antarctica in 1984, and its alleged connection to chlorine atoms freed in the stratosphere by the breakdown of CFCs, generated another assault on the chemical industry. This led 27 industrialized nations, meeting in Montreal, to conclude a treaty in September 1987 that called for a 50 percent reduction in CFC releases by the end of the century.

The persistence of ozone depletion over the South Pole, the persistence of CFCs in the atmosphere, and the flaws of the Montreal Protocol (few developing nations signed it) induced the signatories to go further. Meeting in London in June 1990, they agreed to stop using the five most common CFCs and several other ozone-eating chemicals by the year 2000, and to help Third World countries overcome their dependence on these compounds. By this time, DuPont and Allied-Signal, the two largest manufacturers of CFCs in the United States, announced that they would phase out their production.[24]

Note again that all this was accomplished before any documented harm could be attributed to ozone depletion. Some scientists who forcefully advocated banning CFCs, principally F. Sherwood Rowland, felt the sting of criticism that their science was flawed and that they had lost their objectivity.[25] Yet public policy was made on this incomplete scientific evidence—if "complete" is to mean only actual experience, excluding prediction. Proponents of NW met the same criticism, but failed to alter public policy. (The ozone scientists Crutzen, Molina, and Rowland were honored in 1995 with the Nobel Prize in Chemistry, and in 1989 Crutzen shared the prestigious Tyler Prize for environmental science.[26]) At first, the chemists Rowland and Molina had no professional contacts with atmospheric scientists. Similarly, interdisciplinary contacts were rare among the component sciences of NW, which of course is a major point of chapters 2 and 3.

Another theme in these chapters is the accumulation of relevant skills and knowledge by the nascent TTAPS group. The injection of ozone-eaters into the stratosphere need not, of course, be gradual. As I discussed in chapter 1, MacCracken and Chang investigated the effect of massive nitrogen oxide increases from nuclear fireballs. Another sudden source was the incandescent tail of a meteor as it fell through the atmosphere. A team that included Turco, Toon, and Pollack showed that the estimated 30 million metric tons (tonnes) of nitric oxide produced by the meteor that exploded over the Stony Tunguska River basin in Central Siberia on 30 June 1908 agreed well with measurements that implied an ozone decrease of roughly 30 percent.[27]

Planetary Studies

Studies of the solar system formed a large part of astronomy until the early twentieth century, when interest in galactic astronomy and in the new science of astrophysics, along with distaste for the controversy over the existence of canals on Mars and the inadequacies of available instrumentation for planetary physics, served to marginalize the field. Its return to the mainstream was not easy. The Soviet satellite Sputnik (1957) spurred the United States to comparable space efforts, but the new National Aeronautics and Space Administration found too few astronomers interested in some of its programs. In 1959, for example, NASA was unable to recruit all the space science expertise it wanted for planned lunar and planetary probes. For the first half of the 1960s, NASA's primary focus was on the Apollo lunar landing program. After about 1965, increased attention was directed to planetary missions. To rectify its personnel problems, NASA funded an extensive program of ground-based planetary astronomy, including the construction of high-quality instruments, and supported a large cadre of enthusiastic investigators.[28] Sagan and his students Pollack and Toon were involved in this rebirth of planetary science.

Sagan received a Ph.D. in astronomy and astrophysics from the University of Chicago in 1960. From 1962 to 1968 he was an assistant professor at Harvard University and a staff member of the Smithsonian Astrophysical Observatory in Cambridge, Massachusetts. In 1968 he moved to Cornell University, where he was an associate professor and then professor in the Center for Radiophysics and Space Research and director of the Laboratory for Planetary Studies. Pollack, Sagan's first graduate student, received his doctorate in astronomy from Harvard in 1965 and spent the next 3 years at the nearby Smithsonian Astrophysical Observatory before moving to Cornell (with his mentor) as a senior research associate. In 1970 he became a research scientist at NASA's Ames Research Center. In 1978 he became the chief scientist of the Climate Office at Ames and a member of NASA's Space Science

Advisory Committee. Toon, Pollack's younger colleague at Ames, earned a Ph.D. in physics from Cornell in 1975, served as a research associate at the National Research Council and then at Cornell, and in 1978 joined Ames as a research scientist. In 1997 he became a professor of atmospheric and oceanographic sciences at the University of Colorado. All three men had a long-standing interest in components and properties of planetary atmospheres, including clouds, aerosols, and radiative transfer, and by the time of their NW work Sagan and Pollack were veterans of several Mariner, Viking, and Voyager probes, orbiters, landers, or flybys of Venus, Mars, and the outer solar system.

Among the planets, Mars provided the most useful information for NW studies. Its noted dust storms, for example, could be compared to the dust that would be lofted by nuclear explosions on Earth. Mariner 9, which began orbiting the planet in 1971, carried an infrared spectroscopy experiment that showed large diurnal temperature variations at least to an altitude of 30 km, both during and after the planet-wide dust storm. This implied that the winds possessed a strong tidal component. Atmospheric dust on Mars was found to consist of about 60 percent silicon oxide, comparable to Earth's continental crust.[29]

Photographs of the Martian surface, which showed striking evidence of flowing water at one time in the planet's history, gave credence to earlier speculation by Sagan that Mars oscillates between two quite different climates.[30] In one, there was abundant water, higher temperatures, higher atmospheric pressure, and the possibility of life. At present the planet is in an ice age, with ice caps holding virtually all atmospheric moisture. Sagan, Toon, and another colleague used Mariner 9 data to amplify this argument, looking, for example, at albedo changes in the ice caps as a driving mechanism of Martian climatic instability, with the added possibility of better understanding terrestrial climatic instability.[31]

Because the axis of Mars's rotation is inclined from the perpendicular to its orbital plane, as is that of Earth, Mars experiences seasons. In the Martian spring, the bright areas become progressively brighter, and the dark ones darker. Explanations for this phenomenon included the growth of biological organisms and chemical changes. In 1969 Sagan and Pollack argued for a different process: windblown dust. Dust particle diameter was the source of the photometric differences, they said, and variations were due to particle movement by strong winds.[32] More than a decade later, in their NW work, they would continue this interest in the transport of dust grains of various sizes and the way light is reflected by these particles depending on their sizes.

A team led by Pollack reported in 1976 on its use of a general circulation model to predict Martian winds.[33] In 1977, with Toon and Sagan, he used Mariner 9 orbiter data to infer physical properties of the dust storm particles.[34] Two years later, another Pollack-led group combined such information with optical depth measurements from two Viking landers to define the radiative properties of the suspended dust particles at various wavelengths. (Optical depth, τ, is a measure of the opacity of the atmosphere to radiation of a particular wavelength. The intensity I of the radiation after it passes through a medium is given by the formula $I = I_0/e^\tau$, where I_0 is the initial radiation and e is the base of the natural logarithms. An optical depth of 0 means the medium is transparent. An optical depth of 1 means that light intensity is reduced to $1/e$ of the incident beam, or about 37 percent of the original value.[35]) In one analysis, Pollack and colleagues used these properties in a one-dimensional radiative convective model, finding that the model's predictions matched lander data on the atmospheric temperature structure only when they incorporated the vertical effects of large movements of air masses with those of radiation and thermal convection.[36]

Pollack continued to apply different models to features of the Martian atmosphere, using, for example, a two-dimensional model of the zonal mean circulation (rather than a more complex three-dimensional general circulation model) "to understand the first-order effects of global dust storms on the general circulation."[37] Again, these detailed studies of planetary meteorology, and familiarity in the use of computer circulation models, would prove valuable in the forthcoming NW studies.

Dinosaur Extinction and the Asteroid Impact Hypothesis

From the fossil record, paleontologists had long known that dinosaurs became extinct about 65 million years ago, at the so-called K-T boundary (that is, end of the Cretaceous Period and beginning of the Tertiary Period). What eluded them was an explanation for the event. Speculation—and it was little more than that—centered around a climatic, atmospheric, or sea-level change, a global geomagnetic reversal, or an astronomical event that somehow changed temperatures or destroyed vegetation, killing most creatures outright or condemning them to starvation.

As the understanding of ozone's role in the atmosphere improved, additional conjectures were advanced for the disappearance of many faunal species. In 1974, Malvin Ruderman of Columbia University modified an idea that had first been floated two decades earlier: that a nearby supernova had emitted cosmic rays or x-rays that had markedly increased ionizing radiation in Earth's stratosphere. In the same way that nuclear explosions and hot air from jet aircraft exhausts produce nitric oxides, this radiation had generated these catalytic destroyers of ozone. Earth, as a result, had been bathed in lethal amounts of ultraviolet radiation.[38]

A related mechanism was proposed in 1976 by a group that included Paul Crutzen, then working in Boulder at both the National Oceanic and Atmospheric Administration's Environmental Research Laboratories and the National Center for Atmospheric Research. Evidence had accumulated that showed a connection between the extinction of marine and terrestrial fauna and reversals of Earth's magnetic field. More than a decade earlier, it had been suggested that during these geologically brief changeover periods a much weakened magnetic field would fail to adequately shield Earth's living creatures from galactic cosmic rays. This effect, however, was later calculated to be minor. The new proposal was that protons emitted during solar flares would produce nitric oxide in the stratosphere, leading to ozone depletion and excessive ultraviolet light, as described above. Normally, the effect is minimized because the geomagnetic field deflects protons to the higher latitudes. If an intense proton event in the eleven-year solar cycle coincided with a polarity reversal, however, the ozone shield would be more severely attacked. The group noted that about one-third of living species vanished as the Cretaceous ended, during a period of polarity reversals.[39]

In 1980 the subject of dinosaur extinction got a big boost from a retired nuclear physicist, his geologist son, and two nuclear chemists. Luis Alvarez, Walter Alvarez, Frank Asaro, and Helen Michel, all of the University of California at Berkeley, proposed that an asteroid had smashed into Earth at the end of the Cretaceous Period and had lofted enough dust (10–100 times the mass of the projectile) to darken the skies for several years. Photosynthesis had stopped, they reasoned, plants had died, and many herbiferous and carnivorous species had in turn became extinct. Those that survived into the Tertiary did so due perhaps to hibernation, or to feeding on water-borne nutrients, decaying vegetation, or insects, or by some other marginal means, while some plants regenerated from seeds, spores, and root systems.[40]

What set this proposal apart from previous ones was a healthy measure of credible, hard evidence. Iridium, an element barely found in the crust because of its affinity for iron, which eons ago carried it down into Earth's molten core, appears in unusual abundance in the one-centimeter-thick layer of clay that marks the K-T boundary. Particularly good examples were located in deep-sea limestones now visible in a gorge near the northern Italian town of Gubbio (where Francis of Assisi is said to have talked a fierce wolf out of terrorizing the region), at a site south of Copenhagen, and at a site in New Zealand. Neutron activation analysis and x-ray fluorescence measurements showed that iridium concentration increased in this thin clay layer by a factor of about 30 at Gubbio, 160 in Denmark, and 20 in New Zealand. No terrestrial source or mechanism for concentration could be suggested. But the fact that meteorites have a relatively high percentage of the metal suggested an extraterrestrial origin.[41]

A slow, steady deposition of meteoritic dust would not account for the centimeter-thick layer. Even more, the extinctions, which were worldwide, seemingly demanded a sudden event. The Alvarez group eliminated the possibility of a supernova by showing that plutonium-244, which was expected to be blown off in a supernova explosion, was undetectable in the layer, and that the measured ratio of iridium isotopes had a solar system, not a supernova, value. The most likely scenario, they concluded, was that an asteroid about 10 kilometers in diameter had struck Earth with kinetic energy equivalent to 10^8 megatons of TNT (about 10,000 times the yields in the superpowers' nuclear arsenals), injecting dust from the 200-km-wide impact crater into the stratosphere, where it had then spread around the world. Astronomical data on the many asteroids whose orbits cross that of Earth showed the mean collision time for an asteroid with a diameter of 10 km is 100 million years, an acceptable estimate for the K-T extinction 65 million years ago and for the other four major extinctions in the 570 million years of the fossil record since the Pre-Cambrian period.[42]

So much interest was generated by this proposal that it spawned more than 2,000 articles and books during the next decade.[43] The variety of new information was impressive. One study found that, assuming that 99 percent of sunlight was blocked, the widespread extinction of marine plankton at the end of the Cretaceous would have occurred in 104 days if the impact happened in January, and 33 days if in July or August—well within the several years of darkness predicted by the Alvarez team.[44] Walter Alvarez and his colleagues soon reported that several hundred iridium measurements at 36 sites around the world confirmed the anomalous amounts of the metal at the K-T boundary, and indeed that iridium had been found at extraterrestrial impact sites in the Pliocene and Eocene periods. They added that an unknown oceanic process that might have concentrated iridium was now ruled out by the detection of abnormal quantities in non-marine sediments, and they shortened the predicted period of darkness from a few years to a few months.[45]

Isotopic ratios of other platinum-family elements found at the boundary added support to the idea of an extraterrestrial source.[46] So too did statistical evidence that extinctions occurred about every 26–30 million years, suggesting periodic intersection by Earth with swarms of comets, meteors, and other objects held in orbit by the Sun's gravitational attraction.[47] Not least impressive was the detection of a layer of carbon coincident with the K-T iridium; it appeared that the impact had triggered a global fire.[48]

The idea of a collision would be enhanced if the site of the crater was found. Because most of Earth is covered by oceans with poorly mapped floors, and because considerable areas of the bottom have been subducted under the continental plates since the time of K-T, the task is daunting. Nonetheless, potential sites have been proposed, particularly in the Caribbean Sea (where shocked quartz has been found that could only have been specially deformed by the enormous pressures of an intense blow) and on Mexico's Yucatan Peninsula (where a huge ring of sinkholes associated with a gigantic crater has been mapped).[49] In 1997, geologists claimed to have found the "smoking gun": asteroid debris in sediment cores drilled in 8,500 feet of water off Florida's eastern coast. The debris from an impact in the Gulf of Mexico had washed across the land mass, they said, settling in layers of predicted materials.[50]

The impact concept received further support in 1994 from the collision of Comet Shoemaker-Levy 9 with Jupiter. The comet broke apart as it entered the gaseous planet's envelope, a two-mile-wide fragment creating a stunning explosion estimated by astronomers to have a yield of 6 million megatons. Yet this impact was small relative to the blow that created the 186-mile-wide Chicxulub crater in Yucatan, allegedly the dinosaur extinction event. Eugene Shoemaker estimated the latter projectile as likely three times as large, with 27 times as much energy.[51]

Though the impact hypothesis held by far the most vocal adherents, some specialists (mostly geologists and paleontologists) remained unconvinced. Global iridium anomalies had not been found at the times of all extinctions, for example, and there are impact craters without shocked quartz and without regional extinctions.[52] Another difficulty was that for some species extinction seems to have been too gradual to be explained by a sudden catastrophe; some populations declined over millions of years. Still another obstacle was that iridium might have been concentrated by organic matter and deposited by the mass mortality of plankton.

Volcanism was the alternative mechanism most discussed. In prehistoric times, volcanoes erupted on a scale unseen in historic times. Huge "mantle plumes" of molten rock poured through Earth's crust, depositing 2 million cubic kilometers of lava in the Deccan Traps of India. Iridium might have risen with the magma, for samples of gas from the active Kilauea volcano on Hawaii show concentrations of the element. The killing agent could have been volcanic dust that blocked sunlight, or acids, or fires, although the geological record on this is not clear.[53] Some combination of meteoric impact, volcanic eruption, or another unspecified mechanism might have been responsible for the changes seen at the K-T boundary. By the mid 1990s, it was argued that the impact hypothesis, though fascinating and greatly hyped, had solved a non-problem. The evidence for impact-induced extinctions was claimed to be less and less convincing, while familiar biological, chemical, and environmental changes connected to traditional geology were said to suffice.[54] Further doubt about an asteroid arose in 2004, when a core sample taken from the Yucatan crater suggested that this particular impact had occurred some 300,000 years before the K-T boundary.[55]

This brief survey of recent work on dinosaur extinction depicts the main lines of investigation but necessarily omits many other ideas and discoveries. Its purpose, of course, is to show the subject's usefulness to NW studies. The original concept (1980) of the Alvarez team, with its dust-darkened planet, is quite similar to the early views on NW put forth by the TTAPS group (1983). Additionally, TTAPS members were involved in research on impact phenomena and constructed a unique computer model that was critical to their subsequent work. In 1982, a team of scientists that included all the members of TTAPS except Sagan used this one-dimensional aerosol physics model to study the amount of light reaching Earth through an optically thick dust cloud and the resulting surface temperatures. Most of the dust, they found, would coagulate into micrometer-size particles and descend within 3–6 months. Curiously, this was largely independent of other factors, including "initial altitude, initial particle size, initial mass, atmospheric vertical diffusive mixing rate, or rainout rate." For 1–6 months it would be too dark to see, and photosynthesis would be halted for 2–12 months. Although the oceans' large heat capacity would limit surface cooling of the seas by only a few degrees, continental interiors would fall below freezing for 4–24 months. Obviously these would be prime conditions for continental extinctions, and equally clearly the investigative technique was just as appropriate for NW as for dinosaur extinction.[56] Though the impact concept did not inspire the NW interpretation, it surely gave it much impetus.

No reasonable person would have logically connected spray can propellants, supersonic aircraft, and styrofoam coffee cups. In like manner, no credible scientist in the 1970s would have linked the effects of nuclear weapons, particle microphysics, atmospheric chemistry, fire and smoke research, volcanic eruptions, ozone depletion, planetary studies, and dinosaur extinction. Yet knowledge developed in each of these areas, the ways in which the interactions were seen, and the expertise that jelled around a new breed of atmospheric or space scientists enabled their merger in the spectacular prediction of the NW phenomenon. The whole was indeed greater than the sum of the parts.

II Science, Politics, and Carl Sagan: Through 1983

4 The Origin of Nuclear Winter

As the historian of science Spencer Weart pointed out, humans since prehistoric times have linked severe weather and climatic conditions to human transgressions, such as a violation of a taboo or a failed offering to the gods. The biblical flood punished humans for their sins. Chinese emperors were blamed for terrible floods. Europeans responded to drought with days of penance.

By the middle of the twentieth century, scientists had given the public more serious reason to connect widespread disaster to human activities. Nuclear weapons seemed to pose the possibility that civilization would be destroyed by blast, heat, and radioactivity. Extrapolating from this potential catastrophe, fundamentalist preachers, authors of books that described allegedly real cataclysms in Earth's past, and films involving mutant monsters that were created by radiation were enthusiastically received. Also given respectful hearings were scientific theories of an approaching ice age or, conversely, melting of the Arctic Ocean's ice pack. Increasing levels of carbon dioxide in the atmosphere, causing a greenhouse effect, made sense and were reported widely by the media. Clearly, humans could affect the climate.[1] The credibility given to the possibility of a NW phenomenon surely was conditioned by this context.

Soot

In the 1970s, ozone depletion was the conspicuous new ingredient for those interested in predicting the long-range effects of nuclear weapons. Alarmed by the initial uncertainty, the Arms Control and Disarmament Agency asked the National Academy of Sciences to assess the effects of stratospheric ozone. In 1975 the NAS confirmed the potential for stunning impoverishment of ozone in the stratosphere.[2] Although it was a limited study, giving ecological and agricultural consequences only cursory attention, the report may be considered the first to assess global atmospheric phenomena. The Arms Control and Disarmament Agency publicized these results in a 1976 booklet titled *Worldwide Effects of Nuclear War*.

Ozone remained prominent into the next decade. For example, the dangers for organisms of increased ultraviolet radiation were vividly described to a large audience at a 1980

meeting of Physicians for Social Responsibility in San Francisco, and testimony before
Congress in 1982 largely confirmed the continued validity of the 1975 NAS report's findings
on ozone depletion (despite a trend toward smaller-yield weapons).[3] But dinosaur extinction
made far larger headlines as the 1980s began, and attention to the dust lofted by an
asteroid's impact soon displaced ozone in the calculations of the nuclear-war-effects
community.

Quick to recognize the new significance of dust, Vice Admiral William J. Moran (USN-
Retired) encouraged discussion and preliminary calculations at the NAS in March 1981.
Moran, although not trained as a scientist, was then a staff member of the National Research
Council (NRC), the NAS's operating arm. His long military career included a number of
technical assignments: duty at the Naval Weapons Center in China Lake, California, naval
aide to the assistant secretary of the Navy for research and development, director of the
Navy space program, and director of research, development, testing, and evaluation for the
Navy. Spurred by Moran's enthusiasm, an ad hoc Academy panel met in December 1981
and April 1982.[4]

On a parallel track, Owen Brian Toon of the Ames Research Center presented the work
on dust that he and his colleagues had done to a dinosaur extinction meeting in Snowbird,
Utah, in October 1981. Another NRC staff member, Lee Hunt, was there, and he later invited
Toon to the forthcoming April 1982 NAS meeting. Recognizing that Richard Turco, through
his work for the defense contractor Research and Development Associates (RDA), knew far
more than he about nuclear explosions, Toon deputized his colleague to attend. In preparation, they sought some quantification. Turco estimated the amount of dust a single explosion might loft, Toon entered the number into a model that generated the thickness of a
cloud, and the Ames climatologist Thomas Ackerman calculated the surface temperatures.
To their consternation, "nuclear dust" left Earth just as cold as "dinosaur dust."[5]

At the April 1982 gathering, new concerns about smoke and dust led the group to recommend a full-scale NAS study of their effects; the 1975 NAS report on nuclear war was clearly
out of date. The Defense Nuclear Agency, the DoD's branch specializing in nuclear matters,
agreed to sponsor the investigation. This was a normal pattern: NAS-NRC would suggest a
study and then find a government agency willing to pay for it. Raising the issue of smoke
at the meeting in April 1982 was not mere happenstance. Panel members probably had
heard through the grapevine that *Ambio* (the Royal Swedish Academy of Sciences' journal
of environmental management, technology, and the natural sciences) was about to publish
a special issue on the consequences of nuclear war. Indeed, Turco brought to the meeting
a draft of the *Ambio* issue's most important paper (by Paul Crutzen and John Birks), which
highlighted the danger of massive fires. The *Ambio* issue did not duplicate the recent reports
by the Arms Control and Disarmament Agency, the Office of Technology Assessment, the
Senate, the United Nations, and some individuals. Although various effects of nuclear explosions had been studied for decades, large uncertainties remained, for often the "data" were
little more than best guesses.[6]

Ambio's special issue was the brainchild of its American editor, Jeannie Peterson. At a conference she had attended in 1980, a speaker had labeled the results of nuclear war "unimaginable." This had challenged Peterson to see if they could be specified more concretely than she had found in the host of recent surveys. In particular, she felt that global environmental consequences—"the effects of nuclear war on the land, air and water of the planet"—had not been treated adequately. In retrospect Peterson admitted the presumptuousness of the task, for she had no government agency or academic institute behind her to marshal resources and personnel. Nor was an attempt to raise funds very successful; foundations were uniformly uninterested, and the only external support was $20,000 from the Environment Commission of the Swedish Department of Agriculture. But Peterson was inspired to pick a vigorous advisory board, which in turn selected a strong slate of authors and referees. The advisors posed for the authors a scenario involving about 5,750 MT of nuclear explosions and assumed that the greatest menace to the ecosystem would be from radioactive fallout.[7] The choice of such a war did not, of course, mean that this was the most likely form of future conflict. It merely was a reasonable possibility, one that allowed calculations to be made.

The assumption of fallout's primacy in devastating the environment was challenged by the Crutzen-Birks paper, and had Peterson not been obliged to meet a deadline (a condition for the $20,000 grant) she would have restructured the special issue of *Ambio* around the danger of fire and smoke. Paul Crutzen (the Dutch atmospheric chemist who studied the connection between nitrogen oxides and ozone photochemistry) had moved from the University of Stockholm to Oxford and then to Boulder, and by this time he was director of the Air Chemistry Division of the Max Planck Institute for Chemistry in Mainz, Germany. John Birks was an associate professor of chemistry at the University of Colorado in Boulder and a fellow of that university's Cooperative Institute for Research in Environmental Sciences. As a graduate student at Berkeley he too had been concerned with nitrogen oxides and ozone. The two apparently met in Boulder and had mutual interests strong enough to propel Birks to Mainz as a visiting scientist in 1981–82.[8]

In view of Crutzen's expertise with ozone and his previous residence in Sweden,[9] it was logical for the *Ambio* project to look to him for the latest assessment of the threat to ozone by nuclear war, just as it was reasonable for him to draw Birks into the investigation. They quickly found that, because the explosive yields of nuclear weapons had decreased over the years (as accuracies had increased), *Ambio*'s reference scenario postulated that most warheads detonated would be smaller than a megaton. In such a war, relatively small amounts of nitrogen oxides would be injected into the stratosphere, and the ozone layer would not be directly affected by the explosions. A major new understanding, however, was that ozone concentrations would rise dramatically in the troposphere, with resulting photochemical smog threatening agricultural crops. Yet sunlight was necessary to power the smog reactions, and Cruzen and Birks wondered whether particulate matter from fires would not filter out some light.[10]

With a February 1982 deadline for submission of a draft, Crutzen and Birks decided to look at smoke. They knew that nuclear explosions could ignite fires in both forests and cities, so they searched for scientific reports on aerosol physics and radiative transfer. To their astonishment, they found virtually nothing.[11] By default, they focused on forest fires, for Crutzen, in perhaps his only experimental field endeavor, had studied the atmospheric effects of fires in the tropics. A few years earlier, as a friend jokingly reported, Crutzen "went down to Brazil and then sat in a Jeep directing a graduate student with smoke collectors, telling him to run by that burning tree or between those shrubs."[12] That background was adequate for Crutzen and Birks to point out the potential harm of "the many fires that would be ignited by the thousands of nuclear explosions in cities, forests, agricultural fields, and oil and gas fields."[13]

Lack of time and expertise caused Crutzen and Birks to concentrate largely on forest fire effects and to omit attention to such factors as particle coagulation and proper optical calculations. Yet it must be remembered that their work was a first cut at the problem. Based on the literature, they estimated that a million square kilometers, an area the size of Denmark, Norway, and Sweden combined, would burn in the northern hemisphere. The carbon dioxide from these fires would not be significant relative to amounts normally generated, but atmospheric carbon monoxide would more than double and more nitrogen oxides would be released than are formed in the nuclear fireballs—an amount roughly equal to the annual industrial emission of nitrogen oxides. Since nitrogen oxides (abbreviated NO_x) play a major role in the production of tropospheric ozone (depletion of ozone occurs in the stratosphere), widespread photochemical smog conditions could occur.

The mass of particulate matter generated by these forest fires also was enormous—300 million tonnes. That is comparable to the annual global production, human-caused and by natural fires, of particles smaller than 3 micrometers in diameter. More significantly, its composition was about 55 percent tar, 25 percent soot, and 20 percent ash, indicating a very strong ability to absorb sunlight. Assuming what they felt were reasonable figures for the amount of fossil fuels stored mostly in cities (1.5 billion tonnes), the duration of the fires, size of the particles, and residency time aloft (mostly in the troposphere), Crutzen and Birks dropped their bombshell:

. . . the average sunlight penetration to the ground will be reduced by a factor between 2 and 150 at noontime in the summer. This would imply that much of the Northern Hemisphere would be darkened in the daytime for an extended period of time following the nuclear exchange.[14]

The darkness would devastate agriculture, a conclusion that led to Crutzen's being called "the Jeremiah of nuclear winter."[15] Peaceniks had been saying it all along, but now quantitative science reaffirmed the view that nuclear war was unwinnable.

Surprisingly, this was the first time that smoke's attenuation of sunlight was considered quantitatively in a study of the effects of nuclear war.[16] Why had this insight not been reached earlier? Others had forecast widespread fires in the wake of nuclear explosions, but the logical step to order-of-magnitude calculations of regional and global effects had not been taken. True, the numbers had not been readily available, but there was more to it. Fire researchers, it seems, were a fairly insular group, not used to crossing disciplinary lines, and a principal source of their funding for nuclear-induced fire effects, the Federal Emergency Management Agency, was not an innovative organization.[17] One did not expect bold ventures from this combination.

There was, moreover, the weight of tradition. With the development and testing of fusion weapons, and with their introduction into the arsenal in large numbers in the 1950s, there had been debate within the community of nuclear strategists about the best yardstick of destruction. Blast was selected because a blast always occurred and (if close enough to the ground) would do calculable damage. Prompt radioactive fallout was relegated to a secondary role because its amount was too dependent on local conditions, especially weather, even though long-term fallout was the subject of widespread concern. Fires ignited by the explosion also were placed in a secondary position by defense analysts, largely because their course was believed to be uncertain (although a recent study claims that institutional rigidity was more to blame). The public concurred and exhibited little interest in this effect of nuclear weapons. The scientific community likewise showed little inclination to quantify the consequences of fire.[18]

No person or group had the focus or the mission to gather data on quantities of fuel in cities and the amount of smoke produced, then to distribute it globally, calculate the optical depth, and determine if this was significant. Attention was largely limited to local and regional problems.[19] By the early 1980s, however, time had provided a catalyst for change: the existence of a cadre of atmospheric scientists with some years of experience in dealing with a range of problems in atmospheric chemistry and particle microphysics. They thought globally and quantitatively, were enriched by studies of planetary atmospheres, and benefited from the development, starting in the 1970s, of three-dimensional computer models. With the recent maturity of this scientific specialty, its technical skills could now be applied to new challenges as they arose.

The publication of *Ambio*'s special issue in June 1982 initiated a blizzard of press conferences, news stories, meetings that highlighted the Crutzen-Birks report, reprints of the journal's contents in other languages, further studies, and hearings before a committee of the US House of Representatives.[20] There were critics of the conclusions, to be sure, most slowly raising their voices but some arguing even then that comparable masses of volcanic ejecta had shown relatively minor climatic effects, or that it was unlikely that fires would burn for the 2 months that had been predicted. Others, however, recognized the greater light-absorption property of black smoke and the way in which the absorbed light would heat the surrounding air.[21]The prospect of soot in the atmosphere cast a figurative pall on those who believed in a quick recovery after a nuclear war.

TTAPS

Fanning the spark given to fire research by the Crutzen-Birks paper, a small group of atmo-spheric scientists and astrophysicists also mulled over the problem. Their story began in late 1971, when the Mariner 9 spacecraft, the first artificial satellite to orbit a planet besides Earth, arrived at Mars. Aboard was an instrument to test infrared radiation at different wavelengths. This was fortunate, for Mars was in the midst of a huge, months-long dust storm that obscured television pictures. (Mariner's engineers had predicted the spacecraft would operate only for 3 months; luckily, they were too pessimistic.)

The device that concerns us, an infrared (IR) interferometric spectrometer, earned its keep by metering the intensity of infrared radiation from the planet. These measurements trans-lated into profiles over time of temperatures at the surface and at different elevations. When the dust clouds were thick, atmospheric temperatures were higher than normal and surface temperatures lower—just as one would expect. As the clouds thinned, the atmosphere cooled and the surface warmed—again as expected. Sunlight was the warming agency, and it heated whatever lay in its path.

Carl Sagan (at Cornell) and his former student James Pollack (who recently had moved to the Ames Research Center) were members of the NASA team studying data from Mariner 9. They made preliminary calculations of how much atmospheric warming and surface cooling a specified amount of Martian dust should cause, but they moved on to other experiments when the storm subsided a few months later and the surface was revealed.

Science often progresses by analogies, and Sagan and his students had uncovered much of interest by comparing and contrasting Earth and other planets. Sagan reflected that Mars and Earth bore certain similarities. Atmospheric pressure in Earth's stratosphere is close to that on the surface of Mars, they both rotate once in 24 hours, and their axes are tilted to their orbital planes by about the same amount. It seemed reasonable to test techniques that worked in the investigation of Mars on the study of Earth.

Large volcanic eruptions were known to cause small but measurable declines in global temperature, usually less than a degree Celsius. The stratospheric burden of volcanic aerosols was becoming better understood to be mostly sulfuric acid and silicate particles of known size that remained aloft until gravity slowly pulled them down. Toon, Sagan's student whose investigation of volcanic dust was an important part of his doctoral dissertation, joined his mentor, along with Pollack and others, in confirming that the techniques that specified the Martian dust and temperature relationships worked equally well for the terrestrial tempera-ture dependence on volcanic particles.[22]

This study of volcanoes involved an early use of increasingly sophisticated computer modeling techniques, in this case applied to radiative transfer (heat exchange by radiation) reactions. At intervals over the year, Toon, Pollack, and Sagan discussed applying their techniques to another terrestrial problem—nuclear explosion dust—but its complexities made them bide their time. Aside from the fact that the Ames scientists knew nothing about nuclear weapons, they were not sure how to quantify the materials pumped into the atmosphere by explosions.[23] They were jarred into action by the asteroid-impact hypothesis of dinosaur extinction in 1980. Here was yet another example of sunlight's being attenuated by dust in the atmosphere, and another opportunity to refine their skills.

Sagan was busy filming his *Cosmos* astronomy series for television, but Pollack and Toon were joined in their study of asteroid-impact dust by Richard Turco, Thomas Ackerman, and a few others. After receiving a Ph.D. in electrical engineering from the University of Illinois in 1971, Turco spent most of a year as an NRC postdoctoral fellow at Ames before moving on to the defense contractor Research and Development Associates. In 1986 Turco received a MacArthur Foundation "genius grant" (there is no application; 5 years' handsome support comes as a surprise). In 1988 he became a professor of atmospheric sciences at UCLA. While at Ames, Turco focused on the chemistry and structure of the upper atmosphere and on radiation phenomena. At RDA he became expert in nuclear weapon effects in the atmosphere, while simultaneously continuing his collaboration with Robert Whitten, Pollack, and others at Ames. Of greatest importance, he was involved in a series of reports with Toon on developing and applying the state-of-the-art one-dimensional stratospheric aerosol model that I mentioned in chapter 2.[24]

Similarly, Toon collaborated with Thomas Ackerman, another Ames atmospheric scientist with strong skills in radiation, climate, and computer programming. Ackerman had graduated in 1976 from the University of Washington and then spent 3 years at the Australian Numerical Meteorology Research Center in Melbourne. Pollack and Toon, whose work focused more on stratospheric aerosols, welcomed Ackerman's experience with tropospheric aerosols (air pollution). Having a model for the problem, Ackerman and Toon became interested in the optical properties of an insoluble particle with water condensed on the outside. Fortuitously, their examination of particulate carbon informed them of the combined droplet's behavior before Crutzen and Birks turned everyone's attention to soot from nuclear-ignited fires. Related to this, Ackerman studied the consequences of the Soviet Union's location of a significant amount of coal-burning industry in the Arctic, where the atmosphere is extremely stable. This examination of Arctic haze added yet another dimension to their arsenal of tools to investigate the NW phenomenon. Again, TTAPS without Sagan, primed by computer modeling and studies of Martian and volcanic dust, were able to show that the dust cloud generated by impact of an asteroid could indeed fulfill the conditions of cold and dark that the Alvarez team specified for dinosaur extinction. These results were presented to the second meeting of the ad hoc NAS panel in April 1982.[25] However, in 1981, long before these conclusions were in hand, TTAPS had already decided to tackle the ultimate question: the effects on the atmosphere of nuclear war.[26]

By the early 1980s, Turco had a decade of experience with nuclear explosion phenomena, including access to the best data available on the amount of soil particles lofted by ground bursts and their size distribution. The Ames scientists, volcano experts all, suddenly found themselves occupied with the eruption of El Chichon. Yet it was through wide knowledge and ability, not default, that Turco became the point man of the TTAPS team. In March 1982, at a Defense Nuclear Agency–sponsored meeting at Kaman/TEMPO (a defense think tank in Santa Barbara), he was shown a draft of the Crutzen-Birks paper for *Ambio*. Two weeks later, he and a colleague discussed its conclusions before the ad hoc NAS panel. This led Admiral Moran to write immediately to Frank Press, president of the National Academy of Sciences and chairman of the National Research Council, urging a major review of nuclear effects that would emphasize smoke in addition to dust.[27] The Crutzen-Birks paper, thus, did not instigate the TTAPS investigation but added a crucial dimension to it.

Sagan, too, learned in advance of the Crutzen-Birks work. Early in 1982, while in England attending a meeting of International Physicians for the Prevention of Nuclear War, he heard of it from the British health physicist Joseph Rotblat, who was a member of the *Ambio* advisory panel. Indeed, as is common for those well "plugged in to" the network of scientists in a field, others also provided Sagan with the news.[28]

Clearly, ash and soot must be taken into consideration in TTAPS's calculations. Their efforts received informal encouragement from the NAS ad hoc committee, and Toon and Turco were asked to join the panel preparing the full-scale NAS-NRC report (which appeared in December 1984; the panel first met in March 1983, by which time TTAPS's initial calculations had long been completed).[29]

The TTAPS group congealed in a logical fashion, drawing together people with complimentary skills who were known to one another and available. Yet two things distinguished the team. Their climate model, a radiative-convective model, was not unique; many others had one. But, initially, only they had an aerosol model capable of determining the density of the clouds and their lifetime, developed of course for their earlier planetary atmospheres and volcano work. It was lucky that both models (both one-dimensional) were in the same laboratory. Secondly, unlike Crutzen and Birks, they were able to quantify the mass of urban particulate matter lofted into the atmosphere. Turco's supreme contribution was quantifying smoke production. Sequentially, Toon and Turco made the initial rough calculations for nuclear explosions. Then they were joined by Pollack and Ackerman, who were creating a more sophisticated radiative transfer model for volcano problems than the one that Ackerman had previously used. Sagan, the intellectual parent of the question, was naturally included; he provided ideas, not calculations. Turco upgraded the aerosol model at RDA so it could handle more than one material, such as dust *and* smoke, and they switched to it. While all these models could have been run on a less powerful computer, use of the Cray supercomputer at Ames to crunch numbers for a variety of scenarios made life much easier, and the TTAPS team covered much ground in 1982.[30]

One other factor distinguished the team's spiritual leader. As Sagan's biographer William Poundstone has noted, the problem was of the sort that the astrophysicist pursued throughout his career: searching for small, perhaps unlikely, effects of enormous consequence. Before the Apollo 11 manned mission to the Moon, for example, Sagan argued forcefully that the astronauts should be quarantined upon their return, on the slim chance that lunar microbes might contaminate Earth. So too with NW; we were too ignorant to take chances.[31] NW, for Sagan, thus was *politically* different from his past activities, but not scientifically unique.

A summary of the individual components in their study was prepared by Sagan and Turco. The great variety and mass of data underscored how essential a large-capacity computer was to the project:

properties of urban fires
types and amounts of flammable materials in cities
composition and optical properties of smoke
toxic compounds released by urban fires
heights of smoke plumes and extent of "black rain"
physical and optical properties of nuclear-war-generated dust
nuclear-war/volcanic-eruption analogs
oxides of nitrogen and water vapor content of nuclear clouds
intermediate timescale radioactive fallout
nuclear-war-related ozone depletion and resulting ultraviolet exposure
dust and smoke particle microphysical processes
perturbations of atmospheric visible and infrared radiation fields
changes in air temperatures and light levels
meteorological implications of smoke and dust injection
interhemispheric transport of nuclear-war-generated aerosols
sensitivity of effects to the size of nuclear arsenals and targeting
sensitivity of climatic perturbations to uncertainties in physical parameters
analogs of nuclear winter in phenomena on other planets, especially Martian dust storms.[32]

In short, they first prepared a source model which specified the quantities of soot, dust, toxins, and radioactive debris that would be produced under several different war scenarios. These became the ingredients in a microphysical model that determined cloud density of these aerosols and amount of radioactivity over time. An optical model next examined the opacity of the clouds while a photochemical model looked at ozone and nitrogen oxide levels. Finally, a radiative transport model correlated the opacities with temperature predictions.[33] Turco prepared the smoke and dust estimates and ran the microphysical processes; his colleagues at Ames did much of the radiation and climate work. Ackerman was at the end of the chain. When the others decided what was lofted into the atmosphere, how high it went, and its residence time, he performed the climatology calculations. Once the results began to accumulate, they recognized that, for credibility, they had better become more expert in the composition of the superpowers' arsenals and the types of possible nuclear encounters, or scenarios. Fortunately, Turco was able to tap the expertise of colleagues at RDA in these subjects.[34]

TTAPS (less Ackerman at this point) planned to present their initial results at the American Geophysical Union's meeting in San Francisco, in December 1982, and an abstract of this paper appeared earlier in the journal *Eos*. Under the title "Global consequences of nuclear 'warfare,' " they intended to discuss long-term radioactive fallout, ozone depletion by bomb-generated nitrogen oxides, and climate changes due to large injections into the atmosphere of dust, smoke, and NO_x. They claimed that some consequences were of far greater danger than the immediate effects of nuclear explosions (the familiar blast, heat, immediate gamma and x-ray radiation, and local radioactivity). Surface temperatures could fall 10°C or more, ionizing radiation doses might be in the tens of rems (0.5 rem is the annual maximum recommended for the general population), and ultraviolet radiation could increase tenfold. Added to the social problems of food and water scarcity, lack of shelter and medical care, and disease, these "atmospheric" burdens would result in widespread human death and the possible extinction of some land and water species.[35] However, to the surprise of the audience at the AGU meeting, the paper was not given. The administration of the Ames Research Center forced withdrawal of the report.

Conference in Cambridge, April 1983

Blocked from the scientific forum of the AGU meeting, TTAPS created their own forum. Because their work was so multifaceted and combined concepts and data from so many disciplines, and also because the results had obvious political import, they were more than ordinarily anxious to have it critiqued before submitting it for publication. Usually, one asks a friend to look over a paper. But neither NW's discovery nor its anticipated opposition were normal. Consequently, TTAPS called their own review session (22–26 April 1983), asking participants to maintain the subject's confidentiality until a critical assessment was completed. Expenses were covered by part of an $80,000 grant from the W. Alton Jones Foundation to the Conference on the Long-Term Biological Consequences of Nuclear War[36] (scheduled for later in 1983), for which this April gathering was a first stage. Held over the course of four days at the American Academy of Arts and Sciences in Cambridge, Massachusetts, and attended by about 100 scientists, the assembly was testimony to the enormous tenacity of Sagan. Having had a brush with death in an appendectomy that involved massive internal bleeding and two full-body blood transfusions a month before, he became a man with a mission. Determined that the conference be a success, from his sickbed he telephoned those invited to encourage them to attend.[37] The Ames Research Center did not forbid its members of TTAPS from participating, but insisted that their expenses be paid by private sources.[38]

The first part of the meeting, chaired by Sagan, was a discussion of "Global Atmospheric Consequences of Nuclear War" (commonly called the "Blue Book"). This was a draft of nearly 150 pages on the physical effects of numerous nuclear explosions, prepared by TTAPS for the review, issued by Turco's employer, RDA, and circulated beforehand to many of the participants. An impressive array of physical scientists attended the sessions, including the theoretical physicists Victor Weisskopf of MIT and Freeman Dyson of the Princeton Institute for Advanced Study; the climate modelers Stephen Schneider of the National Center for Atmospheric Research and Vladimir Aleksandrov, G. S. Golitsyn, and N. Moiseyev of Moscow; the arms race specialists John Holdren of UC Berkeley and George Rathjens of MIT; Paul Crutzen and John Birks of *Ambio* paper fame; the applied mathematician and fire specialist George Carrier of Harvard; the atmospheric dynamicist Jerry Mahlman of Princeton; the radiative transfer specialist Robert Cess of SUNY Stony Brook; and the water expert John Harte of the Lawrence Berkeley Laboratory.[39]

Various warfare and physics scenarios—about 50 in all[40]—were postulated, involving different megatonnage, types of targets, mixtures of ground and air bursts, and warhead yields. These produced a range of atmospheric responses, but the common denominator of most was that huge amounts of dust would be injected into the stratosphere and massive quantities of smoke would rise in the troposphere. Together, these would attenuate sunlight enough to lower surface temperatures and reduce visibility strikingly for up to several months. Crutzen and Birks, who had been unable to quantify the consequences of urban and industrial fires, had written of a "twilight at noon" caused by conflagrations that might last months. TTAPS now put numbers on that concept, and the results made "dusk" seem relatively benign.

The second part of the conference, admirably organized in less than 3 months, had mostly a different cast of characters. It consisted of life scientists, just as distinguished and diverse a group as the physical scientists. Among them were the evolutionist Ernst Mayr and the paleontologist Stephen Jay Gould of Harvard, the theoretical ecologist Robert May of Princeton, the agricultural experts David Pimental of Cornell and Anne Ehrlich of Stanford, the population specialist Paul Ehrlich of Stanford, the plant ecologists Harold Mooney and Joseph Berry of Stanford and Fakhri Bazzaz of the University of Illinois, the phytoplankton specialists Christopher McKay and David Milne of NASA, the wetlands ecologist John Teal of Woods Hole, Thomas Lovejoy of the World Wildlife Fund, Mohammed Kassas of Egypt (then president of the International Union for the Conservation of Nature), and the tropical rainforest ecologists Rafael Herrera from Venezuela and Norman Myers from England. This part of the meeting, chaired by the director of the Missouri Botanical Garden, Peter Raven, focused on the long-term worldwide biological consequences of nuclear war.[41] Clearly, these sessions depended heavily on the earlier discussions.

All was not sweetness and light in Cambridge; the attendees argued vigorously for and against points both general and specific. Some felt that two days devoted to a review of the physical effects was inadequate. Several were dismayed at the way TTAPS piled phenomenon on top of phenomenon. They felt that major synergistic effects (where a combination is greater than a simple sum) and feedback effects were being masked. Some believed that the Blue Book simply was not good science: too many assumptions were required for too many processes.[42] The nuclear war specialist Frank von Hippel, who was invited but did not attend, felt that the conference was "pre-packaged" and that the conclusions should have followed the discussion, instead of the reverse.[43]

Freeman Dyson read the Blue Book, "feeling pretty negative about it." "It didn't seem to me they'd done a careful enough job," he later said. Dyson was particularly concerned that TTAPS used the optical properties of dry soot in their calculations, whereas in real life the atmosphere is quite moist. Soot will absorb incoming energy from the Sun at the wavelengths of visible light, but it is transparent to outgoing thermal radiation (the infrared, of longer wavelength) from Earth. Liquid water, on the other hand, absorbs thermal radiation very well, which is why clouds and fog keep the ground warmer at night than does a clear sky. Dyson's point was that, if liquid water adhered to soot particles, a greenhouse-like effect would reduce or reverse nuclear winter cooling. TTAPS had, he felt, unjustifiably used the worst case possible. Dyson argued for experiments to measure the behavior of wet soot, an omission he considered sloppy science. Thus, the theoretical physicist criticized TTAPS's work as "entirely a theoretical effort" and, despite Sagan's argument that freshly generated soot was relatively hydrophobic, continued as late as 1987 to argue for experimental verification.[44]

Stephen Schneider recalled that he, along with Curt Covey, Starley Thompson, and others, reasoned that, while TTAPS's omission of cloud feedback effects and other possible dynamical and infrared radiative effects led to surface cooling, their inclusion might lead even to warming. They felt, too, that warming might occur if the soot did not rise high in the atmosphere or if turbulence mixed the lower atmosphere well. But they had to admit that they were grasping at straws; their criticisms picked at marginal possibilities. The more likely options led straight to TTAPS's conclusions.

Schneider and many others shared a fundamental apprehension that the computer modeling was inadequate for the problem. Sophisticated as it was for its day, the TTAPS model was one-dimensional, giving a vertical profile of the atmosphere but no latitude and longitude variations. And there were other simplifying assumptions: the model could not accommodate day-night and seasonal changes, land-ocean differences, cloud feedback, or heat transported by winds. Were these terribly important real-world factors included, the great temperature decline predicted by TTAPS would be moderated.

But in case after case, when one process was modified in accord with a participant's views, another affected process restored something of the status quo. The TTAPS results seemed surprisingly stable. Representatives from the nuclear weapons laboratories questioned the validity of a 10,000-MT scenario, claiming that it was far larger than anything likely to occur. TTAPS, however, showed that far smaller exchanges would produce not very much less damage. Fires from 1,000 city or ICBM silo targets would generate enough dust and smoke to drop an atmospheric black shroud.

TTAPS's one-dimensional model smoothed out the global distribution of dust and smoke, something many believed would not occur in reality. Instead, they argued, clusters of particles would circulate, leading to greater and lesser degrees of surface darkness and

temperature. This patchiness would have a large effect on growing plants, as enough photosynthesis might occur to keep them alive. Continental temperatures would also not sink
as low. Yet the physical scientists recognized that, dependent on the (not unreasonable)
values assigned to any number of variables, the climatic effects of the scenarios could just
as easily be made worse as better. So much rested on the quantities of dust and smoke produced in nuclear war and the dynamical reaction of the atmosphere.[45]

The biologists looked with alarm at an extended period of land temperatures depressed
by 10–20°C in the Northern Hemisphere, and of light values around 1 percent of normal.
As often noted, this was larger than the temperature change of about 8°C since the last Ice
Age.[46] Paul Ehrlich, another MacArthur Foundation Fellow (1990), pointed out that low
temperatures over just a few days during a growing season are far more significant to plants
than the decrease in mean temperature over longer periods. With the likely targeting of the
United States, the world's largest breadbasket, North America, would be erased. Even if crops
could be harvested, there was little likelihood that they could be transported to market. The
group noted that, though massive extinctions were not certain, both agriculture and wild
flora would be devastated and could take years to recover. Tropical rain forests, Earth's
largest banks of species diversity, would be doomed in the Northern Hemisphere and
severely impacted further south. The consequences of nuclear war had never been regarded
as trivial, but this was the first time that the extinction of some species was considered
likely.[47]

The oceans' productivity also would be impacted, as phytoplankton suffered under the
darkened conditions. Berkeley's John Harte called attention to the circumstance that fresh
water lakes could freeze and take months to melt. Others recognized that coastal fisheries
would be ravaged by radioactivity and other toxins washed off the land. Another significant
point was emphasized: since the dust and smoke clouds were expected to spill into the
tropics and even into the Southern Hemisphere, non-combatant nations would be just as
badly affected as the belligerents. Indeed, because many Third World nations rely on the
developed countries for fertilizers and agricultural technology, they would be severely
impacted even if unaffected by climatic changes. There was widespread agreement among
the biologists about the severity of these effects, should the physical conditions prevail. The
environmental insults were so overwhelming that some could be discounted, such as the
UV radiation that would bathe the surface once the clouds and smog dissipated. Paul Ehrlich
noted that "the overkill from the cold-dark-radiation-smog effects led the biologists to doubt
that there would be much left for the ultraviolet light to damage."[48]

Countering the charges by skeptics that there were too many uncertainties, Sagan underscored that there was no option but to use models and to make theoretical estimations. This
was, after all, "an experiment that can be performed once, at most." Rebutting critics who
faulted use of worst-case assumptions and preferred "more probable" scenarios of nuclear
conflict, Schneider emphasized the minimal need to show merely the plausibility that
agriculture could be devastated in the Northern Hemisphere and part of the Southern

Hemisphere. Should this possibility be accepted, Schneider wrote, "any nuclear planning in [its] absence . . . is sheer madness."[49]

Madness, indeed, entered the discussion. A Harvard psychologist discounted rational behavior by leaders in time of great stress. The gist of the meeting, however, was that nuclear-war-fighting plans should be abandoned before those stressful conditions arose. The UC Berkeley physicist John Holdren, with extensive experience in the nature of the arms race through his long involvement in the Pugwash Conferences, was particularly despondent. It astonished him that analysts who chewed over the billion or so deaths expected from direct blast and radiation in a large nuclear war were deemed to be rational people. He had little hope that their outlook would be affected by the new thought that perhaps four billion humans were doomed by climatic consequences in the aftermath of war.[50]

Sagan and Ehrlich considered the Cambridge meeting to be a positive peer review of their work; no one had shot them down by exposing a critical flaw. Others disagreed, arguing that a serious review could not be accomplished so quickly, by so many people inexpert in the subject, on such a massive topic that was fraught with uncertainties. Though the Cambridge meeting had been an important step in the evolution of TTAPS's views, even Turco admitted that it had not been the "scientific acid test."[51]

5 Publicity

Planning to Go Public with Nuclear Winter

For more than a century, philanthropic foundations have played a significant role in the United States and abroad. Their support has gone into both basic research activities (as when the Rockefeller Foundation underwrote the cost of the 200-inch telescope atop Mount Palomar) and into attacks on social problems (hunger, for example, when the same foundation funded "Green Revolution" research and development). Similarly, unendowed organizations have long existed and pursued comparable goals. Professional scientific societies have looked primarily toward advancing knowledge in their specialties (although in recent decades they have increasingly been involved in social and political matters), while "special-interest groups" (e.g., the National Rifle Association and the National Organization for Women) have focused on matters of particular concern to them. Thus, it is not surprising that numerous non-governmental bodies found it an appropriate function to express concern over the threat of nuclear war in the decades since Hiroshima and Nagasaki. And, just as *Ambio* editor Jeannie Peterson felt that too little attention had been given to the global consequences of such combat, officials of some of these private groups recognized the same oversight. They were, indeed, stimulated in part by *Ambio*'s special issue, which appeared about the time, in June 1982, that they met.

Russell W. Peterson, a Ph.D. textile chemist and an executive at DuPont for over a quarter of a century, who subsequently became governor of Delaware (1969–1973), chairman of the US Council on Environmental Quality (1973–1976), and director of the congressional Office of Technology Assessment (1978–79), was by then president of the National Audubon Society. His colleagues in concern were Robert W. Scrivner, director of the Rockefeller Family Fund, and Robert L. Allen, of the Henry P. Kendall Foundation. Too little information, they felt, was available on how nuclear war might affect the biosphere. What would happen to the soil, water, and air needed for all life?

This was a period of great activism in the environmental movement, spurred in particular by the threatened depredations of the Reagan administration. Why not direct some of this energy toward a better understanding of the nuclear menace to life? With the idea of holding a conference on such extended effects on the planet, they spoke to some scientists and some environmentalists. From Sagan, who was among those consulted, they learned of the TTAPS project then under way, and of the proposed NAS study. Nuclear winter immediately became the focus of their attention. First, they agreed to fund the April 1983 private scientific review in Cambridge. Then, they formed a steering committee to plan the larger public meeting, to be held on 31 October (Halloween) and 1 November 1983, provided that peer review of TTAPS's data and methodology exposed no obvious flaws. The biological consequences of their conclusions were to be emphasized.

For publicity, the Kendall Foundation initially gave $40,000 for a media blitz orchestrated by the public relations firm of Porter and Novelli Associates; their final costs were roughly $100,000. The leading network news programs, morning TV shows, evening discussion programs, metropolitan newspapers, wire services, news magazines, and the international press were targeted, some 25–30 media outlets in all. Before the Halloween meeting, media alerts, press releases, and backgrounders were issued, Sagan was in New York available for interviews the week before, and PR firm chairman Jack Porter expected at least one news magazine cover story. Sensing a story of international importance, he focused on reporters who covered politics rather than science. This strategy for a cover story came to naught, as just days before the meeting President Reagan sent troops to protect American citizens on the island of Grenada. A reporter told Porter: "You're talking about a scientific conference? I got dead marines here!" Still, media coverage was significant.[1] (It is almost unheard of for scientists to hire PR "flaks" to promote their *scientific* ideas, but they do occasionally use these professionals for their political views. For example, immediately after World War II, the Emergency Committee of Atomic Scientists employed such consultants.[2]) By this time, Sagan was more motivated than ever to make nuclear winter a scientific—and a policy— issue. He opposed the Strategic Defense Initiative as poor defense policy, and, as a space scientist, he wanted to keep "space accessible for exploratory purposes." Familiar with the media, he encouraged use of artwork and video clips.[3]

In addition to Sagan, the conference steering committee included Paul Ehrlich, Peter Raven, Walter Orr Roberts (president emeritus of the University Corporation for Atmospheric Research and past president of the American Association for the Advancement of Science), and George M. Woodwell (director of the Ecosystems Center at the Woods Hole Marine Biological Laboratory, an authority on the environmental effects of radiation, and author of a chapter in the special issue of *Ambio*). They decided that the conference must be scientifically credible; it would, therefore, be limited to discussion of physical and biological arguments. The potential impact on nuclear arms acquisition policy, nuclear strategy, arms control, and domestic politics was abundantly clear, and they intended to prevent these issues from upstaging the scientific ideas.

Once the TTAPS Blue Book passed the April 1983 review hurdle, minimally indicating that its predictions could not be dismissed out of hand, the steering committee appointed several dozen scientists from around the world to an advisory board and enlisted the sponsorship of 31 organizations. The latter included scientific societies and establishments (the

American Institute of Biological Sciences, the American Society for Microbiology, the Smithsonian Institution), scientific activist associations (the Federation of American Scientists, the Union of Concerned Scientists), environmental activist organizations (the Sierra Club, Friends of the Earth, the Natural Resources Defense Council), political reform bodies (Common Cause, the United Nations Association of the United States of America), and international assemblies (the International Union for Conservation of Nature and Natural Resources, the International Federation of Institutes for Advanced Study).[4]

A considerable number of these associations were already on record in opposition to the escalating arms race, giving some political coloring to the conference. They might be accused of uncritically endorsing fearful scientific conclusions of global disaster in order to further their arms-control designs. But other groups could be perceived as "objective," and their support in publicizing this investigation would not necessarily be regarded as directed by political agendas. This tension would be evident through the next several years of debate on nuclear winter.

Paul Ehrlich had for some years believed that the environmental consequences of nuclear war were serious, yet were being ignored. A "visible scientist" well known for his earlier crusade to curtail human population growth, Ehrlich wrote and lectured in the early 1980s about the nuclear danger. When mutual friends put him in contact with Sagan, he immediately became the leading spokesman on NW and the life sciences.[5] The American Association for the Advancement of Science had held a Symposium on the Environmental Effects of Nuclear War at its meeting in Detroit in May 1983, but this was recognized as just a beginning.[6]

During the summer of 1983, Ehrlich organized a group of about twenty scientists to elaborate the biological implications of large-area reductions of temperature and light intensity. Meanwhile, TTAPS were busy polishing and distilling the Blue Book into a publishable manuscript. Few journal editors can devote much space to a single article, yet the scientific tradition and concerns about rapid publication mandate that new discoveries appear as articles, not as books. On 4 August they sent the manuscript off to *Science*, their first and only choice. The weekly journal of the AAAS, *Science* was known for its relatively fast production schedule and as the best means of reaching a large fraction of the American scientific community. In the practice followed by virtually all reputable scholarly periodicals, the manuscript was sent by the editor to independent referees (three in this case) and the authors revised their text in light of the comments received. Other changes were based on the "Halloween meeting" discussions. The paper appeared in *Science*'s 23 December 1983 issue.[7]

Halloween 1983: Sagan

NW made its public debut nearly 2 months before the TTAPS paper's publication. The long-planned meeting filled Washington's Sheraton Hotel with about 100 journalists and 500 participants—mostly scientists, but including a sizable number of officials from the United

States and from more than twenty other countries, as well as leaders in the fields of foreign policy, arms control, education, religion, business, and the military. Titled "The World After Nuclear War: The Conference on the Long-Term Biological Consequences of Nuclear War," it was (as I have already noted) held on 31 October and 1 November. (The proceedings were quickly published under the title *The Cold and the Dark: The World After Nuclear War*, and later appeared in German, Swedish, French, Dutch, Portuguese, Spanish, and Japanese translations.[8])

Sagan had jumped the gun with his high-impact article, published in *Parade's* 30 October issue, which gave the media and the conference audience, in addition to the Sunday magazine's huge national distribution, something tangible around which to mold their thinking. Sagan had recently become a contributing editor of *Parade*, his literary agent having been approached by the magazine for a few stories on science each year. When 30 October was proposed as the date for Sagan's first article, he chose NW as the topic, recognizing the value of its coincidence with the meeting.[9] The editor of *Parade* was delighted, since he had perceived Sagan's dedication to the investigation just after his operation early in the year.[10] It was an astute maneuver to direct the debate, but it drew criticism for popularizing scientific conclusions to the public before they had appeared in a refereed journal. None of the TTAPS members from the Ames Research Center traveled to Washington. Aside from the fact that their employer had pressured them not to attend, they felt that it was not really a scientific meeting, and they tried in their personal actions to keep NW as much of a technical problem as possible. At the same time, they felt that Sagan was free to discuss the phenomenon in any way he wished.[11]

In the conference's keynote address, Stanford University's president, Donald Kennedy, quoted a current government pamphlet on the aftermath of nuclear war: "Ecological imbalances that would make normal life impossible are not to be expected."[12] Then the conference proceeded to demolish that position, led by Sagan and Ehrlich, who in turn presented summaries of the atmospheric-climatic and biological consequences of nuclear war. Discussion panels mirrored these two foci, and a six-minute video gave a graphic depiction of the catastrophe.[13]

In his address Sagan emphasized four major effects: (1) Huge amounts of smoke would rise into the troposphere from fires in cities. Should firestorms develop, smoke might ascend to the stratosphere. It would, Sagan argued, be a mistake to believe that cities would be spared destruction, even in attempts at "surgical" strikes. War-supporting facilities would be attacked—the industrial plants, workforce, and transportation hubs—and these usually were situated in or near cities. (2) High-yield explosions (1 MT and larger) at ground level would loft great quantities of fine dust into the upper troposphere and stratosphere. (3) Ground bursts allow radioactive fission fragments from the hydrogen bomb's trigger and third stage to coat vaporized earth. This material returns to the surface as radioactive fallout rather quickly when washed out of the troposphere by rain, and much more slowly when it descends only by gravity from the stratosphere. (4) All nuclear explosions create fireballs which burn atmospheric nitrogen. When the yield is 1 MT or greater, the fireball reaches the stratosphere, where nitrogen oxides consume ozone, allowing biologically dangerous amounts of ultraviolet light from the Sun to reach Earth's surface. Thus, at first, dust and smoke would obscure sunlight, leading to conditions of cold and dark. In time, the atmosphere would clear, only to allow harmful ultraviolet radiation to penetrate it.[14]

The grim picture Sagan painted did not end there. Repeating points made half a year earlier at the meeting in Cambridge, he noted that his Martian studies strongly suggested that smoke and dust clouds would pour over the equator into the Southern Hemisphere, disrupting normal patterns of global circulation. Nuclear effects, thus, would not be restricted to the northern mid latitudes, where the "battle" would be centered; non-combatants the world over would experience the effects. The consequences for plant life in the tropics, a region looked upon as a great reservoir of diverse species, would be devastating. But temperate-zone plants would fare no better, and with a 1°C decrease in average temperature Canada would cease to be a major grower and exporter of wheat. In some places and under certain conditions, it would be pitch black at noon for more than a week, and it would take a year or more for normal light levels to return.[15]

TTAPS had calculated the effects of many scenarios in which the numbers and sizes of weapons, their targets, and the altitudes at which they were detonated were specified. The different conditions of each scenario resulted in unique amounts of dust and soot that were placed at certain levels in the atmosphere. This, of course, controlled the intensity and duration of illumination and temperature effects. At the Washington meeting, Sagan presented only five scenarios, ranging from a high of 10,000 MT detonated to a low of 100 MT, two of them "counterforce" (military targets) only, one "countervalue" (urban, industrial targets) only, and two combinations of targets. In four of the scenarios, temperatures fell below the freezing point of fresh water and stayed below it for at least 75 days; in the one scenario where such profound cold did not occur (a 3,000-MT attack on missile silos with no resulting fires), the lack of smoke was the reason for the difference. Still, temperatures fell 7 or 8 degrees and returned to normal only after a year. In the 5,000-MT baseline scenario (reduced from the 10,000-MT war used as a baseline in the Blue Book), temperatures in mid-continental regions fell to a few tens of degrees below freezing and took months to recover.

Though Sagan recognized the many uncertainties in the data and the deficiencies of the one-dimensional computer model, a consequence stood out that he mentioned briefly in his address but elaborated on in a "political" paper he wrote for the journal *Foreign Affairs*. This was the existence of thresholds. Below a certain level of detonated megatonnage, the atmospheric effects would be minimal; above that level, the effects would be certain. The level was actually a band, and a very fuzzy one at that. But the computer printouts suggested that climatic catastrophe would be certain if 2,000–3,000 warheads were exploded on the ground or low over military targets (dust responsible for most of the effect), or if fires were ignited in 100 or more major cities. The latter scenario was particularly shocking, for it specified a "mere" 100 MT, distributed in 1,000 warheads of 100 KT each. In their nuclear arsenals, this threshold had been crossed by the United States in the early 1950s and the Soviet Union in the mid 1960s. In both cases, the public was unaware of the new danger that war could bring; more unsettling, the military and scientists were equally unsuspecting.[16] Richard Turco put it succinctly: "There's a very high sensitivity to bombs dropped on cities."[17]

Sagan mused that the meeting was held on Halloween for the prosaic reason of hotel-room availability. But the juxtaposition really was quite appropriate. The holiday was, he said,

in pre-Christian times, a Celtic festival [that] marked the beginning of winter. It was celebrated by the lighting of vast bonfires. And it was named after and consecrated to the Lord of the Dead. The original Halloween combines the three essential elements of the TTAPS scenario: fires, winter, and death.[18]

This compelling metaphor, connecting NW to fires, winter, and death, seems to have resonated with scientists as well as with the public, touching deep-seated emotions, and suggests one of the reasons for the initial interest in the discovery.[19]

A question from the audience about the greenhouse effect (the rise in global temperature caused by combustion of fossil fuels) led Sagan to explain that the carbon dioxide released by forest and city fires in a nuclear conflict would be minor relative to the present atmospheric burden. More importantly, greenhouse warming was a slow process, whereas the onset of nuclear winter would be rapid. Superficially, they appeared to have counterbalancing characteristics: greenhouse gases such as carbon dioxide are transparent to visible light but absorb infrared radiation, while smoke does the opposite. But one should not assume that we could accept both hazards without danger, anticipating that they would cancel each other.[20] To many people, NW was an "anti-greenhouse" effect, and one that seemed illogical. The atmosphere's radiative time constant should be hundreds of days, yet TTAPS predicted rapid cooling of Earth's surface. Sagan's explanation was that the heated upper atmosphere would suppress convection, effectively decoupling the atmosphere from the surface.[21]

Another questioner inquired if the well-received 1975 NAS/NRC report titled *Long-Term Worldwide Effects of Multiple Nuclear-Weapons Detonations* was now superseded. Sagan tactfully suggested that the current NAS panel might look at this, but offered some of the more recent insights. Along with ozone, dust had been a major focus of the 1975 study, and conclusions were based on an analogy with the material ejected by Krakatoa. But now it was seen that not only do volcanic ejecta (whose identities were better understood) have a much smaller absorption coefficient for sunlight than black smoke, but the particle size distributions are significantly different. Further, most of the material in the eruption fell close by in the Sunda Straights; it did not remain in the atmosphere. Finally, the simultaneous injection of fine particles from thousands of fires would create quite a different situation than the eruption of a single volcano. TTAPS stood by their interpretations.[22]

Halloween 1983: Ehrlich

Paul Ehrlich then emphasized the remarkable consensus achieved by more than 50 scientists who examined the biological effects of nuclear war, an agreement all the more striking given the obvious political overtones. It was clear to them that the consequences would be grave under *all* scenarios, since Earth's environment would suffer massive assaults. "It would be extremely difficult," Ehrlich said, "to design a major nuclear war that would not lead to a biological catastrophe of unprecedented dimensions."[23] The scientists were, further, convinced that the scope of this danger lay unrecognized by policy planners.

Experienced teacher that he was, Ehrlich explained to his audience that an ecological system—an ecosystem—is "a biological community . . . of the plants, animals, and microbes" in an area, combined with their physical environment. This environment, he noted, includes more than the soil, rocks, and streams; it also includes solar radiation and atmospheric gases. And the heart of the ecosystem is the interaction of all the organisms with their surroundings. Ehrlich then surveyed the nature of the stresses ecosystems would face. Besides cold and darkness, they include wildfires, toxic smog, increased levels of ultraviolet light, radioactive fallout, acid rain, release of poisonous substances into the soil and water, siltation and concentration of sewage in lakes, rivers, and coastal waters, and savage storms along continental edges due to large temperature differences.[24]

Central to Ehrlich's analysis of the threat to ecosystems was the effect of nuclear warfare on green plants. Almost all animals, including humans, are dependent for food on plant life, which requires sunlight for growth (photosynthesis) and storing of nutrients. If nuclear war occurred just before or during the growing season, virtually all land plants in the northern hemisphere would be killed or seriously affected. Perennials in the temperate zone would stand a greater chance of survival after a war in their dormant season, but in the tropics, where plants grow during the entire year, they would be devastated. Suspended photosynthetic activity would result not only from lowered temperatures and light levels. Polluted air, ionizing radiation, and other insults would compound the assault, with devastating effects on the food chain.

Once light levels began to return to normal, the thinned ozone layer in the stratosphere would permit an increase in the intensity of damaging UV radiation that reached the surface. Green plants, Ehrlich explained, once again would be adversely affected, for UV reduces photosynthesis. Even more, leaves that grow under gloomy conditions are more susceptible to UV damage than are leaves grown in bright sunlight. Warm-blooded animals, too, are threatened by UV, which suppresses immunity to disease and causes genetic mutations.[25]

The levels of radioactivity calculated by TTAPS were far higher than those obtained in earlier studies (which had largely ignored effects of intermediate-time-scale washout and fallout from low-yield weapons). Fallout could contaminate as much as 30 percent of the land surface of the Northern Hemisphere's mid latitudes with some 500 rems of radiation.

Such a dose would prove fatal to half the healthy adults exposed. But, of course, people would not be in good health. Quite the opposite would be the case, for their bodies would be stressed to an unusual degree. Ehrlich estimated that between a billion people and all the people in the Northern Hemisphere would be affected by the cumulative effects of fallout: disease, cancer, and genetic damage.

In addition, fallout would particularly affect other mammals, birds, and coniferous trees. Vast stretches of conifers covering more than 2 percent of the land area of the northern hemisphere could be killed, leaving kindling in place for huge wildfires.[26]

The biological report added that toxic gases in large quantities would enter the atmosphere from burning wells, mines, and stores of natural gas, oil, and coal. Such fires could last for months; indeed, some coal seams and peat marsh fires have been known to burn for years. Forest fires, ignited in the dry season in such places as California, could denude large areas, leading to erosion and flooding in the next rainy season. Silt, radioactive rainfall, and toxic runoff would likely kill much river, lake, and sea life, and harm humans and other animals who normally eat fish.

Urban fires and firestorms (whose dynamics were poorly understood) might release a band of smog containing toxic ingredients such as vinyl chlorides. Nitrogen oxides from fireballs and sulfur oxides from other fires would likely cause localized acid rainfall. Elsewhere the disturbed atmosphere could experience a reduction in rainfall. In some combinations, insults to the ecosystems of cold, darkness, UV, radioactivity, smog, fire, drought, and acid rain could lead to the long-term persistence of disease and pests. Synergisms would almost certainly make the effects more severe.[27]

Wild and domesticated animals that did not die of cold would succumb to thirst, since surface water would be frozen, or to starvation. Animals hibernating at the time of conflict would survive, only to emerge into a most inhospitable world. Scavengers form the only group that would benefit from these conditions. With billions of corpses to feed upon, with no predators around, and with their high population growth rates (after the thaw), "rats, roaches, and flies [could quickly become] the most prominent animals shortly after World War III." Soil organisms, since they do not depend directly on photosynthesis, could survive in a dormant state. But many soils would have been ruined through erosion by wind and water.[28]

Agriculture would be devastated. Aside from cereal grains, few foods are stored in quantity. Grain silos, however, are located far from cities, so their contents (if not contaminated by radioactivity) would probably not be available to urban survivors. The disruption of transportation and normal trade also means that people in Third World nations that rely on grain imports would also face starvation. The resumption of agriculture would be problematical. Aside from hostile climatic conditions, fuel for farm machinery and fertilizer for crops would be in very short supply. Seed stocks, not normally preserved each harvest by individual farmers in the US and the USSR, might be destroyed or inadequately available. Their genetic diversity would be reduced by lost stocks, and surviving strains might be unsuited for the new environment. Lowered temperatures were of special concern to agriculture. "A mere 3°C decrease in average July temperature," Ehrlich said, "would push the northern limit of reliable corn production southward several degrees in latitude to southern Iowa and central Illinois."[29]

The fate of the tropics, aquatic systems, and Earth itself would all be jeopardized. Although most nuclear detonations would occur over land areas of the northern temperate zone, cold and dark conditions would likely spill over into (at least) the southern tropic zone. Tropical plants, unused to dormancy in a cold or cool season, would at minimum be stressed. In combination with depressed photosynthetic activity, due to the darkened skies, it could spell the death knell for innumerable species in the world's richest bank of genetic diversity. Many fresh-water organisms would die from the sheet of ice and reduced light levels. In the oceans, the algae (phytoplankton) that are critical to all major food chains would also be devastated by the darkness or weak light. And they would be assaulted further when UV radiation later began to bathe the planet. Should this disruption last long enough to interrupt the food chain, large populations if not entire species of commercially sought fish could be lost.

Ehrlich confessed that he originally doubted that humans could become extinct. More likely, the worst that could occur was a reduction to prehistoric population levels, with humans inhabiting the warmer islands and coastal regions of the southern hemisphere. Now he was not so certain. Prehistoric humans at least were familiar with their environment, growing up in cultures that hunted, fished, gathered wild food, and/or engaged in agriculture. Modern society, by contrast, is so complex and interdependent upon its many components that relatively few people are self-sufficient. "It was the consensus of our group," he concluded, "that, under those conditions, we could not exclude the possibility that the scattered survivors simply would not be able to rebuild their populations, that they would, over a period of decades or even centuries, fade away. In other words, we could not exclude the possibility of a full-scale nuclear war entraining the extinction of *Homo sapiens*."[30] In the words of Ehrlich's wife, Anne, herself a noted ecologist, this was an awesome "environmental impact statement."[31]

Halloween Plus One

The following day was devoted to panels on atmospheric-climatic and biological consequences. Although unhappy with their 10-minute speaking limits, compared to the 2 hours Sagan and Ehrlich each had taken the day before, Stephen Schneider and Paul Crutzen made no public protest. It might seem that TTAPS had done all the work, but the credibility of NW was more important than their egos.[32] Notable among the short presentations was John Holdren's comparison of the TTAPS calculations of radiation doses from intermediate-term (a few days to a month) fallout with the figures of Joseph Knox of the Livermore Laboratory. In the past, fallout from this period had been almost ignored, the immediate and long-term effects capturing most attention. Yet the intensity added significantly to the total dose. Despite inevitable differences in their warfare scenarios, the two estimates were remarkably close.[33]

TTAPS member Richard Turco discussed fires. About one-third of a bomb's energy, when detonated at low altitude, appears as "bomb light." This, he said, has roughly the same frequency spectrum as ordinary sunlight, but can be much more intense. For example, the fireball of a 1-MT low-altitude explosion, at a distance of 10 kilometers, would be 1,000 times brighter than the Sun. The consequences of this brief flash would include third-degree burns to exposed skin and ignition of many materials with low kindling points, such as paper and clothing.

At Hiroshima and Nagasaki, much smaller bombs (12.5 and 20 KT, respectively) had left 13 and 7 square kilometers burned. Within these areas, little combustible material remained. Although some primary fires caused by the bomb light were soon extinguished by the following pressure wave, more secondary fires were kindled as smoking debris was scattered by the explosion and by other effects. Extrapolation of such results from kiloton- to megaton-size weapons was widely accepted as justified, making "the fires envisioned in any future nuclear war . . . unprecedented in scale and much more intense, dwarfing the World War II conflagrations."[34]

Georgiy S. Golitsyn, head of the laboratory at the Institute of Atmospheric Physics in Moscow, an expert on Mars, and a corresponding member (that is, not a full member, or academician) of the Academy of Sciences of the USSR, reemphasized Mars as an analogy for terrestrial phenomena. His main conjecture was that Earth's atmosphere could become so static that rainfall might fail to occur. Golitsyn also revealed that he and his colleagues had developed a simple radiative transfer model which gave results similar to those of TTAPS.[35]

Over the two days of the meeting, a number of speakers had mentioned the many uncertainties of data and approach, yet had claimed that the results were "robust." How could disagreement in detail lead to agreement in general conclusions? Stephen Schneider saw the problem developing and faced it directly. A good example, he said, was the effect of smoke. He took 200 million metric tons (or tonnes) as the amount of smoke spread uniformly between the combat latitudes of 30° and 70° north (which happens to be the most populated region on Earth). The figure, derived from the baseline case used in the fledgling NAS study, was conservative. If the smoke remained in this zone, the optical depth (a number that characterizes the amount of light absorbed by particulate matter in the atmosphere) would be 3. Were the smoke to disperse over the entire Northern Hemisphere, the optical depth would be 1.5, while smoke spread uniformly over the entire planet, without removal, would yield an optical depth of 0.7. Schneider admitted that these numbers covered a significant range, but, he asserted, they showed that, nonetheless, sunlight reaching Earth's surface would be drastically reduced. Robustness was inherent in the NW results because all cases would be catastrophic; indeed, it could be worse if more smoke evolved from the fires.

Schneider also introduced results of his work with an early (it was not interactive) three-dimensional computer model that incorporated seasonal variations and transport of smoke by winds. He and his colleagues Curt Covey and Starley Thompson had found that smoke introduced uniformly into the temperate region of the Northern Hemisphere could result in an 80°C (144°F) rise in atmospheric temperature and a very large decrease in atmospheric temperature under the smoke cloud. These conclusions were compatible with those of TTAPS. If war occurred in July, large pockets of freezing daytime temperatures would be found in the northwestern United States, in central Europe, on the Tibetan plateau, and in parts of the USSR within two days. At first startled by these dramatic changes, they quickly recognized that ordinary nighttime temperatures are 5–20°C lower than those in daytime, and under NW conditions two days was equivalent to four continuous nights. July temperatures could indeed fall below freezing.[36]

Vladimir V. Aleksandrov also had results from a three-dimensional climate model to report. Using a TTAPS war scenario, the head of the Climate Modeling Laboratory of the Computing Center in Moscow had programmed a uniform distribution of dust and soot over the Northern Hemisphere. Surface temperatures, he had found, were an average of 20°C (36°F) below normal at 40 days and remained depressed about 10°C (18°F) 8 months after the war. But the temperatures in specific regions fell more strikingly: at 40 days, as much as a 30°C (54°F) decrease over the western US, a 40°C (72°F) decrease over the northeastern US, and a 50°C (90°F) decrease over Europe. Although the surface would not heat up appreciably over long periods of time, the upper troposphere would. At 8 months the Tibetan plateau's temperature would be as much as 20°C (36°F) higher than normal, while that of the Rocky Mountains would be raised 7°C (13°F). The consequence of this might be the melting of glaciers and snow packs, possibly causing flooding on a continental scale.

Additionally, the vertical air temperature gradient was strongly affected by the dark clouds, perhaps sufficiently to interfere with Earth's general circulation. Simply put, the normal condition of a warm Earth and increasingly cooler temperatures in the troposphere would be reversed. It would be as if the stratosphere started at Earth's surface. Like Golitsyn, Aleksandrov emphasized the potential for a rather static atmosphere in which a lack of rainfall allowed soot and dust to remain aloft. The general validity of his results was supported, he claimed, by overall agreement with Schneider's work, despite the differences in their models and their computers.[37]

Predictions from the biological panel were no less ominous. John Harte, a professor of energy and resources at Berkeley, likened humankind's dependency on the ecosystems to an intensive-care patient's reliance on life-support systems. That being so, the virtual shutdown of the hydrological cycle, the natural processes that remove pollutants from air and water, and the moderation of climate by growing vegetation, among other actions, suggested a difficult future.

Harte provided another interesting insight. He had looked at the effect of lowered temperatures on fresh water and calculated that about a meter of ice would form on surface water in continental interiors. This would lead to death by thirst of humans and animals. For those who survived, it would increase the severity of threatened epidemics, already intensified by lowered resistance due to radiation, by freezing the pipes that normally carry away sewage. Thus, Harte suggested that "synergisms seem to work for you when things are healthy and they turn against you when you and nature are debilitated."[38]

The Stanford University biologist Joseph A. Berry joined in emphasizing the importance of ecological processes. "Photosynthesis," he said, "constitutes the major chemical-energy input into the biosphere and is the major driving force for the operation of natural and agricultural ecosystems." Darkness will affect growing plants far more than those that are dormant, so warfare in spring or summer in the northern hemisphere will have the most severe consequences. Further, recovery of photosynthesis will lag restoration of light—perhaps by decades—since the mass of leaves and algae will have been prodigiously reduced.[39]

The effect on humans was emphasized by Mark A. Harwell of Cornell University. Earth's natural ecosystems—even when healthy—are unable to support the current world population through hunting and gathering of food. Humans rely heavily on managed ecosystems, primarily agricultural, which of course involve tilling, sowing, fertilizing, and (often) irrigating the soil and crops. Society would be so badly disrupted by the immediate effects of nuclear war that agricultural activity would collapse, while the longer-term climatic effects would reduce still further the population capable of being supported by natural ecosystems. Recovery, in which great reliance would be placed on the recuperating natural ecosystems, would be slowed as people harvested plants for consumption rather than allowing them to reproduce.

The session closed with an eloquent plea by Thomas Eisner, Harwell's colleague from Cornell. Biologists, Eisner said, no longer can believe that nuclear warfare is foreign to their professional concerns. Indeed, it is "fundamentally biological." In the United States the gun lobby had popularized the slogan "Guns don't kill people; people kill people." Eisner reversed that catchy syllogism by arguing that "the enemy is not the Soviet Union or the United States, but the nuclear weapons themselves." It is the duty of scientists to speak out: "The issue is not adversarial politics, but biological survival." The consumer advocate Ralph Nader and others in the audience were disconcerted that politics were deliberately not discussed at the Halloween meeting, but in subsequent months and years scientists did popularize the concept of nuclear winter, and politics were never far from center stage.[40]

In Print

As has been noted, the formal paper by Turco, Toon, Ackerman, Pollack, and Sagan appeared in the issue of *Science* dated 23 December 1983. For the first time in a refereed scientific journal, the prediction was made, and limited supporting evidence presented, that nuclear war would likely be followed by severely depressed temperatures lasting for long periods of time: a nuclear winter. Numbers, tables, graphs, explanations, and references fleshed out the more descriptive presentations of the previous months. Uncertainties in the size of many parameters, inadequacies of certain models, and other deficiencies were repeatedly acknowledged, yet the quantities of dust and smoke produced by nuclear explosions and fires, and their calculated effects on the climate, appeared in all cases to be so likely and so large that the TTAPS authors were confident they were on the right track.[41]

Curiously, instead of bringing a sense of order to the growing controversy over NW, the *Science* paper fueled the debate. In retrospect, this seems inevitable. In view of the political implications of the climatic consequences, true believers at both ends of the political spectrum were not about to concede their evaluations of the science that had gone into the TTAPS publication. Additionally, the paper contained some weak points which critics could attack. The most surprising war scenario, for example, in which only 100 MT of nuclear explosions on cities caused NW to descend, was computed using twice the average amount of combustibles in city centers (20 grams per square centimeter) and more than twice the amount of smoke emitted (0.026 gram of smoke per gram of material burned) relative to the values used in the 5,000-MT baseline case. TTAPS might argue that the baseline-case values were conservative, but critics could charge they were manipulating the calculations to maximize the output of smoke.[42]

The TTAPS paper filled ten pages of *Science*, an uncommonly generous commitment of space by the weekly and indicative of the editor's view of its importance. But, given the immense amount of material digested by the authors and the need to explain their nuclear war scenario model, their source terms (how much material is pumped into the atmosphere), their particle microphysics model, and their radiative-convective model (movement of energy by radiation and convection), they were in effect limited to outlining their methods and summarizing their results. In several places, reference was made to another TTAPS paper, still in preparation, that would contain a detailed explanation of how various values of dust, smoke, and soot were determined and used in the calculations.[43] But that paper never appeared. TTAPS might have abandoned the effort, feeling that more recent work of others had superseded their labors; however, for those inclined to be critical, their failure to publish the second paper was viewed as evasion or deception.

Accompanying TTAPS's paper in the 23 December 1983 issue of *Science* was a study of the biological effects of NW. Lead author Paul Ehrlich and nineteen colleagues summarized the effects on organisms of reduced visible light and temperature, and increased ionizing radiation and ultraviolet-B radiation. The predicted consequences for life on land in the temperate regions and tropics, in fresh-water and salt-water ecosystems, and for agriculture everywhere were, of course, appalling. Given the harsh climatic conditions of NW, this largely qualitative report on the biological repercussions was generally believable. Nonetheless, this paper too contained a weak point which the skeptics could criticize. Whereas TTAPS had used a 5,000-MT exchange as their baseline case, the Ehrlich team built their analysis on a reference scenario twice as large, indeed the 10,000-MT figure that had been used for the Cambridge meeting three-quarters of a year earlier. In the paper, Ehrlich and his colleagues explained that they chose the larger figure deliberately, because it was credible and because they wished to impress decision-makers with the seriousness of long-time effects. But to those disposed to be scornful it could appear to be manipulative, as the selection of a "worst case."[44]

Sagan had earlier asked "What other phenomena have we missed?" That was a challenge to the technical expertise and exclusive purview of the government's nuclear weaponeers. With publication of these papers in *Science*, outsiders proved that special knowledge could reside apart from the bureaucracy. Nuclear strategy had had more of a presence beyond the phalanx of the establishment's "defense intellectuals," and those connected to the system were, of course, more influential in the formulation of policy.[45] But here too NW would show that outsiders could become major players in the game.

6 Concern about the Good Name of Science—and with Getting the Message Across

The British historian of science David Knight, writing about an earlier century, nonetheless captured the culture of science as it is in our era:

What is striking about scientific communities is their scepticism. The person who proposes a new interpretation is confronted with disbelief, or perhaps indifference. This is an essential characteristic of science; we are surrounded by a booming, buzzing confusion, and we have to select what we consider relevant—there is not much room for the really unexpected. Men like Darwin and his allies had to struggle to get their ideas across, and there has to be an element of rhetoric about all scientific publications.[1]

By no means was the struggle over NW a battle between the "good guys" and their "evil" or politically reactionary opponents. Generally, as Knight cautions, the picture is rarely so clear: "The light that gleams upon the benighted traveler may be the flicker of the idiot's lantern drawing him further into the boggy wilderness."[2] Or it might be an embarrassing scientific and political truth. How does one decide?

Before World War II, scientists had numerous opportunities to interact with government, the media, and the rest of society, but took advantage of relatively few of them, being rebuffed or disheartened when they could not control the agenda.[3] Notably, in the interwar period, Albert Einstein publicly supported Zionism, Bertrand Russell spoke on morality, and Robert Millikan on religion, but these were rare cases of scientists using their fame to address matters beyond their professional interests.[4] Then the atomic bomb and other wartime inventions thrust scientists into the postwar limelight, and the Cold War made them essential, permanent employees of government and valued part-time advisors. Some, including J. Robert Oppenheimer and Edward Teller, became public figures as well. For a time, scientific societies tried simply to retain their old functions: to uphold the rigorous standards of the discipline, publish a scholarly journal, and organize professional meetings. The pressures for change were too great, however, and American scholarly societies soon found themselves lobbying the federal government for fellowships and research funds for their fields and involving themselves in issues of science policy. Later, they occasionally took stands on such controversial matters as the war in Vietnam and whether to boycott states that refused to pass the Equal Rights Amendment.

To critics who questioned what expertise scientists brought to political questions, scientists could respond that many problems had a technical component and that, further, they could be credited with having minds at least as logical and creative as those of lawyers, bankers, political scientists, and politicians. Indeed, as more and more scientists gained experience in the use of science in support of public policy, their participation in the political process was generally welcomed. But to the old professional ethos of simply doing good science and respecting the mores of the profession, its practitioners now had to add the need to maintain science's good name before the public.[5]

These goals intrinsically had a conservative cast: departures from conventional patterns might be looked at askance. Further, many scientists select their profession because it entails a minimum of interpersonal relations. Few organic bodies and no inorganic bodies talk back. By extension, such scientists avoid real-world applications of their work, for they recognize that they involve distasteful politics of the corporate, administrative, or governmental kind. For them, colleagues who enter the public arena may lose their "scientific virtue"; scientist-citizens, in their eyes, are inadequate scientists. As we shall see, nuclear winter scientists experienced criticism of their behavior for violating such older norms.

Was It Good Science?

A common—and reasonable—response to an unexpected projection is to question the quality of the data and calculations. No scientist is, or should be, immune to such treatment. Persistent and even abusive queries, for example, were addressed to Isaac Newton over his finding that white light is made up of many colors and to Albert Einstein over his theories of relativity. Crutzen and Birks, therefore, experienced predictable criticism when James Hansen, head of the Goddard Institute for Space Studies, opined that "any aerosol or climate impact would be negligible compared to the horrifying direct effects." Noting that a large volcanic eruption would loft a comparable amount of material without comparable reduction of sunlight, he doubted that fires would burn for 2 months and called the light-attenuation numbers used by Crutzen and Birks little more than guesses.[6]

The TTAPS group, too, faced doubters. As early as the April 1983 conference in Cambridge, voices were raised saying that TTAPS had not established their case. The scientific evidence and techniques, some argued, simply did not lead unambiguously to the NW phenomenon. Publicizing such findings, which were sure to be revised, would make scientists appear to accept lower standards of proof. Their stature as advisors would also likely be diminished, and all the more so if politicians and the public sensed that the scientists' political views influenced their work. (Similarly, the question has been asked if financial connections to pharmaceutical companies influenced conclusions of Food and Drug Administration scientists.) Opinions could enter when implications were discussed, but the technical work had to be kept inviolate. The credibility of science must be maintained.[7]

At the Halloween 1983 meeting in Washington, technical differences between TTAPS and Steven Schneider's group from the National Center for Atmospheric Research, whose three-dimensional computer model predicted patchy cooling, showed that the conclusions were by no means clear cut. Critics continued to argue against publication of such "squishy" results.

Also at the Halloween meeting, critics were quick to attack the threshold-of-megatonnage concept. Superficially, the idea was catchy and easy to comprehend. But it backfired by giving opponents a very visible handhold. TTAPS had been careful to qualify their description of the threshold; it certainly was not a sharp line below which civilization was safe. Rather, the calculation was "very approximate" and "extremely rough."[8] Sagan went out of his way to say "We do not know precisely where this threshold is," and that it was not known with "high precision."[9] The point was that horrendous climatic effects could be initiated with what most war gamers considered a relatively small exchange of weapons. Yet to most people Sagan, as spokesman for TTAPS, seemed to be saying that the minimum number of nuclear weapons required to create the NW condition was precisely calculable. (In retrospect, it would have been more accurate and more politic to define the threshold in terms of the optical depth of the smoke. Above a certain atmospheric opacity, OD = 1, NW is likely to occur.[10]) Since it is easy to find fault with the numbers from an early examination of a complex topic, TTAPS were most vulnerable on this point. Schneider felt that the term "threshold" was unfortunate, for it deflected attention away from calculations of the quantity of smoke that would be lofted. In the TTAPS work, moreover, there was "no dynamic feedback . . . the winds don't blow." There were numerous other detailed criticisms that Schneider expected to explore with his own three-dimensional climate model, yet he had to agree with TTAPS on the large picture.[11]

But TTAPS were, in fact, on solid ground regarding professional practice. Perhaps for the same reason that many scientists are uncomfortable with popularization—because the layman wishes to hear certainty, while understanding of Nature is tentative—scientists do not expect every published report to be the last word on a phenomenon. Quite the opposite is true, for a discovery is normally followed by a series of papers that confirm or refute the original claim, add evidence, and refine the analysis. TTAPS clearly recognized this, for they ended their formal paper in *Science* with a reasonable disclaimer:

Our estimates of the physical and chemical impacts of nuclear war are necessarily uncertain because we have used one-dimensional models, because the data base is incomplete, and because the problem is not amenable to experimental investigation. We are also unable to forecast the detailed nature of the changes in atmospheric dynamics and meteorology implied by our nuclear war scenarios, or the effects of such changes on the maintenance or dispersal of the initiating dust and smoke clouds. Nevertheless, the magnitudes of the first-order effects are so large, and the implications so serious, that we hope the scientific issues raised here will be vigorously and critically examined.[12]

Initial use of a one-dimensional radiative-convective model, for example, was altogether proper for that stage of the subject's development. The subsequent use of far more sophisticated three-dimensional global circulation models by TTAPS and by others was entirely to be expected. Were the stakes not so high, it is most likely that TTAPS's methodology would have raised no eyebrows whatever. (Perhaps the same might be said about the controversies that surrounded claims of ozone depletion and CO_2-induced global warming. All implied the need for policy decisions, and easy agreement was not to be anticipated.)

Another criticism that could be laid at TTAPS's feet was that they played the game of "my scientists can lick your scientists."[13] Sagan was said in the *Washington Post* to have secured endorsements of the NW concept from the Nobel laureates Hans Bethe and David Baltimore, from Carson Mark (longtime chief of the Los Alamos National Laboratory's Theoretical Division), and from the famed Harvard sociobiologist Edward O. Wilson.[14] Is such backing meaningful? A scientific idea is generally considered accepted when a consensus forms about it. Total agreement is unnecessary, but reasonably wide support is expected of scientific conclusions. Prominent individuals may provide support or opposition, but in themselves are unlikely to tilt opinions. When a phenomenon is new, supported by only the beginning of data collection and analysis, and also has political baggage attached, public assertions of backing may be little more than encouragement that research continue vigorously. It is hard to accept that such early backers are confirming the ultimate "truth" of a discovery.

But the existence of large numbers of scientists at the Cambridge and Washington conferences who apparently supported NW, many of whom were prominent in their own specialties, seemingly implied that it was correct. This occurred despite the fact that only a tiny number of them actively conducted research on this subject. For most of them it was an intellectual exercise: look for holes in the arguments of their colleagues. If this practice of "endorsement" is faulty, it is nonetheless effective in molding public opinion. Indeed, its use by TTAPS followed a tradition, although that tradition usually applied to political issues. Linus Pauling, for example, gained the signatures of thousands of scientists in the late 1950s to oppose nuclear testing. A few years later, annual meetings of Nobel laureates discussed science and world affairs, and hundreds of scientists (and others) took out full-page newspaper ads to criticize US involvement in Vietnam or to lobby for other causes. Indeed, the tradition is by no means restricted to scientists; it is part of our larger culture, in which movie stars sell jeans and athletes endorse breakfast cereals without being, respectively, experts on textiles or nutrition. Nonetheless, a sense of discomfort remains when scientists support others' scientific conclusions in fields where they have done no specific work themselves.

Another component of the behavior pattern of scientists before a public audience is the tendency to water down or even withhold their criticism of a colleague. This is not so much to keep peace within the fraternity. Quite the opposite, in fact; scientists are conditioned to question experiments, data, and conclusions continually. They know, however, that reporters will highlight disagreements in their articles, for such excitement sells newspapers, even if the scientists are in overall fundamental agreement. It is a form of circling the wagons against potentially hostile outsiders.

In the same issue of *Science* that carried TTAPS's paper on climatic consequences and the Ehrlich team's biological counterpart, William D. Carey wrote a supportive editorial titled "A run worth making." Carey was the publisher and the executive officer of the American Association for the Advancement of Science, so his view carried weight. While affirming scientists' right to design weapons against a feared enemy (a notion the Vatican had recently questioned), he asserted that they must also "look squarely at the consequences of violence in the application of scientific knowledge." Thus, he applauded the authors of the two papers: "It says a good deal for the emergence of the scientific conscience that, in a difficult age of superpower hatreds and technological gusto, the present warning is timely, unvarnished, and stark."[15]

No scientist is known to have lost a job because of NW activities. But applied research is ranked lower in the pecking order than basic research, while the intersection of science and politics carries a pungent odor. The profession makes that clear in subtle and not-so-subtle ways. Starley Thompson, for example, got job offers for his paleoclimate work; NW was not job-marketable. His colleague at the National Center for Atmospheric Research, Curt Covey, was told not to speak about NW in his interview for a position at the University of Miami, on the ground that the interviewers would want to see whether he was a "real" scientist.[16]

The Formality of Publication

Unlike engineers, who aspire to keep their intellectual contributions secret until they can be patented, scientists strive for early publication. Fame (leading to promotions and awards) is their goal, not royalties. The goal is to achieve priority in announcing a discovery. Journals, recognizing the needs of their contributors, usually record the date a paper is received, and this, rather than the date of the issue in which the paper ultimately appears, is accepted as the basis for a priority claim. And virtually all scientific periodicals use referees, who are expected to be reasonably well acquainted with the general subject and to be impartial. Authors, for their part, are expected not to submit a manuscript to more than one journal at a time, and, though they certainly may discuss their work at scientific meetings, it is bad form to release information to the popular media before publication.[17] All this is straightforward and unexceptional. Problems arise, however, when the procedure is modified.

In physics, and even more so in the biomedical field (where there is intense competition for large government grants to fight various diseases, as well as for personal fame), editors of the leading scientific journals have the authority to ban authors who "go public" before publication. This stricture extends to newspapers. Journalists may be given press releases or advance copies of scientific periodicals to enable them to write accurate accounts, but their stories are embargoed until the journals' publication dates.[18] Not only the scientists and reporters but the journals too are competitive; for example, in 1990 the *Journal of the American Medical Association* began to publish each week's issue the day before that of its archrival, the *New England Journal of Medicine*.[19]

Jonas Salk, among biomedical examples, was famous for developing a vaccine against polio. Nonetheless, he was something of an outcast from the scientific community because he used radio and television appearances to air his professional disputes. The conventional venues for such disagreement were, of course, scientific periodicals and scientific meetings. Nominations for Nobel Prizes generally come from one's colleagues, and it is no surprise that Salk never received the prize, although John Enders, Thomas Weller, and Frederick Robbins, who had shown that the virus could be cultured, were so honored (in 1954). It may be argued that the latter three made a basic research discovery, which is more acclaimed in the fraternity, whereas Salk's work was of an applied nature. But Nobels have gone to (allegedly "lower-class") applications of science in all three scientific fields of the award—for example, in physics for color photography (Gabriel Lippmann, 1908) and for a means of illuminating lighthouses and buoys (Nils Gustaf Dalén, 1912), in chemistry for organic chemistry and related help to the chemical industry (Adolf von Baeyer, 1905; Otto Wallach, 1910) and for a fodder-preservation method (Artturi Virtanen, 1945), and in physiology or medicine for discovering the high efficiency of DDT as a pesticide (Paul Hermann Müller, 1948) and for the discovery of the antibiotic streptomycin (Selman Waksman, 1952). Nor was Salk ever elected to the National Academy of Sciences.[20]

In 1986, mathematicians in England and Portugal announced that they had proved the famous Poincaré conjecture in three dimensions. Because of its importance, they said, they revealed the proof in *New Scientist*, a popular science magazine, rather than in a "normal" academic journal, where publication inevitably is much slower. Despite its condemnation, such alternative "publication" has become increasingly common in recent years. Unfortunately for these authors, as sometimes happens when one rushes into print, their proof was flawed.[21]

"Publication" by press conference is another of these alternative forms. The most egregious example in recent years, indeed the most astonishing violation of general community standards, was the announcement in 1989 of "cold fusion." Two prominent electrochemists claimed that they had produced nuclear fusion reactions at room temperature (instead of at the expected millions of degrees Celsius) and in apparatus that fit on a table top (instead of in a huge containment vessel). Their claim was made not in a refereed scientific journal (they had submitted a paper to *Nature* and then withdrew it) but at a news conference. And they declined to give full details of their procedure in deference to a patent application. If their claim had been valid, they would have had found a cheap and clean source of energy, with profound implications for economic, pollution, and political problems that plague the world. The University of Utah received $4.5 million from the state to establish a cold fusion institute, and all the while the two scientists adamantly declined to respond to queries from their colleagues or to provide adequate details of their work. Amidst near-universal disbelief in cold fusion among nuclear physicists, because there was no way to balance the energy equations, the electrochemists' lawyer (who was being paid by the University of Utah) threatened to sue scientists at the same university who intended to publish their own negative results. The university's president (a staunch supporter of cold fusion, since he envisioned institutional greatness in the process, as well as a gold mine in the new technology to be developed) deceitfully funneled funds into the new institute. But the house of cards tumbled fairly quickly as nuclear physicists around the US failed to replicate the phenomenon and the electrochemists continued to stonewall everyone. The lawyer subsequently withdrew his threat, and the president retired after a faculty vote of no confidence. Greed and the bad judgment of the peripheral actors aside, the central characters behaved in remarkably obtuse fashion. They made claims in a branch of science that was unfamiliar to them, declined to accept help from appropriate specialists, and failed to perform the most obvious control experiments. Scientists looked foolish in front of the public.[22]

In two of the examples cited above, the claims happened to be invalid. That, however, is not why I have mentioned them. My object has been to illustrate departures from the norms of the scientific community.

Some critics of NW's validity suggested that TTAPS were as insensitive to the profession's mores as the cold fusionists were several years later. Those critics claimed that TTAPS's work was not properly reviewed and that they committed the sin of doing science in the media.[23] George Rathjens (a political scientist at MIT, but formerly a chemist and chief scientist of the Advanced Research Projects Agency, and one who felt that Sagan was too much a publicist) characteristically did not mince words: ". . . in the scientific community you don't publish first results in *Parade* magazine."[24]

Sagan may have obliquely attempted to defend his behavior in his novel *Contact*, published a few years after the NW controversy erupted. When the fictional American scientists searching for extraterrestrial intelligence received a mysterious message,

At first they . . . tried to keep the findings quiet. After all, they were not absolutely sure it was an extraterrestrial message. A premature or mistaken announcement would be a public relations disaster. But worse than that, it would interfere with data analysis. If the press descended, the science would surely suffer.[25]

But in the novel the press was not kept out, because too many people already knew of the event and were discussing it. Sagan recognized that simple ideals of behavior are often unrealistic in our complex society. NW sounds vaguely similar to the search for extraterrestrial intelligence (SETI), except that a more compelling case can be made for early announcement of the consequences of nuclear explosions: the NW phenomenon can never fully be proved real except by a nuclear war. (In *Contact*, extraterrestrial intelligence was real.) It was appropriate that discussions of national security policy be initiated. Moreover, Sagan and some of his colleagues were veterans of the instant announcements and hype surrounding space probes (for NASA's very political reasons), and their behavior may have been conditioned by this culture.

With their public announcement that NW conditions were a likely consequence of nuclear war, did TTAPS violate the (imprecise) norms of the scientific community? Probably they bent them a little, but not seriously and not very differently than is done by the community's own organizations. The large Halloween-time conference in Washington was not the regular meeting of a scientific society, nor was it an advertised special event of a university, a laboratory, or a research institute, although many prestigious educational bodies willingly joined in sponsoring it. The meeting, further, was less an opportunity for the presentation of research papers than a forum for the publicity of results. In that, it was more like a media event than a scientific congress.

But, as anyone knows who attends the annual meetings of the American Association for the Advancement of Science (America's "umbrella" scientific organization), scientific societies themselves prepare these events primarily for the benefit of the media. Proposed AAAS sessions are preferentially approved if they have "wide" (meaning popular) appeal, and speakers are usually expected to provide multiple copies of their papers to the press office. A meeting's success is measured by the extent to which radio, television, newspapers, and news magazines sing science's praises to the public.

Indeed, positive public relations are so widely pursued by professional societies, universities, corporations, and government agencies that we should not be surprised when individual scientists cultivate their personal images. In *Selling Science: How the Press Covers Science and Technology*, the sociologist of science Dorothy Nelkin wrote about "the gradual development of a veritable public relations industry devoted to promoting science for the press." It has become something of a norm.[26]

The TTAPS paper, submitted to *Science* on 4 August 1983,[27] had been refereed and accepted by the time of the Halloween meeting, although it would be modified as a result of the meeting. Publication in *Science* came 2 months later. The published paper (and the Ehrlich team's biological companion piece) were, of course, only summarized and popularized for the conference in Washington. Though individual journals may have different policies about papers they have accepted, a general rule of thumb is that it is permissible to present a summary of the paper at a meeting, whereas it is impermissible to release information to the public media before publication.[28] (It is not clear if the editor of *Science* followed such a policy, but he did not reject the papers.) This leaves some room for interpretation. In the case of NW, this gray area of behavior allows one to regret that public announcement did not *follow* publication, yet it provides little basis for serious rebuke. The Halloween conference was a legitimate forum, and it is not always possible to coordinate a publication date with a large meeting in Washington. Sagan's article in *Parade*, on the other hand, would seem to be a rather clear violation of the mores of the scientific community, and yet that became almost irrelevant, since the article appeared only a day before a conference that was covered heavily by the press.

In taking their case first to the public, TTAPS appeared less to seek fame or to overcome the rejection of novel ideas by their community and more to advance a political agenda. Their conclusions were of overwhelming importance to mankind, they felt, and must be broadcast quickly. By this time, involvement in political issues by scientists, individually or through their societies, was widely accepted. The American Physical Society, for example, urged greater arms-control efforts, issued influential reports on energy efficiency, reactor safety, and the nuclear fuel cycle, and threw cold water on the Strategic Defense Initiative in the 1980s and on directed-energy weapons in the 1990s. Former FermiLab director Robert R. Wilson, in his 1986 APS presidential address, admitted that different physicists may evaluate a project differently but damned the quality of scientific advice President Reagan received by comparing SDI with Trofim Lysenko's destruction of Soviet genetics under Stalin.[29]

Scientific Personalities

Almost impossible to document, yet fairly abundant anecdotally, is the extent to which personal dislike shapes attitudes. Such aversion can grow from perceived violations of professional norms if the object of disfavor seems to be thumbing his nose at the standards his colleagues choose to obey. This kind of behavior has been discussed above.

Popularization of science is not perceived to be a violation of professional behavior, yet it peculiarly serves to diminish one's stature as much as it might enhance it. Of course, the popularizer usually is more famous than his colleagues and may have an appreciable "outside" income from royalties. Ignoring these factors, and professing the purest of professional reasons, critics may suggest that the publicly appreciated colleague never was, or is no longer, a really reputable scientist. How can he be, when he devotes so much attention to other activities? In England in the 1920s and the 1930s, J. B. S. Haldane, Lancelot Hogben, and Julian Huxley defied the taint of such charges.[30]

But plain, old-fashioned jealousy is surely a source of ill will. Jonas Salk, Carl Sagan, Margaret Mead, Linus Pauling, Paul Ehrlich, B. F. Skinner, Barry Commoner, William Shockley, Robert Oppenheimer, Edward Teller, Albert Einstein, Marie Curie, and others were "visible scientists." Not always popularizers of science in the usual sense, many of them championed controversial science-related policy issues, such as IQ, genetics, overpopulation, energy and food limits, and nuclear arms control.[31] They were famous far beyond the bounds of their discipline; indeed, the public often recognized their names and even their faces. Almost effortlessly, it seems (although manipulation of the media sometimes was involved), many of them appeared on TV talk shows, were quoted in the newspapers, addressed gatherings of non-scientists, and, simply put, were noticeable. Science, a field in which reputation rather than money is the "coinage of the realm," has its share of large egos. Jealously of another's fame is not uncommon, though usually it is disguised. Criticism, as I suggested above, is expressed in terms of allegedly inadequate work, poor presentation of science to the public, mixing science with politics, and so on.

Albert Einstein was disparaged for being too famous. A spokesman for pacifism throughout World War I, he naturally became a foe of the militarists. But the intense hostility he experienced bloomed after the war. During a solar eclipse, starlight was found to bend near a massive object, just as his theory of general relativity predicted. This astonishing result led to his worldwide celebrity. It also inspired virulent condemnation by the German right wing, the anti-Semites, and those who faulted theoretical science. Yet the Berlin Academy of Sciences declined to defend their beleaguered colleague in 1920, its secretary calling the attacks "an essentially political matter" and noting that "the tasteless glorification of the new Archimedes and Newton was distasteful to so many."[32]

Jonas Salk was revered by the populace, his fame having been burnished by the March of Dimes' large public-relations effort (which was in that organization's own interest too). In contrast, Sagan was not beloved by the masses (he had not increased their health or wealth), but he was remarkably well appreciated. Even before his enormously successful *Cosmos* TV series, he had received a Pulitzer Prize (for his book *The Dragons of Eden: Speculations on the Evolution of Human Intelligence*), and he was a media darling. He was a dynamo of activity who wrote delightful prose, spoke in articulate and quotable phrases, was handsome, exuded charm and grace, and participated in spectacular projects, such as the space program and the search for extraterrestrial intelligence. *Cosmos* then put him in the nation's living rooms for 13 weeks in 1980, and repeatedly in following years through re-runs and videos. His turtleneck shirt became recognized as a personal trademark as much as his alleged allusion to "billions and billions" of stars (he denied saying this). Other "visible" scientists of the day—Stephen Jay Gould, Stephen Hawking, and Freeman Dyson, for example—certainly had their fans, but, instantly, Sagan became America's most popular scientist, appreciated for his remarkable ability to explain complex material in simple terms. (When in 1985 the Federation of American Scientists presented him with its Public Service Award, the plaque called him the "Most Visible Member of the Scientific Community of the Planet Earth."[33]) *Cosmos* won Emmy and Peabody awards, and a book drawn from it became the best-selling work of science in English. The novel *Contact* added yet more luster to his obvious talents, and it too reached a mass audience when a film version appeared in 1997.

At the same time, it would seem that Sagan's stock among his peers fell. It is difficult to be a media star while keeping your credentials as a solid, workbench scientist. Some felt that Sagan was indeed quite a good scientist, but not the wizard that his high degree of public recognition implied. Others equated his ever-present visage to that of a television automobile huckster, calling him the "Cal Worthington of science." The columnist William F. Buckley Jr. said Sagan was "so arrogant he might have been confused with, well, me." He was faulted for strutting around on the TV screen, conveying an uncomfortable image for most scientists, one to which they had difficulty relating. One observer (who apparently had never heard of Einstein) gushed: "Never before in the history of science or mass media has a scientist's name, face and voice been as familiar as Brooke Shields' or Bo Derek's."[34]

When Sagan's name became almost synonymous with research on the NW phenomenon, he was perceived by some not only as a not entirely credible scientist, but also as a man who bent his scientific conclusions to support his liberal political agenda.[35] When his name was mentioned in scientific colloquia, it sometimes produced a ripple of sneers and knowing smiles. He was too famous to be taken seriously as a scientist. His colleagues also faulted him for his polemical style, which was designed to persuade as much as to report. A book reviewer scornfully called him a "scientist/self-promoter/public television messiah" and "of course, the smartest man who *ever* lived."

In 1992, when Sagan was nominated for election to the National Academy of Sciences, he was rejected. This is a very rare occurrence, and when it happens it seems to be based on strong feelings that are not entirely related to evaluation of the candidate's scientific accomplishments.[36] In a peculiar (or perhaps apologetic) move 2 years later, the NAS presented Sagan with its Public Welfare Medal, officially noted as the "Academy's highest honor." The medal, recognizing "extraordinary use of science for the public good," had been given in the three most recent years to Jerome Wiesner, Philip Abelson, and Victor Weisskopf. The press release for the 1994 award did not mention nuclear winter.[37] Upon Sagan's death in December 1996, the Harvard zoologist Stephen Jay Gould, himself no slouch in bringing science to the public, lamented Sagan's treatment and called him "the greatest popularizer of the twentieth century, if not of all time."[38]

It seems clear that Sagan's personality was a causal factor in both NW's success and its failure to be believed. Sagan worked energetically to persuade many scientists, officials, and laymen that policy changes were required to avoid the consequences of NW, yet for the doubters he simultaneously became a lightning rod for his alleged self-promotion and disregard of scientific precision. Certainly NW did not rise or fall solely in Sagan's shadow, but he shaped its history far more than any other individual.

The News Media

The news media failed to see NW approaching as one of the year's big stories, whether of science or of politics. No ominous reports were carried by the national press after TTAPS's Cambridge review session in April 1983 (it was not open to the press, but news might have been leaked), or after the International Seminar on Nuclear War, held in Erice, Sicily, that August. The Erice seminar, part of a series that began in 1981, was organized by Edward Teller, Yevgeny Velikhov (vice president of the Soviet Academy of Sciences), and Antonino Zichichi (director of the Ettore Majorana Centre for Scientific Culture). Featured were several papers on the atmospheric effects of nuclear explosions, with scientists from the Lawrence

Livermore National Laboratory prominent on the program.[39] Of particular interest, Michael MacCracken, the climate specialist in the Livermore Lab's Atmospheric and Geophysical Sciences Division (and concurrently since 1993 the director of the Office of the US Global Change Research Program), and Vladimir Aleksandrov, from the Soviet Academy of Sciences' Computing Center in Moscow, both presented preliminary results that showed striking cooling effects.[40] Aleksandrov later spoke at a meeting organized by the Finnish Committee of the Institut de la Vie in Helsinki, in early September,[41] and at the Halloween conference in Washington. NW was international from its origin.

MacCracken, aware of the TTAPS study, initially used a similar one-dimensional radiative-convective computer model. Later, he modified a two-dimensional model (which he had developed for other purposes) to allow for more realistic movement of the smoke. (Aleksandrov's three-dimensional global circulation model had some common ancestry with MacCracken's model, but it was limited in several details.) MacCracken—far more cautious than TTAPS in announcing results (perhaps a characteristic of the weapons laboratories' culture, yet uncharacteristic of Edward Teller, the founder of the applied science program at the Davis campus of the University of California, where MacCracken had studied), and scrupulously candid about the "many assumptions, shortcomings and uncertainties"—nonetheless concluded that smoke from city and industrial targets could lower temperatures significantly in the Northern Hemisphere, lasting from weeks to months. Continental interiors could suffer temperature declines of "a few tens of degrees Celsius."[42]

The media were far more attentive to the Crutzen-Birks paper in *Ambio*[43] and the forthcoming Halloween meeting, which was a public event. *Sierra* and *International Wildlife* primed their readers for disaster, even suggesting that "effects of unforeseen nature and magnitude" would be revealed at the conference, but apparently had no details to report.[44] Indeed, even before the Halloween meeting the media were "cultivated," some would say manipulated. In late October, the *New York Times* (and perhaps other papers) received an advance summary of the NW effect and interviewed Sagan by telephone. The *Times* article appeared on the newsstands as the conference opened, emphasizing faithfully the major points made by Sagan in *Parade*. These were indeed awesome, yet the editors buried the news on page 16, next to a story on two mentally retarded men who were involuntarily kept as farm workers in Michigan.[45]

The next day, 1 November, the *Washington Post* gave the conference front-page attention and a day later placed a related story on page 8. The Soviet work, which predicted an astounding 100°F (56°C) reduction over Russia's Kola Peninsula, and the more conservative estimates by Joseph Knox and Michael MacCracken of Livermore, whose model included the moderating influence on temperature of the oceans, were regarded as independent confirmations of TTAPS's conclusions. The Livermore group, continuing the study MacCracken had presented in Erice, calculated a temperature decrease of around 20°F (11°C) along the coast and one of more than 50°F (28°C) in continental interiors.[46] Such numbers, large on any scale, had a still greater impact when contrasted with the National Academy of Sciences' last estimation (in 1975) of the extent of temperature change in a nuclear war: a few tenths of a degree centigrade due to injected dust and several tenths of a degree from ozone depletion.[47] The novelty of the new figures did not go unobserved.[48] Numerous other stories and editorials were published in the next few weeks, most merely echoing the information presented at the conference. Most writers found the existence of a threshold ominous,[49] although some chose not to mention it.[50]

Though the number of stories on NW never reached a large total, the level of professionalism, especially in those papers and journals with designated science reporters, was very high. Among the best stories were those by Boyce Rensberger and Philip J. Hilts of the *Washington Post*, William J. Broad of the *New York Times*, James Gerstenzang of the *Los Angeles Times*, Barbara G. Levi of *Physics Today*, and R. Jeffrey Smith of *Science*.

Another aspect of media cultivation deserves mention. Knowing that a picture is worth a thousand words, Carl Sagan commissioned for his *Parade* article four paintings by his long-time artistic collaborator Jon Lomberg. The paintings showed Earth from space as the war began, then as the clouds spread, then as the chill descended, and then enveloped in dark mist. Lomberg later used his skills to prepare a videotape on NW that was narrated by Sagan and shown to a number of the world's political leaders.[51] For the Halloween meeting's transcript, quickly published in book form as *The Cold and the Dark*, nine paintings by Rob Wood were used. These were horrifying close-in views of fires, darkness, and devastation to people, flora, and fauna. A film of the climatic consequences of the 5,000-MT baseline scenario also was made and shown at the press conference that followed the Halloween conference.[52]

Paul Ehrlich, lead author of the biological-consequences paper on NW soon to appear in *Science*, was an articulate spokesman to the media. Like Sagan, he was a master of the "sound bite." His research team had concluded, he said, that "when you turn off the lights, turn down the temperature to 40 degrees below zero in the middle of July, and turn up the radiation, you would have an unprecedented biological disaster."[53]

Claims that the human species might become extinct were "eye-catching" for the press. Sagan mentioned that prospect in his *Parade* article, and at the conference Ehrlich and his biological colleagues reluctantly conceded the possibility. This became a controversial issue, all the more, perhaps, because the question of extinction had been tossed around in recent decades in connection with genetic radiation damage. Misused atomic energy had been predicted—and not only in monster movies—to lead to the birth of cripples, dreadful diseases, and ultimately genetic death. These anticipations, although sometimes credible, were considered unlikely.[54] Still more recently, Jonathan Schell's book *The Fate of the Earth* had emphasized the possible end of human life. NW scenarios now reopened the extinction debate, and this provided another personalized connection for laypeople: NW concerned them!

The Halloween meeting's organizers, moreover, made certain that the media would find it irresistible. As if the announcement of NW was not headline material enough, they set up a two-way live satellite-relayed television link with some scientists in Moscow. A last-minute addition to the conference, this was not publicized beforehand, nor was it even noted on the program. A separate handbill listed the American panelists, but labeled the Soviets only as "to be announced."[55] Conceived by steering committee member Robert Allen and a few colleagues, this 90-minute discussion of the climatic and biological outcomes of nuclear war followed the last session of the 1 November 1983 conference. Most of the participants stayed to watch it.[56]

In Washington, the meteorologist Thomas Malone, director emeritus of Butler University's Holcomb Research Institute and former foreign secretary of the US National Academy of Sciences, chaired a panel that consisted of Walter Orr Roberts, Paul Ehrlich, and Carl Sagan. Facing them via satellite were the aforementioned Yevgeny Velikhov (a physicist), the molecular geneticist Alexander Bayev (secretary of the Soviet Academy of Sciences' Biochemical, Biophysical, and Chemical Physiology Department), Yuri Izrael (a corresponding member of the academy, also head of the State Committee on Hydrometeorology and Control of the Natural Environment), and Nikolai Bochkov (an academician of the Medical Academy of Sciences, and the director of the Soviet Academy of Sciences' Institute of Genetics). Earlier they had watched the proceedings in Washington by means of the same "Moscow Link." Like their American counterparts, the Soviet scientists pledged to focus on the scientific issues and avoid political questions.[57]

Little new scientific information was provided from Moscow. Essentially, the speakers said that their own calculations confirmed various predictions that the Americans had made. Yet it appeared that these calculations were from investigations that preceded the NW concept. The work specifically on NW by Aleksandrov and his colleagues was mentioned only in passing. Many comments on both sides, indeed, could be called semi-political: they pertained to international relations, but they were largely unobjectionable. The speakers hoped that the conference would give new impetus to nuclear disarmament efforts; they agreed that nuclear weapons were tools neither of war nor politics; they were comforted by the consensus that nuclear war would be a tragedy for humankind and must be avoided.[58] Each of these remarks was warmly applauded by the audiences in both capitals; participants apparently felt more confident about the future than at any time since Ronald Reagan's election.[59]

The stance on NW taken by various publications could have been predicted fairly well from their editorial policies on other political issues. Environmentalist and liberal journals were generally inclined to accept that NW was a proven phenomenon, while conservative and business publications faulted the science or took a wait-and-see attitude. The environmental agenda, for example, could not help but be galvanized by John Birks's call to arms in *Sierra*: "Nuclear war is the ultimate environmental threat. Unless we solve this problem, all other work on environmental problems will be irrelevant."[60] Nor should it be forgotten that the Halloween conference was called specifically to address the biological consequences of nuclear explosions, a subject far less controversial than the physical climatic effects.

In the other camp, it is hard to find a publication more hostile to the concept of NW than the *Wall Street Journal*, which had long been a venue for arms race hardliners and anti-environmentalists and a locus of right-wing journalistic crusading. Widely praised for its professionally objective treatment of business and economic topics, the *WSJ*'s opinion pages were regularly condemned for bias by scientists, journalists, and officials of activist organizations.[61] *WSJ* editorials and letters to the editor portrayed the TTAPS work as hopelessly flawed, although the *WSJ* also published letters by Sagan and others in response.

Media interest in NW continued for some years, but intense scrutiny lasted only a few weeks. The common criticism of TV and newspapers, that they cater to the sensationalism that most attracts viewers and readers, would seem to be valid here. NW, for example, went virtually unmentioned in the commentary that followed the broadcast of *The Day After*. Was it because NW had been depicted in dispassionate, quantitative fashion, and thus failed to make reporters' stories sizzle? Richard L. Strout, longtime political observer for the *Christian Science Monitor*, thought so.[62] It is difficult, however, to think how else to describe death and destruction that exceeds the carnage of the immediate effects of nuclear war, and to do so without the heightened verbal and visual eloquence of the theater.

The New Yorker complained that the media had missed a chance to show that they could recognize what might have been the most significant event in our lives and describe it well. Not one major newspaper in the United States, *The New Yorker* noted, placed NW across the top of page 1; indeed, only the *Washington Post* carried it on the first page—and then below the fold. Neither did the electronic media acquit themselves well:

ABC gave it a minute and forty seconds, well into the evening news. The NBC Nightly News mentioned it briefly near the end of the broadcast. The CBS Evening News had nothing. The world had just been given the most authoritative warning it has ever had that its doom is an urgent and present danger, but the viewers of this news program never heard a thing about it.

If coverage was inadequate, commentary was worse: "Few columnists or editorialists were stirred to thought by the discovery that mankind threatened to freeze itself to death." Politicians also ignored the issue: "The President had nothing to say. Congress was mute." *The New Yorker* lauded only Ted Koppel, who devoted an entire *Nightline* show to NW.[63]

Koppel also hosted a show on 20 November 1983, after the broadcast of *The Day After*. Many people at home were shocked into silence by the depiction of awesome disaster inflicted on Lawrence and Kansas City by a nuclear warhead. Not so Carl Sagan, one of Koppel's commentators, who faulted the movie for *understating* the enormity of the catastrophe. NW, he claimed, would increase the extent of death and destruction.[64] (Representative Philip M. Crane, chairman of the Republican Study Committee, had unsuccessfully urged President Reagan to make a "preemptive strike" against the film by publicly explaining that his policies—including the impending deployment in Europe of Pershing II missiles—would prevent the pictured holocaust.[65] Nonetheless, the administration was concerned enough about the unprecedented publicity that preceded the film's broadcast, which drew 100 million viewers, and about potential political consequences, to arrange for Secretary of State George Shultz to make a soothing TV appearance immediately after the broadcast.[66])

Sagan got other opportunities to publicize TTAPS's conclusions on television. For example, on 24 March 1984 (and again on 1 April 1984), Ted Turner's cable channel TBS aired a half-hour documentary titled *The World After Nuclear War*, with Sagan as narrator. Much of the show consisted of excerpts from the "Moscow Link"; the rest was Sagan as a "talking head."

Public reaction to these various media events was weak. People may have become blasé about nuclear destruction, uncertain whether NW was indeed a real phenomenon, or somewhat distrustful of both media and scientists—or all of the above. Whereas scientists generally had a good press through the 1940s, the 1950s, and the 1960s, their image as beneficial and omniscient was marred in later decades. Toxic wastes at Love Canal and Times Beach, nuclear reactor accidents at Three Mile Island and Chernobyl, the *Challenger* failure, the chemical plant explosion at Bhopal, cases of scientific fraud, and other conditions and events, before and after NW made its debut, presented new images of scientists as corrupt and often as hired guns for corporate greed and government laxity. The sociologist of science Dorothy Nelkin noted the popular myths that surrounded most intersections of science and society. The public believed, she said, that "science can provide definitive answers about risk, . . . 'facts' speak for themselves rather than being open to interpretation, and . . . decisions about what risks are socially acceptable are scientific rather than political judgments."[67] Perhaps, by the time that the concept of NW was first discussed, the public had become a bit more sophisticated about the unexpected effects on society of science and technology.

7 Politics and the Arms Race

Freeman Dyson, a brilliant physicist and an acclaimed author, has a flair for getting to the heart of the matter. In a 1988 book titled *Infinite in All Directions*, he mused:

Nuclear winter is not primarily a technical problem; it is much more a moral and political problem. It forces us to ask fundamental questions: whether the benefits which we derive from the possession of nuclear weapons are in any way commensurate with the risks; whether the risk of irreparable damage to the fabric of life on Earth can in any way be morally justified.[1]

Dyson was one of just a few who raised the issue of morality in the NW debate. The Roman Catholic bishops, theologians, and scholars who had recently addressed concepts of just war, deterrence, and various aspects of the nuclear arms race were virtually silent regarding NW, though in 1986 Methodist bishops briefly but explicitly mentioned NW in a pastoral letter that strongly condemned the policy of deterrence.[2] Also surprisingly silent were the various American "peace" groups, whose arguments were moralistic to a large degree. They seem to have decided to wait out the technical controversy over NW before jumping into the political fray.

But politics were not to be delayed. Indeed, it was inevitable that politics would enter the nuclear winter picture, and do so at an early date. Not only did many of the scientist-participants look on NW as the "kick in the pants" needed to convince politicians, strategists, and the military that nuclear war could not be won, but any phenomenon that affected battlefield conditions and postwar recovery would have to be part of the political calculus. Additionally, a segment of the American public looked upon citizens who advocated anything less than an all-out arms race as agents or dupes of the Kremlin. Over the years, outspoken physicians, physicists, and theologians were tarred with this disloyalty brush; now biologists who spoke of NW consequences joined them in disrepute. The stakes seemed particularly high in early November 1983, for President Reagan had just sent American forces to Grenada. Surely there was no fear of nuclear combat over this tiny Caribbean island, but as a symbol of the administration's bellicosity it was chilling.[3] The *New York Times* columnist Tom Wicker assessed superpower relations as being "at the lowest level" since the Cuban Missile Crisis.[4] For thematic purposes, the media reception and the political implications of NW are presented separately in this volume, although they were tightly linked.

Political Maneuvering before Halloween 1983

Politics, of course, were always part of the nuclear war picture, and legislators desired to be well informed. When Crutzen and Birks revealed the importance of black smoke to the postwar climate, Congress grew more attentive to the subject. In September 1982, only 3 months after the paper in *Ambio* appeared, the Subcommittee on Investigations and Oversight of the House Committee on Science and Technology held a hearing on "The Consequences of Nuclear War on the Global Environment." Chaired by Representative Albert Gore Jr. (D-Tennessee), the subcommittee was concerned about both the danger of conflict and the conditions in a postwar world. In view of much talk by Secretary of Defense Caspar Weinberger about prevailing in a nuclear war, which surely implied surviving it, the subcommittee wanted to explore whether that was likely. Eight academic physicians and scientists (including John Birks) were called to testify about their new insights. The Department of Defense and its Defense Nuclear Agency were invited but declined to appear, probably because of expected criticism of the Reagan administration's statements and policies.[5]

When asked what sorts of studies needed more funding, witness James P. Friend, a chemistry professor from Drexel University who had been on the 1975 National Academy of Sciences committee that had studied the worldwide effects of nuclear war, cited ultraviolet reaction mechanisms and their effects on specific types of plants, such as crops and oceanic plankton. From the time ozone depletion had first been recognized, Friend said, "biologists have been calling for financial support steadily . . . and have really gotten none. . . . A little money was put forth to do some studies on radiation effects in the environment, and then a lot of that was taken back."[6] Though *A Nuclear Winter's Tale* is not a detailed study of the sources of NW research funding, it is necessary to recognize that the federal government was (and has been since World War II) the source of most research money in the nation, but that the distribution of these funds has always been a matter of controversy.

Friend also provided a useful update of the 1975 NAS report. In the years since then, the arsenals of both the United States and the Soviet Union had undergone changes. Many older warheads had been replaced with "MIRVs" (multiple warheads on the same missile) of greater accuracy and smaller yield. This suggested that a somewhat different mix of surface and altitude detonations over targets would occur, reducing the amount of radioactivity, nitrogen oxides, and dust injected into the troposphere. However, when Julius Chang of the Livermore Laboratory ran the new data through his computer model, he found relatively small changes in the results. The decline in average surface temperature, lasting a few years, remained about half a degree Celsius in this pre-NW calculation.[7] Not until TTAPS brought soot from urban fires into the equation would the temperatures plummet.

Frank von Hippel of Princeton University, president of the Federation of American Scientists, emphasized to the committee that in Sweden minimal funding had produced momentous results. *Ambio*'s editor, Jeannie Peterson, who had commissioned the Crutzen-Birks work, had told von Hippel that publishing the special issue of the journal had cost $35,000. Von Hippel reflected: "That is a pretty small amount compared to the tens of billions of dollars that we and the Soviets are spending each year on developing improved abilities to use these weapons."[8] Among the other scholars who testified on civil defense, UV effects, radioactivity, disease, and medical response were Sidney Drell of the Stanford Linear Accelerator Center and H. Jack Geiger of the City College of New York's School of Biomedical Education.

Congress, of course, was not the only forum for ideas. One of America's most influential molders of public opinion—and even more so of official beliefs—was Edward Teller. Famous for his role in the development of the hydrogen bomb, infamous for his part in convincing the AEC in 1954 to withdraw J. Robert Oppenheimer's security clearance, and notorious once again for beguiling President Reagan in 1983 to launch the Strategic Defense Initiative, Teller worked seriously at pushing his ideas. He was also quite human, in that he criticized others for doing as he did: advocating a national security policy on the basis of a worst-case scenario that itself relied on uncertain scientific data.[9]

In November 1982, *Reader's Digest* gave Teller a forum to warn about several "dangerous myths" concerning nuclear weapons. The TTAPS work, of course, would not be publicized for a year to come and was not mentioned, but Teller was strangely silent about the Crutzen-Birks paper, now out several months. His focus, instead, was primarily on countering arguments for a freeze on the production of nuclear weapons (a position then generating much political support), and secondarily on promoting civil defense measures and continued arms development and minimizing the fears of fallout and ozone depletion. Human life, he insisted, would not be erased by a nuclear conflict.[10] This, one might say, was "vintage" Teller, trying to put the best face on nuclear war. Another venerable refrain was his cry that the data were insufficient. Despite this lack, Teller felt that he could propose a policy position. He focused on the extent of ozone depletion following a large nuclear exchange; this needed more study. Even before such study, however, and "assuming a worst-case scenario" in which about half the superpowers' strategic arsenals were exploded in the atmosphere, with all weapons being at least a megaton in size, Teller accepted a probable 50 percent loss of the Northern Hemisphere's ozone shield. Such damage could be avoided, he said, by limiting warhead yield to 400 KT, since the nitrogen oxides generated in the fireball do not rise to the stratosphere. Teller, steeped in the ways of the bargaining-chip school in dealing with the Soviets, felt that "such a limitation should become an important part of disarmament talks."[11]

In this case, the technological imperative of reducing the weight of MIRVed warheads so as to pack more of them into a missile's nose cone, coupled with less need for large yields due to improved targeting accuracy, made that 400-KT goal a unilaterally large part of the

US arsenal. Regarding policy advocacy, however, before long the pot would call the kettle black.

An abstract of the early work by TTAPS (actually TTPS, since Ackerman was not yet a co-author) was published in *Eos* in advance of the American Geophysical Union's meeting in San Francisco. A paper was to have been read on 9 December 1982 in a session on "Climatic Variations on the Terrestrial Planets," with James Pollack as chairman.[12] But on 8 December, Angelo Gustafero, deputy director of NASA's Ames Research Center, acting on his own initiative, called the AGU to say that the paper could not be presented. His explanation was that, owing to a bureaucratic error, it had not been properly cleared at Ames. The paper was withdrawn.

Toon and Pollack (the two co-authors of the work from Ames) and lead author Richard Turco (from NASA contractor R&D Associates) reluctantly agreed. The management had a legitimate concern, even if it was political and not merely administrative. Indeed, in retrospect they realized that they had been naive. They felt that they had some exciting scientific things to discuss, and they were taken aback by the political storm. "What's the point of working on the earth's climate," Pollack asked, "if you don't want to do a relevant calculation?" NASA earlier had played a leadership role in the ozone-depletion controversy, so the scientists were unprepared for its current timidity. Toon, who traveled to NASA headquarters in Washington to alert officials that NASA scientists were about to discuss nuclear war, learned of the Ames decision while in Washington. When Gustafero asked Turco to present something else, Turco declined, sarcastically saying that he could not tell the audience "Forget about the abstract; I'm going to talk about volcanoes."

Even though the work was not a formally sponsored investigation at Ames, the research on atmospheric phenomena was clearly within the scope of the center's mission, and its Cray supercomputer had been used. In effect, NASA was an unwitting sponsor of this research because it permitted its employees to "moonlight" or "pirate" some of their time for non-programmed research. As such, it was normal procedure to have the paper reviewed "in house," and it had not gone through that evaluation. But, then, neither did a lot of other papers, especially work in progress to be presented at a meeting, well before the stage of submission for publication in a journal.[13]

Indeed, Toon recalled that officials in Washington knew of their NW work (some done at the request of the National Academy of Sciences) as early as the spring of 1982, when he and Pollack submitted a standard form to the program manager indicating how their funds would be spent. Aside from their primary study of volcanoes and climate, they noted that nuclear war would occupy a portion of their time. The canceled paper at the AGU meeting was the first sign of official displeasure. Then, in 1983, headquarters cut their budget, possibly as a sign of disapproval for using NASA money on such a topic, an action that Toon regarded as the bureaucracy covering itself. Or perhaps it was merely part of a larger action by the government to slash budgets in many areas. In any case, by that time the bulk of TTAPS's calculations had been completed.[14]

Carl Sagan regarded the AGU incident as censorship, and was incensed. To Sagan, Gustafero defended his action as a preemptive step to avoid retaliation by the Reagan administration against NASA. Two days before the AGU meeting, the House of Representatives had voted to stop funding the MX missile; one day earlier, someone had tried to blow up the Washington Monument. Gustafero did not want Reagan to hear bad news three days in a row, especially that his *civilian* space agency opposed his nuclear war policies. NASA was not supposed to be in the nuclear weapons business. While Sagan was able to extract from Gustafero a commitment not to deny supercomputer time for the duration of the project, he claimed that the director of Ames, Clarence Syvertson, at one time threatened to close down the entire space sciences division if they persisted in pursuing this subject. Seeking to overcome this fear of offending what he considered an ideological administration, Sagan received assurances from NASA administrator James M. Beggs that NW work would not be suppressed.[15]

Indeed, Ames created a panel of three senior scientists which conducted two reviews of the work.[16] This helped improve its in-house credibility. Ames even provided discretionary laboratory funds to allow completion of the paper for *Science* when NASA bureaucrats in Washington cut funding to the TTAPS members at Ames.[17] Withdrawing the paper at the AGU meeting surprised the audience, particularly Livermore people who wanted to know the contents, but there was no outcry. Cancellation did not go unnoticed by the media: *Aviation Week and Space Technology* reported the withdrawal, printing much of the abstract.[18] As it turned out, the Ames officials need not have feared for their center's future. When NW became headline material a year later, Sagan and Paul Ehrlich were the spokesmen, and no one associated NW with NASA.

This incident highlighted the paranoia to be expected in addressing a topic involved with national security. Turco, not referring to this event specifically, recalled the "tremendous political pressure on us to not get involved." Indeed, many saw the study as non-science; they regarded it as politically motivated.[19] If the NW research could be internationalized, Sagan reasoned, perhaps the level of suspicion that the science was tainted by political beliefs might be lowered. The Soviets, whose warheads were larger and thus more likely to contribute to the creation of a NW, had more to lose if restructuring their nuclear arsenal was necessary. Should the Soviets become convinced that the phenomenon was real and required a response, the expected doubters in the United States might be more open to conviction. If Soviet scientists agreed with TTAPS, it followed that both superpowers should pursue similar nuclear strategies. TTAPS then could not be accused of implicitly advocating unilateral disarmament or any other position that would place the US at a disadvantage. (With the same logic, International Physicians for the Prevention of Nuclear War had recently staged—in June 1982—a television presentation on the medical consequences of nuclear war, by physicians from both the US and the USSR.)

In early 1983, Sagan arranged to see the highest-level Soviet scientist he knew: the physicist Yevgeny Velikhov, vice president of the Soviet Academy of Sciences, who was in

Washington for a meeting of the inter-academy group on national security. Roald Sagdeev, director of the Soviet Institute of Space Research, joined them at the Soviet embassy. Sagan impressed upon them the importance of Soviet participation in the forthcoming April meeting in Cambridge, if only to carry news of the phenomenon back to Moscow. More compelling, though, would be independent study of NW.

Velikhov immediately replied that the perfect person to study the effects of nuclear war on the atmosphere was a young man named Vladimir Aleksandrov, head of the Climate Research Laboratory at the academy's Computing Center in Moscow. Coyly displaying his influence, Velikhov added that the usual requirement for a year or so advance notice of a meeting could be waived. To Sagan's surprise, Aleksandrov came alone to Cambridge, without the expected security agent "handlers." At that meeting, Sagan urged him to make independent calculations with his three-dimensional model. Aleksandrov demurred, saying that computer time was extremely difficult to get in Moscow. He would try, but it would likely take 12–18 months. In fact, he was able to progress much faster: Aleksandrov appeared at the Halloween meeting in Washington, participated in the discussion, and distributed preprints in English of the paper he had presented at Erice the previous August.[20]

Although Sagan took some criticism for working closely with the Soviets, his political sense was correct. The participation of Soviet scientists increased the American public's perception of NW's significance. Aleksandrov, moreover, was an uncommonly appropriate colleague, having spent 6 months in 1978 at the National Center for Atmospheric Research in Boulder, where he used the Cray I supercomputer for climate modeling (and served as Steve Schneider's backyard barbeque chef[21]). Subsequently, Aleksandrov returned to the United States for another half year. This time, he again used the NCAR's Cray at Oregon State University, and he finally did some climate research at the Livermore Laboratory. Indeed, with at least eight trips to the US, he was at the pinnacle of US-Soviet scientific exchanges, and by the mid 1980s, when the Department of Defense sought to limit the Soviet Bloc's access to supercomputers, he may have been the only person from east of the Iron Curtain to have had significant access to these exotic machines.[22]

Also in early 1983, Sagan contacted Robert Cess, a planetary atmospheres scientist at the State University of New York at Stony Brook, because he felt that Cess had good ties to the defense community. Sagan asked him to make an independent, back-of-the-envelope calculation on NW for the conference. Cess presented his results, which largely agreed with TTAPS, at the Cambridge meeting. In particular, he calculated that there would be surface cooling instead of heating. His credibility at the Department of Defense presumably helped underscore the validity of NW. This shows, incidentally, that simple calculations can give reasonable results of some phenomena, even if detailed computations are ultimately required. The reason no one did it sooner was not the lack of the idea (smoke had been named as a problem earlier); it was lack of reasonably good numbers.[23]

The Ames Research Center was not the only employer concerned about its good name (and perhaps retaliation by the Reagan administration). Turco's company had similar apprehensions. R&D Associates thus conducted an internal review of the TTAPS Blue Book, being unhappy with the targeting of cities and finding estimations of superpower arsenal size and configuration, urban area burned, amount of dust lofted, and the population's burden of radioactivity excessive, yet apparently concluding nonetheless that TTAPS's work was solid.[24]

The unusual length to which TTAPS (and Sagan in particular) went to defuse politically based hostility to their work is remarkable. But, as with Sisyphus, the task was never-ending. In the autumn of 1983, after proofs of the paper for *Science* had been corrected, the Ames leadership insisted that there be no discussion of casualties and that the Ames affiliation of Toon, Ackerman, and Pollack not be given if the paper's title included "nuclear war" or "nuclear weapons." They wanted to minimize any suggestion that Ames was working outside its area of expertise, and certainly to avoid waving red flags of terminology. TTAPS picked a substitute title in a conference telephone call, but it was so long that *Science* rejected it. In a second conference call they agreed on Turco's inspired term "nuclear winter." This accommodated Ames's sensitivity, although it perversely allowed the phenomenon to become far more recognizable to a wide public.[25]

Invitations to the Washington conference were mailed by its chairman, George M. Woodwell, to a wide range of people, including many in the federal bureaucracy. The response from officialdom was one of political wariness, and not of enlightened interest in the validity of NW. Typical was NASA administrator James Beggs's note to a colleague in the White House: "The Administration should be aware of what Carl Sagan is up to. No doubt many in the Federal structure will be solicited. Carl is obviously trying to become a leader in the anti-nuke movement."[26] The Reagan White House clearly felt that this was a political issue; the Halloween conference's organizers, for example, rented office space from Gus Speth, of the World Resources Institute, who had been chairman of the Council on Environmental Quality in the Jimmy Carter administration.[27]

The Department of Defense, which already was sponsoring a study of NW by the National Academy of Sciences, also recognized the political dimension. The assistant to the secretary of defense for atomic energy, Richard Wagner, resolved that the DoD should have stated positions on "all upcoming global war media events," including the Halloween meeting and *The Day After*. Further, Wagner felt that someone from the Defense Nuclear Agency should attend the conference in order to be in position to respond to specific questions. Skip Knowles of the office of the secretary of defense volunteered a viewpoint that, in effect, was adopted as the DoD's public position:

. . . to argue technical nuances in an attempt to mollify the outcome of the [NAS] study was ill-advised and might even put us into an awkward PR position of arguing for nuclear war. We should simply reaffirm that the Defense Department recognizes that nuclear war is catastrophic and that all of our policies are directed to preventing war.[28]

Except for Sagan, the members of TTAPS refrained from commenting publicly on the political implications of their work. They tried not to rattle their corporate and laboratory chains. Sagan, however, was under no such constraints. Earlier in his career, he had been mentored or otherwise influenced by some notably outspoken (and distinguished) scientists, including Herman Muller, Harold Urey, and Edward Condon.[29] By now, Sagan was a man with a mission and with the visibility to make the most of it. He willingly began a whirlwind of activity in pursuit of his arms-control goals. Major reductions in the arsenals were necessary, he felt, since we should not rely on the judgment and sanity of political and military leaders.

In October 1983, the American Committee on East-West Accord sponsored a private meeting of fewer than a dozen "of the most knowledgeable and brightest people" to hear Sagan summarize TTAPS's findings and then discuss the policy implications of NW. The president's national security advisor, William Clark, declined his invitation, although he requested a copy of the published paper. "Whatever the conclusions," Clark wrote, "no one can doubt that the consequences of nuclear war are indeed horrible to contemplate. This is why arms control and the challenge of peace in the nuclear age are of foremost concern to the President." Clark's reply illustrated the political conundrum seen with regard to so many topics: the sincerely desired ends were often rather alike, but the means were infuriatingly dissimilar. Peace was everyone's goal, but would it be achieved by military strength or by arms control? Clark's staff had provided him with a sober summary of the new effects predicted to occur after a nuclear war, including this warning: "If the scientific community should reach a consensus that the US or Soviet nuclear arsenals are effectively 'doomsday machines,' that may cause a good deal more public anxiety than we have seen to date."[30]

Still seeking to reach the "movers and shakers," even those not then in office, Sagan and Turco met in Washington with a small group of high-level figures from previous administrations, including W. Averell Harriman and some "senior practitioners of dark arts" (as the astrophysicist called them). After listening to Sagan's impassioned presentation, one practitioner said "Look, if you think that the mere prospect of the end of the world is sufficient to change thinking in Washington and Moscow you clearly haven't spent much time in those places." He cautioned that the only way for new information to effect policy changes was through public discourse.[31]

Political Maneuvering after Halloween 1983

Unwilling to abandon all opportunities for private interchange, Sagan held a personal briefing for some members of both houses of Congress just hours before the Halloween conference opened.[32] But congressmen need not only to be convinced; they require also to be lobbied, to have their constituencies behind them. Television is the modern way to reach such mass audiences, and Sagan, a master of this medium, was now persuaded to make his discourse as public as possible.

On 1 November 1983, after the conference and after the "Moscow Link," Sagan and Ehrlich appeared on Ted Koppel's *Nightline*. With them on stage were Edward Teller and Assistant Secretary of State Richard Burt. On camera in Moscow was the physicist Sergei Kapitsa. In response to one of Koppel's questions, Sagan argued that nuclear war, with its billions of casualties, had long been unthinkable. But he would be glad if recognition of the possibility of nuclear winter—with its *additional* features of the risk of extinction, the low threshold of the phenomenon, the devastation of agriculture, and particularly the danger to non-combatant nations—moved world leaders further to avoid such warfare.

Kapitsa, of the Moscow Physico-Technical Institute and the Institute for Physical Problems, said that calculations and models in the USSR "fully substantiate the message . . . stated by Sagan." Ehrlich emphasized the suicidal nature even of a perfectly executed counterforce attack that destroyed all strategic missiles in the targeted country and (theoretically) killed no one. The climatic consequence, nonetheless, would end grain production in the United States, Canada, and the Soviet Union, leading to mass starvation. The biological conclusions, Ehrlich added, were "enormously robust." If the climatic predictions were accurate, even as little as 100 megatons, "distributed properly," would cause life-supporting systems to collapse.

Teller, when asked by Koppel where he disagreed with NW, digressed to affirm the subject's importance and the seriousness with which it was pursued at the Lawrence Livermore National Laboratory. Indeed, Teller noted, preliminary climatic results obtained at Livermore had been presented in the summer of 1983 at the conference in Erice. Eventually Teller got around to his critique of TTAPS's quantitative predictions. Until there was "thorough international agreement" on the technical matters, he said, politicians could not know the consequences of their decisions. In effect, Teller meant that policy could not be based on this worst-case scenario (although, as related above, he was willing to advocate such behavior when it suited his purposes). When Koppel pushed him by asking whether it really mattered whether the dead would number 1.1 billion or 2.2 billion out of a global population of about 5 billion (as predicted in a recent World Health Organization study[33]), Teller recoiled: "Sir, the distinction, even of one human life, is not academic." Still, Teller thought the numbers were exaggerated.

Some of the climatic effects, Teller maintained, could be produced only by extremely large explosions. Because the USSR had almost all of the giant warheads, it had a special responsibility to avoid nuclear war. Teller made the distinction between aggression and defense and, without specifically mentioning the Strategic Defense Initiative or his paternity of it, added that the US was "turning from retaliation to real defense."[34]

Secretary Burt stated that it had been the United States' policy since just after World War II to avoid nuclear war through deterrence. President Reagan had said repeatedly that a nuclear conflict would produce no winner. Further, the nuclear stockpile in Europe was smaller than at any time in 25 years, and arms-control objectives desired by the public were being reached. Politically, Burt added, the number of deaths from nuclear war, whether 100 million or three times that number, was irrelevant; it would be a political catastrophe, and it must be avoided.

Teller maintained that the calculations of others showed a temperature decline only about one-third that found by TTAPS, but in time scientists would come to an agreement. Sagan, indeed, might be correct, but the "disclosures which have been made today are premature, they are based on incomplete information." Sagan replied heatedly, professing amazement that Teller would minimize the effects found by TTAPS. "But I'm much more amazed," he added, "that he says that he has known about these results for years, because if he has I believe it's unconscionable to have withheld this information from the American and world public." Teller, unperturbed, explained that the early results from Livermore were smaller and thus not widely publicized; officialdom, however, did know of them. Burt added that the politicians were, in fact, ahead of the scientists on this issue, having achieved security through deterrence, and were seeking reductions in the arsenals through negotiations. He hoped that Soviet scientists "have the same access and influence in their society as their American counterparts," since "the Soviet Union is engaging in a massive buildup [while] the United States is unilaterally reducing its nuclear arsenals."[35]

Sagan, Ehrlich, and Teller were among the relatively few scientists consistently able to reach an audience with their views about defense policies. Others only occasionally appeared in newspaper stories. One such was the physicist Joseph Knox, an expert in meteorology who was the longtime head of the Atmospheric and Geophysical Sciences Division at the Livermore National Laboratory—and the boss of Michael MacCracken, the laboratory's leader in NW studies. Like the work done in the Soviet Union and by Stephen Schneider's team at the National Center for Atmospheric Research, the Livermore results agreed in general with those of TTAPS. Cooling was not as drastic, thanks to their ability to program the moderating influence of the oceans into their model, yet it was still striking (tens of degrees). To Knox—who *was* willing to make a policy proposal on the basis of "incomplete" scientific evidence—the political step was obvious: "We should avoid the targeting of cities."[36]

In the weeks after the Halloween meeting, there was a brief "media feeding frenzy" over NW. For journalists it clearly was a political issue, and they tied it to the "freeze" campaign and the imminent deployment of intermediate-range Pershing II missiles in Europe. They recognized, too, that the Reagan administration's actions and hard-line statements had heightened the tension about nuclear war and led opponents to increase their own level of activism. "First it was physicians telling the world that, in the event of a nuclear attack, there could be no adequate medical care for survivors," noted a reporter from *Science*, referring to the efforts of Physicians for Social Responsibility in the early 1980s. "Now biologists and atmospheric physicists, bolstered by new calculations, say that the ecosystem itself would be gravely and permanently damaged by a full-scale nuclear war." *Science* observed that policy issues were not on the agenda at the Halloween meeting, but it was obvious that at least two points stood out: even a unilateral attack would be suicidal, and noncombatant nations could not avoid the climatic consequences.[37] To Victor Weisskopf, who lamented the failure of nuclear physicists of his generation to impress upon the public the destructiveness of nuclear weapons, the reception accorded news of NW must have been encouraging.[38]

The authors of an opinion-page article in the *New York Times* saw in the suicidal nature of the NW threat a means to calm the fears of Europeans that the superpowers would use their continent as a "surrogate battlefield." Their cynicism extended to those who worried whether it would be better to perish or survive a nuclear encounter; now, the question was moot.[39] This was rephrased by some supporters of the Nuclear Freeze movement as "freeze now or freeze later."[40]

Many articles commented on the new danger revealed by TTAPS, or imputed a political agenda to the scientists, or did both. The news weekly *Time* admitted that the news of NW shocked people who had grown jaded by the numerous nuclear war scenarios seen so often in movies and on television. "Disarmament enthusiasts," *Time* added, "promptly predicted that many new adherents will now be won over to their cause."[41]

Not articulated but just below the surface was the distinction between the widespread feeling that it was all right for scientists to petition their government to take stronger steps to avoid nuclear war (as the National Academy of Sciences did at its 1982 annual meeting[42]) and a nagging uncertainty that scientists might be manipulating the data when they cited technical evidence in support of their views. Indeed, to imply that political motives might affect the design of an experiment, the collection of data, or the interpretation of results is to discredit the science severely. To reporters, Sagan strongly defended the purity of TTAPS's work: "In this case I don't think policy drives the science. I think science has to drive the policy."[43] *Newsweek* sought to read between the lines and claimed that "the scientists hope that by demonstrating the futility of a nuclear exchange, they will show the men with their finger on the Button that a nuclear war would be the last war."[44]

Though *Newsweek* was perhaps correct, it was still the case that very few scientists publicly called for specific policy changes. One of the exceptions was Stephen Schneider, who admitted that many of the scientists investigating NW hoped that it would ignite a public debate that would force political leaders to reduce the number of missiles and their megatonnage.[45] But he would have denied that scientists fudged their data. Similarly, the man who first called Schneider's attention to NW, Paul Ehrlich, was cheered that "a lot of busy scientists . . . put aside their more parochial interests to do something directly in the cause of *Homo sapiens*." Ehrlich felt that "if a substantial portion of the global scientific community can be rallied to oppose the nuclear arms race, our chances of survival will increase greatly."[46] It was just this sort of political enthusiasm, however, that led an even-handed reviewer of NW claims to caution that "some authors could unintentionally exaggerate in order to gain attention."[47]

In May 1983, the House of Representatives passed a resolution calling for the United States and the Soviet Union to join in a verifiable freeze on the production and deployment of nuclear weapons. But this statement was watered down from the position earlier proposed by numerous church and peace groups, and these activists looked to the Senate to make a more vigorous statement. In this the Senate failed them, for it voted to table the largely symbolic freeze resolution on 31 October, the first day of the NW conference. Senator Edward Kennedy (D-Massachusetts), co-sponsor of the measure with Senator Mark Hatfield (R-Oregon), argued that "the best way to stop the nuclear arms race is to stop it." Kennedy's opponents agreed with his goal, but not his means. Senator John Tower, for example, supported President Reagan's desire to *reduce* the arsenals, not merely to freeze them, but felt that this must await a better balance, which, he argued, favored the Soviets at the time. A freeze would tie the president's hands in these negotiations.[48]

Pro-freeze forces, led by the Nuclear Freeze Foundation, tried to regain the initiative, using fear of the NW phenomenon as their vehicle. Their efforts stood in sharp contrast to the adjournment in Geneva of superpower arms-control talks, without setting a date to reconvene. The Soviets had walked out in protest of the deployment in Europe by the United States of ground-launched cruise missiles and Pershing II missiles. On 8 December 1983, Kennedy and Hatfield hosted a panel of four scientists from each superpower, all of whom supported the freeze. The meeting was held in the stately Senate Caucus Room. It was a media event, covered by television and print reporters from both the US and the USSR. Sagan and Ehrlich, both authors of NW work, were joined on the American side by H. Jack Geiger (a professor of community medicine at the City College of New York) and by Lewis Thomas (chancellor of the Memorial Sloan-Kettering Cancer Center). Geiger and Thomas were articulate spokesmen on arms-control issues. For the Soviets, Yevgeny Velikhov and Vladimir Aleksandrov were joined by Sergei Kapitsa (who had discussed NW on Ted Koppel's *Nightline*) and by Aleksandr Pavlov, from the Moscow Scientific Institute of Radio-Biology.[49] Some of the panelists pointed to the potential for the worldwide destruction of agriculture, a deliberate slap at a just-released report by the Federal Emergency Management Agency which claimed that, despite loss of half the US population and with crop yields reduced by 50 percent, enough land and rural workers would be left to grow food. A major argument of the study was that livestock and produce needs would be greatly reduced due to massive numbers of human dead.[50] Senator Kennedy, quick to ridicule the report, said: "This kind of thinking makes nuclear war more likely because it makes nuclear war seem more bearable."[51] Kennedy added that a "third world war would be the last world war, for it would be a war against the world itself. In such a conflict the question would be not how many would survive, but how long the dying would take."[52] In this period, after Physicians for Social Responsibility had convincingly emphasized the futility of fallout shelters and "crisis relocation" efforts, and before FEMA's better performance in the aftermath of hurricanes and earthquakes in the early 1990s, the agency, in its civil defense efforts, seemed to many to be ineffective.[53] (Sadly, it restored its reputation for incompetence at the time of Hurricane Katrina in 2005.)

Ehrlich and Pavlov emphasized the certainty of the biological and medical consequences, in view of the dire climatic conditions. There were so many overlapping effects, each one individually capable of massive trauma to plants or animals, that their sum was indeed "overkill." Toxic smog, ultraviolet-B, lack of photosynthesis, high levels of radioactivity, absence of liquid water, infection, disease, a sudden decrease in the oxygen content of the air (from burning of forests), starvation, and other disturbances to the social and environmental fabric would offer little hope to those who survived the war's immediate effects.[54] Ehrlich compared the certainty of the biological consequences of nuclear war to confidence in predicting the medical consequences of firing a double-barreled shotgun into one's mouth.[55]

The worldwide nature of the problem was reaffirmed by Aleksandrov. Conventional wisdom, derived from studies of fallout patterns from large single explosions, showed little mixing of northern and southern hemispheric atmospheres. In contrast, Aleksandrov's three-dimensional general circulation model of the atmosphere, which included a thermodynamic model of the upper level, indicated that the hemispheric barrier would be breached after many simultaneous detonations. A war fought largely in the northern mid latitudes would inject so much soot into the atmosphere that the upper troposphere would absorb most of the Sun's heat and its temperature would increase by more than 100°C. With the resulting great temperature difference between north and south, northern air, with its debris, would pour over the Southern Hemisphere.[56]

Repeating another point that he had made at the Halloween conference, Aleksandrov explained that, with low temperatures at the surface and high temperatures aloft, the atmosphere would become remarkably stable. Vertical air movement would effectively cease, suppressing the hydrological cycle. Dust and soot would not be rained out. Indeed, Aleksandrov said, "the troposphere will disappear, and the stratosphere will start immediately from the surface of Earth."[57] A *Washington Post* reporter saw the Soviets' climatic predictions as more lethal than those of TTAPS.[58]

Kapitsa, host of a popular science program on Soviet television, linked the forum's organizers with the NW phenomenon. "The choice is one freeze or another," he said.[59] In the past, Kapitsa added, it could be argued that deterrence was achieved by the "mutual hostage arrangement between the opposing nuclear powers." But now, with NW in mind, "the whole of the earth and human civilization itself are held hostage." Lewis Thomas, a skilled wordsmith whose books were best sellers, said that wars in the past were fought for land or to impose an ideology on the vanquished. Now, he added, with nuclear war, "it is clear that any territory gained will be, in the end, a barren wasteland." Sagan, a master of one-liners, emphasized that a nuclear war would have so many dire consequences that "it would be an elaborate way of committing suicide." After such a conflict, "the ashes of communism and capitalism will be indistinguishable."[60] With sincerity no doubt, but also perhaps as his entry in the sound-bite competition, Senator Kennedy concluded: "The message of this panel is that the stakes are higher than we ever thought possible—what has been created is a doomsday machine. And what we have to do now is to dismantle it."[61]

Before and after this forum, the Soviet visitors were hosted by the Federation of American Scientists in Washington, in Princeton, and in Boston. A range of arms-control and research issues were discussed. Velikhov and Kapitsa also appeared on NBC's *Today*.[62] And yet, despite the publicity given to NW, traditional peace groups were not noticeably energized by the phenomenon. Organizers of the Nuclear Freeze movement, as we have just seen, used it opportunistically; so did a few others. Most "peaceniks," however, remained focused on protesting deployment of "theater nuclear weapons" in Europe. The Pershing II and ground-launched cruise missiles were "here and now;" they were a reality. NW appeared too hypo-thetical, distant, and even controversial. Probably without any formal decisions, peace groups seem to have placed NW in a "future use" category. An exception was the Council for a Livable World. Founded by the physicist Leo Szilard decades earlier as a fund-raising political action committee to support arms-control-inclined senatorial candidates, and gov-erned largely by scientists, its Education Fund reprinted Sagan's *Parade* article as a handsome booklet. Sagan, a member of the Education Fund's board, willingly permitted this and many other reprintings around the world.[63]

It should be noticed that Sagan did not consult with his peers about his efforts to popu-larize NW and affect strategic policy, but no one who was interviewed in the course of writing this book felt that Sagan had any obligation to do so. They all desired to do the best science they could, and at the same time they were pleased if their discoveries led to better conditions for the citizens of the world. In other words, they were practitioners of the concept of science and social responsibility.[64]

Criticism came from expected sources, namely, those on the political far right in defense and international issues. In addition to Edward Teller, one of the perennials on this scene was Leon Gouré. A political scientist who had been born in Moscow, he specialized in analyses of Soviet military and civil defense policies. Having spent many years at Rand and then some time at the University of Miami, by 1983 he was director of Soviet studies at Science Applications International Corporation, a defense contractor in McLean, Virginia. Though he took swipes at American scientists who "engage in 'doomsday' predictions and advocate an immediate nuclear freeze and disarmament," his primary focus was on the Soviet scientists. They, he said,

do not reflect the findings of independent Soviet research and analysis on nuclear war and its consequences. Instead they merely restate and offer as their own views whatever Western calcul-ations, analyses and conclusions best serve the Soviet objective of promoting an American nuclear freeze.

Gouré criticized the use of worst-case scenarios. Here he was off the mark, since TTAPS had provided a wide range of encounters, and worst-case analysis was a practice long enshrined in the Department of Defense anyway. (In view of the estimated $1 trillion spent to eliminate Y2K computer bugs in the 1990s, it seems that quite a few individuals, corporations, and governments acted on worst-case scenarios.) Gouré was on much firmer ground when he claimed that the work of Soviet scientists was not independent. He pointed out that studies of war scenarios and other activities related to defense were not published in the Soviet Union. Consequently, Soviet authors traditionally used Western data in their analyses seen in the West. This can be of little import if, for example, the conditions of a war scenario (number of explosions, megatonnage, whether surface or air bursts, geographical distribution, etc.) are not controversial; then there is no reason for both sides not to use such data. But when the Soviet scientists could not use their own government's numbers for the critical amount of smoke injected into the atmosphere, and when they used computer models descended from American models, there was some basis for concern over the independence of their results.

Gouré's commentary, however, was not designed to promote discussion. Incapable of attributing honest motives to anyone east of the Iron Curtain, he was heavy handed in stigmatizing his subjects as incompetent (Aleksandrov bragged that his team included no meteorologists), two faced (Velikhov said civil defense was important and then not), sinister (Velikhov was "believed to be a member of the Soviet Secret Police, the KGB"), and intent on furthering the Kremlin's objective, namely "to promote defeatism among the American people and an American freeze." With an article titled "Soviet scientists as shills for a freeze" and with an accompanying cartoon depicting "Carl Sagan's traveling speculation show," Gouré was as much self-identified as a mindless Cold Warrior as Carl Sagan was seen by political conservatives to be a knee-jerk liberal.[65]

8   Policy and the Arms Race

The Government Moves

Soon after the Halloween conference, a Department of Defense official dismissed the significance of the "cold and dark" predictions. "So what," he said; they already were quite well aware that nuclear war would be catastrophic. A spokesman for the Department of State argued that deterrence still worked, even if it was suicidal—as long as the Soviets believed that the United States would use its nuclear weapons. However, the Federal Emergency Management Agency was now concerned. It had earlier dismissed the warning by Physicians for Social Responsibility that medical care would be inadequate, which it thought "exaggerated." But the problem of food supply presented by NW was "even more profound than we had anticipated."[1] Comments by other officials included "What's a little weather?" and "We've blown up civilization . . . what's the big deal?" One had the solution to the food problem: "So it gets cold. We'll just grow the corn somewhere else, like in Mississippi rather than Kansas."[2]

Aside from individual insensitivity, these ramblings suggest that the federal government was hopelessly muddled about NW and politically hostile to anything that might force a reconsideration of its policies. Actually, the military behaved far more responsibly, recognizing quite early the significance of these studies and inclined to obtain honest advice.

By May 1982, the Defense Nuclear Agency was shuttling memos and telephone calls in house and to its contractors about the National Academy of Sciences study—focused primarily on dinosaur-extinction dust, not NW—then being formulated. Aerodyne Research's vice president, Charles E. Kolb, who served as director of the corporation's Applied Sciences Division, advised that the National Academy of Sciences' survey and the parallel "Sagan investigation" would surely attract a lot of public attention. It would be to the DNA's benefit to be able to discuss their conclusions knowledgeably, especially if independently informed by two-dimensional and three-dimensional models of atmospheric chemistry and circulation, studies Kolb offered to undertake.[3]

Eugene Sevin, the assistant to the DNA's deputy director for science and technology, thought that a third study was inappropriate. The DNA might fund the NAS report as the agent of the undersecretary of defense for research and engineering (USDRE), but should do nothing "that would directly support or influence the NAS panel. . . . NAS is responsible totally for the direction and outcome of the study."[4]

USDRE Richard DeLauer, speaking to Vice Admiral William Moran, had informally agreed to the NAS study. We "should all perhaps be a little concerned that we did not recognize a little sooner the importance of the smoke to our calculation of nuclear effects," DeLauer, the Department of Defense's chief scientist, admitted.[5] In June 1982, the NAS's operating agency, the National Research Council, provided formal "terms of reference" to T. K. Jones, DeLauer's deputy undersecretary of defense for research and engineering (strategic and theater nuclear forces).[6] The "terms" specified that classified data on dust lofted in previous weapons tests should be made available, and that the study should take a worst-case approach to the evidence of dust and smoke effects. The cost was estimated at $100,000.[7]

Jones dashed off a note asking for the DNA's evaluation of the need for the study, whether a worst-case approach was appropriate, and whether the available data were "adequate to support any responsible conclusion."[8] The DNA replied that the study might provide valuable information on the interaction of aircraft engines and flight crews with nuclear dust clouds (a potentially serious problem, of the sort that was almost entirely absent in the DoD's later analysis of NW). The worst-case treatment, however, was discomforting to Edward E. Conrad, the DNA's deputy director for science and engineering, since he did not believe that "much of the dust remains aloft for long periods." Data from past tests, Conrad added, "have been thoroughly exploited by DNA," yet there were a few things that might be useful. In closing, he suggested that the DNA join, or even chair, the NAS study group—a proposal which his assistant, Sevin, had warned was improper, and which was not adopted.[9]

The DNA apparently farmed out the NAS terms of reference to some of its contractors for comment. In July 1982, Science Applications Incorporated replied that most of the dust from surface explosions would fall out of the atmosphere within a day. But the size distribution of the smallest particles (those below 50 micrometers, and those of greatest importance in this case) was poorly known, because previous studies, looking at radioactive fallout and reentry-vehicle erosion, had concentrated on larger particles. Pointing to the relationship among the yield of an explosion, the size distribution of particles, and the altitude reached by each size, SAI noted that DNA contractors had employed several "rise models," none of which had been validated. There was a need to merge them with a meteorological model, a task SAI could accomplish within 6 months.[10]

In November 1982, the NAS submitted to the DoD a formal proposal for its study, anticipating a quick start for the one-year task and requesting $187,500 for it (including an overhead rate of 63 percent—higher than that charged by most universities, which have laboratories and libraries to operate). A two-phase approach was planned. First, a committee of "atmospheric physicists, chemists, weapons effects experts, specialists in the optics of aerosols, and climate dynamicists and modelers" would conduct a search of the open and closed literature, and brief each other; then they would engage in an in-depth study of the subject.[11]

The Department of the Navy, always technologically oriented, made its own efforts to keep informed about NW. About a year after the above-mentioned activity to organize an NAS report, Vice Admiral James A. Lyons, the deputy chief of naval operations for plans, policy, and operations, summarized for his boss, the chief of naval operations, the "World After Nuclear War" conference that began on Halloween 1983. Lyons recognized that the newly predicted consequences were far more severe than formerly assessed; the potential for human extinction loomed large in his mind. After learning from Vice Admiral Moran that the NAS study under way would probably come to a "generally similar" conclusion, Lyons judged TTAPS's results likely to be correct and felt that the scientific community would support them.[12]

Lyons was especially impressed with the research done by Vladimir Aleksandrov, who he felt presented "the most significant new scientific work at the conference"—quantitative results from a 3-D model that were far more advanced than those from TTAPS's 1-D model. "It appears," Lyons wrote, "that this problem has gotten high level attention in the Soviet Union. Considerable scientific and computational resources have been devoted to this problem by Soviet academicians and there is clearly an interest in capitalizing on these efforts politically."[13]

The prediction of NW, Lyons believed, "may raise both long term policy issues and short term public relations problems." Policy-issue "overtones" were evident in Soviet support of the NW concept during the conference proper and still more so in the TV satellite link to Moscow that followed. The Soviet Union's intent was to bolster its arms-control goals. In the short term, Lyons expected the Kremlin to raise doubts in the minds of Western Europeans about the wisdom of stationing American Pershing II missiles and ground-launched cruise missiles on their soil. To counter this propaganda—especially an anticipated charge that the Halloween conference was unofficial, evidence of little government interest—the United States could point to the research on NW done in the Department of Energy's Livermore Laboratory and the NAS study sponsored by the Department of Defense. Lyons also suggested that American targeting policy for nuclear weapons be reexamined in light of the new phenomenon. The Navy, however, would defer to the Office of the Secretary of Defense on matters related to NW.[14]

In early December 1983, the assistant to the secretary of defense, Richard Wagner, himself a physicist, was briefed on the NW phenomenon by Michael MacCracken of the Livermore Laboratory and by that lab's former director, Michael May. Though they might quibble over different assumptions and values used by TTAPS, they could not deny that the predictions were to be taken seriously. The Department of Defense, while maintaining a keen interest in further research, continued to refrain from public discussion of NW. The journalist Thomas Powers described the DoD's predicament this way: "The nuclear-winter thesis, if valid, threatens to make nonsense of every notion the planners have managed to come up with, in 40 years of trying to devise a sensible way to fight a nuclear war."[15]

A Search for New Policy

The *New York Times* editorialized a thought that was in the back of many minds: "Doesn't everyone know by now that nuclear disaster is hazardous to human health? Surely every sensible person everywhere believes preventing it is the world's most important cause." How to achieve that goal, the *Times* editorial continued, was the issue, and deterrence based on mutual horror seemed to be the only practical policy. What alternative did the bearers of this expanded horror, NW, propose?[16]

Carl Sagan entered this realm of nuclear theology with a proposal. It was not a new strategy. Leo Szilard had suggested it decades before. Szilard had argued for a force of about 40 nuclear weapons, just enough to inflict unacceptable damage on the Soviet Union.[17] Advocating a version of this "minimal deterrence," Sagan now based it on quantitative calculations rather than best guesses. In early November 1983, speaking to a group of congressional wives brought together by an anti-nuclear organization called Peace Links, Sagan encouraged a "build-down" to the approximate NW threshold level of 100 MT by the end of the century.[18] Then, in a major statement in the policy journal *Foreign Affairs*, he elaborated on this proposition.

Sagan portentously opened his essay with the argument that "apocalyptic predictions require, to be taken seriously, higher standards of evidence than do assertions on other matters where the stakes are not so great."[19] To indicate that he was not a solitary Chicken Little crying nonsense, Sagan prefaced the paper with short quotations of famous physicists (including his nemesis, Teller) who also had experienced visions of global doom:

It is not even impossible to imagine that the effects of an atomic war fought with greatly perfected weapons and pushed by the utmost determination will endanger the survival of man. —Edward Teller (1947)

The extreme danger to mankind inherent in the proposal [to develop thermonuclear weapons] wholly outweighs any military advantage. —J. Robert Oppenheimer et al. (1949)

The fact that no limits exist to the destructiveness of this [thermonuclear] weapon makes its very existence and the knowledge of its construction a danger to humanity. . . . It is . . . an evil thing. —Enrico Fermi and I. I. Rabi (1949)

A very large nuclear war would be a calamity of indescribable proportions and absolutely unpredictable consequences, with the uncertainties tending toward the worse. . . . All-out nuclear war would mean the destruction of contemporary civilization, throw man back centuries, cause the deaths of hundreds of millions or billions of people, and, with a certain degree of probability, would cause man to be destroyed as a biological species. —Andrei Sakharov (1983)[20]

Having placed himself in such distinguished company, Sagan explained that prophets of doomsday, including Nevil Shute (*On the Beach*) and Jonathan Schell (*The Fate of the Earth*), had been dismissed by many policy makers as "alarmist or . . . irrelevant." The policy makers' reasons were partly theoretical (they were not comfortable with questionable extrapolations from limited data) and partly psychological (it was easier for officials to engage in "denial"). Sagan added another interpretation: Should nuclear war really have the potential to end civilization or even the species, "such a finding might be considered a retroactive rebuke to those responsible . . . for the global nuclear arms race."[21]

Sagan next presented a layman's summary of the physical and biological consequences of nuclear war as recently determined by TTAPS and their colleagues. The technical basis for these results, Sagan said, constituted the necessary "higher standards of evidence" for such apocalyptic predictions. Finally, Sagan addressed the main subject of his essay: policy. He described some implications of NW, advanced a miscellany of conceivable strategic responses to it, and offered two policy recommendations.

Seeking to demonstrate that nuclear winter was not just marginally worse than the horrors of nuclear war, Sagan explained that human extinction would eliminate all future generations—possibly some 500 trillion people. NW thus had the potential to be 100,000 times as bad as "ordinary" nuclear war.[22]

The superpowers' arsenals, especially the more accurate and MIRVed missiles, had created an unstable condition in which, some strategists argued, a damage-limiting first strike by the Soviets against American ICBM silos and C^{3}I centers was more likely than before. Indeed, this was the scenario proclaimed by the Committee on the Present Danger in the late 1970s and repeated by Ronald Reagan as he campaigned for the presidency in 1980. Even though a large portion of sea-based American missiles would survive, it was argued that they would not be launched against Soviet cities (they were not accurate enough to pinpoint small, hard targets) out of fear that the remaining Soviet missiles would destroy American cities. This scenario envisioned that the United States would surrender. To avoid that disaster, Reagan embarked on a major arms buildup and especially sought (unsuccessfully) to deploy the highly accurate multiple-warhead MX missile in a mobile mode. An MX that could survive a first strike and threaten Soviet silos would, it was thought, restore stability to deterrence.

With the potential for NW, however, even if the attacked nation did not respond in kind, the attacker would plausibly suffer in a cold and dark environment. Should the attacked nation launch retaliatory salvos, probably aiming them at cities (since many enemy silos would now be empty), the resulting conflagrations would be even more likely to produce the NW effect. A rational aggressor, fearing unintended suicide, would thus eschew a preemptive attack. A further benefit of this NW-driven logic would be reduced pressure in each superpower to expand its arsenals.[23]

But would a nation think that it could initiate an attack that was deliberately below the rough NW threshold of 500–2,000 warheads, trusting that the enemy would not retaliate and thus cause the climatic catastrophe? Sagan thought not, given the inevitable uncertainty of the response by a still well-armed country.[24] Indeed, some critics of NW scenarios said, for example, that the 100-MT war would never happen. If 1,000 fires were to be ignited in cities, the attacking country would surely have fired off a lot more of its arsenal, and the attacked country would likely have responded with an all-out launch. This was an argument made by Turco's colleagues at R&D Associates when reviewing his work.[25] Such analysis, however, seems to have been ineffectual hair splitting. Different scenarios were more or less acceptable to different people. The TTAPS group and many others were impressed by the wide variety of situations that could lead to darkness. It was the diversity of initial war conditions leading to climatic catastrophe that gave the feeling that NW was a valid concept.

In another possible reaction to NW, a nation might believe that the phenomenon could be evaded by making its delivery systems still more accurate, thereby enabling the yields of warheads to be reduced further. Progress of this sort, including remarkable achievements in terminal guidance that can bring a warhead to within a few tens of meters of the target, had in fact been under way for some years, driven by military needs, not by a desire to minimize the number of fires ignited. But if the warheads were redesigned to penetrate the ground before detonating (a technology then being studied), even fewer fires would burn. Sagan recognized that such weapons might preclude NW, yet that very consequence would make their use more likely. The attacked nation, on the other hand, would have less reason to employ these earth-burrowing warheads for retaliation; vengeance is less discriminate. Endeavoring to escape the new instability, both sides would likely abandon the 1972 Strategic Arms Limitation Treaty (SALT I), which contained ABM limits, in order to build large ballistic-missile-defense systems.[26]

In the past, the harshest consequences of nuclear war were thought likely to be fairly well limited to the belligerent nations. Radioactive fallout and the disruption of the world economy were expected to constitute the most serious problems for other countries, with poor states suffering further by the interruption of food and other types of aid. Now, however, the climatic disaster would be a global phenomenon of sufficient intensity to cause the collapse of the majority of nations. Sagan cited preliminary results from a three-dimensional computer simulation by V. V. Aleksandrov and G. L. Stenchikov showing temperature plunges of 15–40°C across much of the planet on day 40. Recognition of the NW threat, Sagan argued, might bring stronger diplomatic and economic pressure for arms control on the five major nuclear powers.[27]

Periodically, the United States had encouraged the construction of shelters for the civilian population. Blast shelters, however, could not be built for large numbers of people, and even fallout shelters were difficult to "sell." Few families constructed them, and the government's efforts to designate communal shelters and stock them with food, water, and other supplies were half-hearted at best. Such shelters were too expensive, were potentially provocative to an enemy who thought the US might believe it really was safe and therefore able to be more belligerent, and would protect (inadequately) only a small fraction of the population. NW magnified the shortcomings of shelters and raised the old issue of the hostile environment that those sheltered would find upon emerging. Sagan surveyed such defects of the shelter concept and pointed out that citizens of non-combatant nations would not have even such marginal sanctuaries.[28]

Ballistic-missile defense (BMD) was much in the news at this time, President Reagan having announced his Strategic Defense Initiative less than a year earlier. Sagan took a pre-emptive swing at BMD, seeing it as some analysts' excuse not to worry about NW: if the incoming warheads could be shot down, NW would be avoided. He pointed out that the full BMD system was not expected to be completed for two or three decades, and even then the shield would allow through enough warheads to cause NW. The enemy, of course, need only build more warheads—a cheaper task—to degrade BMD. Sagan also called attention to the circumstance that some components of BMD would release thermonuclear explosions just a few miles above our own cities. Thus, our defensive system could ignite the fires of our own doom.[29]

Rejecting such strategic responses to NW as were discussed above, Sagan argued for confidence-building measures between the superpowers, including an end to harsh rhetoric, the conversion of MIRVed missiles to carry single warheads, abandonment of the concepts of nuclear war fighting, and an admission that nuclear war would not be limited. All this, however, was only a prelude to Sagan's main proposal: to reduce arsenals below the NW threshold. This was a large step, a reduction of more than 90 percent—greater even than George Kennan's controversial suggestion in 1981 of an initial 50 percent cut, going eventually to more than 84 percent. But according to Sagan there was no rational alternative.[30]

We had, Sagan said, unknowingly created a doomsday machine. It took the recognition of soot's significance in altering the postwar climate to enable us to see that building warheads over the threshold of roughly 500–2,000 had moved us into a "doomsday zone." It was imperative to reduce arsenals so that "no concatenation of computer malfunction, carelessness, unauthorized acts, communications failure, miscalculation and madness in high office could unleash the nuclear winter." Since 1945, counter to conventional belief, more weapons had not purchased more security, Sagan argued. Indeed, factoring NW into the equation, larger arsenals led directly to a decline in security. Rather than trust global civilization to fallible humans and equipment, Sagan wrote, "I would far rather have a world in which the climatic catastrophe cannot happen, independent of the vicissitudes of leaders, institutions and machines. This seems to me elementary planetary hygiene, as well as elementary patriotism."[31]

III   A Cold Day in Hell: Activities and Antagonisms, 1984–85

9   More Publicity

In 1984, Thomas Powers, a well-known journalist who specialized in military, strategic, and intelligence topics, composed an article about the implications of NW. "The invention of nuclear weapons," he warned,

has brought dire warnings aplenty in the past few decades, but this one is on an altogether different scale. It's one thing to say that the United States and the Soviet Union would suffer beyond precedent in a nuclear war, even that a nuclear war "would destroy civilization as we know it." It's our civilization, after all; we built it, and perhaps that gives us the right to destroy it. But we are not our own fathers; we did not create the human race, much less the other forms of life that share the planet with us. A defense policy that threatens life itself on such a scale is simply too crazy to stand.

Maybe, Powers mused, the news is so bad that it's good: "If we finally admit that we can't fight a nuclear war without destroying ourselves . . . then perhaps the time has come to quit preparing to fight one. Even deterrence," he added, "demands a credible threat."[1] In a nutshell, this was the core of the policy debate over NW.

Spreading the Word

The organizers of the Halloween 1983 "World After Nuclear War" conference regrouped after that event to create a body that would provide information on nuclear winter to the media and keep the issue before the public. This was the Center on the Consequences of Nuclear War, located in Washington. It was formed as a project of the Open Space Institute and funded by a $50,000 grant from the W. Alton Jones Foundation.[2] Russell W. Peterson, president of the Audubon Society, chaired the center's steering committee, which consisted of a few lawyers and several scientists, including Paul Ehrlich, Thomas Eisner, John Holdren, Henry Kendall, Thomas Malone, Carl Sagan, Stephen Schneider, Richard Turco, and Gilbert White. In keeping with the Open Space Institute's tax-exempt status, the center advocated no legislation. Its self-defined role was to serve "as a clearinghouse of technical and educational materials . . . including scientific articles, books, videotapes and slides."[3] Serving as the center's executive director was Chaplin B. Barnes, who had held a similar administrative post for the group that orchestrated the Halloween meeting, and who earlier had worked for the National Audubon Society and the Council on Environmental Quality. Jeannie Peterson, who had served as editor of the 1982 *Ambio* issue on nuclear war, interrupted her next position at the United Nations to spend a year at the center as its director of public information.[4]

Public education, though necessary and desirable, was but a step on the way toward public policy. Initially, the Natural Resources Defense Council and the Union of Concerned Scientists, both sponsors of the Halloween meeting and experienced in advocacy, vied to take on the educative role. When, instead, the Center on the Consequences of Nuclear War was established, the NRDC became its policy ally. S. Jacob Scherr, an NRDC attorney who previously had focused on nuclear exports, the breeder reactor, and environmental issues related to the production of nuclear weapons, experienced an emotional reaction that was shared with many other participants in the Halloween conference: a feeling that they were involved in a ground-breaking scientific enterprise. Thus motivated, Scherr spent most of his time at the NRDC on NW activities, as did another attorney, Estelle Rogers. During 1985 and 1986, Scherr also served as executive director of the Center on the Consequences of Nuclear War.[5]

As 1983 turned into 1984, a year made infamous as the title of George Orwell's futuristic novel (published in 1949), the NRDC initiated three efforts: (1) to learn just what the government's response was to NW (for this they filed about 35 Freedom of Information Act requests), (2) to mount pressure on members of Congress, and (3) to compose a booklet called "Nuclear Winter, Silent Spring" to leave no doubt that this climatic consequence of warfare was a valid issue for the environmental movement. The FOIA requests eventually brought forth numerous documents that revealed some of the government's actions. According to Scherr, the NRDC's lobbying, which convinced Congress that the administration was dragging its feet in mobilizing a reaction to the danger of NW, helped to push through legislation that required the Department of Defense to report on the consequences of nuclear war.[6] And the 1984 booklet carried a warning on its back cover: ". . . biologists predict that a nuclear winter would be followed by a spring more silent than Rachel Carson ever imagined."

Jacob Scherr's efforts, and those of others, also succeeded in framing the hearings held in September 1984 by the House Committee on Science and Technology, and in mandating the secretary general of the United Nations to report on the consequences of NW. In Scherr's own estimation, the pinnacle of his work, until the Center expired at the end of 1986, was encouraging the Senate Armed Services Committee to hold hearings in October 1985.[7] There, committee chairman Barry Goldwater (R-Arizona) opened with a statement affirming his strong belief "that there could be such a thing as a nuclear winter"—one of the more positive evaluations to come from Republicans—while William Cohen (R-Maine) and John Warner (R-Virginia), who had run for reelection in 1984, hoping to appeal to environmentalists and to those who supported a strong national defense, maintained their interest in NW the following year.[8]

In September 1984, *Parade* ran another article by Carl Sagan. Titled "We can prevent nuclear winter," it provided Sagan a platform from which to urge anew that the nuclear arsenals be cut massively. The great accuracy of many missiles, he said, which formerly caused us to fear a disarming first strike, was now of lesser significance, since that strike could be suicidal to the aggressor. Self-deterrence was thus increased, and ordinary deterrence would be effective with far fewer weapons. Civil defense shelters and crisis relocation programs, formerly flawed, made even less sense under NW conditions; indeed, there might be "no sanctuaries anywhere on the planet."[9]

Parade revealed that it had received 50,000 (solicited) letters from readers in response to Sagan's October 1983 article "The nuclear winter." Addressed to the American and Soviet presidents, the letters tugged at one's heart. A young woman from St. Paul, Minnesota, fearing for her daughter, wrote: "Don't tell me that I must learn to live with the threat of nuclear war, because it cannot be done without losing what is most precious and human in me." A Chicagoan admonished: "Surely you do not think of yourselves as the murderers of small children. But that you are, if you cannot halt this nuclear madness." From a woman in Bethlehem, Pennsylvania: "No successful world leader would consider suicide as a means to spread ideology." From a physician in Decorah, Iowa: "This issue is not a political issue, nor an issue of power, but an issue of human survival that cuts across all ideological differences." Youth was represented. A 12-year-old in Bloomfield, New Jersey, wrote: "I want a future." A junior high student from Eugene, Oregon, told Ronald Reagan: "My friends are scared. Sometimes they think—Will we wake up to see the world tomorrow?" As an afterthought, he urged "P.S. Please don't make a dumb move. . . ."[10]

Lewis Thomas, an untiring spokesman for the validity of NW, recalled that he "took it to be the greatest piece of good news to emerge from science in the whole twentieth century." He explained this seemingly twisted attitude by claiming that "the weapons are now, in the flattest, most matter-of-fact military sense, *impractical*." This view was emphasized by a striking drawing of a two-barreled revolver with nuclear missiles emerging from barrels bent to point in both directions.[11] Thomas further maintained that science's most urgent concern was to verify the NW phenomenon. The threat of a nuclear holocaust had not been deflected by a balance of terror, nor by humanitarian or moral behavior, nor even by long-running arms-control negotiations, but we might finally escape this scourge by the old-fashioned desire for self-preservation.[12]

The strategic analyst Albert Wohlstetter and other critics of such thinking charged that those who championed the validity of NW wanted the public to believe that nuclear war was so horrible that we would fear to chance it. Thus, to avoid the danger of mass extermination, democracies would be driven to pacifism or surrender, leaving their more callous adversaries to achieve their goals. Former secretary of state Henry Kissinger endorsed the Strategic Defense Initiative with such an argument, saying that it would "mitigate the threat of apocalypse" and deny peaceniks the ability to spread fear.[13]

Responses to Sagan's *Foreign Affairs* Article

The TTAPS paper, and now Sagan's venture into policy matters, were challenges to members of the Establishment, who heretofore had the technical and policy fields largely to themselves. To be sure, there always had been critics of the government's arms-control efforts, but usually they could be ignored as uninformed knee-jerk liberals, ignorant of the way in which the "real world" works. Just what credentials did this self-appointed theorist have? Assistant Secretary of Defense Richard Perle urged Sagan to go back to his laboratory and stop "playing political scientist."[14] This form of denigration was invoked, but NW was too well supported to be so easily dismissed. Additionally, the official arms-control community often had to justify its glacially slow and incremental progress with remarks to the effect that things would be lots worse had they not been around to exert their pressure. Someone who wanted major changes quickly was regarded as an embarrassment; he did not understand how things really worked. This may explain a bit of the aloofness of this community to Sagan.[15]

In its spring 1984 issue, *Foreign Affairs* printed four letters to the editor and Sagan's reply. Resurrecting a long-standing hawk/dove controversy over which was the proper yardstick, the defense analyst Edward Luttwak, of the Center for Strategic and International Studies, pointed out that Sagan had used megatonnage to illustrate the effects of explosions but had used the number of warheads to show the rapid growth of the arms race. Luttwak called this inconsistency "analytical sharp practice," since megatonnage would show a reverse trend: the current US arsenal contained less than one-fourth the yield it had two decades earlier. Sagan professed to be surprised by both the content and the tone of Luttwak's critique. The scenarios he described in his article depended not solely on megatonnage, but on the number of detonations, whether they were surface or air blasts, whether the targets were cities or military installations, the yield of each explosion, and the total yield. Moreover, Sagan had indeed pointed out that the potency of the arsenal could be calibrated in various ways, but that for NW measurements the number of warheads was most appropriate, since a low-yield air burst produced about the same fire damage as a high-yield ground burst, thus marginalizing the value of megatonnage.[16]

A second hostile letter came from Russell Seitz, the director of technology assessment for R. J. Edwards, Inc., an investment banking firm headquartered in Boston. Ignoring Sagan's policy paper in the policy-oriented journal, Seitz levied scorn on the science of the TTAPS paper. For smoke to remain aloft any length of time, he pointed out, it would have to enter the stratosphere, where it could not be rained out. Yet this was an exceedingly rare occurrence, although many large fires occurred in places all around the world each year. Nonetheless, Seitz said that Turco had guessed how much soot would rise to that altitude and *placed* it there; the quantity and location were inputs to, not consequences of, the model. In any case, Seitz emphasized, the one-dimensional computer model used by TTAPS was inadequate for quantitative study of the real world and inappropriate for any policy conclusions regarding nuclear weapons.

Sagan chided Seitz for not noticing, in the *Science* paper, figures showing that NW would come to pass even when no soot reached the stratosphere. Soot located in the high troposphere was sufficient to initiate the optical and climatic effects. Turco, he added, may have had to guess at the fraction of soot lofted into the stratosphere, but it was an educated guess. To illustrate yet another case in which TTAPS and its critics saw the same point differently, Sagan cited Michael MacCracken's work at Livermore with coarse higher-dimensional models. These gave results at variance with TTAPS's conclusions because the inputs were different (such as the initial distribution of soot). However, when the inputs were better matched, "the two sets of conclusions [were] in good agreement."[17]

The only letter in *Foreign Affairs* that dealt with the policy consequences of NW sought to go beyond Sagan's analysis. The political scientists Dan Horowitz (of the Hebrew University of Jerusalem) and Robert J. Lieber (of Georgetown University) saw that a disarming first strike was now an even more remote option than before, because it might be self-destructive. "This logic," they wrote, "introduces a component of self-deterrence into the balance of terror," increasing stability. At the same time, if the threshold for NW could be approximated, and if France, Great Britain, and China built their arsenals to this level, their political influence would increase. Existing policies also would be affected. The US nuclear "umbrella" protecting Europe from Soviet attack by threat of retaliation and NATO's willingness to execute "first use" of nuclear weapons as a deterrent to conventional attack would both lose much credibility. Escalation could not be chanced. In consequence, conventional forces would become more important. Its greater number of troops would seem to favor the USSR, but this might be balanced by the USSR's handicap in having larger-yield weapons than the US. The late Herman Kahn had built his reputation discussing "rational" ways to use nuclear weapons, and this required that they be kept under control. Horowitz and Lieber saw that, once the NW threshold was crossed, control was gone; again, self-restraint was more necessary than ever before.[18]

Whether by Sagan's *Foreign Affairs* article or simply by information on NW they had read in newspapers, some citizens were moved to write to administration officials. They were motivated by the recognition that NW pointed to the need to rethink deterrence strategy,[19] and, indeed, that we must not forget the danger to society of nuclear war: "Nuclear winter," according to one letter, "simply serves to place the exclamation point at the end of the sentence."[20] Neither the aforementioned letter writers nor those who wrote letters to the editors of newspapers were an overwhelming force, but their efforts showed that there was at least a modest political response to NW among the electorate.

10 Inside the Beltway, 1984

Administration Agencies

The scientific response by the Defense Nuclear Agency, in the summer of 1983, to the possibility that NW might be a real phenomenon was prompt and honest. But, as with any government agency, it was impossible to avoid some political overtones. Beyond the real desire to know the likelihood of NW effects, the DNA, on behalf of the Department of Defense, also had to show that it had the administration's view of the national interest at heart. One defense contractor remarked that the potential effect on military equipment was so severe that a "public outcry" would lead Congress to insist on a research program. Since the DNA already had many of the required capabilities, the contractor suggested that the DNA should undertake the effort.[1]

Another consultant also urged DNA activity, since "there is a significant probability that something will hit the fan when either the NAS or the 'Sagan' committee report becomes public."[2] And a third advised: "You need a catchy title, preferably with a good acronym. Possibly 'Environmental' rather than 'Atmospheric' is more user-oriented."[3] Not everyone was concerned with the "spin" the DNA should put on NW (or with disparaging the contributions of others); at least two participants in the DNA's session for contractors and military agencies on 13 July 1983 wrote unflavored responses.[4] Other honest voices were heard in the capital. Charles Zraket, chief operating officer of MITRE, a major defense contractor for C^3I, admitted that "it really is a new thing."[5] And Richard Wagner of the DoD conceded that "not only the Department of Defense but . . . the scientific community in general ought to be a bit chagrined at not realizing that smoke could produce these effects for as long as they do, no question about it."[6]

In March 1984, Russell Peterson, chairman of the Committee on the Consequences of Nuclear War, sought a personal meeting with the president to inform him about NW, but the NSC deflected his request to the Arms Control and Disarmament Agency. The ACDA's director, Kenneth Adelman, welcomed the briefing for himself and his staff. Carl Sagan and the executive director of the Center on the Consequences of Nuclear War, Chaplin Barnes, joined Peterson for this meeting in early June 1984, attended also by representatives from the Department of State, the Department of Defense, the White House Office of Science and Technology Policy, the National Security Council, the Joint Chiefs of Staff, and the Central Intelligence Agency. Reluctant in public to show concern about NW, in private the administration was appropriately engaged.[7] Indeed, even as these administration officials met, a national response was being orchestrated. A report in the *Washington Post* indicated that the president's science advisor, George Keyworth, had approved a three-year program, funded at millions of dollars a year and consisting of both "massive calculations on supercomputers" and city-size fire experiments. Alan Hecht, head of the climate section of the National Oceanic and Atmospheric Administration, would lead the effort.[8] The *Post* was partially correct: all this was being planned, but the details and approvals took until early 1985 to fall into place.

Sagan may be faulted for pushing public discussion of the consequences of NW when he himself recognized the limitations of TTAPS's one-dimensional computer model. Yet, as his colleague Toon explained, a three-dimensional model is such a complex thing that you would not search for phenomena with it. Less sophisticated models were appropriate to identify the event, whereupon general circulation models would logically continue the investigation. The TTAPS paper in *Science*, in Toon's view, was the announcement of an important effect, not the final word.[9] It might have been preferable had Sagan waited perhaps half a year for some solid 3-D results. The threshold would have been seen to be too squishy, temperatures would have been seen to fall less, and human extinction would have been seen to be less likely—all weak points that were attacked by the critics. Without those distractions, Sagan could have highlighted the still dreadful seriousness of NW: a move to smaller arsenals continued to make sense, the temperature decline was still large, and reduction of the human population remained enormous. But Sagan, who felt that the 3-D models would not change the thrust of NW's message, chose to exercise his rights as a citizen to comment on political issues. He correctly sensed that he was riding a wave of media interest. Familiar through his involvement with the Council for a Livable World with the difficulties that anti-Establishment organizations had in getting their message across, Sagan recognized that if he delayed his political campaign for 6 months or so he might miss the opportunity for maximum effect.

Sagan was strongly challenged by those who disagreed with his liberal views on combating the arms race. This was normal politics, except that the critics picked up and used the scientific issues under debate. A more significant question that remains is whether Sagan abused his position as a scientist to urge political changes when the scientific information remained uncertain. Several noted scientists known as advocates of arms control, including Freeman Dyson, George Rathjens, Frank von Hippel, and John Holdren, felt that he was wrong. Other scientists, without apparent arms-control credentials, also mounted in opposition to NW. Among them were Edward Teller, Michael May, and S. Fred Singer.

The National Security Council received a letter from a citizen much concerned about growing public belief in the validity of NW, which he credited to Sagan's vigorous salesmanship. There had been no opportunity for an "adversary peer review" by the nation's atmospheric scientists, most of whom, the letter's author was sure, recognized Sagan's "evasion, stonewalling and dissimulation" over the gaps between computer models and the real world. Aside from bringing Sagan "back to the Hill for further testimony *under oath*," the best chance to discredit him, to "call his bluff" by "hard cross-examination," would come in early December 1984, when the National Academy of Sciences' report was scheduled for release. The unknown author wrote: "We should deploy as many of the skeptics, especially those like Rathjens, as we can." George Carrier, head of the NAS panel, would be there, and Michael McElroy of Harvard had "agreed to cooperate."[10] One hopes that this high degree of paranoia was not mirrored in the NSC. It is hard to think that Sagan—or any scientist, on a scientific issue—would have testified any differently if under oath, and it is an additional measure of the individual's concern that he feared leaving the unveiling of the NAS report unscripted. To those with such political paranoia, Sagan had put his own spin on the NW issue, and it was only natural for them to counter it.

But why was there such concern? The letter writer had a domino theory: New Zealand was using NW to justify its denial of port access to nuclear-powered and nuclear-armed US Navy vessels, a policy that was popular in the region. This reduced American presence in "a million square miles of the Pacific Ocean," and "that's a pretty big chip for a game in which the dealer is using a stacked deck." Aside from weakening the ANZUS (Australia–New Zealand–United States) alliance, the contagion could spread to the NATO countries, where nuclear opponents might elect representatives who equated "the use of theater weapons . . . with the end of the world." Soviet strategists would then interpret this unwillingness to fire "theater nukes" as license to unleash conventional forces to suppress uprisings in Poland or other Eastern European countries, then to continue on into NATO territory. "Dr. Sagan's polemic," the writer opined, "may be the very disease for which it is presumed to be the cure."[11] Geopolitical reasoning such as the above is based on so many "what ifs" that no reliance can be placed on it for the construction of policy. Science cannot answer every question, but its internal process of data gathering, testing, and verification yields far more reliable conclusions than the activities of those who ignorantly fault it.

In addition to its support of NW studies through the Defense Nuclear Agency, the Department of Defense also made use of the Defense Science Board, its highest-level assembly of advisors.[12] The Department of State also expressed interest in NW. The Secretary of State's assistants recommended that the scientific community be allowed to iron out the disputed points, and that State take no policy position. Yet they must be alert to potential consequences if TTAPS's predictions were upheld, or if Congress and the public insisted on some action. There might be, for example, "calls for dramatic reductions in the size of nuclear arsenals, possibly unilateral," or "reduced support for modernization of US nuclear forces—

particularly the increases planned in numbers of nuclear weapons (several thousands)." It was clear to these officials at State that NW posed a specific challenge to policy, and they wished to avoid a governmental "position by default."[13]

Congressional Activity

Sagan continued in his missionary role throughout this period. In mid May 1984, he and Teller appeared before members of the House of Representatives. This private debate in the dining room of the Speaker of the House was sponsored by Representatives Timothy Wirth (D-Colorado) and Newt Gingrich (R-Georgia).[14] That both Sagan and Teller agreed on the need for more information about NW and its consequences impressed a number of people in their audience and led to several proposals.[15]

A few weeks later, in late May 1984, Senator William Proxmire (D-Wisconsin) submitted a bill (S.2693) titled "Comprehensive study on impact of nuclear winter." This was to be an examination by the Department of Defense, not just of the technicalities of NW, but of the effect that NW "would have on the defense capabilities of this country" and on the nation's "defense strategy and doctrine." Proxmire wanted to know how research-and-development and procurement policies should be altered in light of NW. This report would take a year to compose, and Proxmire expected the DoD to coordinate its efforts with the Arms Control and Disarmament Agency and the Federal Emergency Management Agency. Since the DoD had plans not only for a 30-minute "spasm" war but also for limited, protracted, counterforce, countervalue, and other types of conflicts, Proxmire wanted to know how NW affected their conduct "so we do not waste money on weapons and defense strategies that not only do not work, but would be so suicidal that we would not want them to work." He asked particularly if the "air breathing leg [meaning bombers] of our strategic triad [would] function in an atmosphere filled for weeks with smoke, soot, and dust," and also with radioactive debris, and under conditions of ozone depletion and freezing temperatures. He noted that the National Oceanic and Atmospheric Administration and the Defense Nuclear Agency were already studying NW, and that the DoD had asked the Center for Aerospace Doctrine Research and Education to investigate problems for defense policy that were raised by NW.[16] Proxmire asked the right questions, but thorough answers were never provided.

Almost simultaneously, Senator William Cohen (R-Maine) introduced an amendment to the defense authorization bill. This adjustment directed the DoD to issue a report on NW, and it was so similar to Proxmire's bill that the latter seems to have been superseded. Cohen felt it prudent to investigate the consequences of nuclear war and "how those effects should shape our policy."[17] In the final language of its enactment, this addendum specified that the DoD present a thorough review of the science, notably including "atmospheric, climatic, environmental, and biological consequences of nuclear explosions," an evaluation of NW's effect on arms-control and civil defense policies, and an analysis of Soviet activities.[18]

Cohen's addendum, supported by Senators John Warner (R-Virginia) and John Tower (R-Texas), was endorsed by the Senate Armed Services Committee. A similar amendment was filed in the House by Timothy Wirth (the congressman representing Boulder, where the National Center for Atmospheric Research is located). The amendment was supported by Representatives Jim Leach (R-Iowa), Newt Gingrich (R-Georgia), Buddy Roemer (D-Lousiana), and Al Gore Jr. (D-Tennessee). The DoD was instructed to deliver the report to the Armed Services Committees of both houses by 1 March 1985.[19]

The request for such a report was a normal part of legislative activity. By the time Congress adjourned in October 1984, the Department of Defense had been asked for studies on MX and Midgetman missile basing and strategic implications, on the security of communications, on the cost of verifying a ban on chemical and biological weapons, on a means to distinguish between cruise missiles armed with nuclear and conventional explosives, on the survivability of strategic submarines, and on several other topics of current interest.[20] The NW analysis would not be exceptional except (as the Natural Resources Defense Council attorney S. Jacob Scherr pointed out) for the fact that Congress, in effect, had asked the DoD for the "first environmental impact statement on nuclear war."[21]

Although this effort was bipartisan and was supported by some of the more influential members of both houses, it was by no means unanimously endorsed. Representative Samuel Stratton (D-New York) proposed another amendment, one that had the appearance of reasonableness but was regarded as a thinly veiled attempt to cripple the investigation. He sought to limit the DoD's involvement to matters "directly relevant" to military issues. Climatic, environmental, and biological questions, he argued, should not be addressed to the DoD; the National Oceanic and Atmospheric Administration and the Environmental Protection Agency could more appropriately provide answers. Similarly, arms-control and weapons policies were properly subjects for the Department of State, the Arms Control and Disarmament Agency, and the National Security Council. Stratton gave a final twist to his gutting action by adding fiscal conservatism to his amendment, limiting the DoD to a budget of $1.5 million. Representative John Seiberling (D-Ohio) worried that this might be insufficient; funding, he argued, should not be so tightly limited, especially when the DoD's total budget was more than $200 billion. Representative George Brown (D-California)—one of the few members of Congress with technical training, and a long-serving and highly respected authority on defense matters—tried to put things in perspective by noting that the DoD spent "substantially more than $1.5 million to determine the traumatic effect of weapons fire on dogs."[22] Stratton's amendment nevertheless was passed by the House, despite its apparent conflict with the amendment by Wirth.[23] The DoD never cited the Stratton guideline to justify the report it produced the following March, but that was such a minimal effort that it is unlikely they spent even the $1.5 million to which they were constrained. This funding, of course, was distinct from the ongoing support by the Defense Nuclear Agency to the National Academy of Sciences, national laboratories, and contractors, and from support for NW investigations through the Department of Energy and the NOAA.

Joint Congressional Hearings, 11–12 July 1984

The flurry of congressional activity included hearings on NW before the Joint Economic Committee's Subcommittee on International Trade, Finance, and Security Economics. Why, one might ask, were these hearings held before an economics-oriented committee rather than one oriented more toward science, military affairs, civil defense, or foreign policy? NW did, of course, have economic implications, but it is more to the point that this apparent scheduling error occurred because Senator William Proxmire, already interested in NW, was vice chairman of the subcommittee and conducted the hearings. Indeed, some years earlier Proxmire had conducted hearings on the "economic and social consequences of nuclear attacks on the United States." Of the eight-member subcommittee, only Representative Parren J. Mitchell (D-Maryland) attended. Such an empty table apparently was not uncommon in view of the overload of work in the "in" basket of each member of Congress. Senator James Sasser (D-Tennessee) was an interested onlooker.[24]

In a brief opening statement, Senator Proxmire explained the reason for the hearings: not to argue the validity of NW, but to assess the "consequences for public policy." Proxmire was disturbed that neither his colleagues nor the administration were moving very fast. Carl Sagan, the first witness, summarized the TTAPS work and the policy implications. He was followed by Russell Murray of Systems Research and Applications Corporation, who had served as assistant secretary of defense for program analysis and evaluation in the Carter administration. Despite the worsened conditions brought by NW, Murray argued, "thermonuclear war alone should be enough to dictate our policies." He differed from the Reagan administration in his wish list of military hardware (such as nuclear-tipped cruise missiles and new stand-off aircraft to carry them, instead of more expensive B-1 bombers), but he remained a "strong defense" advocate.[25] Apparently, NW made no impact on his views.

Speaking for the American Committee on East-West Accord, Admiral Noel Gayler (USN-Ret.) certified that cities would burn in a nuclear war. Before his retirement, Gayler had been commander in chief of the Pacific Fleet, director of the National Security Agency, and deputy director of the Joint Strategic Target Planning Staff, positions that gave weight to his words. "Most of the deterrent targets," he explained, "are imbedded in cities." Regardless of either superpower's declarative policy, efforts by the USSR to strike the US government would inevitably include an attack on Washington. To destroy the military leadership, Omaha, Norfolk, Honolulu, and Brussels would be hit. To demolish American industry, Los Angeles, New York, Houston, Chicago, San Francisco, Seattle, and dozens of other cities would be hit.

With the existing excess of weapons, even small cities would be deemed "industrial assets." The only important targets that would not ignite urban fires were the ICBM fields in Siberia and on the American plains, but no credible war scenario would limit the conflict to such regions. Gayler, along with many other flag officers, saw no rational military use for nuclear weapons. Further, he felt that, should nuclear conflict occur, it would inevitably escalate, and neither civil defense measures nor a technical advantage such as a missile defense system would provide safety. For Gayler, the best policy choice was to halt all new development of nuclear weapons.[26]

Paul Warnke, who had been a high-profile director of the Arms Control and Disarmament Agency in the Carter administration, professed not to know what the Reagan administration's nuclear policy was. On the one hand, in his State of the Union address the president maintained that nuclear war could not be won and must not be fought. On the other hand, Secretary of Defense Weinberger claimed that nuclear weapons were needed to repulse a conventional attack and to prevail in a nuclear conflict. Like Gayler, Warnke felt that nuclear warfare could not be contained; anticipating what the enemy might launch, you would hit him as hard as you could. For Warnke, therefore, the best policy would be to negotiate massive reductions in the nuclear arsenals, leaving minimal forces that were least provocative and most survivable. Warnke did not argue that small arsenals could be below the NW threshold, though that might be inferred. Nor did he speculate whether nuclear weapons might more readily be used if the combatants felt confident that they could keep below the threshold. For him, NW did not change the goals of arms control.[27]

Proxmire had called critics of the Reagan administration to the first day's session, but aside from Sagan none had thought through the implications of NW. Instead, they suggested policies that predated TTAPS's revelations. This was an example of the inertia that delayed the comprehension of new ideas. On the second day, administration officials defended both their activities and their plans. The assistant to the secretary of defense for atomic energy, the physicist Richard Wagner, pointed to widespread interest in the climatological consequences of fires within government agencies and laboratories, unjustly crediting TTAPS with merely first publication on the subject. The Department of Defense, he claimed, was on top of the matter, pursuing both technical studies of NW and policy implications, the latter through a study commissioned at the War College at Maxwell Air Force Base.

In view of the many uncertainties surrounding NW, Wagner asserted, it was premature even to think of changing policy. The administration continued to believe that the best way to avoid NW, and all other explosion effects, was to prevent nuclear war in the first place. While policies could certainly change as new technical information became available, Wagner was encouraged that the yield and quantity of US nuclear weapons had been decreasing for some years, and that in a conflict strategic defense would reduce the number of explosions. Both steps were pre-NW in conception, yet they served to minimize climatic effects. For now, Wagner emphasized, security depended on the credibility of the deterrent.[28]

For the rest of the morning's session, Wagner and the ACDA's deputy director, David F. Emery, resisted Proxmire's badgering. They defended the administration's desire to avoid nuclear war and its commitment to arms control and the maintenance of a credible deterrent as the centerpieces of a rational policy. Emery surprised the senator by revealing that in June 1984 he and other American officials had met with their Soviet counterparts in Leningrad to discuss the consequences of NW.[29] (There is no evidence that either government took any policy action as a result of that meeting.) The afternoon session focused on civil defense and agriculture. Carl Sagan was given an opportunity to comment on the testimony of all the witnesses, but he had little of substance to add.[30]

These hearings were not given much space in the nation's newspapers, being upstaged by the announcement that the Democratic presidential nominee, Walter Mondale, had selected Geraldine Ferraro as his running mate. The *New York Times*'s short article focused on the qualified agreement of officialdom—in the person of the assistant to the secretary of defense, Richard Wagner, and the deputy director of the ACDA, David Emery—that NW was a real phenomenon and not a liberal fantasy or one based on questionable scientific research.[31]

Hearings in the House of Representatives, 12 September 1984

In anticipation of the administration's budgetary request for the research program that NOAA was cobbling together, the House Committee on Science and Technology's Subcommittee on Natural Resources, Agriculture Research and Environment met in mid September 1984. With Representative James H. Scheuer (D-New York) as chairman, three panels gave testimony on the science, computation, and policy implications of NW. The always eloquent Carl Sagan led off—perhaps a tactic to get the audience into its seats near the planned starting time—and gave a survey of the phenomenon in which he argued that it must be taken seriously, even if the probability of its occurring was small.[32]

Next, the equally articulate Stephen Jay Gould contrasted NW with the biblical darkness that Moses brought over Egypt. The latter lasted only three days before the terrified pharaoh relented. NW, Gould noted, would be much worse, and even more severe than already terrified twentieth-century humanity expected of nuclear warfare. Gould defended the scientific work on NW as entirely credible, even if a major "experiment" to confirm it could not be conducted. Science accepts a variety of approaches to its theories, and there are several scientific fields, such as geology, in which data collection dominates over experimental verification. Gould explained that mass extinctions occur with some regularity, including the famous one at the K-T boundary that killed the dinosaurs, and that they were examples of "nature's plow, clearing away incumbents and making room for the evolution of new creatures." Gould's point was that NW-like experiments probably had been conducted by nature at least a few times. As for the validity of pursuing worst-case scenarios, Gould admonished his audience to "remember the *Titanic*."[33] Again, no new ideas were presented, but this was not the expected forum for them. Congressional hearings served to educate lawmakers and the public about how science works and how its results should be used.

The final witness in this panel was Edward Teller. Attempting to place NW in the context he saw, Teller spoke of the fear of global death from fallout (as in the novel and film *On the Beach*), and of the more recent claim of harm from depletion of the ozone layer. Both were highly exaggerated, he felt. They were serious matters, and worthy of investigation, but neither should play much of a role in considerations of defense strategy. To Teller, NW fell in the same category, all the more so in view of the great uncertainties in the numbers entered into the equations. Teller supported this point by citing some unpublished research that, depending on the quantity of smoke produced, the amount rained out, and other variables, showed the possibility of warming *or* cooling of Earth's surface. He also denigrated the research of NW supporters: they "repeated the same calculations with the same assumptions and found the same results, which shows nothing except that our computing machines are working." This activity, said Teller, "is not science; it is a little deviation from ignorance."[34]

In the discussion that followed, Sagan reiterated the argument he had unsuccessfully made to Keyworth, the president's science advisor, that NW's biological and ecological consequences and its policy implications should be studied simultaneously with the physical, chemical, and meteorological investigations then being planned by the government. If these things were to be studied sequentially, it would be years, Sagan felt, before many serious issues would be addressed. Gould endorsed this view, noting the extraordinary complexity of biological phenomena and the long time needed to gain insights.[35]

There was also testimony from Alan Hecht of NOAA, from Leon Gouré (the "Soviet specialist" at Science Applications International Corporation), and from Theodore Postol of Stanford University's Center for International Security and Arms Control. Gouré and Postol addressed policy issues. Gouré made the interesting point that NW appeared at first to be a deterrent to nuclear warfare, but need not always be so. Aside from scenarios that avoided the NW effect by avoiding the targeting of cities and thus would not deter warfare, the superpowers were likely to have different perceptions of what were unacceptable levels of damage and loss from the immediate effects of explosions. They would similarly differ on the amount of unacceptable climatic consequences. One nation might strike, while the other might hold back. This asymmetry extended to escalation control, especially if a belligerent sought to keep the war's total yield below a poorly defined threshold. Nor did NW mean that cities would be spared entirely; Gouré expected that some would be hit because of counterforce targets in them or nearby. The uncertainty surrounding both the physical phenomenon and the political reactions to it, in his view, made it premature for any strategic planner to be guided by NW.[36]

Postol did not so much address whether it was premature to change policy because of NW as charge that *any* policy, present and apparently future, was based on hopelessly uncertain phenomena. His recently completed two-year tour as assistant for weapons technology in the office of the Chief of Naval Operations had convinced him that politicians and military planners really did not comprehend what they were doing. "The entire structure of our current nuclear policy," he testified, "is beset by misconceptions and problematic and contradictory features." Whether or not NW was valid, Postol urged a reevaluation of this policy. Beyond this, Postol claimed that nuclear effects, besides those associated with NW, were so poorly understood that better knowledge of them could "well result in drastic changes in our military planning and our national policy."[37] Such startling testimony could not have been welcomed by a committee hoping for answers to more limited questions, but the session's scheduled ending time precluded any exploration of Postol's remarks.

As information about NW accumulated, modifying the original TTAPS position but still concluding that the world would experience disaster, some members of Congress grew frustrated that nothing apparently was being done by Congress or by the administration. Senator Proxmire, famous for presenting a "Golden Fleece" award to what he considered to be foolish research projects that nonetheless enjoyed government funding, had no such doubts about the need to explore NW further. On the floor of the Senate in October 1984, he asked rhetorically what the nation's response had been. "Colossal indifference," he replied, employing the term that General Omar Bradley had used to describe the United States' attitude toward general nuclear war. We had made elaborate plans for fighting a nuclear war, Proxmire stated, yet we had ignored difficulties that might be encountered by machinery and by men in a cold, dark, and radioactive environment. Proxmire, also concerned about the ability of the nation to function economically and the ability of people to feed themselves in such conditions, focused not only on major warfare between the superpowers (when such concerns were probably academic) but also on smaller conflicts that still abused the atmosphere.[38] His domestic questions would be answered by studies such as the SCOPE report, but the Department of Defense never (publicly) addressed the obvious military questions.

11 Bureaucracy and Bickering

Most observers would have said that the research goal was to narrow the range of possibilities for the many ingredients of NW. Freeman Dyson disagreed:

I hope the final result of all this work will not be to make the limits of our uncertainty narrower but rather to make the limits wider. We should not claim any ability to predict the effects of nuclear war. We should claim only to have found out that the effects are even more unpredictable than we had believed earlier. In my opinion, the main result of the new work is to strengthen the case for Tolstoy's view that war is in its nature incalculable and incomprehensible and uncontrollable. This is the message which the public needs to hear.[1]

Dyson would have made a good philosopher-king. Americans—indeed, citizens of most nations—however, prefer instead to have leaders who are pragmatists. Being distrustful of idealists, we choose those who can "get the job done." While he believed that nuclear war was so bad that people needed no additional horrific feature of it to insist on avoiding it,[2] Dyson recognized that the thrust of the century was toward greater precision. In the quote above, he thus expressed his wish that we might learn more accurately that the uncertainty was larger. Such fine reasoning would have been lost amidst the general inclination to know with rigor down to the smallest limits. Logic and tradition of course demanded that the NW phenomenon be studied carefully.

Even before 1983 ended, the nuclear winter predictions by TTAPS and others had spawned a flurry of scientific activity. Papers were presented in August (mostly by Livermore scientists) at the international conference in Erice. The International Council of Scientific Unions directed its Scientific Committee on Problems of the Environment to begin a study, and so rapidly did the Scientific Committee on Problems of the Environment (SCOPE) respond that they held a first meeting in Stockholm in November. And the American Geophysical Union, deprived in 1982 of hearing a scheduled paper by Turco, had a special session on global effects in December 1983. Most of the research on NW that followed was conducted in 1984 and 1985.

The National Academy of Sciences Panel: First Draft

The NAS's National Research Council submitted its proposal for a study of nuclear winter to the Defense Nuclear Agency in late 1982. In early 1983, the panel was formed. By the time its chairman, George Carrier, was chosen, most members had been selected by the NAS's president, Frank Press, who also chose the executive director, Lawrence McCray (an NRC staffer who had studied under George Rathjens at MIT). Carrier asked for and got permission to add some others who "represented special knowledge," and this was done. The panel had eighteen members, a normal size.

Carrier, a professor of engineering and applied mathematics at Harvard University and a member of the National Academy of Sciences, was an expert on fire research. He had participated in the two ad hoc meetings called in late 1981 and early 1982 by Admiral Moran, who became vice chairman of the committee. Carrier had been skeptical of the original mechanism for dinosaur extinction which the ad hoc group discussed. The energy of the asteroid or meteor that allegedly caused the creatures to disappear was 10 million times that contained in the world's nuclear arsenals. Were impact dust and explosion dust really comparable?[3]

The unpaid committee members, who received only reimbursement of expenses, included specialists in chemistry, physics, astronomy, geology, atmospheric and Earth sciences, and applications of science to military questions. As nuclear winter, rather than dinosaur extinction, moved to the forefront, Carrier had momentary qualms when he found Birks, Toon, and Turco on his panel, men who might be considered already to hold a viewpoint. He quickly realized, however, that he "didn't want to lose the expertise of a bunch of people who had been thinking very hard about the problem." Nor did he intend that his panel would be "captured by their opinions." At their first meeting, on 7–8 March 1983—which was over a month before the TTAPS Blue Book would be reviewed in Cambridge, an event Carrier attended and from which he emerged unconvinced that NW was real—he asked them for reassurance that, even if the NAS conclusions differed from the expected TTAPS conclusions, they would act as objectively as possible in reaching a consensus. They all agreed.[4]

This, of course, did not mean that everyone held the same viewpoint. "There were people on that committee," Carrier noted, "who it would not be unfair to call zealots." By this he meant those who would do anything to prevent nuclear weapons from being used. Others on the committee "felt . . . this is just another one of those damn threats that people get all excited about . . . and it gets into the political process and does untold damage." The rest of the panel fell between these extremes. Yet the group was able to work satisfactorily as a whole, and those at the ends of the political spectrum nonetheless were able to join in the consensus scientific position.[5]

To reach that position they argued strongly about scientific matters, "not so much about the science as such, but as to the inputs from which the scientifically carried out inferences were drawn. . . . They could only be as good as the input data, and we knew about the uncertainties in the input data." In addition, they were conscious that they must exclude specifics about matters that might be classified, such as the ability of a bomb's radiation to ignite flammables, or their report would receive only limited circulation. Though all the information in the final report came from the open literature, several members of the panel were given security clearance, and the Defense Nuclear Agency gathered secret data on explosions for them. Indeed, until shortly before publication, Carrier observed, they did not know if the study would be classified.[6]

In most NAS investigations the focus is on the scientific literature; the mandate is not to produce new data. That was generally true in this case, but not entirely, for they felt compelled to minimize the "uncertainties that we were swamped in."[7] Consultant Stephen Schneider, who compared the uncertainties to "playing Russian roulette and not knowing if there are one or five bullets in the gun," was strongly motivated by the Cambridge meeting in April 1983 to explore the NW phenomenon with a three-dimensional computer model. The expected dynamic mechanisms were too important to neglect. He had at the National Center for Atmospheric Research a model of this sort and, with colleagues Starley Thompson and Curt Covey, hastened to modify it to his needs. They had less than 3 months before a planned summer meeting of the NAS committee. The model already had seasonal variations built in; now they improved its radiative transfer program. Still, they had time only to provide for total absorption of sunlight by the soot cloud, even though they knew real smoke scatters half the light, and they had to neglect the effects of dust. Using a reasonable optical absorption depth of 3 (meaning that very little light penetrated to Earth's surface), they ran half a dozen simulations, covering the first few weeks after a nuclear war.[8] The results, though tentative, were striking. Heating of the middle troposphere was so rapid, intense, and extensive that winds were radically different from normal conditions. Calculations of soot transport or removal, based on current knowledge, were therefore inadequate. All but low-lying clouds soon vanished, the mid-tropospheric inversion preventing moisture from rising. Climatic effects in the Northern Hemisphere were less significant in January than in July, since it was already cold, but surface temperatures nonetheless fell markedly. A summertime war would create such updrafts along the southern edge of the soot layer that mid-latitude soot would likely spurt southward into the tropics and perhaps into the Southern Hemisphere. Cooled land in Central Asia, even in summertime, would cause air to sink and flow toward the Indian Ocean, potentially reversing monsoon winds and devastating agriculture in South Asia. This could occur even if India was not shrouded by dust and smoke clouds.

Most surprising to Schneider was the "quick freeze" of land surfaces in many places. Simpler climate models treated the atmosphere and surface as a unit, whereas the NCAR model separated these and then subdivided the air into layers. Simpler models had predicted relatively slow cooling. But 24 hours of darkened land was, to the more sophisticated model, the equivalent of two nights, and the normal nighttime temperature decrease of 5–20°C

(9–36°F), when multiplied steadily, would soon lead to freezing. Even a patchy overcast of soot, which some at the Cambridge meeting had said would prevent great cooling, would not protect large areas of the land from transient below-freezing temperatures. "Perhaps no place on earth," Schneider wrote, "could necessarily feel itself immune from temporary severe environmental aftereffects of large scale nuclear war."[9]

In certain areas, such work was a large step beyond the contributions of TTAPS. Yet, although the results were highly plausible, they too lacked the precision required for general confidence in their predictions. In particular, no model yet built was interactive. This meant that the injected dust and smoke did not "modify the heating and therefore the wind structure of the atmosphere. In turn, the smoke [was not] transported and removed by that modified wind structure, thereby [not] feeding back on the atmospheric heating patterns and once again modifying the wind."[10]

New research at the National Center for Atmospheric Research, related computer studies at Los Alamos, and smoke plume calculations done by Carrier and a colleague were exceptions to the general activities of the NAS committee. Though they certainly kept abreast of ongoing research, mostly they looked at what they felt to be missing, the influence of various constituents in the calculations, and how they might enhance the calculations and the models. In short, their task was one of judgment, not of the assimilation of new data.[11]

The NAS expected the study to produce an initial assessment of the literature by the end of 1983. This would be followed by a more penetrating investigation, if recommended.[12] The first phase was completed by mid October 1983, when Carrier, Moran, and McCray presented its conclusions at the Pentagon to Undersecretary of Defense for Research and Engineering Richard DeLauer, members of his staff, and DNA personnel. Carrier emphasized the many unknowns and assumptions throughout the report, yet argued that the conjectures actually were modest. They certainly were not worst-case selections. He cited examples of their modeling choices that led to lesser effects, such as a short cutoff in the ignition range of an explosion's thermal pulse, keeping smoke and soot out of the stratosphere, and not allowing fires to merge.

Still, with a tropospheric smoke loading of 200 million tonnes, considered to be a reasonable amount, the absorption optical depth would be 7. This meant that sunlight reaching Earth's surface would be reduced by three orders of magnitude (e^7). The temperature of land masses, as a result, would decrease by tens of degrees Celsius and remain low for a few months. While Carrier admitted the drawbacks of their calculations, largely based on a one-dimensional model, he doubted that two-dimensional and three-dimensional models would change the conclusions appreciably. NCAR's early approach with a 3-D model supported this view. This work should be done, Carrier felt; however, a large effort was not necessary, only "a few smart people working the problem." The DNA project officer, George Ullrich, was troubled by Carrier's presentation: he seemed to say that the NAS "conclusions and scenarios were more benign and conservative than those of Sagan. Yet as far as I can tell they are virtually identical." Ullrich shared his misgivings with McCray, who agreed that Carrier might have inadvertently misled his audience.[13]

Pentagon Activity

Even before Carrier unveiled the draft of his committee's conclusions to DeLauer and other DoD personnel in October 1983 (and before the Halloween meeting at which NW was publicly revealed), the DoD sought to refine its role. Indeed, the NAS panel's mission was to evaluate the existing literature, while the DNA now looked beyond that to acquire new data. On 13 July 1983, a meeting was held, with Peter Lunn of the DNA as chairman. The group, which included representatives from the DNA, from the Los Alamos National Laboratory, from the office of the chief of naval operations, from the Air Force Geophysics Laboratory, from Harvard University, and from defense contractors such as the Institute for Defense Analyses, Aerodyne Research, Lockheed, Mission Research, and R&D Associates (in the person of Turco), reviewed preliminary results not only from the NAS study but also from the TTAPS team, whose paper for *Science* was being composed at the time. The purpose of the exercise was to "scope out a potential DNA research program to reduce the current uncertainties in global effects for military applications."[14]

While the DNA was responsible for keeping abreast of nuclear explosion effects locally and worldwide, it supported no comprehensive effort. The agency now was concerned that results of both the NAS and TTAPS studies would be "unrealistically pessimistic." There was agreement that computer models that permitted mixing of the atmosphere—three-dimensional global circulation models—would reduce the harsh predictions currently available. Uncertainty concerning dust and fire products also was too great. Better information was needed, they felt, for the present "implications are significant both for habitability and system performance in a protracted conflict." The participants were asked to recommend topics to investigate.[15]

Replies were grouped into scenarios, source functions, and atmospheric responses, which embraced essentially the whole spectrum of subjects examined by TTAPS and the NAS panel. Warfare scenarios to be developed would be "realistic," to set limits on the factors that affected the atmosphere. Imbedded in this proposal was disagreement with TTAPS's focus on high-soot city fires. Desired new source functions would be better quantifications of the materials that perturbed the atmosphere: dust, fire products, and nitrogen oxides produced by fireballs. The final category involved where these products would go in the troposphere and the stratosphere over time, their physical and chemical dynamics, and the extent to which they would veil the sunlight.

Almost all participants urged a significant research program and recommended specific studies that would take 1–3 years. Large projects were not necessary, they believed, and only one or two or three investigators need pursue each subtopic. Contrary to the "sometimes slanted conclusions . . . based on uncertain and incomplete analyses" that appeared to be coming from the TTAPS group and the NAS panel—which, it should be remembered, was funded by the DNA—these new studies would provide "a thoughtful and even-handed interpretation of the results," so one contractor claimed.[16] "It is important to assure that Sagan or equivalent not be in charge," said another.[17] No one explained how anyone could know that TTAPS and NAS conclusions were "sometimes slanted" before they performed their own calculations.

R&D Associates had a computer model, or code, for moving dust clouds by normal winds and circulation, and one of its scientists was then adding soot and water vapor to it. But it was not a three-dimensional model, and this was seen to be required. Only a few such global circulation models existed, one of the best having been composed in Australia and developed further at the US National Center for Atmospheric Research. Robert Malone at the Los Alamos National Laboratory (LANL), had a copy of this general circulation model (GCM). Since he was already supported by the Department of Energy to upgrade the mixing and radiation aspects of the code, it would be cost-effective to give him an equal amount ($200,000) to add soot and dust.[18]

LANL was eager to conduct this research, with special attention to mixing of the Northern and Southern Hemispheres' atmospheres, patchiness in soot distribution, alterations in the stability of the atmosphere, and changes in rainout patterns. This would be an interactive model, with winds able to move aerosols about and scavenging of smoke and dust to occur. Unlike NCAR, Princeton, and the Ames Research Center, which also ran GCMs, LANL claimed to have a "compelling institutional interest in this question." The GCMs, of course, had been designed for the normal atmosphere. (Indeed, their development from the 1960s onward was driven primarily by weather prediction and nuclear explosion research on supercomputers.) While "quick fixes" were possible to transform them to handle the massive additions of explosion and fire debris, as Stephen Schneider at NCAR was doing, "believable answers" required a more "significant modification of the physics package." LANL also proposed to examine the quantities and size distributions of particulate matter. This was a particularly important issue, for most earlier studies had looked at larger particles, while sub-micrometer-size dust and soot were now of greater concern.[19] The "action" was at these smaller dimensions.

The self-puffery of the DoD contractors apparent in the quotes above may be a normal way of doing business, but one wonders if the disparaging allusions to the scientific work of others was because they were mostly academics—who themselves generally look down on scientists in industry and government—or just "others." Scorn was not restricted to the university-connected, however. The Forest Service's fire modeling was thought to be "very rudimentary," and FEMA to be "totally useless."[20]

Conservative Critics

Scientific work, most of its practitioners like to think, is the objective pursuit of knowledge. Fortunately, this is true to a remarkable degree. Scientists are likely to be more honest about their research and practice their trade more ethically than do business executives, laborers, office workers, sales people, lawyers, bankers, politicians, police officers, media people, and those in most other types of employment. But science is not as objective as the public believes. While there is a vast realm of conclusions that are accepted almost universally, there remain many subjects that the specialists continue to debate. They may disagree whether the data really measure accurately the phenomenon in question, or they may accept the data but contest their interpretation. To scientists, this is unexceptional; science generally works like this and in time a consensus usually develops. The participants advocate their positions honestly and are influenced only by their scientific experiences and insights.

On occasion, however, other factors enter the picture: envy, hostility, deceit, and so on. To the extent that these were part of the NW story, they have already largely been described. Here, it is worthwhile to examine another dimension of disagreement—one seemingly influenced by political belief in addition to science. These critics of NW rarely contributed to the research. They improved no computer models, analyzed no banks of data, provided no extensive reworking of the materials, and rarely even made any calculations at all. Their activity consisted of "hand waving," the tossing out of ideas. But most were rightfully regarded as more than crackpots, for they posed some serious scientific questions and they reached important audiences. Further, they often voiced the administration's rationale for making no more than a minimal political response to the climatic consequences of NW.

The geophysicist S. Fred Singer, of the University of Virginia and since mid 1984 of George Mason University, had good connections in Washington, for his career alternated between academic positions and high-level government appointments. He had, for example, been director of the National Weather Satellite Center of the Department of Commerce (1962–1964), deputy assistant secretary for science programs of the Department of the Interior (1967–1970), deputy assistant administrator of the Environmental Protection Agency (1970–71), and chairman of the advisory committee on the environmental effects of the supersonic transport for the Department of Transportation (1971). In 1987 he would return for a while to government service as the DoT's chief scientist. Whether by nature scientifically cautious or because he was politically conservative, Singer often seemed to disparage the claims of those who predicted environmental calamities. Perhaps it is a posture deemed to be suitable for those accustomed to the corridors of power. Thus, his committee found little wrong with the SST in 1971, he was outspoken in minimizing fears of global warming and of ozone depletion in the 1990s, and in between he was a forceful and formidable opponent of the NW hypothesis.[21]

Once TTAPS's ideas were popularized at the Halloween meeting in late 1983, Singer composed a critique, which he ran by about twenty scientific colleagues at a symposium on global environmental problems, and then distributed to, among others, President Reagan's science advisor, George Keyworth. Uncertainty was the name of his game. Indeed, uncertainty was the key note in the hymnology of all the opponents of NW. Could not the debris injected into the atmosphere by nuclear explosions and fires, he asked, retain the heat radiated from Earth by a greenhouse mechanism? And might this not more than compensate for the cooling effect caused by the debris's reflection of incident sunlight? The atmosphere of Venus, full of aerosols, is heated to several hundred degrees Celsius by just such a process, yet TTAPS chose Mars for its analogy, since dust storms there do in fact cause surface cooling. Singer faulted such a selection, since Mars's dust has different optical properties from terrestrial dust, smoke, and soot. He also criticized another TTAPS analogy: surface cooling after large volcanic eruptions. Volcanic ejecta, Singer pointed out, reach the stratosphere and remain there for months or years, while combustion products stay much closer to the ground. "It may become," he noted, "dark and warm instead of dark and freezing."[22]

Elaborating on these ideas, Singer mused that the smoke and soot of fires might not "reflect sunlight back out into space (as Martian dust does)," but instead might "absorb solar radiation and create violent heating of the lower atmosphere." If this occurred, the turbulence could induce heavy precipitation, causing the rain-out of much of the particulate matter and shortening any dark period. If the stratosphere should somehow be affected (which he doubted) and the ozone layer destroyed, this would change the temperature configuration and thus the stability of the stratosphere, turning it into little more than an extension of the troposphere, with its "instability, rapid mixing and clean-up by rain." Whatever the scientific mechanism, Singer saw only short-term climatic effects. He granted that "Sagan's scenario may well be correct, but the range of uncertainty is so great that the prediction is not particularly useful."[23]

After TTAPS's paper appeared in *Science*, Singer reiterated his belief that "changes in the assumptions underlying their analysis can yield quite different climatic consequences." In a January 1984 letter to the editor of *Science* (which was not published), he repeated his arguments above and added that a warming greenhouse effect would be enhanced by water molecules carried into the atmosphere as materials that contained water (such as wood) burned and as other moist sources vaporized.

Singer was further concerned that nuclear war scenarios different from those chosen by TTAPS were more likely to occur, and these would loft different amounts of dust, smoke, and soot to different altitudes, where their times of residence would also vary. On this most critical point of TTAPS's calculations—the types and amounts of particulate matter projected into the atmosphere and their residence time—Singer correctly noted that "this issue cannot be settled by a one-dimensional model but requires a mesoscale approach." Basically, he was of the opinion that the air would quickly be cleansed, and that climatic effects would not be as severe as TTAPS projected because the oceans would moderate land temperatures to a great extent.[24]

The *Wall Street Journal* was more hospitable to Singer's views, printing a guest editorial by him in early February 1984. It was similar to his letter to *Science*, and contained no new points except his doubts (already expressed by others at both the Cambridge review of the

TTAPS Blue Book and the Halloween meeting in 1983) that smoke and dust would spread globally in an even layer, as TTAPS's computer model required. It did, however, add to the language of the subject by predicting a "nuclear summer—dark and hot," if another set of "reasonable" assumptions was chosen. But "whatever the temperature effects," he added, "they are likely to be quite short-lived."[25]

This was Singer's first critique to be aired publicly, and it drew a quick response from Sagan, who chided the geophysicist for his statements "based on no calculations whatever." In contrast, TTAPS had "calculated some 40 different nuclear war cases, with a wide range of parameters, and in none of them is there any significant surface temperature increase." The explanation, Sagan wrote, was because "soot absorbs more light in the visible than in the infrared, where greenhouse opacities must lie." Similarly, TTAPS's computer modeling involved a spectrum of reasonable values for such microphysical processes as particle coagulation, rainout, and scavenging, and the ensuing climatic conditions were not short-lived, as Singer hypothesized.[26] Singer defended himself, pointing to other reputable scientists who saw the possibility of heating, but his main point remained the great uncertainty of the NW effect.[27]

A year later, in January 1985, as the acting chairman of the National Advisory Committee on Oceans and Atmosphere, Singer sang the same song: ". . . uncertainties about the climate consequences of nuclear war still remain as numerous and as large as they were last year. In fact, recent research has uncovered even more uncertainties."[28] Privately, Turco was sharply critical of such "propensity to pontificate" on NW, especially by Singer and John Maddox, "both of whom felt obligated to respond negatively and incompetently to early news of the nuclear winter theory."[29] Singer took another "hit" about a decade later, when Paul and Anne Ehrlich became so annoyed by the "contrarians" that they wrote a book titled *Betrayal of Science and Reason: How Anti-Environmental Rhetoric Threatens Our Future*. They noted that Singer rejected the notion that CFCs could destroy stratospheric ozone and also that global warming was occurring, and implicitly questioned his objectivity by pointing out that he was a paid consultant to ARCO, Exxon, Shell Oil, Sun Oil, and Unocal.[30]

John Maddox was another critic of some stature. As editor of the influential British journal *Nature*, he was appropriately generous with space for NW, accepting articles both pro and con, and occasionally writing editorials on the subject. His bias was that he was reflexively hostile to "prophecies of calamity." A decade before NW, he authored a book titled *The Doomsday Syndrome*, which began with the line: "*This is not* a scholarly work but a complaint." Tired of predictions about the terrible consequences of runaway population growth, pollution, the exhaustion of food and resources, and genetic engineering, he condemned activist-authors such as Rachel Carson, Paul Ehrlich, and Barry Commoner for their alarmist rhetoric. This was not science, he claimed, but pseudo-science, and he faulted the common use of worst-case analyses (he did not discuss their use by military planners). Maddox also criticized scientists for recommending political or social changes to ameliorate a scenario of doom, since these served "chiefly to strengthen the false popular belief that scientists know very little of the real world," and he faulted their often-heated language, which caused not enlightenment but mystification and anxiety.[31]

(Frustration with the "Chicken Littles" may have been more widespread and have had more consequences than was recognized. Lydia Dotto and Harold Schiff, authors of *The Ozone War*, maintained that news about fluorocarbons was slow to reach the public. The media hesitated to print stories, they said, because the *New York Times* had not done so. And the *Times* avoided the subject simply because its science reporter Walter Sullivan felt that there was already too much doomsday talk and was tired of reporting on environmental disasters.[32])

In all these societal dilemmas, Maddox noted, human behavior caused the problems *and* could solve them. In this belief he was a technological optimist. Through several of the postwar decades, with science and technology riding high in the esteem of government officials and the public, the concept of the "technological fix" was popular: if science or technology created a problem, then more science or technology would ultimately overcome it. By the 1970s, however, many had come to recognize that changes in human behavior, not high-tech fixes, would often be necessary.

Maddox, thus, was a self-proclaimed expert on disaster claims, and he reacted to NW with hostility. In January 1984, soon after TTAPS's paper appeared in *Science*, he criticized the "results of the purported recalculations of the long-term consequences of a nuclear war." By calling the work a "recalculation," he belittled the vast amount of new ideas (particularly the effect of soot, which he ignored entirely) in the NW concept, while the word "purported" would never be viewed as an affirmation. Maddox also violated a norm of the scientific world by referring to the TTAPS paper as by "Professor Carl Sagan and a group of associates" and by "Sagan et al." instead of "Turco et al." By denying credit to the paper's lead author, it would seem, this editor (a man immersed in the mores of his vocation) deliberately and unprofessionally sought to tap into the anti-Sagan sentiment that existed. Maddox called attention to a paper in *Nature* on the rather good correlation between frost damage to tree rings and volcanic eruptions. This showed that dust injected into the atmosphere produced climatic effects, which he saw as "exceedingly short-lived." NW was said to be colder and to last longer. Perhaps, Maddox suggested, the discrepancy was due to the greater amount of fine dust Sagan and his colleagues said was lofted, in contrast to the amount specified in the 1975 NAS report, and all could be explained in the next TTAPS paper, said to be "in preparation." The field was replete with uncertainties, as both Sagan and Maddox agreed, and the latter suggested that "conclusions, derived as they are from necessarily crude models and uncertain data, should be plainly stamped with the label QUALITATIVE for fear that their apparent precision may prove spurious."[33]

The dendochronologists whose work Maddox invoked took him to task, not for misrepresenting their paper, but for applying their results only to the NW problem. "Mr. Maddox," they wrote, "seems to have missed the essential point repeatedly made by Turco et al. that smoke, because of its high absorption in the visible light range and low absorption in the infra-red, causes most of the surface cooling."[34] Maddox was, however, correct that TTAPS had promised a more detailed report than their December 1983 paper in *Science*. This study, "in preparation" for a long time, never appeared, perhaps superseded by the work of others. But it was an omission on which critics could focus.

In early March 1984, Maddox again placed his "spin" on the subject with a column titled "Nuclear winter not yet established: Talk of some of the consequences of nuclear warfare had better be postponed until the underlying assumptions are better understood." Reiterating the inadequacies of TTAPS's one-dimensional model of the atmosphere's energy balance and the lack of feedback mechanisms, and complaining again that the "promised detailed discussion of the assumptions remains unpublished," Maddox half-heartedly praised a paper by Covey, Schneider, and Thompson that appeared in the same issue of *Nature*. The NCAR scientists' climate model allowed for movement of clouds in the lower troposphere, even though it was rudimentary to the point that it kept the smoke that caused the circulation stationary after its injection. Maddox, who again focused on dust in the atmosphere, seemingly could not absorb the significance of smoke, but he was gratified that this new work "soften[ed] the results described by Sagan et al. in the expected direction."[35]

Criticism in one of the world's leading scientific periodicals could not go unanswered, although it took more than half a year for TTAPS's protest to appear. They twitted Maddox for failing to note the importance of soot and for misreading much in their paper and in the article by Covey and his colleagues. While agreeing that the climatic effects might be less than they predicted, they also argued that they could be worse. Omitted in their original calculations were such possibilities as a later explosion propelling smoke into the stratosphere, where it would reside longer, and a forest, dried of moisture by a bomb's light, burning more readily. They also had ignored the world total of nearly 35,000 tactical nuclear weapons. In short, they defended their quantitative analysis and pointed out that the American and Soviet governments had both taken the NW prediction seriously enough to commission major investigations.[36]

Maddox nonetheless had his defenders. Sherwood Idso, of the Institute for Biospheric Research in Tempe, Arizona, ridiculed TTAPS for saying in their reply that their climate model was only "partly calibrated." What good is that, he asked? And how could it be calibrated against the dust raised by an asteroid, an event we do not know actually occurred? And why invoke comparisons with volcanic eruptions (whose sulfuric acid aerosols have optical properties different from nuclear dust and soot) and Martian dust storms (on a planet where there is no liquid water)?[37]

Nature and *Science* are weeklies whose rapid publication schedules are attractive to scientists. Their editors must savor their roles as arbiters for many scientific fields, but it is rare for one to depart far from the function of gate-keeper to the pages of his journal to become an opinionated actor in the drama, as Maddox did with NW.

Unlike the others discussed in this section, P. Goldsmith was far more than a "hand waver." He dealt with data and computer simulations, adding to knowledge rather than just commenting on the work of others. Yet, like his fellow critics, he had a consistently negative approach or "posture." This may be a personal scientific style, wherein some push the boundaries of new possibilities while their equally competent colleagues seek to minimize the consequences. It could be due to personality, training, workplace tradition, political attitude, or a combination of such factors. In 1973, when the effect of supersonic aircraft exhaust on stratospheric ozone was hotly debated, Goldsmith led a team from the British Meteorological Office in Bracknell, Berkshire, that reported the Concorde would alter ozone levels far less than done by previous nuclear testing, which itself, they found, had no clear effect on these levels (another controversial matter).[38]

By early 1986, Goldsmith was at the European Space Agency in Paris. In work submitted the previous year, co-authored by colleagues at Bracknell, he again found reason to be a nay-sayer. Early studies of NW, while numerous and varied, had not used models able to incorporate the initial patchiness of the smoke. Taking advantage of a model developed by the Meteorological Office to help forecast the weather, which employed a latitude and longitude grid of 15 kilometers (far finer than that found on GCMs), it appeared to them that radiative cooling would induce sufficient turmoil in the smoke plume to build clouds. Rainfall then would wash out much of the smoke from the atmosphere, minimizing its diffusion to continental-scale overcast, thus likely precluding NW effects.[39]

Liberal Critics

In the section above, critics of NW, consciously or unconsciously, were seen shielding their politically conservative positions with scientific analyses of the phenomenon. Here, politically liberal critics are shown to have used similar scientific rhetoric. In neither case is there any doubt of each scientist's intellectual honesty. In the latter, however, there must have been some tension between strong feelings that the case for NW had not been made and recognition that it might yet be a powerful engine for arms control. Indeed, the major critics of NW who can be called politically liberal were all prominent spokesmen for arms reduction.

George Rathjens, whose outspoken contempt for Sagan's use of *Parade* to reveal NW to the public has already been mentioned, had earlier dealings with the astrophysicist. These too concerned style: while planning a TV series on nuclear war, Sagan wanted to introduce catchy media effects that Rathjens rejected as unscientific. The April 1983 conference in Cambridge was another bone of contention, for Rathjens considered it not to be a peer review session, while Sagan claimed it as such. They also disagreed on disseminating the work. "Sagan and company, particularly Sagan and Turco," Rathjens remarked, "were disposed . . . to present . . . results in an alarmist and not appropriately qualified way for scientific discussion. They did it in ways that would command headlines . . . and I found that offensive." Indeed, Rathjens recalled, "Turco and I, and Sagan and I, really had at each other."[40]

Before the publication of Sagan's policy piece in *Foreign Affairs*, Rathjens privately reviewed a draft for the author. NW simply was not terribly significant in his mind. He could "not get much concerned about the possibility of extinction or near extinction," after the "over-whelming catastrophe" of civilization's destruction. While the NW phenomenon, if real, was interesting scientifically, it had little significance for policy. Thus, he did not comment on the newly revealed suicidal nature of nuclear war or on the increased vulnerability of non-combatant nations. The uncertainties were so large, Rathjens felt, that worst-case sce-narios had little meaning, and neither opposition to certain weapons programs nor support of certain arms-control initiatives made much sense.[41]

Rathjens, in addition, had specific criticisms. While TTAPS used the word "robust" almost like a mantra to describe its modeling, he saw it as quite the opposite. You could get any answer you wanted, he felt. Such quantities as the amount of fuel available, the altitude reached by smoke, the uniformity of soot distribution (a feature of the primitive model), and targeting scenarios were just guesses, he claimed, and poor ones at that. Nor was "con-firmation" by other scientists meaningful, for they used similar assumptions.[42] The way in which TTAPS's program inserted soot instantaneously particularly bothered him, for it was obvious that real-world winds would require time to achieve such homogeneity, time in which aerosols would likely be removed. Other corrections also would reduce climatic con-sequences significantly.[43]

At a public discussion about NW held on the Berkeley campus of the University of California on 3 October 1984, Rathjens objected to TTAPS's doubling the quantity of smoke in its 100-MT scenario, when compared with smoke production in the baseline case. The Berkeley physicist-turned-ecologist John Harte replied that that had been done because the targets were only cities, which do have higher fuel loadings. In this Harte missed the point that the doubling was of baseline *city-center* smoke. Turco explained elsewhere that in this scenario they had roughly doubled both the average burden of combustible material and the smoke emission factor for city-center fires to less conservative but still realistic values.[44] TTAPS had been candid about this in their *Science* paper, calling attention to the different values. No doubt they wished to enhance the NW effect for their minimalistic 100-MT case. But to critics it appeared as manipulative and special pleading. Rathjens also doubted that all asphalt, fuels, and plastics would burn, and these were major sources of soot. Thus, he felt that the numbers were squishy.[45]

Rathjens further charged that the Ehrlich et al. companion to Turco et al. was "a lot more irresponsible than the TTAPS paper." Because they used a 10,000-MT severe case, not the 5,000-MT baseline of TTAPS, Rathjens noted, Ehrlich et al. "wouldn't even buy off on the TTAPS central case as the basis for their analysis. . . . They picked a different scenario."[46] Perhaps this criticism was only made orally, for no one seems to have felt the need to answer it. Indeed, in their paper, Ehrlich and his collaborators had explicitly defended their choice of the larger figure: "We believe . . . that decision-makers should be fully apprised of the potential consequences of the scenarios most likely to trigger long-term effects."[47]

Returning to the TTAPS work, Rathjens felt that its publicity was "overblown" and that there was an "extraordinary callousness of it all". While he admitted that the authors probably could not have done better with the computer models available to them, he felt that they should have held back publication until they had better data. "You know that the results you have are wrong because you make simplifying assumptions that drive the conclusion in one direction." These should not have been portrayed as the best values, he argued.[48]

What we see here are different understandings of the scientific process: Rathjens desired a highly precise standard, while TTAPS followed a more common practice. Many scientists publish early data on a discovery, fully expecting that they will later be refined. TTAPS, it should be noted, never claimed that their results would resist modification. The inclination to publish may be a subtle thing, based on the author's trust in the data and results. If they are believed to be shaky, it would be deceitful to publish them, but there is no evidence that TTAPS doubted their work.

On certain points, Rathjens was measured in his criticism of TTAPS's paper. While he felt that it should never have been published, he allowed that it was a reasonable first cut at a scientific problem. "People would have had minor caveats, and that sort of thing," but the paper raised interesting issues. Rathjens remained bothered, though, about "a reference to a paper that was supposed to be the backup analytical paper for the *Science* magazine . . . no such paper existed."[49] Other critics of NW also cited this omission, since a footnote in *Science* indicated that it was "in preparation," yet it never appeared. Turco privately explained later that "reference 15 exists as an available and widely distributed draft report," meaning the Blue Book.[50] Either TTAPS were unable to find a journal for it or they felt that subsequent work by others superseded it.

Besides specific scientific criticisms, Rathjens's hostility appears based on an understanding that the logic of NW required steps toward smaller and more accurate warheads, earth penetrators, and missile defense—all involving a ratcheting up of the arms race. This was a pity, because both he and Sagan advocated smaller numbers of weapons. However, new policies, whether they increased or decreased the arsenal, had costs associated with them. For the case of NW, besides changes in weaponry, there might be civil defense expenses, such as stockpiling of food, a difficult task for the United States but an impossible burden for developing nations. Such actions, Rathjens insisted, should not be taken on the basis of such an uncertain theory. That policy changes did not ensue, however, is more likely a consequence of the Reagan administration's disinterest in NW. Rathjens, finally, was irate that the more popular articles and talks of Sagan and others discussed NW effects in terms of "would" and "will" happen, instead of "might" or "could" occur.[51]

Another liberal critic was the Princeton University physicist Frank von Hippel, an authority on science policy and on nuclear arms control. Like Rathjens, he had left his scientific career to pursue his interests on the border of science and politics. Long active in the Federation of American Scientists, a think tank and lobby with a liberal persuasion, he chaired the organization from 1979 to 1984, and again from 2000 to 2003. In 1993–94, von Hippel served the Clinton administration as assistant director for national security in the White House Office of Science and Technology Policy. Another of the MacArthur "genius" fellows who parade through these chapters, von Hippel also received the American Physical Society's 1977 Forum Award, with Joel Primack, for their book, *Advice and Dissent: Scientists in the Political Arena*, and the 1989 FAS Public Service Award.

More sad about than hostile to the concept of NW, von Hippel declined to criticize Sagan overmuch. Each generation, he felt, had to be reminded of the terror of nuclear war. But the initial NW emphasis on extinction was "strange." It had never made that much of a difference to von Hippel whether half or the whole human race was killed, for neither was acceptable. Nor did he think much of the revelation that NW could be suicidal to the nation that initiated the war, for he believed that the inability of either superpower to launch a successful first strike already made nuclear war suicidal. And yet, if the publicity had some impact in India and countries in the Southern Hemisphere, mustering pressure for arms control, it might be regarded as a good thing politically. So even if Sagan's public utterances irritated him, and even though he felt that the recent activities of Physicians for Social Responsibility had already "inoculated" the public against the arms race, von Hippel was grateful for the renewed attention to the threat of nuclear weapons.[52]

Indeed, in the decade or two that von Hippel had spent publicizing the effects of nuclear war, he never ceased to be amazed by the amount of self-deception in which government people engaged. They sanitized the situations, he felt. Words such as "counterforce" and "fratricide" spoke to action of weapons on weapons, not on people. He feared that policy makers would get so out of touch with the human consequences of nuclear weapons that inhibitions against their use would be lowered.[53]

Yet von Hippel, like many others, was uncomfortable with the technical uncertainties in the TTAPS report and in subsequent research. He was equally dubious of the way in which Sagan turned popularization of NW into a one-man show. Were Sagan to "make himself into our leader and then lead us all into catastrophe" (if NW were discredited), scientists might be marginalized in their other battles for arms control. Scornfully, von Hippel noted that it was acceptable for Edward Teller (who was associated with the national labs, the DoE, and the DoD) or for the government itself to lose its credibility every day by overstating cases. They were going to be there the next day, they were in charge, and you had to deal with them. Outsider scientists, however, must be concerned about being defined as insignificant. They could lose their credibility only once, for others would not let anyone forget it. Von Hippel's attitude, apparently widespread, helps to explain why the scientific community and its organizations did not jump on the NW bandwagon. A better approach was to critique the research, so as to force more solid work. Consequently, von Hippel and

Rathjens became the "loyal opposition," disbelieving the reality of NW but never wavering in their support for arms control.[54]

Von Hippel's successor as chairman of the FAS (1984–1986) was the Berkeley environmental physicist John Holdren, another MacArthur Foundation fellowship recipient. Also well known for his expertise in nuclear weapons and in arms control, Holdren was naturally interested in NW. But he too felt that the phenomenon's reality was unproven, and did not encourage the FAS to take a policy position with respect to it. Besides, most arms-control groups had other concerns that were more pressing. Opposition to Reagan's Strategic Defense Initiative and support for the Intermediate Nuclear Forces Treaty were paramount. Holdren argued that the immediate effects of nuclear war were so horrible that, if they were not enough to make people avoid that danger, the addition of NW would not change anything. Nor did NW alter the strategic balance. A first strike by either superpower was not feasible, because enough retaliatory force would remain to destroy the attacker—with or without a climatic catastrophe. The goal, Holdren believed, was to prevent nuclear war, not to find an illusory threshold below which such combat could occur.[55]

Rathjens, von Hippel, and Holdren were highly respected arms-control advocates of long standing. In contrast, Sagan had not been especially prominent in this field before NW. He had signed some petitions, had devoted part of an episode of his *Cosmos* TV series to the dangers of nuclear war, had quit the Scientific Advisory Board of the Air Force in protest of the Vietnam War, and was on the boards of the Council for a Livable World Education Fund and the FAS.[56] Sagan was a relative Johnny-come-lately to anti-nuclear-weapons activism.

Though Stephen Schneider was not a critic of NW, his activities should be mentioned. Angry with Sagan for springing the concept of thresholds on his colleagues at the Halloween 1983 meeting (where the participants had earlier sorted out their contributions, to avoid public conflict), he was unhappy too with the way that Sagan and Ehrlich minimized the uncertainties when presenting NW to the public. He agreed with others that scientific credibility was endangered. Any errors that were subsequently publicized might poison the well of public confidence in the nation's scientists. Even more, he specifically feared that the credibility of NW would be eroded. Thus, he consciously carved out a role for himself. To his skeptical colleagues, he vocally criticized the weak parts of the TTAPS paper, emphasizing uncertainties and showing that he was not being led by his political views. Then he discussed his own results, which, while more moderate than TTAPS's conclusions, were bad enough, and thereby helped to convince other scientists that the problem was real.[57]

Brian Martin, a perceptive observer in the Department of Science and Technology Studies at the University of Wollongong in Australia, noted that this debate was similar to other controversies involving the "impacts of technological development of the environment." "In nearly every case," he wrote, "individual assumptions about the fragility or resilience of ecosystems have remained the same." Martin pointed to Paul Ehrlich and population growth, and to Carl Sagan to a lesser extent. On the other side, he saw John Maddox, who had long been a critic of environmental Chicken Littles; Edward Teller, whose fame was built on his enthusiasm for nuclear weapons and whose concept of deterrence required a willingness to use them, who thus had an incentive to downplay possible NW effects; S. Fred Singer, who denied claims that SSTs would deplete stratospheric ozone; and P. Goldsmith, who defended the Concorde against environmentalists. "That there is continuity in the perspective that an individual has on the world should be neither surprising nor especially worrying," Martin concluded. "It does not mean that what a scientist has to say is necessarily wrong. But it does indicate that scientists come to scientific problems with various preconceptions, preferred methods of analysis and background concerns which can shape the way they define the problem, select evidence, build models, treat uncertainties and present results."[58] Likewise, the great complexity of NW permitted a wide range of choices of both technical parameters and war-fighting scenarios, a circumstance that gave more of a free rein to the participants' predilections than might have been the case in some other field.

More Reaction to the TTAPS Work

In the year following the appearance of TTAPS's paper, *Science* published two news stories, one editorial, and seven letters to the editor on NW, certainly not a spirited response. More to the point, not one of them was a direct rejoinder to the TTAPS article itself. These surfaced elsewhere. S. Fred Singer, with perhaps unaccustomed evenhandedness, noted that "the TTAPS paper has virtues and faults." He admitted that it was the most extensive climatic study of nuclear war, incorporating a significant range of phenomena and models. But all this made it "easiest to criticize." Singer would have preferred that the limits of uncertainty be indicated at the outset, for he recognized that, in the normal scientific course of events, questions would be posed, new data would be provided, and TTAPS's predictions would be modified or supplanted.[59]

In mid 1984, Edward Teller contributed a long and detailed commentary to *Nature*, arguing that the feared after-effects of nuclear war had been found, upon study, to be not as serious as first predicted. Radioactive fallout, ozone depletion, and the effects of dust—dangers discussed in past years—could be tolerated, especially in the non-belligerent nations. This was the context into which Teller placed the recent TTAPS work, saying that the "preliminary and uncertain nature of their findings deserves clarification." To Teller, TTAPS's conclusions were "inconclusive," although "Sagan calls them scientifically robust." Teller correctly pointed out that the meteorological phenomena involving smoke were more complex and less understood than the other processes, and that computer modeling was not yet adequate for the full task.[60]

In particular, Teller focused on the two weeks it would take for smoke to be uniformly distributed in the upper atmosphere. He wondered if this dispersal would occur. Water vapor has an average residence time in the atmosphere of a little more than one week, meaning that rainfall continually washes dust from the skies. The weight of water vapor and droplets in the northern mid latitudes, moreover, is 10,000 times the 225 million tonnes of smoke in TTAPS's baseline case. Unless the smoke quickly rose higher than the mass of water and remained there, it seemed logical that most would be washed out. Summing up the "uncertainties and omissions in the theory on which nuclear winter is based," Teller concluded that "the concept of a severe climatic change must be considered dubious rather than robust." "Nonetheless," he added, "the *possibility* of nuclear winter has not been excluded." Teller ended eloquently with the statement already presented in the preface of this book: "Highly speculative theories of worldwide destruction—even the end of life on Earth—used as a call for a particular kind of political action serve neither the good reputation of science nor dispassionate political thought."[61]

The TTAPS and Ehrlich-group papers, published in *Science* at the end of 1983, elicited some thoughtful commentary. In the *Los Angeles Times*, the science writer George Alexander emphasized how surprised the scientists involved—particularly Birks and Turco—were by their own discoveries. By quantifying the fire products, they recognized that "as much as 400 million tons of thick, greasy smoke would be pumped into the lower atmosphere." Dust, which scatters but does not absorb sunlight, would reach the stratosphere, while the lower-lying soot, weight for weight 10 times as efficient in blocking incoming solar radiation by absorbing it, would shut down normal and necessary photochemical reactions in the atmosphere. Storms generated at the land-sea interface would be unusually violent, and "there would be weather [patterns] like no one has ever seen before." Survivors would breathe a smog of carbon monoxide, hydrogen sulfide, hydrogen chloride, methane, ammonia, nitrogen oxides, and hydrocarbons. Whether surface temperatures fell by 40–60°F (as calculated by TTAPS) or 20–30°F (as Michael MacCracken obtained by averaging land and ocean cooling), MacCracken concurred that they were in "qualitative agreement." Alexander saw the disagreements more as reflections of the intricacies of computer models than as contentions about the phenomena involved.[62]

Indeed, MacCracken and his Livermore colleague George Bing, while most unhappy with Sagan's and Ehrlich's overly simplified and overly alarmist popularizations of NW, credited TTAPS with a fine piece of work. MacCracken admitted that there was "no smoking gun sitting here . . . the fatal flaw that pulls the whole theory apart." Bing commented: "For a problem as multifaceted, it is one of the more impressive syntheses that you'll ever see. In terms of looking at all the elements, picking a central value, recognizing there's great uncertainty. It's all there. . . . There are places where they've put a little body English in. . . . And it's survived quite nicely . . . if you like baseline points of departure."[63]

Just as Carl Sagan had sought to reach a wider audience with his policy paper in *Foreign Affairs*, Paul Ehrlich painted a multifaceted and astonishing portrait of Earth after nuclear war in the magazine *Natural History*. In his conjectured scenario, it was the little, previously ignored things that caught one's eye: those insect pollinators that survived would be disoriented by the ultraviolet light, which is visible to them, and be less effective in their role, and "the once endangered bald eagle" would outlast and even dine on "the species that had endangered them."[64]

In August 1984, the TTAPS group published a popular article on "The climatic effects of nuclear war" in *Scientific American*, for a long time a venue for discussions of the arms race. They emphasized that NW was a *combination* of conditions, not just "prolonged darkness [and] abnormally low temperatures" but also "violent windstorms, toxic smog and persistent radioactive fallout." They also allowed themselves to range beyond scientific issues, noting such social catastrophes as "the widespread breakdown of transportation systems, power grids, agricultural production, food processing, medical care, sanitation, civil services and central government." They even raised the possibility of human extinction (soon to be abandoned as unlikely). Essentially, however, the *Scientific American* article was little more than a popularization of TTAPS's December 1983 report in *Science*, and as such it was the first attempt by TTAPS themselves to reach a large, lay audience. They went beyond their own original paper only in noting a more recent (and larger) estimate of smoke lofted and in discussing the first assortment of two- and three-dimensional atmospheric circulation models, whose results modified but did not overturn their own 1-D conclusions.[65]

The *Scientific American* article elicited a letter to the editor on a point that must have bothered many people whose concept of climate was rudimentary. Just as few laymen in developed nations knew much about the atom before 1945 but quickly became familiar with fission, plutonium, and uranium-235 after the bombings of Hiroshima and Nagasaki, concepts of ozone depletion, the greenhouse effect, and other consequences of climate change became popular only in the 1980s. After condemning *Scientific American* for printing Sagan's politicized views and citing a *Wall Street Journal* piece by S. Fred Singer as confirmation of their speculative nature, the writer dismissed the value of weather prediction in general:

To this day atmospheric scientists and weather experts, using all the worldwide weather data available with the most modern theories and algorithms in the most powerful computers, cannot reliably and accurately predict the weather.

With barely concealed condescension, TTAPS replied that weather, a downpour for example, is indeed not yet predictable with great accuracy. But it differs from climate, such as recognition that it is cold in winter, about which there is much better understanding and quantitative predictability. They emphasized that their findings could be tested by objective means and were "independent of political predispositions." TTAPS also denied that NW was a "scare tactic" or a "political issue." Rather, they called it a fact that politicians must keep in mind when discussing nuclear arsenals and war. It was possible that they overestimated the severity of NW, but it was more likely that they underestimated it, for example, by omitting considerations of the world's tens of thousands of tactical nuclear weapons. TTAPS also rejected Singer's belief that a warming—a greenhouse effect—was possible, referring dismissively to deficiencies in his understanding that had already been cited in the *Wall Street Journal*.[66] Stung by this criticism, Singer wrote his own letter to the editor of *Scientific American*, complaining that it was Sagan, hardly an unbiased observer, who had provided the *WSJ* critique of him.[67]

The Cold and the Dark, a book consisting of a transcript of the Halloween conference proceedings plus reprints of TTAPS's and the Ehrlich team's papers in *Science*, was published in 1984, was soon translated into German, Swedish, Dutch, French, Portuguese, Spanish, and Japanese, and was widely reviewed. An expectedly hostile review appeared in *Survival*, the journal of the International Institute for Strategic Studies. Authored by George Rathjens and his graduate student Ronald Siegel, the review took as its "text" another review that had appeared in the *San Francisco Chronicle*. " 'Conceivably, *The Cold and the Dark: the World after Nuclear War*, might be the most important book ever written,' one whose contents 'may have more influence on human history than the Odyssey, the Bible, the Koran, or the collected works of William Shakespeare,' " Rathjens and Siegel quoted. To the contrary, they admonished, "the book represents a triumph of merchandising and showmanship." Conceding that the TTAPS authors "deserved great credit" for their "pioneering work," and that the NW research was "only a crude first approximation," Rathjens and Siegel nonetheless criticized various values assumed. "When all these concerns are combined, it appears that the temperature decrease may not exceed a few degrees. This would not add very much to the terrible destructiveness of an all-out nuclear war."[68] They also repeated their criticism of the Ehrlich team's paper on biological consequences on the ground that it used a 10,000-MT scenario (twice as many megatons as the TTAPS baseline case) and other assumptions that made its conclusions harsher. "When one adds it all up," Rathjens and Siegel observed, this is "an example of 'worst case' analysis run wild, inadequately qualified by discussions of uncertainties." Without criticizing all use of such analysis, they faulted Sagan's *Foreign Affairs* policy piece for ignoring the costs of risk avoidance, such as civil defense and new military weapons, both defensive and offensive.

The participants in this debate were separated by the fault line of their philosophical or methodological positions on evidence. TTAPS, the Ehrlich group, and other supporters of NW were initially concerned merely to show that severe climatic effects were possible under conceivable circumstances. They had no reservations about using worst-case scenarios and selecting physical data as long as they were in the range of possible to probable. Worst-case analyses, as mentioned before, had become so enshrined in many think tank and government agency planning activities that this stance could be regarded as unexceptional. Their opponents, on the other hand, prided themselves on living in the "real world," a world in which some events were far more likely to occur and some technical values more likely to be correct, than others. They criticized NW for a range of possibilities that was so broad as to encompass almost everything. For them, greater certainty was required. If everything is possible, they asked, have we really learned something of value? Should we even try to respond to extreme predictions? In a world of limited resources, they naturally concluded, we should focus on conditions deemed most likely. No action should be taken with so much uncertainty remaining.

Another controversy surrounded the appropriateness of both input data and their treatment. The nuclear war-fighting scenarios that established the quantities of smoke and dust were contested, the physical and chemical processes that then occurred were challenged, and the validity of computer simulations of the atmospheric response was argued. Simulations, in particular, were worrisome, because their use was a relatively new way of doing science. Except for the rare case when a measured value was available, inputs were based on comparable examples of known phenomena, such as volcanic eruptions, Martian dust storms, forest and city fires, and nuclear explosions (which were of limited value, since existing data were from individual events only). How closely did they approach NW phenomena? But this is what science is about: "pushing the edge of the envelope" to seek answers to questions about nature. It made sense to invoke the most reasonable and testable analogues.

NOAA Coordinates the Government's Investigations

Through 1983 and well into 1984, most of the cash supporting the investigation of NW came from "discretionary" funds: money in the budgets of various agencies that could be used, with little bureaucratic bother, for unplanned investigations. The Department of Energy (through the Livermore and Los Alamos laboratories), the Department of Defense (through the Defense Nuclear Agency), the National Aeronautics and Space Administration (through the Ames Research Center), and the National Science Foundation (through the National Center for Atmospheric Research) were the agencies most involved. When the private Natural Resources Defense Council revealed, from documents obtained via the Freedom of Information Act, that the government's response to NW remained overwhelmingly ad hoc, the activity in Congress sent a message to the White House that it was time for an organized approach.[1]

The gestation of an organized response actually began earlier, in February 1984, when the administrator of the National Oceanic and Atmospheric Administration, John Byrne, and the director of NOAA's National Climate Project Office, Alan Hecht, received orders from George Keyworth to fashion a plan. Byrne headed the interagency committee; Hecht was point man for the work. A twenty-member committee, drawn from government agencies, national laboratories, and universities, composed a list of research priorities, which was then submitted to a broad panel of referees. The process, which included a large fraction of those who had published on NW, reached conceptual completion in early May 1984.[2] Public announcement of the program later that month[3] moved Sagan to contact Keyworth, the president's science advisor (and, surely unknown to Sagan, an official for whose job Sagan had been recommended[4]). The NW work, Sagan felt, should not be limited to physical and chemical investigations, but should *simultaneously* examine biological and ecological consequences and doctrine and policy implications. Should the NW phenomenon be "severe and prolonged," the biological and ecological studies could be somewhat rough, since it was already clear that most systems would die under such stress. But if NW was relatively mild, detailed investigations would be needed. The new knowledge generated would be valuable in itself, but would additionally serve to silence voices that were critical of the national program on the basis that we already knew that the consequences of nuclear war were terrible and public funds should not be wasted gathering further details of the horror.[5]

Keyworth replied genially, noting that "decisionmakers have necessarily become inured, and therefore tend to move very cautiously, on recommendations based upon doomsday predictions, regardless of how well initially documented." To make policy, they require consensus among well-informed technical experts, time to ponder the issues, and some reasonable "alternatives from which to choose." It would be "drastically premature," Keyworth argued, to preface the climatological research, to be led by NOAA in fiscal year 1985, with doctrine and policy discussions; that would look like prejudging the outcome. But a biological-and-ecological investigation had value beyond its connection to NW, and might be done independently of what Keyworth expected would be a "very controversial climatological study."[6]

Unwilling to drop the matter, Sagan replied that policy analysis should not be postponed. It could be parameterized, just as for the scientific inquiries: "Let the uncertainties vary over their plausible range, and see what policy implications emerge for the various parameter choices." The Department of Defense traditionally did this, and no pre-judgment was implied. Sagan felt that the matter was urgent, in that the risk of NW must be minimized as soon as possible.[7] Keyworth, however, remained adamant that basic science was needed first, to reduce the uncertainties. The recently published report (in December 1984) on NW by the National Academy of Sciences underscored the need to know far more accurately the basic climate mechanisms.[8]

Planning within a presidential administration is customarily lubricated by interagency committees on which the various interested departments, agencies, councils, administrations, and offices are represented. This genius of democratic government may be slow and inefficient, and it provides many opportunities for opponents to sabotage an initiative, but under the best conditions it allows for a wide range of inputs. The announcement in May 1984 really concerned only the plan's research program. Who was to do what, and who would pay for specific investigations, remained to be decided.

The Nuclear Winter Policy Planning meeting in the New Executive Office Building on 30 October 1984 seems to have been rather ordinary; indeed, it revealed how little had been accomplished since May. Looked at from another perspective, however, it was exactly a year from the date when NW had received its first public airing, at the 1983 Halloween conference. This was reasonably good speed for the federal bureaucracy. Representatives of the National Security Council, the Office of Management and Budget, the Office of Science and Technology Policy, and the National Oceanic and Atmospheric Administration still debated the program's cost, which agencies would pay for it, and when it would begin. They expected to decide within a month. Alan Hecht would take the leading role in briefing the NSC, the OSTP, and the Department of State on the USSR's NW activities, would develop management options for guiding the research effort, and would brief the "policy Mafia" (apparently in the NSC) on this effort.[9]

Much was accomplished before the meeting scheduled for 30 November 1984—a meeting designed to parade the research plan before Keyworth. Based on an annual budget of $7.5 million for fiscal year 1985, of which $4 million was an increase beyond existing allocations, funds would be apportioned as follows:

Department of Defense	25%
Department of Energy	20%
National Oceanic and Atmospheric Administration	10%
National Aeronautics and Space Administration	8%
National Science Foundation	20%
National Bureau of Standards	12%
National Forest Service	5%

Fire research, including the number and location of fires, how much smoke was generated and where it went, and the smoke's optical properties, would receive $4 million. Computer modeling, of both mesoscale (that is, 10–100 km) and global-scale phenomena, was budgeted at $2.95 million. In view of the criticism levied later about the government's lack of interest in the biological consequences, it is interesting to see that $150,000 was designated for initial assessment of the problem and preparation of a research plan. Similarly, toxicology and chemistry were scheduled for $400,000, in recognition that these subjects too could present serious problems. About 25 percent of the total would support research in universities, while most of the work would be conducted in national laboratories.[10] Since Congress a month before had approved a Department of Defense budget that included an 11 percent increase in funds for research and development (giving the DoD authority over two-thirds of federal R&D appropriations), research on the NW phenomenon should be well supported.[11] These plans, as with other research efforts by government agencies, appeared to be serious attempts to gather information. When science veered off into the political realm, however, manipulation was to be expected.

To coordinate the research program, comprising both the new efforts and the ongoing activities in the Department of Defense and in the Department of Energy, the OSTP was asked to charter a Joint Program Management Office, to be headed by Alan Hecht. Other options, including setting up a research center, placing NW investigations in a civilian agency, and placing them in the OSTP or in a joint DoD-DoE office, were rejected because of a likely perception of bias, potential awkwardness in dealing with the scientific community, reluctance to place an agency on the "hot seat," belief that the office was too close to the administration, and yet other management factors that were less political in tone.

Among Hecht's first chores were to review the forthcoming NAS report to assure that there were no "surprises" in the academy's press release and to compose a government statement on it. The DNA and the OSTP were simultaneously to prepare a question-and-answer sheet on NW for distribution to government agencies. That done, Hecht could return to the NW study plan, which was scheduled for official White House acceptance in mid January 1985. This was to be a media event, with plan handouts, press releases, and more question-and-answer sheets for various government offices, including US embassies. The last task on Hecht's short-term horizon was to coordinate testimony with the DoD for their anticipated appearance at a congressional hearing on NW in March.[12]

It must be emphasized, however, that from the end of November 1984 extending well into January 1985 almost all these plans remained unsettled. Toon, in disgust, said that the United States had a national "non-program."[13] Michael MacCracken observed that additional money from the DoD in 1984 essentially bought into work already under way.[14] But bureaucracies move slowly. The need to assure the credibility of the national research effort made the National Center for Atmospheric Research and its sponsor, the National Science Foundation, both of which had excellent relations with the academic scientific community, strong contenders for the management role. NSF, which virtually never conducted programs itself, was nonetheless willing to take charge if it had a free hand in staffing the effort and adequate funds were assured. NSF was further concerned that other agencies agreed with the management and plans, and that the results would be unclassified. Hecht (director of the National Climate Project Office) was instrumental in drafting the program, but there was apparent reluctance to place real power in his hands. His office had even less experience than NSF to draw on in running operational programs, and the National Oceanic and Atmospheric Administration (the NCPO's parent agency) and the Department of Commerce (its grandparent) would be reluctant to be drawn into the arena of nuclear issues, where they had no expertise. Another unsettled point was the level of funding. The Office of Management and Budget was willing to go along with a $4 million program, while the drafting committee felt that $15 million was appropriate. High-level policy and political decisions were necessary.[15]

The program jelled at a meeting on 17 January 1985, attended by representatives of the DoD, the DoE, the NSC, the NSF, the DoC, the OMB, and the OSTP. This alphabet soup was turned into an interagency coordinating committee, chaired by the OSTP, which advised on the administration's scientific efforts. Real authority was left to the agencies paying for the research. The OSTP entered the meeting hoping to get a commitment of $2 million each from the DoD and the DoE, beyond what they already spent, plus $500,000 from the NSF. Its lowest expectation was for an augmentation of $1 million from each of the departments. No longer planning for fiscal year 1985, they achieved a *total* budget of $500,000 from NSF and $2.5 million each from the DoD and the DoE for fiscal year 1986. Since the two departments together already funded $3.5 million worth of research in fiscal year 1985, the augmentation seems to have been even less than the OSTP's bottom line. Also, $5.5 million was less than the $8 million originally desired for fiscal year 1985, so only $2 million more was to be spent for this much-hyped new initiative than was allocated in the past. Finally, the government's effort was renamed the Interagency Research Program, with no mention of nuclear winter in the title and with policy explicitly beyond its purview.[16] (Additional budgetary information was provided in the secretary of defense's 1985 report to Congress on NW: the DoD spent $400,000 in fiscal year 1983, $1.1 million in fiscal year 1984, $1.5 million in fiscal year 1985, and $2.5 million in fiscal year 1986.[17])

Alan Hecht's parting NW effort[18] was to chair the committee that drafted the NCPO's account to the OSTP describing the government's plan, titled "Interagency research report for assessing climatic effects of nuclear war." The committee included such NW heavyweights as John Birks, Michael MacCracken, Robert Malone, James Pollack, Starley Thompson, and Owen Brian Toon. Its report, released on 5 February 1985, less than 2 months after the NAS report appeared, was influenced by the NAS panel's conclusions. The NAS panel had indicated somewhat generally the types of information that were needed to reduce the uncertainties of NW. Hecht's interagency committee took this a step further by more precisely detailing the data required. Theoretical studies, laboratory and field experiments, and computer modeling improvements were suggested with enough specificity that interested scientists could design their work. Especially useful was an appendix (prepared by Michael MacCracken) that presented the ranges of uncertainties that surrounded the commonly used values in many calculations, with brief notes explaining what the variable depended on.[19] The focus of the NAS report was the status of knowledge about NW, while the interagency report provided marching directions. It is notable that in both documents the research agenda and discussion followed closely the pioneering work of the TTAPS team. Use of the word "uncertainties" was not infrequent, but the specific objections of critics were virtually unmentioned, most likely a measure of their evaluation by the scientific community.

To reduce uncertainties about "source inputs," new data were needed on the area and intensity of fires, their distribution, and the combustibles available. From these the quantity of particles lofted and their optical properties could better be determined. For example, a dense smoke cloud, especially one filled with soot from synthetics, might lead to rapid coagulation of the particles and more optical transparency. But this was not a certainty, and data had never been collected from urban and large forest fires. The height to which smoke and excavated debris were carried by heated air depended on the temperature, humidity, and winds of the ambient air, and on the degree of turbulence within the plume and the amount of unheated air it entrapped. Most ash would stay within the troposphere, but intense firestorms could carry as much as 20 percent into the stratosphere. The altitude of injection also depended on microphysical processes such as coagulation of particles and on interaction of the plume with moist clouds. Understanding of such contacts and the circulation over mesoscale distances (10–100 km) was inadequate. Scaling experiments were needed to determine if data from laboratory and small fires could be extrapolated to large urban and forest fires.[20]

Scientists could study the effects of planned burns under different environmental conditions, and satellites were proposed to identify "fires of opportunity," track their smoke
plumes, and test their optical properties. Slash-and-burn fires in the tropics and desert dust
storms were regarded as the closest analogues of NW. At a minimum, the authors of the
interagency research report believed that the government's plan should yield data on urban
and non-urban fuel loading, better estimates of smoke lofted, and an improved match of
physical and optical properties of smoke with types of fires. When plugged into interactive
computer models that better mimicked the real atmosphere, such data would yield climate
changes within narrower limits and a more precise range of policy options.[21]

The government thus had a solid research program planned, with marginally adequate—
certainly not opulent—funding. Hecht had served well to get the activity organized, but
his base, NOAA, would have been chosen as lead agency only if there was a cynical goal
to accomplish as little as possible. NOAA was a troubled body, incapable of providing
strong leadership. Its proposed new administrator was opposed by powerful groups in
Congress, the White House, and NOAA itself. Moreover, the agency mission was unclear
and its staff demoralized: interest in NOAA by its parent, the Department of Commerce,
was weak, and the Reagan administration tried repeatedly to slash its budget. Indeed, it
would be hard to find an agency better situated to be ignored.[22] On top of this, the NCPO
was a tiny office in NOAA, with only nine positions and a relatively meager budget of $1.1
million, half of which went to support research in universities. Choosing its director, Hecht,
to administer the nation's NW research program would have affected the NCPO's ongoing
labors.[23]

The Interagency Research Program seemed sound, but its funding and execution were
not. R. Jeffrey Smith, a reporter for *Science*, correctly noted that the proposed budget of $5.5
million for one year only was far less than the plan, initially floated, of $50 million of *new
money* over 5 years. When asked to explain this disparity, OSTP officials declined to comment.
Others concluded that the several agencies involved were reluctant to provide the new funds
from their existing budgets and that the OSTP lacked the clout or incentive to force the
issue. Hovering in the background, the Office of Management and Budget was "in the midst
of a budget-cutting binge."[24] Thus, the multi-year plan that was considered necessary was
not funded, and desired laboratory experiments and field observations of fires would be
severely constrained.

In September 1985, in what could hardly have been more than political posturing,
however sincere, Representative Timothy Wirth (D-Colorado), of the House Science and
Technology Committee, asked Keyworth why so few new projects had been started. Little
was being done in independent and university laboratories, Wirth claimed, and not much
was of an experimental or field data-gathering nature. The $5.5 million level of support
particularly galled Wirth, especially when compared to the president's Strategic Defense
Initiative, budgeted at $2.7 billion: "[T]here is no justification for the gross inequity in
research funding for theories of arguably comparable importance." (Wirth could have stated

the amazing disparity even more dramatically by comparing the five-year NW plan of $50 million with the 1983 Fletcher Report, which called for SDI research to the tune of $18–27 billion over a similar period, or with the multi-billion-dollar budgets for the Superconducting Super Collider and the Space Station.[25])

Indeed, it appears that the government's new initiative for NW research petered out. Some very good work was accomplished with government funding, but it would likely have been done even without this initiative. Little new research of significant magnitude was apparent. But no opportunity for cosmetic touch-ups was lost. For example, Keyworth asked the administrator of the Environmental Protection Agency if he had any ongoing programs that could be listed under the government's NW activities, so Congress and the public could see "the Administration's continued commitment to this important research effort."[26]

The DoD's 1985 Report

Despite the government's plans to fund new research, its continued funding of investigations in the national laboratories, and its continued commitment to the ongoing NAS study (all of which implied that the government was keeping an open mind about the validity of NW predictions), administration spokesmen emphasized the uncertainty of the phenomenon in most public comments through 1984. Then, at a press conference on 11 February 1985, President Reagan spoke of NW in terms that seemed to signify acceptance of its likelihood: "And they called it the year [1816] in which there was no summer. Now if one volcano can do that, what are we talking about with the whole nuclear exchange, the nuclear winter that scientists have been talking about?"[27] By the following month, when the DoD report required by Congress was issued, the administration had all but embraced NW, yet duplicitously strove to use it for its own purposes. With amazing cheek, Secretary of Defense Caspar Weinberger asserted that the new geophysical conditions nuclear war might bring changed no current policies but instead supported them. The Department of Defense co-opted NW.

In a sense, the Department of Defense threw up its hands and claimed nothing could or should be done because the data were so unclear. The department's external scientific advisors, the Defense Science Board, had organized a Task Force on Atmospheric Obscuration, chaired by Harold Lewis (a physicist) and including Stephen Schneider. This body decided that predictions of NW were valid, but that the phenomenon was exaggerated by the 1-D model used. Although the task force issued no final report, Lewis informally told Weinberger that research should be supported and coordinated, but that it was too early to think about changing weapons and strategies, "since we were all doing our damnedest to avoid nuclear war anyway."[28] Weinberger accepted these recommendations, and the DoD's study (like the NAS's report issued 3 months earlier) emphasized the huge uncertainties in estimates of climatic responses to nuclear explosions:

At this time, for a postulated nuclear attack and for a specific point on the earth, we cannot predict quantitatively the materials that may be injected into the atmosphere, or how long they will react there. Consequently, for any major nuclear war, some decrease in temperature may occur over at least the northern mid-latitudes. But what this change will be, how long it will last, what its spatial distribution will be, and, of much more importance, whether it will lead to effects of equal or more significance than the horrific destruction associated with the short-term effects of a nuclear war, and the other long-term effects such as radioactivity, currently is beyond our ability to predict, even in gross terms.[29]

The DoD chose as its foil the TTAPS paper, published more than a year earlier, instead of work done more recently. Thus, the report could disparage the "large number of poorly-known variables" used to calculate the results of explosions, and insinuate that a truism (recognized and treated quantitatively by TTAPS) was somehow a disability: "In actuality, the same yield weapon could produce vastly different amounts of smoke over different target areas and under different meteorological conditions."[30] The DoD did, however, cite new work when it furthered its own position or served to discredit the opposition. A yet unpublished report from the Pacific-Sierra Research Corporation (a defense contractor) found that nuclear attacks on 3,500 *non-urban* targets would produce only 1/30 as much smoke as TTAPS had estimated if the war occurred in July, and about 1/300 as much if it occurred in January.[31] (The main thrust of the TTAPS paper was, of course, the number of *city* fires.) Also noted were early results from three-dimensional computer models which suggested that a "substantial" amount of smoke would be scavenged from the lower atmosphere and would not be available to obscure sunlight, although the remaining smoke would be lofted to higher altitudes as a result of solar heating.[32]

Those who had hoped that NW might incline the DoD to rethink its nuclear war policies and the size and configuration of its arsenal were disappointed. Given the many uncertainties surrounding NW, the DoD claimed to see no reason to alter the nation's strategic policies. Even if NW were found to be a valid prediction, the report maintained that the Reagan administration's approach was appropriate: missile defense would reduce the number of American cities ignited, while escalation control and the US targeting practice of avoiding urban areas would minimize the number of Soviet cities in flames.[33]

Additionally, those who argued that the USSR would simply increase the number of its warheads in response to missile defenses in the US had it wrong, Weinberger maintained, for, since the ABM Treaty of 1972, the Soviet arsenal had multiplied fourfold anyway (much of this was in response to the installation of multiple warheads on many US missiles, but the report ignored this point).[34] As for the US arsenal, Weinberger deemed that modernization plans under way (fewer, smaller, and more accurate weapons, enhanced C[3]I capabilities, and, in the future, possibly earth-penetrating weapons and non-nuclear warheads) were appropriate responses to the NW phenomenon.[35] The "basic imperative of US national security policy," Weinberger wrote, was "that nuclear war must be prevented. For over three decades, we have achieved this objective through deterrence and in the past 20 years we have sought to support it through arms control. Now, through the Strategic Defense Initiative, we are seeking a third path to reduce the threat of nuclear devastation."[36]

The *New York Times* reported the DoD's concession in a story headlined "Pentagon agrees nuclear warfare could block sun, freezing Earth," and the British scientific weekly *Nature* summarized the Reagan administration's response to NW as "so what?"[37]

Since an informal interagency group had been created to discuss policy issues relating to NW, the report presumably had the imprimatur of more than the Department of Defense.[38] The government's (not just the DoD's) dismissive attitude, then, may not have surprised those who scoffed at politics, yet it is perplexing that the DoD itself showed so little interest in its own ability to conduct military operations. In congressional testimony almost a year earlier, Weinberger's own assistant for atomic energy, Richard Wagner, had said that NW's effect on forces and equipment would be examined.[39] But in the DoD report, commentary was either inadequate or nonexistent concerning the effect of low temperatures, low visibility, and atmospheric contaminants on aircraft engines and other equipment, the functioning of satellites and other components of C^3I, troop movements, logistics, the health and morale of personnel, and other aspects of modern warfare. The report, moreover, failed to respond to the law, which specified that environmental, biological, and policy issues be addressed, in addition to atmospheric and climatic effects. The ostriches in the Pentagon had carried the day.

After reading a draft of the DoD report in February, Ronald Reagan's own science advisor and head of the Office of Science and Technology Policy was dismayed. George Keyworth, who had worked at Los Alamos and had a keen appreciation for nuclear issues, typed on a memo he attached to the report's cover "It's mostly mush."[40] Once the report was issued, criticism of it became stronger.

The report's primary congressional sponsors, Senator William Cohen and Representative Timothy Wirth, expressed disappointment that the DoD virtually ignored some issues, such as civil defense, saying in the document only that it was "impractical" to spend funds in attempts to defend the population against NW until more was known about the climatic impact. Especially irritating was the use of NW to promote the Strategic Defense Initiative. "All the Pentagon has done is use this as a soapbox for defending 'Star Wars,'" Wirth commented. "Clearly, the obvious response is to reduce the number of nuclear weapons, not increase them." Sagan was of like mind, noting that if merely "1 percent of the Soviet missiles came through the [SDI] net, you'd have a nuclear winter."[41]

An aid to Senator William Proxmire called the study "shallow" and bemoaned its cynicism. "This is a serious business," he said, "and to have the Pentagon just come back and manipulate it to justify their nuclear weapons modernization, the 'Star Wars' program, and their arms control position is just not serious." Jacob Scherr of the NRDC agreed, calling the report "totally deficient—17 pages of promotion."[42] Scherr was irked that the report focused on the atmospheric and climatic effects and cavalierly dismissed the environmental and biological consequences of nuclear war. Paraphrasing the NAS report, Secretary of

Defense Weinberger contented himself with the observation that "if the climatic effect is severe, the impact on the surviving population and on the biosphere could be correspondingly severe."[43] This generality substituted for concrete analyses of the effects on people, the infrastructure of society, and the environment.

In the hope of forcing the DoD to comply fully with the congressional requirements for the study's scope, Scherr asked the Washington legal firm of Wilmer, Cutler, and Pickering to consider if the secretary of defense had met his obligations. These attorneys concluded that Weinberger had indeed disregarded the lawmakers' intent, not only by omitting some scientific topics and a considered analysis of policy implications but also because the abbreviated report could not adequately inform the public and guide congressional action.[44] Scherr's suit went nowhere, however, largely because he lacked standing in the matter. It was up to Congress to rectify the report's inadequacies.[45]

Senator Dan Quayle (R-Indiana) was among the few to praise the DoD's report. It offered, he said in the Senate on 14 March 1985, "yet another reason to avoid targeting cities and to reduce our arsenal's indiscriminate destructiveness." The previous reasons—fear of retaliation in kind, desire to spare civilians, belief that such threats were not credible anyway—had only partially sufficed to steer targeting from cities. Now, despite the uncertainties about NW's severity that the report emphasized, it made good sense, Quayle said, to avoid aiming at cities and even to rethink the targeting of military and industrial facilities located near cities. If these must be destroyed, he argued, precision conventional or low-yield nuclear devices should be employed. Quayle thus endorsed the DoD's desire to increase the accuracy of its weapons. This reconfiguration of the arsenal, he felt, was a step also toward reducing the likelihood of war, since smaller weapons would be mobile and more secure.[46] Similarly, the *Wall Street Journal* endorsed the report, but used it more as a vehicle to criticize scientists for using their technical credentials to debate political questions.[47]

By the end of March 1985, Representative Tim Wirth had more reason to express his frustration with the DoD report. Although the secretary of defense had acknowledged the NW concept to be valid, Wirth felt that he was hiding behind the alleged rudimentary nature of the initial computer programs used by TTAPS, claiming the predictions were too uncertain to be the basis for planning. Recent work using sophisticated three-dimensional computer models, however, had affirmed the threat to the climate. Wirth called attention to a symposium on NW (sponsored by the National Academy of Sciences) that had just ended. Stephen Schneider of the National Center for Atmospheric Research had described there the quick freezes from even a limited nuclear exchange that could destroy agriculture in and near the zone of combat, and freezes from a larger exchange that could interrupt food production in non-combatant regions such as Japan and India. Robert Malone of the Los Alamos National Laboratory, using a computer model that diced the atmosphere into more boxes, thus providing finer resolution, showed that a large percentage of the smoke would not be scavenged by rain. Heated by the Sun, it would instead rise to the stratosphere, where it would remain for months, blocking sunlight from Earth's surface. These conclusions, Wirth argued, pointed to the need for analysis of the impact of NW on civil defense, conventional deterrence, extended deterrence, strategic nuclear targeting, effects of NW on non-combatants, and other policies and programs, none of which the DoD seemed inclined to address.[48]

Senator Christopher Dodd (D-Connecticut) took as a hopeful sign the DoD's recognition that NW was potentially a credible threat (the report, after all, was titled "The potential effects of nuclear war on the climate"), and urged the superpowers to agree to reduce their arsenals.[49] Jacob Scherr of the Natural Resources Defense Council, less willing to see the cup as half full, filed a Freedom of Information Act request to see the documents he felt must have been created when deciding to exclude biological and environmental effects, but Weinberger's office produced nothing.[50]

In June 1985, with bipartisan support, the House of Representatives added to the 1986 defense authorization bill the requirement that the DoD prepare an annual report on knowledge about NW and its policy implications.[51] In the same month, Senators William Proxmire and Mark Hatfield introduced an amendment to the 1986 State Department Authorization Act asking the president to propose joint NW research with the Soviet Union. They called for analysis of the implications for national security, as well as of the climatic, atmospheric, environmental, and biological consequences.[52]

Hearing in the House of Representatives, 14 March 1985

A hearing intended to provide a major forum for discussion of the just-released DoD report was held by the Subcommittee on Natural Resources, Agriculture Research, and Environment of the House Committee on Science and Technology, jointly with the Subcommittee on Energy and the Environment of the House Committee on Interior and Insular Affairs. The tone was set by Morris Udall (D-Arizona), chairman of the latter subcommittee, when he opened the morning session. Noting that the NW phenomenon had surprised the analysts, which suggested how little we knew, Udall professed skepticism that the Strategic Defense Initiative, then the most prominent weapon in the DoD's R&D register, would work as proclaimed. It was "strategic snake oil," he said, to believe that the path to peace was "through a never-ending succession of weapons systems disguised as bargaining chips."[53]

James Scheuer (D-New York), chairman of the other subcommittee, attacked Caspar Weinberger's 17-page report on NW as terribly inadequate and called attention to the meager $2.5 million requested for NW research out of a Department of Defense R&D budget of more than $39 billion.[54] Manuel Lujan of New Mexico, the ranking Republican on Udall's subcommittee, posed several statements and questions worthy of discussion: The USSR was not taking NW as seriously as the United States was. Were the warfare scenarios and climatic consequences credible? What sort of research would best help along the arms-control negotiations then under way in Geneva? Was SDI the best way to defend the United States? The

Democrats (then the majority party in the House) got in the last of the opening statements. Representative Wirth pointed out that the DoD had agreed to the validity of NW yet had failed to follow through with a discussion of the implications. This hearing, Wirth hoped, would remedy that deficiency.[55] Partisan posturing aside, all the remarks suggested a well-informed and serious congressional panel.

Carl Sagan was the first friendly witness before this initially friendly hearing. When NW was first revealed, he said, it was denounced as "liberal propaganda or distortions invented by proponents of a nuclear freeze." Since then, however, the National Academy of Sciences, the Royal Society of Canada, the Pontifical Academy of Sciences, President Reagan, and now the Department of Defense had acknowledged the real possibility of danger. But what was the DoD's response, he asked? Essentially nothing. Scornfully, Sagan lectured: "Nuclear war is bad for Government, bad for labor, bad for business, bad for people on a scale that remains unreflected, as far as I can see, in this administration's policies." The blindness to consequences ranged from purely military matters, such as the ability of air-breathing engines to function in soot and dust, to long-range human survival.

Sagan noted that not only the DoD report but also the administration's new multi-year program of research ignored such questions as the ability of agriculture to continue in North America. He deplored the large cut that the $50 million plan for 5 years had already suffered. The administration might be charged with being disingenuous, Sagan suggested, since it was not clear "how much of that is really new money and how much of that is simply relabeling money that has been already programmed to study areas of this sort." The program, moreover, might be misconstrued as overly in-house and therefore biased, since the National Science Foundation's share of the funding, the only source for scientists unconnected to the government, was small.[56]

The testimony sizzled when Representative John McCain (R-Arizona) awarded Sagan a grade of F for disparaging Reagan's and his administration's sincerity about arms control. As the essayist Anne Taylor Fleming perceptively noted 15 years later, McCain had a "temperament with a temper in it, a need not just to win but to vanquish."[57]

The hearing then degenerated into ad hominem attacks as the Reagan administration's "pit bull" on defense issues, Richard Perle, called Sagan's critique a "shallow, demagogic, rambling policy pronouncement," not scientific analysis, and in his view worthy of a failing academic grade. Not that the assistant secretary of defense for international security policy was unprovoked. Sagan had just denounced the current doctrine of deterrence and first-strike capability, and said that the DoD report on NW would have received a grade of D in his graduate seminar. "Peculiarly," Sagan remarked, "nuclear winter turns out to justify all the policies that the administration has just embarked on. Remarkable coincidence. There are no agonizing reappraisals. There are no changes in doctrine or policy. From their point of view, the discovery of a doomsday machine hiding in the arsenals of the United States and the Soviet Union hardly matters at all. It doesn't change anything."

Sagan's sarcasm continued as he pointedly protested the DoD's use of nuclear winter as a rationale for promoting the Strategic Defense Initiative, which he ridiculed as a "Maginot Line in the sky," easily circumvented by the enemy.[58]

In keeping with the thrust of Weinberger's report, Perle did not deny the possibility of NW, but effectively and articulately maintained that the administration's defense policies, including its Strategic Modernization Program, its arms-reduction efforts, the elimination of intermediate-range nuclear forces, and the Strategic Defense Initiative, were the best deterrent to that catastrophe. The Department of Defense, Perle said, had long recognized that nuclear war would be a tragedy, and the discovery that it might be still worse did not change its view that war must be avoided. Greater knowledge of the biological and agricultural consequences of protracted low temperatures, for example, would not alter the DoD's efforts to prevent war. Perle thus denied any need for a reevaluation of defense policies. He also saw no value in a joint US-USSR research project, arguing that Soviet scientists contaminated their conclusions with politics. However, he noted that it was beneficial to all to share American data with the Soviets.[59]

The other witnesses at this hearing provided testimony that was tamer, or at least more mannerly. Jeremy Stone, director of the Federation of American Scientists (an organization that grew out of the Manhattan Project and maintained its concern with nuclear weapons throughout the following decades), proclaimed his support of arms reduction and opposition to both the Strategic Defense Initiative and Reagan's arms-modernization program. But new treaties and new policies would take time to implement and were not the salient response to NW. For Stone, it would be wise immediately to review the Single Integrated Operational Plan (SIOP) of strategic targets, removing urban areas. Of course, the plan already contained city-avoiding options, but NW suggested the need for closer scrutiny. Moreover, the Soviets had exactly the same motivation to avoid the boomerang effect by deleting their US urban targets.[60]

George Rathjens, admitting to being an advocate of nuclear disarmament and at the same time a critic of NW for being over-hyped and unproven, testified that NW (even if valid) would not lead to smaller arsenals and less carnage. "Any war," he said, "that could conceivably produce serious nuclear winter effects would be utterly catastrophic in any case," and the likely changes in warhead yield and detonation altitude would mean that more nuclear weapons, not fewer, would be built. NW, thus, would not lead to arms reduction, nor would missile defense reduce the number of explosions on US soil.[61]

Another who saw nuclear war as already sufficiently horrible was David Williamson, a senior fellow in space and technology policy at Georgetown University's Center for Strategic and International Studies. Containing aggression, not trying "to tailor policies that look toward less sooty targets," was his recipe, for the latter path would be a diversion from reality. By this Williamson meant that Americans were too fond of "facts and precision," which in this case he felt were a substitute for the major problem of deterrence. And deterrence, he explained, involved perceptions of the enemy's (and one's own) behavior. Should NW be widely accepted as valid, it might increase self-deterrence. But should it be theoretically proved nonexistent, this might perversely make nuclear war seem more acceptable. Exploring the consequences of the former attitude, Williamson predicted greater emphasis on defense over offense in future force structures, incorporation of fewer nuclear systems in new weaponry, and an overall reduction in existing nuclear weapons.[62]

As the last witness of the day, Stephen Schneider of the National Center for Atmospheric Research, called himself the "junkman," gathering and presenting the bits and pieces of information left over by the others. He also brought a refreshing breeze of common sense to the hearing, insisting that NW be viewed probabilistically. "Uncertainty is not the same thing as no effect," he said, adding that "there is a higher probability of lower consequences and a lower probability of higher consequences." Thus, even with wars much smaller than the baselines of TTAPS or the NAS committee, patches of smoke could cause freezing temperatures locally. This would not be a trivial event, Schneider noted, comparing it to the devastation visited periodically on the Florida citrus industry by transient freezes. He also argued for biological and social research even before the physical investigations, not only as good policy but also because they might identify additional points for physical research. In all this, he suggested, it was better to involve Soviet scientists, not to ignore them as Perle recommended, for they must understand the phenomenon well enough to advise their leaders. When asked to evaluate the DoD report, Williamson, Rathjens, and Schneider rated the sections on the state of physical science highly, and that on policy very low.[63]

This hearing in the House of Representatives on 14 March 1985, almost a year and a half after the public first heard of NW at the Halloween meeting, was notable in a few ways. It was scheduled to discuss the report Congress required from the Department of Defense, a mark of the legislature's oversight responsibility on a topic considered important. Scientific findings and policy consequences showed considerable sophistication and progress in this period. But one would be hard pressed to recognize these advances in the political presentations before Congress. The DoD's report and the testimony remained tied overwhelmingly to the TTAPS paper and a few other early responses. Apparently, it was more profitable politically to criticize data from the debut of NW.

Hearings in the Senate, 2–3 October 1985

Ostensibly another follow-up to the March 1985 DoD report, the last congressional hearing on NW followed closely on the heels of the last major report written on NW, by the Scientific Committee on Problems of the Environment (SCOPE). The nineteen-member Senate Committee on Armed Services, chaired by Barry Goldwater (R-Arizona), included Strom Thurmond (R-South Carolina), John Warner (R-Virginia), William Cohen (R-Maine), Dan Quayle (R-Indiana), Pete Wilson (R-California), Phil Gramm (R-Texas), Sam Nunn (D-Georgia), John Stennis (D-Mississippi), Gary Hart (D-Colorado), Carl Levin (D-Michigan),

Edward Kennedy (D-Massachusetts), and John Glenn (D-Ohio). Most of these senators attended the hearings, escorted by assistants.

The witness list was short, with three out of four on the first day clearly in the "it's too early to do much" camp. For the final session, the two verbal antagonists of the House hearings held half a year earlier, Carl Sagan and Richard Perle, offered to provide heat if not light. Goldwater opened the hearings by stating that he was "a firm believer that there could be such a thing as a nuclear winter," a conviction based on recent discussions with the physicist Luis Alvarez about the asteroid that had killed the dinosaurs. While not a "bomb-shell," since both the president and secretary of defense had already leaned in this direction, this public positioning was still noteworthy.[64]

C. M. Gillespie, an assistant to the Defense Nuclear Agency's deputy director for testing, opened by explaining that the DNA had "no position on the science of nuclear winter, much less on the policy implications that flow from those science considerations." The DNA's role was, rather, to "manage scientific research into the climatological effects." (The DNA's determination that NW be an unclassified subject and its policy of not politically influencing the scientific work was affirmed by Michael MacCracken and George Bing of Livermore.[65]) In his summary of the current state of that research, Gillespie noted that recent work had made transport of smoke into the Southern Hemisphere "very credible," and that the SCOPE report was the "first very careful, thorough approach" to ecological and agricultural problems. Additionally, toxic chemicals from burning plastics and other hydrocarbons were acknowledged as a real threat, along with the increased incidence of ultraviolet light. Discounted were the danger of a new ice age, human extinction, and any significant difference in the amount of global radioactive fallout expected.

Among the significant uncertainties, Gillespie listed the warfare scenarios. He regarded the baseline cases used by TTAPS, the NAS, and SCOPE as upper limits of megatonnage, since each side would initially aim at the other's weapons and would destroy many of them. Smoke production from urban areas was still a large question mark (the only important advance in fire knowledge being a study of wildland targets, in which the mass of particulates was much smaller). Other uncertainties were the spreading and removal of smoke, with research showing the likelihood of patchiness, and the ability of smoke to absorb solar radiation, which depended on the chemical and physical properties of the particulates. Gillespie estimated the sum of the uncertainties to be larger than a factor of 10, meaning that the total effect could be more than 10 times larger or 10 times smaller than that of the baseline case. Larger was meaningless, since the surface darkness, the lowered temperature, and the duration were already nearly as great as they could be. In the other direction, a factor of 4 or 5 smaller would change NW conditions significantly.[66]

As a spokesman for SCOPE, in addition to reporting on his own work, Mark Harwell, of Cornell University's Center for Environmental Research, provided an interesting counter-point to Gillespie's testimony. Many of the uncertainties the DNA's representative just cited were not important, he said, because the "biological systems, especially agricultural production and distribution systems, [are] so sensitive to the sorts of perturbations we are talking about." Indeed, Harwell continued, "the indirect effects of nuclear war could be more consequential than the direct effects." By this he meant that the 1–4 billion fatalities due to NW would far exceed the several hundred million casualties expected from nuclear war directly. Mass starvation would be more lethal than blast, heat, and radiation.

Natural ecological systems, Harwell added, even if perfectly healthy, could support less than 1 percent of the current world's population. Humans depended overwhelmingly on farming, and agriculture was highly susceptible to decreases in temperature, light, and precipitation and to a diminished growing season. A major war in spring or summer could easily cause the loss of a growing season in the Northern Hemisphere, and chronic environmental and social conditions would reduce growth in following years. Harwell observed that exceedingly few countries had even a year's supply of food, so the calendar worked against humanity.[67]

The other two speakers on the first day of the hearings were Leon Sloss (a policy advisor on nuclear targeting who headed his own consulting company and who seemed singularly uninformed about NW effects) and Leon Gouré (director of the Center for Soviet Studies at Science Applications International Corporation). Gouré typically overstated his case, but he was fundamentally correct that Soviet scientists lacked enough computer power to make significant advances, and that their research could not be considered an independent verification of NW work in the West, despite their public statements that it was. He cautioned that Soviet scientists were really propagandists, that NW had changed the views on policy of no one in the Soviet military, and that there was no public debate of the significance of NW in the USSR.[68] Carl Sagan, in contrast, considered the Soviet people reasonably well exposed to the idea of NW. It had, he said, "been repeatedly discussed in Soviet newspapers, including *Pravda*, on all-Union prime time television programs, and in technical papers and books." Sagan had himself spoken about it on Soviet television, and the TTAPS article from the August 1984 issue of *Scientific American* had been published in *V. Mire Nauki* (October 1984), a comparably popular magazine.[69]

In the discussion that followed, Senator Levin extracted from Gillespie the admission that no one from the DoD had pressed for greater funding than the $5.5 million total allotted to NW research for fiscal year 1986. This was 1/500 of the budget for SDI, and Levin wondered if NW was not a greater deterrent to a first strike. Levin also learned from Harwell that Soviet scientists had indeed made independent contributions. Though Soviet atmospheric modelers were forced to use Western values for smoke production (they lacked the data and knowledge to calculate them themselves), they nevertheless modified their antique programs to move the smoke around and to explore ocean-atmosphere interactions. Even more, biologists conducted a very large program of original research, going in directions not covered by the SCOPE report.[70]

Senator Glenn expressed his concern in a monologue. "We are truly in a new era," he said. "It is the first time in the history of mankind that war may affect every single person on Earth, not just combat participants."[71]

In the rapid alternation between science and policy, the TTAPS paper was warmly praised. For a first look at a very complex problem, Harwell and Gillespie agreed, its authors had produced a remarkably solid analysis and were open about its limitations. More sophisticated research and reviews, including the NAS and SCOPE reports, had subsequently modified many factors, but had reinforced, not overturned, the plausibility of severe climatic effects.[72] After considerable battering by critics of the NW predictions over almost 2 years, it was somewhat novel to hear TTAPS lauded for their scientific strength, not condemned for their allegedly hidden political agenda.

In a written reply to questions he could not adequately answer during the hearings, Gillespie displayed familiarity with the biological issues and a recognition of important questions that should be answered. This seems to be the first modestly extensive commentary on ecological and agricultural problems—and societal issues also—by a government official. Even though official policy foreswore funding such investigations, the DNA continued to show its scientific professionalism.[73]

The final session failed to produce many sparks between Sagan and Perle, largely because they responded to questions and had little opportunity to provoke one another, but also because the discussion revolved around SDI more than around NW. Among the few point of interest were Sagan's continued use of the concept of a NW threshold (though properly fuzzy) and his assertion that France's nuclear *force de frappe*, if targeted on the USSR's cities, as Sagan believed it was, would probably suffice to cross that threshold, making NW more than a superpower problem. Sagan characteristically got off a memorable one-liner, calling NW "an extremely expensive and elaborate way to commit national suicide." Perle consistently argued that the Reagan administration's steps to enhance deterrence were the best way to avoid NW; Sagan just as determinedly insisted that SDI was worthless and that the solution was to greatly reduce the arsenals.[74]

The four congressional hearings on NW seemed to result in little. Aside from requiring the secretary of defense to prepare a few annual reports on the phenomenon, no legislation emerged, nor did the administration act on requests for joint research with Soviet scientists. Moreover, members of the various committees seemed often to be of two minds about NW: while expressing belief in its validity, they were unable to act on its logic, and they maintained their support of a nuclear war-fighting capability against the Soviet Union.[75] No one in the US Congress composed legislation that used the NW phenomenon as the argument for huge reductions in the nuclear arsenal.[76] The minimal newspaper coverage of the hearings increased only when there were verbal clashes between witnesses, and then the headlines focused on these fireworks and rarely on policy matters. At best, the hearings informed members of Congress, and some, such as Senator Alan Cranston of California, alerted their constituents,[77] but it seems that only a small percentage were intellectually engaged, Tim Wirth and William Cohen being the leading examples.

13 A Frenzy of Research

New Physical Research: Computer Modeling

Because some of the computer models used in NW research were derived from others, there was concern that many scientists were starting with the same assumptions and data, feeding them into similar programs, and inevitably coming to the same conclusions. How independent, then, was the work?

In general, the participants who examined the war scenarios, the physical and chemical effects, and the climatic consequences felt that their research was independent to a highly satisfactory degree, and this allowed them to be confident of its direction. The programmers of a general circulation model did not just plug in a mass of smoke and press the "on" button. They distributed the smoke at different elevations, with certain optical coefficients. Then they might try one-third the amount of smoke, and move it higher and lower. Such simulations were sensitivity tests of the program. Similarly, the modelers of fire plumes tried fires of various intensities, sizes, and locations. The variety of approaches and educated guesses was sufficiently great that the models were convincingly different to most people. When results from one-dimensional and three-dimensional models were compared, the differences were reasonable and the similarities striking. Indeed, 3-D general circulation models, which were capable of showing the oceans as huge heat sources, confirmed TTAPS's 1-D finding of freezing continental temperatures and the prediction that northern smoke would be blown into the Southern Hemisphere. While these models incorporated many "best guesses" for different numbers, such value judgments had the redeeming qualities of being educated guesses and of being "subject to scientific test and validation."[1]

Another issue besides the independence of models was their intrinsic value. Were they worth believing? In a paper published in *Science*, the historian of science Naomi Oreskes and two colleagues pointed out that confirmation of numerical models is inherently partial. This necessarily follows the understanding that Earth and its atmosphere are too complex; their "systems are never closed." Phenomena, thus, cannot be described fully. But that does not mean models are worthless. Indeed, they can suggest the consequences of differing inputs with enough confidence (a value judgment) for policy decisions.[2]

The early atmospheric models were, as expected, somewhat primitive. They suffered from the defect that certain quantities of smoke or dust were all-of-a-sudden distributed and the absorption of solar radiation then observed, while the particulates unrealistically could not be scavenged or move about, except for a programmed reduction over time. The models also ignored scattering of sunlight and the particles' effect on the thermal infrared wavelengths. Additionally, modelers made different choices: TTAPS, for example, injected smoke into different layers of the atmosphere (1–7 km for urban fires, 1–5 km for wildfires, and 0–2 km for long-term fires), with denser smoke in the upper level, an option that led to stronger climatic effects. The NAS panel, in contrast, used a constant smoke density up to 9 km. More fundamentally, both proponents and opponents of NW recognized that no model, however sophisticated, could ever match the complexity and fine structure of the real atmosphere.

Further, NW conditions would so perturb the normal atmosphere that another degree of uncertainty entered the picture. There was no way that a model could be validated by matching its predictions against data gathered from observations. "Clearly," George Carrier observed, "it is eminently sensible to use these models to estimate the order of magnitude of the temperature change caused by smoke, but the results can only be regarded as suggestive. They are definitely not predictions."[3] Nonetheless, because the models increasingly provided calculations that conformed to actual measurements where possible (seasonal variations and temperature decreases due to forest fires are good examples), they more and more earned the confidence of those who used them.

Between the 1-D radiative-convective climate models used by TTAPS and Michael MacCracken and the desired interactive 3-D models that everyone recognized as necessary was MacCracken's 2-D atmospheric circulation model. It lacked longitudinal inputs, but it resolved latitude into 10° increments and cut the vertical atmosphere up to 35 km into nine layers. MacCracken placed smoke in the atmosphere at four locations—likely target areas of the southwestern US, the Ohio River basin, the Rhine Valley, and Moscow—and allowed it to spread in a calculated pattern, to simulate thermal mixing. When this model's results were combined with those from a 1-D radiative-convective model, MacCracken found cooling over the northern hemisphere's land surfaces that averaged 10–15°C in just a few days. The 1-D model alone had temperatures plummet more than 30°C in about ten days, corresponding well to TTAPS's results.

MacCracken, more than most others, fretted over the "many assumptions, shortcomings and uncertainties" in such complex modeling. He recognized that "such a model must treat space scales from a few to thousands of kilometers and from hours to months, radiative, dispersive convective processes acting on and affected by the injected aerosol, and land and ocean surface interactions." There were, he noted, no "verified models formulated to deal with all of these processes and scales simultaneously." Still, that was no excuse to be idle; it was worthwhile to estimate if one could not fully assess.[4]

Another 2-D model, with 15 vertical layers up to 30 kilometers altitude and 5° resolution in latitude, was used by a group consisting of Robert Haberle, Thomas Ackerman, and Owen Brian Toon (of the Ames Research Center) and Jeffery Hollingsworth (of Oregon State University). Sponsored by the Defense Nuclear Agency, this research was one of a number of examples of NW investigations by Ames personnel, despite laboratory administrators' earlier misgivings about the subject. In an attempt to study the heating of a large smoke cloud by solar radiation, Haberle et al. showed both smoke being lofted into the stratosphere and smoke pouring into the Southern Hemisphere. The results were handicapped, however, by the model's inability to predict precipitation, which had to be prescribed.[5]

At the August 1983 seminar in Erice, where MacCracken described his 2-D work, Aleksandrov presented results from a primitive 3-D general circulation model. This GCM was based on the Mintz-Arakawa model, modified more than 10 years earlier at the Rand Corporation and more recently at Oregon State University. Aleksandrov accepted the *Ambio* scenario for the optical thickness of the atmosphere and included no chemical reactions and no ozone effects. This first attempt considered the atmosphere solely as a simple gas and examined its hydrodynamics. The soot, once inserted, could not move about, but it could change temperature and circulation patterns in the troposphere. Nonetheless, Aleksandrov's results were in reasonable agreement with those reported in TTAPS's Blue Book earlier in 1983.[6]

In subsequent work, Aleksandrov and his colleague Georgi L. Stenchikov, a senior researcher in the Soviet Academy's Computing Center, used a coarser model than comparable American models. This was much in the long tradition of the arms race, wherein the Soviets used brute force to launch giant rockets, while the more sophisticated scientists and engineers in the United States microminiaturized their hardware. The troposphere was cut into only two layers, and the geographical grid had a resolution of 12° in longitude and an unrefined 15° in latitude—something approaching the area of Mexico or of Norway and Sweden together, and unrealistically giving such vast regions uniform physical properties. Still, Aleksandrov and Stenchikov's model incorporated an approximation of the continents and recognized the thermal effects of the oceans, sea ice, and continental snow and ice. The model was designed to describe the "large-scale motion of the air mass, which occurs due to non-homogeneous liberation of energy in the troposphere"—largely incoming solar and outgoing infrared radiation, which is affected by the presence of clouds.[7] In a sense, Aleksandrov and Stenchikov, and all other NW modelers, abused their models by entering information for which these programs were not originally designed. This, indeed, was a point raised by NW critics, who objected to the immediate insertion of massive amounts of soot and dust, arguing that the models would respond erratically.[8] Yet within a few years this charge largely vanished as different climatologists reported reasonably congruent conclusions.

Thus, Aleksandrov and Stenchikov instantaneously filled the troposphere north of 12° latitude uniformly with soot and the stratosphere with dust. Their model incorporated no dynamic feedback, but used accepted formulas to track the growth and decay of various phenomena. The seasons were averaged. Calculations to model one year's atmospheric activity required some 40 hours on their BESM-6 computer. They found that solar radiation reaching Earth was attenuated by a factor of 400. Air above the continental surfaces cooled rapidly an average of more than 15°C. For 6 months, the troposphere as a whole heated and then slowly cooled. An important consequence of this was that, in the Northern Hemisphere, air temperature increased with altitude, whereas normally it decreased. This meant that hot air would not rise. In this unusually stable atmosphere, there would be little precipitation, and soot would stay aloft much longer. Temperatures changed far less in the Southern Hemisphere, but this imbalance induced growth of an inter-hemispheric circulation cell that transferred pollutants to the south. When the Soviet climatologists looked at specific geographical locations 40 days after the start, the results were stunning:

. . . the temperature in Alaska drops by 36°C, in central and [e]astern America by 34° and 40°C, in central Europe by 51°C, in the Kola Peninsula by 56°C, and in Kamchatka by 41°C. The most intensive drop in temperature at low latitudes, by 51°C, occurs on the Arabian Peninsula.

At 243 days, continental temperatures generally rose slowly, but above mountain ranges the rise was striking. Tibet, for example, experienced a rise of almost 20°C. Massive flooding was possible as snow fields and glaciers melted.[9]

Another paper reporting results from a three-dimensional GCM appeared in early March 1984. Authored by Curt Covey, Stephen Schneider, and Starley Thompson of the National Center for Atmospheric Research, it showed that model development had come a long way but still had further to go. Schneider, in his late thirties and the "old man" of the group, had received a Ph.D. in mechanical engineering from Columbia University in 1971 and had spent almost all of his early career at NCAR. His interests ranged from technical studies of climate changes due to human and natural causes to science policy and popularization. Covey was a 1982 UCLA Ph.D. in geophysics and space physics, next a postdoc at NCAR, then (from 1984 to 1987) an assistant professor in the Meteorology and Physical Oceanography Division of the University of Miami's Rosenstiel School of Marine and Atmospheric Science. Thompson, who only a few months earlier had received a Ph.D. in atmospheric sciences from the University of Washington, was already a veteran of about 7 years of theoretical climatology work. At the time he was a research scientist in Schneider's Advanced Study Program at NCAR, where he has remained.

The trio had been thinking about the climatic effects of nuclear weapons since May 1982, when Schneider had attended a conference on atmospheric chemistry in Berlin. As a referee of Paul Crutzen and John Birks's manuscript, Schneider gave Crutzen some last-minute suggestions for changes while the *Ambio* article was in the proof stage. Recognizing that climate modeling was not his field, Crutzen urged Schneider to continue the investigation.

The latter, now more a manager than a researcher, was agreeable, but wondered who he would get to do it. His boss advised that he was not saying Schneider shouldn't pursue this politically "dangerous" subject, but warned that he should be very careful—meaning accurate. Regular staff members were unavailable or uninterested, but postdocs were free to do whatever they wished. At the time, Covey was looking at paleoclimates and the atmosphere of Venus, and Thompson wanted some rest after completing his dissertation. Schneider employed his considerable skills of persuasion, and the three formed a team. They first tried a simple model built by a colleague, because it was handy. This gave them some experience, but since the model had no vertical resolution, it was as inappropriate for looking at smoke in the upper troposphere as it could be. With the atmosphere a single vertical box, they got warming. Meanwhile, the TTAPS group conducted its first run of the problem, got surface cooling, and was disturbed to hear that NCAR got warming.

Covey, Schneider, and Thompson wanted to run a general circulation model, but it belonged to others at NCAR who were leery of the political "baggage" attached to nuclear war scenarios. Covey was told that the climatic effects *must* be trivial, and that the president would then be able to say that scientists had shown that nuclear war was not so destructive. This mindset, that scientists should avoid political involvement, was widespread. Another mindset, that fires could not be very important, kept a number of competent scientists from quantifying the matter years earlier. Working with remarkable speed, Thompson constructed a radiative-convective model over a weekend. By the time of the April 1983 TTAPS review conference in Cambridge, they had supportive results that went further, by including seasonal and land and sea effects (the lack of which had been limitations of TTAPS's effort). Motivated by the meeting (and, no doubt, by the head of the NAS investigation, George Carrier), Schneider obtained a version of the NCAR general circulation model from a colleague. He cajoled help from some associates with special expertise (particularly Veerabhadran ("Ram") Ramanathan, well known for his work in radiative transfer), and eventually they removed many bugs from lines of code as they modified the GCM for their purposes. (An unintended benefit that mollified their NCAR colleagues was this cleanup of the GCM.)[10]

In their GCM, Covey, Schneider, and Thompson sliced the vertical atmosphere into nine layers, versus only two (of the troposphere only) in the work of Aleksandrov and Stenchikov. They resolved horizontal directions into 4.5° in latitude and 7.5° in longitude—treating as a single cell an area comparable to that of the states of New York and Pennsylvania combined—versus 12° latitude and 15° longitude in the Moscow model. This was by far the finest grid to date; the vertical cuts were essential to tracking significant atmospheric movements due to heated smoke. As in the Aleksandrov-Stenchikov model, Covey and his colleagues could observe changes in wind patterns but were not able to have these winds redistribute the smoke or remove it (theirs was a "stabilized smoke cloud"). Nor could the model track fully the consequences of energy transfers. They ignored some processes (such as infrared absorption and emission of aerosols) that would only marginally affect the results, and they chose not to treat dust. They well understood that their work was only a first-order approximation.

At the direct request of the NAS panel,[11] Covey et al. adopted the 6,500-megaton scenario used in the NAS study then in progress; they also rounded off the panel's value for the quantity of smoke generated, making it 200 teragrams. (1 teragram = 10^{12} grams = 10^{6} metric tons = 1 million tonnes.) Further research might show that injection and removal processes would lead to a mass of smoke different than 200 million tonnes, but this number was the best available then. Again paralleling the academy study, the NCAR team inserted this mass of smoke almost uniformly between 30° and 70° north latitude, and between 1 and 10 kilometers in altitude. This would be the condition at their model's time zero, reached about a week after the fires were ignited. Use of a standard absorption coefficient for smoke gave them an optical depth of 3.0, which meant that the model absorbed almost all solar radiation at upper-tropospheric levels and virtually no light reached Earth's surface.

Model simulations of 20 days were run for winter, spring, and summer conditions. As was expected, summer, when greater quantities of solar radiation are available to heat the aerosols, showed the largest effect: within 10 days, sub-freezing temperatures descended from the Arctic across much of the North American and Asian land masses. Soon, smoke streamers spilled across the equator. Strong surface winds developed, bringing warmer oceanic air to the western sides of the continents, a process that halved the average land cooling predicted earlier by the TTAPS group (from 30–40°C to 15–20°C). Smaller but discernible effects were seen for the other seasons. Since areas with sub-freezing temperatures were found after only two days, the authors concluded that in the real atmosphere, with the likelihood of comparably dense clouds of smoke in various locations shortly after ignition, there could be surface freezing under these "transient patches." The most critical need, they felt, was for better data on fuel inventories in cities and forests, and on the dynamics of burning. Nonetheless, they were confident that their conclusions ("strong land surface cooling, mid-atmospheric warming, and profound changes in circulation"), which confirmed and expanded the work of others, were robust. "Patchy, transient subfreezing outbreaks," ranked by Covey et al. only as plausible, was the novelty that caught many eyes. They had seen it thanks to their model's fine slices of the vertical atmosphere. It was missed by TTAPS, whose lower atmospheric layer was 2 kilometers thick (and which naturally lacked crucial wind activity since it was 1-D). Schneider interpreted patchiness to mean that even limited nuclear wars (seemingly endorsed by Secretary of Defense Weinberger) could have environmental effects.[12]

While to some it appeared that the NCAR group was casting cold water on extreme predictions by TTAPS, Turco and Toon were encouraged by the results from Boulder. Assuming that the GCM reasonably represented the real world, these results showed that their 1-D model also mimicked reality. Quick freezes, they felt, were valid. These were of little moment for the Northern Hemisphere, where great cooling would come a few days sooner or later. The tropics, however, would suffer inordinately from transient freezes.[13] Less certain, Tom

Ackerman noted that GCMs thus far ignored the diurnal cycle, using weakly unstable diurnal averages at the boundary layer between earth and atmosphere, instead of real-world stable conditions at night and unstable conditions during daylight. He wondered if quick freezes were an artifact of the model.[14]

Almost a year after the Halloween 1983 announcement of NW, Janet Raloff offered this observation in *Science News*: "Most scientists now concede that based on existing data, TTAPS appears to have flagged a valid threat to the global environment. But that qualification, 'based on existing data,' was a big one." The lack of hard numbers in many areas was worrisome. Besides experiments to obtain desired data, computer sensitivity tests could be conducted. Most climate models used a fixed or static Sun, and in a particular test a rise of 5°C in air temperature was observed. If, however, a more realistic moving Sun was programmed, the temperature change reversed in sign.[15] As Ackerman noted, improved GCMs as well as better data were needed.

Alan Robock, a meteorologist at the University of Maryland, introduced a new idea into the study of NW effects by looking at temperatures over a period of several years. His "seasonal energy balance climate model," like all other models, contained a normal number of simplifications, but had the advantage of explicitly looking at snow and ice feedbacks. These became significant after about a year, when the pall of smoke and dust had thinned. At mid and higher latitudes, the additional snow on land that resulted from lowered temperatures reflected more sunlight, causing temperatures to decline further. This albedo effect was most prominent in summer, when the insolation was greatest. Something similar occurred over sea ice, again in summer, but was masked by an even greater effect in winter. Initial NW cooling produced more sea ice, which made the thermal inertia of the ocean stronger. The ocean, now less responsive than usual, slowed restoration to pre-war temperatures. If TTAPS and the other modelers were correct about the many critical measures they used, and their models at least approximated reality, then the climatic impact of NW would last longer.[16]

Thus, when roughly the same initial conditions (basically, injection of about 200 million tonnes of black smoke into the Northern Hemisphere's troposphere) were employed, the different computer models gave rather similar results. Still not independently determined, however, were such matters as quantity of smoke, injection height, its optical properties, and scavenging processes. Moreover, none of these models was interactive—that is, able to determine the spread of the smoke cloud, its effect on the weather, and the consequential scavenging of the airborne debris. This last point should be emphasized. All these models incorporated *normal* conditions of precipitation. Yet, since rainout of aerosols was a major factor in determining if NW would occur, and precipitation patterns were widely expected to be altered in this assault on the atmosphere, it is clear that the computer programmers still had much work to accomplish in matching their models to the real world.

Nature's editor, John Maddox, had titled one of his own columns "Nuclear winter not yet established."[17] That column had been published in the issue dated 1 March 1984. In August of the same year, *Nature* published the critical analysis by Edward Teller described in chapter 11 above and (on the very next page) an article by S. Fred Singer titled "Is the 'nuclear winter' real?" Singer's target now was not the TTAPS paper but the more recent study by Covey, Schneider, and Thompson. Singer still questioned whether a long-lasting, major cooling of the continental interiors would occur. As far as he was concerned, by inserting a fairly uniform layer of smoke with an optical depth of 3.0 into their model, the NCAR team had "accept[ed] the physical model of Turco et al. and, not surprisingly, [got] a similar answer."

If, however, the smoke was not as transparent to infrared radiation from Earth as assumed (by increasing particle size through coagulation, for example), there could be a greenhouse effect. Indeed, if the smoke rose higher than the moisture in the atmosphere, the water-rich layer would trap and re-emit even more IR radiation back to the land. Further, he argued, atmospheric moisture would be increased substantially beyond its normal amount, since dry mass (hydrocarbons) that is burned is oxidized to form H_2O. Add to this the ground heat from smoldering combustion and Singer saw the likelihood of only a few degrees of cooling, rather than tens of degrees, and even the possibility of a slight increase in temperature. He also maintained that the relatively coarse scale of the NCAR model missed important mesoscale activity, such as thunderstorms and rain squalls, that would reduce the atmosphere's burden of particulates.[18]

The reply by Thompson, Schneider, and Covey emphasized that, rather than mimic TTAPS's numbers, they used the conservative value for lofted smoke that was adopted by the National Academy of Sciences committee investigating NW, and its equally conservative optical depth. Their results were, in fact, not the same as those of TTAPS, but that was understandable in view of the differences between their models. Of great significance, their 3-D model separated the temperatures of the surface and lower atmosphere, revealing just as much land cooling (40°C or more in July) as had TTAPS, but occurring more quickly—in a few days. This showed that adding detail, as they had done, would not necessarily remove the NW effect. Solar heating of high-altitude smoke, which would have a long lifetime, would dominate IR emissions from moisture at lower altitudes, making the latter of minor importance. As for Singer's other energy-balance arguments, in case after case, they and others had done calculations that did not support his views. The subject was beyond the stage where qualitative hand waving was useful; quantitative investigations were required. Among the things that would have to be investigated was the significance of mesoscale effects on washing smoke from the atmosphere, but that could not yet be calculated.[19]

Before the end of 1984, scientists at Livermore began to incorporate interactive phenomena into their model. Michael MacCracken and John Walton coupled a simple two-layer GCM that had been developed at Oregon State University with GRANTOUR (a 3-D model, built at Livermore, that handled trace materials and microphysics in the atmosphere). GRANTOUR—essentially an upgrade of MacCracken's 2-D model—simulated the movement of particles, including scavenging by rainfall. Selecting a July scenario, MacCracken and Walton allowed 150 million tonnes of smoke from city fires to "spread slowly by the winds rather than instantaneously dispersed as in previous calculations." Their scavenging treatment was uncertain, since there were no global data on particle removal to compare with it, nor were they content with the model's height distribution of rain clouds. Aerosol properties, moreover, were taken as unchanging, although coagulation and other processes were in fact likely to alter them. Despite these limitations, their experiment was a singular technical advance. They found minor cooling of land in regions where the presence of smoke was tardy, and significant cooling—more than 15°C after several weeks—under dense plumes of smoke. This compared well with the results of MacCracken's 2-D non-interactive model.[20]

About the same time, Aleksandrov and Stenchikov also revised their GCM to be interactive. Both the Moscow model and the Livermore model showed less patchiness and more uniformity in the distribution of smoke than anticipated, and a movement of smoke from higher latitudes toward the tropics, confirming earlier indications that smoke would flow to the south. For a major conflict, at day 99, the interactive or "coupled" model halved the cooling over the Northern Hemisphere shown by the fixed-smoke or "uncoupled" model, but dramatically increased the cooling at lower latitudes. Central America suffered a cooling of 60°C, northern South America 40°C, and Central Africa 50°C.[21]

Another team from Moscow teased new insights from their own model. Expanding on work reported at the 1983 Halloween meeting, G. S. Golitsyn and A. S. Ginsburg of the Institute of Atmospheric Physics found surface and atmospheric temperatures to vary little when the solar radiation optical depths were about 2 or larger, whereas these temperatures were most sensitive to changes in the OD when it was 1 or smaller. They noted also that the smoke-filled atmosphere over the oceans might be as much as 20°C warmer than air over the continents, thanks to the sea's large heat capacity continuing to pump thermal radiation into the overlying clouds. Reiterating the prediction made in Washington of an attenuated hydrological cycle, Golitsyn and Ginsburg explained that air over the oceans is normally cleaner than air over land, resulting in larger raindrops. The addition of NW aerosols, providing more nuclei for water vapor to condense upon, would lead to smaller raindrops everywhere these particulates were found, reducing the drops' scavenging ability.[22]

At the beginning of 1985, better results from interactive models appeared. Such third-generation models succeeded the one-dimensional representation used in the first exploration by TTAPS and the second generation's two- and three-dimensional models, which lacked the ability to move smoke around. About two years earlier, about the time that the NAS panel and the TTAPS meeting in Cambridge were being organized, scientists at the Los Alamos National Laboratory also began thinking about NW. Hans Bethe, one of the twentieth century's great physicists and a consultant to the Los Alamos Lab, remembered the modeling ability of Robert Malone, a former student, and urged him to investigate NW.

Funding was casual: Malone became a half-time administrator so money could be released to hire a programmer. Politics were equally relaxed: lab director Donald Kerr told him to ignore any political pressure and just do good work.[23]

Malone, Lawrence Auer, Gary Glatzmaier, and Michael Wood (all of the Los Alamos National Laboratory's Earth and Space Sciences Division) and Toon (of the Ames Research Center) presented their most newsworthy results at a March 1985 symposium on NW organized by the National Academy of Sciences. They had started with the NCAR Community Climate Model, which meant that they had diced the atmosphere in the same way that Covey, Schneider, and Thompson had. To this they had added aerosol transport in three dimensions, an advance beyond models that inserted aerosols in various places and moved them in prescribed ways. Malone et al. allowed 170 million metric tons of smoke (close to the NAS report's lowered baseline case of 180 million tonnes) to move horizontally by winds and vertically as it was heated by sunlight and washed out by GCM-predicted rainfall. Through a feedback loop, the smoke could be affected by the very changes it induced in the atmosphere. The model's significant feature was that the rate of smoke removal was *not* prescribed.

TTAPS had assumed that carbon was hydrophobic—an assumption criticized by Freeman Dyson but defended by TTAPS. Malone's group assumed the aggregation of carbon and other aerosols, and that the clusters would be hydrophilic. This meant that they would be scavenged sooner. Indeed, much smoke in the model was washed out by rainfall: at day 40, 85–95 percent in winter, but only about 64 percent in summer, when solar heating caused the plumes to rise above most moisture. A large part of the remaining one-third of the smoke, buoyant from the sunlight, was lofted to the higher levels of the troposphere, where it resided for extended periods. Indeed, the tropopause re-formed beneath the region of heated smoke, down from an altitude of 9–13 kilometers to about half that height, thereby shrinking the zone in which precipitation could occur. Critics of NW could still argue that fuel loading of cities, particle size, small-scale and mesoscale atmospheric phenomena, and other inputs remained too uncertain, but Malone and his colleagues had undercut their contention that insufficient smoke to cause NW would remain aloft.

Whereas a wintertime war would lower temperatures only a few degrees (if the smoke did not last until spring), a summertime war would cause temperatures to fall 15–25°C within two weeks over the North American and Eurasian interiors, and about four weeks later temperatures would remain depressed by 5–15°C. This was not as low as normal winter temperatures for such regions, but in summer it would be catastrophic for plant and animal life.[24] Early notice of this research supporting the NW concept appeared simultaneously with the dismissive 1985 political report about its significance by Secretary of Defense Caspar Weinberger. The god of coincidences has a wicked sense of humor.

Support for the Malone team's position was published a few months later by William Cotton, a professor of atmospheric science at Colorado State University in Fort Collins. Since clouds normally form in buoyant plumes once they attain the height of a kilometer, Cotton incorporated cloud processes in his firestorm simulation. The model was actually for thunderstorms, and it was capable of accounting for the scavenging of aerosol particles by precipitation particles. If a city the size of Denver burned, Cotton calculated, the intensity of the urban firestorm would be about twice that of a natural cumulonimbus cloud. Violent updrafts would carry elemental carbon particles high into the troposphere, and even into the lower stratosphere, where inefficient scavenging processes would allow a long residence.[25]

Table 13.1 gives some details of various computer models used in NW research. (The models had different features and inputs, so an exact comparison of results would be misleading. To a first approximation, however, comparable results affirmed the nuclear winter concept.)

Further insights were offered by a number of other investigators as they altered inputs to test a model's sensitivity. The size of aerosols, the injection height of smoke and dust, optical depth, and other variables were examined.[26] Robert Cess and his colleagues sought to determine the amount of smoke that would cause the normal combination of surface cooling by tropospheric convection and surface heating by solar radiation to cease and surface cooling to begin. In other words, this was the point at which the surface and troposphere were decoupled. Their purpose was not to look at various war scenarios, but to "obtain a qualitative understanding as to how a GCM responds to a most unusual climate forcing mechanism." Among other factors, they found infrared radiation from the surface to play "a key role with respect to climatic change induced by atmospheric smoke."[27]

Two scientists at the National Center for Atmospheric Research performed other sensitivity tests. Assuming homogeneous spherical dust and smoke particles and a reasonable size distribution to simplify the calculations, Venkatachalam Ramaswamy and Jeffrey Kiehl

Table 13.1

		Latitude box	Longitude box	Vertical layers	Temperature decrease
TTAPS (urban)	1-D				30–40°C
MacCracken	1-D				>30°C
MacCracken	2-D	10°		9	10–15°C
Haberle et al.	2-D	5°		15	
Aleksandrov	3-D	15°	12°	2	>15°C
Covey et al.	3-D	4.5°	7.5°	9	15–20°C
MacCracken	3-D				>15°C
Malone et al.	3-D	4.5°	7.5°	9	15–25°C
NAS Report					10–25°C
SCOPE Report					20–40°C
Thompson and Schneider					12°C

learned that aerosol dimensions and location were critically important. Smoke particles larger than a micrometer were far less effective in absorbing sunlight, while the radiation absorbed increased with the smoke cloud's height above the ground. A layer of dust in the stratosphere reduced solar absorption in the troposphere.[28]

Additional confirmation of the work of Malone et al. was published in 1985. Starley Thompson refined the GCM that he and his NCAR colleagues Curt Covey and Stephen Schneider had used so that it would incorporate interactive transport of the smoke. Massive amounts, Thompson found, would move "upward and equatorward" after a July war, and the solar-heated smoke would largely evade rainout to remain aloft longer than previously believed.[29] This was enough to convince John Maddox that NW was real.[30]

New Physical Research: Fire Studies

Attention was refocused on smoke by Crutzen and Birks in 1982. The startling climatic consequences of urban fires that emerged from the TTAPS scenarios followed. Soon, other scientists pushed and squeezed the data in independent efforts to verify or challenge these findings, among them the climate modelers mentioned in the preceding section. They had a difficult path to follow, for fire modeling was primitive.

In 1984, Paul Crutzen and Christoph Brühl (both of the Air Chemistry Division of the Max-Planck-Institute for Chemistry in Mainz, Germany) and Ian Galbally (of the Commonwealth Scientific and Industrial Research Organization's Division of Atmospheric Research, in Victoria, Australia) focused particularly on urban, industrial, and forest fires. Solely from laboratory test fires, they assembled a large data bank on the quantities of fuel in a given area ("fuel loading"), the fraction of this fuel that would be consumed in a fire, the fraction of this consumed material that was injected into the atmosphere as particulate matter, and other variables. With the by-then-standard disclaimer that there probably would be errors in scaling small fires to mass-fire size, several notices of simplifications, and the common assertion that, where a choice existed, values were selected that gave the least serious effect, they used a modification of the 1982 *Ambio* scenario (namely, a smaller war) in a rather elementary global average climate model that had only three atmospheric layers. They concluded that 100 million tonnes of black smoke might be produced in urban and industrial fires—an amount comparable to that used by the modelers—and this cloud of particles might absorb enough sunlight to freeze large areas of the continents for weeks.[31]

In 1984, Crutzen's famous 1982 paper with Birks was criticized by two members of Galbally's division who charged that they had overstated their case in a number of ways. While admitting that "the atmospheric effects of a nuclear war would indeed be observable (presuming of course that anyone would care)," Ian J. Barton and Garth W. Paltridge argued that "it is not likely that the effects would be as drastic as those envisaged." Barton and Paltridge accepted the quantity of fire-produced aerosol used in the *Ambio* paper, granting that Crutzen and Birks's "guess is as good as that of anyone else," but focused on the size of the smoke and soot particles. This dimension was of extreme importance, since it was of the same order (radius 0.05 micrometer) as the incident radiation's wavelength and thus a most sensitive factor in determining the cloud's opacity. Their point was that coagulation of the particles would occur quickly, giving them a larger radius and lowering their efficiency in blocking optical wavelengths. Calculations by the Aussies showed that solar radiation reaching Earth's surface at noon, five days after the smoke was inserted into the atmosphere, would be 15 percent of normal—not less than 1 percent, as claimed by Crutzen and Birks.[32]

Barton and Paltridge also took issue with the assertions from several sources that the atmosphere might become more stable because of the absorption of radiation and that rainfall might decrease due to an overabundance of condensation nuclei. Not so, they said. The smoke and soot would not be spread uniformly across the Northern Hemisphere (as many computer models required). Solar radiation absorbed by these aerosols would "ensure differential heating of the atmosphere of one geographical region relative to another." If anything, circulation of the atmosphere would increase.[33]

Crutzen replied with a mea culpa to the effect that in 1982 he had not been an expert in "aerosol and radiative transfer research" and that he had been astonished to find no literature on the atmospheric effects of soot. Thus, particle coagulation and optical depth calculations had been omitted. Now he cited authorities to argue that coagulation would occur much more slowly and that the mass of smoke and soot in the atmosphere could be much greater than originally stated, the combination allowing his figure for sunlight transmission of less than 1 percent to stand. Crutzen also criticized the claim by Barton and Paltridge that noontime light of 15 percent of normal was not terribly serious. That illumination would occur only in the tropics, with the Sun overhead; a global average for the transmission of sunlight gave only 2 percent, and less if scattering were included. Also, since Earth's surface would cool while the troposphere warmed, owing to clouds of smoke and soot in it, Crutzen maintained his belief that the atmosphere would become remarkably stable. In these conditions, he wrote, "it is hard to escape the general suspicion that for most survivors of a nuclear holocaust and for life on earth as a whole, the environment might become extremely hostile, because of hitherto overlooked changes in the composition of the atmosphere."[34]

At the Livermore Laboratory, a plan for the experimental investigation of large-scale fires was drafted. Laboratory and field tests, its authors felt, might yield necessary information about some very basic processes involving smoke generation, lofting, and removal. Learning what went up and what came down may sound like an easy task, but it was in fact quite complex. It depended on the substances that burned, the size and temperature of the fire, the distribution of ignition points, the fraction of the fuel that was consumed, the locations of fire breaks, the meteorological conditions, and numerous other factors. The NW phenomenon depended critically on the quantity of smoke lofted. TTAPS had estimated a few hundred million tonnes of smoke (225 million tonnes in their baseline case), had injected it into the mid troposphere, and had not allowed the solar-heated smoke to rise buoyantly. These were considered conservative choices, but TTAPS recognized that better data were needed. To gain such quantitative information, many experiments would be required.[35]

While city fires were regarded as the prime culprit in initiating NW, forest fires remained of great interest. This was both because forest fires were likely to occur in a nuclear war and because they could be studied in peacetime. In the summer of 1984, at a Conference on Large Scale Fire Phenomenology sponsored by the National Bureau of Standards, a forest fire consultant named Craig Chandler provided some anecdotal information. He took issue with a widely accepted estimate of the area that might burn in a nuclear war—20 times the sum of wildfire acreage in a year—saying that the latter blazes occur only on days when they *can* occur. By this he meant that such fires never are ignited "when the ground is snow covered, during a rain or whenever the amount of water in the fuel . . . exceeds the amount of dry matter." Who could say that a nuclear war would start during the burning season?

Chandler was equally critical of the fraction of living biomass claimed to burn. A mature forest, he said, contained about 22 kilograms of biomass per square meter. Yet 80 percent of this is found in the tree trunks, which not only rarely burn but which serve "as heat sinks, absorbing more calories of thermal radiation than their outer layers liberate when they char." His estimate for the biomass that would burn was 2.6 kg/m^2. This would be increased by 1–2 kg/m^2 from the dead debris on the forest floor and reduced by the smaller size of the trees in Russian and Canadian forests. It would be reduced still more by "steam shielding," the explosive release of moisture in the foliage that keeps the dry fuel below the kindling temperature.[36]

Experiments were needed to determine the quantity of smoke and soot produced in a variety of fires. The experimenters would examine the optical properties of the smoke in the visible and infrared regions of the spectrum, and also observe differences over time, a process called "aging." The top and bottom of the mass of smoke, called a "plume," and its dynamical behavior would be measured. Finally, the life of the plume would be tracked to determine the extent of cloud-induced coagulation, rainout, and aging of the aerosols. Direct answers were needed to such questions as whether a large, intense fire produced more or less smoke than smaller, calmer fires that burned the same quantity of fuel.

Dense smoke from large fires would, seemingly, have little optical transparency. But if density of the aerosols encouraged particle coagulation and their subsequent removal by rain and gravity, such fires might not lead to the NW effect. Coagulation in the plume clearly was in need of study. Proven models of plume rise existed for smokestacks and volcanoes, but there were none for large fires and it was unlikely that one could extrapolate from so small to so large a source. Scaling experiments were needed to create models for urban fires and wildfires of giant size, in particular to determine whether smoke would be confined to the troposphere, where it would be rained out in days, or rise to the stratosphere and have a lifetime of years. Many variables would have to be measured, "since they are not easily calculated from first principles." Ultimately, of course, the likelihood of NW could not be measured, but would have to be extrapolated or modeled. Thus, Livermore scientists felt that the experiments should be planned by teams of experimentalists and modelers to maximize the value of the data.[37]

Cresson Kearny, a retired engineer at the Oak Ridge National Laboratory was another critic who focused on forest fires in order to cast doubt on TTAPS's calculations of urban fires. He charged that TTAPS, in their 5,000-MT baseline case, had used air bursts to maximize the area that would burn, while they had the same weapons explode on or near the ground to maximize radioactive fallout. Another overestimate, he said, resulted from the TTAPS condition that each weapon produced a unique ignition area, without any overlap. In reality, Kearny noted, each silo in the six Minuteman ICBM bases in the United States was expected to be targeted by at least two warheads. Owing to the geographic plan of these bases, only about 10 percent of the area specified by TTAPS would be ignited. These regions, moreover, contained relatively little fuel; they consisted mostly of desert, range, and farmland.

Kearny, like Craig Chandler, also called attention to the shielding action of a forest's foliage, an effect that had been documented in above-ground tests during the 1950s. Forests were also much less likely to burn than the 50 percent possibility estimated by TTAPS, due to snow, rain, and other conditions. In all, Kearny concluded, less than 10 percent of TTAPS's predicted amount of non-urban smoke would be produced. TTAPS's forecasts of city fires were no more reliable, he claimed. Without tall structures still standing to help generate a chimney effect, even combustible rubble would be more likely to smolder than to blaze. Tall city buildings, too, would shield many lower structures from the thermal pulse. Urban smoke, Kearny claimed, like smoke from non-urban sources, was overestimated. TTAPS, rebutting Kearny's contentions in a letter to *Science*, defended the calculations in their original article and, in a rare departure (for they published no further research papers), presented new data on wildland ignition.[38]

George Rathjens and Ronald Siegel (introduced in chapter 11 above) were among the more effective critics of TTAPS's calculations on smoke. Hostile to the claim that TTAPS's work was "robust" and unhappy that the NAS report overstated (in their view) the possible climatic consequences of NW, they used the NAS's journal *Issues in Science and Technology* to argue for uncertainty. They were driven by the belief that government action should be taken on the best evaluation of risk, rather than on the assumption that NW must be valid if it could not be disproved. With such large uncertainties, this was not the time for worst-case analysis.[39]

Using data from the literature and performing their own calculations, Rathjens and Siegel argued "that there would likely be about four times less smoke and eight times less soot" than the NAS assumed, and that the plume would rise to lower altitudes than the NAS concluded. This would permit more rapid rainout of the particles, but then again it might not—an example of the uncertainty that permeated the problem. Rathjens and Siegel also criticized the procedure—standard with the computer models—of starting with the smoke spread uniformly over a wide band of latitude. In reality, the plumes would rise from point sources and would be subjected to westerly winds from oceans to continents and warm air flowing northward. Such movement of air, Rathjens and Siegel reasoned, would halve the amount of cooling that was predicted. "These deficiencies and omissions in the various models," they wrote, led them to conclude that continental temperatures might fall 0–5°C but not 10–40°C. They praised the many papers published in scientific journals by NW investigators, noting that the conclusions generally were "appropriately qualified," but they disparaged the severity of the phenomenon and its inevitability that was asserted in popular accounts.[40]

Beyond the several qualitative critiques, insightful though they were, was some number crunching. Joyce Penner of the Livermore Lab was one of the stalwarts of this activity. Working with Leonard Haselman, Penner performed some sensitivity tests for smoke. These showed that the altitude smoke reached was highly dependent on the intensity of the fire, and that smoke's ability to attenuate sunlight depended greatly on particle radius, decreasing as the size grew by coagulation. These processes could be modified if, for example, there was moisture in the air, for then the latent heat of condensation released would impart more buoyancy to the plume. Penner and Haselman found, however, that two or three times the amount of water needed for rainfall was condensed in high-intensity fires, suggesting that much smoke might be washed out of the atmosphere before NW effects could occur.

Another adjustment in the atmosphere's microphysical processes that Penner and Haselman noted was the slowing of coagulation as the density of particles thinned in the expanding plume. This was of particular significance, since most computer modelers, restricted by the relatively primitive state of their one-, two-, and three-dimensional programs, necessarily inserted smoke instantly and uniformly (and thus somewhat sparsely) throughout large portions of the troposphere. This, of course, differed from real-world conditions, in which burning point sources would yield soot particles in close proximity to one another, encouraging coagulation. Nor did any model track the evolution of smoke from scattered targets to a more or less uniform spread; indeed, no model was yet able to employ cells with horizontal sides smaller than a few hundred kilometers.[41]

Interestingly, fire research was not limited to fire. Seasonal Arctic haze, traced to industrial pollution from the Soviet Union and even from the British Isles, absorbed solar energy. Covering an area comparable to that of North America, the effect of haze on temperature was being studied from Barrow, Alaska.[42]

The overwhelming percentage of NW research was conducted in government laboratories. Universities received little funding for such work. Even Richard Turco's employment by R&D Associates was no indicator of strong involvement by defense contractors, for he, not the company, initiated the work, and the Defense Nuclear Agency seems to have farmed few studies out to such think tanks. Pacific-Sierra Research Corporation was one of the rare exceptions. With funding from the DNA, Richard Small and Brian Bush examined smoke production from nuclear-ignited wildland fires. While city fires were expected to produce most of the wartime smoke, several studies had estimated that as much as half the quantity might be generated from non-urban fires. Especially if belligerents adopted a city-avoiding targeting strategy, it would be a good idea to know the implications for NW.

Using unclassified information, Small and Bush listed missile complexes, airfields, radar sites, C^3I facilities, weapons bunkers, and other major military bases of the nuclear powers— some 3,500 in all—that would conceivably be targeted by an enemy, but only if they were distant enough from a city that no urban fire would be ignited upon their being attacked. For each of these "rural" targets, they determined the local vegetation and the weather. Their clever analysis showed that 60 percent of the targets were located in farmed areas and 20 percent in grasslands. Only 14 percent had neighboring forests, and the remaining 6 percent were in wastelands. Even with the assumption that all targets were hit and all combustible matter was consumed, far less smoke would be lofted than specified in the earlier studies by Crutzen et al. and by TTAPS, both of whom used (higher) hemispheric averages of fuel loadings.

But there were other factors that drove the quantity down further. Weather affects the moisture content of fuel, the clarity of the atmosphere, and wind velocity and direction, and these determine ignition radius and fire spread. Using data from numerous weather stations, Small and Bush charted the area likely to burn at different times of the year. This proved less than the average of 500 square kilometers per megaton of explosive estimated by TTAPS. Whereas Crutzen and Birks had calculated 200–400 million tonnes of smoke from non-urban fires, TTAPS 80 million tonnes, and the NAS report 30 million tonnes, Small and Bush calculated only 0.3–3 million tonnes.[43] The issue remained controversial, as the reduction in rural fuel of 10–100 times that Small and Bush estimated was challenged by the authors of the physical science volume of the SCOPE report, who saw about ten times as much fuel available as the Pacific-Sierra team did.[44]

In addition to the theoretical studies, experiments were conducted. Obviously cities could not deliberately be torched, but controlled burning of forests and of lumber piled to simulate cities was expected to provide valuable information. Data of this sort would be especially useful in evaluating analyses such as that by Small and Bush. In early August 1985, eight American and Canadian scientists, including Richard Turco and Richard Small, observed the burning of 1,600 acres of balsam fir trees that had been killed by an infestation of spruce budworm. The fire, near the town of Chapleau in northern Ontario, was one of about 50 fires set each year in Canada to clear away deadwood in preparation for reforestation. As a helicopter flew in a spiral pattern over the bulldozed trees, a suspended drip torch was used to ignite them. A plume of thick, white smoke rose above 20,000 feet.[45] Unfortunately, the American scientists came away with impressionistic "results" only, since Ontario's Ministry of Natural Resources had denied them the opportunity to collect data. The officials were anxious not to appear to be cooperating with the US weapons program, yet professed to be willing to reconsider the issue in the future. One of the impressions was of surprise that rain did *not* occur in the huge, anvil-shaped cloud to wash out some of the smoke.[46]

Many these investigations concerning fire were considered newsworthy by the nation's media. In one investigation that received unusual attention, the University of Chicago chemists Edward Anders and Roy Lewis assigned the task of looking for traces of neon and xenon in the clays of the Cretaceous-Tertiary boundary to Wendy Wolbach, a graduate student. Like iridium, which led to the Alvarez et al. dinosaur-extinction hypothesis, the isotopic abundance of these gases provides signatures of an extra-terrestrial body, and might distinguish between a comet and a stony meteorite. The noble gases were absent, but Wolbach saw an astounding quantity of elemental carbon—about 10,000 times as much as expected. Her scanning electron microscope revealed this carbon to be in the form of fluffy clusters of a kind that are formed only in flames or hot gases. It appeared that vegetation that burned in gigantic fires produced far more soot than had been estimated in previous studies. The distribution was large and fairly uniform. Samples from New Zealand, Spain, and Denmark suggested that the dinosaurs' extinction was due to worldwide fires and the resulting shroud of soot rather than to rock dust kicked up by the impact of a meteorite or a comet. Wolbach and her colleagues saw a close analogy to NW, yet noted the possibility that the many NW scenarios discussed in the literature might be optimistic, since they predicted smaller quantities of soot. Reporters made the same connection.[47]

New Biological and Ecological Research

The extinction of the human species, a possibility that Paul Ehrlich had raised at the Halloween meeting and again in the paper published in the 23 December 1983 issue of *Science* as a companion to TTAPS's article, was a persistent specter. Even more, the apparition of extinction resonated with visions presented in Jonathan Schell's 1982 book *The Fate of the Earth*. Surely, one would think, any investigation of NW would include further study of its biological consequences. The administration's strategy, however, was different. It preferred to study NW sequentially: climatic phenomena, then biological effects, and finally (if ever) policy. This was perhaps marginally less expensive economically. By delaying the presentation of potentially dire results to the public, however, it certainly was cheaper politically.

In prepared testimony given to a congressional committee in July 1984, Richard Wagner, the assistant to the secretary of defense for atomic energy, called biological research "essential." "We are," he claimed, "augmenting our research into the biological consequences of prolonged temperature depressions, reduced sunlight and the radiological environment."[48] This augmentation, unfortunately, was hard to detect. The government, in fact, had a tradition of being far more interested in the physical consequences of nuclear weapons than their biological effects. The Federal Emergency Management Agency and its predecessors commonly published pollyanna views of the aftermath of war that were, Ehrlich noted, "rooted in the pervasive ignorance of ecology that has always been endemic in certain circles in Washington."[49] Even the National Academy of Sciences' 1975 report, *Long-Term World-wide Effects of Multiple Nuclear-Weapons Detonations*, which featured a look at ozone destruction, still paid inadequate attention to the resulting ecological problems.

In retrospect, the blame should not be placed entirely on "officialdom." Biologists themselves, even those few who, before 1983, wrote about climate changes caused by the fires of nuclear war, limited themselves to far smaller effects than predicted by the NW scenarios.[50] It takes an inspired intellectual leap—and evidence—to see much further than your nose. And, in any case, biologists knew that nuclear war would be bad for living organisms and were not overly interested in quantifying such consequences. For a different reason, John Harte of the Lawrence Berkeley Laboratory was at first disinclined to join Ehrlich's team; he felt it would be a waste of time. "Only a damn fool would believe that the potential political gains from a nuclear war could possibly outweigh the terrible costs to humanity." He changed his mind when he came to believe that there were such people, including some in high political office.[51]

Upon publication of the National Academy of Sciences' final report, in December 1984, the American Institute of Biological Sciences issued a statement urging policy makers to recognize the possibility of NW. A sponsor of the Halloween meeting a year earlier, the AIBS now argued that the NW scenario had been legitimized. Of course, research should continue, but it was not too early for policy changes. Interestingly, of the research topics the AIBS specified, none was in the biological sciences.[52]

In September 1985, the Institute of Medicine conducted a Symposium on the Medical Implications of Nuclear War in Washington. Lynn Anspaugh, leader of the Livermore Laboratory's Environmental Sciences Division, participated in a panel on long-term consequences and prospects for recovery. For him, "long-term" meant years or even hundreds of years, the time it would take large, native ecosystems to restabilize after experiencing the major climatic changes of NW. The difficulties in predicting such an event more than mirrored the problems faced by the atmospheric scientists in analyzing NW. Just as there were numerous uncertainties among the many factors inserted into the GCMs, and the inadequacies of the models themselves to mimic the real atmosphere were acknowledged, the biological sciences were handicapped on the same two counts. Anspaugh noted: "We simply don't have a long-range and broadly-based program that attempts to model ecological systems on a sufficiently large scale." Such efforts were far behind those modeling climate.[53]

At best, biologists and ecologists had community-scale models that functioned on ranges measured in tens of feet. Such models were driven by empirical data rather than by an understanding of the processes, and thus it was difficult to make predictions that required extrapolation. Moreover, processes such as extinctions and migrations were not incorporated, another indication of the low level of sophistication of the models.

Early papers on NW, Anspaugh said, predicted plummeting temperatures, a condition that made it relatively easy to anticipate the biological consequences. More recent NW research showed smaller declines in temperature, which increased the difficulty of judging the effect on living things. Ehrlich et al., in their 1983 *Science* article, had raised the possibility of human extinction. The SCOPE study focused instead on the destruction of agriculture, and on the widespread starvation that would ensue. Anspaugh saw this as an advance in understanding and noted that more was known about agricultural crops than about native ecosystems, but he remained skeptical of results: "... we don't have a good basis to predict changes in plant and animal populations." Nor were the temperature-driven physiological response models for agricultural crops programmed for a simultaneous decrease in the amount of sunlight.[54]

Still, progress was being made. At the Institute of Medicine's symposium and at a workshop sponsored by Livermore Lab and Stanford University, biological research agendas were discussed. Quantitative predictive ability was not expected soon, but there was confidence that it would be possible to "classify ecosystems as to their sensitivity and resilience." (The ecosystem most sensitive and least likely to recover was the tropical rain forest.) Anspaugh advocated the development of numerous new models to process new data. Experiments, he proposed, should be conducted under controlled conditions, even to the point of constructing large enclosures over native ecosystems. Notably, Anspaugh mentioned a physiological investigation of pine trees, wheat, potatoes, and soybeans contracted by Livermore Lab to the University of Wisconsin.[55] Despite virtually no enthusiasm from Washington, Livermore, it seemed, was one of the few laboratories engaged in biological and ecological experiments.

In October 1985, *BioScience*, the journal of the American Institute of Biological Sciences, published a special issue on nuclear war that was based on a 1984 symposium of the Ecological Society of America but was significantly informed by the recent SCOPE report. Two SCOPE scientists, Herbert Grover of the University of New Mexico and Mark Harwell of Cornell University, had contributed a particularly alarming paper in which they claimed that the "biosphere's structural and functional integrity [was] at risk." This was more than the human disaster from the cold and dark of TTAPS's scenarios; it was even a step beyond the collapse of agriculture in the Northern Hemisphere that SCOPE forecast. Looking past the plight of humans, it predicted long-term if not permanent damage to the environment.[56] Blast, heat, nuclear and ultraviolet radiation, pyrotoxins, reduced sunlight and temperatures, increased tropospheric ozone levels, and further consequences of nuclear explosions individually would behave as biocidal agents toward certain species, while simultaneously benefiting others. In hard-hit areas, it was possible that no higher life forms would survive, and recovery from outside would be glacially slow or would not occur at all. Echoing remarks mentioned above, Grover and Harwell decried the almost complete lack of mathematical models that could be used to describe the "mosaic of ecosystems." This reduced them to "extrapolat[ing] far beyond our normal frame of reference." Neither the explosions in Japan nor weapons tests in the Pacific and in Nevada were particularly helpful, because "population-, community-, and ecosystem-level interactions were often not looked at."

Further, ecophysiological researchers had previously had no reason to study plants and animals under conditions of extremely low light and temperature. Yet there had been numerous studies conducted whose relevance in a larger picture was now apparent. Radio-active fallout and its passage through the food chain had been tracked to a considerable degree. Ionizing radiation was known to cause cellular mutations. Photosynthesis was pro-portional to sunlight. Plants that normally tolerated winter weather could survive if cold arrived in the proper season. Light quality provided the cue to many plants for dor-mancy, development of fruit and flowers, and other aspects of growth. Unusual conditions, such as quick chills, would more strongly affect species with short lifetimes and species not normally subjected to a wide range of conditions. Marine phytoplankton growth could be smothered by intense UV-B radiation. It was like fitting together the pieces of a picture puzzle.[57]

The few ecosystem-simulation models that existed, Grover and Harwell noted, were modi-fied for strongly perturbed conditions. A growth model for the mixed conifer and hardwood forests of the southern Appalachians showed an 85 percent decline in forest biomass in the several years after a baseline-level war when programmed for average annual temperatures 6°C and 9°C lower. Recovery was far from complete after 50 years, and the forest's mix of species changed considerably. The same reduced temperatures gave biomass levels 30 and 50 percent lower when programmed into a grassland model. A marine model was used to determine that darkness lasting about 30 days in summer or about 100 days in winter destroyed the oceanic food chain, as zooplankton exhausted their phytoplankton food supply.[58]

Mass extinctions were known to have occurred in the geological past, yet the steps in their development were not clear, which made NW predictions difficult. Another complica-tion was that earlier nuclear war studies had assumed that Earth's surface was highly resilient and that things ultimately would return to something approaching "normal." Now, however, it was recognized that the situation was far more complex, and that life could be interrupted if, for example, there were no pollinators left to perform their customary task, or if a link in a food chain was missing, or if seedlings that sprouted were killed by overdoses of ultra-violet radiation. Although there would be some form of recovery, Grover and Harwell pleaded that research should be done to explore the possibilities.[59]

Harwell, who was associate director of Cornell's Ecosystems Research Center and a senior research associate of the Center for Environmental Research, had earlier taken a working paper on biological effects of nuclear war that was prepared by a committee of scientists for the Halloween 1983 conference and refashioned it into a book titled *Nuclear Winter: The*

Human and Environmental Consequences of Nuclear War (1984). In this first substantial report on biology to be published, he had laid out the cost to humans and to ecosystems, addressed the question of food availability, and speculated on psychological damage.[60] A year later, Harwell, who led SCOPE's biological analysis, co-authored (with Thomas Hutchinson) the SCOPE report on this work. With marginal support from the US government, American scientists and colleagues in the international community pushed ahead with their investigations of the biological effects of nuclear war.

The NAS's Final Report, 11 December 1984

For a phenomenon predicted by computer models and not by observed evidence, and one that divided many scientists and the public along deep political fissures, it was inevitable that the National Academy of Sciences' balanced and cautious final report on nuclear winter would be claimed as a victory by everyone. The *New York Times* columnist Tom Wicker wrote that NW was given "legitimacy" by the study, and quoted George Carrier's opinion that his committee's results were "quite consistent" with previous investigations.[1] In contrast, Wicker's editors, reading elsewhere in the document, thought that NW appeared "increasingly uncertain." The editorial writers charged that the original TTAPS work presented "only the worst possible outcome." Now, they seemed relieved that, although "a severe postwar freeze might seize the earth for months . . . its effects are so far impossible to define." Further study, the editors hoped, would pinpoint the consequences of massive soot injections into the atmosphere as being somewhere between "the full nuclear-winter scenario [and] almost nothing." The editors rejected worst-case analyses, but offered no recommendations for action while awaiting scientific enlightenment.[2]

Ronald Reagan's National Security Council summarized the report's findings as follows:

(1) The uncertainties that pervade the quantitative assessment of the atmospheric effects of a nuclear exchange are so numerous and so large that no definitive description of those effects is possible at this time. Nevertheless:
(2) The model calculations that can be made suggest temperature changes of a size that could have devastating consequences. This possibility cannot and must not be ignored. Therefore:
(3) It is incumbent on agencies having resources that can be allocated to such matters and on appropriate members of the scientific and technological community to support and conduct investigations that can narrow many of the uncertainties. Only in this way can we approach a posture from which a more definitive assessment can be made.[3]

Because the NAS report's first draft was completed in October 1983, its final publication in December 1984 raised some eyebrows. Committee member O. B. Toon explained some causes of the delay. The NAS, aware of TTAPS's work and concerned about doing something independent of it, nonetheless was slow in establishing the review panel. Then, from the time the Carrier committee commenced operations in early 1983 to the completion of its draft report, the committee found itself in the middle of an evolving field. This was unusual. An NAS review more commonly surveys a large, somewhat stable body of literature. Moreover, the committee was asked to review a subject that was not well developed.

The draft was sent to more than 100 referees, who conscientiously returned copious comments. These took much time to incorporate. In the meantime, new information became available. The redraft then had to be refereed. George Rathjens, for example, sent in eight pages of technical comments expressing general satisfaction with many changes but still questioning a great number of values and the committee's tone of confidence. It was these multiple stages that so delayed the final report's appearance.[4] Stephen Schneider explained, less diplomatically, that, in addition to some valid criticisms, there were "a hundred brutal, vicious, largely irrelevant attacks" by individuals angry at Sagan's publicity-seeking.[5]

Committee members were a cross-section of scientific disciplines and ranged from believers in NW to skeptics. In addition to Birks, Toon, and Turco, there were fifteen other distinguished representatives of chemistry, physics, geology, engineering, astronomy, and geophysics. Vice Admiral William Moran was joined by Vice Admiral Levering Smith, the NAS supplied a nuclear warfare expert in the person of Spurgeon Keeny, and defense contractors were represented by Conrad Longmire of Mission Research Corporation. There were no biologists; as Frank Press, president of the NAS, explained in his cover letter, the current task was to examine atmospheric effects, leaving the consequences to life for future study.[6] Conway Leovy, a member of the panel, was highly dubious when his former student Thomas Ackerman became a member of the TTAPS team. A cautious man, Leovy was far less doubtful when the report was completed, although he still had many questions.[7]

The committee's chairman, George Carrier, also maintained an equivocal stance, recognizing that NW was possible but kept by the many uncertainties from becoming a believer. This was reflected in the "yes, but" tone of the report. Severe climatic effects "could" occur, but there were "enormous uncertainties involved in the calculations." The estimates provided a rough "indication of the seriousness of what might occur," but the committee could not "subscribe with confidence to any specific quantitative conclusions drawn from calculations based on current scientific knowledge." This might seem to be a wishy-washy approach, but it was in fact a careful, cautious, and realistic analysis. The panel recognized the unsettled state of knowledge in this new field, yet acknowledged that there was a real possibility of disastrous consequences if the atmosphere became laden with soot and dust. The danger was tangible enough that these uncertainties should be attacked by a major scientific effort.[8]

A baseline case was chosen that was similar to, but not identical with, the *Ambio* and TTAPS baselines. This was done to sidestep criticism that the earlier scenarios were not realistic, and the baseline was selected with some input from the military.[9] About half the total world arsenal of 50,000 nuclear weapons was used, equally divided between strategic and tactical types. The 12,500 strategic weapons detonated provided 6,000 MT of explosive yield (an average of 480 KT each) and the same number of tactical arms contributed 500 MT (an average of 40 KT each). The total of 6,500 MT was expended between latitudes 30° N and 70° N, 1,500 MT of this at ground level and the other 5,000 MT at various altitudes to maximize blast damage.

Implicitly rejecting the argument that the United States did not deliberately target cities, 1,500 MT were aimed at "military, economic, and political targets that coincidentally lie in or near about 1,000 of [NATO's and the Warsaw Pact's] largest urban areas." There were other choices to be made, in order to calculate the effects of this war. These were the physical parameters used in the equations or models. In such cases they lay "well within the spectrum of scientifically plausible values."[10]

For the critical calculation of soot, a conservative three-fourths of the combustible material struck by 20 or more calories per square centimeter (easily adequate for ignition) from the 5,000 MT of air bursts would burn. Cautiously, the fires were not permitted to spread to areas with fresh fuel. From a probable range of 1–6 percent, the committee chose 4 percent as the portion of consumed fuel that was converted to smoke particles of sub-micrometer size, the most efficient diameter for the absorption of sunlight. In all, about 180 million tonnes (180 teragrams) of smoke were emitted (150 Tg from urban fires and 30 Tg from forest fires), with graphitic carbon, or soot, constituting 20 percent of the urban smoke. Conservatism appeared also in the stipulation that half the urban smoke was scavenged by coagulation or rainout. Much of the smoke that remained aloft would rise higher than the usual level of 4 kilometers for fire products, propelled up to as much as 9 kilometers by the solar-heated buoyant fire plume. It would reside in the upper troposphere longer than at lower levels, with about half being scavenged in 30 days or longer. The recognized weak point was using such figures in climate models, even three-dimensional ones. Since there was little in the way of hard data from actual events in which huge amounts of aerosols had poured into the atmosphere, everyone had to rely on computer simulations. The models, however, were validated over small perturbations only, not over the massive changes now being programmed into them.[11]

Carrier was truly uncomfortable with the reliance on computer modeling which, he observed, varied all over the lot. When predictions can be tested, as in engineering, one can be very sure of the validity of the model. But, Carrier noted, "you cannot model the atmosphere in the laboratory; you absolutely cannot."[12]

In the 193 pages of the report, these factors and doubts were further explained, analyzed, varied, and treated with circumspection. Some reviewers of earlier drafts suggested that no quantitative conclusions be drawn, fearful that they might be misinterpreted or believing that, truly, it was not possible to predict the atmospheric effects. The committee disagreed, deciding that the issue was so important to the world's security that it would be unfitting to vacillate, that a vacuous report would appear to deny the valid science in work already published, and that numbers provided the best way to further a systematic analysis of the problem. Even more, quantification helped to identify the most important of the variables for future research.[13]

The report concluded that nuclear-lofted dust could cause climatic problems. But the shroud of smoke that could initially obscure 99 percent of sunlight over large areas was the more serious of these two particulates. The megatonnage exploded over urban areas, rather than the total yield of the conflict, was the crucial factor in kindling fires. A war much smaller than the baseline case, therefore, could still generate a severe climatic response. Temperatures in continental interiors could plummet 10–25°C (18–45°F) after a summertime conflict, and this brutal chill could persist for weeks, while it could take months for temperatures to return to normal. Under these conditions, the northern tropics and the Southern Hemisphere would experience lesser but noticeable effects.[14]

Nowhere in the text (except in citations) was the term "nuclear winter" used. Perhaps this denoted the NAS's desire to present both the perception and the reality of a report independent of TTAPS and the political tinge Sagan had given to the team. Still, to a large degree, the NAS report vindicated TTAPS (as well as the Livermore, NCAR, and Moscow groups). Quantitative predictions were not congruent, but there was no reason for them to be, since somewhat different assumptions and initial values had been used. The gross predictions by TTAPS were, however, affirmed: cities would burn, huge quantities of smoke would be lofted, soot would attenuate sunlight, and Earth's surface would suffer severe cooling for lengthy periods of time.

There was cause for concern. George Carrier admitted as much: "When one makes plausible estimates, the results look very worrisome and one can't rule out the possibility that the impact might be very severe."[15] Yet the report itself somewhat undercut this view: "the pervasive uncertainties in the data and the limited validity of the atmospheric models used to date imply that some future study . . . could produce quite different analyses and conclusions."[16] The totality of such guarded comments and views lent support to those who doubted NW. Frank Press, president of the NAS, echoed this inconclusive-but-credible tone: "There's great uncertainty. . . . But it's not implausible."[17]

Carrier was sensitive to the apparent ambiguity of the report. Although his committee members had used the most likely numbers in their effort to provide quantitative results, the report was, he felt, "unusual in that the range of uncertainty was enormous." They simply did not know accurately the portion of fuel that would ignite, the portion that would turn to soot, the portion of soot that would be lofted relatively high, and the portion that would be scavenged quickly by moisture. Even the oft-cited case of fire-bombed Dresden, where much soot was rained out, was a questionable example because it was unknown how usual this was. Carrier had had a "responsible person" draft each chapter, usually the leader of the subgroup studying that topic, and then the entire committee had argued over the text. It appears that consensus, not full agreement, had led to the conclusion that NW could occur, but the committee had no confidence in specific quantitative conclusions.[18]

Reaction to the NAS Report

For those who saw the NAS report as validation of the NW phenomenon, it also served to support their long-held opposition to the arms race. Their view of the military uselessness of nuclear weapons was reaffirmed, while the weapons' diplomatic value remained for them a weak reed to lean upon. Indeed, with national suicide now a potential outcome, the credibility of deterrence was seen as reduced. Good sense called for a reduction in the arsenal, not an increase.[19] The Reagan administration's efforts to pry funds from Congress for 21 more MX intercontinental ballistic missiles and its pressure on reluctant Belgium and the Netherlands to accept deployment of cruise missiles seemed all the more dangerous.[20]

Nuclear weapons jumped still higher in the public's consciousness in January 1985 when the United States and the Soviet Union resumed long-stalled arms-control negotiations in Geneva. More than 12 years earlier, the Nixon administration had struggled to convince the Soviets that unrestrained efforts to build ballistic-missile defenses meant an unlimited arms race. Success was codified in the 1972 ABM Treaty, which denied either side more than two anti-missile sites, along with other controls. Mutual assured destruction (MAD), a consequence of this policy, was, however, increasingly criticized in subsequent years as immoral: unprotected populations were hostages to good behavior. Reagan's Strategic Defense Initiative was designed to provide that protection, but its development and testing was expected to violate provisions of the ABM Treaty. Thus, positions were switched by 1985, as the Soviets sought now to preserve limits on missile defenses, while the United States envisioned new, exotic defensive assets located in space, on land, and in the sea. Ronald Reagan sent Secretary of State George Shultz to Geneva to plan negotiations on mid-range and long-range offensive weapons, but he was instructed to keep SDI off the table.[21]

The media, always inclined to boost their ratings with sensational and controversial topics, were more than happy when their mercenary tastes corresponded with real news. The discussion of NW on CBS's "Face the Nation" program on 16 December 1984 provided such an occasion. The guests included Senator William Proxmire (D-Wisconsin) and Carl Sagan, representing the nuclear-winter-is-real-and-we-must-do-something-about-it-quickly position. George Carrier, the Harvard applied mathematician who chaired the NAS panel that wrote the report, was there; he may be characterized as cautiously believing in the possibility of NW. Representing the it-doesn't-change-a-thing school was former secretary of defense James Schlesinger. Substituting for moderator Lesley Stahl was Fred Graham, also of CBS News. The guests argued their positions with grace and wit but presented nothing that was new.[22]

Indeed, the NAS report received minimal attention, and the show could almost have aired a year earlier.

Scientific American titled its news story about the NAS report "No taps for TTAPS." The less alliterative *BioScience* bannered its story "NRC report backs nuclear winter theory." The *New York Times* similarly put a positive spin on the NAS report and headlined its story "'Nuclear winter' is seen as possible: Panel, stressing uncertainty, finds theory of a climatic upheaval seems sound." Whereas TTAPS had initially been disparaged as alarmist, the study commissioned by the government now gave the phenomenon credibility. The *Los Angeles Times*, while offering its readers only a single paragraph about the report, headlined it "Effects of A-war affirmed." The *Washington Post* gave Union Carbide's Bhopal gas leak tragedy higher billing, yet still found space on page 1 for the affirming headline "National Academy of Sciences backs nuclear-winter theory." Richard Turco, a member of both the TTAPS team and the NAS committee, remarked: "This legitimizes the problem. It shows that this isn't some wild idea of a bunch of left-wing, liberal college professors. This was a balanced panel and we're saying there really is cause for concern." To R. Jeffrey Smith of *Science*, Michael MacCracken commented: "It was easy for many people to dismiss the phenomenon of nuclear winter when it was first envisioned." But not now, for "there is no fatal flaw that negates the work performed to date."[23]

After the news reporters wrote their stories, the editorial writers and columnists got busy. The *Los Angeles Times* acknowledged the panel's belief in the "clear possibility" of NW despite the report's "uncertainties." The likelihood of an "ultraviolet spring" after the winter also caught its attention. These consequences made nuclear weapons even less useful, deterrence being their only purpose—until a better means of avoiding war was conceived. The conflicting stances of the *Times*'s columnist Tom Wicker and its editorial writer were noted in the opening of this chapter.[24]

In a letter to the editors of the *New York Times*, Carl Sagan complimented them on their grudging acceptance of NW; it was, he said, slightly better than their position a year earlier. But he protested their comment that NW might make the aftermath of war only marginally worse. Nations outside the northern mid-latitude battleground, he noted, would share in the suffering. There were steps that should be taken to avoid NW. In response, Jonathan Katz, a physicist at Washington University in St. Louis who was a member of the Carrier committee, deplored Sagan's claim that the NAS report supported TTAPS's work, arguing that uncertainties prevailed. Indeed, George Rathjens, one of those who had critiqued the first draft extensively, perceptively noted that the final report's executive summary had been rewritten to reflect criticisms and now was quite reasonable. However, Rathjens charged that it was not consistent with the rest of the text. The body of the report thus emphasized how bad things could be, while the summary emphasized how uncertain things were—a situation that permitted anyone to find something he approved.[25]

The biological perspective had been excluded from the NAS report and, except for commentary by Paul Ehrlich, continued to be overlooked by the media. Ehrlich, however, poured oil on the turbulent controversy over the extent of uncertainty, showing that it mattered less. "Uncertainty in the debate," he observed, "is dampened by the extraordinary sensitivity of living organisms."[26] Plant and animal life could be affected by *any* change in climate.

One of the editorial writers for the *Los Angeles Times* disagreed so strongly with the consensus of his colleagues that he wrote his own by-lined column. "What does the description of a 'nuclear winter' tell us that we didn't know before?" asked Lee Dembart. "It is already clear, and it has been clear for years, that nuclear war would be a catastrophe that must be avoided at all costs." Complaining that "the nuclear winter alarm is just more hand-wringing about the sword of Damocles that hangs over civilization," Dembart argued that our knowledge of NW did not "suddenly make nuclear war unacceptable." Further, the dilemma about what to do with the weapons "remains intractable, and it will not be solved with bumper-sticker slogans."[27] Exhibiting a surprising anti-science bias, Dembart perhaps spoke for many who knew there was a problem but cared little for the details. By extrapolation, it would seem that one needed to know nothing about prompt radiation, radioactive fallout, EMP, ozone depletion, or the ability of military forces and equipment to function in cold and dark conditions; awareness of blast and thermal effects presumably would suffice to form an adequate, though uninformed, opinion about nuclear weapons.

Thus, in the majority of what the "educated layman" read, the validity of NW was largely affirmed, yet for anyone who had an opinion about NW beforehand (or those like Dembart who thought the matter irrelevant), the NAS report seems not to have changed such views appreciably. One of the latter was *Nature* editor John Maddox. Upon publication of the NAS report, he poked fun at Carl Sagan in a survey of the literature, noting that the first popularization of NW seemed to be the astrophysicist's article in "the supermarket magazine *Parade*." In addition, Maddox continued his spat with Richard Turco over whether TTAPS's paper had been "hyped." When he turned to the report, Maddox could not deny that the NAS said that NW could occur. Still, he explained that the uncertainties were detailed to an unusual extent. And in what may have been half an olive branch extended to TTAPS, Maddox admitted that in "any attempt to predict the behaviour of a system as complicated as the atmosphere, it is natural that the starkness of first approximations should be relieved when refinements are introduced."[28]

In the next issue of *Nature*, Maddox returned to the NAS account, seemingly trying to minimize its significance by calling it a "second approximation to reality" (ignoring all other work on NW). The first approximation, TTAPS's paper, was "qualitatively confirmed," he said, "but hedged around with so many qualifications that a null outcome could well be compatible with the academy committee's analysis." It was to be expected that the NAS would call for more research, and with this Maddox agreed. He felt, however, that it need not be done under the NW rubric. Atmospheric physics would be most appropriate, especially since the greatest challenge would be to learn more about the dynamics of cloud formation and be able to incorporate individual clouds into models, rather than insert uniform cloudiness. The Australian atmospheric scientist A. Barrie Pittock cut through Maddox's equivocation to claim that the NAS report solidly refuted the anti-NW papers by John Maddox, S. Fred Singer, and Edward Teller in the pages of *Nature*.[29]

The NAS report spurred S. Fred Singer to write privately to presidential science advisor George Keyworth. As acting chairman of the National Advisory Committee on Oceans and Atmosphere (NACOA), and with his extensive experience in government, Singer sought to place his views where they might best affect policy. NACOA commented on matters that the NAS treated minimally, if at all. These involved, for example, estimates by others of the amounts of urban and forest fire smoke that were an order of magnitude smaller than figures the NAS panel used. Another topic was inadequate attention to atmospheric instability, which would lead to faster washout or even "snow-out" of smoke particles. And yet another was the old Singer concept of warming rather than cooling, brought about by conglomeration of particles and a resulting large infrared opacity of smoke clouds. In some of these cases Singer's group simply was second-guessing the NAS panel, but in others they may have offered valid suggestions for further research.[30] But it seems to have been Singer's fate to be ignored.

Official Washington had awaited the NAS report with some trepidation. Policy makers in the Department of State believed that "the implications for US policy . . . could be profound if the Administration-sponsored studies agree with the TTAPS conclusions and/or if, by default, congressional and public attitudes are molded by those results."[31] The report *did* basically agree with TTAPS, but the groundswell of legislative and public concern never materialized. The NAS study thus affirmed the credibility of NW, but left the subject with essentially the same questions as before: How much smoke would be generated? To what altitude would it be lofted? How long would it remain there? How long would the climatic consequences last?

Royal Society of Canada Report, January 1985; Royal Society of New Zealand Report, May 1985; UN Report, October 1985

Canadians had reason to be as apprehensive as any people upon the announcement of NW. Not only did they share a continent with the United States, but American ICBM bases targeted by the USSR were located upwind across the border. Ian Carr, a pathologist from Winnipeg who headed Physicians for Social Responsibility in Canada, noted that temperature decreases that had been predicted would doom the wheat crop. William Snarr, head of Emergency Planning Canada, a government agency comparable to the Federal Emergency Management Agency, wondered aloud about the wisdom of planning if there would be no survivors. In Canada as in the United States, officialdom (in this case the minister of the environment) sought advice from the scientific elite (in this case the Royal Society of Canada, counterpart to the National Academy of Sciences).[32]

The Royal Society's investigation, which began in the summer of 1984, occurred amidst controversy over an invitation to the Canadians to participate in the Strategic Defense Initiative and the Reagan administration's argument that SDI was needed to deter nuclear war.[33] The Canadian report, issued at the end of January 1985, opened with a routine letter of transmittal from committee chairman Kenneth Hare (a climatologist at the University of Toronto) to the president of the Royal Society. This letter, however, contained a most uncustomary sentence, one that foretold the study's content: "If we have gone beyond the Society's usual norms [of demanding exact proof of statements], we have done so only because we feel strongly that the Canadian government must be made aware of the macabre predictions being made by responsible scientists."[34]

Committee members, led by the study's scientific director and chief author, Andrew Forester (an environmental scientist at the University of Toronto), admitted the inadequacy of computers, models, and the data they processed, but felt obliged to accept the evidence at hand, which was from research done mostly abroad. Teller's, Singer's, and Maddox's criticisms of NW were examined and considered less persuasive than the quantitative studies that endorsed the NW concept. The computer models, they felt, were credible, and they accepted the plausibility of NW. While reluctant to jump into the debate over deterrence (especially since Canada, as a member of NATO, participated in this strategy), they found it impossible to avoid this issue and still comply with the minister's request for advice. Deterrence was no longer viable, they believed, because NW changed the equation: the climatic effects would cause global havoc ("there would be few spectators"), and a superpower's first strike could bring NW on itself even if the enemy did not respond.[35]

The authors of the Royal Society of New Zealand's 83-page report, issued in May 1985, were aware that the "intrusion" of scientists into political questions remained controversial. Thus, they premised their report on the obligation of scientists to examine the consequences of technical work. To laypersons the social responsibility of scientists may have seemed novel, but within the profession it was a strong, if minor, current dating at least from the development of poison gases in World War I, and given a huge kick by the bombing of Hiroshima and Nagasaki in the next global war. Indeed, by the time of the war in Vietnam, not just individual scientists but their professional societies at times took formal (often contentious) positions on such issues as weapon systems and nuclear strategy.[36]

The Kiwis' report was less an analysis of NW than a primer on nuclear warfare. In a surprising echo of former US President Dwight D. Eisenhower's farewell address, it also contained a long chapter warning of the roles of the military-industrial complex and the scientific-technical elite in furthering the arms race. The authors accepted the validity of the US National Academy of Sciences report, and expected that in the event of a war New Zealand would receive radioactive fallout from explosions in Australia, to windward, and smoke as it poured into the Southern Hemisphere.[37] Designed to educate their countrymen on the effects of conflict in the Antipodes, the report seems to have had little impact. A survey of popular responses to New Zealand's policies on nuclear weapons, for example, failed to mention NW at all.[38] This is all the more surprising in view of the fact that New Zealand's prime minister, David Lange, an advocate of a nuclear-free zone in the South Pacific, had highlighted NW in remarks he made to the UN General Assembly in September 1984.[39]

In December 1984, the United Nations expressed official interest in NW when the General Assembly asked the secretary-general for a report. Delivered in October of the following year, the report was an impressive selection of excerpts from many articles and reports, carefully organized by topic. The General Assembly thereupon asked that a committee of experts be appointed to study the climatic effects (specifically including socio-economic consequences) of nuclear war, and specified that a report was due in 2 years. The United States, consistently opposed to research on anything but physical effects, cast the resolution's only negative vote. Israel, Grenada, Luxembourg, and seven NATO allies abstained. The price tag of more than half a million dollars, coupled with the UN's ongoing financial crisis (caused largely by the persistent unwillingness of the United States to pay all its obligated dues to an organization whose members too often failed to vote as Washington desired) forced Secretary-General Javier Pérez de Cuéllar to delay work on the report for a year.[40]

Pérez de Cuéllar appointed an international committee of eleven members, of whom G. S. Golitsyn (from the USSR) was the only one actually to have done NW research. They were briefed by leading investigators from the United States and Canada, and they sat in on a workshop of the SCOPE group. The committee produced a short but accurate survey of atmospheric and climatic consequences of nuclear war, the effects on natural ecosystems and agriculture, and health and socio-economic effects. Avoiding the phrase "nuclear winter" on the notion that the effects were more far-ranging, the scientists concluded that the climatic consequences would be severe, even within the range of the uncertainties. Since no natural disasters of such global dimensions had been recorded in history, and with no "outside" help possible, the time for recovery was uncertain.[41]

This study, however, did not appear until the end of 1988, by which time it had little impact. Other, more elaborate, reports covering the same material, particularly that by SCOPE in 1985, had preceded it, and the subject was fading from public attention. Despite the report's grim conclusion that "the direct effects of a major nuclear exchange could kill hundreds of millions; the indirect effects could kill billions," the General Assembly, in the dry bureaucratic language of resolutions, merely thanked the secretary-general and his team of experts and requested wide distribution of the report.[42] From this project's start in 1984 to its finish in 1988, the *New York Times* (America's "newspaper of record" and the UN's "hometown" paper) paid no attention. Perhaps this indifference was due to a lack of concern about "motherhood" resolutions by the world body, or perhaps it was because the report was based on other studies, and was not original research.[43]

SCOPE Report, September 1985

The International Council of Scientific Unions (ICSU) traces its ancestry back to 1899, when the International Association of Academies (IAA) was founded. The IAA, which orchestrated the collaborative activities of many national academies (including the US National

Academy of Sciences) in such fields as seismology, geodesy, astronomy, meteorology, and oceanography, where national borders were irrelevant, succumbed to the schisms of World War I. It was replaced by the International Research Council (IRC), an organization that initially excluded Germany from membership. In 1931, the IRC became the ICSU, which survived World War II and went on to play a distinguished role in international science for the rest of the century. Among the many projects it sponsored, the International Geophysical Year (IGY) in 1957–58 was easily the most famous. The 1985 report on NW by the ICSU's Scientific Committee on Problems of the Environment (SCOPE) was another occasion when the council was uncommonly thrust into the limelight.[44]

The ICSU, as its name implies, is an umbrella for many unions which embrace most areas of science. At the time of the SCOPE report, the International Astronomical Union, the International Union of Pure and Applied Chemistry, and the International Union of Pure and Applied Physics were among the twenty unions in existence. Reflecting its IAA origins, there were 74 national academies also under the umbrella. Forming a third branch were 26 other groupings called Scientific Associates. Rounding out the organization were (in 1985) ten Scientific Committees created to address a particular problem or area of research. SCOPE was the thirteenth such committee upon its foundation in 1969, and from the beginning it had a particular mandate to study the effect of human activity on the environment. Within a decade its efforts were so broad that subcommittees sometimes were formed. This was the case for NW. In 1982, SCOPE and the ICSU established a Committee for the Assessment of the Environmental Consequences of Nuclear War, which took the acronym ENUWAR.

Similar in behavior to committees of the US National Academy of Sciences-National Research Council, in that it reviewed existing research, rather than engage in bench or field work itself, ENUWAR conducted its activities through a worldwide series of workshops. Chaired by Sir Frederick Warner (a chemical engineer at Essex University who also was treasurer of SCOPE), ENUWAR tapped the expertise of about 300 scientists from more than 30 countries. This was both the largest of SCOPE's projects and the only one, of some dozens, involving weapons.[45] (From another perspective, this was just more of the "numerology of credibility,"[46] similar to the way TTAPS claimed that the 100 scientists who attended its closed meeting in April 1983 supported NW's validity. But there was a real difference: SCOPE authors labored to reach consensus positions.)

ENUWAR's steering committee included Sir Frederick Warner, Paul Crutzen, Sune Bergström of the Karolinska Institute in Stockholm (who in 1984 chaired a committee that produced the World Health Organization's report on health and health services following a nuclear war[47]), and Thomas Malone of Butler University (a former foreign secretary of the US National Academy of Sciences, secretary general of SCOPE from 1971 to 1976, and treasurer of the ICSU, who had chaired the televised "Moscow Link" that followed the 1983 Halloween meeting). ENUWAR's leadership included such familiar faces as Richard Turco, Thomas Ackerman, and Michael MacCracken, which made it seem that the "old boy network" from TTAPS and the Livermore Lab formed an interlocking directorship to guide all studies, regardless of the sponsor. But the membership actually extended to virtually everyone who had made a research contribution to the subject, and, just as George Carrier concluded when organizing his NAS panel, it would have been foolhardy now to exclude the most knowledgeable scientists. In any case, the numerous other members of the panel were expected to be capable of independent judgment.[48]

Funding and other support was provided by the ICSU, the Carnegie Corporation of New York, the General Service Foundation, the Andrew W. Mellon Foundation, the W. Alton Jones Foundation, the MacArthur Foundation, the Rockefeller Brothers Fund, and other institutes and societies,[49] including the national academies of Sweden, Great Britain, the Soviet Union, India, the Netherlands, France, Japan, Canada, Venezuela, Australia, New Zealand, and the United States.[50]

On a $600,000 budget, after 2 years and nine major technical workshops held in cities around the world, the scientists produced two volumes of their findings, amounting to nearly 900 pages. A sense of awed satisfaction prevailed as the books' principal authors, who had not known the outcome beforehand, witnessed the distillation of initially varied points of view into an unusually strong consensus. A pre-publication conference to discuss the study was held on 12 September 1985 at the National Press Club in Washington. Scientists were becoming increasingly adept at ministering to the media. Similarly, SCOPE (this term will be used hereafter, instead of the less familiar ENUWAR) employed the talented science writer Lydia Dotto to distill a thin popular version from the two thick technical volumes.[51]

The first tome of the report (often called "SCOPE 28," meaning the 28th report issued since SCOPE's creation) discussed the physical and atmospheric effects of nuclear war. Its principal authors were A. Barrie Pittock (of Australia's Commonwealth Scientific and Industrial Research Organization), Thomas Ackerman, Paul Crutzen, Michael MacCracken, Charles Shapiro (of San Francisco State University), and Richard Turco. Ackerman served as coordinating editor in the final months of the project, while MacCracken was responsible for final editing and production.[52] Since the cycle of SCOPE's work occurred about 9 months after that of the NAS committee, they benefited from the more recent and thus more advanced computer models. In particular, interactive smoke rising from specific targets in the Northern Hemisphere replaced smoke that was inserted uniformly in position and was unable to be moved by the atmospheric changes it caused.

For a summertime conflict, continental temperatures could fall about 20–40°C (35–70°F). In a scenario that involved the detonation of half the superpowers' arsenals and the ignition of 25–30 percent of the urban flammables in these countries and in Europe, the SCOPE scientists calculated that a minimum of 50–150 million tonnes of smoke would be lofted. While this figure was somewhat smaller than that used in most other studies (for example, the NAS used 180 million tonnes in its baseline case, and TTAPS estimated 225 million tonnes), the smoke was deemed to be richer in light-absorbing elemental carbon. Oil and coal storage sites and asphalt paving in cities were the richest sources of sooty smoke. Half the particulates would be washed out in the first day, but much of the remainder would be heated by summertime solar energy and quickly soar above a depressed tropopause (as low as 5 kilometers) and would thus be above the weather. The normal decrease in temperature with increase in altitude would be reversed by the warmed sooty clouds. The inversion thus created would disrupt familiar weather patterns, leaving a remarkably stable troposphere—one with minimal rainfall.

Recent arguments by Edward Teller, S. Fred Singer, and Jonathan Katz[53] to the effect that far more moisture would condense and wash out greater quantities of soot and dust were rejected. The SCOPE scientists believed that condensation would occur at a lower rate. Temperatures would plummet as 99 percent of sunlight was blocked under many relatively small but dense patches of smoke, and in a few weeks the deprivation would stand at 90 percent as the smoke spread uniformly across the Northern Hemisphere. Global cooling effects might last months or years. The concept of a NW threshold was rejected, with no minimum amount of smoke unable to cause some cooling. The term "nuclear winter" also was discarded, as evoking too limited a vision of the consequences stemming from nuclear war.[54]

Though the first SCOPE volume differed somewhat from earlier efforts in methodology, assessing the consequences of the burning of different percentages of the flammables available rather than exploring specific (and tendentious) scenarios of war, the conclusions were much in line with those of previous reports. Nothing new had been found to deny that "severe environmental effects" could occur. Indeed, lofting of solar-heated smoke made the effects more likely. Of course, uncertainties remained, and these could push the consequences in either direction. Atmosphere-ocean interaction was one of these.[55]

In contrast to the steady accretion of physical and climatic knowledge presented in SCOPE's first volume, the second volume was a novelty. It was perhaps the only commissioned report to deal extensively with biological effects. One might say that this was the report the US government disdained to request. There was novelty too in the interaction among scientists. Physical scientists, who generally sought answers to global problems, were forced now to think locally, as biologists asked "about effects on coastal zones, islands, the wheat belt, and so forth."[56] The methodology started with physical stresses on the environment: acute and chronic climate change, global and local fallout, ultraviolet light, toxic aerosols, and so on. The next step was to understand better the effects of such wartime and postwar strains on natural ecosystems and agriculture, with emphasis on the latter because of its importance for humans and its greater sensitivity. The goal was to evaluate the vulnerability of humans to disruptions in the availability of food.

Natural ecosystems, the SCOPE biologists determined, were inadequate by themselves to feed Earth's human inhabitants. Less than 1 percent of the current population could survive without agricultural efforts. Some 200 biologists, meeting in seven workshops, carefully investigated a wide variety of crops. They noted their vulnerability to temperature changes and studied records of production and consumption, the reliance of humans on them (for example, rice consists of more than 80 percent of the diet of nearly 2 billion people), and patterns of imports and exports. The scientists then detailed the specific effects of NW on agriculture in fifteen diverse countries that contained about 65 percent of humanity.

The report's most shocking findings concerned the future of the human race. Darkness and cooler temperatures were but preludes to the collapse of agriculture in the Northern Hemisphere. If the war occurred in the spring or summer, the next growing season would be lost. Lesser, but still dramatic, agricultural losses would follow an autumn or winter conflict. A freeze would of course destroy many growing plants. But even if temperatures fell only 3–4°C, far less than the 35°C or so predicted in TTAPS's report, this would sharply limit the growing season and curtail the cultivation of wheat in Canada, in the northern parts of the United States, and in the Soviet Union. Corn, soybean, and rice yields would suffer similarly from modest reductions in temperature at critical times in the growing season. Additionally, drought would affect many regions. Monsoon rains, for example, would be disrupted, the moisture falling mostly at sea and along coastlines. Water would be denied to crops in the African Sahel, in India, in Southeast Asia, in China, and in Japan. Indeed, non-combatant India would suffer more fatalities from mass starvation than would the two belligerents combined from the bombs' direct effects. More people would die in Africa than in Europe. Rice production would be eliminated in the Northern Hemisphere and possibly in the Southern Hemisphere also. Where agriculture continued, it would be handicapped by uncontrolled fires and radioactivity, and by increased ultraviolet radiation, the degree depending on the extent to which stratospheric ozone was depleted. Humanity would not perish, but with 1–4 billion people thrust into starvation (out of an estimated global population of 4.6 billion) it would experience the most staggering blow in its history. Forget Hiroshima and Nagasaki, co-leader of the biologists Mark Harwell counseled. The more valid images of nuclear war were those of famine-stricken Sudan and Ethiopia. Said another way, the immediate effects of nuclear explosions—the blast, heat, and radiation—awesome as they were (with 500 million estimated deaths), seemed minor compared to the long-term consequences.[57]

The "traditional" view of nuclear war, involving immense numbers of casualties and vast destruction of human artifacts, still imagined Earth as an enduring home to the many species that would survive. Ecologists were among the few who recognized how delicate was the incredibly thin layer of the planet's surface and atmosphere. NW showed that a material as tenuous as smoke could wreak havoc on a far greater fraction of Earth's living creatures than previously believed.

Earlier papers and reports in these chapters described serious potential blows to agriculture, but they were largely related to initial predictions of huge temperature decreases and the cutoff of seeds and supplies from developed to developing nations. Now, it appeared, even with lesser temperature changes, the damage would be far worse. "What emerges," wrote the science reporter Janet Raloff, "is a new perspective on the fragility of the agricultural systems that feed our planet." Temperature was the most important variable, and it could affect plants in a number of ways. Cold could interfere with metabolism (by preventing synthesis of chlorophyll, or by the growth of ice crystals within the cells), or hinder germination, or prevent fruit from setting. When imposed suddenly, it could kill plants which normally "harden" over a period of declining temperatures, a process that enables them to endure the winter (cold snaps, for example, familiarly pose a danger to orange groves). Dry seeds and dormant plants were most likely to survive. Darkness added to plant problems; light levels below about ten percent of normal were insufficient for adequate photosynthesis to occur. A variety of toxic gases produced in the conflagration posed another threat to plant growth. The persistence of this collapse was also striking: even if climatic conditions returned to normal in a year, the lack of seed stocks, farm animals, pollinators, fertilizer, pesticides, tractor fuel, irrigation equipment, and other farming needs could easily condemn agriculture to a slower revival—on the order of several years.[58]

SCOPE scientists also examined food stores in many countries. Only in very few was there an indefinite supply. These were the grain-exporting nations, such as the United States and Canada, where the surviving population could exist on the surviving stores. For the majority of the world's nations and population, stored food would last 6 months at most and, with imports inevitably curtailed, the next harvest would likely be too far in the future. Australia and New Zealand would fare better than most other nations. Their oceanic surroundings would moderate climatic changes, as would their location in the Southern Hemisphere, while their self-sufficient populations of relatively small size would lessen food problems. Predictions were dire for countries with large populations that relied heavily on food imports, such as Japan and many states in Asia and Africa. Mass starvation seemed inevitable.[59]

A thin World Health Organization report on the effects of nuclear war, written after the Crutzen-Birks article in *Ambio* appeared but before the TTAPS group revealed its calculations, emphasized the failure of agriculture in its estimate of 1.15 billion deaths and 1.1 billion injured—about half of Earth's population.[60] The SCOPE report nearly 2 years later did not alter the scale of the calamity, but it showcased agriculture even more and fleshed out the details convincingly. There would be no escape from the collapse of the global system by which food is grown and distributed.

The report's principal authors, Mark Harwell (of Cornell University's Center for Environmental Research) and Thomas Hutchinson (of the University of Toronto's Institute for Environmental Studies), insisted that it presented far more quantitative information on the biological consequences of a large nuclear war than had been gathered before. And its findings were solid. Yet, just as "uncertainty" was almost a mantra when discussing physical and atmospheric phenomena, the biologists did not claim to know everything. Their report was not the final word, but a first step toward understanding how many people could be fed under certain conditions, how small a temperature change would alter interactions in an ecosystem, what steps of a civil defense nature were desirable (such as increasing variety of seeds and quantity of grain stored in the Southern Hemisphere), and other questions rarely asked before.[61]

If the long-term consequences of nuclear war looked bad for humans, the short-term effects also appeared worse. Government estimates of casualties had customarily been made by extrapolating the deaths and injuries from the atomic bomb's blast at Hiroshima on 6 August 1945. At the National Academy of Science's Institute of Medicine's symposium, held in Washington just ten days after the SCOPE report was publicized, recalculations by the Stanford physicist Theodore Postol that included other effects besides blast showed two to four times the fatalities of previous assessments. The importance of fire was greatly increased, owing to weapons in the arsenal that were larger than those of 1945. Superfires had the ability to produce winds of hurricane velocity and extreme temperatures, as well as to generate smoke and toxic gases, and they would consume many of those humans previously classified as merely injured.

Aside from the huge shortfall in the number of burn-treatment centers and critical-care beds in the nation's hospitals, overwhelmed physicians and nurses who survived would encounter patients with more problems than previously anticipated. According to David Greer, dean of medicine at Brown University, and his co-author Lawrence Rifkin, radiation (both ionizing and ultraviolet), fire burns, trauma, malnutrition, stress, and depression would attack the T cells of the immune system, leading to its suppression, with remarkable similarity to the acquired immune deficiency syndrome. In addition to all its known horrors, nuclear war could spread something akin to the epidemic of AIDS.[62]

The SCOPE report qualified many of its conclusions, recognizing the continuing inadequacies of GCMs to handle mesoscale units of the atmosphere, uncertainties involving urban smoke production and its rainout, and the early stage of development of ecosystem models. Nonetheless, the authors were convinced to sound the alarm because, even at best, small temperature changes were to be expected and these would suffice for the devastation of agriculture.[63] "Why study these issues?" Mark Harwell asked rhetorically. "Aren't the consequences of direct effects bad enough?" These were the wrong questions, Harwell argued: "Our premise is that consequences to the global human population are precisely what we should focus upon; the other [physical] studies are but intermediate steps in making that evaluation. . . . There will always be uncertainties [in the physical investigations]. . . . Delaying biological assessments until physical uncertainties are resolved, then, is never to do them."[64]

Reaction to the SCOPE Report

Toward the end of 1984, *Scientific American*'s "Science and the Citizen" columnist wrote: "The findings of the SCOPE review panel can be expected to influence the future course of all such longer-term research efforts." More expansively, at a meeting in Paris during the same period, a SCOPE scientist anticipated that the final report was "likely to be one of the most momentous environmental impact statements ever prepared."[65] In that exciting period, when research contributions were published from many scientists and the US government was gearing up for an expanded effort, this expectation seemed reasonable.

When SCOPE's report appeared, 9 months later, it received much attention and was praised as ambitious and insightful. Though the report avoided policy recommendations, many participants, including the chairman, Sir Frederick Warner, vocally urged others to draw them. Mimicking the title *The Day After*, Laura Tangley, *BioScience*'s features editor, titled her review "The Year After" and noted the widespread feeling among SCOPE scientists that policy changes were mandatory. One scientist commented on the futility of planning for nuclear war: "The emperor has no clothes; it's time we stopped discussing the fabric of those clothes." Even before the work was published, the International Council of Scientific Unions circulated it to officials of several governments, and SCOPE arranged for its public unveiling to be orchestrated by the Washington-based Center on the Consequences of Nuclear War, an organization known for its support of the NW concept.[66]

Mark Harwell, one of the most prominent of the scientists involved in the SCOPE project, and certainly one of the most eloquent, explained how previous thinking had gone astray: "Hiroshima is a dangerously misleading example of what the next nuclear war would be like—misleading because of differences of scale." By current standards, the atomic bombs dropped on Hiroshima and Nagasaki would be classified as tactical weapons. Not only yield but numbers were hugely different, with about 17,000 strategic and 30,000 tactical warheads distributed among the arsenals. Quantitative extrapolations from Hiroshima's experience were thus inadequate; there were major qualitative differences. Modern conflict would be "war against the global environment itself," placing humans everywhere in as much risk as citizens of the belligerents. Not the plausibility of NW, Harwell argued, but only its degree remained uncertain, and even a small atmospheric perturbation would be devastating; ". . . after the next nuclear war, there would be no Peace Memorial Park like the one at Hiroshima, no one collecting the names of the victims under a cenotaph, no one engraving an inscription to the dead to 'sleep peacefully; these mistakes will never be repeated.' "[67]

In an unsigned editorial, *Nature* praised the openness of the SCOPE process and called its findings, which were marginally on the "cheerful side of those of Turco et al.," not importantly different. "For the time being, the nuclear winter must firmly be listed among the consequences of substantial nuclear wars. . . ." A section in the report on radioactive fallout (now called more serious than previous studies had called it) was praised. The need to investigate mesoscale processes, so as to understand the behavior of individual smoke plumes, instead of assigning uniformity to a GCM cell of many miles to a side, was emphasized. The "actual release" of SCOPE's report by "publicity managers more free with press releases than with copies of the full text (not yet available)" was condemned and was said to be "probably best explained by the need in the United States to shout even to be heard."

Nature assumed that small nuclear wars were still very possible—indeed, the most likely nuclear-war scenario—and that NW's effect on non-belligerent nations would do little to alter the superpowers' behavior. Most surprisingly, the editorial criticized the scientists' clear effort to present only a technical report and leave its policy implications to the politicians. This, of course, was long-standing behavior, invoked to insulate scientists from charges of having a political agenda. Yet, with the technical details of nuclear warfare so relevant to military decisions, the SCOPE committee "might have taken its courage in both hands and said that the two activities cannot be separated." What, *Nature* asked, were the policy implications?[68]

Nature certainly seemed now more conciliatory toward NW, yet retained the touch of a typically feisty, unpredictable, and error-prone Maddox—who, the previous December, had criticized SCOPE for issuing a statement condemning space-based defenses and proclaiming the need for profoundly different international relations.[69] For this Maddox was taken to task by the ICSU's executive secretary, who pointed out that those political comments were made not by SCOPE but by an ad hoc group of scientists and religious leaders.[70]

The *New York Times* was in less of a quandary over policy than *Nature* was. In an editorial scornful of the Reagan administration's contention "that the debate is irrelevant to policy," the *Times* argued that it was incumbent on governments to understand what the failure of deterrence would mean. The "lesson will not have been learned if strategists merely reallocate their targets and change the design of warheads." Instead, the *Times* urged large reductions in the nuclear arsenals.[71]

Thomas Powers, a prominent reporter and author on the arms race, was struck by the great potential for ecological disaster. It reminded him of Jonathan Schell's forecast of a "republic of insects and grass" (in *The Fate of the Earth*), the surviving fauna and flora being those most resistant to radiation and climatic stress. The SCOPE report's analysis of food stores in various countries caught Powers's eye, and he wondered what would happen in a nation with a six-month supply. Would half the population be given rations for a year, until the next harvest, or would the entire nation eat for half a year and then starve? With history showing famine often associated with siege, Powers had no doubt.[72]

The ecologist Arthur H. Westing called the SCOPE biological sciences report "both more ambitious and less satisfactory" than the physical sciences report. While applauding the way in which environmental consequences of nuclear war were highlighted, he pointed to the relatively primitive state of the ecological research, questioning the strength of conclusions about agricultural devastation.[73] The overall reaction to the entire SCOPE report, nonetheless, was that it was a resounding affirmation of the possibility that a nuclear war would have severe climatic consequences, and, if severe climatic consequences occurred, of the near certainty of widespread biological collapse. While individual doubters sniped at NW throughout its years in the limelight (often with legitimate arguments, for much remained uncertain), every formal report by a group of scientists upheld the potential for a climatic catastrophe.

Despite the promotional activity surrounding the SCOPE report's release, its intrinsic worth, and the favorable reviews it received, it failed surprisingly to encourage or direct additional investigations. Why? Carl Sagan, in his review praising the SCOPE study, noted that the Department of State authorization bill that Congress had passed and the president had signed called for a significant joint US-USSR study of NW. But the administration had already scaled back its proposed $50 million, 5-year research effort, allocating only $5.5 million for the first fiscal year, and biological investigations were never included in that program.[74]

The US government thus continued to profess its belief in the reality of some climatic consequences of nuclear war, but maintained that its military policies already served to prevent that war. Nor was there any noticeable pressure from abroad for change. Foreign governments generally were silent, while news of public protests failed to penetrate the American media. It was a good example of bureaucratic stonewalling with a sympathetic smile on the administration's face. Research would continue at an unhurried pace; the sense of urgency that characterized the period 1984–1985 would be gone.

In a sense, the SCOPE report left its public in the same place as it had been before. While changing the emphasis from cold-and-dark to the demise of agriculture, and providing new technical details and a sense of independent analysis from this international committee, there remained the still-valid criticism of much uncertainty surrounding NW. Joseph Knox of the Livermore Lab, for example, cited the doubt that undercut the report's apparent finality. "A lot depends," he argued, "on how much soot survives its first six hours in the atmosphere." If most was scavenged during that period, we might have just a "transient chill, the kind of thing man has survived before in history."[75]

In addition to the reports described in this chapter, several books appeared on the subject of NW. Mark Harwell's *Nuclear Winter: The Human and Environmental Consequences of Nuclear War*[76] was something of a preview of his contribution to the SCOPE report. Published in 1984, this was the first monograph to treat extensively the damage to plants, animals, ecosystems, humans, and society of reduced temperatures and light levels. Also in 1984, Julius London and Gilbert White published an edited volume, titled *The Environmental Effects of Nuclear War*, that comprised presentations from a symposium at the annual meeting of the American Association for the Advancement of Science.[77] In 1985, three British scientists, Owen Greene, Ian Percival, and Irene Ridge, published *Nuclear Winter: The Evidence and the Risks*, a highly readable technical primer for the layman that presented extensive discussions of both physical and biological issues.[78] In 1986, Peter Sederberg published *Nuclear Winter, Deterrence, and the Prevention of Nuclear War*, an edited volume of conference papers that focused almost entirely on policy issues.[79] Also in 1986, Lester Grinspoon published *The Long Darkness: Psychological and Moral Perspectives on Nuclear Winter*, another edited volume.[80] Together with *Planet Earth in Jeopardy: Environmental Consequences of Nuclear War*, Lydia Dotto's condensation and popularization of the two-volume SCOPE report,[81] these books showed the interest of publishers in NW, and by extension the interest of the public.

Further, some organizations published popular summaries for their readers. For example, in early 1986 Earthscan (a self-described "editorially-independent global news and information service on development and environment issues," supported by the UN and various other international and national agencies) issued a press briefing document titled "No Place to Hide: Nuclear Winter and the Third World." Funding for this document was provided by the Center on the Consequences of Nuclear War.[82]

In 1984 and 1985, the pace of investigation, review, and popularization was breathless. An impressive amount of solid research on NW was accomplished. Much remained uncertain, however, and all recognized how much more they had to learn. Robert Cess (of Stony Brook) saw the cup as half empty: "Never has so much been said about a field in which so little has been done."[83] From another perspective, Paul Crutzen downplayed the uncertainties: "The high sensitivity of agricultural productivity to relatively small alterations in climate conditions indicates that the unresolved issues in the physical sciences may not be of great consequence."[84]

15 Looking at Moscow

Squeezing the Bear for Information

In the United States, the news media gave much attention to NW in the months following the October 1983 public announcement of the phenomenon. In the Soviet Union, however, television, the newspapers *Pravda* and *Izvestiya*, and other mass outlets kept their audiences informed only in small quanta of information until mid 1984. Then they improved markedly, but still their shows and stories seem to have been composed mostly for an elite audience. This shift was attributed to increasing concern about the climatic consequences of nuclear war by the USSR's political leaders.[1]

The reactions of the superpowers' top leaderships also differed. In late 1983, Yevgeny Velikhov, vice president of the Soviet Academy of Sciences, briefed Defense Minister Dimitri Ustinov and Foreign Minister Andrei Gromyko on the dangers to climate posed by nuclear war. Gromyko subsequently discussed the phenomenon with President (that is, chairman of the Supreme Soviet, and also general secretary of the Communist Party) Yuri Andropov and with Premier (that is, chairman of the Council of Ministers) Nikolai Tikhonov. A reported 5–10 million rubles was budgeted for research.[2] The Soviet leaders seem to have taken the evidence for NW seriously. Indeed, their receptiveness, if not their actions, was warmer than that found in Washington, where Secretary of State George Shultz and Secretary of Defense Caspar Weinberger seem not to have been briefed.

The cosmonaut Alexsei Leonov later observed that Carl Sagan

came to Moscow, to the Central Committee [of the Communist Party] and . . . briefed them on Nuclear Winter. After he left, a dozen men on the General Staff looked around at each other, and they said, "Well, it's all over, isn't it? The nuclear arms race doesn't make any sense any more, does it? We can't do this any more. The threat of massive retaliation isn't credible anymore. It jeopardizes too much of what is precious to us.[3]

In May 1983, in response to heightened tensions caused by Reagan's plans for a Strategic Defense Initiative and the cavalier attitude his administration seemed to take toward nuclear war, an unusual organization was created in Moscow. The Soviet Scientists' Committee for the Defense of Peace Against Nuclear Threat (SSC) emerged from a conference called by the Soviet Academy of Sciences. It was not meant to replace the academy's own efforts, but rather to educate a younger generation of Soviet scientists in arms-control issues. Senior academicians participated in this effort, which focused primarily on ballistic-missile defenses, but NW was also studied. As an action-oriented group, the SSC may be compared to the Federation of American Scientists or the more activist Union of Concerned Scientists. Along with these and other organizations, such as the Soviet Committee of Physicians for the Prevention of Nuclear War (part of the international group that was awarded the Nobel Peace Prize in 1985), the goal of the SSC was to convince the public that nuclear war was not a realistic option.

Whether the SSC's views marked a degree of domestic liberalization in the rudderless final days of the ailing Andropov, who died in February 1984 and was succeeded as general secretary of the Communist Party of the Soviet Union by an equally infirm Konstantin Chernenko, or whether it merely reflected the government's positions, is not apparent, but the group did approach current issues vigorously. That its chairman, Velikhov, was the academy's vice president gave the committee immediate stature. One of the first studies it sponsored was by Vladimir Aleksandrov and G. L. Stenchikov of the academy's Computing Center, who used a three-dimensional computer model of Earth's climate. Their results, which agreed largely with those of TTAPS, were presented in 1983, first in Erice and then, 2 months later, at both the Halloween meeting and the Nuclear Freeze forum in Washington.[4]

Another impressive publication of the SSC was a fat survey of NW titled *The Night After . . . Scientists' Warning: Climatic and Biological Consequences of a Nuclear War*, which appeared in English translation in 1985. Although marred by several vitriolic condemnations of an imperialist US, it was overwhelmingly a thoughtful review of scientific information, based on work done in both the Soviet Union and the United States.[5]

Despite this activity, Soviet research on NW offered few if any new ideas to the debate and was regarded by all points on the political spectrum in the West largely to be derivative of findings in the United States. The American investigators nonetheless appreciated any fresh insights on their own results. Further, they wished to gain access to Soviet data that could help refine their calculations. During the "Moscow Link," which followed the Halloween 1983 conference, Sagan tried to put his fellow panelists on the spot. "Do our Soviet colleagues," he asked, "think it possible that they might supply data on the particle size distribution function of debris from Soviet nuclear weapons tests before the 1963 Limited Test Ban Treaty, and information on particle sizes and absorption coefficients from large fires in the Soviet Union? Also, will they eventually give us a range of nuclear war scenarios that they consider likely?"[6] Sagan's queries were awkwardly deflected. When repeated on subsequent occasions, they continued to be ignored.

Richard Turco was quickly disillusioned by the Soviets' behavior. At first they seemed eager to cooperate with American scientists, who were anxious to see their information from fire experiments. Particle size was critical for the absorption or transmission of solar radiation. But when new experiments never occurred and old data were withheld, the basis for real collaboration (with some exceptions) vanished. When Aleksandrov and Stenchikov were lauded for using the first 3-D computer model, an exasperated Turco remarked that it was "a very weak piece of work, crude and seriously flawed." Their model, he added, was "a primitive rendition of an obsolete US model." Unburdening himself to *Science* reporter R. Jeffrey Smith, Turco charged that "the Soviets have contributed little to the international 'nuclear winter' study effort thus far, and quite a few people are extremely disappointed." Starley Thompson joined in the criticism of the Moscow model: it "was developed in the United States in the early 1970s," it "contains a number of defects," and "one of [Aleksandrov's] major conclusions is apparently incorrect."

Their pique peaked after a mid-1984 visit to Leningrad by nearly two dozen American scientists. At a conference sponsored by the International Council of Scientific Unions, they anticipated learning details of Soviet nuclear tests in the atmosphere. Such data, or at least parts of such data, were generally unclassified in the West. Additionally, they expected to receive information collected from Siberian forest fires and hear of the planning for a large fire experiment. In all these areas they felt stonewalled; possibly, Turco mused, the Soviets were incapable of real contributions to NW, or planned only to manipulate NW for political purposes.[7]

Such indelicate remarks about other scientists are seldom placed "on the record," and an immediate protest by Aleksandrov forced the Americans to back-pedal a bit. Aleksandrov admitted that his was a "relatively simple climate model," and that his computer, although ten times faster than an IBM personal computer, had less memory. Certainly, he was capable of less than the NCAR model (and its supercomputer), but nonetheless he had produced results that supported TTAPS's findings. These results had been presented at no fewer than half a dozen international meetings, and neither Turco nor Thompson, who were at some of these meetings, had taken exception to his work.[8]

Thompson then showered Aleksandrov with compliments for his leading role in Soviet NW studies, recognized the limitations of his computing facility, and admitted that all models have defects—"weaknesses would be a better word." The defect to which he had originally referred was Aleksandrov's simplifying assumption that the smoke would decrease in stepwise fashion. This sudden removal of smoke, Thompson believed, led to an excessive warming of the surface. Turco was equally contrite, explaining that his critical remarks were taken out of the context of a wide-ranging discussion of NW research by the Soviets. He cautioned, however, that the work in Moscow "contained flaws not properly acknowledged or promptly corrected," and that Aleksandrov seemed not to be moving beyond the limitations of his model. Turco then took aim at the academicians who participated in the "Moscow Link" on 1 November 1983, for they had claimed an independent solution of the NW problem. "Nevertheless," he wrote, "during the subsequent 8-month period, no substantive physical data, and little evidence of objective scientific analyses, were forthcoming.

It would be artificial," he added, "not to be skeptical under such circumstances."[9] By the end of 1984, no one seemed to expect hard data or serious cooperation to be offered by the Soviet Union. At the SCOPE meeting in Paris, for example, a desired joint large-fire experiment was noticeably off the agenda.[10]

The US government tried to mount a coordinated national effort, but never quite succeeded. It is not clear whether the Soviet government ever made such an attempt. Their researchers also seem to have acted as individuals or groups within their several bureaucracies.[11]

The View from the United States

Written in the accusatory style of the first Reagan administration, when the Soviet Union was called the "evil empire," the 1985 DoD report on NW maintained that the USSR had conducted no independent research on the phenomenon, and indeed that Soviet scientists "show no evidence of regarding the whole matter as anything more than an opportunity for propaganda."[12] Soviet scientists, the report elaborated, "have neither used independent scenarios nor provided independent values of the essential parameters characterizing the key ingredients (soot, ash, and dust) on which the hypothesis principally depends." Moreover, they used a borrowed and now obsolete model developed in the United States.[13]

In a written statement submitted to a congressional hearing, Assistant Secretary of Defense Richard Perle elaborated on this view. The Soviets, he confided, "have used the nuclear winter issue to request access to US super-computers, software models and modeling techniques. Here lies an ultimate irony—that in the guise of expressing concern about the climatic danger of nuclear war the Soviets are seeking to steal Western technology to improve their nuclear arsenal."[14] Another irony, that of criticizing the quality of the Soviet research but denying them the equipment requested to improve their work, went unremarked.[15]

These indictments by Weinberger and Perle made a number of valid points, even if they overstated the case. Alan Robock, a University of Maryland meteorologist who had worked with Soviet scientists for 6 years, pointed out that "three-dimensional climate modeling was invented in the United States," so it was natural for others to base their work on the American contributions. Nonetheless, the first 3-D GCM experiment to be published was by Aleksandrov and Stenchikov. If their work was allegedly "crude" and "flawed," the same could be said of every paper published, for all attempted to remove some uncertainties from a hugely complex situation. Given the relatively poor computer facilities in Moscow, they properly simplified their model so it could be run in a reasonable time; it was by no means obsolete. That their results agreed with those of Americans showed the model's workability. Robock had given perhaps the first public lecture on NW in Leningrad (on 4 July 1984), to an audience of more than 100 people, and was convinced that the Soviet government was not interfering with scientific discussion of the subject. He further rebutted Perle's claim that Soviet interest in NW was a pretext to gain access to US technology. Under a decade-old environmental protection agreement, Soviet scientists already had such access, and NW provided no more. The charge that they were propagandists was untrue, Robock believed; he had never seen anyone misrepresenting scientific results for political purposes.[16]

To savvy political observers, the anti-Soviet comments by Weinberger and Perle probably were expected, if disappointing. Thus, in early April 1985, in sensible disregard of the Department of Defense's hostility, both houses of Congress offered resolutions urging the president to ask the Soviet government to create a joint commission to investigate the physical and biological effects of NW and the implications of such consequences for each superpower's security. (As I mention in chapter 12, the State Department Authorization Act of 1986 also asked the president to propose joint research with the Soviet Union.) The goal was both to influence the Soviets' actions and to learn more about what their investigations had uncovered. Senators William Proxmire and Mark Hatfield (R-Oregon) and Representatives Jerry Huckaby (D-Lousiana) and Morris Udall (D-Arizona), who led these efforts in their respective chambers, felt that it was in the self interest of each nation to participate. In time, the other declared nuclear powers—the United Kingdom, France, and the People's Republic of China—should be invited to join the commission. Two years later, however, Huckaby and Udall were still offering their unsuccessful resolution.[17]

The Department of State, despite Soviet enthusiasm for joint research, was seemingly intent on avoiding any expansion of scientific contact with the Soviet Union.[18] It replied that interchange under the 1972 bilateral Agreement on Cooperation on Environmental Protection already "meets the spirit of the resolution." In a memo revealed by Representative Edward Markey (D-Massachusetts) in a House hearing, State argued that a joint study of a large-scale set forest fire in Siberia was not considered because "some may believe it politically difficult for the United States to engage in such an experiment under the environmental exchange agreement since nuclear freeze advocates are so closely linked with the nuclear winter advocates."[19] The National Security Council, a bit more sensitive to the profundity of the NW prediction, commented that State "treats this issue more as if it were a US-Soviet project to investigate tornadoes than nuclear war." The NSC sought to assure Congress that it recognized the connection between NW and the policy choices one had with strategic weapons. Specifically, in support of missile-defense efforts, the NSC felt "it is extremely important to support our research into strategic defenses and other technologies that could reduce our dependence on nuclear offensive weapons," and, adopting some peacenik jargon and goals (to which it also could legitimately make a claim), "to continue to seek deep, verifiable reductions in the offensive arsenals of both the US and Soviet Union."[20]

Even the Environmental Protection Agency's administrator, Lee M. Thomas, was drawn into discussion of NW, although he had "no regulatory or research interest in the nuclear winter problem." He was the co-chair of the US-USSR Joint Committee on Cooperation in the Field of Environmental Protection, with a long-avoided first meeting of Reagan's presidency scheduled in the fall of 1985. Thomas expected the Soviet representatives to propose joint atmospheric research on NW, of the sort already planned in the US national program. Should the US be willing to cooperate, that would not greatly enlarge such efforts. But it was likely that the Soviets would also press to include "secondary and tertiary effects," such as "disruption of food chains and ecosystemic responses," and investigations of this kind would depart from US plans. Keyworth forwarded Thomas's concerns to the National Security Council, with a sympathetic cover letter, but no bilateral research program ever rose above the horizon.[21]

The US administration thus concentrated more on image than substance. Nonetheless, American scientists continued their unofficial contacts with counterparts in the USSR, both informally and when the latter acted through the Soviet Academy of Sciences. That this was possible is a reflection on the remarkable, if not unprecedented, circumstance that this research on nuclear weapons' effects almost entirely avoided the shroud of security classification. Why this was so is not entirely clear, for there is a tradition of technical subjects being "born secret," to the point that some were even taken away from their discoverers who happened to lack clearance. NW was not enveloped in such secrecy, perhaps because its high visibility would have made a blackout poor politics.

Contacts between American and Soviet scientists continued also because both governments recognized that the long series of Pugwash meetings, the many talks sponsored by the Federation of American Scientists, and numerous other interchanges provided valuable ideas for containing the arms race. Since June 1981, for example, members of the National Academy of Sciences' Committee on International Security and Arms Control, chaired by Caltech president Marvin Goldberger, had been meeting to discuss (successfully) a ban on anti-satellite systems with their counterparts in the Soviet Academy of Sciences.[22]

S. Fred Singer saw nothing but duplicity in the Soviet interest in NW. The phenomenon, he felt, had been given widespread coverage in the USSR, and prominent scientists who believed in NW had been made available for various international meetings, both to further their government's plot to constrict the US arsenal.[23] Soviet specialist Leon Gouré was of the same mind. Moscow, he emphasized, gave much publicity to NW, just as it did to other worst-case scenarios of nuclear warfare conceived in the West. The purpose was "to influence Western public opinion and US defense programs." Soviet defense policies, he noted, had not been affected by the NW concept.[24] (Nor had US policies. For example, an intense battle between Secretary of State Shultz and Secretary of Defense Weinberger, pro and con, respectively, over whether to adhere to the provisions of the unratified SALT II treaty, despite frequent charges that the Soviets repeatedly violated it, was decided by the president in favor of State, without NW entering the discussion.[25])

Gouré also argued that the unanimity of scientific opinion in the USSR, on a subject embedded with uncertainties, surely suggested that propaganda ruled over research.[26] This was disputed by Stephen Shenfield of the University of Birmingham's Centre for Russian and East European Studies. He admitted that Soviet scientists might use their NW research for propaganda, but insisted that their work was "genuine, substantive and relatively autonomous," with a likely impact on their political leaders.[27] Even Stephen Schneider and Richard Turco, who saw no conspiracy among Soviet scientists, explained to Aleksandrov that the lack of debate in his country left them unclear about the role of propaganda.[28] Stirring the pot further, Brian Martin (of the Department of Science and Technology Studies at Australia's University of Wollongong) concluded that Soviet scientists emphasized the worst effects of NW even more than Westerners, clearly a propaganda effort.[29] The Soviet public also was exposed to positive expositions of NW and criticism of those Americans who minimized its seriousness.[30]

Soviet scientists, naturally, saw nothing sinister in their own behavior. And they were refreshingly open in admitting their goal, more so than most of their American colleagues. Presumably, this was because it was politically acceptable for them, while politically indelicate for the Americans. Frank von Hippel, who traveled to Moscow in the fall of 1983, easily signed up Yevgeny Velikhov and Sergei Kapitsa for the Nuclear Freeze forum in Washington at the end of that year.[31] In a review of Soviet research, published by the prestigious Stockholm International Peace Research Institute (SIPRI) in its 1985 yearbook *World Armaments and Disarmament*, A. S. Ginsburg, G. S. Golitsyn, and A. A. Vasiliev placed themselves in a tradition that dated from the end of World War II: ". . . the efforts of scholars in many countries and various scientific fields, trying to investigate thoroughly and expose the results of a nuclear conflict, are a logical continuation of the anti-war activities of scientists."[32]

Most American scientists tried to keep their political comments (as when writing for the *Bulletin of the Atomic Scientists*) separate from reports of their technical work. By so doing, they felt themselves honest in defending their research as high-quality science, unmotivated by political aims. Regardless of Moscow's (or Washington's) machinations, they felt that it was wiser to learn as much as possible of Soviet accomplishments than to ignore them. Nor should the political aspect of the Soviet work be discounted: if concern about the phenomenon carried to the highest levels in the Kremlin, it gave the US government another reason to treat NW seriously. Michael May, the Livermore Laboratory's former director and at that time an associate director at large, consulted with administration leaders (the National Climate Program Office's Alan Hecht in this case) to convey semi-official information to Moscow. There, May discussed fire research with the Soviet Academy of Sciences' vice president, Yevgeny Velikhov, in mid 1984.[33]

Even Edward Teller was on record in favor of joint research on the effects of a large-scale nuclear war.[34] So too was the Soviet Scientists' Committee for the Defense of Peace Against Nuclear Threat, whose vice chairman Roald Sagdeev (also the director of the Soviet Institute of Space Research) warmly endorsed collaboration.[35] Little if anything came of such appeals. While the US and the USSR could work together on a range of basic research endeavors involving scientists visiting each other's laboratories, other events, such as the International Geophysical Year in the 1950s, during which Cold War attitudes prevented real cooperation, showed the difficulties of joint work when issues of hegemony were involved.[36] In this light, the major national security implications of NW made it an unlikely vehicle for such an exchange. Moreover, American scientists generally had a low opinion of Soviet research on NW, a judgment that would have been reinforced by the lackluster SIPRI review of their work cited above.

Soviet Activities

Scientists in the USSR nonetheless were not unprepared for NW investigations. Nikita N. Moiseyev had installed a planetary climate modeling program at the Computing Center in Moscow, and Georgi S. Golitsyn had examined Martian dust storms for the past decade.[37] Climate modeling seems to have been the Soviets' greatest strength, but they could not compete with the resources of the West. The Computing Center was stuck with its GCM that coarsely diced the atmosphere into two vertical layers and horizontal dimensions of 12° in longitude and 15° in latitude. It took more than a year, for example, to respond to criticisms that the early 3-D work by Vladimir Aleksandrov and Georgi Stenchikov over-stated by far the megatonnage of a conflict and removed smoke in an unrealistic stepwise fashion over time. The former pumped more smoke into the atmosphere and lengthened the duration of cooling; the latter accounted for a spurt of excessive warming.

In 1985, Stenchikov and P. Carl (of the Central Institute of Electron Physics in the German Democratic Republic—that is, East Germany), looked at the same 10,000-MT and 100-MT scenarios as before (which had been adopted from the several described by TTAPS), but modified their program to allow the previously stationary aerosols to move about. With more realistic smoke removal, temperature declines were somewhat reduced, but the geographical pattern of this effect was much the same as before. They also emphasized how similar the temperature decreases after about a month were in the two scenarios, indicating that both cut off almost all sunlight to the surface.[38] While the accuracy of the conclusions was almost immediately superseded by parallel work in the West, this research had the merit of being one of the relatively few examples of a new investigation and not a survey (however worthwhile).

In 1984, the Soviet Scientists' Committee for the Defense of Peace Against Nuclear Threat published not a research report but a technical primer designed to educate other scientists. Golitsyn, chief of the climate theory section of the Institute of Atmospheric Physics in Moscow (and elevated to the 47-member presidium of the Soviet Academy in October 1988),[39] and A. S. Ginsburg, deputy chief of the climate theory laboratory at the same institute, surveyed 10 years' work on atmospheric physics, including dust storms on Mars, ozone depletion, dinosaur extinction, and the concept of NW. Soviet research was emphasized, but appropriate foreign sources were noted.[40]

Another publication of the SSC in the same year bore more marks of original thought. Anatoly A. Gromyko, director of the Institute of African Studies, chaired a group of more than a dozen scholars that focused on the effects of NW on developing countries. Although the text opened with a propagandistic statement ("In the early 1980s the international situation took a sharp turn for the worse through the fault of the more adventuristic and aggressive circles in the West"), it continued with a straightforward review of climatic and biological consequences that seemed largely derived from the 1983 TTAPS paper and the counterpart study by Paul Ehrlich and his colleagues.

New ground was broken in assembling information about developing nations, such as the fact that these countries, although poor, are nonetheless part of the world economy. The states of tropical Africa, for example, require technical and food aid valued at 50 percent more than their gross output. Nuclear war, and especially the consequences of NW, would throw these economies into chaos, also bringing political, social, cultural, and medical turmoil. Famine would affect the 180 million Africans living in urban areas, as food imports ceased. North Africa would be particularly hard hit, as more than half the population dwell in cities. Lacking fuel, industry and transportation would come to a halt. Export of cash crops, such as coffee and cotton, would cease, as markets vanished. Even subsistence agriculture would be seriously affected by the hostile climatic conditions. This devastating picture painted for the Third World was notable not for its conclusions, for they were duplicated in far greater detail in other studies, such as the 1985 SCOPE report, but for its early attempt at such an assessment. A point not seen in other studies noted the additional vulnerability of developing nations: because they hosted a large percentage of the 1,500 American military bases distributed in 32 countries on all continents except Antarctica, they were potential targets of a Soviet retaliatory strike.[41]

Another climatological work that emphasized Soviet contributions was a thin volume published in Leningrad in 1986. Because that work was too technical for popular reading, and because it extended to natural catastrophes as well as nuclear ones, it is difficult to define its intended audience. But it was authoritative, with the distinguished Michael I. Budyko, of the State Hydrological Institute in Leningrad, as chief author, and Georgi S. Golitsyn and Yuri A. Izrael, of the State Committee on Hydrometeorology and Control of Natural Environment in Moscow, as co-authors. Golitsyn had attended both the April 1983 conference in Cambridge, organized by Sagan, and the Halloween meeting in Washington later that year. Izrael had participated in the televised "Moscow Link," conducted immediately after the Halloween sessions ended.

A reasonable survey of NW conclusions, the book is notable for a surprising number of priority claims. Soviet scientists, the authors stated, were in the forefront when the new discipline of physical climatology began to develop in the late 1960s. "In particular," they maintained, "the theory of aerosol climatic catastrophe appeared in studies by Soviet scientists more than 10 years earlier than similar conclusions in other countries." NW was another first: "This conclusion was discussed at a number of national and international meetings in the early 1980s just before the appearance of the first publications on this problem."[42] Of course, climate changes were also discussed at meetings in the West before publication. Whether these priority claims—almost a staple of Soviet behavior—are legitimate or not, they have not been supported by a documented trail of specific research results and their dates.

Like their Western counterparts, the authors were concerned about uncertainties, such as phenomena that occurred on micro and meso scales being represented in GCMs of far larger scales. Still, they remained confident in the reality of NW: "Almost all scientists concerned with the problem of climatic change after a nuclear war support the conclusion of the likelihood of a great aerosol catastrophe."[43]

As in the West, scientists from the Institute of Atmospheric Physics and the Karpov Physico-Chemical Institute burned numerous materials under laboratory conditions, determining the smoke yield from each and various microphysical and optical properties. Such values provided greater confidence in their GCM calculations. Soviet scientists also participated actively in the SCOPE study, hosting three working meetings in the USSR. In addition, they led in preparing two reports for the World Meteorological Organization and engaged in work by the European Physical Society.[44]

This sketch of Soviet activity involving NW, in addition to the research I described in chapter 13, draws a picture of relatively limited capabilities, constrained efforts, and minimal results. Confirmation of work done in the West seems to have been its chief characteristic. The Kremlin may have been more interested in NW than the White House, but there is no evidence of manpower and resources ever being directed massively at the study. NW was, nonetheless, occasionally used for political purposes. On 18 August 1986, for example, General Secretary Mikhail Gorbachev proclaimed a unilateral extension, to 1 January 1987, of the Soviet moratorium on nuclear testing (not matched by the United States). As part of his explanation, he asserted: "If someone still dares make a first nuclear strike, he will doom himself to agonizing death—not even from a retaliatory strike but from the consequences of the explosion of his own warheads."[45] Although he avoided using the term "nuclear winter," Gorbachev could not have been referring to anything else. Also, by calling it a "reality," his endorsement of the concept could not have been stronger. Scientists in the United States, nonetheless, seem to have been better able to manipulate a more flexible (and better equipped) scientific structure within the government, even when the bureaucrats were somewhat hostile.

Aleksandrov

In 1985, disaster struck the Soviet NW program. Its leading investigator, a major publicist of NW and a man who had endeared himself to his American counterparts, disappeared in Spain. Amid unsubstantiated speculation that Vladimir Aleksandrov (a) had been kidnapped by the KGB, perhaps preemptively because they suspected he had plans to defect to the

West, or because he had rubbed them the wrong way by requesting medical treatment for his wife in England, or (b) that he had successfully defected to the CIA with results from his earlier work on the plasma surrounding reentry vehicles from space, or (c) that his jokes and erratic behavior cost him access to American supercomputers and then an American visa, infuriating his political superiors, who had wanted him to remain internationally visible, or (d) that his lack of research progress, as others in the West refined NW, hurt his credibility, or even (e) that he was assassinated by unknown persons trying to sabotage any arms-control steps that might be taken if the climatic catastrophe was more solidly assured, a frantic search failed to find him.

Aleksandrov had spoken at a political meeting in Córdoba, Spain, in March 1985, and returned by car to Madrid, but never appeared for an appointment at the Soviet embassy. Although not a heavy drinker, both before and after his talk he had gotten roaring drunk, a sin he must have known was commonly punished by ending travel privileges. Portending criminal assault or defection, his passport and airline tickets were found in a trash receptacle. Defection seemed unlikely, lacking any evidence of disillusionment with communism. Moreover, he was trusted well enough to travel frequently outside the Soviet Union, and he appeared to be close to his wife and daughter, who were still in Moscow. Foul play remained an unsupported possibility, but Spanish authorities found no evidence of it.[46]

Nor did anyone ever find Aleksandrov. One apparent repercussion of his disappearance was the unexplained failure of the Soviet delegation to make its customary appearance at the International Seminar on Nuclear War, held annually in Erice.[47] Another consequence was the absence of Aleksandrov's name from the volume *The Night After*, in which his work nevertheless was cited. This purge resembled a Stalin-era rewriting of history. A further effect was the obvious embarrassment of the delegation to the June 1985 SCOPE symposium at the University of Essex. Though that was not the last event dealing with NW attended by Soviet scientists—Golitsyn, for example, spoke at an ICSU conference in Berne, Switzerland in September 1986—the era of jet travel to NW meetings was on the decline. *Literaturnaya Gazeta* claimed that Aleksandrov's disappearance caused this break,[48] but it is more likely that SCOPE's work now was mostly done and its further international conferences were regarded as of lesser importance (although Moscow hosted one in March 1988). All told, the hope that NW would provide a vehicle for technical cooperation between the superpowers, in an area dealing with national security and promoting better diplomatic relations, faded away.

The public did not become excited about NW. No gripping *On the Beach*-type novels were written, no delightfully sarcastic and humorous songs of the Tom Lehrer variety were composed, no blockbuster movies used NW as a theme.[1] The closest approach to popular culture was a passing mention of NW in the boring 1996 science-fiction film *Independence Day*. But the advent of NW was an occasion for nuclear analysts and policy wonks to think seriously about the issues.

Carl Sagan and other NW proponents ultimately failed in their endeavors to move the US government to study the political consequences of the phenomenon. But NW generated a large and rich outpouring of policy ideas and analyses anyway. The subject gave planners numerous options: it could be taken as a rationale for arms expansion (such as offensive earth penetrators and defensive ballistic-missile defense), for arms control (for example, Sagan's proposals in *Foreign Affairs*), and for doing nothing. It provided an array of policy choices in times of conflict, ranging from a first strike of yield just below the threshold for NW (assuming the target nation would not respond), to non-urban targeting, to nuclear abstinence. Along this spectrum, there was a sophisticated and multifaceted assortment of nuances to policy. A number of policy issues have already been presented in the unfolding of the historical development of the debate. Here, some issues are addressed again, while others are introduced.

Asymmetries and Slow Changes

For all his alleged faults as a biased gadfly, S. Fred Singer was a practiced and thoughtful analyst. In mid 1984 he ruminated about a threshold for climatic effects. This was not the relatively well-defined and strikingly minimal megatonnage championed by Sagan that had been ridiculed so strongly. Singer did not try to specify when it might occur, for he recognized that the threshold "cannot be a very precise number in terms of megatons or warheads exploded, but will depend on how they are exploded, at what altitude, at what time of the year, against what targets, etc." While a threshold had to exist, he fully expected it to be very broad, and this had strategic implications.[2]

The "effects on the US and USSR are *not* symmetric," Singer reasoned; indeed, the Soviets were actually disadvantaged. Their dominance in large-yield weapons would be a handicap, for they produce a greater environmental effect while having little more advantage against hard targets than smaller but more accurate American warheads. Moscow might therefore be hesitant to fire its weapons, but Washington would operate under less restraint, since its weapons would ignite fewer fires, especially in often-snow-covered Russia.[3] (Including the energy required to melt one inch of snow, Singer calculated it would take at least 700 times as much energy to ignite flammables than in dry conditions.[4])

There were still other asymmetries, Singer continued. These included smaller quantities of fuel stored in the Soviet Union that might be ignited by explosions, their far more unstable agricultural system, and the minimal moderation of that nation's climate by oceanic heat sinks. Earlier in the Cold War, Russia's large geographic extent with sparse population might have served to "dilute" the effects of radioactive fallout. In a hemispheric chill, however, this would be of no advantage. Now, too, urban dwellers would find civil defense preparations inadequate against low temperatures. From Singer's perspective, NW was far worse news for the USSR than for the US.[5] In this, Michael May concurred. The Livermore Laboratory's former director argued that the fates of the US and the USSR would differ: the Pacific Ocean, which cannot burn, is upwind of the United States, while a flammable Europe is upwind of the Soviet Union.[6]

These differences would be apparent, Singer noted, after an exchange of strategic nuclear weapons. But what about tactical nuclear weapons? Many in both superpowers believed that in reality there was no difference between the use of these two types of nuclear weapons. Since neither side would wish to lose a battle, escalation would inexorably occur, leading to a major war. With NW, however, Singer saw a "decoupling" between tactical and strategic employment of nuclear weapons, because the small explosions would present little threat of widespread fires. If tactical weapons of the enhanced-radiation variety (often called neutron bombs) were employed, their suppressed blast and heat effects would reduce any NW consequences still further. The United States could then continue its tactical nuclear plans to thwart a Warsaw Pact tank thrust through northern Europe. The Soviet military and political leadership seemed to have accepted the reality of the NW phenomenon, but Singer now wondered if they would disown it once they recognized their disadvantage under its scenarios.[7]

Changes in Third World thinking must also flow from NW, Singer wrote. Rogue states such as Khomeini's Iran and Qaddafi's Libya, and even more responsible nations such as China, it was believed, had looked to their ascendancy following war between the superpowers. In similar anticipation, some strategists in the United States had hoped for a Soviet-Chinese confrontation. Now, since NW might bring hemispheric, if not global, tragedy, self-interest should impel even the non-superpowers to urge the avoidance of nuclear war.[8]

At the end of 1984, Philip Romero, a graduate fellow at the Rand Corporation's Graduate Institute in Santa Monica, provided a thoughtful, sober analysis of war strategies. Assuming little change in the arsenals, Romero felt, "there will be no 'overnight revolutions' in doctrine or force postures."[9] But thought would be given to changes that might increase chances of survival. Warfare below NW's rough threshold would be examined, such as avoiding highly flammable targets and using as few weapons as possible.

Cities were already a low priority, Romero noted—it made more sense to destroy first an enemy's weapons that could harm you—and threats against them came to be regarded over recent decades as both immoral and not credible. (Unless, as TTAPS argued, they contained military and industrial sites targeted in the first launch of missiles.) Should the war get to the second launch, possible targets might be the less flammable suburbs upwind of cities, and then urban inhabitants would experience radioactive fallout instead of flames. Also, if fewer warheads were employed, the conflict could continue over an extended period of time. Some military experts had previously claimed that nuclear war could not be limited; rapid escalation was inevitable. NW, Romero pointed out, "would *guarantee* protraction in the future," and advantage would go to the side with logistics and C^3I for its strategic forces that were capable of the greatest endurance.[10]

In a time of crisis, these logistical and C^3I assets, as well as mobile ICBMs and missile-firing submarines (in harbors) might be deployed within cities. Similarly, troops might surround themselves with huge amounts of combustible materials. Both steps would constitute a form of doomsday machine to ward off a first strike that could boomerang on the attacker.

On the far horizon, say in a few decades, Romero saw some reconfiguration of the arsenals. Still more accurate guidance systems coupled with earth-penetrating nuclear warheads would minimize fire ignition and lofting of dust. At some point, conventional explosives, and chemical and biological weapons, delivered with precision, would suffice to destroy their targets. Protection would involve concealment and mobility, with the enemy's satellite reconnaissance systems fated for early attack. Overall, Romero believed that fear of NW would make nations more reluctant to employ nuclear weapons, thereby enhancing stability in crises and reducing the carnage should the fuses ever be lit. Interestingly, research and development already under way pointed in the direction Romero described, while the strategic policy of neither superpower needed to change very much.[11]

From the Rand Corporation's office in Washington came another policy study. J. J. Gertler argued that discussion of short- and long-term consequences should not be delayed while waiting for scientific validation of the phenomenon's reality. *Perception* would mold the behavior of nations if they accepted the possibility of NW. Like Romero, Gertler believed that the existing reluctance to use nuclear weapons would intensify. NATO allies, which depended on a US pledge to regard an attack on them as an attack on the US, and which had accepted the willingness of the US to use nuclear weapons in such circumstances, would then doubt the credibility of this "nuclear umbrella." Should World War III occur and NW follow, Gertler continued, the Southern Hemisphere would suffer relatively less. The United States would be wise now to polish its relations with these potential bread-basket countries south of the Equator (who would not be well disposed toward the superpowers in any case). Because the NW scenario might be initiated by a relatively small number of weapons, other nuclear powers than the United States and the Soviet Union might be the combatants. This possibility could lead to a much more interventionist foreign policy by Washington and Moscow, as they sought to restrain the rivalries of other countries, even to the point of disarming them. (Had Gertler been writing 10 years later, he likely would have cited India and Pakistan as prime examples.) Allies such as Great Britain and France were already, or soon would be, capable of destroying all large Soviet cities. This tended to make the US nuclear umbrella superfluous; the Europeans themselves could cause NW. This might lead to "calls on both sides of the Atlantic for a decoupling of the US strategic arsenal from European defense (making NATO a conventional-defense-only treaty) and so would drive another wedge into the gap between the allies." The positive spin on NW was that it could lead to stronger non-proliferation efforts.[12]

Gertler criticized those who claimed that NW was "just another horror." This implied that nuclear war was already as bad as conflict could possibly get, which meant, he said, that the US would do anything to avoid it. Such an attitude completely devalued the credibility of the nuclear deterrent, for an enemy would conclude that the threat to use these weapons was a paper tiger. Also devalued was the "window of vulnerability" argument upon which Ronald Reagan rode to the presidency. In that scenario, fashioned by the Committee on the Present Danger, the Soviets would deliver a disabling first strike on American strategic forces, leaving intact only the less accurate (and harder to find) submarine-launched ballistic missiles. The United States would be reluctant to retaliate against Soviet cities since that would invite similar devastation in North America. In the late 1970s, the solution proposed was to increase the US arsenal mightily, so enough of it would escape destruction in the initial spasm of war. By the mid 1980s, NW made a first strike suicidal, even without retaliation.[13]

Another political scientist who cast his gaze upon NW was George Quester, a distinguished nuclear analyst at the University of Maryland. "Perhaps," he wrote, "we should indeed heave a sigh of relief at all the additional complications for civil defense and postwar recovery that continue to be uncovered, for each of these complications simply amounts to one more reinforcement of strategic stability and deterrence, one more argument against anyone's wishing to grasp for a sneak-attack nuclear victory or fearing that the other side was contemplating such a move."[14]

Quester found the concept of a doomsday machine intriguing. He pointed out that such a device is of no value unless the enemy knows of its existence; being so informed, he will behave with caution. It was not the threat of unbearable destruction that maintained global apprehension, Quester suggested, but the contrary arguments of some analysts who felt that civil defense or other actions could deny the "assured" part of mutual assured destruction. Now, NW might reaffirm widespread destruction, removing incentives to try to beat the odds. Even more, NW might confirm belief that the deterrents were adequate.[15]

Strategic Defense

When Cold Warriors looked at NW, they saw another reason for pursuing Reagan's Strategic Defense Initiative. In early 1984, Keith Payne and Colin Gray, respectively executive vice president and president of the private National Institute for Public Policy, wrote a long and positive analysis of ballistic-missile defense for the prominent policy journal *Foreign Affairs*. As icing on their argument, they maintained that "strategic defense is the only candidate answer to this potential threat to humanity [that is, NW]." It was "incredible," they felt, to expect that arms-control negotiations could ever reduce the huge arsenals to a point where the climatic catastrophe was impossible. Spaced-based defenses, however, could intercept Soviet missiles in their launch and mid-course phases, before they released their MIRVed warheads, while ground-based defenses would destroy whatever leaked through the outer parts of the shield. Together these barriers would reduce to almost nothing the possibility of damage to the United States. Nuclear deterrence based on offensive weapons, Payne and Gray maintained, could never offer the kind of security and freedom from fear desired by most people, but deterrence based on a many-layered and effective defensive system could provide that stability. For them it was a "moral imperative" to seek such a strategic policy.[16]

Carl Sagan, usually enthusiastic for NASA's glittering gadgets, was not a technological optimist when it came to missile defense. Unlike Payne and Gray, he saw SDI as a threat, not a solution. Even under the best of circumstances, the system would be sufficiently porous to incoming warheads for them to destroy the United States as a functioning society. But if the US went ahead with this shield, the Soviets' inevitable response would be to increase their offensive missile arsenal greatly. And this was exactly the wrong move to force on them, for it amplified the likely effects of NW.[17]

Just the opposite was called for. Turco and Sagan argued that, since NW strengthened nuclear deterrence and reinforced the movement toward minimum deterrent forces (Sagan liked to call it "minimum sufficient deterrence," a better sound bite for the public), these forces could be structured to minimize (or avoid) potential environmental effects. They believed that tactical nuclear weapons should be eliminated completely, since they could lead to escalation, and conventional forces had to be equalized. SDI, they felt, was inconsistent with US goals; it offered only a marginal amount of protection, while raising too many problems.[18]

Colin Gray, convinced that there would always be uncertainties about warfare, dismissed NW's usefulness: ". . . nuclear winter is, and is likely long to remain, a 'wild card' inherently resistant to analysts looking for relevant advice for operational policy." What, he asked, would an American president do if he truly believed in the validity of NW? He could attempt to negotiate, with all members of the nuclear club, severe reductions in their arsenals. But would Britain, France, and China agree to a tiny number of weapons? Might not nations hide away a few bombs or missiles? Alternatively, the president might unilaterally choose to reduce the US arsenal below the level at which NW was a threat. Would the allies of the US then choose to build up their own arsenals, creating new instabilities? A pragmatist, Gray argued that "the key question in strategy is not 'is it right,' rather it is 'will it work.'" A third presidential choice was the only realistic one in Gray's opinion: technological steps, particularly SDI.[19]

The strategic analysts Francis Hoeber and Robert Squire echoed Gertler on the importance for policy of a nation's perception of NW, and, like Payne and Gray, embraced the value of strategic defense. (Hoeber, an alumnus of several think tanks, was at the time president of his own consulting company; Squire, with a background at the Livermore Lab and in the DoD hierarchy, was at the time a defense contractor.) There were so many uncertainties surrounding NW, they noted in the summer 1985 issue of *Strategic Review*, that opponents felt free to fault any belief in the phenomenon. But these same uncertainties made it impossible to deny the validity of NW. Thus, while scientists sought to achieve some consensus on this issue, it was useful, they said, to examine the political implications of the view that NW was real. In a way, the reality of NW was irrelevant (until the warheads exploded), since governments act on beliefs, not absolute knowledge. If NW was *accepted* as legitimate, policy would incorporate it. This was logical, since nuclear warfare, even without NW, was filled with uncertainties and yet governments constructed policies.[20]

An understanding of crucial concern was that the United States would never really know what Soviet planners believed about NW. The best we could do was to observe their actions and largely ignore their rhetoric—as we had been doing all along. Hoeber and Squire made the interesting observation that no policy alterations had been detected in the Kremlin, despite Soviet expressions of belief in NW. Was this, they wondered, an example of "dezinformatsia"?[21]

Centrist Thoughts

A short time after the National Academy of Sciences' report appeared, its theme of "possible but uncertain" was carried into the academy's new policy journal, *Issues in Science and Technology*, which featured NW in its winter 1985 issue. Articles by George Carrier, who admitted that extreme climatic effects were possible, and the DoD's Richard Wagner, who urged further research but found no basis for changing defense policies, presented expected views. So too did MIT's George Rathjens and his graduate student Ronald Siegel, in criticizing the research done on smoke. More novel was the analysis of Livermore's Michael May, who agreed with Wagner that it was "too soon to assess what influence the global climatic effects of fires started in a nuclear war should have on targeting policy, weapons acquisition, arms-control policy, and other strategic matters," but nonetheless extracted some substance from the current situation.[22]

The weapons used in a war and the manner in which they are employed, May noted, are highly variable. Similarly, season, weather, and geography offer their own set of constraints on the severity of the smoke's effects. Doomsday would, thus, not automatically ensue from a large exchange; the consequences would depend strongly on the conditions. This meant that a single threshold could not be specified. It also meant that NW might not be avoided merely by reducing the yield of the weapons used. Such uncertainties inherent in NW would deprive strategic planners of the ability to incorporate the phenomenon into their calculus of warfare. While this might at first glance seem unacceptable, May pointed out that radioactive fallout and ozone depletion also proved to be incommensurable with planning (as well as less serious than first believed).[23] We learned to live (in matters of defense) with these uncertainties by ignoring them!

Al Gore Jr., recently elected to the Senate, offered political insights. Perfect arms control and perfect defenses were simplistic and unachievable. Indeed, an attempt to build a missile defense system would perversely induce other nations to expand their arsenals, potentially making any future war worse. Politics being the art of the possible, Gore sought a middle path, a blend of avoiding nuclear war but minimizing its consequences should it occur. To achieve this, both arms-control efforts and weapons acquisitions should conform to the principle that neither side need fear a first strike. The goal of arms control should be not merely parity but mutual stability. Gore was open to discussion of various policy and hardware choices and, since other nations would be affected by NW, he provocatively suggested that it might be wise to offer them "a voice in our deliberations."[24]

Rathjens and Siegel expressed interest in the much-discussed earth-penetrating weapons and the option to fuse other warheads to explode at low, rather than high, altitude. Both would reduce the incidence of fire, although radioactivity would increase in the large amounts of dust lofted. Their most interesting insight concerned Third World nations that contained no targets but would be imperiled by NW. Should the risk of NW prove to be severe, such countries could survive by stockpiling food and fuel, and by providing appropriate shelter for their populations. "People do, after all, live through long, cold, dark winters with no great difficulty, *if* they are prepared." Sadly, though, these were the nations least able to finance the needed effort.[25]

The military analyst and physicist Theodore Postol saw little reason to expect a change in the US-USSR relationship. Since deterrence was based on the concept of mutual assured destruction, NW added only marginally to the superpowers' concern, for an attack on a city was already homicidal and suicidal. NW would, however, affect the conduct of the war. In addition to military matters, if nuclear smoke and dust degraded the early warning and reconnaissance ability of satellites, the fog of war would be literal. The information needed for escalation control would be absent and the ability to limit the nuclear exchange would be an early casualty.[26]

For somewhat different reasons, Jeremy Stone, president of the Federation of American Scientists, agreed that NW would have little effect on defense policy. Since the United States had always looked more to its own security than to that of the world (a charge valid for any nation), and its overriding concern in the nuclear era was to avoid uncontrolled escalation should war occur, Stone believed that enormous constraints to both conflict and its intensification already existed. In these views he differed little from those of the administration. But Stone agreed with Sagan that the stakes now were much higher, and that we should think more in terms of the planet's well-being. A review of war policy surely was justified, particularly those parts of the Single Integrated Operational Plan that weakened constraints on aiming warheads at cities. In October 1980, Stone related, the Carter administration abandoned the strategic requirement that the United States be able to destroy 70 percent of Soviet military and war-supporting industrial assets. Yet, Stone continued, the best analyst of the SIOP, Desmond Ball, found that the 300 largest urban-industrial areas of the Soviet Union would still receive about the same nuclear blows as before and suffer the same damage. NW, Stone felt, might also serve the useful function of convincing American planners that their country's vaunted science and technology would be inadequate to monitor the progress of a war and to control military forces. We now had an opportunity to collaborate with the Soviets, by convincing them that it was suicidal for them to target North American cities. Stone charged that the DoD seemed more intent on preventing NW from undermining its own plans than in exploring ways to remove our cities from Soviet crosshairs.[27]

The political scientist Allen Lynch distinguished between "existential deterrence"—the need to avoid using nuclear weapons because both sides had them (also termed "mutual assured destruction")—and "deterrence as doctrine." The latter involved planning how to employ the weapons for foreign policy goals, using presumably credible scenarios that would convince opponents and reassure allies that nuclear explosives really might be used. NATO's insistence on a strategy in which it might use nuclear weapons first is an example of deterrence as doctrine. Lynch saw little or no impact of NW on existential deterrence, for it only reinforced the view that these weapons could not be used. NW did, however, have potential effect on deterrence as doctrine, because it removed the possibility of "victory" in nuclear war. The execution of a perfect first strike, for example, no longer assured victory, but instead brought the climatic catastrophe upon the aggressor's own head. NW thus could undercut the credibility of deterrence as doctrine.[28]

Nuclear Winter as a Diversion

Albert Wohlstetter, a well-known strategic analyst, recalled a celebrated 1958 exchange between Bertrand Russell and Sidney Hook. The two philosophers had argued whether it was better to be Red or dead, a phrase that became a shorthand cue for the perpetual dove-versus-hawk debate. Wohlstetter saw the latest incarnation of the "Red" side of this divide in current apocalyptic visions of nuclear warfare, such as *The Day After* and the NW phenomenon. "Does that possibility," Wohlstetter asked in *Foreign Affairs*, "require us to subordinate all considerations of freedom to survival and to dismiss any possibility of responding justly to a nuclear attack—or at least without committing suicide?"[29]

In Wohlstetter's view, the political establishment felt that deterrence worked because the alternative was so ghastly; indeed, "the more horror the better," which explained the popularity of the reaffirming TV shows and the TTAPS report. In consequence, public attitudes had drifted toward a position of "deterrence only," which he defined as surrender if deterrence failed. "It appears then," he wrote, "that we may be faced with a choice between darkness at noon in the political sense of Koestler or darkness at noon in the literal sense." Yet such options were often too starkly presented. Despite the strident cries of Manhattan Project scientists after World War II that the choice was only between one world or none, and that deterrence was too fragile a reed to lean upon, Soviet behavior had removed the possibility of a world in harmony and the United States had learned that the alternative was not "none." Tactical nuclear weapons, civil defense, and air defense against enemy bombers were some of the programs pursued in the 1950s to cope with the threat of nuclear war.[30]

By the end of the 1950s, however, fusion weapons atop ballistic missiles, with their inaccuracies in targeting, had led both to the belief that nuclear war could not be contained and to the belief that cities (which were larger than military assets) must be targeted. A consequence of this was the long-lived concept of mutual assured destruction, whose extreme potential would later fit the thinking of the NW theorists. Wohlstetter scornfully noted that for such people it was evil to develop "more discriminately effective offense and defense weapons or any preparations to respond to attack in ways that would confine destruction to military targets." TTAPS, he charged, skewed the debate toward their preferred goals by deliberately choosing scenarios that invoked "enormous collateral damage both local and global."[31]

In his summer 1985 paper, Wohlstetter used his formidable powers of argument to parade the now-familiar uncertainties of TTAPS's work—and to criticize most US strategic planning, especially mutual assured destruction. MAD (never a sensible policy in his eyes, because the targets were urban populations) made even less sense if one accepted the possibility of NW. Believing that nuclear wars would be fought by rational people capable of avoiding escalation, Wohlstetter deplored the TTAPS and NAS baseline cases for their assumption that the adversaries would behave in ways harmful to themselves by such large exchanges. Especially if the superpowers believed in NW, it was even less credible that they would fight in such ways under its "shadow." Recent scenarios suggested by the Swedish Academy of Sciences (publisher of *Ambio*) and the World Health Organization also were faulty, Wohlstetter felt, for they involved unrealistically large megaton attacks on numerous Third World cities and in the Southern Hemisphere. Even TTAPS's "small" 100-MT war, Wohlstetter argued, though restricted to NATO and Warsaw Pact cities, was unreasonable: it was *not* small and it was not an example of limiting collateral damage when attacking military targets. By having the protagonists fight mindlessly and in ways that maximized the climatic effects, Sagan calculated a meaningless threshold and then arrived at arms reduction recommendations so enormous that they were not likely ever to be adopted. "Nuclear winter theorists propose such Utopian solutions," wrote Wohlstetter, because they reject the idea that an attacker could use nuclear weapons for some military purpose and yet confine the effects substantially to military targets." Nor did Wohlstetter think much of the concept that NW could be suicidal to the attacker, who would then foreswear the attack.[32]

Wohlstetter (always interesting to read) failed to destroy the NW theorists' position. He argued eloquently that Soviet leaders would behave rationally in time of crisis and against inevitable escalation from tactical to theater to strategic weapons. But he could not erase the *possibility* of the opposite occurring, and that was all the NW theorists felt was necessary for strategic policy to be overhauled.

Wohlstetter's recommendations incorporated some of the ideas of those he criticized, showing a little convergence of the two sides on some issues. The West, said Wohlstetter, "should make clear that we will not respond to an attack in any way that would have a substantial chance of causing a nuclear winter." He inclined toward the use of earth-penetrating weapons, aimed preferentially at military, not urban, targets. And defensive weapons, he argued, should be just as discriminating as offensive ones, referring particularly to nonnuclear means of destroying incoming enemy warheads (such as SDI). Convinced that massive and indiscriminate attacks were improbable, Wohlstetter felt that NW with its climatic holocaust was far less likely to occur and was thus a diversion.[33]

Opportunity for Reevaluation

To Dan Horowitz (a professor of political science at the Hebrew University of Jerusalem) and Robert Lieber (a professor of government at Georgetown University), the reality of NW was uncertain but surely no diversion. They wrote in the summer 1985 issue of the *Washington Quarterly* that "even if the nuclear winter phenomenon ultimately proves doubtful, the subject deserves closer consideration." For them, NW provided a useful opportunity to reevaluate the role of nuclear weapons in the policies of both the US and the USSR, as much as had recent controversies. These latter included public debate over deployment of intermediate-range missiles in Europe and first-strike-capable missiles aboard submarines, research and development for SDI, whether a no-first-use policy should be adopted, and nuclear freeze proposals then current.[34]

Horowitz and Lieber focused on unique consequences of NW, namely that "such a conflict would appear to offer no sanctuary" and that "there would be an unavoidable loss of control." Recalling that the nuclear theorist Herman Kahn had said that "uncontrollable weapons cannot be rationally utilized," they opined that the doomsday-machine nature of nuclear weapons, once the threshold was crossed to ignite NW, made contemplation of their use irrational. Additionally, they pointed to the paradox that an attacker would have to maintain greater confidence in its enemy's self-restraint than in that opponent's faithfulness to arms-control agreements. More was risked on the less likely condition.[35]

The United States' refusal to adopt a no-first-use nuclear pledge (the ambiguity being seen as deterring Soviet conventional attacks, especially in Europe) was now regarded by Horowitz and Lieber as less meaningful, for a nuclear response was less credible. NATO allies desired the US nuclear umbrella as long as it served as a deterrent, for neither conventional war nor first strikes with tactical nuclear weapons were palatable options in congested Europe. But an American president's perceived willingness to employ such weapons, as long as they could be limited to European territory, would be undercut by NW's global reach. The balance of conventional forces, Horowitz and Lieber noted, would be of increasing significance, and this in turn would require increased spending on conventional arms. This would mean reversing the nuclear preference, which dated from the Eisenhower administration, that gave "more bang for the buck." An active defense might have to replace the more cost-effective deterrence. The draft might have to be reintroduced.[36]

In the area of arms control, Horowitz and Lieber suggested, stability would rely more on self-deterrence than on a second-strike capability. Nuclear superiority would have even less meaning than many felt it had before. The Soviets' greater number of launchers and their larger-yield warheads were least likely to be used. But as arsenals got smaller, the Soviets might fear a first strike on their land-based ICBMs. Greater stability would thus be achieved as the two countries' arsenals grew to resemble each other.[37]

The question of human extinction continued to arise occasionally. Edward Cornish, president of the World Futures Society, asked a nuclear weapons expert if these weapons could put an end to mankind, with or without NW. "We simply don't have the power to wipe out the human race," he was told. "But we're working on it." Cornish, not oblivious to the dry humor in this remark, nonetheless advocated space exploration and development of colonies on the planets, on the Moon, and elsewhere in the cosmos as a means of ensuring humankind's survival.[38] In response to the popular argument that, if Western society might be destroyed in a nuclear war, then such weapons must be abandoned, the Harvard political scientist Joseph Nye asked "Is defending our way of life worth raising the risk that the species will be destroyed from one in 10,000 to one in 1,000, for a certain period of time?"[39]

Admirably introspective, the climatologist Stephen Schneider pondered whether the NW investigators, himself included, might inadvertently inform strategists when would be the "best" time to start a nuclear war? For example, the climatic effect is smaller in winter than in summer, suggesting less danger. But such an unwanted policy consequence of the research was unlikely. The variables were still huge, leading to great uncertainties. In the wintertime case just cited, a smaller amount of seasonal rainfall might allow smoke to remain aloft much longer, yielding effects that were initially thought avoidable. Nor would one side believe that any geographical disparity in the damage inflicted by NW was great enough to risk the phenomenon; the climatic effects predicted were all too similar. More-over, the awesome destruction in nuclear war from the initial effects of blast, heat, and radiation would continue to suppress the urge to pull the trigger. NW, Schneider felt, would not be the deciding factor whether to go to war.[40]

Carl Sagan, who had unleashed much of this blizzard of analysis with his article in *Foreign Affairs*, remained an interested onlooker. He noted that the question whether extended deterrence was still credible remained unanswered. Would the United States defend its allies with nuclear weapons against a conventional attack by the Soviet Union, chancing that NW might be triggered? Sagan also observed that no one discussed proliferation of nuclear weapons to other nations in the context of NW. If a small arsenal was capable of initiating NW, proliferation was of much more serious concern. The current nuclear powers alone provided a dangerous situation, for the arsenals of Britain, France, and China were largely targeted on Soviet cities.[41] More fundamentally, if simplistically, Sagan reiterated his view that "the aggressor can 'win' a nuclear war for about two weeks, until the soot and dust circle the globe."[42]

17 More Policy Questions

Military Concerns

Diplomatic and strategic consequences were not the only issues brought to light in the policy discussions surrounding NW. Large- and small-scale military concerns also followed. If the NW phenomenon was real, any idea of a large, preemptive first strike had to be abandoned, for the by-now-familiar reason that the initiating nation was also doomed. However, since NW could perhaps be set off by far smaller exchanges, involving many weapons of relatively low kiloton yield, the line separating strategic weapons from the "lesser" theater and tactical varieties became meaningless. They all had global significance. How, then, to prevail in conflict?

J. J. Gertler of the Rand Corporation suggested that sophisticated conventional weapons might find increasing favor on the battlefield. A move back to conventional arms, however, had the disadvantage of playing to the Soviets' greater numerical strength. Yet if nuclear weapons were still to be employed, very small and accurate warheads could be aimed at command, communication, and control facilities, denying the enemy the ability to operate, while limiting potential environmental effects. Alternatively, a high-altitude explosion that created an electromagnetic pulse (EMP) might disable these C^3 assets. Should enemy troops be desirable targets, enhanced radiation weapons would be most suitable (although their reduced ability to ignite fires was debatable), along with chemical weapons.

The military's Single Integrated Operational Plan (SIOP), the complex menu that prioritized nuclear targets, would become more complicated still, with the additional factor of NW concerns. Oil refineries, for example, might be deleted as targets. Gertler suggested the value of designating "high-winter" targets and "low-winter" targets, depending on the likely severity of their contribution to smoke and dust. A mobile missile launcher hidden in a forest would be "high," while the same launcher on an open plain turned to "low." An airfield near a city of steel and concrete would be lower than a base near an older metropolis constructed largely of wood. Military commanders might, on the one hand, hesitate to use their nuclear weapons, believing that damage would boomerang on their own country. On the other hand, they might expect that NW was coming anyway, and thus have no incentive not to launch their weapons. These psychological options argued for the National Command Authority to design clear rules of engagement.[1]

Echoing Gertler, two political scientists saw both the United States and the Soviet Union moving toward smaller and more accurate warheads. In a paper filled with perhaps a touch of excessive numerical dexterity, Michael Altfeld (of Michigan State University, and more recently affiliated with a "Beltway Bandit") and Stephen Cimbala (of the Pennsylvania State University at Media) analyzed the trend toward precision-guided warheads. They calculated that explosive yields as small as about 1 kiloton could soon be able to destroy many hard-ened targets, such as missile silos. Whereas TTAPS described a 3,000-MT counterforce attack on ICBMs, Altfeld and Cimbala maintained that the same attack could be conducted using only 1/1,000 of that yield. The reduced danger to the climate was obvious, and this held even if cities were targeted, for there was less likelihood of large fires. A consequence of this, Altfeld and Cimbala maintained, was that belief in NW would make nuclear warfare *more* plausible, not less, as Sagan and others argued, for NW inspired the technological imperative toward improved weaponry.

NW also would inspire greater efforts in ballistic-missile defense (already under way with SDI) and in civil defense. Altfeld and Cimbala explained that the United States had never felt able to defend its population against explosions, so the only shelters constructed in the past were protection against radioactive fallout. With a new generation of tiny warheads, blast shelters would be conceivable. Thus, "the possibility of nuclear winter may improve the case for active and passive defenses instead of rendering them futile."[2]

Whenever nuclear attacks upon cities were described, some defense planner claimed to be insulted by the prediction that cities would burn. "It would be immoral to target urban areas" was the mantra. That may have been technically correct, in that populations per se were not countervalue targets in a SIOP. But the planner's argument was disingenuous, for government agencies, Communist Party offices, military headquarters, intelligence facilities, armament factories and repair shops, and transportation centers most certainly were in or near many cities (co-located), and military aircraft could well be dispersed to municipal airports. Urban areas thus would be hit and they would burn. Joseph Nye asserted that 60 targets within Moscow's limits were specified in the current SIOP.[3]

Moreover, planners in the USSR were expected to act in precisely the same way as their American counterparts. "Think of the aerospace targets in Los Angeles," mused Michael May. "Are [the Soviets] going to leave those alone even if they have the best of intentions for the Angelenos?"[4] Note also that neither superpower believed that the other would refrain from targeting cities, for each had some form of civil defense evacuation plan.

With nuclear war fighting arguably feasible, it was important to observe that military operations could be affected by the changed physical conditions, and all the more so if mid-1980s-type weapons were used. On the basis of the experiences of aircraft flying though the volcanic dust clouds after the eruptions of Mount St. Helens (in Washington State) and Galunggung (in Indonesia), it was apparent to Theodore Postol that the thin veil of dust from nuclear explosions would cause problems. Nuclear fireballs, for example, would melt dust into glass, and glass-laden air might tear apart the air-breathing engines of bombers, tankers, airborne command posts, and cruise missiles. These particulates might even abrade reentry vehicles containing warheads. The dust could also interfere with satellite reconnaissance, from infrared wavelengths through the visible spectrum to the ultraviolet band. Optical and electronic (for example, radar) devices for fire control of everything from aircraft bombsights to ballistic-missile defenses might be blinded in the particle-laden atmosphere. Postol suggested, too, that high levels of radioactivity in the dust clouds might block electronic communications, and also present a dangerous environment to the crews of post-attack survey aircraft.

These war-fighting problems were not, however, unique to nuclear winter—which indeed was Postol's point. They could occur in any "old-fashioned" nuclear conflict. The additional burdens of NW that had to be addressed concerned the lengthy cold and dark conditions. The engines of trucks, tanks, and ships, whose performance normally could be degraded by nuclear dust at ground level, would bear the further constraint of operating in unaccustomed low temperatures. Would they even start? Troops would have to be fed, clothed, billeted, and supplied in darkness, and be prepared to fight without seeing the enemy or the terrain. While professing belief in the possibility of NW, neither the military chiefs nor the civilian leaders in the Department of Defense gave any visible attention to the novelties of battle after the onset of NW.[5] Carl Sagan, who claimed to have conferred widely with members of the military and intelligence communities, thought that the dismissive views of NW by the DoD's civilian leadership inclined their subordinates to be silent.[6] George Carrier, explaining the lack of much commentary by scientists close to the military, felt that they already had enough trouble getting their ideas accepted and weapons developed, and regarded NW as just another hassle.[7]

Only marginally related to the problems of fighting in the cold and dark conditions of NW was another military concern. Astonishingly, NW might be initiated by non-nuclear means. The powerful chemical or free-electron lasers planned for President Reagan's Strategic Defense Initiative were expected to burn holes in the casings of Soviet missile as they rose from their silos in the boost phase. Alternatively, they might melt components of the separated warheads as they traveled on their ballistic trajectories, in one way or another rendering them harmless. But these narrow beams, whether from ground-based lasers reflected off orbiting mirrors or space-based lasers, would contain so much concentrated energy that a mere tenth of a second's illumination of combustible material on the ground would send it soaring well above its kindling temperature. Beams could be slewed rapidly from one city to another, igniting their funeral pyres even more efficiently than by nuclear explosives. "Fires engulfing a million people would be started in a few minutes. . . . From such a near-simultaneous high density of ignition points a fire storm would almost certainly develop," maintained Albert Latter and Ernest Martinelli.[8] Both physicists worked at R&D Associates (where Richard Turco also was employed) and had made rough but reasonable numerical calculations of the possibility of such laser ignition. They noted that the president's desire for deterrence by defense could quickly be superseded by the long-despised deterrence by retaliation: instead of protecting cities, directed-energy weapons could be used to attack them.

Caroline Herzenberg, a physicist at the Argonne National Laboratory, soon provided more detailed analysis of this possibility, pointing out that the TTAPS paper had specified that 80 joules of radiant energy exposure per square centimeter were needed for the ignition of urban fires, while 10,000 joules/cm^2 of laser energy was the goal for burning through the skin of a missile. Before long, T. S. Trowbridge of the Red Mesa Research Company in Los Angeles confirmed this ability. Whereas very powerful lasers heat their paths, causing a "thermal bloom" that disrupts the beam, lower-power lasers should be able to deliver enough energy to Earth's surface to ignite combustibles. Cities thus were endangered by this "laser winter" potential of SDI.[9] And as with so many other features of the arms race, American technology would soon be matched by Soviet achievements.

In September 1985, the *Los Angeles Times* reported that it had used the Freedom of Information Act to force the Department of Defense to release a 73-page study that had been prepared for the Defense Nuclear Agency by the Palomar Corporation, a defense contractor. This "think piece" was apparently the first independent policy analysis of NW commissioned by the DoD. Planners currently did not take into account the smoke and dust that would be lofted by nuclear explosions, the report charged. Yet reconnaissance to provide damage assessment that might discourage escalation and even help to end the conflict could be blinded. Another insight offered was that a "decapitating attack" on the leadership and C^{3}I might be more attractive than a massive strike against military hardware if the latter threatened to initiate NW. Stronger, deeper shelters might therefore be desirable.

NW, further, introduced new uncertainties to the already incalculable fog of war, and this might make decision makers more reluctant to engage in battle. Should conflict begin, missiles carrying a single, smaller-yield warhead were to be preferred over the giant ten-warhead MX missile currently in the arsenal. By the same token, the Soviet Union's massive ten-warhead SS-18 was less likely to be a credible threat if its employment was thought to lead to NW. Reagan's pet project, SDI, would suffer degradation of its optical sensors, guidance controls, and target systems (an important point ignored by SDI enthusiasts). And while SDI might lower the likelihood of NW by destroying incoming warheads, its presence might actually provoke the climatic catastrophe if the enemy sought to overcome this defense by a massive volley of warheads. Overall, the options to use nuclear weapons seemed to be reduced.[10] Palomar also questioned whether the US should "identify, categorize, and set priorities for military targets based on their smoke and dust creating potential and their colocation with such areas."[11] The US government's lack of serious attention to all these military concerns was a striking failure of policy. By not acknowledging them, the administration seemed to wish them to vanish.

Civil Defense

Edward Teller, long an advocate of civil defense, wrote an op-ed article on the subject for the *New York Times* in early 1984. This drew an angry rebuttal, whose writer noted that Teller had ignored the NW phenomenon. The expected cold and dark would soon kill those who survived the radioactive fallout in shelters, making "calls for civil defense . . . absurd, irresponsible and the ultimate waste of money, intellect and time."[12] Representative Parren Mitchell (D-Maryland) felt that the Federal Emergency Management Agency was "not worth a damn in a nuclear war, that the dimensions of the thing are just so enormous that it's foolish."[13] While more moderate in his language, Charles Zraket of the MITRE Corporation agreed. NW, he said, "will reinforce the existing belief that a first strike makes no sense, because it may be suicidal. And it renders the notion of a real civil defense program, which is already in disrepute, even more disreputable."[14]

In its bureaucratic language, the December 1984 NAS report concurred with these attacks on civil defense: "Long-term atmospheric consequences imply additional problems that are not easily mitigated by prior preparedness and that are not in harmony with any notions of rapid postwar restoration of social structure."[15] More pithily, Turco commented: "Nuclear winter has severe implications for civil defense planning. You're dealing with a lot more than just a few blown-out windows." Sagan asserted that "even if the superpowers had adequate shelters, it would be a hostile act against developing nations."[16]

Civil defense, however, was not without its supporters. Based on the natural human instinct for survival, it was only sensible to prepare for possible disaster. Indeed, such preparations allegedly would provide the USSR with fewer worthwhile targets, reducing its ability to blackmail the US into concessions. Arthur Broyles (a physicist at the University of Florida in Gainesville) and Conrad Chester (a chemical engineer at the Oak Ridge National Laboratory) condemned the pre-SDI policy of mutual assured destruction, which, by abjuring construction of nation-wide missile defenses, left populations hostage to an attack. This vulnerability supposedly reduced one's own incentive to launch an attack, but it cursed the people to a life in fear. Defense, both active (ballistic-missile defense) and passive (shelters, evacuation of cities), would reduce the terror and improve the climate in which a stable peace might be sought. Since the USSR had a far more extensive civil defense program than the US, the US was currently at a disadvantage. Citing studies, Broyles and Chester claimed that the distribution of food would likely be the most serious problem facing the survivors of a nuclear war. They recommended that the government should stockpile a year's supply of edibles in many locations. This was, in fact, a worldwide problem, since many countries relied on the US for food imports. A global response was desirable. Additionally, if low temperatures were to make agriculture difficult, Broyles and Chester suggested that seeds of crops that require lower than normal amounts of light should be distributed. Education should include training in primitive lifestyles, such as the crude preparation of clothing and food—grinding wheat, for example. Other precautions they suggested were the widespread provision of flashlights and warm clothing. These recommendations may seem unsophisticated and even banal, but they constituted one of the few attempts to build a civil defense response to NW.[17]

Howard Maccabee was another supporter of civil defense measures. A radiation therapy specialist, he was president of Doctors for Disaster Preparedness from 1982 to 1984. Viscerally opposed to what he saw as the "political misuse of science," he pointed to Rachel Carson's *Silent Spring*, Paul Ehrlich's pleas to control population, the Club of Rome's predictions of resource depletion, and Samuel Epstein's book *The Politics of Cancer*. All were warnings about disasters that did not happen, while the authors nonetheless called for stringent government controls. NW, Maccabee said, was another prophecy of doom, one supported by "various groups advocating unilateral nuclear disarmament, accommodation with the Soviet Union, and the nuclear-freeze movement." (Though there is little or no evidence of any groups other than the Freeze advocates supporting NW, the larger claim can be taken as normal rhetoric.) What makes Maccabee's statement interesting is that he was one of relatively few physicians to oppose the stance of the highly visible Physicians for Social Responsibility, who argued that medical care—indeed survival—was unlikely in the target area after a nuclear attack. In contrast, Maccabee believed that urban targets could largely be avoided, and that SDI would reduce the numbers of incoming warheads.[18]

Sagan, who was not unalterably opposed to civil defense measures, agreed that they would be justified for a single nuclear explosion on American territory. He objected, however, to the political objective of the Federal Emergency Management Agency: "to give [citizens] some hope of survivability after nuclear war." "The net result," Sagan continued, "is that people then don't worry about nuclear war as much." Soviet planners had told him that their high-profile civil defense program was designed to achieve such confidence. Edward Teller had recently suggested, as a civil defense response to NW, that food be stockpiled. Sagan asked how that would look to nations that could not engage in such a luxury.[19] George Rathjens, who came from Alaska, felt that Americans could be educated to insulate their houses better and to stockpile food; one *could* survive cold weather. But Rathjens too recognized that the poor nations of the world could not be expected to do the same.[20]

Charlie Martin, a former employee of the Livermore Lab, took the argument a step further. In a letter to the editor of the *Washington Post*, he pointed out that Eskimos live in small enclosures (igloos) and benefit from the great insulating properties of snow. Martin's larger point was that civil defense *is* moral, and he was replying to a syndicated column in which Ellen Goodman ridiculed the FEMA report that said that agriculture would survive nuclear war. To Goodman, survival was illusory, and thus civil defense was immoral.[21] Martin unfortunately did not elaborate on the training and acculturation needed to survive in the cold and dark. Could FEMA train millions of people to build igloos? Aside from the skill needed, what if snowfall was inadequate? And even if this construction enabled large populations to survive, what would they eat (surely not whale blubber) and what would they wear while waiting for better weather and the reconstruction of society?

Leon Gouré was yet another advocate of stockpiling food and fuel supplies, adjusting agricultural production, and planning medical care in advance of any nuclear war. NW suggested the need for additional attention to heating and water supplies, and means for their delivery. While posing increased problems, they were soluble. After all, Gouré noted, people around the world, including some in the United States, live parts of the year in sub-freezing temperatures.[22] Gouré noted ominously that NW had no visible effect on Soviet civil defense, strategic, or targeting policies. NW, he said, was ignored in the Soviet literature of these topics.[23]

A lot of cold water was poured over civil defense in September 1985 in the Palomar Corporation report mentioned above. Evacuation of urban residents to rural areas, a mainstay of Reagan's civil defense ideas, was said to be irrelevant for long-time survival. Shelter, fuel, food, water, and other necessaries, for periods far longer than the days or weeks currently envisioned, would have to be provided for large numbers of people. While not an impossible task, that was well beyond FEMA's mandate at the time.[24]

The debate concerning what mitigating actions to take before NW actually occurred, such as civil defense measures or food stockpiling, was low-key. Virtually no attention was given to reducing the flammable materials in cities, no doubt because that would have involved the reconstruction of urban centers. Far more thought was given to analysis of measures to avoid NW in the first place. And here the dichotomy was fairly clear: massive weaponry, including SDI, to continue the four decades of deterrence, or massive reductions in the nuclear arsenals to minimize the damage from nuclear war.[25]

On the Fringe

Of course, not everyone who commented on NW fully understood its details or significance—nor was that necessary. Moralists, for example, had comprehended the basic points about nuclear war since 1945. The theologian John C. Bennett, writing in *Christianity and Crisis*, felt that, as a result of the NW discovery, "political decision makers and military strategists . . . may come to realize that it is essential to abandon their trust in nuclear weapons even as a deterrent." The suicidal possibility of damaging our own Earth and atmospheric support systems should force a "convergence of religious and moral persuasion and the pressure of the realities," and "of God's persuasion and God's judgment."[26]

In other cases, an understanding of the details mattered. The author of a letter to the editor of the *New York Times* failed to grasp the difference between dust and soot, especially in smoke from urban fires. He wrote that all a nation had now to do was detonate 100 MT on its *own* soil and let the winds blow. A technological optimist, he anticipated a race to develop a "stratosphere sweep" method to clear the air and deny an aggressor the ability to inflict NW. To those who might think this a fantastic proposal, the writer cited the once-utopian tasks of containing an oil spill and seeding clouds with iodide crystals. Civil defense also came under his wide-ranging gaze. Wars were now likely to be limited, making shelters and stockpiles of food more manageable. Cheerfully assuming that agriculture could be quickly resumed, he felt that people could "outwait a . . . period of crop shortages." Paraphrasing Shelley, he asked, "if a nuclear Winter comes, can Spring be far behind?"[27]

Not so easily dismissed, because he published in William F. Buckley's influential journal of conservative opinion *National Review* and lectured at the even more right-wing Heritage Foundation, was Brad Sparks. The director of the Political Freedom Legal Defense Fund in Berkeley, Sparks called NW a scandal and asked why there were no such alterations of the climate at Hiroshima and Nagasaki. Where were the reports of darkness at noon, quick freezes, and frostbite? Continuing in his derisive tone, Sparks paraded other events which, he claimed, should have produced NW effects: the meteor or comet that exploded over Siberia in 1908, and the World War II firestorms in Hamburg and Dresden. It was clear, he charged, that "a number of prestigious scientists have used their standing to promote, for political reasons, a theory that cannot be justified scientifically." In addition, these "winterists," he argued, "persistently ignored, evaded, and even suppressed [contradictory] evidence." The larger scientific community was "too meek or simply too naive and inexperienced" to protest effectively.[28]

For his many factual errors and his diatribe in repeating numerous criticisms of NW (already presented in this book), Sparks was taken to task in a letter to *National Review*'s editor by Richard Turco, Owen Brian Toon, and Thomas Ackerman, and in another by the atmospheric scientist Robert Whitten. Scientists who supported NW treated Sparks as if he was intellectually unhinged. True, he did seem to rant and rave a bit, but his fundamental arguments were no different than those advanced by S. Fred Singer and other reputable scientists. The TTAPS members asserted that proper science went into their work, which was extensively reviewed before publication.[29] Whitten cited the lack of data from World War II events and the possibility of non-linear responses by the atmosphere to explain the lack of NW effects at that time. He also emphasized the agreement by the two weapons laboratories, NCAR, and the formal reviews by the NAS and SCOPE that NW was a real possibility.[30]

Although he was one of Sparks's primary critical sources, Russell Seitz also decried his misconstruals and misconceptions. The Tunguska meteor ignited no fire, he pointed out, hence there was no reason for NW effects. But he cited a large Siberian fire in 1915, that produced a mass of smoke in the NW realm, and yet "twilight at noon co-existed with a heat wave." Seitz also interpreted the NAS report as being nearly dismissive of NW, because it never used the term: "What its authors couldn't quantify they disdained to name."[31] Singer wrote to praise Sparks for exposing the political as well as the scientific background to NW. But his real purpose was to argue that the NAS report could be read to discredit the NW concept. Indeed, if dense clouds of smoke arose over burning cities and were not rained out (as he claimed occurred over the German and Japanese cities in WWII), they might serve as a heat blanket, making plausible a slight warming—his "nuclear summer."[32]

Russell Seitz (already mentioned in chapter 9 as the author of a letter hostile to Sagan's article in *Foreign Affairs*) was the most talented and serious of the (surprisingly few) NW skeptics who were "on the fringe." Rathjens, von Hippel, Dyson, Singer, and others were Ph.D. scientists with some basis for credibility in the various subjects that melded into NW investigations. Seitz, in contrast, had some physics training, but was without a doctoral degree. He was director of technology assessment at R. J. Edwards investment bankers in Boston, and later a visiting scholar and associate at Harvard's Center for International Affairs. His lack of appropriate credentials led NW supporters to dismiss his criticisms, but he was hard to keep down.[33]

Seitz sought to highlight flaws and inconsistencies in the arguments for NW. One familiar disparity he noted was that in 1983 TTAPS used a baseline scenario of 5,000 MT, while the Ehrlich team of biologists worked with 10,000 MT. This was stacking the deck toward more dire consequences, Seitz charged, echoing George Rathjens. But this issue had been dealt with long before Seitz seized it, the biologists declaring that they deliberately provided a worst-case analysis.[34]

Seitz also wrote under the auspices of the American Security Council Foundation, a private group of "Cold Warriors" located in Boston, Virginia. A clever man with wide-ranging interests, Seitz could be depended on to present provocative challenges to NW. Fossil fuels such as coal, oil shale, and peat, he noted, were located in shallow deposits across much of Earth, such that the "carbon budget" of these sources vastly exceeded the fuel loadings calculated for NW scenarios. Massive volcanism in these areas should have injected enormous amounts of carbonaceous plasma and particulate matter high into the atmosphere at intervals of less than 10 million years. If such gigantic NW events did occur, he asked, how could humans now populate the globe?[35]

Continuing to address smoke production, which he recognized as the most important factor in fostering climate change, Seitz returned his attention to the great Siberian fire of July and August 1915. During the most extreme drought since records began to be kept in that region, fire consumed not only many trees, covering upwards of a million square kilometers, but an extensive layer of peat to a depth of two meters over an area of 500,000 square kilometers (roughly the size of France). From on-site reports and from his own back-of-the-envelope calculations, Seitz concluded that the amount of smoke (surely more than 20 million and perhaps as much as 180 million tonnes), the visibility (less than 100 meters over an area larger than 4 million square kilometers), cooling (about 10°C), and the duration of such conditions (an average of 51 days) were strikingly similar to the values that were emerging from recent three-dimensional interactive GCM studies of NW. Yet the Siberian smoke did not travel beyond Asian borders and remained inhomogeneous. Additionally, there was a notable absence of hard frost and harvests were only somewhat delayed and slightly smaller than normal. In a paper published in *Nature*, Seitz claimed to show that the hemispheric or global reach predicted for NW was not a necessary consequence of the scenarios examined by NW proponents. There remained much to learn.[36] At a conference in early 1986, sponsored by the Defense Nuclear Agency at the Ames Research Center, Seitz spoke about this 1915 fire. Turco dismissed the data as overly anecdotal, the only scientific study showing 140,000 square kilometers burned, and facetiously suggested taking up a collection to send Seitz to Siberia for better information.[37] Alexander Ginsburg of the Soviet Academy of Sciences' Institute of Atmospheric Physics suggested elsewhere that weather conditions at the time of most large forest fires prevent the smoke from rising high in the atmosphere, a level that would make NW effects more likely.[38]

Switching from a scientific periodical to a journal of opinion—*The National Interest* (published by Irving Kristol, with the prominent conservatives Samuel Huntington, Jeane Kirkpatrick, Henry Kissinger, and Daniel Pipes on its advisory board)—Seitz declared that NW had been "laid to rest," along with the "Energy Crisis" and the "Population Bomb." Its demise, he maintained, was due to a "notorious lack of scientific integrity." Within 4 years the theory had "unraveled under scrutiny." Seitz's article was a selective history of NW research and marketing, made all the more readable by colorful language and an alleged conspiracy among leading liberal scientists. The latest research showing NW to be virtually nonexistent, Seitz claimed, was ignored by the media, which continued to highlight old videos of apocalyptic climatic change. Seitz lamented the lack of objectivity shown by the scientific community, but his own polemics suggested that the kettle was calling the pot black.[39]

The *National Interest* broadside was condensed and reworked for the editorial pages of the *Wall Street Journal*. Stephen Schneider, whose research with Starley Thompson was the basis for Seitz's claim that NW had unraveled, protested strongly. Although the average temperature decrease that Schneider and Thompson found was smaller than TTAPS's, Schneider pointed out that farmers are concerned not with seasonal averages but with freezes on a particular night. Such ruinous frosts, Schneider affirmed, remained sporadically in his computer model. Although Schneider and Thompson had suggested that "nuclear winter" might now be relabeled "nuclear fall," this was no cause for relief, as mass starvation still was possible. Schneider reemphasized his belief that nuclear arsenals should be reduced for greater strategic stability and that NW continued to be a valid part of that argument. He also made the point, presented all too infrequently to non-scientific audiences, that "the process of science is to step from simple ideas to more complex calculations," and that the NW case was one of "normal scientific evolution."[40]

Behaving as if only experts could play the game, TTAPS responded to Seitz's criticism, pointing out his lack of academic credentials. Indeed, they went so far as to call him a "crackpot," and a "disappointed suitor of nuclear winter" (since his analogy to NW about the likely ignition of coal seams by volcanic eruptions had found no support).[41] The editors of the *Wall Street Journal* deleted these personal references to Seitz, but printed a still-long and detailed letter from TTAPS. They depicted his attack as "mean-spirited" and "based

almost entirely on gossip, innuendo and misinformation," revealing "a superficial understanding of the facts." They challenged the slurs on NW that Seitz attributed to distinguished
scientists, having received disclaimers from most of those very scientists. They emphasized
their own achievements and awards, and denied the alleged hijacking of science by a liberal
cabal, pointing out that NASA, the DoD, and the NAS, all supporters of NW research, were
not usually counted among the "inner circle of disarmament activists." And, typically
emphasizing that their approach was scientific and not politically inspired, they recited a
long list of phenomena predicted in their first paper that had been confirmed, to greater or
lesser extent, by subsequent research. The *Journal*, they said, had unfortunately given Seitz
"a platform to spread his political biases and personal invective."[42]

Seitz's "did too" rebuttal to TTAPS's "did not" letter failed to advance the argument
much.[43] Both sides made some valid points, but they were largely incapable of any construc-
tive interaction. Proponents of NW believed it was necessary to show only the possibility
of climatic catastrophe, often a worst-case situation; opponents insisted that NW be shown
as likely under "reasonable" scenarios. Seitz also behaved as if the flawed TTAPS paper of
1983 remained the appropriate focus of reproach, especially as TTAPS had never published
the data in its "Blue Book." (Turco explained that this large document was quickly superseded by the frenzy of research after 1983, using 2-D and 3-D models, and it made little
sense to revise it for publication. Instead, he mailed the original version to anyone who
asked for a copy.[44]) Each side could pick appropriate quotations from the NAS and other
reports to bolster its position, and could not appreciate the other's belief that the mores of
science required different behavior.

However, even without an academic seal of approval, Seitz was a brilliant amateur, able
to gain occasional employment in some Cambridge-area labs and to win the respect of
prominent scientists at Harvard and MIT. He had real talent in technical matters and was
fertile with ideas. In 1990, for example, he co-authored a paper that suggested the comet
or asteroid that ended the Cretaceous period and caused the extinction of dinosaurs (see
chapter 3 above) had hit south of western Cuba, and charged that General Electric had
stolen his idea of making isotopically pure carbon-12 diamonds. Twelve years later, he led
an expedition that found the Guatemalan sources of the Olmec Empire's blue jade.[45]

Seitz had to be taken more seriously than Brad Sparks. He seems to have been motivated
by his own political views as much as he claimed Sagan had been. But the battle over NW
was fought in the realm of politics and the mass media, not just on the scientific front, and
Seitz was adept in gaining space in reputable (if partial) newspapers and policy journals,
and even in the occasional scientific periodical. NW scientists felt obliged to respond to
him. Nonetheless, Seitz was on the fringe because, like virtually all the opponents of
NW, he did little more than criticize details, offering no research on NW that could be
published in a refereed scientific journal. In addition, his lack of professional status made
it easy to dismiss even his reasonable arguments. Scientists reject amateurs as much as
dentists do.[46]

As we have seen, the significance of NW was in the eye of the beholder. If NW's reality was disbelieved or regarded as far too uncertain, it made sense not to change strategic policy because of it. If it was deemed to be likely, there were civil defense, tactical, strategic, and political choices that could be made. Some looked to NW as the unforeseen doomsday weapon that would force the nuclear powers to cut their arsenals severely. Others sought ways to circumvent the danger of nuclear winter by altering warheads, by tweaking targeting doctrine, and by creating a missile-defense system. Some even suggested that NW could be used as an offensive weapon, given the asymmetries in climatic responses over the continents. It was a rich debate, enlivened by widely opposed political views.

18 Other Voices, and Some Echoes

Where Have All the Peaceniks Gone?

In the 1980s, the peace movement and the environmental movement recognized many similarities of interest and made common cause. The Audubon Society played a part in organizing the Halloween meeting at which NW was publicly revealed, and the Council for a Livable World Education Fund reprinted Carl Sagan's *Parade* article. On a more long-term basis, the Natural Resources Defense Council supported public education of NW. Attention was drawn to the presentation to Sagan of the 1984 SANE Peace Award for his NW efforts and to the presentation to Paul Crutzen of the 1984 *Discover*-Rolex Scientist of the Year Award. A 1985 report issued by ten conservation groups criticized the US government's positions on clean air, automobile fuel efficiency, and nuclear weapons (and specifically mentioned NW),[1] and occasionally an article on NW appeared in *Sierra* or *Environment*. But for neither the peace movement nor the environmental movement was NW an overwhelmingly significant issue.

The explanation for this may lie in the nature of groups that, after all, exist largely to protest government or industry policies. Their vision may be long-range, but their resources are not. Funding is never adequate, the number and variety of problems are overwhelming, and great reliance is placed on unpaid members. These constraints make such organizations far more effective on issues of great immediacy than on issues whose consequences are uncertain or will occur in the distant future. Thus, "peaceniks" rallied against the Anti-Ballistic Missile around 1970, the war in Vietnam in the 1960s and the 1970s, and deployment of intermediate-range missiles in Europe in the early 1980s, and environmentalists protested the use of DDT in the 1970s, the capture of dolphins in tuna nets from the 1960s onward, and global warming from the 1990s on. These issues were "here and now," and there were petitions to sign, politicians to lobby, rallies to attend, letters to the editor to write, and even (in the case of global warming) international treaties to support. In January 1985, the short-lived organization Beyond War took a monumentally different tack by endeavoring to change the way in which people thought, rather than by focusing on a specific weapon or policy step. Beyond War drew 72 United Nations ambassadors to a NW conference addressed by Carl Sagan and Sergei Kapitsa, yet did not make NW a continuing theme of its activities.[2]

NW suffered from the fact that peaceniks had already been protesting against nuclear weapons and the arms race for decades. Was there really much more to add? Well, yes. NW would give the lie to the argument that nuclear war was winnable. If nuclear war was a suicidal gesture (since the initiator would experience severe climatic consequences too), and if non-combatants would suffer horribly, it was irrational to contemplate such conflict. The physician Lewis Thomas expressed a common pre-NW sense of frustration: "I thought that every reason for abandoning nuclear weapons had been discussed often enough and publicly enough." And yet the stockpiles remained huge. Now, NW's appearance as a newly predicted consequence of nuclear war changed Thomas's despair to hope. As I noted in chapter 9, Thomas argued that NW was a *good* discovery: "The weapons have turned out to be not just homicidal and genocidal. The wonderful thing about them, which changes everything for the future of arms control and arms limitation negotiations, is that they are suicidal." Common sense or the instinct for self-preservation, he thought, would make NW pivotal to a change in attitude and policy.[3]

Thomas was wrong. NW's novel twists received no special prominence. Moreover, despite a lot of talk, the Reagan administration's conviction of the wisdom of its strategic policies left little flexibility to accommodate new ideas. Its conspicuous endeavor to improve nuclear weapons draped over the NW issue a sense of futility for the public. Could a massive reversal of the nuclear stockpile be initiated? As I said above, neither individuals nor "peacenik" organizations chose to make NW the centerpiece for a major campaign.

Not that some didn't try. NW was given a measure of publicity at the April 1985 meeting of the American Physical Society in Crystal City, Virginia. There the APS's Forum on Physics and Society presented its prestigious Leo Szilard Award (honoring applications of physics for the benefit of society) to Paul Crutzen, John Birks, and the members of TTAPS.[4] In addition, some authors and editors completed books on different aspects of the NW phenomenon and its consequences. Besides the several mentioned in chapter 14, there were David Fisher's *Fire and Ice: The Greenhouse Effect, Ozone Depletion, and Nuclear Winter* (1990) and Carl Sagan and Richard Turco's *A Path Where No Man Thought: Nuclear Winter and the End of the Arms Race* (1990), whose title was borrowed from a line in Euripides' *Medea*.[5] Though all these books were reviewed, and though there was an audience for them, none of them rose to the best-seller level or motivated a movement.

Carl Sagan was a one-man whirlwind of NW promotion. He carried his message about NW not only through the halls of Congress and other corridors of power in Washington, but throughout the United States and even abroad. He championed a petition (eventually signed by 98 Nobel laureates) that was directed to all nuclear states and those with the potential to acquire such weapons. He spoke before committees of legislators and military planners in the Soviet Union, to the public in Japan and several other countries, to Pope John Paul II, and to heads of government in Argentina, Canada, Greece, France, India, Mexico, New Zealand, Sweden, and Tanzania.[6]

Other scientists involved in atmospheric science did far less lobbying but clearly were concerned with the policy implications of NW. Paul Crutzen, for example, was quoted as saying:

Although I do not consider [the NW] idea among my greatest achievements . . . I am convinced that, from a political point of view, it is by far the most important, because it magnifies and highlights the dangers of a nuclear war and convinces me that in the long run humankind can only escape such horrific consequences if nuclear weapons are totally abolished by international agreement.[7]

Religious leaders should logically gravitate towards the "peacenik" camp, except that the term "peace" long ago acquired a connotation of describing those opposed to the US government's national security policies. With the democratic West in ideological battle against atheistic communism, many churches learned, if not to like the bomb, at least to live with it. Nonetheless, theologians debated such concepts as nuclear deterrence, and on significant occasions took moral positions. Only 2 months after the Halloween 1983 debut of NW, the Vatican hosted twenty scientists from around the world to meet Pope John Paul II and draft a warning that nuclear war must be avoided. Stephen Jay Gould, a participant, approved this NW-inspired combination of scientific and moral deterrents.[8]

Another religiously inspired conference took place at Thanksgiving-time 1984, in the Villa Serbelloni, the Rockefeller Foundation's intellectual retreat at Bellagio on the shores of Lake Como. Chaired by the president of the University of Notre Dame, Theodore Hesburgh, a group of two dozen religious leaders and technical experts met to discuss nuclear war. NW was at center stage. Familiar faces on the NW scene in attendance were Carl Sagan, Paul Crutzen, and George Rathjens. Other scientists included George Skryabin, general scientific secretary of the Soviet Academy of Sciences, Roald Sagdeev, head of the Soviet Space Research Institute, and Lord Solly Zuckerman, former science advisor to the British Ministry of Defence. Among the theologians were Bishop Roger Mahony of Stockton, California (soon to be archbishop of Los Angeles, and later a cardinal), Rabbi Balfour Brickner of New York, Secretary-General Inamullah Khan of the Karachi-based World Muslim Congress, and Archbishop Kirill, rector of the Leningrad Theological Academy. In all, ten countries were represented.

Stirred by a showing of the BBC film *Threads*, which depicted a nuclear attack on Great Britain and the agonies of survival afterward, the group had no conflict over its goal. Avoiding nuclear conflagration, of course, was everyone's desire. Securing that, and gaining a world without the likelihood or fear of war, was the difficult part. A Chinese physicist, Tao Shi-yan, looked at records going back to the fifteenth century and reported a strong correlation between dust storms and reduced temperatures. This was a rare indication of interest in NW in the People's Republic of China. Sagan, an agnostic, pushed the theologians for help in conceiving new ways to achieve their goal, but nothing novel emerged.[9] Although such dialog between religion and science (more properly, between religion and politics) may not produce clear, immediate results, the circulation of ideas is beneficial and may on rare occasion reach policy makers.

Still, neither theologians nor scientists, in any numbers, rallied in opposing the threat of NW by urging new policy. Stephen Jay Gould, Lewis Thomas, and a few other scientists did so, but as citizens hopeful of a more sane future and not as research participants. Of those engaged in the calculations of NW, only Carl Sagan and Paul Ehrlich spoke often about policy. The lack of a large "movement" behind efforts to investigate and publicize the NW phenomenon surprised some observers who inferred that research that highlighted the dangers of nuclear war must be inspired by arms-control "groupies"—who were singularly invisible. Toon felt that he and his TTAPS colleagues were improperly regarded as left-wing disarmament "freaks."[10]

World leaders also were conspicuously silent about NW. When, in May 1984, six heads of government called on the nuclear powers to "halt all testing, production and deployment of nuclear weapons and their delivery systems, to be immediately followed by substantial reductions in nuclear forces," it was not clear if NW was on their minds. The statement by prime ministers Indira Gandhi of India, Olof Palme of Sweden, and Andreas Papandreou of Greece and presidents Julius Nyerere of Tanzania, Miguel de la Madrid of Mexico, and Raúl Alfonsin of Argentina included references to "death and destruction to all peoples," "global suicide," and the threat to "human survival," all high on the list of NW concerns. Yet the term "nuclear winter" was nowhere mentioned. While UN Secretary General Javier Perez de Cuellar and Pope John Paul II praised this effort, a US Department of State spokesman said the requested freeze "would not enhance stability or reduce the risk of war." He explained that the USSR's massive buildup had created "dangerous disparities" that would have to be removed before a "stable strategic balance" could be achieved.[11]

Half a year later, with Rajiv Gandhi replacing his assassinated mother, the same leaders issued the "Delhi Declaration" on the same topic of nuclear weapons. This time they explicitly referred to NW.[12] Yet little occurred that could be called a follow-up. Only in the Antipodes was there a continuing protest of NW by government leaders, scientists, and laypeople.

Among DoD planners, Thomas Powers found "a wistful hope that 'more study' will make the nuclear-winter problem go away, embarrassment at having overlooked it for nearly 40 years, resentment that the peacenik doom-mongers might have been right all these years, even if they didn't know why they were." "Above all," Powers continued, "one finds frank dismay at what the nuclear-winter problem does to a defense policy heavily based on nuclear weapons."[13]

Concern in the Antipodes

In the 1950s and the 1960s, a number of North Americans considered moving to the Antipodes in hopes of escaping the nuclear war that seemed to loom in the Northern Hemisphere. Seeking to benefit from its geography, Australia attracted teachers by placing advertisements in American magazines showing young men and women on beautiful beaches, wearing bathing suits and mortarboards. Nevil Shute's 1957 novel *On the Beach* erased for many the image that war would be confined north of the Equator. In the 1980s, NW reaffirmed the likelihood that global residents beyond the neighborhood of the super-powers would be affected far more strongly by nuclear war than earlier believed. S. Fred Singer commented: "After being exposed to megaton blasts, incineration, radioactive fall-out, etc., people may not care if the weather turns cold. But to the Third World, dependent on United States grain exports and other assistance, a nuclear winter scenario, even a minor one, may spell the difference between life and death."[14]

Concern was not, however, limited to Third World nations dependent on the United States for commerce or aid. Despite their geographic isolation, well before the public ever heard of the NW phenomenon, people in the South Pacific had developed a strong nuclear phobia, stirred not least by the long series of test explosions by the United States (at Bikini and Eniwetok) and later by France (at Mururoa and Fangataufa). This anti-nuclear sentiment, consistent over the years but never stronger than interest in domestic issues, was tapped by David Lange, whose Labour Party rose to power in the July 1984 elections in New Zealand.

As prime minister, Lange barred from his country's ports all ships powered by nuclear reactors or carrying nuclear weapons.[15] Since the US Navy had a policy of not confirming whether a vessel had such weapons aboard, port calls in New Zealand were effectively ended when a conventionally powered American destroyer, the USS *Buchanan*, was denied entry in early 1985. While the US government sniffed about an anti-American tilt by one of its ANZUS (Australia-New Zealand-United States) allies and suspended military obligations under the treaty, the Kiwis emphasized that they were anti-nuclear, not anti-American.[16] New Zealanders preferred to adhere still to the 1951 security treaty, toothless as they thought it to be, but felt that they were a partner, not a client state. As such, they could legitimately protest the "continuing and deadly competition in [the] production [of nuclear weapons], their refinement and their deployment."[17]

NW recast the concept of nuclear deterrence for the worse, Lange told the United Nations General Assembly in September 1984, for southern nations could also experience the plum-meting temperatures. He argued that, even if the danger was later shown to be only a frac-tion of that now predicted, it was "incumbent upon the nuclear weapon states to do everything possible to avoid . . . use [of these explosives]." Toward this end, a proposal by Australia to create a South Pacific Nuclear Free Zone was endorsed less than a month before by the eleven countries of the South Pacific Forum; a treaty was signed at Rarotonga in 1985. The agreement forbade any use, testing, or stationing of such weapons in their region.[18] This initiative was consolidated by the New Zealand Nuclear Free, Disarmament and Arms Control Act, passed by Parliament in 1987. Popular support for such action—a combination of self-interest and idealism—had crystallized after agents of the French government blew up the Greenpeace ship *Rainbow Warrior* in Auckland Harbor in 1985, and the world witnessed with dread the Chernobyl nuclear plant explosion in 1986.[19]

The New Zealand Ecological Society reacted specifically to the publications on NW by Crutzen and Birks, TTAPS, and others with a call for more study of the climatic effects on plants and animals in the Southern Hemisphere. The society's council took the possibility of danger seriously.[20] So did the Royal Society of New Zealand. Also active were the New Zealand Association of Scientists, the New Zealand branch of International Physicians for the Prevention of Nuclear War, Scientists Against Nuclear Arms, Engineers for Social Responsibility, Computer People for the Prevention of Nuclear War, Librarians for Nuclear Disarmament, Architects Against Nuclear Arms, and Students and Teachers Organizing for Peace.[21]

The New Zealand government, reacting positively to the SCOPE report's call for more intensive study of the indirect societal, economic, and environmental impacts of a major nuclear war in the Northern Hemisphere, funded such an analysis (using money the French government paid as compensation for blowing up the *Rainbow Warrior*). It appeared in 1987. Assuming no local nuclear explosions (except in one scenario: the effects of an electromagnetic pulse from a blast closer to Australia) and at most a temperature decline of a few degrees, the consequences nonetheless would be staggering. Expanding on the Royal Society's economic analysis, the authors noted that, with loss of the 80 percent of trade overseas that was concentrated north of the Equator, imports of fuels, materials, and machines would cease. Without ball bearings, spare parts, computers, lubricants, and other industrial needs, and with a marginal domestic ability to provide substitutes, the economy would falter. For one reason or another, the nation's sole oil refinery, which provided 55 percent of transportation fuel needs, would fail. This would lead to an unemployment rate of 40–50 percent. Society would be further impacted by the absence of pharmaceutical imports and, when electrical generators inevitably broke down, the inability of pumps to move water and sewage. Food production would decline, but would still be adequate for the population. However, moving produce from farm to consumer would be problematical. At best, the report said, Kiwis would revert to subsistence living. Its authors called for widespread education of the danger and for the government to begin planning ways to minimize such threats.[22]

These outposts of Western civilization in the South Pacific, it should be noted, were not "nuclear virgins." New Zealand had long provided the United States with military, naval, and communications stations—which, in the post-World War II world, meant potential involvement in a nuclear war. Aside from port facilities useful to the US Navy, the US Air Force's Military Air Command used the Harewood Air Base near Christchurch, while the US Navy had, also at Harewood, a communications facility for submarines which served as a backup to another at North West Cape Station, Australia. There were, in addition, a station of the US Naval Observatory at Black Birch that provided celestial data useful for precise global positioning, and underwater acoustic arrays to detect Soviet submarines.[23] The island nation had also provided help, in a minor way, to British nuclear tests near Christmas Island in the 1950s.[24] In view of these past nuclear connections, the New Zealand Labour Party's

1984 move to ban nuclear weapons on its land and in its waters was in some degree an attempt to gain credibility for its opposition to nuclear testing and radioactive waste disposal in the Pacific.[25]

Australia was even more connected to the outside world, having its own security concerns about Indonesia, and providing the United States with satellite surveillance stations at Pine Gap, near Alice Springs in the Northern Territory, and Nurrungar, some 300 miles north-west of Adelaide in South Australia. These facilities could relay to and from the US data on missile launches from the Soviet Union and China as well as targeting information. A naval communications station at North West Cape in Western Australia was a vital link to American forces worldwide, especially to nuclear-armed submarines while under water. And Australia provided other military assets to the United States, including a satellite tracking station in Smithfield, South Australia, that provided geographic location information to American submarines; an Omega very low frequency navigation station, also useful to position submarines, in Gippsland, Victoria; passive sonar listening arrays to detect Soviet submarines, off Christmas Island; the Oak Tree seismic station to identify underground nuclear tests, at Alice Springs; and port facilities at Cockburn Sound, near Perth in West Australia.[26]

This was also a land in which uranium was mined and which was the site for a series of British nuclear tests in the 1950s, at Monte Bello Island, Western Australia, and Maralinga, South Australia.[27] The continent's location, just about half a world away from the United States, gave the United States global electronic coverage. Australia was indeed "a suitable piece of real estate," in the words of the analyst Desmond Ball, and its contribution to the command, control, communications, and intelligence aspects of American national security efforts made it a probable target in any superpower confrontation.[28]

But Australia's anti-nuclear sentiments, like New Zealand's, went back three decades. Led by clergy, churchgoers, and intellectuals, and eventually by unions and the Labor Party, a majority of the population became convinced that nuclear testing should be suspended worldwide: a 1957 poll showed 50 percent in favor and 38 percent opposed. Some 360 scientists in Australia agreed, and signed Linus Pauling's petition to this end.[29] Australia, too, had some abrasive encounters with the "non-disclosure" policy of the United States in the early 1980s. The B-52 bombers that landed at an Air Force base near Darwin while conducting navigation training flights certainly had nuclear capability. A growing controversy was finessed by an unsigned but valid statement by both governments that assured the aircraft would be unarmed and that Australian consent would be required to change that status. Opposition to port visits by nuclear-powered or nuclear-armed warships also surfaced, but was contained by governments that were convinced of the value of the ANZUS Treaty, despite a widespread perception that it made Australia a wartime target yet provided no guarantee of American assistance.[30]

By the 1980s, incensed by a belief that their leaders knew little about the American installations on their soil, and angered by revelations that facilities alleged to be run by the US military were covers for the Central Intelligence Agency, the National Security Agency, the National Reconnaissance Office, and other "spook" outfits, Australians protested the form of these arrangements, if not their need itself. Fundamentally, and just like the Kiwis, they desired to be a partner with the United States, not just a lackey.[31]

During World War I, Great Britain had created the Department of Scientific and Industrial Research (DSIR) in recognition of the government's need for technical expertise. This idea was exported to various Commonwealth countries, with New Zealand and Australia establishing particularly strong agencies. The Commonwealth Scientific and Industrial Research Organization (CSIRO), as it was called in Australia, employed Ian Galbally as a principal research scientist in its Division of Atmospheric Research. Following the pioneering 1982 paper in *Ambio* by Crutzen and Birks, but before the public announcement of NW research in late 1983, Galbally was joined by Crutzen and H. Rodhe, a professor of chemical meteorology at the University of Stockholm, in a study of the effects of nuclear explosions on the atmosphere over his native Australia. This was an early follow-up to the work of Crutzen and Birks, attempting further quantification, and the first to focus strongly on the Southern Hemisphere. It also illustrated the strong capabilities of "Down Under" in atmospheric sciences. The authors took war scenarios published by the US National Academy of Sciences in 1975 and by *Ambio* (with some modifications) and examined the disruption of sunlight and the penetration of harmful UV radiation at Earth's surface. With appropriate disclaimers about the accuracy of their values for such factors as fuel loading, and looking particularly at oil storage tanks and oil wells (whose down-hole safety valves were notoriously prone to failure), and at the rapid drying effect on tropical forests of radioactive fallout, they calculated an atmospheric burden of about 10 million tonnes of aerosols, versus approximately 200 million tonnes in the Northern Hemisphere. This would reduce sunlight by 80 percent or more, and was clearly a hazard.[32] Further study would require the use of various computer models, which is what the TTAPS team and others provided.

A. Barrie Pittock was another principal research scientist in CSIRO's Division of Atmospheric Research. He was not only a scientist familiar with NW from the time of its public unveiling, but a man with a social conscience. For Pittock, the organizers of the Halloween conference erred in their desire to avoid politics, in order that their scientific message would be more readily accepted. "By not raising such questions," he wrote, "scientists betray a lack of conviction about the reality of their scientific findings as these apply to their very own future existence."[33]

Recognizing that there were many who thought that nuclear war was an acceptable risk, Pittock hoped that the newly revealed climatic effects would change their minds. He accepted the notion "that the action or inaction of scientists on this issue has political implications, as do their conclusions." "Inevitably," he added, "this must raise the question as to whether scientists can (or even should) be objective on such an issue." Pointing to examples in which scientists divided on matters of public policy, such as the desired response to the effect of fluorocarbons on the ozone layer, the carbon dioxide greenhouse effect, and the safety of nuclear reactors, he acknowledged the potential for bias by scientists and their employers. Similar polarization existed among those who wrote about the environmental effects of nuclear war, with Edward Teller and Helen Caldecott (a leader of Physicians for Social Responsibility) as polar examples. Pittock's point was not that this was unusual, but rather that he and his colleagues, as scientists and citizens, must recognize the influences to which they were subjected, and endeavor to be objective; "it will not do us any good to distort the scientific facts."[34]

As the lead author of the well-received *Environmental Consequences of Nuclear War*, the SCOPE Report's first volume, on the physical effects of NW, Pittock brought his expertise to bear locally. The effects of conflict in the Northern Hemisphere, he recognized, would be moderated in the Southern Hemisphere by distance and by buffering of temperature changes by the larger areas of ocean. Nonetheless, the consequences could be severe. War in the northern springtime or summer would loft smoke high in the atmosphere. Simultaneously, the lower atmosphere would become remarkably stable, curtailing much precipitation. In the tropics, for example, the attenuated sunlight would lower surface temperatures over continental areas, canceling the monsoon mechanism that brings rain to southern and southeastern Asia. Smoke would pour further southward, lowering temperatures and rainfall over Australia, where agriculture depends heavily on precipitation. Still further south, in Tasmania and New Zealand, crops would be affected more by temperature changes. Australia, New Zealand, and Argentina might see their food surpluses reduced but, Pittock felt, they could survive. Mass starvation, however, would likely hit densely populated southern Africa, as well as Asia.[35]

With his scientific expertise and moral enthusiasm, Pittock became something of a policy force with the publication of his book *Beyond Darkness: Nuclear Winter in Australia and New Zealand* (1987). If the American bases were closed, he argued, Soviet and Chinese warheads would be retargeted. Australia and New Zealand would thus become more likely to survive a nuclear conflict, and would assume "the mantle of civilization in the aftermath of a war which had devastated the Northern Hemisphere [and] would, in a real sense, be like Noah preparing for the Flood." Another consequence of NW, he thought, was that allies of the superpowers might become more insistent about having a voice in their strategic and political decisions. Indeed, rejection of the US's nuclear umbrella by its allies might be a desirable move toward greater peace by allowing the superpowers to negotiate larger disarmament steps.[36]

Australia had long been home to nuclear activities that evoked controversy. These were primarily the mining of its vast uranium resources and the American military bases, called "joint facilities." Opponents of mining argued that the safest thing was to leave the ore in the ground. Additionally, they feared environmental degradation and yet another assault on Aboriginal lands. Governments, both Liberal and Labor, defended mining, saying that uranium sales were carefully controlled by provisions of the nuclear Non-Proliferation Treaty (NPT). Purchasers could no doubt buy the processed ore elsewhere from less scrupulous nations, an action that would do damage to the primary goal of the treaty: curtailing weapons proliferation. Moreover, the NPT gave nations that renounced the option to develop weapons the right to purchase materials. Should the supply of uranium diminish markedly, it would make breeder reactors more appealing economically, and this would lead directly to a "plutonium economy," with large quantities of this bomb material in circulation as fuel for this type of reactor.

As for the joint facilities, governments claimed that Australians were kept fully informed of American activities, and that they served not offensive, but defensive, postures of the United States. By monitoring nuclear and missile tests in China and the USSR, they deterred Soviet aggression and contributed to international stability. A 1984 position paper by the Australian Department of Foreign Affairs, headed by Labor's Bill Hayden, showed that realists, not idealists, were in charge. While the "Australian Government is committed to complete nuclear disarmament," they did not expect this to happen in the near future. Deterrence was not a long-term solution, but it was the only viable option at the moment. Interestingly, the ministry pursued a worst-case analysis in acknowledging that nuclear war just might destroy the world, and completely accepted the possibility that the NW phenomenon was valid, making the targeting of joint facilities irrelevant in the threat to the nation. "Even if the war was confined to the northern hemisphere, even if Australia was not hit by a single nuclear weapon, we would still suffer a nuclear winter effect in the southern hemisphere."[37] This acknowledgment of interest in NW was followed by at least one research grant to the CSIRO, in 1986, for $140,000.[38]

Aside from people in the United States and the Soviet Union, citizens of Australia and New Zealand seemed most concerned about the climatic consequences of nuclear war. Despite their distance from the superpowers, they had not been insulated from weapons tests in the Pacific or, indeed, on Australian soil, or from other nuclear connections. Both nations had a tradition of strong opposition to nuclear dangers and minor concern with international communism. Notably, too, the Aussies could boast of some first-rate atmospheric scientists with social consciences. A sense of independence and the shock of the newly revealed NW danger seemingly led these nations to focus on NW as a vehicle to express their frustration with the superpowers' inability to curtail the arms race.

Perhaps, however, there is less need to seek enlightenment on why these countries expressed lasting concern about NW and more need to understand its absence elsewhere. Despite reports on NW by the Royal Society of Canada, the United Nations, and the ICSU's Scientific Committee on Problems of the Environment, which marshaled about 300 contributors from dozens of countries, and a workshop by the European Physical Society, there was little significant interest in NW shown by virtually all nations on Earth. Great Britain, a leader in world science, saw several papers emerge from its Meteorological Office, and a few elsewhere, but its scientific community can not be said to have been actively engaged. Public funds for research were conspicuous in their absence outside the superpowers. Perhaps that was as it should have been, the US and the USSR having caused most, if not all, of the threat. The lack of supercomputers, atmospheric models, and trained personnel in many nations, and the political dominance of the superpowers, presumably were important in molding the widespread non-response. Another perspective was illustrated by China, where Ye Du Zhang, a meteorologist who had been trained at the University of Chicago in the 1940s, was aware of the NW phenomenon and accepted its reality. Yet this former vice president of the Chinese Academy of Sciences felt that it was not necessary to warn his government because he doubted that a large nuclear war would ever occur. "So why bother?"[39] Still, New Zealand showed that it could be a presence on the world stage, even without a cast of atmospheric scientists. It took a belief that it was necessary to respond to potential threats of disaster.

The Debate Continues

NW did not inspire measured commentary. The level of polarization remained high, in both scholarly and popular periodicals, and more than a few authors questioned the motives of those who believed, or failed to believe, in NW. Paleontologists who disagreed with the asteroid-impact explanation for the demise of the dinosaurs (and who may have had their noses bent a bit out of shape by physicists invading their turf) complained that they had difficulty getting grants and having papers accepted by journals, if their reviewers favored the impact theory. Even more, they complained that they were "being branded as militarists, on the grounds that their skepticism undermine[d] the nuclear winter thesis."[40]

In a two-page diatribe that must have disconcerted the one-paragraph preference of *USA Today* readers, Herbert London of New York University and the Hudson Institute charged that Sagan and his accomplices had "produced a moral play of nuclear war." The professor of social studies and host of the NBC-TV show *Myths That Rule America* enumerated a number of technical uncertainties before querying why the "Sagan report" (presumably the TTAPS paper in the August 1984 issue of *Scientific American*) was released. Surely, he felt, it was "designed to produce disarmament by pointing out the horrendous consequences of nuclear exchange." Our Soviet adversaries, in contrast, "will emphasize the need to be vigilant in the face of Western threats." London called the Sagan report the "scientific equivalent of the film *Testament* and the television program *The Day After*." These were scare tactics, designed to "destroy national resolve by suggesting that our enemy is nuclear weapons, not the Soviet Union." He railed against unilateral disarmament (which had not been advocated by anyone) and urged the maintenance of a credible deterrent. "If it were up to our doomsday prophets," he intoned, "national defense would be the sacrificial lamb for their new social order." "Fortunately," he added, "most prophets have been Cassandras and most have been wrong. There is no reason to believe that Sagan and his friends are any different from their predecessors."[41] (Cassandra, London forgot, had warned about the Trojan horse and had been correct.)

Even S. Fred Singer, normally a strong but sensible partisan, came intemperately close to Red-baiting in an autumn 1984 article in the United Nations journal *Disarmament*. Criticizing the nuclear freeze movement as a "standstill" rather than a "build down" (freeze advocates, of course, preferred the latter, but despaired achieving it under Reagan), he wrote: "I do not want to suggest that the average supporter of a nuclear freeze is a witting or unwitting Soviet agent, but there is no question of the parallelism between a freeze and Soviet political aims."[42]

One of the most persistent critics of NW was George Rathjens of MIT. His technical arguments were mentioned in chapter 11; he also had extensive policy experience—he had been, for example, special assistant to the director of the US Arms Control and Disarmament Agency. If the pre-NW prediction of more than 2 billion deaths in a nuclear war had failed to reduce the superpowers' stockpiles, he asked, why should a climatic change do so now? NW was irrelevant for policy; at most, targeting might be changed still more away from cities. Even without NW, Rathjens felt, people recognized that war is terrible; NW was but a small perturbation in its horror.[43]

Not all agreed with this view. Public perception of yet further horrors to result from nuclear war, they felt, might finally cause governments to turn the arms race around. Pressure from non-combatants, who formerly thought themselves out of danger, might also force policy changes. With puckish humor, the Berkeley physicist Gene Rochlin wondered if it were worthwhile, even if the science predicting NW was flawed, to "debunk a scientific myth which may perform positive historical functions."[44] Freeman Dyson searched his soul over the same point: "As a scientist I want to rip the theory of nuclear winter apart, but as a human being I want to believe in it. . . . What does a scientist do when science and humanity pull in opposite directions?"[45]

Rathjens had no doubts. His realist approach matched that of the two other distinguished arms-control activists with backgrounds in physics who were discussed in chapter 11, John Holdren and Frank von Hippel. All doubted the quality of TTAPS's science, and all apparently were influenced by a desire not to see the role of scientific advice discredited in furthering the goal of arms reductions.[46] Opposed to these views were Carl Sagan, Paul Ehrlich, and Jonathan Schell, idealists who in their early statements emphasized the danger of human extinction—a concept that is almost unfathomable and therefore perhaps unarguable. For them, the circumstances had been altered decidedly, and a worst-case analysis demanded action.

Rathjens, a colorful personality, seemed at times a bit intemperate. At an October 1984 meeting in Berkeley, some in the audience were startled at his call for NW scientists to be "discredited" for "misinforming the public."[47] Speculation followed that his hostility, which bordered on the personal, reflected Sagan's elevation to preeminence as the nation's leading anti-Establishment arms controller, over many who had spent years in the trenches. Indeed, except for the concluding show in the *Cosmos* television series, in which he spoke eloquently against the danger of nuclear war,[48] Sagan had not before been seen as a major player on this field, while Rathjens had labored long, effectively, and publicly. A specific irritant between the two occurred when Sagan, on the board of the Council for a Livable World's Education Fund, allowed it to republish his *Parade* article as a handsome booklet. Rathjens, who chaired the Council for a Livable World and disdained the article, was not informed; he was "furious."[49]

Reflecting on that period, Rathjens noted that many long-time comrades in the effort to contain the nuclear arsenals were appalled by his criticism of NW work. To those who recognized that fear of NW could be used as a tool to "fight pernicious public policy," his behavior seemed counterproductive. Some shared his low opinion of TTAPS's work (he named Freeman Dyson and Victor Weisskopf), but they chose not to express their views publicly.[50] Dyson did later explain his behavior. Of the three options available—demand scientific accuracy, encourage anything that leads to arms control, or refrain from comment— he chose the last, joining the majority of scientists who shrank from appearing to say in public that "after all, nuclear war may not be so bad." Admitting that it was "an unheroic compromise," Dyson believed that "it is good to be honest but it is often better to remain silent."[51]

In October 1985, Sagan was given four pages of *Nature* for a "Commentary" column to rebuke Edward Teller, who, he felt, minimized the consequences of nuclear war and the relevance of NW. Citing the NAS-NRC, SCOPE, and Royal Society of Canada reports, Sagan claimed widespread support for the possibility of severe climatic effects from city fires. In congressional testimony and published articles, Teller had argued that radioactive fallout, ozone depletion, and NW effects from nuclear warfare were "exaggerated." Not so, said Sagan, marshalling data and arguments. In particular, he noted that the trend in weaponry—toward warheads smaller than 1 MT and construction of a missile-defense system—would do nothing to divert NW: A 100-KT air burst would be a very efficient match to ignite cities, and a missile-defense system would provoke the USSR to expand its arsenal.[52]

Teller's sanctimonious remark in *Nature*, a year earlier, that "highly speculative theories of worldwide destruction—even the end of life on Earth—used as a call for a particular kind of political action serve neither the good reputation of science nor dispassionate political thought"[53] particularly irked Sagan. Before the dangers of fallout, ozone depletion, and NW were recognized, Sagan said, we were not warned that "the alleged *absence* of widespread or long-term effects was speculative." He continued: "However, when a range of scientific evidence suggests that these effects are real, with grave biological and social consequences, then Teller comes forth to minimize the possible consequences, reminding us that not all the evidence is in." This, Sagan claimed, was "a clear double standard of scientific evidence at work," and it would lead to its own "particular kind of political action."[54]

In Tellerian style, Teller responded to Sagan's charges circuitously. First he chided Sagan for not mentioning some mitigating features of the SCOPE report and imputed that Sagan still insisted on the full accuracy of the TTAPS paper (Sagan had called it a "valid first-order assessment"). Then he took issue with Sagan's call in *Foreign Affairs* for reducing the nuclear arsenals of the superpowers. Not only did Teller doubt that we could trust the Soviets to comply with treaties, but since 1965, as the stockpiles were modernized and increasingly oriented toward MIRVed missiles, the United States had unilaterally reduced the number of weapons by 30 percent and their megatonnage by 75 percent anyway. To this process of limiting the devastation of war, defensive measures (SDI) should be added. Finally, Teller invoked the global fire that was ignited by the asteroid 65 million years ago (indicated by the layer of carbon alongside the band of iridium), which produced 1,000 times as much smoke as in the NW calculations. He conceded that this K-T event obviously swamped the rainout ability of the atmosphere's moisture, but argued that it was unlikely to happen when cities burned. The carnage would be great, but not total: "The survival of approximately half the living genera witnesses the toughness of life on Earth."[55]

Clearly, these bitter antagonists moved but microscopically toward one another. But during 1984 and 1985, as reports by the National Academy of Sciences, SCOPE, and other bodies appeared, something of a consensus on the science developed in the wider community. It was a weak agreement, more to the effect that NW *can* occur, not that it *will* occur. As models were refined, the severity of cooling was reduced. Paradoxically, however, the impact on humans was expanded, as the consequences on agriculture of even these moderated temperatures were probed. Scenarios considered unreasonable, such as the World Health Organization's estimate of 2 billion injuries and deaths in targets that included cities of the Third World and the Southern Hemisphere, were ignored. Human extinction gave way to the possibility of near-extinction. But danger of the destruction of civilization remained, and this was not limited to the states that comprised the battlefield.

In 2 years of intense investigation and debate on NW, much new information was added to the store of knowledge and many new insights were discussed. Despite the scientific consensus just mentioned, virtually all actors and commentators enlisted in one of the two political camps (presented here as polar opposites). The one camp consisted of those who believed that the danger of climatic disaster was so great that changes in the arsenals must be made immediately. The other camp embraced those who felt that NW was too uncertain a reed to lean upon, so existing peace-through-strength policies must be maintained. Few people changed their NW loyalties—which seemed largely to match their pre-NW political sympathies. Nor should this be seen as surprising, since the debate was about the interpretation of scientific evidence and national policy, and to a far lesser extent about the correctness of scientific "facts."

Moreover, by this time, if not much earlier, it was recognized that, in addition to searching for objective "truth," scientists were motivated to promote their careers and increase the importance of their disciplines. This could make them emotional, egotistical, ambitious, and nasty—much like the rest of us. (Political orientation colored views on other science-related matters. For example, opinion polls frequently track the political affiliation of respondents on various issues. In 1997, Democrats, seen as tending toward greater concern about the environment, believed strongly in the evidence for global warming, while Republicans, seen as concerned more with the needs of business, were far less alarmed.[56])

The debate over the validity and significance of NW predictions largely positioned individuals against individuals. Virtually no professional society or citizen's organization or professional interest group, claiming to represent some body of organized scientific or enlightened opinion, took a side. Such polarization had occurred during debates over the supersonic transport, the Anti-Ballistic Missile, and the Strategic Defense Initiative, among various environmental and weapon controversies. Neither the Committee for a Sane Nuclear Policy, the Union of Concerned Scientists, the Federation of American Scientists, the Sierra Club, nor the American Physical Society (which protested SDI) embraced NW as an issue of great concern.[57] This limited the political intensity of the debate, leaving it to individuals to convince Congress to require annual reports on NW from the Department of Defense. And even Congress's muscle turned flabby, as it accepted the public relations travesties that the secretary of defense palmed off as serious reports in 1985 and 1986. Throughout the period, Carl Sagan's voice remained the strongest and most committed for NW-inspired cuts in the nuclear arsenals. A powerful call to rationality, it was nonetheless scientifically suspect by some; it suffered additionally from antipathy to his perceived arrogance and alleged tendency toward self-promotion.

The TTAPS group did not hold together much beyond 1984, which may help to explain why they never published the extensive details of their calculations, as promised in their December 1983 paper in *Science*. Nor did any of them contribute much new research to the ongoing debate over NW. They made little progress converting their work to a GCM. Sagan was preoccupied with his crusade, Turco spent much of his time going to meetings, Ackerman divided his time between meetings and research on radiative transfer and remote sensing, Pollack returned to planetary studies, and Toon investigated Saharan sand storms.[58]

As 1985 ended, Edwin M. Yoder Jr. presented one of the year's few commentaries on NW by a syndicated columnist. In his "New Year litany," Yoder wrote:

From ghoulies and ghosties and long-leggedy beasties, and things that go bump in the night, especially Carl Sagan's redundant warnings against nuclear weapons and nuclear winters,

Good Lord, deliver us.[59]

IV Smoldering Issues: 1986 and Afterward

19 Scientific Progress and Controversy

The Conference Circuit

In addition to attending meetings of the bodies that produced the several studies mentioned in previous chapters, NW scientists ran up frequent-flier miles on the lecture and conference circuit. Turco and Toon, for example, were in Tokyo for a SCOPE session in February 1985 (and to inform Japanese scientists about their work, though the Japanese produced no significant research on NW), and were in Santa Barbara later that month, attending a three-day conference sponsored by the Defense Nuclear Agency. Contemptuous though many scientists seemed to be toward the US government's nuclear weapons policies, and dismissive even of Defense Nuclear Agency gatherings that seemed to showcase old news, they felt obliged to be present in case something novel was announced.[1] Attendance also was a means of parading each laboratory's accomplishments, as at a fashion show, with the DNA the sole customer.

A year later, in February 1986, the DNA sponsored a successor meeting, held at Moffett Field, California (home of the Ames Research Center), showing both its dedication to bringing NW participants together and its continued wisdom in selecting California as a winter venue. More than 50 papers were on the agenda, indicating the large community of scientists now contributing to NW information, the variety of their university and government labs, and the sprinkling of defense contractors interested. Mark Harwell led off the program with a review of his volume of the SCOPE report, mischievously remarking that biologists were usually at the tail of the agenda. In a way, this showed the DNA's interest in biology, even if the political masters declined to fund its investigation.

Toon noted the flexibility of the model he was developing at Ames, which could be adapted to a variety of geographical projections and which would be able to incorporate wet smoke and dust particles, coagulation, and condensation. The National Center for Atmospheric Research, Stephen Schneider reported, also was concerned with the degree to which carbon was hydrophilic or hydrophobic, and with processes that occurred on a scale far smaller than the latitude-longitude-altitude bins of current 3-D GCMs. Smaller units could be chosen, but the cost in time and money was considerable. Schneider's team was improving a number of factors, including aerosol properties, scattering of sunlight, and the effect on smoke lofting of a higher dust layer that shielded it from some solar radiation. Starley Thompson added that GCM improvement had considerably reduced the area of quick freezes from what had been announced a year earlier. Thompson also sketched the progression of temperature decreases, from 1-D models that gave a temperature decline of 35°C through interactive 3-D models (capable of removing aerosols) that yielded a temperature decline of 12°C.

Richard Small of the Pacific-Sierra Research Corporation, who earlier had looked at wild-land fires, now was working on cities. Defining an "urban" area as one with at least 25,000 people, he found about 4,300 targets in the Soviet Union, such as military facilities, ports, power stations, and refineries, that were co-located in urban areas. Interestingly, Soviet and American cities differed in some relevant ways. In the USSR, apartments were of the order of 300–400 square feet, much smaller than those in the US. This probably meant that fuel loadings were higher there, as more furniture and books were packed into these spaces. On the other hand, Soviet cities had many wide streets, constructed deliberately to minimize the spread of fire.

Fuel loading was the "hot" subject discussed by several scientists at this meeting. With more attention now being given to fire studies, better data were becoming available. George Bing of the Livermore Lab looked at Warsaw Pact and NATO cities and concluded that their burnable inventories were about half those calculated by others. Still, NW, or "nuclear chill," did not go away. Turco, defending his own estimates in the TTAPS paper, criticized Bing for minimizing the contribution of certain sources, such as plastics. David Simonett, a geographer at the University of California at Santa Barbara, was in the process of more systematically examining such tools and ingredients as aerial photo interpretation, census data, land-use maps, floor-space use, the number of buildings per unit area, the number of floors in a building, and firebreaks for cities representative of the United States, Western Europe, and India. His early finding for the largely suburban California city of San José was 10 kilograms of fuel per square meter, rather less than the 40 kg/m^2 value used in the NAS report. This figure was in line with an analysis Turco presented at a National Academy of Sciences seminar in March 1985: 2–10 kg/m^2 in suburban areas, 20–40 kg/m^2 in central cities, and 100–300 kg/m^2 in dense urban cores.[2]

Politics, like biology, was not funded by the DoD, but it was represented nonetheless on this DNA program in the person of Leon Gouré. He remarked that the Soviet Union had given indications that it lacked the computer capability to model large fires. This was surely not a great surprise to the audience, but it helped to explain the stonewalling faced by American scientists when they asked for such information. Gouré also noted that it was forbidden in Soviet publications to discuss the effects of attacks on targets in their country; the examples given were always of NATO targets. Most of Gouré's address was directed at the way in which the Kremlin used NW for propaganda purposes, the reliance of Soviet scientists on Western data and models, and the absence of any real contributions from the

Soviet Union. Turco called Gouré's remarks "non-objective political propaganda," and Schneider and others joined the criticism. A defensive Gouré admitted that he had written his paper in mid 1984 and had not revised it in the nearly 2 years since then.[3]

The next month, March 1986, the Virginia Polytechnic Institute and State University hosted a conference on the strategic and diplomatic implications of NW. A representative cast of characters attended—among them Thomas Ackerman, George Carrier, Mark Harwell, Alan Hecht, Michael MacCracken, Russell Seitz, Richard Small, Thomas Malone, and George Rathjens—and said (mostly) predictable things.[4]

Arthur Broyles, of the Livermore Lab, addressed the ranges of uncertainties in many of the ingredients that entered fire calculations: "Multiplying these uncertainty factors together implies that the maximum amount of smoke produced could exceed the minimum amount by a factor of 86,000, a ridiculous number." And this did not even take into consideration the reality of warfare scenarios and other variables. Broyles's approach was a good example of the continuing gap between those who proposed inaction (via more research to reduce the uncertainties) and those who embraced political action based on a not-ridiculous possibility of a climatic catastrophe.[5]

Broyles's Livermore colleague Joseph Knox, a consistent voice of common sense, disdained the discordance over the plausibility or doubtfulness of NW. He urged others to accept that "the most important characteristics of nuclear winter are its inherent uncertainty, untestability, and the unknowability of details." Because scenario outcomes were sensitive to variations in inputs, Knox suggested that reducing the number of nuclear warheads by a few factors "could make an important difference in the climatic consequences" predicted, especially if fewer weapons were targeted on cities. Other measures to reduce damage and ensure larger numbers of survivors, none of them new by this time, were smaller-yield warheads, increased targeting accuracy, earth-penetrating warheads to minimize fires, "revitalized" civil defense efforts, and even a "less than perfect strategic defense shield." Knox appeared ambivalent about strategic defense, however, suggesting that, with negotiations, it might be unnecessary.[6]

Colonel Gary Betourne, the military assistant to the DoD's director for strategic forces policy, emphasized that the DoD opposed both House and Senate Concurrent Resolutions to establish a joint US-USSR scientific study of NW. These resolutions, introduced a year earlier, were languishing and ultimately died. Betourne asserted that the Soviets were more interested in scoring propaganda points and in gaining access to advanced US computer technology. The proper channel for joint research, he asserted, was the existing program run by the Environmental Protection Agency. In this he was supported by Gary Waxmonsky of the US Environmental Protection Agency, who revealed that during high-level discussions in Moscow in November 1985 Hydromet chairman Yuriy Izrael had shown a willingness to collaborate on NW at whatever pace the United States wished. Much of what the United States knew of Soviet research, Waxmonsky claimed, came via this environmental agreement (a claim poorly substantiated either in the literature or in statements by American scientists). In any case, it appears that the EPA link supported little or no new research on NW.[7]

Not all meetings occurred in the United States or were dominated by American scientists. The Second All-Union Conference of Scientists on Problems of Peace and Prevention of Nuclear War took place in Moscow in May 1986, and the published SCOPE report was formally presented to the ICSU in mid September 1986 in Berne, Switzerland.[8] Still, Americans did lead the study of NW and North America is where the action was.

The Defense Nuclear Agency, still admirably doing its job, held yet another conference, in April 1987, again in Santa Barbara. David Simonett of the University of California at Santa Barbara reported on his continuing study of the amount of combustible materials in cities, with San José as his focus. Simonett's student Howard Veregin examined the cities of NATO and Warsaw Pact countries. Aerial photographs were Simonett's principal means of calculating the built-up area, and from that the fuel loading, but his conclusions were still to be regarded as tentative. Average urban fuel loadings were double Simonett's estimate of the previous year (now about 20 kg/m^2), but fossil fuel stores were excluded from the count, and San José was notably a city of one- and two-story buildings. By the time of publication, in 1988, Simonett had reduced his estimates to slightly below 10 kg/m^2 for built-up areas. Also reduced, in a report from the Pacific-Sierra Research Corporation, was the amount of smoke produced by a 3,000-MT nuclear attack on the United States: 39 million tonnes in July, 36 million in January.[9]

Sandia National Laboratories in Albuquerque (which specialized in the non-nuclear components of nuclear weapons) reported on two large pool fires that had been set (using jet fuel) to collect data on the fires and their smoke plumes. Similarly, scientists at the Lawrence Berkeley Laboratory observed burning Douglas fir, plywood, and asphalt roofing shingles, noting in particular the fraction of black carbon particles emitted. Researchers at the Georgia Institute of Technology ignited three types of plastic materials. Sandia also tested the changing characteristics of smoke as it aged. Scavenging of aerosol particles from the atmosphere by increased motion, by serving as cloud condensation nuclei, and by ice crystals was studied both theoretically and experimentally at several institutions.

In his overview of the two DNA volumes from this meeting, Turco noted that "burning petroleum, plastics and related materials can emit 5% or more of their mass as soot," while wood burned with limited oxygen can yield as much as 2% soot. Smoke thus would be blacker than believed previously. Turco also suggested that the fraction of soot from oil refineries and cities, though still uncertain, would likely be larger. Of the soot lofted, Turco noted, probably less than half would be rained out immediately, "because of its poor nucleation properties relative to other materials, and because of the likely overseeding and reduced precipitation efficiencies of smoke clouds." In addition to these papers, there were reports on particle microphysics, on the dynamics of smoke plumes, on mesoscale phenomena, on GCMs, and on results from a fire set in Lodi Canyon. In all, more than 50 papers were presented.[10]

Computer Modeling

The SCOPE report, published in late 1985, indicated a number of topics that should be investigated further, as did the NAS account, which appeared almost a year earlier. The NAS mandate, however, expired with its report, while SCOPE continued for another 3 years, holding more workshops and issuing a revised edition of its study in 1989. Aside from a valuable preface that surveyed recent developments, the second edition was identical to the first.[11]

Adhering to their original methodology of avoiding the contentious subject of warfare scenarios, SCOPE scientists, meeting in Bangkok in February 1987, decided to examine three Northern-Hemisphere smoke scenarios. Injection into the atmosphere of 15, 50, and 150 million tonnes of dark smoke uniformly and immediately gave absorption optical depths of 0.3, 1.0, and 3.0, numbers subsequently used by several GCM programmers. For a climatically sensitive summertime conflict, land areas between 30° N and 70° N suffered daytime temperature reductions of about 5°C, 13°C, and 22°C, respectively. Precipitation over land was reduced to one-fourth of normal in each of the three cases, and was only marginally better in the region down to the Equator; the Asian monsoon season disappeared. Light levels plunged 40, 70, and 90 percent in the upper band and 0, 30, and 50 percent in the range from the Equator to 20° N. Humans had never experienced such changes over large parts of Earth. These GCM studies provided finer detail than available just a few years earlier, but they still had weaknesses. Richard Small, in particular, encouraged more research on smoke injection profiles. Each major study (except NCAR's) inserted smoke of uniform density into one or more altitude bands, a condition that might prevail a week or more after a nuclear war. But this differed from conditions *immediately* after a war, when smoke would rise from numerous geographically separated sources. Modeling of precipitation also needed refinement, while the fundamental uncertainty remained of using GCMs so far out of the range for which they were constructed. Nonetheless, the new work did nothing to challenge the conclusions of the first SCOPE report.[12]

Although scientists at a number of institutions worked with GCMs, most NW studies were conducted in four places. The National Center for Atmospheric Research and the Los Alamos National Laboratory used variants of the Community Climate Model, while the Lawrence Livermore National Laboratory and the Computing Centre of the USSR Academy of Sciences applied variants of the Oregon State University tropospheric GCM. Comparisons between LLNL and NCAR provided reasonably similar results. No one GCM treated all phenomena, but by the end of 1986, in general, they accounted for "the transport and dispersion of smoke, coupling of smoke removal to model-predicted precipitation, varying particle size, coagulation, diurnal variation, scattering of solar radiation, and absorption and emission of thermal radiation by smoke particles." What they lacked, to varying degrees, were adequate treatment of the surface boundary layer, seasonal changes (represented by varying ocean temperatures), particle scavenging, consensus on a mathematical approach to smoke transport, atmospheric chemistry, and chemical scavenging.[13]

In 1985 and 1986, Robert Malone and his colleagues at Los Alamos had used an interactive GCM model to show that optically dense smoke layers could absorb solar radiation and rise higher in the troposphere than earlier believed, and even into the stratosphere. With this immunity to rainout, the smoke was capable of remaining aloft for months or years, a finding that was the greatest novelty of this research. When the "Bangkok scenarios" were tested, after 30 days the low smoke case showed that 25–40 percent of the original smoke mass had stabilized aloft, 35–40 percent in the 50 million tonnes case, and about 55 percent when 150 million tonnes was considered. The smoke pall spread within weeks over the Northern Hemisphere and into the Southern Hemisphere. In each case the smoke had a lifetime of one year, allowing it enough time to induce marked climatic effects that persisted into the second growing season. In addition, smoke that rose into the stratosphere reduced the ozone layer by an average of 40 percent, half by chemical decomposition and half by displacing ozone toward the Southern Hemisphere. UV-B radiation would stream through this ozone hole for an extended period.[14]

Curt Covey, at the University of Miami, tweaked his GCM to test other variables. Current models prescribed an ocean surface temperature and existence of sea ice that remained fixed. This was unrealistic under NW conditions, and increasingly so over the duration of a long-term study. Covey therefore relaxed those conditions and tested the response over 4 months of simulated time, finding contradictory effects: an increase in formation of sea ice in some locations and land surface warming in others. The more extensive ice contributed to cooling of downwind North America and Europe, while land south of the assumed smoke cloud saw temperatures moderated by heat transported from smoke-filled, solar-warmed air in the upper troposphere.[15]

With Starley Thompson and V. Ramaswamy, Covey fine-tuned the optical properties of smoke, using a range of values to test previous assumptions about the absorption and scattering of solar radiation and its transparency to infrared radiation. Surface temperatures proved to be sensitive to these changes, indicating the need to incorporate them in future GCM simulations. At Livermore, Steven Ghan, Michael MacCracken, and John Walton conducted other sensitivity studies, noting the strong curtailment of rainfall over land even for smaller amounts of smoke. This was likely caused by reduced evaporation of surface moisture because there was less convective mixing of the boundary air layer and the upper troposphere. Tests were made using varying masses of smoke placed at different altitudes, smoke particles of different sizes, conflict at different seasons, and so forth. An intuitive conclusion was confirmed: "For modest injections [of smoke] the land surface cooling in the first few weeks is found to be proportional to the smoke loading, while for larger injections the amount of smoke affects only the duration of the surface cooling."[16] Such research did not, and could not, specify precisely the climatic responses of a nuclear war, for there remained too many variables, but it went far in showing the limits of uncertainty and in affirming that changes would be substantial.

The "mesoscale problem"—referring to distances in the range 10–100 kilometers—persisted. With GCMs dicing the atmosphere into blocks that were far larger than meteorological activity such as a cloud, and necessarily treating each slab as uniform, some scientists doubted that real behavior was being predicted. B.W. Golding, P. Goldsmith, and their colleagues used a British Meteorological Office weather model with a grid of 15 kilometers that predicted significant rainout of smoke. Schneider, Thompson, and Covey, whose GCM had a grid of about 550 kilometers, welcomed attention to such smaller phenomena, but noted that the UK mesoscale model failed to include "the most controversial and important aspects in the entire early removal debate." Schneider et al. referred to the manner in which individual smoke particles would be "processed" by convective movement in plumes and clouds. This microphysical problem left the early removal of smoke to range from 10 percent to 90 percent of the amount generated. (The NAS report had arbitrarily assumed 50 percent removal.) Running a NW computer model with small grids was prohibitively expensive.[17]

Under NW conditions, land would cool much more than the oceans, presumably bringing strong winds and enhanced precipitation along the coastline of continents. Charles Molenkamp of the Livermore Lab, using an improved mesoscale model, instead found little difference in the land and sea temperatures and slight air flow, as far as 90 kilometers inland, thanks to fog and clouds.[18]

These numerous studies suggested that in the first two weeks of a summertime war the mid latitudes of the Northern Hemisphere would experience a decline of as much as 15–20°C, with continental interior temperatures falling as much as 30°C, including occasional freezing experiences. Prolonged freezing, however, was extremely unlikely. As temperatures in the temperate regions moderated, sub-tropical areas, such as India and southern China, might face a 5–10°C decline, with the temperature rarely going below 15°C, a temperature that is critical at a certain stage in the growth of rice. For the tropics and the Southern Hemisphere, different authors came to different conclusions. G. S. Golitsyn and Michael MacCracken, in a major review for the World Climate Programme, predicted minor temperature decreases (unless the amount of smoke lofted was extreme); Barrie Pittock thought the tropics could see cooling of 10–15°C and Southern Hemisphere inland areas about 5°C.

Under even moderately opaque skies and with moderate cooling of Earth's surface, however, the troposphere could become unusually stable. This would lead to a great reduction in convective activity and rainfall. The Asian and African summer monsoons are normally driven by heated air rising in the interiors, drawing in moist air from the nearby oceans. With lowered inland temperatures (caused by as little as 10 million tonnes of soot), the monsoon circulation could be suppressed over densely populated regions. In the period beyond one month of the smoke plumes' rising into the atmosphere, the acute NW effects were expected to moderate, but to an unknown extent. With perhaps half of the smoke lofted into the high troposphere or the stratosphere, above the weather, lowered temperatures could persist for months or even years. Ocean temperature, sea ice, dust, chemical toxins, and radioactive materials would contribute further to changes that were largely qualitative at that time. Both a CSIRO team led by Barrie Pittock and a rump TTAPS group consisting of Ackerman, Turco, and Toon considered that the smoke that stabilized in the stratosphere would have a residence time of half a year or more. Absorption optical depths of 1 to 3 over large parts of the Northern Hemisphere within weeks of the outbreak of war would decline to about 0.2 by the second growing season, while the Southern Hemisphere would experience an optical depth of 0.2 during the first 6 months. This would be sufficient for noticeable temperature effects.[19]

As most atmospheric scientists moved toward consensus, not all critics were prepared to accept their conclusions. In 1988, S. Fred Singer, who had been quiet for some time, re-entered the lists on the same horse. As before, Singer argued that, if there were any NW cooling, it would be short-lived and of minor amount, due to rapid rainout of much smoke and heating by a greenhouse effect. The novelty of Singer's case now was his analysis of the NAS report. He disagreed with the warfare scenarios used by the NAS (and by TTAPS and in the *Ambio* paper), asserting that they maximized smoke and, consequently, climatic effects. However, for argument's sake Singer was willing to accept them. His current attention focused on physical phenomena. The NAS, he complained, looked at such immediate effects as the lofting of dust, vaporization and lofting of surface water, lofting of atmospheric water vapor, and the creation and rise of nitrogen oxides by the fireball. However, the report ignored condensation of the considerable amount of water vapor now in the atmosphere from both nuclear explosions and subsequent fires, and the likelihood that cirrus clouds (ice crystals) might be formed from water vapor propelled to high altitude by explosions. The cirrus clouds could produce a strong greenhouse effect on the smoke below, and also reflect considerable solar radiation back into space.

Also inadequately treated, Singer charged, were the injection of smoke into the atmosphere over the course of hours or days, the inhomogeneity of the smoke, the scavenging of smoke by sinking dust clouds, and the smoke particles' coagulation. All would lead to a lesser ability to absorb sunlight, a greater opacity to infrared radiation (which would slow cooling), and speedier fallout. Singer also faulted the inability of GCMs to deal with mesoscale processes and their use of a diurnally averaged Sun instead of true day/night conditions. The latter was of particular concern, as Singer suggested that night-time cooling might lower smoke clouds. Interesting and provocative as always, Singer failed to make any observable impression on the atmospheric scientists doing the modeling. Perhaps they disagreed with his arguments because their calculations of scavenging and particle size yielded different degrees of infrared opaqueness and visible transmission than Singer estimated. Indeed, Stephen Schneider called Singer's emphasis on heating an "infrared herring."[20]

When Turco, Toon, Ackerman, Pollack, and Sagan published their blockbuster paper on NW in *Science* in December 1983, the journal gave them a very generous 10 pages. In January 1990, as research on the phenomenon dwindled, *Science* provided TTAPS with 11 pages to survey the current state of the field (or perhaps to wrap it up). Much had happened in the intervening period. TTAPS focused on climate and smoke. Inventories of lumber were significantly lower than they first calculated, but oil and petrochemical stocks were about the same and these provided most of the soot. The areas burned in various war scenarios also were roughly comparable, but it was recognized that far more soot would be produced and considerably less would be washed out of the atmosphere by rain. The original TTAPS assessment that most of the smoke would be injected at a height of 4–6 km still seemed valid, as was their estimate of the minor effect of aging and the significant absorption of light by soot.

Smoke plumes were still predicted to spread widely over the Northern Hemisphere within a week or two, although by 1990 TTAPS recognized that the pattern would be patchy instead of homogeneous. Nonetheless, the hemispheric average smoke absorption optical depth would be roughly doubled from their earlier figure. Smaller than originally calculated but still significant, land surface cooling (now 10–20°C, instead of a 15–25°C decline for the baseline scenario) would occur for a spring or summer war over a range of optical depths, during both the acute phase of the first 3 months and the chronic phase of up to 3 years. The upper atmosphere would be heated and stabilized, rainfall strikingly reduced, and stratospheric ozone and the Southern Hemisphere markedly affected.

Despite an enormous amount of new and detailed information over 6 years, despite the application of increasingly sophisticated computer models, despite a changed focus from darkness and cooling to the destruction of agriculture, and even if one wished to regard this paper as self-justification by TTAPS of their original work, the authors clearly had identified a likely phenomenon in 1983, and had pointed to a reasonable variety of scenarios and effects.[21]

Fire Studies

From 1986 to 1990, much additional work was accomplished, but the end results changed little. The earlier estimates of fuel inventories (by Crutzen and Birks in their 1982 *Ambio* paper, by TTAPS in 1983, and in a 1984 study by Crutzen, Galbally, and Brühl) were trimmed by a factor of 2 or 3 in later studies by Joyce Penner, the TTAPS group, and the Pacific-Sierra Research Corporation team of R. D. Small, B. W. Bush, and M. A. Dore. Yet the several techniques of determining these inventories remained controversial. Another variable was that fuels seemed to provide less smoke as ventilation (oxygen) was increased. Most of the reductions, however, were assigned to sources that contributed minimally to the production of soot. Inventories of petroleum and its products, asphalt roofing, and plastics, the major sources of elemental carbon (which constituted 90–95 percent of a soot particle's mass), were now better documented but remained largely unchanged.[22] In 1987, W. Einfeld and his colleagues ignited these petrochemicals under different conditions of combustion in laboratory tests and found the smoke contained 70–90 percent soot, more than previously thought. While these products made up only about 10 percent of urban fuels (wood products contributed about 90 percent), they dominated soot production, an insight recognized as increasingly important. Studies in the United States and in the Soviet Union now estimated that a major nuclear war between the superpowers would yield about 80 million tonnes of sooty smoke. Although this was less than half the NAS's example of 180 million tonnes, its increased soot content left atmospheric conditions largely unchanged. Work by Yu. A. Gostintsev and his colleagues showed that an explosion's thermal radiation can turn organic matter into a considerable amount of soot without burning (a process called pyrolysis). Potentially, forests could contribute a significant amount of smoke by this mechanism. Small, however, added a word of caution: "We have never seen an area fire from a megaton explosion. The amount of smoke generated by such fires and its properties are only poorly estimated."[23]

The fraction of smoke that was removed from the atmosphere by precipitation immediately (called "black rain" because of entrained debris) or over the next few days was yet another important component in determining the opacity of the clouds of soot. Many estimates ranged between 30 and 50 percent, but were considered "soft." Joyce Penner and Charles Molenkamp, both of Livermore, showed just how soft they were. In an analysis that looked at additional scavenging pathways, they concluded that the fraction washed out was between 10 percent and 90 percent. Adding to the imprecision, experiments suggested that the blackest, sootiest smoke resisted scavenging more successfully than previously believed, while coagulation of particles, leading both to faster removal from the atmosphere and less absorption of light, seemed to occur sooner. Much more needed to be known about phenomena in the first few hours and the first few days after the smoke plume rose.[24]

Properties of soot remained of interest. Micrographs showed the particles were irregular in shape, like badly torn snowflakes. They absorbed sunlight about equally well across the visible spectrum (roughly 0.35–1.0 micrometer), seemed not to change their optical properties much over time (a modest decrease in light attenuation), and the measurements appeared consistent with new understandings of fractal aggregates. When the fractal shape of soot particles (as shown in electron micrographs) replaced the formerly used spherical shape in calculations, temperatures fell a few degrees. This occurred because the convoluted shape of soot particles allowed more atoms of carbon to be near the surface, where they were better able to absorb solar energy. This insight led Stephen Schneider to remark ruefully that "the scenario is creeping back from nuclear autumn to early winter." Whereas a great number of wood smoke particles (25–75 percent) served as cloud condensation nuclei (CCN) when fresh or aged, the numbers were far lower for liquid fuels. Jet fuel, for example, yielded only about 1 percent of soot particles to serve as CCN. Heavy diesel fuel, crude oil, and kerosene generated far more, all bearing on the rainout of particles. Once aloft and above the rain, soot particles were decomposed by ozone more slowly than had been believed, on a scale of years or decades, making turbulence, gravity, and perhaps microphysical processes the more likely means of their removal. Re-evaporation of water droplets, the huge contribution of CCNs from wood, and the efficacy of cloud electrification were scavenging mechanisms that needed more study.[25]

As was mentioned above, Robert Malone and others had found that solar-heated smoke could rise buoyantly. Tropospheric altitudes of 5–10 kilometers, and in some mid-latitude cases a stratospheric 15 kilometers, were reached in simulations. Nor did the blaze have to be very large—an observed fire of one square kilometer produced a plume that pierced the tropopause. Freeman Dyson's persistent belief that wet soot had different optical properties than the dry material was challenged by laboratory tests in which smoke was aged for 16 hours in supersaturated air; the differences were negligible. Curt Covey, however, pointed out that, whereas elemental carbon was hydrophobic, man-made carbonaceous materials might be hydrophilic. In field observations in May 1987, daytime temperatures fell 2–6°C in Alaska; this was attributed to smoke from a large forest fire in China. Similarly, wildfires in southern Oregon and northern California, in September 1987, lowered daytime temperatures 15°C in one rural town; blacker urban smoke would have a greater effect. It was also notable that the smoke was at a lower level of the atmosphere, where it was not expected to cause such surface cooling. But an inversion kept it in place and the smoke shielded the surface from sunlight.[26]

The effect of smoke aloft on radiation transfer was, of course, the most important factor in determining the extent of NW conditions. Optical properties of smoke, dependent on the size, configuration, and makeup of the particles, were examined in a range of scattering and absorption studies. Increased attention was given to oil refineries and storage facilities. For urban and petroleum fires, SCOPE suggested, smoke was about twice as absorbing as had been assumed in the 1985 NAS report's baseline case. The optical properties of thermal infrared radiation were re-examined, as the simplifying assumption that soot particles were spherical (made to enable use of a known formula), applied poorly to the ragged shape of real particles. In consequence, it was likely that temperatures in the upper atmosphere would be a few degrees higher, while surface values might be comparably lower. Possibly counterbalancing some of these changes was recognition that about half of the Sun's energy lies in the near infrared range, a circumstance that might moderate the radiative disturbance. Experimental studies of large fire plumes would be valuable to resolve differences in laboratory tests.[27]

The prescribed forest fire set in August 1985 near Chapleau, Ontario was beset with political setbacks that restricted collection of data. In another attempt, the Defense Nuclear Agency added significant research to a plan by the US Forest Service to set ablaze about 1,000 acres of chaparral in the San Gabriel Mountains, about 30 miles northeast of central Los Angeles. Such controlled burns were normal means of reducing the dense fuel near urban areas, especially when winter rains caused lush growth that turned tinder-dry in hot summers. This burn was to be the most instrumented fire in history, with studies planned of air pollution, of erosion due to fire, and of global warming. A U-2 flying at 65,000 feet would test an infrared camera intended for satellite reconnaissance of forest fires worldwide. Dozens of scientists and eight aircraft were in place on 3 December 1986 to monitor the blaze and, in the NW portion of this multi-faceted experiment, to collect samples of smoke to determine the size of its particles. Wind and rain had delayed the $750,000 project a dozen times over the previous 3 months. Now it came literally crashing to a halt. A Los Angeles County Fire Department helicopter ignited a small part of the canyon, to test the vegetation moisture level, using a suspended 55-gallon drum of jellied gasoline.. An electric spark lit the fuel as it dripped from the drum. The helicopter then rose above the canyon ridge, snagged its cable on a telephone line, and crashed. The small test burn was extinguished and the participants dispersed, uncertain if and when to try again. Ten days later, however, weather, equipment, and personnel succeeded in igniting more than 500 acres of brush and in studying the consequences. A recent rain kept the chaparral from burning as intensely as hoped, and the smoke topped at about 8,000 feet, which was half the height desired to see if a rain-inducing capping cloud would form.[28]

Half a year later, in June 1987, scientists and fire crews returned to the San Gabriel Mountains, and at the cost of $500,000 ignited about 300 acres and conducted numerous experiments. Toward summer's end, DNA-funded scientists from Sandia National Laboratories took advantage of forest fires ignited by lightning in southern Oregon and northern California to gather smoke samples. With more than 900,000 acres burned, the fires provided valuable regional data, as contrasted with the far smaller sources of earlier studies. Smoke plumes soared to 15,000–20,000 feet. A University of Washington aircraft tracked one plume the unprecedented distance of 400 miles, gathering information that suggested it would take longer than expected for particles to coagulate and fall. Richard Turco volunteered the opinion that the overabundance of particles led to formation only of fog droplets instead of raindrops (which would wash out smoke faster). The fractions of sunlight and reflected heat that were absorbed by smoke particles and the amount scattered were also studied, and cumulus clouds that formed over smoke plumes were sampled for the first time.[29]

At about the same time in 1990 that the TTAPS group surveyed current NW knowledge and found much that reinforced their 1983 paper, George Carrier looked at the 1985 report of the National Academy of Sciences committee that he had chaired and found still too much uncertainty in their understanding of NW phenomena. Carrier, an expert on fires, pointed to the lack of knowledge of combustion in mixes of fuel and rubble that contained concrete, steel, and plaster. Many individual phenomena were entered into the GCM programs, he noted. Each had an uncertainty range in which the largest number was a few or several times the smallest. Individually, this was normal and reasonable. But when one multiplied these uncertainty factors for a "total" uncertainty, the result was an enormous number, so big as to embrace everything—from no climatic effect to a calamity. Carrier emphasized that the warfare scenarios and figures, such as smoke lofted, were not the most likely events and values, but simply credible guides to enable calculation of the atmospheric response. Yet this calculation suffered further from the uncertainty of the computer programs used, particularly for processes that occurred in small volumes of the atmosphere, volumes far smaller than any of the GCM grids. Establishing the credibility of these calculations was important. Despite his reservations, Carrier was impressed by the danger to agriculture posited in the SCOPE report, and concluded that "no recent refinements of knowledge and understanding have diminished the truth of the qualitative conclusion of the [NAS] study that says, in effect: there is a clear possibility that the atmospheric modification accompanying a major nuclear exchange could be of serious concern, even in regions somewhat remote from those in which detonations would occur."[30]

Biological and Ecological Research

The SCOPE report's revision (1989) described efforts to mesh global circulation models (where the best grid resolution was about 500 kilometers on a side) with agricultural models, such as those developed by the International Benchmark Sites for Agrotechnology Transfer (where grids were often only a kilometer or two on a side). GCMs, moreover, incorporated time averages of phenomena, whereas biological responses often depended on the amplitude of, say, a temperature swing or the abrupt change of a region affected by a monsoon from dry to wet. The dialogue was only beginning and results relied to an unusual degree on historical analogy, existing data from controlled experiments on plant and animal responses to varied environmental conditions, and personal judgment. But the effort was promising.[31]

Similarly, biological models in other areas remained less sophisticated than those in the physical sciences. Indeed, this could justly be called their infancy. Aside from ecological studies of regions immediately downwind from nuclear explosions (before the Limited Test Ban Treaty of 1963), governments provided meager support to examine the biological effects of nuclear war. "Biological responses to stress are functions of the scale and intensity of the stresses," Mark Harwell and Ann Freeman wrote in 1988, "yet no ecosystems-level experiments have been conducted using nuclear-war-projected climatic changes." Nonetheless, SCOPE workshops held in Bangkok, Moscow, Geneva, and Beijing after the first edition was published reaffirmed the original findings. This was so despite recent predictions of temperature declines considerably smaller than those from the early days of NW research. Agriculture was the most sensitive ecosystem to the types of physical stresses and societal disruptions predicted from nuclear war. It would still fail, Harwell and Hutchinson concluded, because "the uncertainties in these [lesser] effects . . . are not significant for the biological conclusions."[32]

Contrary to the comment by Harwell and Freeman about the lack of ecosystem-level experiments, a team from Syracuse University and Colorado State University at Fort Collins attempted a more quantitative study than was common. Looking at the Serengeti region of Tanzania and Kenya, where the grazing ecosystem might become a significant food-production area for humans, they had a Grassland Research and Serengeti Systems Model already well developed. Their major conclusion was that severe changes to the ecosystem occurred sharply when temperatures fell more than 10°C and light levels more than 28 percent. But so much uncertainty had to be accorded any predictions that "ecological unpredictability itself could be one of the most damaging consequences of post-war climatic effects."[33]

There were other modifications, the major one since SCOPE's first edition concerning devastation of the stratospheric ozone layer. As was mentioned in the section on modeling above, about half of the ozone could be removed. This might lead to an increase in ultraviolet-B radiation by a factor of 5 or more. Harwell and Freeman observed that even with a radiation increase of 10–50 percent "many marine phytoplankton, zooplankton, and larval fish populations" would suffer damage, "with potential alterations in marine biological diversity, pelagic community structure, and fisheries yields."

After 1988 (when SCOPE's efforts ended), Mark Harwell's Global Environmental Program at Cornell used the network of scientists to coordinate national case studies. These investigations in Sub-Saharan Africa, Australia, the People's Republic of China, India, Japan, and Venezuela were hoped to be specific enough to rivet the attention of political leaders, far better than hemispheric averages of effects might do. National studies would have the additional benefit of examining many problems already familiar to society—"habitat destruction, air pollution, sedimentation, radiation, ozone depletion, climatic alteration, acid precipitation, toxic chemicals, species extinction, human exploitation"—albeit "on a scale and at an intensity of unprecedented proportions."[34]

In July 1986, almost a year after the media were briefed on the conclusions of the original SCOPE report, the Reagan administration seemingly reversed its stubborn refusal to support any biological or policy studies of NW until the physical consequences of nuclear war shed their uncertainties. The US Department of Agriculture wanted to know if food supplies would be curtailed as severely as predicted by the SCOPE scientists. Mary Carter, the associate administrator of the Agricultural Research Service, requested a review of the second volume of the SCOPE report (the volume on the ecological and agricultural effects of nuclear war). The Committee on Interagency Radiation Research and Policy Coordination (CIRRPC), an obscure group handicapped by an unmemorable name and an unpronounceable acronym, gathered three USDA scientists, three university professors, and an executive of the private environmental group Resources for the Future to do the study. In November 1987, the results were sent to CIRRPC's parent agency, the Office of Science and Technology Policy. In March 1988, OSTP's director, William R. Graham (who also served as science advisor to the president), transmitted it to USDA's assistant secretary for science and education for release.

The study team examined the SCOPE data, methodology, and conclusions, and conducted its own simulation studies, using new soybean and corn growth models. They agreed that crops in the northern mid latitudes could be lost or severely limited for at least the first growing season following conflict, assuming that temperatures would fall, even briefly, by 5–15°C. However, they criticized SCOPE's inadequate treatment of several important topics. These included the long-term near-eradication of animal agriculture, the likely increase of carbon dioxide in the atmosphere, the loss of agricultural land flooded when dams were breached or parched when water from aquifers could no longer be pumped, radioactive contamination of food supplies, and the inability to produce, process, and distribute food when the infrastructure of the United States (electricity, refrigeration, transportation, and so forth) was demolished. They found fault, too, with SCOPE's inattention to potential synergisms of low light and temperatures and stress from drought. In short, the CIRRPC team argued that modern agriculture was far more complex than presented in the SCOPE report, and predicted even more hostile conditions than did SCOPE's scientists. "The worst case scenario in Volume II," they wrote, "may be a gross underestimation of the likely effects of a nuclear war on human populations."[35]

This stunning rebuke of the Reagan administration's intent to forestall federally sponsored studies of the biological and policy consequences of NW raises interesting but seemingly unanswerable questions. Why was the effort not quashed when first commissioned? Was there debate about releasing the report when it concluded that NW's consequences would be even more severe than had been thought? Since the OSTP (and therefore CIRRPC) is administratively located in the Executive Office of the President, this suggests that the report received authorization at quite a high level. Why and by whom? The report presents still another peculiarity: though it was seemingly at odds with most of the administration's behavior toward NW, and therefore a piece of "red meat" for the media, no newspaper or journal stories appear to have been published. Except for the preface to the second edition of the SCOPE report and a boxed note in a 1990 book by Sagan and Turco, it elicited no comment. It is as if the only study by the government that strongly *supported* some aspect of NW fell into the same media black hole that consumed the unbiased 1986 General Accounting Office report and the 1986 Department of Defense non-report (both to be described in the next chapter).[36]

The GAO's Report to Congress

In March 1986, the General Accounting Office issued a report to Congress titled "Nuclear winter: Uncertainties surround the long-term effects of nuclear war." The focus on uncertainties was surely in keeping with the Reagan administration's posture regarding NW, but the report was uncommonly even-handed in such a politically charged atmosphere. Ostensibly written to provide Congress with knowledge of the state of research and debate before the release of the Department of Defense's second annual report on NW, it was drafted by a committee headed by Alan Hecht of NOAA and including several scientists already prominent in these chapters. No one could have forgotten Congress' anger at the triviality of the DoD's first report in March 1985 and Caspar Weinberger's omission of subjects the legislators explicitly wanted discussed. The GAO's timing was appropriate also for the government's Interagency Research Program (begun in fiscal year 1986), which had provided $2 million dollars more for research (for a total of $5.5 million) than had been diverted from the previous year's DoD, DoE, and NSF budgets.

In addition to an overview of the technical uncertainties still found in the war scenarios, fire products, atmospheric effects, and computer modeling of NW research, the report fairly presented the basic arguments for and against conducting simultaneously with the physical investigations the officially neglected biological research and policy analysis. Other agencies involved with NW were asked informally to review the GAO's draft report. The Defense Nuclear Agency merely said that it was technically accurate. Only the Office of Science and Technology Policy was asked for formal comments, since it coordinated the government's NW efforts. John P. McTague, acting presidential science advisor and head of the OSTP, requested changes in the tenor of the GAO's draft. He argued that, by discussing possible policy implications, it presented NW in a more favorable light than was deserved. Whether the GAO had more clout or whether the matter was not considered overly serious, the GAO (which anyway reported to Congress, not the executive branch) declined to make such changes. Neither the report nor McTague's displeasure seem to have caught the eye of the national news media, although an Associated Press account was carried in a handful of newspapers.[1]

The DoD's 1986 Report

In March, Sharon Begley of *Newsweek*, presumably privy to pre-publication drafts of a *Foreign Affairs* summer 1986 essay by Starley Thompson and Stephen Schneider and the (May) 1986 DoD report to Congress, laid out the new terrain. In a way, it appeared to be little more than a rearrangement of the *Titanic*'s deck chairs, but Begley was astute in highlighting changed nuances. She quoted George Rathjens, at a recent conference, disparaging NW as "the worst example in my memory of results being misrepresented to the public." This illustrated that the *Titanic* still had chairs. But then she described the furniture's reshuffle. She recounted that C. Milton Gillespie, who led NW research at the Defense Nuclear Agency and thus had more than minor input to the DoD's annual report, summed current attitudes by saying that "the climatic effects look to be less than we thought, but that it probably takes less than we thought to have an impact on the global environment." This referred both to the catchy comment by Thompson and Schneider that temperature decreases predicted by NCAR's GCM of only about half the initial TTAPS value (about 22°F, or 12°C) made the climatic impact more of a "nuclear fall" than a nuclear winter, and the SCOPE report's estimation that agriculture would be devastated over vast regions of Earth if chills of only a few degrees occurred during the growing season. Indeed, Mark Harwell noted that the exact magnitude of the decrease was "essentially irrelevant."

Begley also reported cracks in the phalanx of the DoD's leadership. While maintaining publicly that a better understanding of physical phenomena was required before policy issues could be addressed, a view held by the secretary of defense's assistant for atomic energy, Richard Wagner, others felt a need to act. Powerful bureaucrats—Fred Iklé, the undersecretary of defense, and Richard Perle, an assistant secretary—argued for new missiles of smaller yield and higher accuracy, and for a rapid conversion from offensive to defensive hardware, namely SDI. Was limited nuclear war still an option?[2]

Unlike the CIRRPC report that claimed an even greater threat to agriculture than found by SCOPE, Secretary of Defense Caspar Weinberger's congressionally mandated annual report on NW for 1986 (due 1 March but distributed 9 May) contained no surprises and reflected none of the DoD's internal debate. Taking as a given that uncertainties of many sorts still were too large, the DoD dismissively referred readers to the attached 1985 report for its unchanged views on NW's effect on nuclear policy and Soviet behavior. The DoD's belief in deterrence through threat of retaliation was reaffirmed. Indeed, new material in the 1986 report consisted solely of a "technical issues update." Several subjects were surveyed in this update, without any citations of literature. The most recent understanding, it was claimed, sometimes increased the severity of climatic changes and sometimes decreased it. In no case, however, was anything sufficiently definite to be used as the basis for action.[3]

While expected of this administration, observers felt that it was hypocritical for an agency that dealt daily with uncertainty about low-probability events to claim to be so allergic to uncertainty and to invoke it for inaction. The report also was strikingly superficial and gave a surprisingly inaccurate account of the status of NW. On fuel distribution, on height of smoke injections into the atmosphere, on smoke's attraction or rejection of moisture, on smoke removal, and on temperature reductions the DoD's statements were criticized as inaccurate, unsupported, and/or misleading.[4]

The DoD's 1985 report, consisting of 17 pages of text, had drawn howls of outrage from Congress, the media, and the public for its cursory treatment of a serious matter. The 1986 report, limited to a technical update, was only five pages long, and it ignored Congress's specific demand for an evaluation of NW's implications for "strategy, targetting, planning, command, control, procurement, and deployment; the nuclear arms control policy of the United States; and the civil defense policy" and for its biological consequences. The DoD, it seemed, was focused far more on other concerns, such as a major reorganization plan being considered by Congress.[5]

Senator William Cohen, who helped direct congressional interest in NW, was confounded that the DoD ignored the legislators' previous criticism. Representative Timothy Wirth, who also had shown keen interest earlier, called the 1986 report "five pages of filler" and asked a rhetorical question: "If the General Accounting Office and the International Council of Scientific Unions [SCOPE] can produce detailed responsible reports on this issue, why can't the Pentagon?" Senator William Proxmire likened it to "a term paper an undergrad hastily writes the night before it is due."[6]

The legislators' critical remarks apparently failed to make it into the *Congressional Record*.[7] The *Washington Post* judged news of the report undeserving of a proper story, and merely mentioned it in a smorgasbord of government chit-chat called "Talking Points."[8] Beyond the Beltway there was even less response in the mainstream media to the report's appearance. The *New York Times*, the *Wall Street Journal*, the *Los Angeles Times*, and other newspapers ignored it.[9] When the Defense Authorization Act for fiscal year 1987 once again asked for an analysis of NW, the secretary of defense replied to Senate Arms Services Committee chairman Sam Nunn that, despite advancing technical research, uncertainties remained so large that the DoD's 1985 report, coupled with the NAS report, would be their best reply.[10]

NW, it seems, was fast becoming "yesterday's" concern. The nuclear reactor catastrophe at Chernobyl on 26 April 1986 deflected world attention from the military atom to the civilian atom, and from sooty urban fires to ionizing radiation emitted by air-borne radioactive debris, for a considerable period. NW lost what little audience it had. One of the few actions that went beyond posturing was Stephen Schneider's stillborn request to Frank Press (president of the National Academy of Sciences) for a new study of NW. Enough research, Schneider argued, had been accomplished since the NAS report of December 1984 appeared to justify another critical analysis.[11] (Gilbert White, a past president of SCOPE and a professor emeritus of geography at the University of Colorado, counseled Schneider that this was an international problem that should be pursued under the auspices of the International Council of Scientific Unions or the UN General Assembly, although the latter would likely lack the funds for it.[12])

Nuclear Fall

Starley Thompson, with help from Stephen Schneider, kept improving the NCAR GCM, which was interactive and incorporated land/sea and seasonal features.[13] By early 1986, as mentioned above, they concluded that a summertime war would lead to a temperature decline in the Northern Hemisphere of about 12°C (22°F), which they compared to autumn, not winter. As was true of all models, there were "imperfections" that opened them to criticism. In this particular case, heat from the oceans caused more convection currents over land than expected by others, who anticipated greater suppression of vertical mixing. Additionally, the smoke was inserted rather low, permitting a greater amount of rainout. These characteristics of the model inclined it toward smaller reductions in surface temperature. The point here is that modelers necessarily made choices in how to represent atmospheric phenomena, and not everyone agreed with those options.[14]

The TTAPS one-dimensional model, with its portrayal of an all-land planet, was an antique by now, but Carl Sagan continued to advocate the arms-control measures, based on its results, that he had proposed in *Foreign Affairs* at the end of 1983. While to a degree he backed away from thresholds involving megatonnage and recognized the increased importance that the SCOPE report gave to the potential loss of agriculture, Sagan saw no reason to alter his policy proposals. He persistently campaigned for a minimal deterrent. Schneider and Thompson, who shared most of Sagan's political goals, nonetheless felt that he was too glib with technical matters, and they drew somewhat different policy conclusions from their work. What better venue to challenge Sagan and parade their own views than *Foreign Affairs*? This they did in its summer 1986 issue.

NW, said Schneider and Thompson, had initially been accepted by many as a scientifically sound prophecy: weeks of sub-freezing temperatures on a hemispheric scale, with the attacker likely committing suicide and the existence of the human race threatened. TTAPS's articulation of a rough threshold below which the NW would not occur both suggested that lesser nuclear wars could be fought and supported an argument for a vastly smaller arsenal.[15]

In the *Boulder Camera*, a reporter named Robert Ebisch vividly portrayed the early TTAPS vision: "Thermonuclear explosions and the resulting firestorms, radiation, social collapse and mass starvation would kill only part of the human race; nuclear winter would come down like a great black pillow over the face of the planet and snuff out the rest."[16] Now, that apparition was challenged.

The subsequent policy debate, described extensively in previous chapters, was summarized by Thompson and Schneider, who proposed "to show that on scientific grounds the global apocalyptic conclusions of the initial nuclear winter hypothesis can now be relegated to a vanishingly low level of probability." This meant that NW alone was no longer a justification for major cuts in weaponry. At the same time, students of nuclear warfare should refocus away from blast, heat, and radiation as the only primary results of explosions and consider the consequences of environmental effects.[17]

Thompson and Schneider dismissed Sagan's argument that the existence of a low threshold mandated a small nuclear arsenal. The NCAR GCM, "using geographically realistic models," showed such great variability in the effects of any given war scenario that "it became clear that the elegant and strategically compelling idea of a threshold was an artifact of a simplified model." Alternatively, Schneider opined that climatic effects of nuclear war covered a "continuous spectrum," a view he had articulated as far back as the Halloween conference in 1983.[18]

Thompson and Schneider also criticized Sagan's endorsement of worst-case-scenario thinking, noting that neither the NAS nor SCOPE reports had spent time analyzing war scenarios. This seemed a distinction without a difference, for NAS and SCOPE inserted amounts of smoke into the atmosphere that were comparable to the quantity used in TTAPS's baseline scenario. Their point, however, was that something less than a worst case could reveal serious problems—as SCOPE had shown regarding agriculture. Such disturbances were of greater interest scientifically, for the biologists helped the physical scientists to focus on answers to their questions. Thompson and Schneider also pointedly noted that SCOPE did not even bother to address the issue of human extinction, and asserted that "two unique conclusions of the original nuclear winter ideas with the most important implications for policy [a threshold, extinction] have been removed."[19]

True. But Thompson and Schneider's presentation seemed to imply that this was a fresh conclusion, oddly suggesting that readers of *Foreign Affairs* had been tuned out of NW discussions since Sagan's paper appeared in their journal 2½ years earlier. Were these readers really oblivious that the issues of threshold and extinction had been seriously criticized and were no longer very prominent? Moreover, the SCOPE report, which preceded the Thompson-Schneider article by nearly a year, may have given less attention to war scenarios than TTAPS, but it did assume a multi-stage conflict, with specific megatonnage exploded at surface and at altitude. And some of its conclusions could well be described as apocalyptic. It also emphasized that global horror could occur without worst-case thinking.[20]

The heart of Thompson and Schneider's revisionism was the NCAR GCM's prediction of a temperature decrease of 12°C, lasting a few weeks rather than months, using their baseline insertion of 180 million tonnes of smoke into the atmosphere. Other models had different characteristics, making comparisons difficult and imprecise, yet with roughly similar

Table 20.1
Predicted temperature decreases.

TTAPS	30–40°C
Aleksandrov and Stenchikov	>15°C
NAS report	10–25°C
LLNL	>15°C
SCOPE report	20–40°C
LANL	15–25°C
NCAR	12°C

amounts of smoke and, where possible, looking at a summertime war, the previous work led to the decreases in temperature shown in table 20.1.

The NCAR findings, thus, were at the low end of predictions. In themselves, they might not have elicited overmuch attention, especially as Thompson and Schneider agreed with others that "climatic disturbances, radioactive fallout, ozone depletions and the interruption of basic societal services, when taken together, could threaten more people *globally* than the direct effects of explosions in a large nuclear war." Though the acute effects would last a shorter time (days or weeks), the chronic effects of a large nuclear war would extend to months or years.[21] Importantly, however, this smaller temperature decrease kept continental interiors largely above freezing for a summertime war and, in the eyes of many commentators, this erased the iconic picture of a glaciated wasteland. For much of the public, out of touch with the developing scientific understanding, NW continued to mean extreme cold and dark, a perception that carried into the early 1990s. In 1986, however, Thompson and Schneider's astute descriptor of "nuclear fall" for their overall image (much like Turco's inspired term "nuclear winter") was a media blessing.[22]

The press (and thus the attentive public), still tuned to its first impression of NW, now heard largely what it wished to hear. Headlines emphasized such phrases as "less drastic theory," "global freeze . . . is moderated," and "towards a mild nuclear winter?" Nuclear warfare, while still terrible, was not as horrible as recently argued. In an extreme example of muddle-headed journalism, the *Detroit News* exulted that NW was now "downgraded" to a nuclear fall "of far less frightening consequences," and warned of "a hidden political agenda behind the scare-mongering scenarios so confidently put forth in the name of 'science.'" Were the US to reduce its arsenal and fear to use it even in a limited war, while the USSR maintained its larger stockpile, the US would be unable to deter aggression. The editorial concluded that "the threat of a 'nuclear fall' is not, on its own account, a strong enough reason to cuckold this country into the kind of unilateral disarmament that is so ardently sought by Mr. Sagan and company. Thompson and Schneider saved us from that." Thompson and Schneider, taken aback, felt that the newspaper misrepresented much. Sagan, to the best of their knowledge, had never advocated unilateral disarmament. And, while they disagreed with him over the extent to which the arsenals should be cut, they fully endorsed major reductions and opposed anything that would make nuclear war more acceptable. In short, their differences with Sagan were "generally over numerical issues, not so much over questions of principle."[23]

In response to the article by Thompson and Schneider, letters to the editor of *Foreign Affairs* appeared in the next issue. In their original scientific paper, Carl Sagan wrote, TTAPS had been forced by their 1-D model to compute temperatures for a fictitious all-land planet, but they had stated even then that continental interior temperatures would likely be about half of what they calculated. More recent 3-D analyses, Sagan believed, led to results that were not terribly dissimilar. Correcting for several technical differences in their models, Thompson and Schneider begged to disagree: their temperature decrease was only about one-third that of the TTAPS paper. Sagan defended his use of the adjective "apocalyptic" to describe the climatic consequences of a major nuclear war, even if humanity escaped extinction; Thompson and Schneider had equated that word to extinction and asserted its improbability.

In his letter, Richard Turco noted that "devastating global climatic perturbations" were possible consequences of nuclear war. Even if temperatures were to fall only 5–10°C, SCOPE had shown that agriculture would fail. Thus, "in any sizable nuclear exchange, massive indirect human casualties should be expected with a substantial probability." In the past, "government planning and decision-making [in the uncertain area of nuclear conflict] have always prudently reflected all of the potentially serious outcomes." Why, then, Turco asked, "should nuclear winter be an exception?"—a question no NW critic ever seriously answered. For Turco, large force reductions should be coupled with conversion to single-warhead ICBMs and various confidence-building steps. Thompson and Schneider in general agreed with his goals, but not that they were "impelled" by NW. For them, nuclear war in itself would so disrupt global society that mass starvation would occur, while the milder NW they predicted would then be an "added burden."

George Rathjens and Ronald Siegel decried the lack of "qualification or differentiation" in discussions of NW over the past few years, during which the better models had predicted smaller temperature declines. They welcomed the term "nuclear fall," even if they thought it "overstate[d] things somewhat." Underlying these views was their long-held perception that there would be far less black smoke generated in a war than the amount used in most models. Rathjens and Siegel also believed that the conditions of nuclear fall might not lead to the collapse of agriculture south of 30° N, and that the work of Thompson and Schneider, while welcomed, was not in itself an argument for fewer nuclear weapons. This debate in print, by some of the major players in the NW tale, illustrates the insuperable computer and data inadequacies, the differences in interpretation of model predictions, and diverse views on what all this meant for strategic policy. Despite better information and technology, steps that narrowed uncertainties, absent nuclear war itself there could never be proof of the extent of the predicted climatic catastrophe.[24]

Before the publication of their paper, Thompson and Schneider circulated the text to several scientific colleagues, including Sagan. This led to several modifications, including some made in a frustrating post-deadline frenzy. More serious was the advice of colleagues who felt, correctly, that Thompson and Schneider would be perceived by the public as largely invalidating NW and implying that one could worry less about nuclear war. The two authors anticipated such misrepresentation, but hoped that a careful and honest reading of their words would demonstrate their continued belief in environmental effects that would cause untold misery. Their goal, they asserted, was to elevate the debate with increased scientific accuracy, thus ensuring the credibility of climate modelers.

Credibility was a major concern for Schneider, as he was thinking not only of NW but also of global warming, another controversy in which he participated. By authoritative research, and by focusing on more likely if less dramatic events, he and Thompson hoped to convince the policy circle that read *Foreign Affairs* that scientists must always participate in the debate. The consequences of nuclear war were more severe than the planners thought, and they could not be used to justify SDI, as Assistant Secretary of Defense Richard Perle sought to do. Stunned by the "incomplete reporting or even outright distortion of our views" in the next 6 months, Schneider decried the false dichotomy alleged between his and Sagan's views, but maintained that the *Foreign Affairs* publication was a positive contribution to the debate over NW.[25]

Not the concepts of thresholds and human extinction, as highlighted by Thompson and Schneider, but the public's persistently held vision of darkness and ice was the reason the paper by Thompson and Schneider attracted so much attention. Another argument that struck a responsive chord was that NW now mattered much less in the realm of strategic policy.[26] The irony of "nuclear fall" is that, had it appeared *before* the TTAPS paper shocked the world with that arctic winter vision, its 12°C decrease would have been regarded as frighteningly large and terribly serious, as indeed it was. Only in comparison to TTAPS's first cut, and despite strong denials by Thompson and Schneider, did it seem moderate: Who worries about autumn?

Debate Continues

The American media long ago recognized that controversy, violence, sex, and outrageous charges piqued readers' and viewers' interest. "Yellow journalism" did not refer to the color of brittle, old, newsprint. One has only to glance at most television and newspaper offerings today to recognize that this tradition remains strong. Earlier in the twentieth century, when science was of minor interest to the public, it rarely received sensational treatment (Einstein's theory of general relativity was one of the few exceptions). But after World War II, things changed. With the contribution of science to national security so prominent, with some hi-tech ventures such as landing men on the Moon so exciting, and with the widespread attacks by medical researchers on many diseases so hopeful, science was enticing game for the pundits. Some reporters, however, looked upon scientists as little more than members of just another special-interest group, prone to extol its successes and cover up its failures, rather like any other self-centered association.

Thus, in 1990 a dubious editorial writer for the McClatchy Newspapers in Sacramento, California, listed nuclear winter and global warming, along with charges that large numbers of people were getting cancer from drinking water and eating apples, as examples of exaggerated claims. Environmentalists, he stated, ignored scientific objectivity to peddle fear, attract attention, and sell their books.[27] He failed to see that he was committing the evil he condemned (by his own exaggerated criticism), nor did he give credit to those authors who may have believed in their own words. For our purposes, this illustration serves to establish the existence of an unknown percentage (no polls seem to have asked this question[28]) of the general public that was hostile to the concept of NW. Even more interesting, NW may have suffered by its association with the environmental movement, for "eco-extremists" had antagonized many Americans who saw no compromise between forestry jobs and spotted owls or agricultural water and maintaining wetlands.

Despite the remaining uncertainties, toward the end of the 1980s a consensus could be seen among the scientists. The NAS and SCOPE reports that appeared in 1984 and 1985, both of which affirmed the possibility of the NW phenomenon, and the SCOPE revision 3 years later, which gave greater precision to some variables, could not be denied. Notwithstanding the prediction of inadequate funding, a report commissioned by the United Nations General Assembly echoed the consensus in 1988.

No report, however, was sufficiently authoritative, or attended to all the controversial details of NW policy, to suppress debate. Little was added in subsequent years to the policy arguments already surveyed, although some new voices were heard. These included Fred Schwarz of the Christian Anti-Communism Crusade, who reasoned that the Soviets were not suicidal and who thus was confident that neither NW nor nuclear war itself would occur.[29] The psychiatrist Robert Jay Lifton, famous for his study of the survivors of Hiroshima, posited that "nuclear winter tells us loud and clear that hope lies only in prevention. There is no hope in preparation. And that's a very valuable message."[30] The George Mason University physicist Robert Ehrlich also looked at psychological reactions. He counseled that the public would do well to learn to live with ambiguity, thereby not being inclined to precipitous (and unlikely) actions while still making more acceptable, less risky, steady progress in arms control.[31]

Heedless of the Department of Defense's inclination to minimize discussion of NW's policy implications, a team at the US Air University's Center for Aerospace Doctrine, Research, and Education (CADRE, located at Maxwell Air Force Base in Alabama), led by Lieutenant Colonel Dennis M. Drew, made a substantial analysis of the effect of NW on national security. This is another of the few examples of actions that ran counter to Reagan administration principles, and may merely illustrate the inability to impose absolute

conformity in a country as large as the United States. Their perhaps counter-intuitive conclusion was that a large war required little policy change, because the superpowers were
already inhibited from such conflict and would not likely undertake revisions of policy just
because NW brought disaster to non-combatants.

If, however, NW could occur as a result of a small exchange of nuclear weapons, there
were more policy questions raised. These involved such matters as the potential intent of
other nations to become nuclear powers; a disincentive to use nuclear weapons at all,
leading possibly to unilateral disarmament; whether the American "nuclear umbrella"
would continue to protect allies (would we protect Paris if it meant the bombing of New
York or, worse, much of the Western world?); whether nuclear wars could be fought over
a protracted period of time, to prevent the accumulation of sufficient smoke to produce dire
climatic effects; and whether nuclear warheads would be replaced by conventional weapons,
with their additional costs, manpower and deployment needs, and poor track record in
keeping the peace before the advent of the nuclear age.[32]

Half a year after Thompson and Schneider's *Foreign Affairs* article on nuclear fall appeared,
a survey of the current scene was printed in *Science* magazine's "News and Comment"
section, and it was clear that controversy was still heated. The caption for an accompanying
photograph of Sagan described him as a "celebrity" (arguably a prejudicial term in a scientific periodical) and quoted him as saying that the recent NW studies presented "nothing
new" in the way of reduced danger. George Rathjens asked rhetorically "Is this another case
of Lysenkoism?" and answered his own question pretty much in the affirmative. To maintain the validity of the original NW model—which Sagan was not exactly doing—was to
Rathjens "the greatest fraud we've seen in a long time." Russell Seitz was quoted repeating
his political conspiracy theory that NW had been cooked up in 1982 to frighten people into
supporting the nuclear freeze campaign.[33] The same sort of fireworks illuminated the annual
meeting of the American Association for the Advancement of Science in February 1987,
which featured an impassioned session on NW.[34]

Curt Covey tried to restore some rationality to the debate. From the beginning, he conceded, TTAPS acknowledged that their one-dimensional model lacked important features
that were incorporated in later three-dimensional models, and that its all-land Earth, which
yielded a temperature drop of 35°C, would be much reduced when more realistic geography
was introduced. Covey did not fault TTAPS's science, but he disliked the "provocative phrase
'nuclear winter'" and reasoned that the "TTAPS group is guilty at least of lack of energy in
combating distorted reporting of their model's results, as well as a tendency . . . to imply
that their original findings are as good as inscribed on stone tablets." Nonetheless, the NW
debate, Covey concluded, was useful because it forced people to focus on the consequences
of war.[35]

In a similar vein, the physicist Harold Lewis, who chaired a Defense Science Board
committee advisory to Caspar Weinberger, chided prominent scientists whose opposition
to nuclear war seemed to have arisen only when potential climatic effects were revealed. As

Lewis (of the University of California at Santa Barbara) had told the secretary of defense 5 years earlier, there remained many unanswered questions. But in that half-decade a lot had been learned. Of course the first predictions from 1-D models were modified once 3-D models were introduced, but, wrote Lewis, even these smaller predicted effects "are still alarming, because the underlying theory of the effect is surely right." NW, he concluded, "is real, but one of the less important reasons to work at the prevention of nuclear war."[36]

The University of Vermont zoologist Bernd Heinrich was baffled that the United States was spending $5.5 million to learn if severe climatic consequences would follow the annihilation of major cities in the Northern Hemisphere and provoke widespread starvation due to interrupted trade in food and agricultural supplies.[37] This was a question asked persistently by those who felt we already knew that nuclear war must be avoided. There was no simple answer, for the question involved political, military, social, and scientific issues. Some, for example, felt that knowledge of the additional climatic effects might spur currently inadequate disarmament efforts. Others accepted the possibility that such conflict might be initiated and wished to know what offensive and defensive preparations were possible. Still others recognized the high quality of the science, which need not be restricted to NW investigations. The religious community continued in its apparent indifference to NW, with only an occasional article appearing.[38]

Turco kept the pot boiling. At a news conference in May 1987, he emphasized the confirmation of serious NW effects by SCOPE and by the many papers presented at the DNA Global Effects Program conference in Santa Barbara the previous month. Urban areas contained adequate fuel. Indeed, some common fuels were sources of more sooty smoke than earlier estimated, and this soot would be washed out by rain less efficiently. Oil refineries alone, Turco revealed, contained enough fuel to cause global effects. He contrasted the confused national priorities of war and peace by noting that NW's budget amounted to the equivalent of only 0.1 percent of SDI funding, and 0.001 percent of the DoD budget.[39]

Concerned with more than the optical effects of smoke, Turco, with his brilliance in putting things into perspective, examined the consequences of the 1986 nuclear reactor accident at Chernobyl. As measured by the biologically important radioisotopes iodine-131 and cesium-137, the release of radioactivity from Chernobyl was about as much as would be dispersed from a nuclear explosion of 0.01 kiloton. (Hiroshima was 12.5 KT, Nagasaki was about 20 KT, and most of the strategic weapons in the superpowers' arsenals were hundreds of KT.) Since Europeans were terrified by this relatively tiny amount of contamination, Turco suggested that the potential for social upheaval after a far "dirtier" nuclear war be studied, particularly short-term and long-term medical problems.[40]

Nature's editor, John Maddox, while praising a 1988 paper by Schneider and Thompson in the same issue, was unable to refrain from commenting more widely on NW. With his standard mixture of sarcasm and questionable facts, Maddox implied that the authors of the 1983 Turco et al. paper in *Science* were renamed TTAPS for the egotistical advantage of instant name recognition, and that the late Mrs. Gandhi was somehow wrong or misled for "complaining that a nuclear war between the superpowers might destroy others than themselves." Essentially, Maddox spurned the "bandwagon" of press conferences and publicity that had been successfully designed to make an "impact."[41]

In late 1989, the Swedish environmental journal *Ambio*, which in 1982 had published the paper by Paul Crutzen and John Birks that had given great impetus to the study of NW, bemoaned the general loss of interest in the subject. Scientific journals were still publishing some articles on the topic, but citations of such articles in the press and in popular magazines were increasingly rare. Nuclear arsenals, however, were still absurdly large. To draw renewed attention to the environmental effects of nuclear war, *Ambio* again published a special issue, drawing especially on papers presented at a conference in August 1988, devoted to policy questions. In this issue, Crutzen reiterated the need for avoiding the climatic catastrophe, noting that, while his earlier *Ambio* paper gave him quite the opposite of the "aesthetic satisfaction" he derived from most of his atmospheric research, he considered it by far his "most important scientific paper."[42]

The University of Maryland meteorologist Alan Robock rejected the concept of deterrence, since it was based on the threat of actually using nuclear weapons. Robock, who had been sensitized to the concerns of other nations years earlier by service in the Peace Corps, was currently an exchange scientist in the US-USSR Agreement on Cooperation in the Field of Environmental Protection. He emphasized that public education, represented by such publications as the UN report, the *Ambio* issue, and a recent special issue of the journal *Environment*, was essential to change the old views of politicians and the military.[43]

The Australian atmospheric scientist A. Barrie Pittock argued that the "environmental effects have raised the stakes in a possible failure of nuclear deterrence," and thus "the search for safer strategies [is] more urgent." He agreed with Robock that deterrence no longer made sense, but he suggested that it would take some time for the military to admit it publicly and find some alternative. Pittock also anticipated more pressure from Third World nations, citing the Delhi Declaration, New Zealand's exclusion of nuclear powered or armed warships, and recent discussions about a South East Asia nuclear-free zone.[44]

Pittock hoped for universal rejection of nuclear weapons, but recognized the political and military instabilities that would arise while reaching that goal. Progress would be made in small, less threatening, steps. In contrast, Turco and Sagan, impatient with the existing danger, called for rapid changes. They sought the elimination of all nuclear-equipped bombers, land-based and sea-based multiple-warhead missiles, and tactical nuclear weapons, and a reduction and balancing of conventional forces in Europe. In the place of these military assets, each superpower would erect a "Canonical Deterrent Force" (CDF) of 100–300 weapons, each with a single warhead, and contained in hardened or mobile delivery systems to assure their survivability. An attempted first strike to disable an enemy was already potentially suicidal, Turco and Sagan maintained, and it would be ineffective once the CDFs were in place. Space-based defenses would be abandoned, and the military would emphasize defensive rather than offensive practices. Stability was Turco and Sagan's goal, with the much-doubted NW threshold suggesting the appropriate number of strategic weapons. No longer could military forces be designed by political aspirations; scientific predictions of the effects of war must also be considered. Turco and Sagan argued that NW had already made an impact on political leaders, with many of them referring publicly to the phenomenon, and with a decrease in blustery statements about nuclear war fighting, prevailing, and limited exchanges.[45]

In 1990, Sagan and Turco elaborated on a path toward each superpower's Canonical Deterrent Force. By the year 2015, they hoped, strategic warheads would be cut back greatly from the total of 20,000 that existed, and tactical weapons would be phased out entirely. In addition to the goals mentioned in the paragraph above, Sagan and Turco expected that the explosive yield of remaining weapons would be in the 100-KT range, and that testing would be ended. With such arsenals, the danger of NW would be minimal, while both the US and the USSR would retain the ability to defend themselves.[46]

Oil Well Fires in Kuwait

In 1991, NW theory gave way to experiment. The Persian Gulf War ended with Iraq torching most of the 1,250 oil wells in Kuwait. Some refused to burn, and low internal pressure in others caused the fires to die within a few weeks. Firefighters were faced with 550 wells burning fiercely, and these blazes took 9 months to extinguish. In the process, about 60 million barrels of oil flowed uncontrollably, producing the largest oil spill in history (more than 200 times the amount leaked in Alaska by the *Exxon Valdez*). Each day another 6 million barrels of oil burned, a quantity equivalent to about a million tons. Aside from sulfur dioxide and carbon dioxide, about 100,000 tons of sooty smoke bellowed skyward daily. This was consistent with Turco's prewar estimate, and identical to a figure given by American scientists who flew through the smoke plume. Sagan, Turco, and others warned of the danger of a nuclear-winter-like effect. Indeed, regional temperatures fell by about 10°C. This was, however, a localized effect, not the globe-circling catastrophe envisioned by the term "nuclear winter."[47]

Did the Kuwait fires invalidate the NW concept? It depends on the "expert." Those who accepted that the NW phenomenon was valid pointed to the cooler temperatures of the winter war, suggesting that, had the same smoke and soot been lofted higher in the hot summer, the climatic effect would have been larger. India, about 1,300 miles downwind, experienced slightly lowered temperatures and soot fell on Himalayan snow. The physicist and climatologist Adam Trombly (a member of Friends of the Earth) noted that the smoke rose above the very low altitudes that the US government first predicted. Critics of NW, in contrast, claimed vindication. George Ullrich, deputy director of the Defense Nuclear Agency, argued that "the data suggest a considerably more benign assessment of the nuclear winter scenario." Kuwait therefore serves as an interesting example of an event that provided ambiguous data and served to alter no preconceptions. Justifiably, it had no effect on policy; but that was not surprising, since NW had faded from the policy horizon 3–4 years earlier—an eternity within the Beltway.[48]

21 Evaluation

In a 1985 article in *Science Digest*, Andrew Revkin mused that after "three congressional hearings, dozens of scientific meetings, several international conferences and at least four books later, *nuclear winter* has taken its place—somewhere between *megaton* and *overkill*—in the burgeoning lexicon of terms spawned by the study of nuclear war."[1]

NW certainly was given attention. In the *1985 Britannica Book of the Year*, a survey of significant recent events, Stephen Schneider reinforced that conclusion: "No recent topic in the atmospheric sciences has been more talked about, more controversial, and—to many—more important than nuclear winter."[2] So what happened?

Real (Not "Junk") Science

Whether one believed in the phenomenon or not, nuclear winter was a product of scientific research—and, remarkably, this research was initiated by scientists who did *not* work at nuclear weapons laboratories. As already described, several scientific disciplines—weapons effects, particle microphysics, atmospheric chemistry, fire and smoke studies, volcanic eruptions, ozone depletion, planetary studies, and dinosaur extinction—came together to reveal the potential effects of nuclear-explosion-ignited fires. The phenomenon had remained undetected until data and techniques from these several scientific specialties were integrated. This was an illustration of the increasing interdisciplinarity of science, although in most other cases the phenomenon is discovered first and its investigation and possible explanation—again requiring contributions from several specialties—come later. (An example would be the sea-surface temperature anomalies in the tropical Pacific Ocean known as El Niño.[3])

Initially a great debate about data, the scientific controversy over NW was waged largely around two issues: methodology and uncertainties. Because a sizable number of scientists ultimately published refereed papers in respectable journals, and because prestigious scientific bodies published serious reports that treated NW as potentially very real, the carping over technical issues failed to convince the layman that NW was bad science. The critics of NW thus continued their disparaging analyses, but often invoked politics also. To many of them, the believers in NW had a political agenda, and this made for polluted science. That their own political beliefs were quite different generally went unmentioned—but not always, for there were some scientists, political scientists, and government officials, sympathetic to the perceived goals but not the means, who chose to challenge the policy recommendations of Sagan and others.[4]

NW is a good illustration of the way in which a multifaceted research project was created. It was largely through individual initiative—a from-the-ground-up approach, rather than a top-down legislative or administrative command. This may be the preferable mode, as the scientists themselves defined what was important and (in this case) made the links to other technical disciplines. Since the $50 million federally concocted program never materialized, we cannot know if its higher degree of management would have proved worthwhile.

NW research was conducted overwhelmingly in government laboratories and not on university campuses; corporate research facilities were even less involved. This is not to say that institutions of higher education lacked professors, or industry lacked scientists, with the interest and skills needed. It was more a matter that the "culture" of the labs favored their response. Scientists in the national labs work within divisions and groups, with management coordination. The complex geophysical problems of NW required multidisciplinary team efforts, common in the labs, while university people are more independent-minded. Industry, further, saw no large construction project in the offing, nor perhaps even the opportunity for a significant part of computer programming, and lobbied only a little for inclusion. The most powerful computers, too, were at the national labs, where research funds could more quickly be reallocated from one project to another. Like astronomers in large observatories, many people working with general circulation models find it difficult to alter their long-range programs, making them less responsive to "targets of opportunity." Thus, Richard Turco, working for a defense contractor in Marina del Rey, could not interest the atmospheric scientists at nearby UCLA, who had a GCM that Turco admired and wished to use. In addition, meteorology was not a topic pursued at many universities, few of which had supercomputers. While a number of university scientists had radiative transfer codes that enabled them to perform climate calculations, they needed much data of other kinds before they could begin NW work meaningfully.[5]

Funding opportunities also favored the government labs. They, and defense contractors, can generate research proposals far more rapidly than can most academics. Moreover, in the case of NW, the traditional source of grants for much university investigation, the National Science Foundation, had far less money than the Department of Energy and the Defense Nuclear Agency. Indeed, university scientists were barely visible on the horizon of the DoE (which funded research at national laboratories) or of the DNA (which looked primarily to defense industry contractors). Nonetheless, in the case of NW, the DNA provided almost the only funding available to university scientists—about $2.5 million per fiscal year in 1986–1988, and funding effectively ended in 1989. Historically and critically, research on aerosols in relation to air pollution had been far better funded than studies of aerosols connected to climate, but the latter was the more important in understanding the effects of NW. The Ames Research Center was the only laboratory in the United States with a substantial program in aerosols and climate. Still, NW research was not very expensive; computer time and salaries were the major costs, and only Turco's time at R&D Associates might have amounted to a large sum.[6]

At the national laboratories, scientists with weapons expertise were on the sidelines of NW research; those with knowledge of fires and of climate predominated. Hardly any women scientists contributed to NW research, Livermore's Joyce Penner being the only prominent female. This is likely a reflection of the small fraction of women found in the atmospheric sciences and in the sciences that led to the revelation of the NW phenomenon, relative to their percentage in other sciences. The same gender bias seems to exist among strategic policy analysts.[7]

NW research became an identifiable field. One could say "I'm investigating the nuclear winter phenomenon" and be understood. Though contributions came from many areas of science, NW would best be called a subdiscipline of atmospheric science. No journals specializing in NW were founded, in part because the subject was not pursued for more than several years, but many established journals were hospitable to publishing papers. There appear to have been numerous opportunities for NW experts to gather, whether in special sessions at meetings of larger societies or in private conferences devoted solely to NW. The field benefited from new technology, particularly three-dimensional models on supercomputers, but this was a double-edged sword, for the relative novelty of the methodology gave NW doubters a weakness to attack.

The NW phenomenon achieved public notice far more quickly than most other scientific subjects, and it also rapidly polarized those involved. The popularization and the controversy, which were symbiotic, clearly resulted from the startling predictions of climatic catastrophe, the efforts made to rally public interest, and the lobbying for changes in governmental policies. Since the public had been aware for some time that humans could produce large-scale effects on the environment (global radioactive fallout, pollution of the sea and air, and even global warming), the concept that huge amounts of sooty smoke placed high in the atmosphere could lower temperatures was not seen as alien or far-fetched. In its technical and institutional development, for most scientists and the public this was real, not junk, science.

A Remarkably Healthy Debate

After World War II, the physicist Leo Szilard, reflecting on his nuclear fission experiments with Enrico Fermi in 1939, mused:

Fermi thought that the conservative thing was to play down the possibility that [a chain reaction] may happen, and I thought the conservative thing was to assume that it would happen and take the necessary precautions.[8]

Each, of course, thought that he was correct, and in a sense each *was* right. But Fermi was thinking of a scientific phenomenon, while Szilard had progressed to the political consequences of fission. These two levels of concern have been the basis for this volume's discussion of NW: Is it scientifically correct? If so, what action should be taken to avoid the consequences?

Beyond this, subsidiary questions abound. Were scientists suitable persons to play the part of advisors to government? On technical issues, they were of course indispensable. But had they the breadth of knowledge and experience to advise on the political (and even moral) consequences of technical steps? World War II, often called a physicist's war, showed the importance of science to national security. During that conflict, Vannevar Bush, an engineer, and James B. Conant, a chemist, headed the government's organization of science for military purposes and showed that scientists could valuably be on top, as well as on tap. At the same time, scientists working on the Manhattan Project, who felt that their position gave them unique understanding of the way in which nuclear weapons would change the world, volunteered their advice. The [James] Franck Report and Leo Szilard's petition were pre-Hiroshima efforts to alert the government to the consequences of bombing Japan. Officials thus became used to receiving both solicited and unsolicited advice.[9]

These dual tracks continued in the postwar period, with J. Robert Oppenheimer a ubiquitous advisor to the US government and with mostly young and not famous scientists forming a "movement" that lobbied for a civilian US Atomic Energy Commission and a similar body in the United Nations.[10] Public debate over the boundaries of scientific advice occurred in the decade or two following World War II,[11] reaching the point where scientists' role was little contested. For the rest of the twentieth century, scientists continued to offer unsolicited advice to the nation through such vehicles as the Federation of American Scientists, the *Bulletin of the Atomic Scientists*, and the Union of Concerned Scientists. Thus, Carl Sagan's public and private lobbying in the case of NW was not an aberration; playing a political role had been an accepted activity in the culture of science for half a century.

To be sure, there remained some critics of any "outside" role for scientists. The biologist Jacques Monod, for example, wrote that "any mingling of knowledge with values is unlawful, forbidden." Yet Monod acknowledged that this desire for objective knowledge was itself not objective, but an ethical guideline.[12] The physicist Freeman Dyson found himself more in the mainstream, at some distance from Monod on this spectrum of scientific mores: "We are scientists second, and human beings first. We become politically involved because knowledge implies responsibility. We fight as best we can for what we believe to be right."[13]

Thus, granting that differences of opinion remained, for most people, by the 1980s, the circumstance that scientists were discussing policy questions raised few eyebrows. They had been around government long enough that their expertise and independence were rarely questioned. Though some may have believed that Sagan violated the norm of this analytical world by being emotional (he spoke of deaths, not of body counts), it seems that very few felt that Sagan, who was neither a politician nor a political scientist, abused his scientific prestige in speaking out on political issues. (Whether they agreed with him is another matter.) Moreover, Sagan's advice was directly connected to a scientific discovery in which he participated.

Just as scientists had learned to operate within the corridors of power, government had adopted its own rules of behavior. Federal funds paid for virtually all NW research, but there is no evidence of any attempt to direct it toward certain conclusions. Individual investigators conducted their work honestly, even if sometimes their superiors wished they would drop the subject. Most significantly, there seems to have been no inclination by the government to place a security classification on NW research, a subject that might have seen the censor's stamp. And the many research papers, reports, and conferences were covered by a knowledgeable body of journalists, especially those who wrote for scientific magazines.

Although President Reagan had a scientific advisor, he was far less influential than scientific advisors had been in some previous administrations. The question thus arises whether an effective scientific advisor would have made any difference in the government's response to NW. That seems unlikely, since the highest levels of government would not have had any better technical resources than the authors of the NAS and SCOPE reports, and in any case the policy consequences were openly and widely debated.

On the border between a scientific and a political question was the issue whether to release preliminary data and conclusions. Those with confidence in the early work were buoyed by a concern to inform the world of this previously hidden danger. Those who felt the initial investigation to be poor science also were frequently motivated by political agendas (for example, some feared for the good name of science). Such a conundrum is not, of course, exclusive to NW. Medical research sees it frequently: Shall unconfirmed reports of helpful or harmful drugs be publicized?

Determining what action to take in light of NW was not a scientific matter at all. As with so many other issues in the political realm, it was a choice, a value judgment. Certainly, evaluation of the technical evidence and one's political philosophy were major components in any projected reaction. But there were other ingredients: economics (the cost of new weapons systems), morality (should we not try to ensure that NW is avoided? should we not avoid imperiling non-combatants?), and psychology (should a government leave its citizens feeling unprotected?). Encouraging such interest in policy, the environmental movement had matured, and the public was attuned to asking such questions.

Scientists do not expect universal consensus on many questions. The healthy attitude of skepticism in science generally precludes this. Wide agreement may be even more difficult to achieve in fields where traditional experimental and theoretical techniques are supplemented in major ways by the still-new approach of computer simulation. In the case of NW, where a full-scale laboratory test was of course unthinkable, it was understandable that doubts existed concerning whether the simulations accurately modeled the real atmosphere when it was greatly perturbed. Given this relatively messy—but normal—situation within science, it was not surprising that many politicians hesitated to act.

And yet, it is the customary fate of politicians to be forced to act without the benefit of "total" knowledge. It is their task to balance some possible future disaster against near-term economic, political, or defense constraints. Based on their evaluation of whatever "facts" are placed before them, and the political pressures on them, they do take positions.

One need only recall how Rachel Carson's *Silent Spring* led to a ban on the pesticide DDT and to other environmental legislation. Similarly, the Montreal Protocol of 1987 obliged nations to limit production of chlorofluorocarbons and other compounds in an effort to reverse the depletion of stratospheric ozone, and the Kyoto Protocol of 1997 placed limits on the emission of greenhouse gases, hoping to stabilize the global warming trend. In 1988, an advisory panel to California's state government concluded that a link exists between alcohol consumption and cancer, and wrangling began about the warnings to be placed on beverage labels.[14] All these steps were fought strenuously, with the opponents charging that shaky or even bad science underlay the allegations of alarming events. Nonetheless, governments did act. Recognizing that the scientific evidence could never be "complete," politicians seemed to be satisfied with the overwhelming support within the scientific community, and perhaps they grew to see the role of the opponents as one of obfuscation and obstruction, often based on vested interests.

In the case of NW, the US Congress held several hearings, a number of senators and representatives were vocal about the issue, and the Reagan administration investigated the phenomenon but did *not* act. Substitute pesticides were found for DDT. Substitute compounds were found for CFCs. Substitute technologies (zero-emission vehicles, conservation, recycling, and electricity generated by wind or by nuclear reactors) are available or being developed to reduce greenhouse gases. To banish the threat of NW, however, it was clear that nuclear arsenals should be eliminated or at least vastly reduced, but there was no obvious substitute for them. Some combination of President Reagan's missile-defense system, earth-penetrating warheads, smaller-yield warheads with greater accuracy, nuclear arms control, and preference for conventional weapons was recognized as likely to reduce the number of urban nuclear fires.

Whether severe NW effects could be avoided by the above-mentioned options was arguable. While disarmament was a futuristic goal, there simply were insufficient political pressure and will in the 1980s and the 1990s to dismantle the nuclear arsenals. Deterrence was regarded as fundamental to the national security of the United States; nothing else could be relied upon. Moreover, the public never became energized (almost a prerequisite for action) about NW. The nuclear freeze movement had reinforced the public's accurate comprehension of the horrors of war and its view that such conflict was "unwinnable, unsurvivable,"[15] yet NW was too new, or too uncertain, to marshal a "NW movement." Prominent legislators flirted briefly with NW and then went on to the next political controversy. The media behaved similarly. Politically well-connected individuals found that the issue had surprisingly little purchase.[16]

Those who believed in NW depicted images of burned-out cities, a cold and dark landscape (at least initially), and surviving populations suffering from starvation and disease. There was no need to compose fiction or relate human-interest stories of personalities in such trying times, as John Hersey famously did for some real survivors of Hiroshima. Hersey compassionately described individuals, not the more amorphous Japanese society or population, and in so doing changed Americans' attitude toward the former enemy. By the 1980s, however, the public knew so much about nuclear explosions that such a literary approach was unnecessary to gain converts. It was all too easy to comprehend the consequences of the NW climatic catastrophe. We did not have to imagine the stature and features of foreign victims; Pogo's remark had become true: "We have met the enemy, and it is us."[17]

The Strategic Defense Initiative gave the Reagan administration a major argument that it was taking action to limit the damage from a nuclear war, or even preventing it from occurring. Using SDI to undercut the NW argument was clever, but it should be regarded as an example of common political behavior. In September 2000, for example, President Bill Clinton performed a similar feat. Explaining his rationale for postponing the decision whether to begin construction of a National Missile Defense system (a descendant of SDI), Clinton said that diplomatic steps were being taken to reduce the threat from potentially hostile nations. Threat reduction was the common theme in avoiding hard decisions about the consequences of NW and NMD.[18] During Reagan's presidency, however, there were more differences than commonalities between NW and SDI. Unlike NW's fairly cool reception in Washington, SDI exposed heated, conflicting positions held by the Department of State and the Department of Defense, an alleged violation of an existing treaty (the Outer Space Treaty of 1967), big-budget pressures by the DoD and NASA, and an unsuccessful summit at Reykjavik in 1986, where Gorbachev tried to explain to Reagan the Soviet belief that SDI was an offensive weapon. Not only was SDI a program that demanded attention for both domestic and international reasons, while NW forecasts did not, but it was the fond pathway to security of the president. SDI, additionally, was a new class of weapons, involving not only particle, laser, and electromagnetic beams but also a third generation of nuclear weapons (some beams might be generated by focused nuclear explosions). For all these reasons, SDI rose to the level of high politics; discussion of NW, in contrast, barely made it above the Washington haze.[19]

The end of the Cold War and the collapse of the Soviet Union in the late 1980s and the early 1990s was something of a historical joke in that it was unpredicted. Or, some might say, it was predicted but not anticipated soon.[20] Amidst the euphoria of that period, with the dramatic decrease in the likelihood of nuclear war, the level of interest in NW fell even lower than it had been. Then, Iraq invaded the tiny sheikdom of Kuwait in 1991, and provoked great concern when its retreating troops torched hundreds of oil wells. Black smoke rose to moderate heights in the cool winter weather, causing modest environmental consequences and leaving NW predictions invalidated or inconclusive, depending on one's persuasion.

Security concerns subsequently turned to proliferation, terrorism, and other Third World conflicts. Deterrence between the superpowers almost seemed a thing of the past. Indeed, the nuclear arsenals of the United States and the former Soviet Union are being reduced under the terms of the START I and START II accords. But even if these goals are achieved in the early twenty-first century, the United States and Russia will each have 1,700–2,200 deployed strategic nuclear weapons, and Great Britain, France, and China will possess smaller but still substantial inventories of such arms. Israel, India, and Pakistan—and perhaps North Korea and Iran—will contribute further to the numbers. Unilateral action or perhaps negotiations may reduce the American and Russian arsenals further, but America's withdrawal in 2002 from the 1972 Anti-Ballistic Missile Treaty, in order to proceed with a National Missile Defense, may spark another arms race. The world, thus, is not free from the specter of NW, yet it is tied more tightly together by that image.

The technical debate among those who actually did calculations on NW was, for the most part, polite and friendly, even when they disagreed. Crutzen and Birks, the TTAPS team, and many who followed did brilliant work in defining and exploring a new phenomenon. This was science at its healthy best, with the sharing of information. When venom was injected into the controversy, it came largely from the peripheral figures, those called "hand wavers" by the centrists. Yet they too played a proper and useful role in the advancement of science, for they raised many questions that had to be answered.[21] Happily, there are no known cases of any scientists' having been demoted for taking a position for or against the evidence for NW. Many, in fact, went on to better posts.

Was NW research influenced by the spotlight of media attention? Critics claimed that TTAPS's inputs and outputs were massaged to yield consequences of nuclear war even more horrific than those detailed earlier, but the evidence for this is slim. That the several panel studies which followed used similar data, with increasingly sophisticated treatment, suggests strongly that TTAPS did good science for its stage of the research. This view is reinforced by the striking lack of criticism of most post-TTAPS work. Though no study has been conducted seeking to determine any effect of the print and electronic media on research, there is no obvious evidence of it.

The NW political divide meandered more through the liberal-conservative terrain than through the positions of the Democratic and Republican parties (to the extent that such a distinction can be made). Representatives and senators expressed their views as individuals, those engaged enough to speak out usually inclining to accept the reality of NW. Nor were they motivated by regionalism, as often occurred when there were legislative debates about the siting of a major technical facility, such as the Superconducting Super Collider. Overall, NW was a political episode explored far more through its intrinsic merits than through partisan politics, economic interests, Cold War ideology, or personal egotism. Even the

Reagan administration's successful action in constraining NW research and sidelining discussion of its political consequences seems to have been motivated by honest doubts about the phenomenon and preference for its own policy choices.

Congress, too, acquitted itself reasonably well in dealing with an unusual situation. Most commonly, the legislature has a known issue to deal with and tries to carve out a policy. NW, in contrast, was thrust upon a surprised government, which was told, in effect, "you should do something." The information presented to the congressional committees was not very technical or difficult to comprehend, nor need it have been so. But all too often the presentations assumed an adversarial tone, suggesting strongly that the advice was not impartial. This was at odds with the tradition of disinterested scientific advice formed in the decades after World War II, and might not have helped convince the uncommitted. Still, even though the scientific advice offered by NW believers was not accepted by the legislative or executive branches of government, overall, the hydra-headed (or cobbled-together) scientific advisory system did work quite well.[22]

But working well and working wisely are not necessarily the same. Was it sensible to marginalize NW research and policy? In view of the remarkably low cost of the research (especially relative to other defense programs), it seems foolish to have starved the laboratory effort and short-sighted to have dismissed the need to explore new plans. The Reagan administration, however, had no wish for the potential disruption to its policies that real acceptance of NW could bring. NW advocates, consequently, never really reached the point of submitting specific research proposals and budgets to funding agencies.

Conclusion

"Environmental warfare" has a long and inglorious history. Laying waste to the land was attempted in the past, on both small and large scales. Its purpose was to deny food, shelter, and communication to an enemy, to demoralize its population, to punish them, to force the transfer of resources from combat to mitigation of the harm, or, when self-inflicted, to deny the enemy territory. It could also be an accidental result, as with ozone depletion and global warming. Militarily, salting the earth (done at Carthage by the Romans), dumping corpses down wells (done in numerous wars), flooding their own country (done by the Dutch at the end of the seventeenth century, and threatened in World War II), Sherman's march to the sea in the American Civil War, Japanese attempts to ignite American forests by incendiary balloons in World War II, the Soviet scorched-earth practice in World War II, the American threat in the 1950s to lay a band of radioactive waste across Korea to keep out Chinese troops, the use of defoliants in Vietnam, and continuing research on weather modification are some examples of deliberate behavior.

NW is yet another environmental "insult," notable for its potential global reach. Just as we must cautiously approach activities of civilization that span huge regions (such as free-trade zones, multinational corporations, an international stock market, and even cultural imperialism) because of untoward and unexpected consequences, NW should give us pause to avoid a nuclear war that could be far worse than previously anticipated. From the birth of nuclear weapons in 1945, there have been calls to face political problems globally, to think broadly of civilization, rather than in narrow, nationalistic terms.[23] The history of the last half of the twentieth century shows the general failure of these visionaries, except in the unhappy international rivalry of the superpowers and in First World economic domination, both being global behavior at odds with global interests. To be sure, there have been a few successes (such as activities of the United Nations, some international environmental accords, the Internet, and possibly some multinational corporations), but the story of the world remains dominated by nation-state concerns. The non-response to the threat of NW may be counted among the failures to act globally.

In the past, and even to this date, Western Civilization has relied largely on its scientific and technological prowess. This high-tech exuberance often is called a "technological fix." It means that people seek to solve problems created by science and technology by throwing more science and technology at them. This has often been practicable, as with the development of synthetics to replace depleted natural materials, with the Green Revolution increasing world food supply, and with the drive to reduce dependency on petroleum by building nuclear reactors (not that these activities are without their own problems). But the successful efforts usually fall into the category of "man against Nature." Ingenuity and creativity can accomplish some remarkable things. Once, however, the contest turns to "man against man," complexities increase. Humans do not behave as consistently as does Nature—and the search for technological fixes is far less appropriate. Thus, for example, SDI or its contemporary incarnation, NMD, is doomed to failure, since a fraction of incoming warheads will always penetrate the defenses, and these relative few will be enough to harm American society unacceptably. Other defenses against nuclear weapons (for example, duck-and-cover, evacuation of cities, blast and fallout shelters) were properly regarded by the American public as inadequate, and were never strongly supported. (They also lacked the glamour of high technology.)

The argument that attempts at a technological fix work less well in man-against-man situations is not meant to imply that man-against-Nature efforts invariably succeed. CFC production threatened to destroy stratospheric ozone and therefore had to be halted; no "end run" solution was possible. Similarly, global warming will not succumb to a palliative; its causes must be reversed. NW should also be placed in this final category. If NW is physically possible, no combination of greater warhead accuracy, missile-silo targeting, earth-penetrating warheads, or wintertime attack will likely prevent cities from burning in a major nuclear war. We will not be saved by a technological fix.

We should also recognize the limitations of "expert" knowledge. It was not nuclear explosion experts who uncovered the NW phenomenon, but a bunch of atmospheric scientists. In an area well plowed with federal funding and with a near monopoly by the federal government, a few competent civilian scientists were able to make a major discovery.

Expertise in unexpected areas can be serendipitous; the people closest to a subject are not always the most knowledgeable. NW also was somewhat unusual in being part of a new style of science in which computer simulations take the place of experiments that cannot be conducted. Greenhouse warming is perhaps another such field. These scientific specialties embrace a new wave of thinking on a global scale, using interdisciplinary tools and integrating disparate data.

Worst-case analyses are, of course, made and justified all the time, often for good reason. When suitable for one's political purposes, it is common to criticize an opponent for such an approach. In 1993, defending his tenure as secretary of defense, Caspar Weinberger pointedly responded to criticism from the General Accounting Office that the Department of Defense had misled Congress about the cost, performance, and necessity of several nuclear delivery systems, including the B-1B and B-2 bombers and the cruise and MX missiles. Calling the report "revisionist history written by accountants," Weinberger said: "This analysis was done without any understanding of how it looked to us in 1981. Yes, we used a worst-case analysis. You should always use a worst-case analysis in this business. You can't afford to be wrong. In the end, we won the Cold War, and if we won by too much, if it was overkill, so be it."[24]

Also in the early 1980s, and based on the capabilities of the computer models and on the various quantitative data that went into NW, the TTAPS conclusion was valid. It was good science. The authors never claimed that their work was the last word; rather, it was a first cut at a phenomenon that would improve with increasingly refined models and numbers. That they had discovered a possible climatic catastrophe was validated by the inability of the NAS and SCOPE reports to deny it. During the course of about 5 years, TTAPS's predictions were modified, as expected, yielding less severe climatic disturbances, but devastation that was still awesome. The political action urged by Sagan and others was respectable public policy, something that the superpowers hoped eventually to achieve.

It was the critics of NW, not its proponents, whose behavior might be questioned. They condemned the concept, but they failed to provide models and data that could be used to generate alternative climatic results. But it was not these scientific censors who succeeded in marginalizing NW. Rather, it was an administration marching to its own concept of arms control, followed by an out-of-sight-out-of-mind attitude when the Cold War ended. The US government accepted the possibility of NW, then ignored it. Suppressing NW in this fashion was politically effective; it took the wind out of the sails that Sagan tried so hard to inflate.

To this administration, the source of advice, surprisingly, seemed to matter little. The foci of NW research were the Lawrence Livermore National Laboratory, the Los Alamos National Laboratory, the National Center for Atmospheric Research, the Ames Research Center, the Computing Centre of the USSR Academy of Sciences, the Institute for Atmospheric Sciences of the USSR Academy of Sciences, the United Kingdom Meteorological Office, and the Australian Commonwealth Scientific and Industrial Research Organization—every one of them a government unit. If the political masters chose to ignore advice from such "insiders," why would they listen to unwanted suggestions from "outsiders"? Thus, research agendas withered, and no plans were made for food, shelter, medical care, rebuilding, or replanting under changed climatic conditions. The largely null effect from the oil well fires of Kuwait, whether significant in invalidating NW or not, was the coup de grace to most interest in NW.

It would have taken action by the office of the president to change course. Reagan, interestingly, showed that he was capable of startling innovations with his nearly unilateral command to adopt the Strategic Defense Initiative. But this escalating, high-tech, and defensive response (its offensive aspects were largely ignored by politicians) to the nuclear threat was more in line with Reagan's thinking and emotions than the cooperative, no-tech, and massive cut in the arsenals that Sagan urged. This leads, effectively, to the truism that technical advice is usually accepted only when it meshes with political goals.

By and large, the media behaved creditably. Stories on NW appeared in newspapers, news magazines, science periodicals, popular science magazines, journals and magazines of opinion, and the magazines of environmental societies. Reporters covered stories as they broke and were generally accurate in their writing. The bias came more in the form of editorial decisions whether to run a story or not. Periodicals with known political orientations did not disappoint their readers, particularly the *Wall Street Journal* on one side and *Sierra* and *Environment* on the other. But professional standards were maintained even here, with opposing letters to the editor printed. Aside from an occasional interview show on TV, such as that hosted by Ted Koppel, radio and television virtually ignored NW. Its announcement in 1983 would be topical for a sound bite, but little thereafter was sensational enough for the evening news.

The Soviet Union dissolved in the early 1990s, and the threat of nuclear war is lower than it has been for half a century. So why should we still be concerned about NW? It is because both the United States and Russia still have thousands of nuclear weapons, and several other nations have smaller but still significant numbers in their arsenals. If the NW believers are correct, the danger of a climatic catastrophe continues to exist. Even if the NW skeptics are right, both the minor cost of funding research and rapid steps toward a proposed minimal nuclear deterrent appear to be cautious and sensible policies.

Policy never made it to first base in the case of NW. Placing non-combatant nations on the front lines was insufficient to mobilize the Third World against the potential danger of NW. Nor were the nuclear states moved to change any policies by the threat of suicide if they used their arsenals. In the first instance, there was little action of a concrete nature that poor countries could take, aside from the few protests recounted in these chapters. They lacked funds for daily requirements, and they could not stockpile the needed food and warm clothing anticipated. In the second instance, most bureaucrats did not see NW as significantly worse than the horror of nuclear war that they already had known they must avoid.

American bureaucrats displayed a surprisingly callous attitude toward knowledge, with the notable exception of the Defense Nuclear Agency, which continued to fund a substantial amount of US research on NW for several years. Officialdom chose to be disdainful of biological and policy consequences until the physical effects were proved to their satisfaction. That this knowledge would have cost remarkably little relative to many other government programs confirms that the Reagan administration wished to encounter no political challenges to its plans for military hardware and policies. Scientific advice was offered and effectively ignored. The advisory system worked well, but the officials, as was their right, unwisely declined the advice. This was, of course, a decision, but one by default. NW, thus, withered as a topic of inquiry.

A Nuclear Winter's Tale illustrates the political and cultural bias in American society. When faced with uncertainty in its relations with the Soviet Union, Americans had little difficulty in assuming the worst and acting upon that presumption. Invariably, this meant improving the nuclear arsenal and being willing to spend trillions of dollars to do so. The Soviets, of course, responded in kind. Whether the United States became safer in the process is doubtful. Arms control and disarmament goals were pursued over many decades, and some valuable treaties were signed and ratified. But the scale of these efforts towards peace by negotiation was minuscule compared to the labors that enhanced America's "weapons culture." The self-defeating behavior of the United States has been caricaturized vividly—as a man striking matches while standing in a pool of gasoline, or (for the US and USSR) as two scorpions in a bottle—but Americans seem incapable of stopping or separating. This is not a technical problem, nor even a military problem. It is a lack of political courage to lead public opinion away from genocidal, fratricidal, and now possibly suicidal conditions. Americans still live in the mental state of the pre-nuclear world, wherein security was measured in terms of arms and patriotism by bellicosity.

Cassandra, the daughter of Priam and Hecuba and the sister of Hector and Paris, had the gift of prophecy. She warned against allowing the Greeks' wooden horse behind the walls of Troy, but to no avail. Chicken Little was perhaps the first "scientific Cassandra," calling attention to an atmospheric phenomenon. Her cry that the sky was falling was based on faulty evidence (it was an acorn), yet the king, who was grateful that she assisted in ridding the land of a wolf, gave her an umbrella. Stretching the comparison, her umbrella served as a personal SDI-like missile shield. Acting as a Cassandra is, in effect, being one who supports worst-case analyses. Just as the Department of Defense often used such prophecies when it suited the war planners (and when it came time to present its annual budget request to Congress), Sagan invoked it for his own purposes. There need not be any connotation of duplicity about this practice; those involved can be credited with an honest belief in the wisdom of advocating action that is based on extreme conditions.

George Rathjens, in contrast to Sagan, had far more experience as an analyst and recognized that there are costs associated with action and with inaction. In the case of NW, he felt that the uncertainties were too large to accept the cost of hedging against the prediction.[25] Rathjens's position was the one that prevailed. Nonetheless, Sagan, his TTAPS colleagues, and other NW scientists succeeded in moving defense intellectuals, congressmen, scientists, and the public to think beyond the immediate casualties of nuclear war and reexamine the potential long-term effects. They may also be credited with prying off the lid of confidence in deterrence—at least a bit—and forcing people to think—at least a bit—about the suicidal nature of nuclear war.

For the most part, however, the public, over several decades, had become inured to (or tolerant of) the threat of mass destruction—not only to its enemies but to itself. While discouraging, it is no surprise, then, that NW inspired so little outrage. Even the additional danger to non-combatants provoked minor response. The subtitle of Stanley Kubrick's classic anti-war film *Dr. Strangelove* (1964) accurately described this condition: "How I learned to stop worrying and love the bomb."

Epilogue

By the end of the Reagan administration, in 1989, there was no evidence that NW had affected policy. With the demise of the Soviet Union, NW even disappeared from discussions of strategy. For example, in 1993 the Center for Defense Information published an issue of its *Defense Monitor* devoted to the question "Does the United States need nuclear weapons?" The consequences of explosions were mentioned only superficially and only twice (once in terms of devastation, once in terms of radioactive contamination). There was no hint of climatic effects, suicidal action, or the destruction of agriculture.[1] Other commentators on nuclear issues similarly ignored NW in their analyses of the diminished arms race.[2]

Some NW scientists, however, offered circumstantial evidence to assert that NW *did* have an effect on policy. They noted that the number of nuclear warheads in the Soviet Union peaked in 1986, and that the American stockpile had been in a slow decline for many years. However, the total number of warheads in the *combined* arsenals was highest in 1986.[3] After that year, both countries reduced their nuclear arsenals dramatically, such that the total in 2002 was only about one-third that in 1986. During this period, the Intermediate Nuclear Forces Treaty and the Strategic Arms Reduction Treaty were signed. NW, of course, was revealed in 1983. Did fear of the nuclear winter phenomenon help to push the superpowers to sharply reduce their nuclear stockpiles? The timing is suggestive and it is an interesting argument. But as yet the connection is unproven.

Toon, Robock, Stenchikov, Turco, and other scientists (who suggested the above connection) continued their investigation of NW, using (perhaps for the first time) a GCM able to couple the atmosphere and oceans to study the effects of soot from nuclear-ignited fires. Cities in the subtropics, such as those of nuclear-armed Israel, India, and Pakistan, have adequately high fuel loadings. With strong heating by the Sun, smoke clouds from this part of the world could be lofted significantly higher than predicted before, into the high stratosphere. There they would disperse slowly. While the amount of smoke used in this model (5 teragrams) was far smaller than amounts used in previous investigations, its persistence made it effective. Global average surface air temperatures fell about 1.25°C in the first year and were about 0.5°C cooler than normal a decade later; precipitation followed a similar path. This work, published in 2006, claimed that a regional war, a conflict with far fewer weapons than earlier considered (a "mere" fifty 15-KT bombs on each side) might provoke a global climate change of long duration, with great harm to agriculture.[4]

Is NW a real phenomenon? This is not for a historian to decide. But the overwhelming sense of the scientific community—voiced in many research papers, articulated in the NAS, SCOPE, and other reports, not disproved in the skies over Kuwait, and reinforced by studies nearly a quarter of a century after the announcement of nuclear winter—is that the phenomenon is possible. We ignore calamitous warnings at our peril.

Notes

Chapter 1

1. S. McNaughton, R. Ruess, and M. Coughenour, "Ecological consequences of nuclear war," *Nature* 321 (29 May 1986), 483–487, on 483.

2. C. Sagan, "The nuclear winter," *Parade*, 30 Oct. 1983, 4–7.

3. H. Rosenberg, *Atomic Soldiers: American Victims of Nuclear Experiments* (Beacon, 1980); T. Saffer and O. Kelly, *Countdown Zero: GI Victims of US Atomic Testing* (Putnam, 1982); H. Ball, *Justice Downwind: America's Atomic Testing Program in the 1950s* (Oxford University Press, 1986); R. Lindsey, "Veterans agency is penalized over data ordered by court," *New York Times*, 12 June 1987; anon., "New rules on benefits for disabled veterans," *New York Times*, 22 May 1988. See also the following articles in the *Los Angeles Times*: "Trial to seek truth behind early US nuclear testing" (13 Sept. 1982); "Deception's high cost" [editorial], 19 Sept. 1982; "Cancer suit tied to Nevada A-tests ends" (18 Dec. 1982); "US is ordered to pay victims of nuclear tests" (11 May 1984); "'Atomic veterans' push claims campaign" (28 Aug. 1986); "A-test victims can't sue US, court decides" (23 June 1987); "Compensation for radiation victims OKd" (28 Sept. 1990); "They were told there was no danger" (1 Oct. 1990).

4. R. Abramson, "US, Russ arms accord reached," *Los Angeles Times*, 10 May 1979; "Treaty based on Soviet honor, critics say," *Los Angeles Times*, 20 Mar. 1979; S. Talbott, *Endgame: The Inside Story of SALT II* (Harper and Row, 1979).

5. Anon., "Carter sinks SALT 2," *Star* [Christchurch, New Zealand], 4 Jan. 1980.

6. D. Yankelovich and J. Doble, "The public mood: Nuclear weapons and the USSR," *Foreign Affairs* 63 (fall 1984), 33–46, quote on 44.

7. W. Isaacson, "Fighting the backbiting," *Time* 118 (16 Nov. 1981), 22–23; D. Alpern, "There they go again," *Newsweek* 98 (16 Nov. 1981), 32–33.

8. T. Draper, "Dear Mr. Weinberger: An open reply to an open letter," *New York Review of Books* 29 (4 Nov. 1982), 26–31; "On nuclear war: An exchange with the Secretary of Defense," *New York Review of Books* 30 (18 Aug. 1983), 27–33.

9. "Reckoning with Armageddon" [editorial], *New York Times*, 25 Oct. 1984.

10. M. Katz, *Ban the Bomb: A History of SANE, the Committee for a Sane Nuclear Policy, 1957–1985* (Greenwood, 1986), esp. 154; D. Cortright, *Peace Works: The Citizen's Role in Ending the Cold War* (Westview, 1993); Robert R. Bland, Development Director of the Union of Concerned Scientists, letter to L. Badash, 28 Dec. 1989; Gene R. La Rocque, Director of Center for Defense Information, letter to L. Badash, 8 Jan. 1990; John Loretz, Director of Communications of Physicians for Social Responsibility, letter to L. Badash, 9 Mar. 1990.

11. Of 126 organizations listed, 63 were founded between 1981 and 1984. See D. Burek et al., *Encyclopedia of Associations, 1990*, volume 1: *National Organizations of the U.S.* (Gale Research, 1989), section 9: public affairs organizations.

12. J. Schell, *The Fate of the Earth* (Knopf, 1982).

13. This view was widely held. For example, General Bernard W. Rogers, while NATO Supreme Commander in 1983, said: "We are not going to contain a nuclear war in Western Europe. A nuclear war in Western Europe is going to escalate to a strategic exchange. I feel the war would escalate quickly." (quoted in *Defense Monitor* 17, no. 3 (1988), 2) A similar statement made by the US National Academy of Sciences was reported in "Scientists urge more effort to cut atom risk," *New York Times*, 28 Apr. 1982. Colonel-General Makhmut Gareyev, Deputy Chief of the General Staff of the Armed Forces of the Soviet Union, added: "We do not believe that a controlled nuclear war is possible. A nuclear war will not be fought at a limited level." (Gareyev, "The revised Soviet military doctrine," *Bulletin of the Atomic Scientists* 44, Dec. 1988, 30–34, quote on 30) A poll conducted in 1981 revealed that 50% of the public believed conflict between the superpowers would become all-out war, 21% felt the war could be limited, 16% said the war would be fought with conventional weapons only, and 13% had no opinion ("A Gallup poll on nuclear war," *Newsweek* 98, 5 Oct. 1981, 35). For further discussion, see D. Ball, *Can Nuclear War Be Controlled?* (International Institute for Strategic Studies, 1981), 30–35. See also D. Holloway, *Stalin and the Bomb: The Soviet Union and Atomic Energy, 1939–1956* (Yale University Press, 1994).

14. H. Smith, "MX panel proposes basing 100 missiles in Minuteman silos," *New York Times*, 12 Apr. 1983; remarks by Marshal Sergei F. Akhromeyev, Chief of Staff of the Soviet armed forces and First Deputy Defense Minister, at press briefing held before special conference of Communist Party, as reported in M. Parks, "Soviets admit foreign policy, defense errors," *Los Angeles Times*, 26 June 1988.

15. S. Talbott, *Deadly Gambits: The Reagan Administration and the Stalemate in Nuclear Arms Control* (Knopf, 1984). See also R. Powaski, *March to Armageddon* (Oxford University Press, 1987), 193–194.

16. G. Kennan, "A modest proposal," *New York Review of Books* 28 (16 July 1981), 14–16. Note that the US, somewhat offhandedly, had earlier advanced a similar proposal: "On a reciprocal basis we are willing now to reduce them by 10 per cent, 20 per cent or even 50 per cent" ("Address by President Carter to the United Nations General Assembly, October 4, 1977," *Documents on Disarmament, 1977*, US Arms Control and Disarmament Agency, 1979, 605).

17. S. Weisman, "Reagan proposes U.S. seek new way to block missiles," *New York Times*, 24 Mar. 1983; S. Lakoff and H. York, *A Shield in Space? Technology, Politics, and the Strategic Defense Initiative* (University of California Press, 1989).

18. P. Boyer, *By the Bomb's Early Light: American Thought and Culture at the Dawn of the Atomic Age* (Pantheon, 1985); I. Gitlin, "Radio and atomic-energy education," *Journal of Educational Sociology* 22 (Jan. 1949), 327–330.

19. For an eloquent essay on nuclear strategy, morality, and related issues published just at the debut of nuclear winter, see J. Schell, "The abolition," *The New Yorker* 59 (2 and 9 Jan. 1984), 36–75 and 43–94.

20. L. Badash, E. Hodes, and A. Tiddens, "Nuclear fission: Reaction to the discovery in 1939," *Proceedings of the American Philosophical Society* 130 (June 1986), 196–231. See also L. Badash, *Scientists and the Development of Nuclear Weapons: From Fission to the Limited Test Ban Treaty, 1939–1963* (Humanities Press, 1995).

21. Hans Bethe, letter to L. Badash, 20 Nov. 1990; Bethe, "Can air or water be exploded?" *Bulletin of the Atomic Scientists* 1 (15 Mar. 1946), 2, 14; Bethe, "Ultimate catastrophe?" *Bulletin of the Atomic Scientists* 32 (June 1976), 36–37; A. Compton, *Atomic Quest: A Personal Narrative* (Oxford University Press, 1956), 127–128.

22. Edward Teller, "Comments on the historical presentation in the television production 'Day One' based on Peter Wyden's book, *Day One: Before Hiroshima and After*," typescript (1989), obtained through the courtesy of Dr. Teller and Dr. George Bing. I have followed Teller's recollections about the 1944 study, because they seem to be consistent with the secret report, but not about the 1942 events, where he is contradicted by Bethe and Compton (see preceding note). In this typescript he says that "Oppenheimer's trip to Compton was not made because of the possible ignition of the atmosphere. . . . The question was not an issue in Berkeley." A slightly different story is told, without citations of sources, by G. Goncharov ("Thermonuclear milestones," *Physics Today* 49 (Nov. 1996), 44–61, esp. 45). See also E. Konopinski, C. Marvin, and E. Teller, "Ignition of the atmosphere with nuclear bombs," Los Alamos report LA-602, 14 Aug. 1946, declassified 2 Feb. 1973; "Manhattan District History," Book 8, Vol. 2, Project Y, History, Technical, in US National Archives.

23. P. Bridgman, undated letter to H. Bethe, reproduced in Norris Bradbury, telegram to Gen. Leslie Groves, 13 Mar. 1946; Bethe, reply, 13 Feb. 1946; [no initials given] Gee, telegram to N. Bradbury, 12 Mar. 1946. These documents are preserved in the Los Alamos National Laboratory Records Center/Archives. See also H. Bethe, "The hydrogen bomb: II," *Scientific American* 182 (Apr. 1950), 18–23; J. Mark, "A short account of Los Alamos theoretical work on thermonuclear weapons, 1946–1950," Los Alamos report LA-5647-MS, July 1974 (abridged version of a still-secret document first issued on 1 Oct. 1954).

24. President's Commission on the Accident at Three Mile Island, *The Need for Change: The Legacy of TMI* (Government Printing Office, 1979); D. Sills, C. Wolf, and V. Shelanski, eds., *Accident at Three Mile Island: The Human Dimensions* (Westview, 1982).

25. Reuters News Service, "Chernobyl toll was 300, Soviet lawmaker says," *Los Angeles Times*, 26 Apr. 1990.

26. E. Marshall, "Recalculating the cost of Chernobyl," *Science* 236 (8 May 1987), 658–659; R. Wilson, "A visit to Chernobyl," *Science* 236 (26 June 1987), 1636–1640.

27. O. Frisch and R. Peierls, "Memorandum on the construction of a 'super-bomb; ' based on a nuclear chain reaction in uranium," published as appendix in M. Gowing, *Britain and Atomic Energy, 1939–1945* (Macmillan, 1964), 389–393.

28. B. Hacker, *The Dragon's Tail: Radiation Safety in the Manhattan Project, 1942–1946* (University of California Press, 1987), 86–108.

29. J. Hirschfelder, "The scientific and technological miracle at Los Alamos," in L. Badash et al., eds., *Reminiscences of Los Alamos, 1943–1945* (Reidel, 1980); J. Webb, "The fogging of photographic film by radioactive contaminants in cardboard packaging materials," *Physical Review* 76 (1 Aug. 1949), 375–380.

30. R. Lapp, *My Life with Radiation: Hiroshima Plus Fifty Years* (Cogito, 1995), 28–29.

31. R. Hewlett and F. Duncan, *Atomic Shield, 1947/1952: Volume II of a History of the United States Atomic Energy Commission* (Pennsylvania State University Press, 1969), 362–364.

32. "USAEC General Advisory Committee Report on the 'Super,' October 30, 1949," USAEC GAC records, US Department of Energy, Germantown, Maryland. The text is published in R. Williams and P. Cantelon, eds., *The American Atom: A Documentary History of Nuclear Policies from the Discovery of Fission to the Present, 1939–1984* (University of Pennsylvania Press, 1984), 120–127, quote on 126. On the hydrogen bomb's development, see H. York, *The Advisors: Oppenheimer, Teller, and the Superbomb* (Freeman, 1976); R. Rhodes, *Dark Sun: The Making of the Hydrogen Bomb* (Simon and Schuster, 1995).

33. Y. Smirnov and V. Zubok, "Nuclear weapons after Stalin's death: Moscow enters the H-bomb age," *Cold War International History Project Bulletin* no. 4 (fall 1994), 14.

34. J. Hirschfelder et al., eds., *The Effects of Atomic Weapons* (Department of Defense and Atomic Energy Commission, 1950), 273–275.

35. S. Glasstone, ed., *The Effects of Nuclear Weapons* (Department of Defense and Atomic Energy Commission, 1957), 446–454.

36. Ibid., 423–427; York, *The Advisors*, 75–87, 108; R. Lapp, *The Voyage of the Lucky Dragon* (Harper, 1958). Lapp is also credited with authoring the first detailed public description of the dangers of radioactive fallout: "Civil defense faces new peril," *Bulletin of the Atomic Scientists* 10 (Nov. 1959), 349–351.

37. Stockholm International Peace Research Institute, *World Armaments and Disarmament: SIPRI Yearbook 1976* (MIT Press, 1976), 416.

38. B. Commoner, *The Closing Circle: Nature, Man, and Technology* (Knopf, 1971), 49–56. See also B. Hacker, *Elements of Controversy: The Atomic Energy Commission and Radiation Safety in Nuclear Weapons Testing, 1947–1974* (University of California Press, 1994).

39. L. Pauling, "Science and peace," in F. Haberman, ed., *Nobel Lectures: Peace, 1951–1970* (Elsevier, 1972), 257–292; Pauling, *No More War!* (Dodd, Mead, 1958).

40. Katz, *Ban the Bomb*, 14–44; C. Driver, *The Disarmers: A Study in Protest* (Hodder and Stoughton, 1964); F. Myers, "British peace politics: The Campaign for Nuclear Disarmament and the Committee

of 100, 1957–1962," doctoral dissertation, Columbia University, 1965; R. Taylor and C. Pritchard, *The Protest Makers: The British Nuclear Disarmament Movement of 1958–1965, Twenty Years On* (Pergamon, 1980).

41. R. Divine, *Blowing on the Wind: The Nuclear Test Ban Debate, 1954–1960* (Oxford University Press, 1978); G. Seaborg, *Kennedy, Khrushchev, and the Test Ban* (University of California Press, 1981); L. Wittner, *One World or None: A History of the World Nuclear Disarmament Movement, through 1953* (Stanford University Press, 1993); Wittner, *Resisting the Bomb: A History of the World Nuclear Disarmament Movement, 1954–1970* (Stanford University Press, 1997).

42. *SIPRI Yearbook 1976*, 416.

43. W. Broad, "Nuclear pulse (I): Awakening to the chaos factor," *Science* 212 (29 May 1981), 1009–1012; "Nuclear pulse (II): Ensuring delivery of the doomsday signal," *Science* 212 (5 June 1981), 1116–1120; "Nuclear pulse (III): Playing a wild card," *Science* 212 (12 June 1981), 1248–1251; S. Glasstone and P. Dolan, *The Effects of Nuclear Weapons* (Department of Defense and Energy Research and Development Administration, 1977), 77–78.

44. L. Ricketts et al., *EMP Radiation and Protective Techniques* (Wiley, 1976), 3–5.

45. W. Broad, "Military grapples with the chaos factor," *Science* 213 (11 Sept. 1981), 1228–1229.

46. Broad, "Nuclear pulse (I)" and "Military grapples with the chaos factor."

47. Ibid.

48. J. Campbell, *Rutherford: Scientist Supreme* (AAS Publications, 1999), 149–150.

49. S. Chapman, "A theory of upper-atmospheric ozone," *Memoirs of the Royal Meteorological Society* 3, no. 26 (June 1930), 103–125.

50. J. Levine, "Earth, atmosphere," in S. Maran, ed., *The Astronomy and Astrophysics Encyclopedia* (Van Nostrand Reinhold, 1992); A. Jursa, ed., *Handbook of Geophysics and the Space Environment* (US Air Force Geophysics Laboratory, 1985), 21–2, 21–3, 22–4. L. Dotto and H. Schiff (*The Ozone Wars*, Doubleday, 1978, 35) specify ozone's presence as one-tenth that given above, or less than one part per million in the stratosphere.

51. S. Stephens and J. Birks, "After nuclear war: Perturbations in atmospheric chemistry," *BioScience* 35 (Oct. 1985), 557–562, on 559.

52. Glasstone and Dolan, *The Effects of Nuclear Weapons*, 77–78.

53. F. Rowland, "Stratospheric ozone depletion," *Annual Review of Physical Chemistry* 42 (1991), 731–768, on 731.

54. A. Nier et al., *Long-Term Worldwide Effects of Multiple Nuclear-Weapons Detonations* (National Academy of Sciences, 1975), 5; F. Gilmore, "The production of nitrogen oxides by low-altitude nuclear explosions," *Journal of Geophysical Research* 80 (20 Nov. 1975), 4553–4554.

55. P. Crutzen, "The influence of nitrogen oxides on the atmospheric ozone content," *Quarterly Journal of the Royal Meteorological Society* 96 (Apr. 1970), 320–325.

56. H. Johnston, "Reduction of stratospheric ozone by nitrogen oxide catalysts from supersonic transport exhaust," *Science* 173 (6 Aug. 1971), 517–522.

57. H. Foley and M. Ruderman, "Stratospheric NO production from past nuclear explosions," *Journal of Geophysical Research* 78 (20 July 1973), 4441–4450.

58. H. Johnston, G. Whitten, and J. Birks, "Effect of nuclear explosions on stratospheric nitric oxide and ozone," *Journal of Geophysical Research* 78 (20 Sept. 1973), 6107–6135. Their conclusions were not universally accepted; less than a month earlier a British team argued the opposite. See P. Goldsmith et al., "Nitrogen oxides, nuclear weapon testing, Concorde and stratospheric ozone," *Nature* 244 (31 Aug. 1973), 545–551.

59. J. Hampson, "Photochemical war on the atmosphere," *Nature* 250 (19 July 1974), 189–191, quote on 190.

60. M. MacCracken and J. Chang, "A preliminary study of the potential chemical and climatic effects of atmospheric nuclear explosions," Lawrence Livermore Laboratory Report UCRL-51653, 25 Apr. 1975.

61. The ACDA request was made on 4 Apr. 1974. For Philip Handler's letter to Fred Iklé, 12 Aug. 1975, published as the preface to this work, see Nier, *Long-Term Worldwide Effects*, 1.

62. Nier, *Long-Term Worldwide Effects*, 5–7, 25, 38–39, 51–53, 60; P. Handler, "Nuclear war's effects might last 25 years," *Los Angeles Times*, 5 Oct. 1975.

63. Glasstone, *The Effects of Nuclear Weapons*, 69–71.

64. T. Stonier, *Nuclear Disaster* (World, 1964), 136–152.

65. Hampson "Photochemical war." See also R. Whitten, W. Borucki, and R. Turco, "Possible ozone depletions following nuclear explosions," *Nature* 257 (4 Sept. 1975), 38–39.

66. P. Ehrlich and A. Ehrlich, *Population, Resources, Environment: Issues in Human Ecology* (Freeman, 1970), 192.

67. P. Ehrlich, A. Ehrlich, and J. Holdren, *Ecoscience: Population, Resources, Environment* (Freeman, 1977), 640.

68. S. Schneider, *The Genesis Strategy: Climate and Global Survival* (Plenum, 1976), 203–205, quote on 204. See also S. Schneider and R. Londer, *The Coevolution of Climate and Life* (Sierra Club Books, 1984).

69. Nier, *Long-Term Worldwide Effects*, 6–7, 60, quote on 7.

70. K. Lewis, "The prompt and delayed effects of nuclear war," *Scientific American* 241 (July 1979), 35–47.

71. US Congress, Senate, Committee on Foreign Relations, Subcommittee on Arms Control, International Organizations and Security Agreements, *Analyses of Effects of Limited Nuclear Warfare*, Committee Print, 94th Congress, 1st Session, Sept. 1975, 155.

72. Ibid., 155–156.

73. J. Mark, "Global consequences of nuclear weaponry," *Annual Review of Nuclear Science* 26 (1976), 51–87, quote on 82.

74. A. Sakharov and E. Henry, "Scientists and nuclear war," in S. Cohen, ed., *An End to Silence: Uncensored Opinion in the Soviet Union* (Norton, 1982); D. Holloway, *The Soviet Union and the Arms Race* (Yale University Press, 1983), 165–166.

Chapter 2

1. Leo Szilard, testimony, in US Congress, Senate, Special Committee on Atomic Energy, *Atomic Energy*, hearings, 79th Congress, 1st Session, 27 Nov. 1945–15 Feb. 1946, 291.

2. Examples: D. Ball, *Can Nuclear War Be Controlled?* (International Institute for Strategic Studies, 1981); P. Bracken and M. Shubik, "Strategic war: What are the questions and who should ask them?" *Technology in Society* 4 (1982), 155–179; US Congress, Joint Committee on Defense Production, *Economic and Social Consequences of Nuclear Attacks on the United States*, Committee Print, 96th Congress, 1st Session, Mar. 1979. For a bibliography of several of these topics, see M. Riordan, ed., *The Day After Midnight: The Effects of Nuclear War* (Cheshire, 1982), 130–132. (*The Day After Midnight* is based almost entirely on *The Effects of Nuclear War*, published by the congressional Office of Technology Assessment in 1979.)

3. F. Walkhoff, "Unsichtbare, photographisch wirksame Strahlen," *Photographische Rundschau*, Oct. 1900, 189–191; H. Becquerel, "Recherches sur une propriété nouvelle de la matière," *Mémoires de l'Académie des Sciences, Paris* 46 (1903), 263–266.

4. L. Badash, *Radioactivity in America: Growth and Decay of a Science* (Johns Hopkins University Press, 1979), 125–134.

5. R. Evans, "Radium poisoning, a review of present knowledge," *American Journal of Public Health* 23 (1933), 1017–1023; D. Lang, "A most valuable accident," *The New Yorker*, 2 May 1959, 49ff.; C. Caufield, *Multiple Exposures: Chronicles of the Radiation Age* (Secker and Warburg, 1989), 29–37.

6. Hacker, *Elements of Controversy*.

7. R. Hewlett and F. Duncan, *Atomic Shield, 1947/1952: Volume II of a History of the United States Atomic Energy Commission* (Pennsylvania State University Press, 1969), 499–500.

8. Hirschfelder, *The Effects of Atomic Weapons*, 267–268, 436–437.

9. R. Norris, T. Cochran, and W. Arkin, "History of the nuclear stockpile," *Bulletin of the Atomic Scientists* 41 (Aug. 1985), 106–109.

10. USAEC and USAF Project Rand, "Worldwide effects of atomic weapons: Project Sunshine," report R-251-AEC, amended (Rand Corporation, 1953), 2–8. The recommended sampling, using gummed film to hold particles deposited upon it, is described in M. Eisenbud and J. Harley, "Long-term fallout," *Science* 128 (22 Aug. 1958), 399–402. Eisenbud and Harley's results for strontium activity are of the same order of magnitude as the numbers used in the Sunshine estimates.

11. See, e.g., US Congress, Joint Committee on Atomic Energy, Special Subcommittee on Radiation, *The Nature of Radioactive Fallout and its Effects on Man*, hearings, 85th Congress, 1st Session, 27 May-7 June 1957; *Report of the United Nations Scientific Committee on the Effects of Atomic Radiation*, General Assembly, 13th Session, Supplement 17 (A/3838) (United Nations, 1958); National Academy of Sciences-National Research Council, *The Biological Effects of Atomic Radiation*, Summary Reports (NAS, 1956 and 1960).

12. C. Comar, "Biological aspects of nuclear weapons," *American Scientist* 50 (June 1962), 339–353.

13. Ibid.

14. See, e.g., J. Mark, "Global consequences of nuclear weaponry," *Annual Review of Nuclear Science* 26 (1976), 51–87.

15. "Project Sunshine," 23–36, 83–87.

16. L. Machta and D. Harris, "Effects of atomic explosions on weather," *Science* 121 (21 Jan. 1955), 75–81, quote on 76.

17. Ibid.

18. E. Batten, "The effects of nuclear war on the weather and climate," Memorandum RM-4989-TAB, Rand Corporation, Aug. 1966.

19. R. Ayres, *Environmental Effects of Nuclear Weapons*, report no. HI-518-RR (Hudson Institute, 1 Dec. 1965), vol. 1, 3–1, 3–12, E-14. Nearly a quarter-century later, Ayres provided some further interesting comparisons in "Global effects of nuclear exchange," in S. Singer, ed., *Global Climate Change: Human and Natural Influences* (Paragon House, 1989): 100 MT of ground bursts or 10,000 MT of air bursts could inject 10^{11} metric tons of dust into the stratosphere—more than the 10^{10} metric tons lofted by Krakatoa.

20. See, e.g., Nier, *Long-Term Worldwide Effects*; US Congress, Senate, Committee on Foreign Relations, Subcommittee on Arms Control, International Organizations and Security Agreements, *Analyses of Effects of Limited Nuclear Warfare*, Committee Print, 94th Congress, 1st Session, Sept. 1975; Mark, "Global consequences of nuclear weaponry;" Office of Technology Assessment, *The Effects of Nuclear War* (1979); US Congress, *Economic and Social Consequences* (Mar. 1979); US Arms Control and Disarmament Agency, *Effects of Nuclear War* (Apr. 1979); K. Lewis, "The prompt and delayed effects of nuclear war," *Scientific American* 241 (July 1979), 35–47; H. Kendall, "Second strike," *Bulletin of the Atomic Scientists* 35 (Sept. 1979), 32–37.

21. "Project Sunshine," 17–21, 69–82; M. Nathans, R. Thews, and I. Russell, "The particle size distribution of nuclear cloud samples," *Advances in Chemistry Series* 93 (1970), 360–380.

22. Ayres, *Environmental Effects of Nuclear Weapons*, 3–4 and 3–5.

23. J. McCormick, *Reclaiming Paradise: The Global Environmental Movement* (Indiana University Press, 1989).

24. J. Twitty and J. Weinman, "Radiative properties of carbonaceous aerosols," *Journal of Applied Meteorology* 10 (Aug. 1971), 725–731.

25. J. Ogren, "Deposition of particulate elemental carbon from the atmosphere," in G. Wolff and R. Klimisch, eds., *Particulate Carbon: Atmospheric Life Cycle* (Plenum, 1982).

26. R. Turco, O. Toon, R. Whitten, J. Pollack, and P. Hamill, "The global cycle of particulate elemental carbon: A theoretical assessment," in H. Pruppacher et al., eds., *Precipitation Scavenging, Dry Deposition and Resuspension* (Elsevier, 1983). (Toon is usually called Brian by his friends and co-workers.)

27. W. Gray et al., "Weather modification by carbon dust absorption of solar energy," *Journal of Applied Meteorology* 15 (Apr. 1976), 355–386.

28. M. MacCracken and J. Chang, "A preliminary study of the potential chemical and climatic effects of atmospheric nuclear explosions," Lawrence Livermore Laboratory Report UCRL-51653, 25 Apr. 1975, quote on 3.

29. For some aspects of the history of computing, see the special issue of *Physics Today* titled "50 years of computers and physicists" 49 (Oct. 1996).

30. R. Turco, P. Hamill, O. Toon, R. Whitten, and C. Kiang, "The NASA-Ames Research Center stratospheric aerosol model. I. Physical processes and computational analogs," NASA Technical Paper 1362 (1979); Turco, Hamill, Toon, Whitten, and Kiang, "A one-dimensional model describing aerosol formation and evolution in the stratosphere: I. Physical processes and mathematical analogs," *Journal of Atmospheric Sciences* 36 (Apr. 1979), 699–717; Toon, Turco, Hamill, Kiang, and Whitten, "The NASA-Ames Research Center stratospheric aerosol model. II. Sensitivity studies and comparison with observations," NASA Technical Paper 1363 (1979); Toon, Turco, Hamill, Kiang, and Whitten, "A one-dimensional model describing aerosol formation and evolution in the stratosphere: II. Sensitivity studies and comparison with observations," *Journal of Atmospheric Sciences* 36 (Apr. 1979), 718–736.

31. R. Turco, R. Whitten, and O. Toon, "Stratospheric aerosols: Observation and theory," *Reviews of Geophysics and Space Physics* 20 (May 1982), 233–279, quote on 273.

32. C. Sagan, O. Toon, and J. Pollack, "Anthropogenic albedo changes and the Earth's climate," *Science* 206 (21 Dec. 1979), 1363–1368.

33. O. Toon and T. Ackerman, "Algorithms for the calculation of scattering by stratified spheres," *Applied Optics* 20 (15 Oct. 1981), 3657–3660; Ackerman and Toon, "Absorption of visible radiation in atmosphere containing mixtures of absorbing and nonabsorbing particles," *Applied Optics* 20 (15 Oct. 1981), 3661–3667.

34. R. Turco, O. Toon, P. Hamill, and R. Whitten, "Effects of meteoric debris on stratospheric aerosols and gases," *Journal of Geophysical Research* 86 (20 Feb. 1981), 1113–1128.

35. Ayres, *Environmental Effects of Nuclear Weapons*, E-14–E-17.

36. Batten, "The effects of nuclear war on the weather and climate," 39–40.

37. T. Powers, "Nuclear winter and nuclear strategy," *Atlantic Monthly* 254 (Nov. 1984), 53–64.

38. A. Broido, "Mass fires following nuclear attack," *Bulletin of the Atomic Scientists* 16 (Dec. 1960), 409–413.

39. Ibid., 410.

40. Ibid., 411.

41. Federal Emergency Management Agency, *FEMA Attack Environment Manual*, CPG 2-1A3 (FEMA, June 1973, reprinted May 1982), chapter 3, panel 7.

42. Ibid., chapter 3, panels 9–14.

43. *Analyses of Effects of Limited Nuclear Warfare*, 15. On Project Flambeau, see A. Revkin, "Hard facts about nuclear winter," *Science Digest* 93 (Mar. 1985), 62–68, 77, 81, 83, esp. 81.

44. R. Eagan, P. Hobbs, and L. Radke, "Measurement of cloud condensation nuclei and cloud droplet size distributions in the vicinity of forest fires," *Journal of Applied Meteorology* 13 (Aug. 1974), 553–557.

45. D. Sandberg, J. Pierovich, D. Fox, and E. Ross, "Effects of fire on air: A state-of-knowledge review," General Technical Report WO-9, US Department of Agriculture, Forest Service, 1979, 3, 16, 18, quote on 3.

46. L. Eden, *Whole World on Fire: Organizations, Knowledge, and Nuclear Weapons Devastation* (Cornell University Press, 2004), 2, 223–225.

47. D. Larson and R. Small, "Analysis of the large urban fire environment. Part II. Parametric analysis and model city simulations," PSR Report 1210 for National Preparedness Programs, FEMA, Nov. 1982 (Pacific-Sierra Research Corporation, 1982), 1–4, 64–66.

48. W. Arkin and R. Fieldhouse, *Nuclear Battlefields: Global Links in the Arms Race* (Ballinger, 1985), 94.

49. Ibid., 95. For a more recent analysis of city fires, using Washington as the example, see L. Eden, "City on fire," *Bulletin of the Atomic Scientists* 60 (Feb. 2004), 32–43.

Chapter 3

1. US Arms Control and Disarmament Agency, *Worldwide Effects of Nuclear War . . . Some Perspectives* (1976), 17. This booklet is a condensation of the conclusions of Nier, *Long-Term Worldwide Effects*. See also S. Winchester, *Krakatoa: The Day the World Exploded, Aug. 27, 1883* (HarperCollins, 2003); M. Dörries, "Global science: The Eruption of Krakatau," *Endeavour* 27 (Sept. 2003), 113–116.

2. S. Schneider and C. Mass, "Volcanic dust, sunspots, and temperature trends," *Science* 190 (21 Nov. 1975), 741–746.

3. Ibid.

4. H. Landsberg and J. Albert, "The summer of 1816 and volcanism," *Weatherwise* 27 (Apr. 1974), 63–66; H. Stommel and E. Stommel, "The year without a summer," *Scientific American* 240 (June 1979), 176–186; R. Stothers, "The great Tambora eruption in 1815 and its aftermath," *Science* 224 (15 June 1984), 1191–1198.

5. Landsberg and Albert, "The summer of 1816." For the argument that unusual movement of arctic air southward into Hudson Bay played at least a role in the lowered temperatures of 1816, see S. Schneider, "Volcanic dust veils and climate: How clear is the connection?—an editorial," *Climatic Change* 5 (1983), 111–113; A. Catchpole and M. Faurer, "Summer sea ice severity in Hudson Strait, 1751–1870," *Climate Change* 5 (1983), 115–139, esp. 135–137.

6. Stothers, "The great Tambora eruption," 1196–1197.

7. W. Rose et al., "Small particles in volcanic eruption clouds," *American Journal of Science* 280 (Oct. 1980), 671–696.

8. G. Walker, "Generation and dispersal of fine ash and dust by volcanic eruptions," *Journal of Volcanology and Geothermal Research* 11 (1981), 81–92; S. Carey and H. Sigurdsson, "Influence of particle aggregation on deposition of distal tephra from the May 18, 1980, eruption of Mount St. Helens volcano," *Journal of Geophysical Research* 87 (10 Aug. 1982), 7061–7072; S. Brazier et al., "Bimodal grain size distribution and secondary thickening in air-fall ash layers," *Nature* 301 (13 Jan. 1983), 115–119.

9. J. Pollack, O. Toon, C. Sagan, A. Summers, B. Baldwin, and W. Van Camp, "Volcanic explosions and climatic change: A theoretical assessment," *Journal of Geophysical Research* 81 (20 Feb. 1976), 1071–1083, quote on 1072.

10. B. Baldwin et al., "Stratospheric aerosols and climatic change," *Nature* 263 (14 Oct. 1976), 551–555.

11. R. Turco, O. Toon, R. Whitten, P. Hamill, and R. Keesee, "The 1980 eruptions of Mount St. Helens: Physical and chemical processes in the stratospheric clouds," *Journal of Geophysical Research* 88 (20 June 1983), 5299–5318.

12. C. Sagan, "The atmospheric and climatic consequences of nuclear war," in P. Ehrlich, C. Sagan, D. Kennedy, and W. Roberts, *The Cold and the Dark: The World After Nuclear War* (Norton, 1984).

13. M. Rampino, R. Stothers, and S. Self, "Climatic effects of volcanic eruptions," *Nature* 313 (24 Jan. 1985), 272.

14. "Final report of the ad hoc supersonic transport review committee of the Office of Science and Technology," 30 Mar. 1969, quote in cover letter.

15. Ibid., 6, 10.

16. Congressional Record, 92nd Cong., 1st session, vol. 117, 18 Mar. 1971, 7023–7024, and 24 Mar. 1971, 7828–7829. See also W. Shurcliff, *S/S/T and Sonic Boom Handbook* (Ballantine, 1970); M. Horwitch, *Clipped Wings: The American SST Conflict* (MIT Press, 1982).

17. A. Grobecker, S. Coroniti, and R. Cannon, "The effects of stratospheric pollution by aircraft," final report to Congress by Department of Transportation's Climatic Impact Assessment Program, Dec. 1974.

18. J. Gribbin, *The Hole in the Sky: Man's Threat to the Ozone Layer* (Bantam, 1988), 26–27; L. Dotto and H. Schiff, *The Ozone War* (Doubleday, 1978); S. Roan, *The Ozone Crisis: The Fifteen Year Evolution of a Sudden Global Emergency* (Wiley, 1989).

19. M. Molina and F. Rowland, "Stratospheric sink for chlorofluoromethanes: Chlorine atom-catalysed destruction of ozone," *Nature* 249 (28 June 1974), 810–812; M. Clyne, "Destruction of atmospheric ozone?" *Nature* 249 (28 June 1974), 796–797.

20. D. Meadows et al., *The Limits of Growth: A Report for the Club of Rome's Project on the Predicament of Mankind* (Universe, 1972); E. Schumacher, *Small Is Beautiful: A Study of Economics As If People Mattered* (Blond and Briggs, 1973).

21. L. Carter, "The global environment: M.I.T. study looks for danger signs," *Science* 169 (14 Aug. 1970), 660–662.

22. Gribbin, *The Hole in the Sky*, ix–xii, 39; Dotto and Schiff, *The Ozone War*; S. Mitchell, "The politics of freon," *The Nation* 220 (28 June 1975), 775–778.

23. Gribbin, *The Hole in the Sky*, 40; Dotto and Schiff, *The Ozone War*, 146; Mitchell, "The politics of freon."

24. Gribbin, *The Hole in the Sky*, ix, 56–61, 107–141, 163–181; L. Stammer, "53 nations pledge to ban ozone destroyers by 2000," *Los Angeles Times*, 30 June 1990; D. Meadows, "New ozone accord is one giant step for mankind," *Los Angeles Times*, 8 July 1990; M. Cone, "Chemicals still stratospheric problem, expert says," *Los Angeles Times*, 4 Dec. 1990. Cynics will be fortified by the claim that DuPont and its counterparts in other countries led the fight to ban CFCs because the old patents had almost expired and the companies had ready more expensive replacements; see G. Kauffman, "Earth Day and costly exaggeration," *Fresno Bee*, 20 Apr. 1990. In 1992, meeting in Copenhagen, the signatory nations hastened their goal by requiring the end of CFC production by 1996; see J. Abbatt and M. Molina, "Status of stratospheric ozone depletion," *Annual Review of Energy and the Environment* 18 (1993), 1–29; R. Benedick, *Ozone Diplomacy: New Directions in Safeguarding the Planet* (Harvard University Press, 1991).

25. L. Jones, "He sounded alarm, paid heavy price," *Los Angeles Times*, 14 July 1988.

26. B. Levi, "Nobel chemistry prize gives a stratospheric boost to atmospheric scientists," *Physics Today* 48 (Dec. 1995), 21–22; L. Monroe, "UC San Diego sea expert will share science award," *Los Angeles Times*, 5 May 1989.

27. R. Turco, O. Toon, C. Park, R. Whitten, J. Pollack, and P. Noerdlinger, "Tunguska Meteor fall of 1908: Effects on stratospheric ozone," *Science* 214 (2 Oct. 1981), 19–23.

28. J. Tatarewicz, *Space Technology and Planetary Astronomy* (Indiana University Press, 1990), xi–xvi.

29. R. Hanel et al., "Investigation of the martian environment by infrared spectroscopy on Mariner 9," *Icarus* 17 (Oct. 1972), 423–442.

30. C. Sagan, "The long winter model of martian biology: A speculation," *Icarus* 15 (Dec. 1971), 511–514.

31. C. Sagan, O. Toon, and P. Gierasch, "Climatic change on Mars," *Science* 181 (14 Sept. 1973), 1045–1049.

32. C. Sagan and J. Pollack, "Windblown dust on Mars," *Nature* 223 (23 Aug. 1969), 791–794.

33. J. Pollack et al., "Winds on Mars during the Viking season: Predictions based on a general circulation model with topography," *Geophysical Research Letters* 3 (Aug. 1976), 479–482.

34. O. Toon, J. Pollack, and C. Sagan, "Physical properties of the particles composing the martian dust storm of 1971–72," *Icarus* 30 (Apr. 1977), 663–696.

35. V. Illingworth, ed., *The Facts on File Dictionary of Astronomy* (Facts on File, 1979), 229.

36. J. Pollack et al., "Properties and effects of dust particles suspended in the martian atmosphere," *Journal of Geophysical Research* 84 (10 June 1979), 2929–2945.

37. R. Haberle, C. Leovy, and J. Pollack, "Some effects of global dust storms on the atmospheric circulation of Mars," *Icarus* 50 (May-June 1982), 322–367.

38. M. Ruderman, "Possible consequences of nearby supernova explosions for atmospheric ozone and terrestrial life," *Science* 184 (7 June 1974), 1079–1081.

39. G. Reid, I. Isaksen, T. Holzer, and P. Crutzen, "Influence of ancient solar-proton events on the evolution of life," *Nature* 259 (22 Jan. 1976), 177–179.

40. L. Alvarez, W. Alvarez, F. Asaro, and H. Michel, "Extraterrestrial cause for the Cretaceous-Tertiary extinction," *Science* 208 (6 June 1980), 1095–1108. For an interim report on the concept, see anon., "Dinosaur extinction due to asteroid?" *Physics Today* 35 (May 1982), 19–21. For a later summary of developments, see L. Alvarez, "Mass extinctions caused by large bolide impacts," *Physics Today* 40 (July 1987), 24–33.

41. Alvarez, "Extraterrestrial cause."

42. Ibid.; "Dinosaur extinction due to asteroid?" *Physics Today* 35 (May 1982), 19–21.

43. W. Glen, "What killed the dinosaurs?" *American Scientist* 78 (July-Aug. 1990), 354–370, esp. 354.

44. D. Milne and C. McKay, "Response of marine plankton communities to a global atmospheric darkening," Geological Society of America Special Paper 190 (1982), 297–303.

45. W. Alvarez et al., "Current status of the impact theory for the terminal Cretaceous extinction," Geological Society of America Special Paper 190 (1982), 305–315.

46. R. Kerr, "Isotopes add support for asteroid impact," *Science* 222 (11 Nov. 1983), 603–604; J. Luck and K. Turekian, "Osmium-187/osmium-186 in manganese nodules and the Cretaceous-Tertiary boundary," *Science* 222 (11 Nov. 1983), 613–615.

47. D. Raup and J. Sepkoski, "Periodicity of extinctions in the geologic past," *Proceedings of the National Academy of Sciences* 81 (Feb. 1984), 801–805; H. Shipman, "Astronomical causes of biological extinctions," *Physics Today* 38 (Jan. 1985), s10–s11.

48. W. Wolbach, R. Lewis, and E. Anders, "Cretaceous extinctions: Evidence for wildfires and search for meteoric material," *Science* 230 (11 Oct. 1985), 167–170; W. Wolbach et al., "Global fire at the Cretaceous-Tertiary boundary," *Nature* 334 (25 Aug. 1988), 665–669.

49. R. Kerr, "Asteroid impact gets more support," *Science* 236 (8 May 1987), 666–668; B. Bohor, P. Modreski, and E. Foord, "Shocked quartz in the Cretaceous-Tertiary boundary clays: Evidence for a global distribution," *Science* 236 (8 May 1987), 705–709; B. Bohor and R. Seitz, "Cuban K/T catastrophe," *Nature* 344 (12 Apr. 1990), 593; R. Kerr, "Dinosaurs' death blow in the Caribbean Sea?" *Science* 248 (18 May 1990), 815; A. Hildebrand and W. Boynton, "Proximal Cretaceous-Tertiary boundary impact deposits in the Caribbean," *Science* 248 (18 May 1990), 843–847; T. Maugh, "Findings bolster meteorite theory," *Los Angeles Times*, 10 May 1991. For surveys that include some more recent interpretations of the K-T event, see B. Levi, "Twelve-year trail of clues leads to impact crater from the K-T boundary," *Physics Today* 45 (Dec. 1992), 17–19; W. Alvarez, *T. Rex and the Crater of Doom* (Princeton University Press, 1997).

50. Associated Press, "Samples from Atlantic floor prove huge asteroid hit Earth, experts say," *Los Angeles Times*, 17 Feb. 1997.

51. R. Hotz, "Force of comet impact amazes astronomers," *Los Angeles Times*, 18 July 1994; "Jupiter takes huge blow from comet," *Los Angeles Times*, 19 July 1994; "Sliver of dinosaur-killing asteroid is believed found," *Los Angeles Times*, 19 Nov. 1998.

52. R. Kerr, "Beyond the K-T boundary," *Science* 236 (8 May 1987), 667; C. Officer and J. Page, *The Great Dinosaur Extinction Controversy* (Addison-Wesley, 1996).

53. A. Hallam, "End-Cretaceous mass extinction event: Argument for terrestrial causation," *Science* 238 (27 Nov. 1987), 1237–1242; R. Kerr, "Huge impact is favored K-T boundary killer," *Science* 242 (11 Nov. 1988), 865–867; Kerr, "Did a volcano help kill off the dinosaurs?" *Science* 252 (14 June 1991), 1496–1497; K. McDonald, "New data suggesting an asteroid impact inflame debate over dinosaurs' demise," *Chronicle of Higher Education* 39 (28 Oct. 1992), A7–A9.

54. Officer and Page, *The Great Dinosaur Extinction Controversy*. For an article suggesting that a meteor-induced cold period, if it did occur, must have been quite short, based on similar plant life on both sides of the K-T boundary, see "Dinosaur winter," *New York Times*, 4 Mar. 1986.

55. Anon., "New doubts raised over what killed off dinosaurs," *Los Angeles Times*, 6 Mar. 2004.

56. O. Toon, J. Pollack, T. Ackerman, R. Turco, C. McKay, and M. Liu, "Evolution of an impact-generated dust cloud and its effects on the atmosphere," Geological Society of America Special Paper 190 (1982), 187–200, quote on 187; J. Pollack, O. Toon, T. Ackerman, C. McKay, and R. Turco, "Environmental effects of an impact-generated dust cloud: Implications for the Cretaceous-Tertiary extinctions," *Science* 219 (21 Jan. 1983), 287–289.

Chapter 4

1. S. Weart, "The public and climate change," July 2007, at http://www.aip.org. Also see Weart, *Nuclear Fear: A History of Images* (Harvard University Press, 1988) and *The Discovery of Global Warming* (Harvard University Press, 2003).

2. Nier, *Long-Term Worldwide Effects*.

3. Presentation by Kosta Tsipis in *The Last Epidemic* (film of 1980 meeting of Physicians for Social Responsibility); James P. Friend, testimony, in US Congress, House, Committee on Science and Technology, Subcommittee on Investigations and Oversight, *The Consequences of Nuclear War on the Global Environment,* hearing, 97th Congress, 2nd Session, 15 Sept. 1982, 113.

4. G. Carrier et al., *The Effects on the Atmosphere of a Major Nuclear Exchange* (National Academy Press, 1985), 186; R. Turco, interview by L. Badash and B. Kirtman, 20 Feb. 1985.

5. O. Toon, interview by L. Badash and B. Kirtman, 6 Mar. 1985.

6. Arms Control and Disarmament Agency, *The Effects of Nuclear War* (1979); Office of Technology Assessment, *The Effects of Nuclear War* (1980); US Senate, Committee on Banking, Housing, and Urban Affairs, *Economic and Social Consequences of Nuclear Attacks on the United States* (Government Printing Office, 1979); United Nations, *Comprehensive Study on Nuclear Weapons* (1981); E. Chivian et al., eds., *Last Aid: The Medical Dimensions of Nuclear War* (Freeman, 1982); A. Katz, *Life After Nuclear War: The Economic and Social Impacts of Nuclear Attacks on the United States* (Ballinger, 1982); C. Sagan and R. Turco, *A Path Where No Man Thought: Nuclear Winter and the End of the Arms Race* (Random House, 1990), 459.

7. Jeannie Peterson, letter to L. Badash, 23 Jan. 1985; *Ambio* (entire issue) 11, no. 2–3 (June 1982). The *Ambio* issue was also published as J. Peterson, ed., *The Aftermath: The Human and Ecological Consequences of Nuclear War* (Pantheon, 1983).

8. Peterson, letter to Badash, 23 Jan. 1985; Peterson, *The Aftermath*, 193–194.

9. P. Crutzen, comment at conference on NW sponsored by the Defense Nuclear Agency, Santa Barbara, 12 Feb. 1985.

10. P. Crutzen and J. Birks, "The atmosphere after a nuclear war: Twilight at noon," *Ambio* 11, no. 2–3 (June 1982), 114–125. The authors originally planned to use the title "Darkness at noon" (source: Stephen Schneider, interview by L. Badash, 13 Feb. 1985). See also Crutzen, "Atmospheric pollution effects following a nuclear war," presented at 1983 conference in Erice, Sicily, and published in W. Newman and S. Stipcich, eds., *International Seminar on Nuclear War, 3rd Session: The Technical Basis for Peace* (World Scientific, 1992), 129–152.

11. P. Crutzen, "Darkness after a nuclear war," *Ambio* 13, no. 1 (1984), 52–54.

12. S. Schneider, quoted in D. Overbye, "Prophet of the cold and dark," *Discover* 6 (Jan. 1985), 24–32, quote on 28.

13. Crutzen and Birks, "The atmosphere after a nuclear war," 115.

14. Ibid., 115–117.

15. Overbye, "Prophet of the cold and dark," 26.

16. J. Birks, testimony, in hearing, 15 Sept. 1982, 124.

17. C. Covey, S. Schneider, and S. Thompson, "Global atmospheric effects of massive smoke injections from a nuclear war: Results from general circulation model simulations," *Nature* 308 (1 Mar. 1984), 21–25; C. Sagan, interview by L. Badash, 26 Dec. 1984.

18. Carrier, *The Effects on the Atmosphere*, 185. For a strong argument that the uncertainties of fire damage were no more taxing for nuclear planning than were the other forms of destruction, see L. Eden, *Whole World on Fire: Organizations, Knowledge, and Nuclear Weapons Devastation* (Cornell University Press, 2004).

19. Turco, interview by Badash and Kirtman, 20 Feb. 1985.

20. Peterson, letter to Badash, 23 Jan. 1985.

21. J. Schmidt, "Global atmospheric effects of nuclear-war fires," *Physics Today* 35 (Oct. 1982), 17–20.

22. C. Sagan, "The atmospheric and climatic consequences of nuclear war," in Ehrlich, *The Cold and the Dark*; Sagan and Turco, *Path*, 455–457; J. Pollack, O. Toon, C. Sagan, A. Summers, B. Baldwin, and W. Van Camp, "Volcanic explosions and climatic change: A theoretical assessment," *Journal of Geophysical Research* 81 (20 Feb. 1976), 1071–1083; B. Baldwin et al., "Stratospheric aerosols and climatic change," *Nature* 263 (14 Oct. 1976), 551–555.

23. Sagan, "The atmospheric and climatic consequences of nuclear war," 3–5; Sagan, interview by Badash, 26 Dec. 1984; Toon, interview by Badash and Kirtman, 6 Mar. 1985.

24. Turco, interview by Badash and Kirtman, 20 Feb. 1985.

25. O. Toon, J. Pollack, T. Ackerman, R. Turco, C. McKay, and M. Liu, "Evolution of an impact-generated dust cloud and its effects on the atmosphere," Geological Society of America Special Paper 190 (1982), 187–200; J. Pollack, O. Toon, T. Ackerman, C. McKay, and R. Turco, "Environmental effects of an impact-generated dust cloud: Implications for the Cretaceous-Tertiary extinctions," *Science* 219 (21 Jan. 1983), 287–289; Sagan and Turco, *Path*, 457–458; T. Ackerman and O. Toon, "Absorption of visible radiation in atmosphere containing mixtures of absorbing and nonabsorbing particles," *Applied Optics* 20 (15 Oct. 1981), 3661–3667; T. Ackerman, interview by L. Badash and B. Kirtman, 6 Mar. 1985.

26. Sagan, "The atmospheric and climatic consequences of nuclear war," 5.

27. Carrier, *The Effects on the Atmosphere*, 185–186; Sagan and Turco, *Path*, 458–459; Overbye, "Prophet of the cold and dark," 29; Turco, interview by Badash and Kirtman, 20 Feb. 1985; Toon, interview by Badash and Kirtman, 6 Mar. 1985.

28. Sagan, interview by Badash, 26 Dec. 1984; Sagan and Turco, *Path*, 460.

29. R. Turco, O. Toon, T. Ackerman, J. Pollack, and C. Sagan, "The climatic effects of nuclear war," *Scientific American* 251 (Aug. 1984), 33–43; Carrier, *The Effects on the Atmosphere*, v; Sagan and Turco, *Path*, 459–460.

30. Turco, interview by Badash and Kirtman, 20 Feb. 1985; O. Toon and J. Pollack, interviews by L. Badash and B. Kirtman, 6 Mar. 1985.

31. W. Poundstone, *Carl Sagan: A Life in the Cosmos* (Holt, 1999), 121–122.

32. Sagan and Turco, *Path*, 460–461.

33. R. Turco, O. Toon, J. Pollack, T. Ackerman, and C. Sagan, "Global consequences of nuclear 'war': Preliminary summary," nine-page typescript, undated (this document, apparently written in early 1983,

was obtained from the government via a Freedom of Information Act request by the Natural Resources Defense Council in 1984, and was provided by NRDC attorney S. Jacob Scherr); Pollack, interview by Badash and Kirtman, 6 Mar. 1985.

34. Turco, interview by Badash and Kirtman, 20 Feb. 1985; Ackerman, interview by Badash and Kirtman, 6 Mar. 1985.

35. R. Turco, O. Toon, J. Pollack, and C. Sagan, "Global consequences of nuclear 'warfare,'" *Eos* 63 (9 Nov. 1982), 1018.

36. R. Turco, O. Toon, T. Ackerman, J. Pollack, and C. Sagan, "Nuclear winter: Global consequences of multiple nuclear explosions," *Science* 222 (23 Dec. 1983), 1283–1292, on 1292; W. Alton Jones Foundation, *Annual Report, 1983*, 8.

37. Sagan, interview by Badash, 26 Dec. 1984; Sagan, form letter to "Dear Colleague," 31 Mar. 1983, inviting comments on the Blue Book; correspondence provided by Professor Freeman Dyson.

38. Toon, interview by Badash and Kirtman, 6 Mar. 1985.

39. P. Ehrlich, "The nuclear winter: Discovering the ecology of nuclear war," *Amicus Journal* 5 (winter 1984), 20–30; T. Malone, "Preventing nuclear war" [letter to editor], *Science* 223 (27 Jan. 1984), 340.

40. Sagan and Turco, *Path*, 21.

41. Ehrlich, "The nuclear winter."

42. George Carrier, interview by L. Badash, 11 Feb. 1993.

43. F. von Hippel, interview by L. Badash, 8 Feb. 1993.

44. Freeman Dyson, interview by L. Badash, 9 Feb. 1993 (quotes are from this interview); Sagan, letter to Dyson, 4 Mar. 1987; Dyson, letters to Sagan, 25 Apr. 1983, 10 Feb. 1987 and 9 Mar. 1987. Correspondence provided by Professor Dyson.

45. Schneider and Londer, *The Coevolution of Climate and Life*, 352–357.

46. A. Pittock et al., *Environmental Consequences of Nuclear War*, volume 1: *Physical and Atmospheric Effects* (Wiley, 1985), 157. Note that I give the difference in temperature from the last Ice Age as about 5–15°C in chapter 1 and as about 8°C in chapter 3, an indication that this is a "ballpark figure" and not a precise measurement.

47. Schneider and Londer, *Coevolution*. For eloquent musings on continuity and extinction, see S. Gould, "Continuity," *Natural History* 93 (Apr. 1984), 4, 6, 10.

48. Schneider and Londer, *Coevolution*; Ehrlich, "The nuclear winter," quote on 28.

49. Schneider and Londer, *Coevolution*, 357.

50. Ibid., 357.

51. Turco, interview by Badash and Kirtman, 20 Feb. 1985. George Carrier was among those who felt that the meeting did not endorse the soundness of the NW prediction (Carrier, interview by Badash, 11 Feb. 1993).

Chapter 5

1. H. Lewis, "How 'nuclear winter' got on page one" [interview of Jack Porter], *Newsletter of the National Association of Science Writers* 32 (Apr. 1984), 7–8, quote on 8.

2. Urey Papers, University of California, San Diego, box 29, folder 21, Eileen A. Fry, secretary-treasurer of Harold L. Oram, Inc., consultants in public relations and fund raising, letter to Harold Urey, 29 June 1946; Urey Papers, box 29, folder 23, Advertising Council, Inc., letter to Joseph Schaffner (of the Emergency Committee), 10 Oct. 1946.

3. C. Sagan, "Nuclear war: The perspective of a planetary astronomer" (Nuclear Age Peace Foundation, 1994), 4; Sagan, interview by Badash, 26 Dec. 1984; Sagan, letter to Badash, 8 Sept. 1986.

4. Source: Ehrlich, *The Cold and the Dark*, xiii–xvii.

5. A. Ehrlich, "Nuclear winter: A forecast of the climatic and biological effects of nuclear war," *Bulletin of the Atomic Scientists* 40 (Apr. 1984), 1s–16s, on 12s.

6. G. White and J. London, "Nuclear winter scenario" [letter to editor], *Science* 224 (13 Apr. 1984), 110.

7. Ehrlich, *The Cold and the Dark*, xviii; Sagan and Turco, *Path*, 465; Sagan, interview by Badash, 26 Dec. 1984.

8. Ehrlich, *The Cold and the Dark*. For a summary of the promotion of NW research and publicity during 1982 and 1983, see Russell W. Peterson's foreword to M. Harwell, *Nuclear Winter: The Human and Environmental Consequences of Nuclear War* (Springer-Verlag, 1984).

9. Sagan, letter to Badash, 8 Sept. 1986.

10. W. Anderson [editor of *Parade*], "Science and the press," in Y. Terzian and E. Bilson, eds., *Carl Sagan's Universe* (Cambridge University Press, 1977).

11. Toon and Ackerman, interviews by Badash and Kirtman, 6 Mar. 1985; Sagan and Turco, *Path*, 465.

12. P. Hilts, "Scientists say nuclear war could cause climatic disaster," *Washington Post*, 1 Nov. 1983.

13. Ehrlich, *The Cold and the Dark*, see especially p. xvii. The video is mentioned in Russell W. Peterson, letter to Ronald Reagan, 30 Mar. 1984, in Ronald Reagan Library, file PR007–224659.

14. Sagan, in Ehrlich, *The Cold and the Dark*, 7–11.

15. Ibid., 14–19.

16. Ibid., 15–27, 134–135.

17. R. Turco, "The final season: Nuclear winter," part 1, quoted from 1983 radio show *Prescription for Survival*, Pacifica Radio Archive.

18. Sagan, in Ehrlich, *The Cold and the Dark*, 27.

19. M. Curry, "Beyond nuclear winter: On the limitations of science in political debate," *Antipode* 18 (Dec. 1986), 244–267, on 263.

20. Sagan, in Ehrlich, *The Cold and the Dark*, 30–31.

21. Toon, interview by Badash and Kirtman, 6 Mar. 1985.

22. Sagan, in Ehrlich, *The Cold and the Dark*, 31–32.

23. P. Ehrlich, in Ehrlich, *The Cold and the Dark*, quote on 44.

24. Ibid., quote on 45.

25. Ibid., 46–51.

26. Ibid., 51–52.

27. Ibid., 52–53.

28. Ibid., 54.

29. Ibid., quote on 55.

30. Ibid., quote on 59.

31. A. Ehrlich, "Nuclear winter," quote on 3s.

32. Schneider, interview by Badash, 13 Feb. 1985.

33. Panel discussion, in Ehrlich, *The Cold and the Dark*, 78–81.

34. Ibid., 81–83.

35. Ibid., 87–89.

36. Ibid., 89–94.

37. Ibid., 95–100. See also V. Aleksandrov, "Climate response to global injections," presented at 1983 conference in Erice and published in *International Seminar on Nuclear War, 3rd Session* (World Scientific, 1992). In the first reference Aleksandrov said he used the TTAPS baseline scenario (5,000 MT); in the second he referred to the *Ambio* baseline case (5,742 MT).

38. Panel discussion, in Ehrlich, *The Cold and the Dark*, quote on 112.

39. Ibid., quote on 118.

40. Ibid., quotes on 129; Sagan, letter to Badash, 8 Sept. 1986, re Nader.

41. R. Turco, O. Toon, T. Ackerman, J. Pollack, and C. Sagan, "Nuclear winter: Global consequences of multiple nuclear explosions," *Science* 222 (23 Dec. 1983), 1283–1292.

42. Ibid., 1285.

43. This report is cited in note 15 of Turco, "Nuclear winter."

44. P. Ehrlich et al., "Long-term biological consequences of nuclear war," *Science* 222 (23 Dec. 1983), 1293–1300.

45. See, e.g., G. Herken, *Councils of War* (Oxford University Press, 1987).

Chapter 6

1. D. Knight, *The Age of Science: The Scientific World-View in the Nineteenth Century* (Blackwell, 1986), 69.

2. Ibid., 68.

3. Marcel LaFollette, personal communication, 29 July 2002.

4. J. Gregory and S. Miller, *Science in Public: Communication, Culture, and Credibility* (Plenum, 1998), 29.

5. For surveys of science policy, see B. Smith, *American Science Policy Since World War II* (Brookings Institution, 1990); Smith, *The Advisers: Scientists in the Policy Process* (Brookings Institution, 1992); J. Stine, *A History of Science Policy in the United States, 1940–1985*, Science Policy Study Background Report no. 1, Task Force on Science Policy, US Congress, House of Representatives, Committee on Science and Technology, 99th Congress, 2nd session, 1986.

6. J. Schmidt, "Global atmospheric effects of nuclear-war fires," *Physics Today* 35 (Oct. 1982), 17–20, quote on 18.

7. Carrier, interview by Badash, 11 Feb. 1993.

8. C. Sagan, "The atmospheric and climatic consequences of nuclear war," in Ehrlich, *The Cold and the Dark*.

9. C. Sagan et al., "Nuclear winter: The world-wide consequences of nuclear war," *UNESCO Courier* 38 (May 1985), 26–31, quotes on 28. This is an abridged transcript of the 8 Dec. 1983 forum in the Senate Caucus Room.

10. Toon, interview by Badash and Kirtman, 6 Mar. 1985.

11. J. Raloff, "Beyond Armageddon," *Science News* 124 (12 Nov. 1983), 314–317, quote on 316; Schneider, interview by Badash, 13 Feb. 1985.

12. Turco, "Nuclear winter," quote on 1290.

13. E. Mesthene, "Can only scientists make government science policy?" *Science* 145 (17 July 1964), 237–240, on 239.

14. P. Hilts, "Scientists say nuclear war could cause climatic disaster," *Washington Post*, 1 Nov. 1983.

15. W. Carey, "A run worth making," *Science* 222 (23 Dec. 1983), 1281.

16. Schneider, interview by Badash, 15 June 1986.

17. For some problems concerning the author-editor relationship, see B. Culliton, "Journals and data disclosure," *Science* 242 (11 Nov. 1988), 857. For a plea to return to the old practices, see V. Fitch, "An APS president reflects on his two-year term," *Physics Today* 42 (Dec. 1989), 49–53, on 53. For a discussion of editorial policies, see Dorothy Nelkin, *Selling Science: How the Press Covers Science and Technology* (Freeman, 1987), 161–162. On the peer-review process, see J. Burnham, "The evolution of editorial peer review," *Journal of the American Medical Association* 263 (9 Mar. 1990), 1323–1329; E. Knoll, "The communities of scientists and journal peer review," *Journal of the American Medical Association* 263 (9 Mar. 1990), 1330–1332. On the interaction of science with non-scientific society, see Gregory and Miller, *Science in Public*.

18. V. Kiernan, "Ingelfinger, embargoes, and other controls on the dissemination of science news," *Science Communication* 18 (June 1997), 297–319; Kiernan, "Changing embargoes and the *New York Times'* coverage of the *Journal of the American Medical Association*," *Science Communication* 19 (Mar. 1998), 212–221.

19. J. Scott, "Medical journals: Eye on the scoop," *Los Angeles Times*, 26 Feb. 1990.

20. J. Smith, *Patenting the Sun: Polio, the Salk Vaccine, and the Children of the Baby Boom* (Morrow, 1990).

21. Anon., "The burden of proof," *Los Angeles Times*, 4 Dec. 1986.

22. F. Close, *Too Hot to Handle: The Race for Cold Fusion* (Princeton University Press, 1991); G. Taubes, *Bad Science: The Short Life and Weird Times of Cold Fusion* (Random House, 1993); K. McDonald, "U. of Utah president plans to retire; decision follows criticism of handling of cold-fusion controversy," *Chronicle of Higher Education* 36 (20 June 1990), A15.

23. See, e.g., K. Emanuel, "Towards a scientific exercise," *Nature* 319 (23 Jan. 1986), 259.

24. G. Rathjens, interview by L. Badash, 11 Feb. 1993.

25. C. Sagan, *Contact* (Pocket Books, 1986), 75.

26. Nelkin, *Selling Science*, quote on 133.

27. Sagan and Turco, *Path*, 465.

28. In January 1978 the editors of several biomedical journals created the International Committee of Medical Journal Editors, whose purpose was to establish uniform requirements for manuscripts submitted to them. The committee's instructions can be found, for example, in *The Lancet* 348 (6 July 1996), opp. 68.

29. Anon., "Public policy studies by the American Physical Society," *Physics Today* 52 (Mar. 1999), 32; H. Lustig, "To advance and diffuse the knowledge of physics: An account of the 100-year history of the American Physical Society," *American Journal of Physics* 68 (July 2000), 595–636, esp. 606–611; R. Wilson, "The sentiment of the unity of physics," *Physics Today* 39 (July 1986), 26–30, on 28.

30. Gregory and Miller, *Science in Public*, 31–32.

31. R. Goodell, *The Visible Scientists* (Little, Brown, 1977).

32. Gustave Roethe, letter to Max Planck, 10 Sept. 1920, quoted in J. Heilbron, *The Dilemmas of an Upright Man: Max Planck as Spokesman for German Science* (University of California Press, 1986), 116.

33. *FAS Public Interest Report* 39 (Jan.-Feb. 1986), 36.

34. W. Buckley Jr., "The specter of nuclear war," *Washington Post*, 22 Apr. 1985; B. Beyette, "Carl Sagan is a busy man in the universe," *Los Angeles Times*, 3 Apr. 1985. For another commentary on Sagan, see T. Ferris, "The risks and rewards of popularizing science," *Chronicle of Higher Education* 43 (4 Apr. 1997), B6.

35. See, e.g., Cornel Sarosdy, letter to editor, *Scientific American* 252 (Jan. 1985), 9.

36. F. Flam, "What should it take to join science's most exclusive club?" *Science* 256 (15 May 1992), 860–861; Freeman Dyson, interview by L. Badash, 9 Feb. 1993. The quotes are from J. Queenan, "Apocalypse again," *Wall Street Journal*, 3 Jan. 1991.

37. NAS press release dated 29 Nov. 1993. The medal was presented on 25 Apr. 1994.

38. S. Gould, "Bright star among billions" [guest editorial], *Science* 275 (31 Jan. 1997), 599. For an interesting quantitative discussion of Gould's admirers and detractors, with mention of the "Sagan effect" (one's stock as a scientist decreases as one's fame as a popularizer grows), see M. Shermer, "Stephen Jay Gould as historian of science and scientific historian, popular scientist and scientific popularizer," *Social Studies of Science* 32 (Aug. 2002), 489–524. For full-length biographies, see K. Davidson, *Carl Sagan: A Life* (Wiley, 1999); Poundstone, *Carl Sagan: A Life in the Cosmos*. For a review of these two biographies, see R. Hotz, "Star trek," *Los Angeles Times Book Review*, 16 Jan. 2000.

39. Anon., "Atmospheric calculations suggest a nuclear winter," *Physics Today* 37 (Feb. 1984), 17–20; anon., "Sicily establishes large award for scientific culture," *Physics Today* 43 (Feb. 1990), 116; M. McGrory, "Ain't gonna study war no more," *Washington Post*, 18 Sept. 1983.

40. V. Aleksandrov and G. Stenchikov, "On the modeling of the climatic consequences of nuclear war," USSR Academy of Sciences Computing Center, Moscow, 1983; Aleksandrov, letter to editor, *Science* 225 (7 Sept. 1984), 978.

41. P. Harries-Jones, "The nuclear winter hypothesis: A broadened definition," paper appended to *Nuclear Winter and Associated Effects: A Canadian Appraisal of the Environmental Impact of Nuclear War* (Royal Society of Canada, 1985), on 375.

42. M. MacCracken, "Nuclear war: Preliminary estimates of the climatic effects of a nuclear exchange," Lawrence Livermore National Laboratory preprint UCRL-89770 (Oct. 1983), quotes on 1–2; MacCracken, interview by L. Badash, 13 Feb. 1985.

43. See, e.g., Schmidt, "Global atmospheric effects."

44. A. Nord, "The world after nuclear war," *Sierra* 68 (Sept.-Oct. 1983), 36–38, quote on 37; S. Iker, "No place to hide," *International Wildlife* 13 (Sept.-Oct. 1983), 44–47.

45. P. Shabecoff, "Grimmer view is given of nuclear war effects," *New York Times*, 31 Oct. 1983. Insofar as the story was filed on 30 Oct., the day Sagan's *Parade* article appeared nationwide, it could not be considered much of a scoop.

46. Hilts, "Scientists say"; Hilts, "'Nuclear winter' catastrophe confirmed by Soviet scientists," *Washington Post*, 2 Nov. 1983.

47. Nier, *Long-Term Worldwide Effects*, 6.

48. "The winter after the bomb" [editorial], *New York Times*, 6 Nov. 1983.

49. Ibid.

50. See, e.g., anon., "US and Soviet scientists join in nuclear warning," *Times* (London), 3 Nov. 1983; S. Begley, "Nuclear war: The long view," *Time* 102 (7 Nov. 1983), 137.

51. Sagan, letter to Badash, 8 Sept. 1986. *Parade*'s editor noted that it is the largest-circulation publication in the world. The 1983 circulation of 20 million translated to more than 40 million readers. See W. Anderson, "Science and the press," in Terzian and E. Bilson, eds., *Carl Sagan's Universe*. See also J. Lomberg, "The visual presentation of science," in ibid.

52. M. McGrory, "Biologists paint an icy picture of how the world could end," *Washington Post*, 1 Nov. 1983.

53. R. Strout, "Scientists weigh aftermath of nuclear war," *Christian Science Monitor*, 4 Nov. 1983.

54. B. Wallace and T. Dobzhansky, *Radiation, Genes, and Man* (Holt, 1959), 166–167, 174–177. The risk of human extinction is not negligible, although not high, according to J. Leslie (*The End of the World: The Science and Ethics of Human Extinction*, Routledge, 1996). Leslie discussed numerous potential causes, such as depletion of the ozone layer, pollution, biological warfare, nuclear warfare (including NW), the greenhouse effect, disease, asteroid impact, and a nearby supernova.

55. J. Lyons, "Memorandum for the Chief of Naval Operations: 'The World After Nuclear War,'" 7 Nov. 1983, 65B Memo 393/A112102–07 and two enclosures. This document was obtained via a Freedom of Information Act request by the Natural Resources Defense Council (hereafter NRDC file) in 1984, and was provided by NRDC attorney S. Jacob Scherr.

56. Ehrlich, *The Cold and the Dark*, xviii–xx.

57. Transcript of the "Moscow Link," in Ehrlich, *The Cold and the Dark*.

58. Ibid., 133–153.

59. L. Tangley, "After nuclear war—a nuclear winter," *BioScience* 34 (Jan. 1984), 6–9.

60. J. Birks, "Darkness at noon: The environmental effects of nuclear war," *Sierra* 68 (May-June 1983), 58–61, quote on 61.

61. See, e.g., J. Gleick, "A cold shoulder to science" (review of G. Taubes, *Bad Science*), *Los Angeles Times Book Review*, 22 Aug. 1993; P. Ehrlich and A. Ehrlich, *Betrayal of Science and Reason: How Anti-Environmental Rhetoric Threatens Our Future* (Island, 1996), 40; C. Pope, "Science at war with itself," *Sierra* 83 (Mar.-Apr. 1998), 18–19. Also see remarks on the *WSJ*'s criticism of the American Physical Society's directed-energy weapons study by V. Fitch, "An APS president reflects," 50. Regarding a *WSJ* attack on opponents of the Strategic Defense Initiative, see F. von Hippel, "Attacks on Star Wars critics a

diversion," in L. Ackland and S. McGuire, eds., *Assessing the Nuclear Age* (Educational Foundation for Nuclear Science, 1986). Regarding *WSJ* criticism that "yellow rain" was not bee excrement but a communist biological agent, see "Bees in South-East Asia," *Nature* 317 (19 Sept. 1985), 190. For labeling of the *WSJ* as "the leading bulletin board for conservatives," see R. Brownstein, "Still a few dots to connect in Iraq domino theory," *Los Angeles Times*, 23 Sept. 2002. On denial of global warming, see D. Kennedy, "Climate: Game over" [editorial], *Science* 317 (27 July 2007), 425.

62. R. Strout, "Tale of two eras: Harding, nuclear winter," *Christian Science Monitor*, 8 Feb. 1985.

63. Anon., "The talk of the town," *The New Yorker* 59 (21 Nov. 1983), 41–42 (reprinted as "The last headline," *Audubon* 86, Jan. 1984, 32–33).

64. D. Sullivan, "After the shock of 'The Day After,'" *Los Angeles Times*, 22 Nov. 1983. See also W. Broad, "Scientists say TV film understates possible devastation of nuclear attack," *New York Times*, 21 Nov. 1983; anon., "The real day after would be worse," *People* 20 (21 Nov. 1983), 50.

65. Philip M. Crane, letter to Ronald Reagan, 26 Oct. 1983, Ronald Reagan Library, file PR016–01176096.

66. G. Lometti, "Broadcast preparations for and consequences of 'The Day After,'" in J. Wober, ed., *Television and Nuclear Power: Making the Public Mind* (Ablex, 1992), 3–17, esp. 5–6, 11. The media frenzy over the film led to predictions that it would serve as a strong deterrent to nuclear war. This was reminiscent of similar predictions made about Stanley Kramer's 1959 movie *On the Beach*. In both cases, these forecasts were wrong; indeed, public opinion barely changed in 1983, despite survey results showing that 80% agreed with Sagan that the consequences of nuclear war would be worse than depicted. This relative lack of impact was explained as follows: *The Day After* showed many survivors, which viewers thought unrealistic; it deliberately bore no political baggage, and thus failed to stir up Cold War ideologies into a frenzy; and it wasn't very gripping theatrically. See R. Kubey, "US opinion and politics before and after 'The Day After': Television movie as Rorschach," in Wober, *Television and Nuclear Power*.

67. Nelkin, *Selling Science*, quote on 59.

Chapter 7

1. F. Dyson, *Infinite in All Directions* (Harper and Row, 1988), 264.

2. J. Goldman, "Methodists reject nuclear deterrence," *Los Angeles Times*, 30 Apr. 1986. See also E. Pace, "Methodist bishops back pastoral letter denouncing rise of nuclear arms," *New York Times*, 30 Apr. 1986; M. Hyer, "Methodist bishops blast SDI, A-arms," *Washington Post*, 30 Apr. 1986. The American Catholic bishops' pastoral letter "The challenge of peace: God's promise and our response," issued 3 May 1983, is reprinted in J. Castelli, *The Bishops and the Bomb: Waging Peace in a Nuclear Age* (Doubleday, 1983). The Catholic bishops called deterrence a "transitional strategy" that was morally acceptable only as a step toward progressive disarmament. They were also skeptical of limited nuclear war and insisted that population centers not be targeted.

3. E. Goodman, "Can world survive another Reagan term?" *Los Angeles Times*, 4 Nov. 1983.

4. T. Wicker, "A grim agreement," *New York Times*, 12 Dec. 1983.

5. US Congress, House, Committee on Science and Technology, Subcommittee on Investigations and Oversight, *The Consequences of Nuclear War on the Global Environment*, hearing, 97th Congress, 2nd Session, 15 Sept. 1982, iii, 164, 176–177.

6. Friend, testimony, ibid., 150.

7. Friend, ibid., 115–121.

8. F. von Hippel, testimony, ibid., 162.

9. Edward Teller apparently was not above misrepresenting technical data to achieve his own political goals. Whistleblowers at the Livermore Laboratory charged him with presenting glowing progress reports to the White House on the x-ray laser, a major component of the Strategic Defense Initiative, while simultaneously receiving internal reports detailing enormous problems with no obvious solutions to them. See D. Morain and R. Meyer, "Teller gave flawed data on x-ray laser, scientist says," *Los Angeles Times*, 21 Oct. 1987; D. Blum, McClatchy News Service, "Probe reveals letter: Document says scientist misrepresented progress on 'Star Wars,'" *Daily Nexus* [University of California, Santa Barbara], 2 Mar. 1988. See also W. Broad, *Teller's War: The Top-Secret Story Behind the Star Wars Deception* (Simon and Schuster, 1992). For another example of Teller's willingness to employ worst-case considerations (this in connection with incoming missiles and decoys overwhelming SDI computers), see E. Teller, "Peaceful applications and the world laboratory," in W. Newman and S. Stipcich, eds., *International Seminar on Nuclear War, 5th Session* (World Scientific, 1992).

10. E. Teller, "Dangerous myths about nuclear arms," *Reader's Digest* 121 (Nov. 1982), 139–144.

11. Ibid., 143. The phrase "best face on nuclear war" was used by Richard Turco in the 20 Feb. 1985 interview by Badash and Kirtman.

12. R. Turco et al., "Global consequences of nuclear 'warfare,'" *Eos* 63 (9 Nov. 1982), 1018.

13. Sagan, interview by Badash, 26 Dec. 1984; Turco, interview by Badash and Kirtman, 20 Feb. 1985; Toon, Ackerman, and Pollack, interviews by Badash and Kirtman, 6 Mar. 1985.

14. Toon, interview by Badash and Kirtman, 6 Mar. 1985.

15. Sagan, interview by Badash, 26 Dec. 1984; Sagan and Turco, *Path*, 461–462. On the events in Washington, see R. Halloran, "President is grim," *New York Times*, 8 Dec. 1982; D. Shribman, "Man slain in capital monument threat," *New York Times*, 9 Dec. 1982.

16. R. Turco, O. Toon, and T. Ackerman, letter to editor, *National Review* 38 (31 Jan. 1986), 4, 10.

17. Sagan and Turco, *Path*, 461–462.

18. Anon., "NASA withdraws presentation," *Aviation Week and Space Technology* 117 (20 Dec. 1982), 67; Turco, interview by Badash and Kirtman, 20 Feb. 1985; Toon, interview by Badash and Kirtman, 6 Mar. 1985.

19. R. Turco, interview on radio program "Fire and ice: Nuclear winter, part 2," no. 17 in the series *Prescription for Survival*, Pacifica Radio Archive, 1983.

20. Sagan, interview by Badash, 26 Dec. 1984.

21. Schneider, interview by Badash, 13 Feb. 1985.

22. Alan Robock, written testimony, in US Congress, House of Representatives, Committee on Science and Technology, Subcommittee on Natural Resources, Agriculture Research, and Environment, and Committee on Interior and Insular Affairs, Subcommittee on Energy and the Environment, *Nuclear Winter*, joint hearing, 99th Congress, 1st Session, 14 Mar. 1985, 274–277, on 277. See also A. Revkin, "Missing: The curious case of Vladimir Alexandrov," *Science Digest* 94 (July 1986), 32–43.

23. Sagan, interview by Badash, 26 Dec. 1984; Toon, interview by Badash and Kirtman, 6 Mar. 1985.

24. Sagan and Turco, *Path*, 463; R. D. Speed to A. Field, "Review of Global Consequences of Nuclear 'War,'" R&D Associates interoffice correspondence, 13 Apr. 1983, NRDC file; Turco, interview by Badash and Kirtman, 20 Feb. 1985.

25. Sagan, interview by Badash, 26 Dec. 1984; Sagan and Turco, *Path*, 465; Turco, interview by Badash and Kirtman, 20 Feb. 1985; Pollack, interview by Badash and Kirtman, 6 Mar. 1985.

26. J. Beggs, letter to Craig Fuller, 23 Aug. 1983, attached to G. W. Woodwell, letter to Hans Mark, 11 July 1983, Ronald Reagan Library, WHORM Subject File ND018 167459.

27. Al Hill, Council on Environmental Quality, memo to William Clark, NSC, and others, 13 July 1983, Ronald Reagan Library, WHORM Subject File, MC 156598.

28. George Ullrich [DNA project officer], "Memorandum for the record: National Academy of Sciences study on global nuclear war," 14 Oct. 1983, NRDC file.

29. Poundstone, *Carl Sagan: A Life in the Cosmos*.

30. Jeanne Vaughn Mattison and Adm. Noel Gayler (USN-Ret.), letter to William Clark, 27 Sept. 1983; Ray Pollock, memo to W. Clark, 5 Oct. 1983; W. Clark, letter to J. Mattison, undated (Oct. 1983), Ronald Reagan Library, WHORM Subject File FG006–01 182481.

31. Sagan, interview by Badash, 26 Dec. 1984. Slightly different wording is found in Sagan's testimony in US Congress, House of Representatives, Committee on Science and Technology, Subcommittee on Natural Resources, Agriculture Research, and Environment, and Committee on Interior and Insular Affairs, Subcommittee on Energy and the Environment, *Nuclear Winter*, joint hearing, 99th Congress, 1st Session, 14 Mar. 1985, 19.

32. C. Sagan, "The atmospheric and climatic consequences of nuclear war," in Ehrlich, *The Cold and the Dark*.

33. S. Bergström et al., *Effects of Nuclear War on Health and Health Services: Report of the International Committee of Experts in Medical Sciences and Public Health to Implement Resolution WHA34.38* (World Health Organization, 1984). This report was criticized for its heavy emphasis on city attacks around the globe: far less megatonnage fell on the US and the USSR than on Asia. This scenario was not an impossible war, but an incredible one, according to the Livermore Lab physicist George Bing (interview by L. Badash, 13 Feb. 1985).

34. On the Strategic Defense Initiative, see W. Broad, *Star Warriors* (Simon and Schuster, 1985); G. Herken, *Counsels of War*, expanded edition (Oxford University Press, 1987), 331–357.

35. Transcript of *Nightline*, 1 Nov. 1983, provided by ABC.

36. P. Hilts, "'Nuclear winter' catastrophe confirmed by Soviet scientists," *Washington Post*, 2 Nov. 1983.

37. C. Holden, "Scientists describe 'nuclear winter,'" *Science* 222 (18 Nov. 1983), 822–823, quotes on 822.

38. J. Evans, "The big chill: Learning about 'nuclear winter,'" *Commonweal* 111 (20 Apr. 1984), 231–232.

39. R. Lieber and D. Horowitz, "Live, die: Moot point," *New York Times*, 20 Nov. 1983.

40. R. Turco, "Fire and ice" [radio interview].

41. Anon., "A cold, dark apocalypse," *Time* 122 (14 Nov. 1983), 43.

42. R. Reinhold, "Scientists urge more effort to cut atom risk," *New York Times*, 28 Apr. 1982.

43. L. Tangley, "After nuclear war—a nuclear winter," *BioScience* 34 (Jan. 1984), 6–9, quote on 9.

44. S. Begley, "Nuclear war: The long view," *Newsweek* 102 (7 Nov. 1983), 137.

45. Schneider and Londer, *Coevolution*, 361.

46. P. Ehrlich, "The nuclear winter: Discovering the ecology of nuclear war," *Amicus Journal* 5 (winter 1984), 20–30, quote on 20.

47. H. Rodhe, "A nuclear winter," *Ambio* 13: 1 (1984), 43–44, quote on 44. On the increasing political activity of scientists, see R. Lapp, *The New Priesthood: The Scientific Elite and the Uses of Power* (Harper and Row, 1965), esp. chapter 9.

48. D. Shribman, "Senate rejects move to make nuclear freeze an immediate goal," *New York Times*, 1 Nov. 1983.

49. P. Shabecoff, "US-Soviet panel sees no hope in an atomic war," *New York Times*, 9 Dec. 1983; L. Silverman, "US and Soviet experts say nuclear war would destroy human race," *Los Angeles Times*, 9 Dec. 1983; C. Sagan et al., "Nuclear winter: The world-wide consequences of nuclear war," *UNESCO Courier* 38 (May 1985), 26–31. The preceding is an abridged transcript of the 8 Dec. 1983 forum in the Senate Caucus Room. For a longer but still abridged transcript, see "Washington Forum on the World-Wide Consequences of Nuclear War," *Disarmament* 7 (autumn 1984), 32–62.

50. Anon., "Atom attack impact assayed," *New York Times*, 7 Dec. 1983.

51. J. Fox, "Will there be life on the farm after the bomb?" *Science* 222 (23 Dec. 1983), 1308.

52. Y. Velikhov, ed., *The Night After . . . Scientists' Warning: Climatic and Biological Consequences of a Nuclear War* (Mir, 1985), quote on 8.

53. An example of the criticism is J. Leaning and L. Keyes, eds., *The Counterfeit Ark: Crisis Relocation for Nuclear War* (Ballinger, 1984). This book was sponsored by Physicians for Social Responsibility.

54. Sagan, "Nuclear winter: The world-wide consequences of nuclear war," 29–31.

55. T. Wicker, "A grim agreement," *New York Times*, 12 Dec. 1983.

56. Sagan, "Nuclear winter: The world-wide consequences of nuclear war," 28–29.

57. "Washington Forum on the World-Wide Consequences of Nuclear War," 41.

58. A. Horne, "Nuclear climate more lethal than predicted, Soviets say," *Washington Post*, 9 Dec. 1983.

59. Anon., "US–Soviet forum on nuclear winter," *F.A.S. Public Interest Report* 37 (Jan. 1984), 1.

60. Shabecoff, "US-Soviet panel sees no hope in an atomic war"; Silverman, "US and Soviet experts say nuclear war would destroy human race."

61. "US–Soviet forum on nuclear winter."

62. Ibid.

63. Sagan, interview by Badash, 26 Dec. 1984.

64. John Harte, interview by L. Badash, 3 Oct. 1984; Turco, interview by Badash and Kirtman, 20 Feb. 1985; Toon, Ackerman, and Pollack, interviews by Badash and Kirtman, 6 Mar. 1985.

65. L. Gouré, "Soviet scientists as shills for a freeze," *Washington Times*, 19 Dec. 1983.

Chapter 8

1. C. Holden, "Scientists describe 'nuclear winter,'" *Science* 222 (18 Nov. 1983), 822–823, quotes on 823.

2. Turco, interview by Badash and Kirtman, 20 Feb. 1985.

3. G. Ullrich, memo (apparently to himself), 11 May 1982, NRDC file.

4. G. Ullrich, memo, 12 May 1982, NRDC file.

5. R. DeLauer, letter to C. Sagan, quoted in R. Smith, "Nuclear winter attracts additional scrutiny," *Science* 225 (6 July 1984), 30–32, quote on 30.

6. See R. Scheer, *With Enough Shovels: Reagan, Bush and Nuclear War* (Random House, 1982).

7. Lee M. Hunt, executive director, Naval Studies Board, NRC, letter to T. K. Jones, 11 June 1982, NRDC file.

8. T. K. Jones, memo to Gordon Soper, 21 June 1982, NRDC file.

9. Edward E. Conrad, memo to T. K. Jones, 5 Aug. 1982, NRDC file.

10. J. McGahan, SAI, memos to D. Auton, DNA, 22 and 28 July 1982, NRDC file.

11. NAS Proposal for the Support of the Workshop on Atmospheric Effects of Nuclear Weapons Detonations, 15 Nov. 1982, NRDC file.

12. J. Lyons, "Memorandum for the Chief of Naval Operations: 'The World After Nuclear War,'" 7 Nov. 1983, 65B Memo 393/A112102–07 and two enclosures, NRDC file.

13. Ibid.

14. Ibid.

15. Powers, "Nuclear winter and nuclear strategy," quote on 59.

16. "The winter after the bomb" [editorial], *New York Times*, 6 Nov. 1983.

17. L. Szilard, "'Minimal deterrent' vs. saturation parity," *Bulletin of the Atomic Scientists* 20 (Mar. 1964), 6–12.

18. J. Mann, "Threshold," *Washington Post*, 11 Nov. 1983.

19. C. Sagan, "Nuclear war and climatic catastrophe: Some policy implications," *Foreign Affairs* 62 (winter 1983–84), 257–292, quote on 257–258.

20. Ibid., 257.

21. Ibid., 258.

22. Ibid., 275.

23. Ibid., 275–277.

24. Ibid., 275, 277–278.

25. Powers, "Nuclear winter and nuclear strategy," 58.

26. Sagan, "Nuclear war and climatic catastrophe," 279–280.

27. Ibid., 280–281.

28. Ibid., 281–282.

29. Ibid., 282–283.

30. Ibid., 283–285. With the major caveat that the Cold War had ended, three influential analysts argued in 1991 that virtually all of the world's more than 25,000 tactical nuclear warheads could be dismantled as unneeded, leaving more than another 25,000 strategic warheads (97% in the hands of the US and the USSR) in the arsenals. Security could adequately be maintained, they said, if each side kept only 1,000 of these. This would be fewer than the 3,000–3,500 set by the still-unratified START II Treaty. See C. Kaysen, R. McNamara, and G. Rathjens, "Nuclear weapons after the Cold War," *Foreign Affairs* 70 (fall 1991), 95–110. In 1995, Herbert York, the Livermore Lab's founding director and subsequently a top Department of Defense official, suggested that about 100 nuclear weapons would suffice

(a number comparable to the proposals of previous decades, despite the proliferation of enemy targets). See H. York, *Arms and the Physicist* (American Institute of Physics Press, 1995), 273–277.

31. Sagan, "Nuclear war and climatic catastrophe," 285–286.

Chapter 9

1. Powers, "Nuclear winter and nuclear strategy," quotes on 55.

2. W. Alton Jones Foundation, *Annual Report, 1984.*

3. Source: *Nuclear Winter* [newsletter of Center on the Consequences of Nuclear War], summer 1984, 4.

4. Ibid.; S. Jacob Scherr, interview by L. Badash, 21 Apr. 1987; Peterson, letter to Badash, 23 Jan. 1985.

5. Scherr, interview by Badash, 21 Apr. 1987.

6. Ibid.

7. Ibid.

8. US Congress, Senate, Committee on Armed Services, *Nuclear Winter and its Implications*, hearings, 99th Congress, 1st Session, 2–3 Oct. 1985, quote on 2.

9. C. Sagan, "We can prevent nuclear winter," *Parade*, 30 Sept. 1984, 13–15, quote on 15.

10. "The people speak," *Parade*, 30 Sept. 1984, 15–17.

11. L. Thomas, "Nuclear winter, again," *Discover* 5 (Oct. 1984), 57–58. The artist was Victor Juhasz.

12. L. Thomas, "A new agenda for science," *SIPIscope* 12 (spring 1984), 9–11.

13. H. Kissinger, "Faulting US posture for negotiations with Soviets," *Los Angeles Times*, 8 Mar. 1987.

14. R. Perle, testimony, in US House of Representatives, Committee on Science and Technology, Subcommittee on Natural Resources, Agriculture Research, and Environment, jointly with Committee on Interior and Insular Affairs, Subcommittee on Energy and the Environment, *Nuclear Winter*, hearing, 99th Congress, 1st Session, 14 Mar. 1985, 54.

15. This certainly was Sagan's impression (Sagan, interview by Badash, 26 Dec. 1984).

16. E. Luttwak, letter to editor, and C. Sagan, reply, *Foreign Affairs* 62 (spring 1984), 995–1002, quote on 997.

17. R. Seitz, letter to editor, and C. Sagan, reply, *Foreign Affairs* 62 (spring 1984), 995–1002, quote on 1000.

18. D. Horowitz and R. Lieber, letter to editor, and C. Sagan, reply, *Foreign Affairs* 62 (spring 1984), 995–1002, quote on 995.

19. Richard C. Raymond, letter to Ronald Reagan, 5 Mar. 1984, Ronald Reagan Library, WH Staff File, Keyworth, box 23, folder NW#1.

20. D. Curtis and John Rangus, letter to G. Keyworth, 20 Aug. 1984, Ronald Reagan Library, WH Staff File, Keyworth, box 23, folder NW#3.

Chapter 10

1. David Sowle, Mission Research Corporation, statement to Peter Lunn, undated but probably mid July 1983, NRDC file.

2. Dale Sappenfield, Los Alamos National Laboratory, statement to Peter Lunn, undated but probably mid July 1983, NRDC file.

3. Ernest Bauer, Institute for Defense Analyses, letter to Peter Lunn, 18 July 1983, NRDC file.

4. Theodore A. Postol, office of the chief of naval operations, letter to Peter Lunn, 14 July 1983, and R. Turco, R&D Associates, note to Peter Lunn, undated but probably mid July 1983, both in NRDC file.

5. R. Smith, "Nuclear winter attracts additional scrutiny," *Science* 225 (6 July 1984), 30–32, quote on 30.

6. R. Wagner, testimony, in US Congress, Joint Economics Committee, Subcommittee on International Trade, Finance, and Security Economics, *The Consequences of Nuclear War*, hearings, 98th Congress, 2nd Session, 11–12 July 1984, 123.

7. R. Peterson, letter to Ronald Reagan, 30 Mar. 1984, and Robert M. Kimmitt, NSC staff, memo to Frederick J. Ryan, director of presidential appointments and scheduling, 14 Apr. 1984, Ronald Reagan Library, both in WHORM Subject File, PR007 224659; K. L. Adelman, letter to R. Peterson, 14 May 1984, WHORM Subject File, ND018 205297; *Nuclear Winter* [newsletter of Center on the Consequences of Nuclear War], summer 1984, 3; R. Peterson, *Rebel with a Conscience* (University of Delaware Press, 1999), 396–397.

8. P. Hilts, "US begins study of possible climatic disaster in nuclear war," *Washington Post*, 29 May 1984. See also W. Broad, "US weighs risk that atom war could bring fatal nuclear winter," *New York Times*, 5 Aug. 1984.

9. Toon, interview by Badash and Kirtman, 6 Mar. 1985.

10. Unknown author (possibly Russell Seitz, since the page is among papers he sent to NSC), memo to John M. Fisher, undated but about Oct. 1984, Ronald Reagan Library, WH Office File, European and Soviet Affairs Directorate, National Security Council, box 91037, folder Nuclear Winter.

11. Ibid.

12. Harold Lewis, letter to L. Badash, 16 Jan. 1990.

13. Jonathan T. Howe, information memo to the secretary of state, 7 Mar. 1984; John T. Chain, information memo to the secretary of state, 16 Aug. 1984, both in NRDC file. Quotes are from the second memo.

14. *Congressional Record—House* 130 (16 May 1984), H3997.

15. *Congressional Record—House* 130 (31 May 1984), H14670.

16. *Congressional Record—Senate* 130 (22 May 1984), S13141– S13142, quotes on 13141.

17. W. Cohen, "Cohen seeks study of 'nuclear winter,'" press release, 4 May 1984, cited in S. Scherr, "Coming to grips with nuclear winter," *Environment* 27 (Oct. 1985), 4–5, 40–41, quote on 4.

18. The Department of Defense Authorization Act, 1985 (House of Representatives Report No. 1080, 98th Congress, 2nd Session) was finally passed on 26 Sept. 1984. Section 1107 contains the instructions for the report on NW. See Public Law 98–525, 19 Oct. 1984, in *United States Statutes at Large*, 98 STAT. 2583.

19. *Congressional Record—House* 130 (31 May 1984), H14668–14671.

20. R. Smith, "Congress approves nuclear weapons buildup," *Science* 226 (26 Oct. 1984), 422–423.

21. Scherr, "Coming to grips with nuclear winter," 4; Department of Defense Authorization Act, 1985.

22. *Congressional Record—House* 130 (30 May 1984), H14461.

23. Ibid., H14670.

24. Hearings, 11–12 July 1984, ii, 1–2.

25. Russell Murray, testimony, hearings, 11–12 July 1984, 1–12, 51–55, quotes on 1, 2, and 51.

26. Noel Gayler, testimony, hearings, 11–12 July 1984, 55–58, quote on 56.

27. Paul Warnke, testimony and prepared statement, hearings, 11–12 July 1984, 63–66, 73, 85.

28. Richard L. Wagner, testimony, hearings, 11–12 July 1984, 100–104.

29. David F. Emery, testimony, hearings, 11–12 July 1984, 125, 130.

30. Sagan, testimony, hearings, 11–12 July 1984, 129–130, 180–181; afternoon session, 144–198.

31. Anon., "Pentagon aides agree on a 'nuclear winter,'" *New York Times*, 13 July 1984.

32. Sagan, testimony, in US Congress, House of Representatives, Committee on Science and Technology, Subcommittee on Natural Resources, Agriculture Research and Environment, *The Climatic, Biological, and Strategic Effects of Nuclear War*, hearings, 98th Congress, 2nd Session, 12 Sept. 1984, 4–7.

33. Stephen Jay Gould, testimony, hearings, 12 Sept. 1984, 8–11, quotes on 9, 10.

34. E. Teller, testimony, hearings, 12 Sept. 1984, 18–23, 40–41, quotes on 22, 40.

35. Sagan and Gould, testimony, hearings, 12 Sept. 1984, 38.

36. Leon Gouré, testimony, hearings, 12 Sept. 1984, 60–72.

37. Theodore S. Postol, testimony, hearings, 12 Sept. 1984, 72–105, quotes on 72.

38. *Congressional Record—Senate* 130 (10 Oct. 1984), S13980.

Chapter 11

1. F. Dyson, letter to C. Sagan, 25 Apr. 1983. A copy was provided by Professor Dyson.

2. Dyson, interview by Badash, 9 Feb. 1993; F. Dyson, *Infinite in All Directions* (Harper and Row, 1988), 260–261.

3. Carrier, interview by Badash, 11 Feb. 1993.

4. Ibid.; Committee on the Atmospheric Effects of Nuclear Explosions, "Agenda: Organizational meeting," 7–8 Mar. 1983, NRDC file.

5. Carrier, interview by Badash, 11 Feb. 1993.

6. Ibid.; Richard A. Vaaler, letter to Defense Industrial Security Clearance Office, 23 Mar. 1983, NRDC file.

7. Carrier, interview by Badash, 11 Feb. 1993.

8. Schneider and Londer, *Coevolution*, 357–358. The research was published as C. Covey, S. Schneider, and S. Thompson, "Global atmospheric effects of massive smoke injections from a nuclear war: Results from general circulation model simulations," *Nature* 308 (1 Mar. 1984), 21–25. See W. Broad, "US weighs risk that atom war could bring fatal nuclear winter," *New York Times*, 5 Aug. 1984, for the quote.

9. Schneider and Londer, *Coevolution*, quote on 360.

10. Ibid., quote on 361.

11. Carrier, interview by Badash, 11 Feb. 1993.

12. G. Ullrich, "Weekly activity report," 19 Apr. 1983, NRDC file.

13. G. Ullrich, "Memorandum for the record: National Academy of Sciences study on global nuclear war," 14 Oct. 1983, NRDC file.

14. Peter Lunn, "Memorandum to DNA Deputy Director for Science and Technology: Atmospheric effects of global nuclear war," 6 Sept. 1983, NRDC file.

15. Ibid.

16. Forrest Gilmore of R&D Associates, letter to Peter Lunn, 26 Aug. 1983, NRDC file.

17. Undated notes by DNA of conversation with David Sowle of Mission Research, NRDC file.

18. Gilmore, letter to Lunn, 26 Aug. 1983.

19. E. Jones of LANL, statement to Peter Lunn, 13 July 1983, NRDC file.

20. Notes of conversation with Sowle.

21. In addition to standard biographical directories, information about Singer has been found in the following articles: I. Goodwin, "Washington reports," *Physics Today* 40 (Dec. 1987), 61; C. Holden, "Random samples," *Science* 260 (30 Apr. 1993), 618–619; R. Archibold, "Nobel winner unfazed by backlash," *Los Angeles Times*, 20 Oct. 1997.

22. S. Fred Singer, typescript titled "Nuclear winter on the day after?" 25 Nov. 1983, Ronald Reagan Library, WH Staff File, Keyworth, box 23, folder NW #4.

23. Ibid.

24. S. Singer, typescript titled "Letter to the editor *Science* magazine," 12 Jan. 1984, Ronald Reagan Library, WH Staff File, Keyworth, box 23, folder NW #4.

25. S. Singer, "The big chill? Challenging a nuclear scenario," *Wall Street Journal*, 3 Feb. 1984.

26. C. Sagan, "The chilling aftermath of a nuclear war," *Wall Street Journal*, 16 Feb. 1984.

27. S. Singer, letter to editor, *Scientific American* 252 (Apr. 1985), 8.

28. S. Singer, letter to G. Keyworth, 25 Jan. 1985, and attached "NACOA statement on nuclear winter research," 25 Jan. 1985, Ronald Reagan Library, WH Staff File, Keyworth, box 23, folder NW#1. See also Singer, letter to editor, *Science* 227 (25 Jan. 1985), 356, and reply by Turco et al. on 358–362.

29. Richard Turco, letter to Tony Rothman, 15 Mar. 1985, commenting on Rothman's draft of an article titled "A memoir on nuclear winter." This was published as chapter 5 in Rothman's book *Science à la Mode: Physical Fashions and Fictions* (Princeton University Press, 1989). Both authors provided copies of the letter and the draft.

30. P. Ehrlich and A. Ehrlich, *Betrayal of Science and Reason: How Anti-Environmental Rhetoric Threatens Our Future* (Island, 1996), 36–37.

31. J. Maddox, *The Doomsday Syndrome* (McGraw-Hill, 1972), quotes on v–vi.

32. L. Dotto and H. Schiff, *The Ozone War* (Doubleday, 1978), 21.

33. J. Maddox, "From Santorini to Armageddon," *Nature* 307 (12 Jan. 1984), 107.

34. V. LaMarche Jr. and K. Hirschboeck, "Nuclear war models," *Nature* 309 (17 May 1984), 203.

35. J. Maddox, "Nuclear winter not yet established," *Nature* 308 (1 Mar. 1984), 11.

36. R. Turco, O. Toon, T. Ackerman, J. Pollack, and C. Sagan, "'Nuclear winter' to be taken seriously," *Nature* 311 (27 Sept. 1984), 307–308. The world total of tactical nuclear weapons, given elsewhere as about 25,000, was obviously an approximation, as nuclear powers rarely, if ever, gave precise numbers.

37. S. Idso, "Calibrations for nuclear winter" [letter to editor], *Nature* 312 (29 Nov. 1984), 407. Idso was another "contrarian," well known for his disbelief in carbon dioxide's effect on global warming. See Schneider and Londer, *Coevolution*, 328–330. For a defense of simulations, see F. Hauser and M. Kotva, "Aftermath of nuclear war," *Nature* 313 (28 Feb. 1985), 732. For TTAPS's reply to Idso and

other critics, see R. Turco et al., "Ozone, dust, smoke and humidity in nuclear winter," *Nature* 317 (5 Sept. 1985), 21–22.

38. P. Goldsmith et al., "Nitrogen oxides, nuclear weapon testing, Concorde and stratospheric ozone," *Nature* 244 (31 Aug. 1973), 545–551.

39. B. Golding, P. Goldsmith, N. Machin, and A. Slingo, "Importance of local mesoscale factors in any assessment of nuclear winter," *Nature* 319 (23 Jan. 1986), 301–303.

40. Rathjens, interview by Badash, 11 Feb. 1993.

41. G. Rathjens, letter to C. Sagan, 8 Nov. 1983; Rathjens, letter to Lawrence McCray, NAS-NRC staff, 4 Jan. 1984. Copies of both letters were provided by Professor Rathjens.

42. George Rathjens, comments in panel on "Nuclear winter" held by California Workshop on American Foreign and Defense Policy at University of California, Berkeley, 3 Oct. 1984.

43. Rathjens, interview by Badash, 11 Feb. 1993.

44. Richard Turco, letter to Tony Rothman, 15 Mar. 1985. See R. Turco et al., "Nuclear winter: Global consequences of multiple nuclear explosions," *Science* 222 (23 Dec. 1983), 1283–1292, esp. 1285.

45. Rathjens, comments in panel on 3 Oct. 1984.

46. Rathjens, interview by Badash, 11 Feb. 1993.

47. P. Ehrlich et al., "Long-term biological consequences of nuclear war," *Science* 222 (23 Dec. 1983), 1293–1300, quote on 1294. In a letter to L. Badash dated 14 Aug. 2001, Ehrlich expressed surprise at the allegation of duplicity, noting that there were too many authors involved for any kind of conspiratorial behavior.

48. Rathjens, interview by Badash, 11 Feb. 1993.

49. Ibid.

50. Turco, letter to Rothman, 15 Mar. 1985.

51. George Rathjens, "A critique of discussion of nuclear winter," typed abstract of his comments at meeting of the American Physical Society, 24 Apr. 1985 (a copy of this document was provided by Professor Rathjens; Rathjens reiterated his many critiques in the interview; he especially objected to the words "would" and "will," instead of the conditional "might" and "could"); Rathjens, interview by Badash, 11 Feb. 1993.

52. Von Hippel, interview by Badash, 8 Feb. 1993.

53. Ibid.

54. Ibid.

55. Holdren, comments in panel on 3 Oct. 1984.

56. Sagan, interview by Badash, 26 Dec. 1984.

57. Schneider, interview by Badash, 13 Feb. 1985.

58. B. Martin, "Nuclear winter: Science and politics," *Science and Public Policy* 15 (Oct. 1988), 321–334, quotes on 324–325.

59. S. Singer, "Nuclear winter and nuclear strategy" (typescript, 7 June 1984), p. 4. The typescript is attached to Singer, letter to Edward Teller, 26 July 1984, Ronald Reagan Library, WH Staff File, Keyworth, box 23, folder NW#1.

60. E. Teller, "Widespread after-effects of nuclear war," *Nature* 310 (23 Aug. 1984), 621–624, quotes on 621–622. This paper was presented at a 1984 conference in Erice and was published in W. Newman and C. Stipcich, eds., *International Seminar on Nuclear War, 4th Session* (World Scientific, 1992).

61. Ibid., quotes on 624.

62. G. Alexander, "Nuclear winter scenario startled its discoverers" and "Piecing together grim scenario of the aftermath was a complicated problem," *Los Angeles Times*, 22 Jan. 1984.

63. M. MacCracken and G. Bing, interviews by L. Badash, 13 Feb. 1985.

64. P. Ehrlich, "North America after the war," *Natural History* 93 (Mar. 1984), 4–8, quote on 6. For another biology-oriented popularization, see H. Grover, "The climatic and biological consequences of nuclear war," *Environment* 26 (May 1984), 6–13, 34–38.

65. R. Turco, O. Toon, T. Ackerman, J. Pollack, and C. Sagan, "The climatic effects of nuclear war," *Scientific American* 251 (Aug. 1984), 33–43, quotes on 33.

66. Cornel Sarosdy, letter to editor, and reply by Turco et al., *Scientific American* 252 (Jan. 1985), 9.

67. Singer, letter to editor, *Scientific American* 252. The *WSJ* articles in dispute were those by Singer ("The big chill?") and Sagan ("The chilling aftermath").

68. G. Rathjens and R. Siegel, review of *The Cold and the Dark* in *Survival* 27 (Jan.-Feb. 1985), 43–44; R. Graham, review of same book, *San Francisco Chronicle*, 5 Aug. 1984.

Chapter 12

1. R. Smith, "Nuclear winter attracts additional scrutiny," *Science* 225 (6 July 1984), 30–32.

2. A. Hecht, testimony, in US Congress, House of Representatives, Committee on Science and Technology, Subcommittee on Natural Resources, Agriculture Research, and Environment, *The Climatic, Biological, and Strategic Effects of Nuclear War*, hearings, 98th Congress, 2nd Session, 12 Sept. 1984, 46–47, 51–52.

3. P. Hilts, "US begins study of possible climatic disaster in nuclear war," *Washington Post*, 29 May 1984.

4. F. David Plummer, letter to Ronald Reagan, 27 Jan. 1985, Ronald Reagan Library, WHORM Alpha File.

5. C. Sagan, letter to G. Keyworth, 9 Sept. 1984, Ronald Reagan Library, WH Staff File, Keyworth, box 23, folder NW#2. To illustrate the critics' views, Sagan enclosed an op-ed piece by William Turner (a Baptist pastor): "Federal study of nuclear winter theory wastes time and money," *Herald-Leader* [Lexington, Kentucky], 19 Aug. 1984.

6. Keyworth, letter to Sagan, 9 Oct. 1984, Ronald Reagan Library, WH Staff File, Keyworth, box 23, folder NW#2.

7. Sagan, letter to Keyworth, 6 Nov. 1984, Ronald Reagan Library, WH Staff File, Keyworth, box 23, folder NW#3.

8. Keyworth, letter to Sagan, 20 Dec. 1984, Ronald Reagan Library, WH Staff File, Keyworth, box 23, folder NW#3.

9. "Action items for policy related to nuclear winter," undated but early Nov. 1984, Ronald Reagan Library, WH Staff File, Keyworth, box 23, folder NW#2. See also T. Beardsley, "US plans for studies proliferate," *Nature* 311 (27 Sept. 1984), 287.

10. Maurie Roesch, OSTP assistant director for defense programs, memo to G. Keyworth, 29 Nov. 1984, Ronald Reagan Library, WH Staff File, Keyworth, box 23, folder NW#4.

11. R. Smith, "Congress approves nuclear weapon buildup," *Science* 226 (26 Oct. 1984), 422–423.

12. Roesch, memo to Keyworth.

13. O. Toon, comment at DNA-sponsored conference on NW, Santa Barbara, 12 Feb. 1985.

14. M. MacCracken, interview by L. Badash, 13 Feb. 1985.

15. "Nuclear winter research program management options," 29 Nov. 1984, Ronald Reagan Library, WH Staff File, Keyworth, box 23, folder NW#3; G. Keyworth, memo to Erich Bloch, NSF director, 20 Dec. 1984, box 23, folder NW#3; Bloch, letter to Keyworth, 7 Jan. 1985, box 22, folder NSF 1984/1985, #5.

16. Maurie Roesch, memo to G. Keyworth, 16 Jan. 1985, Ronald Reagan Library, WH Staff File, Keyworth, box 23, folder NW#1; Keyworth, letter to Clarence J. Brown, deputy secretary of commerce, 25 Jan. 1985, with attached Keyworth, memo for distribution, 25 Jan. 1985, box 23, folder NW#2; Keyworth, letter to Richard H. Stallings, House Committee on Science and Technology, 18 June 1985, box 23, folder NW#1.

17. C. Weinberger, "The potential effects of nuclear war on the climate: A report to the United States Congress," Department of Defense, Mar. 1985, 7.

18. G. Keyworth, letter to A. Hecht, 8 Mar. 1985, Ronald Reagan Library, WH Staff File, Keyworth, box 23, folder NW#2.

19. *Interagency Research Report for Assessing Climatic Effects of Nuclear War* (National Climate Program Office, NOAA, 5 Feb. 1985).

20. Ibid., 1–3, 17.

21. Ibid., 1–3, quote on 3. For another analysis of research that was needed, see C. Covey, S. Thompson, and S. Schneider, "'Nuclear winter': A diagnosis of atmospheric general circulation model simulations," *Journal of Geophysical Research* 90 (20 June 1985), 5615–5628. See also remarks by DNA's program manager for global effects research: P. Lunn, "Global effects: Where do we go from here?" in W. Newman and S. Stipcich, eds., *International Seminar on Nuclear War, 5th Session* (World Scientific, 1992).

22. Colin Norman, "Turbulent times for NOAA," *Science* 226 (7 Dec. 1984), 1172–1174.

23. "Nuclear winter research program management options," 29 Nov. 1984.

24. R. Smith, "'Nuclear winter' feels budgetary chill," *Science* 227 (22 Feb. 1985), 94–95, quote on 94.

25. Rep. Timothy Wirth, letter to G. Keyworth, 9 Sept. 1985, Ronald Reagan Library, WH Staff file, Keyworth, box 23, folder NW#1; F. FitzGerald, *Way Out There in the Blue: Reagan, Star Wars, and the End of the Cold War* (Simon and Schuster, 2000), 371–372; M. Riordan, "The demise of the Superconducting Super Collider," *Physics in Perspective* 2 (Dec. 2000), 411–425.

26. G. Keyworth, letter to Lee M. Thomas, EPA administrator, 12 Nov. 1985, Ronald Reagan Library, WH Staff File, Keyworth, box 23, folder Nuclear War—Climatic Effects.

27. "Transcript of interview with president on a range of issues," *New York Times*, 12 Feb. 1985.

28. H. Lewis, letter to L. Badash, 16 Jan. 1990; H. Lewis, interview by L. Badash, 13 Feb. 1990; John V. Ello, executive director of the Defense Science Board, letter to L. Badash, 14 Jan. 1994, enclosing memo from Office of the Under Secretary of Defense to chairman, DSB, 5 Mar. 1984, asking that a task force be established to study NW.

29. Weinberger, "Potential effects," 2. See also J. Gerstenzang, "Pentagon study uncertain of risks of 'nuclear winter,'" *Los Angeles Times*, 3 Mar. 1985; M. Weisskopf, "Pentagon says nuclear winter justifies arms," *Washington Post*, 3 Mar. 1985; S. Budiansky, "Pentagon says yes, it may happen, but 'so what?'" *Nature* 314 (14 Mar. 1985), 121; R. Smith, "DoD says 'nuclear winter' bolsters its plans," *Science* 227 (15 Mar. 1985), 1320.

30. Weinberger, "Potential effects," 4.

31. Ibid. The report was published as R. Small and B. Bush, "Smoke production from multiple nuclear explosions in nonurban areas" *Science* 229 (2 Aug. 1985), 465–469.

32. Weinberger, "Potential effects," 5–6.

33. Ibid., 10–11, 13.

34. Ibid., 14. The point about MIRVing is from Budiansky, "Pentagon says yes."

35. Weinberger, "Potential effects," 12, 15.

36. Ibid., 10.

37. W. Biddle, "Pentagon agrees nuclear warfare could block sun, freezing Earth," *New York Times*, 2 Mar. 1985; Budiansky, "Pentagon says yes."

38. Bill Wright and Bob Linhard, NSC staff, memo to Admiral John M. Poindexter, deputy assistant to the president for national security affairs, 3 Jan. 1985, Ronald Reagan Library, WHORM Subject File, ND018 270562.

39. R. Wagner, testimony, in US Congress, Joint Economics Committee, Subcommittee on International Trade, Finance, and Security Economics, *The Consequences of Nuclear War,* hearings, 98th Congress, 2nd Session, 11–12 July 1984, 139.

40. G. Keyworth, memo to "Dave," 28 Feb. 1985, Ronald Reagan Library, Keyworth, White House Staff File, box 23, folder NW#2.

41. Weisskopf, "Pentagon says."

42. R. Smith, "DoD says."

43. Weinberger, "Potential effects," 9.

44. Wilmer, Cutler, and Pickering, memo to Natural Resources Defense Council, 11 Apr. 1985. This document was provided by NRDC attorney S. Jacob Scherr.

45. Scherr, interview by Badash, 21 Apr. 1987.

46. *Congressional Record—Senate* 131 (14 Mar. 1985), S2979–S2980.

47. "Scientific deep freeze" [editorial], *Wall Street Journal*, 18 Mar. 1985.

48. *Congressional Record—House* 131 (28 Mar. 1985), H1656–H1657.

49. *Congressional Record—Senate* 131 (28 Mar. 1985), S3729.

50. S. Scherr, "Coming to grips with nuclear winter," *Environment* 27 (Oct. 1985), 4–5, 40–41, on 5.

51. *Congressional Record—House* 131 (26 June 1985), H17473, and 131 (27 June 1985), H17970.

52. Anon., "Senate, House act on nuclear winter," *Nuclear Winter* [newsletter of the Center on the Consequences of Nuclear War], summer 1985, 1.

53. Rep. Morris Udall, remarks, US Congress, House of Representatives, Committee on Science and Technology, Subcommittee on Natural Resources, Agriculture Research, and Environment, and Committee on Interior and Insular Affairs, Subcommittee on Energy and the Environment, *Nuclear Winter*, joint hearing, 99th Congress, 1st Session, 14 Mar. 1985, 2.

54. Scheuer, remarks, ibid., 6.

55. Lujan and Wirth, remarks, ibid., 11–12.

56. Sagan, testimony, ibid., 19–37, quotes on 19, 20, 23.

57. J. McCain, remarks, ibid., 36–37, 66; A. Fleming, "McCain: 'Manliness' is what matters most," *Los Angeles Times*, 13 Feb. 2000.

58. R. Perle,, testimony, ibid., 37–68, quote on 37; Sagan, testimony, ibid., 19–37, quotes on 19, 20, 24.

59. Perle, testimony, ibid., 37–68. See also J. Dickenson, "Sagan, defense official clash on nuclear winter," *Washington Post*, 15 Mar. 1985; B. Secter, "Sagan clashes with defense official on 'nuclear winter' study," *Los Angeles Times*, 15 Mar. 1985.

60. J. Stone, testimony, ibid., 69–70. See also Stone, "Nuclear winter: Self-interest in avoiding revenge?" *F.A.S. Public Interest Report* 38 (Apr. 1985), 1, 4–5.

61. G. Rathjens, testimony, ibid., 81–83, quote on 82.

62. D. Williamson, oral and written testimony, ibid., 93–96, quotes on 93.

63. S. Schneider and others, testimony, ibid., 125–127, 151–153, quotes on 125.

64. Sen. Barry Goldwater, remarks in US Congress, Senate, Committee on Armed Services, *Nuclear Winter and Its Implications*, hearings, 99th Congress, 1st Session, 2–3 Oct. 1985, 2.

65. MacCracken and Bing, interviews by Badash, 13 Feb. 1985.

66. C. Gillespie, testimony, Senate, Committee on Armed Services, *Nuclear Winter and Its Implications*, hearings, 99th Congress, 1st Session, 2–3 Oct. 1985, 3–10, quotes on 3 and 6.

67. M. Harwell, testimony, ibid., 14–18, quotes on 15.

68. L. Sloss and L. Gouré, testimony, ibid., 61–62, 64–67, 110.

69. Sagan, written reply to questions, ibid., 208–209.

70. Discussion, ibid., 95–96, 108.

71. Sen. John Glenn, comments, ibid., 97.

72. Gillespie and Harwell, testimony, ibid., 104–106.

73. C. Gillespie, written testimony, ibid., 115–117.

74. Sagan and Perle, testimony, ibid., 123–157, esp. 140.

75. Scherr, interview by Badash, 21 Apr. 1987. Scherr made this observation about illogical behavior.

76. M. Clarke, "Nuclear winter: US arms control policy doubts," *Nature* 317 (10 Oct. 1985), 466.

77. *Senator Alan Cranston Reports to California* [occasional newsletter to his constituents], not dated but Dec. 1985.

Chapter 13

1. Turco, interview by Badash and Kirtman, 20 Feb. 1985. For a detailed survey of models, from 1-D to interactive 3-D, see A. Pittock et al., *Environmental Consequences of Nuclear War*, volume 1: *Physical and Atmospheric Effects* (Wiley, 1986), 149–215. See also P. Edwards, "A brief history of atmospheric general circulation modeling," in D. Randall, ed., *General Circulation Model Development* (Academic, 2000). For a discussion of the early models by one who felt they were rather similar, see W. Hahm, "Nuclear winter: A review of the models," Rand Graduate Institute Paper P-7121-RGI (July 1985).

2. N. Oreskes, K. Shrader-Frechette, and K. Belitz, "Verification, validation, and confirmation of numerical models in the earth sciences," *Science* 263 (4 Feb. 1994), 641–646, quote on 641. See also Oreskes, "The role of quantitative models in science," in C. Canham et al., eds., *Models in Ecosystem Science* (Princeton University Press, 2003).

3. G. Carrier, "Nuclear winter: The state of the science," *Issues in Science and Technology* 1 (winter 1985), 114–117, quote on 116.

4. M. MacCracken, "Nuclear war: Preliminary estimates of the climatic effects of a nuclear exchange," presented at 1983 conference in Erice and published in W. Newman and S. Stipcich, eds., *International Seminar on Nuclear War, 3rd Session* (World Scientific, 1992), quotes on 162, 165. See also B. Levi, "Atmospheric calculations suggest a nuclear winter," *Physics Today* 37 (Feb. 1984), 17–20; NOAA *Interagency Research Report*, 5 Feb. 1985, 10–11.

5. R. Haberle, T. Ackerman, O. Toon, and J. Hollingsworth, "Global transport of atmospheric smoke following a major nuclear exchange," *Geophysical Research Letters* 12 (June 1985), 405–408.

6. V. Aleksandrov, "Climate response to global injections," presented at 1983 conference in Erice and published in *International Seminar on Nuclear War, 3rd Session*.

7. V. Aleksandrov and G. Stenchikov, "Numerical simulation of the climatic consequences of a nuclear war," *USSR Computational Mathematics and Mathematical Physics* 24 (1984), 87–90, quote on 87. For an overview of Soviet computer capabilities, see anon., "Soviet computing," *Jane's Defence Weekly* 4 (19 Oct. 1985), 866–867.

8. This point was made by Joseph Smagorinsky, retired head of Princeton's geophysical fluid dynamics laboratory (as quoted in anon., "The nuclear-winter threat," *Discover* 5, Jan. 1984, 10–11).

9. Aleksandrov and Stenchikov, "Numerical simulation," quote on 89. See also Levi, "Atmospheric calculations suggest"; NOAA *Interagency Research Report*, 5 Feb. 1985.

10. Schneider, interview by Badash, 13 Feb. 1985; Schneider, letter to Badash, 16 Oct. 1986.

11. S. Schneider, testimony, in US House of Representatives, Committee on Science and Technology, Subcommittee on Natural Resources, Agriculture Research, and Environment, jointly with Committee on Interior and Insular Affairs, Subcommittee on Energy and the Environment, *Nuclear Winter*, hearing, 99th Congress, 1st Session, 14 Mar. 1985, 133.

12. C. Covey, S. Schneider, and S. Thompson, "Global atmospheric effects of massive smoke injections from a nuclear war: Results from general circulation model simulations," *Nature* 308 (1 Mar. 1984), 21–25, esp. 25; Schneider, interview by Badash, 13 Feb. 1985. For a comparison of the first two GCMs (of NCAR and of Moscow) and a discussion of their results, see S. Thompson, V. Aleksandrov, G. Stenchikov, S. Schneider, C. Covey, and R. Chervin, "Global climatic consequences of nuclear war: Simulations with three dimensional models," *Ambio* 13: 4 (1984), 236–243. For other comparisons of early models, see R. Cess, "Nuclear war: Illustrative effects of atmospheric smoke and dust upon solar radiation," *Climatic Change* 7 (June 1985), 237–251; C. Covey, "Climatic effects of nuclear war," *BioScience* 35 (Oct. 1985), 563–569.

13. Turco, interview by Badash and Kirtman, 20 Feb. 1985; Toon, interview by Badash and Kirtman, 6 Mar. 1985.

14. Ackerman, interview by Badash and Kirtman, 6 Mar. 1985.

15. J. Raloff, "'Nuclear winter' research heats up," *Science News* 126 (22 Sept. 1984), 182.

16. A. Robock, "Snow and ice feedbacks prolong effects of nuclear winter," *Nature* 310 (23 Aug. 1984), 667–670. See also D. Green, "Nuclear winter," *Nature* 313 (31 Jan. 1985), 343.

17. J. Maddox, "Nuclear winter not yet established," *Nature* 308 (1 Mar. 1984), 11.

18. S. Singer, "Is the 'nuclear winter' real?" *Nature* 310 (23 Aug. 1984), 625.

19. S. Thompson, S. Schneider, and C. Covey, reply to Singer ["Is the 'nuclear winter' real?"], *Nature* 310 (23 Aug. 1984), 625–626.

20. M. MacCracken and J. Walton, "The effects of interactive transport and scavenging of smoke on the calculated temperature change resulting from large amounts of smoke," presented at 1984 conference in Erice and published in W. Newman and S. Stipcich, eds., *International Seminar on Nuclear War, 4th Session* (World Scientific, 1992), quote on 260. See also George Bing, "Global effects of nuclear war: Background and current status" [informal report, Lawrence Livermore National Laboratory], July 1984, esp. p. 14.

21. V. Aleksandrov, "Update of climatic impacts of nuclear exchange," in *International Seminar on Nuclear War, 4th Session*. See also J. Raloff, "New Soviet 'nuclear winter' maps," *Science News* 126 (29 Sept. 1984), 204.

22. G. Golitsyn and A. Ginsburg, "Comparative estimates of climatic consequences of Martian dust storms and of possible nuclear war," *Tellus* 37B (1985), 173–181.

23. R. Malone, interview by L. Badash, 13 Feb. 1986.

24. R. Malone, L. Auer, G. Glatzmaier, M. Wood, and O. Toon, "Influence of solar heating and prescription scavenging on the simulated lifetime of post-nuclear war smoke," *Science* 230 (18 Oct. 1985), 317–319; Malone, public lecture at University of California, Santa Barbara, and interview by Badash, 13 Feb. 1986. See also B. Rensberger, "New studies support nuclear winter theory," *Washington Post*, 27 Mar. 1985; R. Kerr, "Nuclear winter won't blow away," *Science* 228 (12 Apr. 1985), 163; M. MacCracken, "Nuclear winter: Recent results from climate models," *Physics and Society* 14 (July 1985), 9.

25. W. Cotton, "Atmospheric convection and nuclear winter," *American Scientist* 73 (May-June 1985), 275–280.

26. See, e.g., V. Ramaswamy and J. Kiehl, "Sensitivities of the radiative forcing due to large loadings of smoke and dust aerosols," *Journal of Geophysical Research* 90 (20 June 1985), 5597–5613; R. Cess, "Nuclear war: Illustrative effects of atmospheric smoke and dust upon solar radiation," *Climatic Change* 7 (June 1985), 237–251; G. Stenchikov and P. Carl, "Climatic consequences of nuclear war: Sensitivity against large-scale inhomogeneities in the initial atmospheric pollutions," report of Physical Society of the German Democratic Republic, Oct. 1985.

27. R. Cess, G. Potter, S. Ghan, and W. Gates, "The climatic effects of large injections of atmospheric smoke and dust: A study of climate feedback mechanisms with one- and three-dimensional climate models," *Journal of Geophysical Research* 90 (20 Dec. 1985), 12,937–12,950, quotes on 12,946 and 12,948. For a survey of model sensitivity and of future research needs, see J. Knox, "Climatic consequences of nuclear war: New findings, 1985," and "Climatic consequences of nuclear war: Working group #1," both in W. Newman and S. Stipcich, eds., *International Seminar on Nuclear War, 5th Session* (World Scientific, 1992).

28. Ramaswamy and Kiehl, "Sensitivities."

29. S. Thompson, "Global interactive transport simulations of nuclear war smoke," *Nature* 317 (5 Sept. 1985), 35–39, quote on 35.

30. J. Maddox, "Nuclear winter can cross equator," *Nature* 317 (5 Sept. 1985), 11.

31. P. Crutzen, I. Galbally, and C. Brühl, "Atmospheric effects from post-nuclear fires," *Climatic Change* 6 (1984), 323–364. In their 1982 *Ambio* paper, Crutzen and Birks had calculated 200–400 million tonnes of smoke from forest fires. See also Crutzen, "Atmospheric pollution effects following a nuclear war," presented at 1983 conference in Erice and published in *International Seminar on Nuclear War, 3rd Session: The Technical Basis for Peace* (World Scientific, 1992).

32. I. Barton and G. Paltridge, " 'Twilight at noon' overstated," *Ambio* 13: 1 (1984), 49–51, quotes on 49.

33. Ibid., quote on 51.

34. P. Crutzen, "Darkness after a nuclear war," *Ambio* 13: 1 (1984), 52–54, quote on 54.

35. "Uncertainties in the generation and evolution of the atmospheric smoke burden," manuscript dated 24 May 1984, attached to Michael M. May, letter to Alan D. Hecht, 24 May 1984, Ronald Reagan Library, WH Staff File, Keyworth, box 23, folder NW#1, quote on p. 1; Toon, interview by Badash and Kirtman, 6 Mar. 1985. For a review of the status of research, which focused on fire and included some calculations by the authors, see B. Levi and T. Rothman, "Nuclear winter: A matter of degrees," *Physics Today* 38 (Sept. 1985), 58–65. For yet another research review, typical of the author's thoroughness and objectivity, see M. MacCracken, "Global atmospheric effects of nuclear war," *Energy and Technology Review* (Lawrence Livermore National Laboratory), May 1985, 10–35.

36. C. Chandler, quoted in J. Raloff, "Estimating nuclear forest fires," *Science News* 126 (29 Sept. 1984), 204.

37. "Uncertainties in the generation and evolution of the atmospheric smoke burden," quote on p. 5.

38. C. Kearny, "Fire emissions and some of their uncertainties," in *International Seminar on Nuclear War, 4th Session*; Kearny, letter to editor, *Science* 227 (25 Jan. 1985), 356–358; reply by Turco et al. on 358–362.

39. G. Rathjens and R. Siegel, "Nuclear winter: Strategic significance," *Issues in Science and Technology* 1 (winter 1985), 123–128.

40. Ibid., quotes on 124 and 125.

41. J. Penner and L. Haselman, "Smoke inputs to climate models: Optical properties and height distribution for nuclear winter studies," in *International Seminar on Nuclear War, 4th Session*.

42. B. Curry, "World climate change feared in 'Arctic haze,'" *Los Angeles Times*, 25 Nov. 1984.

43. R. Small and B. Bush, "Smoke production from multiple nuclear explosions in nonurban areas," *Science* 229 (2 Aug. 1985), 465–469. For a historical survey of city fires, see H. Brode and R. Small, "A review of the physics of large urban fires," in F. Solomon and R. Marston, eds., *The Medical Implications of Nuclear War* (National Academy Press, 1986).

44. R. Turco, "Recent assessments of the environmental consequences of nuclear war," in Solomon and Marston, eds., *The Medical Implications of Nuclear War*.

45. H. Denton, "Forest fire to test theory on nuclear war," *Washington Post*, 3 Aug. 1985; anon., "Scientists test theory of 'nuclear winter,'" *New York Times*, 5 Aug. 1985; T. Beardsley, "Canadian forest burn as model," *Nature* 316 (8 Aug. 1985), 479.

46. P. Giffen, "Experimenting with 'nuclear winter,'" *Macleans* 98 (19 Aug. 1985), 46; anon., "Ontario fire sparks DNA research proposals," *Nuclear Winter* [newsletter of Center on the Consequences of Nuclear War], fall-winter 1985, 6.

47. W. Wolbach, R. Lewis, and E. Anders, "Cretaceous extinctions: Evidence for wildfires and search for meteoric material," *Science* 230 (11 Oct. 1985), 167–170; J. Wilford, "Findings back idea that pall over Earth killed dinosaurs," *New York Times*, 4 Oct. 1985; P. Osterlund, "Chicago team offers its explanation of why dinosaurs disappeared," *Christian Science Monitor*, 4 Oct. 1985; J. Bishop, "Scientific research suggests soot once blanketed Earth," *Wall Street Journal*, 4 Oct. 1985; anon., "Report ties dinosaur's demise to firestorm from comet crash," *Los Angeles Times*, 5 Oct. 1985; "Dinosaurs and nuclear winter" [editorial], *Los Angeles Times*, 7 Oct. 1985; S. Begley, "An ancient 'nuclear winter,'" *Newsweek* 106 (14 Oct. 1985), 106; N. Angier, "Comet fire," *Time* 126 (14 Oct. 1985), 92. See also three letters to the editor in *Science* 234 (17 Oct. 1986), 261–264.

48. R. Wagner, statement, in US Congress, Joint Economics Committee, Subcommittee on International Trade, Finance, and Security Economics, *The Consequences of Nuclear War*, hearings, 98th Congress, 2nd Session, 11–12 July 1984, 105–111, quotes on 109.

49. P. Ehrlich, "When light is put away: Ecological effects of nuclear war," in J. Leaning and L. Keyes, eds., *The Counterfeit Ark: Crisis Relocation for Nuclear War* (Ballinger, 1984), quote on 249.

50. P. Ehrlich, "The nuclear winter: Discovering the ecology of nuclear war," *Amicus Journal* 5 (winter 1984), 20–30.

51. J. Harte, comments in panel on "Nuclear winter," California Workshop on American Foreign and Defense Policy, University of California, Berkeley, 3 Oct. 1984.

52. Anon., "AIBS issues nuclear winter statement," *BioScience* 35 (Feb. 1985), 77.

53. L. Anspaugh, "Panel: Long-term consequences and prospects for recovery," prepared for the Symposium on the Medical Implications of Nuclear War, Washington, 20–22 Sept. 1985, Livermore

Laboratory publication UCRL-93656, quote on 2. This paper appeared as "Long-term consequences of and prospects for recovery from nuclear war: Two views," in Solomon and Marston, eds., *The Medical Implications of Nuclear War.*

54. Anspaugh, "Panel," quote on 6.

55. Ibid., quote on 6.

56. H. Grover and M. Harwell, "Biological effects of nuclear war, II: Impact on the biosphere," *BioScience* 35 (Oct. 1985), 576–583, quote on 576.

57. Ibid., quotes on 576.

58. Ibid., quotes on 579.

59. Ibid., quotes on 580–581.

60. M. Harwell, *Nuclear Winter: The Human and Environmental Consequences of Nuclear War* (Springer-Verlag, 1984). For a review of this book, see P. Kelly, "In the aftermath," *Nature* 315 (9 May 1985), 161.

Chapter 14

1. T. Wicker, "Tambora's lesson," *New York Times*, 14 Dec. 1984.

2. "Nuclear winter, Star Wars" [editorial], *New York Times*, 14 Dec. 1984.

3. Bill Wright and Bob Linhard, NSC staffers, memo to Robert C. McFarlane, assistant to the president for national security affairs, 10 Dec. 1984, Ronald Reagan Library, WHORM Subject File, ND018 308386.

4. Toon, interview by Badash and Kirtman, 6 Mar. 1985; George Rathjens, letter to Lawrence McCray, NAS-NRC staff member, 8 Sept. 1984 (a copy of this letter was provided by Professor Rathjens). See also A. Pittock, "Report on reports," *Environment* 27 (Apr. 1985), 25–29; S. Budiansky, "US National Academy urges greater caution," *Nature* 312 (20–27 Dec. 1984), 683.

5. Schneider, interview by Badash, 13 Feb. 1985.

6. Carrier, *The Effects on the Atmosphere*, iii. See also "Nuclear winter report excerpts," *Bulletin of the Atomic Scientists* 41 (Mar. 1985), 39–40.

7. Ackerman, interview by Badash and Kirtman, 6 Mar. 1985.

8. Carrier, *The Effects on the Atmosphere*, 1. See also Budiansky, "US National Academy urges greater caution."

9. Carrier, interview by Badash, 11 Feb. 1993.

10. Carrier, *The Effects on the Atmosphere*, 2, 13–16, quotes on 2.

11. Ibid., 3–4, 37–38, 58–62, 75–76. See also anon., "Uncertainties of climatic change," *Nature* 312 (20–27 Dec. 1984), 683.

12. Carrier, interview by Badash, 11 Feb. 1993.

13. Carrier, *The Effects on the Atmosphere*, 5.

14. Ibid., 6–9.

15. R. Smith, "NRC panel envisions potential nuclear winter," *Science* 226 (21 Dec. 1984), 1403.

16. Carrier, *The Effects on the Atmosphere*, quote on 5.

17. W. Broad, " 'Nuclear winter' is seen as possible," *New York Times*, 12 Dec. 1984.

18. Carrier, interview by Badash, 11 Feb. 1993.

19. See, e.g., Wicker, "Tambora's lesson."

20. See, e.g., B. Keller, "President mounts campaign for MX; bars compromise," *New York Times*, 27 Feb. 1985; J. Tagliabue, "Dutch parliament backs a proposal to delay missiles," *New York Times*, 14 June 1984; R. Bernstein, "Belgium announces decision to accept nuclear missiles," *New York Times*, 16 Mar. 1985.

21. L. Gelb, "Arms role reversal," *New York Times*, 6 Jan. 1985; B. Gwertzman, "Shultz urges US not to cut back on arms outlays," *New York Times*, 11 Jan. 1985.

22. Transcript of CBS Television Network's *Face the Nation*, 16 Dec. 1984. A copy is preserved in the Ronald Reagan Library, WH Staff File, Lehman, box 90570, folder Nuclear Winter.

23. Anon., "No taps for TTAPS," *Scientific American* 252 (Feb. 1985), 61–62; J. Wortman, "NRC report backs nuclear winter theory," *BioScience* 35 (Feb. 1985), 77; W. Broad, " 'Nuclear winter' is seen as possible," *New York Times*, 12 Dec. 1984; anon., "Effects of A-war affirmed," *Los Angeles Times*, 12 Dec. 1984; B. Rensberger, "National Academy of Sciences backs nuclear-winter theory," *Washington Post*, 12 Dec. 1984; R. Smith, "NRC panel envisions potential nuclear winter," *Science* 226 (21 Dec. 1984), 1403. See also P. Grier, "Study backs theory that nuclear war would alter world climate," *Christian Science Monitor*, 12 Dec. 1984; N. Angier, "Debate over a frozen planet: A major study supports the grim prediction of nuclear winter," *Time* 124 (24 Dec. 1984), 56–57.

24. "In the chill, in the shadow" [editorial], *Los Angeles Times*, 13 Dec. 1984; "Nuclear winter, Star Wars" [editorial], *New York Times*, 14 Dec. 1984; Wicker, "Tambora's lesson."

25. C. Sagan, "A nuclear theory that can't be tested" [letter to editor], *New York Times*, 29 Dec. 1984; J. Katz, "Nuclear winter effects not settled" [letter to editor], *New York Times*, 5 Jan. 1985; Rathjens, interview by Badash, 11 Feb. 1993.

26. P. Ehrlich, quoted in Rensberger, "National Academy of Sciences backs nuclear-winter theory."

27. L. Dembart, "Nuclear proliferation is an even icier prospect than nuclear winter," *Los Angeles Times*, 14 Dec. 1984.

28. J. Maddox, "Nuclear winter and carbon dioxide," *Nature* 312 (13 Dec. 1984), 593.

29. J. Maddox, "Where now with nuclear winter?" *Nature* 312 (20–27 Dec. 1984), 696; Pittock, "Report on reports."

30. S. Singer, letter to G. Keyworth, 25 Jan. 1985, with attached "NACOA statement on nuclear winter research," 25 Jan. 1985, Ronald Reagan Library, WH Staff File, Keyworth, box 23, folder NW#1.

31. John T. Chain Jr., memo to secretary of state, 16 Aug. 1984, declassified and released 21 Dec. 1984, and quoted in T. Malone, "International scientists on nuclear winter," *Bulletin of the Atomic Scientists* 41 (Dec. 1985), 52–55, quote on 53.

32. D. Lees, "A closer look at the bomb," *Macleans* 97 (20 Aug. 1984), 48.

33. H. Denton, "Forest fire to test theory on nuclear war," *Washington Post*, 3 Aug. 1985.

34. F. Kenneth Hare, letter to the society's president, 14 Jan. 1985, in *Nuclear Winter and Associated Effects: A Canadian Appraisal of the Environmental Impact of Nuclear War* (Royal Society of Canada, 1985), 2.

35. *Nuclear Winter and Associated Effects*, 17–18, 32–34, 52–53, quote on 52.

36. For an example of a controversy, see the 23 Jan. 1983 resolution on nuclear warfare passed by the council of the American Physical Society: "APS Council adopts nuclear-war resolution," *Physics Today* 36 (Mar. 1983), 63–64, and a critical response by presidential science advisor (and APS member) G. Keyworth: "APS steps into a political vortex," *Physics Today* 36 (May 1983), 8, 101.

37. E. Bollard et al., *The Threat of Nuclear War: A New Zealand Perspective* (Royal Society of New Zealand, 1985), 17.

38. P. Reynolds, "Popular responses to the New Zealand government's nuclear weapons policy: 1984–1986," *Politics: Journal of the Australasian Political Studies Association* 22 (May 1987), 60–66.

39. Statement by the Honourable David Lange, Prime Minister of New Zealand, on 25 September 1984, to the UN General Assembly. A copy is preserved in the Ronald Reagan Library, WH Office File, European and Soviet Affairs Directorate, National Security Council, box 91037, folder Nuclear Winter.

40. General Assembly Resolution 39/148F of 17 Dec. 1984; Secretary-General, *Climatic Effects of Nuclear War, Including Nuclear Winter*, Report A/40/449 of 28 Oct. 1985, and A/40/449/corrigendum 2 (a bibliography) of 23 Dec. 1985; General Assembly Resolution 40/152G of 16 Dec. 1985; General Assembly, "Programme budget implications of the draft resolution contained in document A/C.1/41/L.36/Rev. 1," A/C.1/41/L.79 of 11 Nov. 1986; General Assembly Resolution 41/86H of 4 Dec. 1986. See also *United Nations Disarmament Yearbook* 9 (1984), 149–152, and 10 (1985), 498–501.

41. H. Nix et al., *Study on the Climatic and Other Nuclear Effects of Nuclear War: Report of the Secretary General*, UN Report A/43/351 (May 1988; a printed version bore the date 1989), esp. 45–48. A 14-page condensation of the report also appeared, under the title *Climate and Other Global Effects of Nuclear War: Summary of a United Nations Study* (United Nations, 1989). See also S. Bergström et al., "The climatic and other global effects of nuclear war," *Environment* 30 (June 1988), 42–45; anon., "The nuclear twilight," *UN Chronicle* 25 (Sept. 1988), 16–17.

42. General Assembly Resolution 43/78D of 7 Dec. 1988; *United Nations Disarmament Yearbook* 12 (1987), 385–386. The UN quote is from M. Harwell and T. Hutchinson, *Environmental Consequences of Nuclear War*, volume 2: *Ecological and Agricultural Effects*, second edition (Wiley, 1989), xl.

43. No stories were found in the *New York Times Index* for the years 1985–1990.

44. F. Greenaway, *Science International: A History of the International Council of Scientific Unions* (Cambridge University Press, 1996). In 1998 the ICSU changed its name to International Council for Science.

45. Ibid., 176–182; G. White, "SCOPE: The first sixteen years," *Environmental Conservation* 14 (spring 1987), 7–13; V. Ploco, "Teenage SCOPE," *Nature* 318 (21 Nov. 1985), 204; A. Pittock et al., *Environmental Consequences of Nuclear War*, volume 1: *Physical and Atmospheric Effects*, second edition (Wiley, 1989), ix–x.

46. Schneider, interview by Badash, 25 Feb. 1986.

47. S. Bergström et al., *Effects of Nuclear War on Health and Health Services: Report of the International Committee of Experts in Medical Sciences and Public Health to Implement Resolution WHA34.38* (World Health Organization, 1984). This is sometimes cited as WHO Report A36.12 of 1983.

48. P. Crutzen, "The global environment after nuclear war," *Environment* 27 (Oct. 1985), 6–11, 34–37, esp. 37; Malone, "International scientists on nuclear winter"; Pittock, *Environmental Consequences*, volume 1, xxvii, 323–348. For a profile of Malone, see *Nuclear Winter* [newsletter of Center on the Consequences of Nuclear War], summer 1985, 2.

49. Crutzen, "The global environment," 37; Pittock, *Environmental Consequences*, volume 1, xxiii.

50. L. Dotto, *Planet Earth in Jeopardy: Environmental Consequences of Nuclear War* (Wiley, 1986), v; F. Warner, "Environmental consequences of nuclear war," *Science and Public Policy* 16 (Feb. 1989), 53–55.

51. Pittock, *Environmental Consequences*, volume 1, xxii; P. Gambles, "Cautious support from SCOPE," *Nature* 315 (13 June 1985), 534–535; B. Rensberger, "Study says billions might die in a 'nuclear winter' famine," *Washington Post*, 13 Sept. 1985; J. Gerstenzang, "'Nuclear winter' seen killing more than atomic blasts," *Los Angeles Times*, 13 Sept. 1985; T. Beardsley, "International committee echoes gloomy forecasts," *Nature* 317 (19 Sept. 1985), 191–192; R. Smith, "A grim portrait of the postwar world," *Science* 229 (20 Sept. 1985), 1245–1246; L. Tangley, "The year after," *BioScience* 35 (Oct. 1985), 536–540; Dotto, *Planet Earth in Jeopardy*; White, "SCOPE: The first sixteen years," 11.

52. Pittock, *Environmental Consequences*, volume 1, x.

53. E. Teller, "Widespread after-effects of nuclear war," *Nature* 310 (23 Aug. 1984), 621–624; S. Singer, "Is the 'nuclear winter' real?" *Nature* 310 (23 Aug. 1984), 625; J. Katz, "Atmospheric humidity in the nuclear winter," *Nature* 311 (4 Oct. 1984), 417; Pittock, *Environmental Consequences*, volume 1, 204.

54. Pittock, *Environmental Consequences*, volume 1, xi, xxi–xl, 194–214.

55. Ibid., 36, quote on 196–197.

56. Thomas Ackerman, quoted in Tangley, "The year after," 537.

57. Harwell and Hutchinson, *Environmental Consequences*, volume 2 (1985), ix, 480; second edition (1989), xxxiv; Rensberger, "Study says"; Gerstenzang, "'Nuclear winter' seen"; Smith, "A grim portrait";

M. Harwell, testimony, in US Congress, Senate, Committee on Armed Services, *Nuclear Winter and Its Implications*, hearings, 99th Congress, 1st Session, 2–3 Oct. 1985, 18.

58. J. Raloff, "Nuclear winter: Shutting down the farm?" *Science News* 128 (14 Sept. 1985), 171–173, quote on 171; Tangley, "The year after"; Harwell and Hutchinson, *Environmental Consequences*, volume 2, 338–347, 485–491.

59. Raloff, "Shutting down the farm?"; Tangley, "The year after."

60. Bergström, *Effects of Nuclear War on Health and Health Services*.

61. Harwell and Hutchinson, *Environmental Consequences*, volume 2, 501–503; Raloff, "Shutting down the farm?"

62. G. Lardner Jr., "Nuclear war effects said underestimated," *Washington Post*, 22 Sept. 1985; T. Postol, "Possible fatalities from superfires following nuclear attacks in or near urban areas," in F. Solomon and R. Marston, eds., *The Medical Implications of Nuclear War* (National Academy Press, 1986); D. Greer and L. Rifkin, "The immunological impact of nuclear war," in ibid.

63. Malone, "International scientists," 54; Harwell and Hutchinson, *Environmental Consequences*, volume 2, xxvi–xxix.

64. M. Harwell, "Nuclear winter—Why study the biological effects of nuclear war?" *Nuclear Winter* [newsletter of Center on the Consequences of Nuclear War], summer 1985, 3–4.

65. "Nuclear winter in Paris" [Science and the Citizen column], *Scientific American* 251 (Dec. 1984), 68.

66. Tangley, "The year after," 540; Rensberger, "Study says"; Gerstenzang, "'Nuclear winter' seen"; Beardsley, "International committee echoes"; T. Beardsley, "Mechanics of SCOPE report," *Nature* 317 (19 Sept. 1985), 192.

67. M. Harwell, "Sleep peacefully," *BioScience* 35 (Oct. 1985), 530–531. See also H. Grover and G. White, "Toward understanding the effects of nuclear war," *BioScience* 35 (Oct. 1985), 552–556.

68. "What to make of nuclear winter" [editorial], *Nature* 317 (19 Sept. 1985), 189–190.

69. Maddox, "Where now."

70. F. Baker, "SCOPE and nuclear war," *Nature* 313 (21 Feb. 1985), 619. See also F. Warner, "SCOPE response," *Nature* 317 (24 Oct. 1985), 666.

71. "Rethinking nuclear war" [editorial], *New York Times*, 29 Sept. 1985.

72. T. Powers, "Nuclear winter: Forecasts uncertain," *Los Angeles Times*, 29 Sept. 1985.

73. A. Westing, review of SCOPE volumes 1 and 2, and of L. Dotto's *Planet Earth in Jeopardy* in *Environmental Conservation* 13 (autumn 1986), 280–281, quote on 281. For another review of these and a few other volumes, see *Physics Today* 40 (Nov. 1987), 97–98.

74. C. Sagan, "Nuclear winter: A report from the world scientific community," *Environment* 27 (Oct. 1985), 12–15, 38–39, esp. 39.

75. Joseph Knox, quoted in Rensberger, "Study says."

76. M. Harwell, *Nuclear Winter: The Human and Environmental Consequences of Nuclear War* (Springer-Verlag, 1984).

77. J. London and G. White, eds., *The Environmental Effects of Nuclear War* (American Association for the Advancement of Science, 1984).

78. O. Greene, I. Percival, and I. Ridge, *Nuclear Winter: The Evidence and the Risks* (Blackwell, 1985).

79. P. Sederberg, ed., *Nuclear Winter, Deterrence, and the Prevention of Nuclear War* (Praeger, 1986).

80. L. Grinspoon, ed., *The Long Darkness: Psychological and Moral Perspectives on Nuclear Winter* (Yale University Press, 1986).

81. Dotto, *Planet Earth in Jeopardy*.

82. P. Kelly and J. Karas, "No Place to Hide: Nuclear Winter and the Third World" (press briefing document 43, Earthscan, London, 1986).

83. Robert Cess, quoted in A. Revkin, "Hard facts about nuclear winter," *Science Digest* 93 (Mar. 1985), 62–68, 77, 81, 83, quote on 64. For surveys of the major accomplishments and reports, through 1985, see J. Peterson, "Scientific studies of the unthinkable—the physical and biological effects of nuclear war," *Ambio* 15 (1986), 60–69; G. Golitsyn and N. Phillips, "Possible climatic consequences of a major nuclear war," World Climate Programme report 113 (World Meteorological Organization, Feb. 1986).

84. M. Chown, "Nuclear war: The spectators will starve," *New Scientist* 109 (2 Jan. 1986), 14–15, quote on 15.

Chapter 15

1. C. Sagan and V. Aleksandrov, testimony, in US Congress, House of Representatives, Committee on Science and Technology, Subcommittee on Natural Resources, Agriculture Research and Environment, *The Climatic, Biological, and Strategic Effects of Nuclear War*, hearings, 98th Congress, 2nd Session, 12 Sept. 1984, 45, 52–53. In a written response to questions from this same congressional committee, Leon Gouré claimed that public discussion of NW in the Soviet Union was sparse, most media attention being propaganda directed toward international opinion; in these hearings, 197. For a survey of Soviet work on NW, see S. Shenfield, "Nuclear winter and the USSR," *Millennium* 15 (summer 1986), 197–208, esp. 202–203.

2. C. Sagan, testimony, in US Congress, Joint Economics Committee, Subcommittee on International Trade, Finance, and Security Economics, *The Consequences of Nuclear War*, hearings, 98th Congress, 2nd Session, 11–12 July 1984, 94, 97; Sagan, "We can prevent nuclear winter," *Parade*, 30 Sept. 1984, 13–15; Turco et al., letter to editor, *Science* 227 (25 Jan. 1985), 358–362. Sagan later claimed that the Soviet budget for NW research was 2 million rubles; see his testimony in US House of Representatives, Committee on Science and Technology, Subcommittee on Natural Resources, Agriculture Research, and Environment, jointly with Committee on Interior and Insular Affairs, Subcommittee on Energy and the Environment, *Nuclear Winter*, hearing, 99th Congress, 1st Session, 14 Mar. 1985, 28. There was no

official rate of exchange, but a ruble was worth somewhat more than a dollar in Moscow, while "on the street" one could get perhaps 20–30 rubles for a dollar.

3. Quoted on p. 166 of A. Druyan, "Does science need to be popularized?" in Y. Terzian and E. Bilson, eds., *Carl Sagan's Universe* (Cambridge University Press, 1997). (Druyan was Sagan's wife.) Even before NW was publicized, the Soviet public and apparently some of its high officials exhibited a heightened level of fear of nuclear war. Much was caused by the Reagan administration's bellicosity. For the chief of the Soviet general staff, Marshal Nikolai V. Ogarkov, the American television film *The Day After* portrayed a real danger, and the superpowers' arsenals constituted "nuclear madness." See J. Burns, "Comments by Soviet marshal point up public's war jitters," *New York Times*, 11 Dec. 1983.

4. F. von Hippel, "The Committee of Soviet Scientists Against the Nuclear Threat," *F.A.S. Public Interest Report* 37 (Jan. 1984), 1–4, 8; von Hippel, "Arms control physics: The new Soviet connection," *Physics Today* 42 (Nov. 1989), 39–46, on 40. See also B. Levi, "US and USSR scientists jointly study arms control," *Physics Today* 37 (Feb. 1984), 18.

5. Y. Velikhov, ed., *The Night After . . . Scientists' Warning: Climatic and Biological Consequences of a Nuclear War* (Mir, 1985). Passages critical of the US are found on 113ff, 153–154, and 158–160.

6. C. Sagan, comments, in P. Ehrlich, *The Cold and the Dark*, 146.

7. R. Smith, "Soviets offer little help," *Science* 225 (6 July 1984), 31; Turco, interview by Badash and Kirtman, 20 Feb. 1985.

8. V. Aleksandrov, letter to editor, *Science* 225 (7 Sept. 1984), 978.

9. S. Thompson and R. Turco, letters to editor, *Science* 225 (7 Sept. 1984), 978–980.

10. "Nuclear winter in Paris," *Scientific American* 251 (Dec. 1984), 68.

11. For a valuable survey of Soviet activities, citing several Russian sources, see A. Lynch, *Political and Military Implications of the "Nuclear Winter" Theory* (Institute for East-West Security Studies, 1987), 17–25.

12. Caspar W. Weinberger, "The potential effects of nuclear war on the climate: A report to the United States Congress," Department of Defense, Mar. 1985, 10. The charge of propaganda cannot simply be dismissed. For example, the speech by physicist Sergei Kapitsa before the United Nations in January 1985 (S. Kapitsa, "A Soviet view of nuclear winter," *Bulletin of the Atomic Scientists* 41, Oct. 1985, 37–39) was thick in pious platitudes but thin in information and it endorsed a no-first-use pledge, the cessation of nuclear testing, and a reduction in the size of the arsenals.

13. Weinberger, "The potential effects," 16.

14. R. Perle, written testimony, in hearing, 14 Mar. 1985, 52.

15. D. Sanger, "Curb on campus computers: Pentagon vs. academia," *New York Times*, 17 Aug. 1985; Sanger, "US to restrict supercomputer use by Soviet scholars," *New York Times*, 10 Feb. 1986.

16. A. Robock, written testimony, in hearing, 14 Mar. 1985, 274–277, quote on 275; A. Robock, interview by L. Badash, 26 Feb. 1986.

Notes to Chapter 15

17. *Congressional Record—Senate* 131 (2 Apr. 1985), S3829. *Congressional Record—House* 131 (3 Apr. 1985), E1314; "Foreign Relations Authorization Act, 1986 and 1987," Public Law 99–93, 16 Aug. 1985, in *United States Statutes at Large*, 99 STAT. 448; US Congress, House of Representatives, Committee on Science, Space, and Technology, Subcommittee on International Scientific Cooperation, *To Examine US-Soviet Science and Technology Exchanges*, hearings, 100th Congress, 1st Session, 23 and 25 June 1987, 4–10.

18. John T. Chain, information memo to the secretary of state, 16 Aug. 1984, NRDC file.

19. William L. Ball III, assistant secretary of state, legislative and intergovernmental affairs, letter to Richard C. Lugar, chairman, Senate Committee on Foreign Relations, undated but April or early May 1985, Ronald Reagan Library, WHORM Subject File CO 165 325593; Edward Markey, comments, in hearing, 14 Mar. 1985, 35.

20. Stephen P. Rosen, NSC staff, memo to Robert M. Kimmitt, NSC staff, 23 May 1985; Robert M. Kimmitt, memo to Ronald K. Peterson, OMB staff, 28 May 1985, Ronald Reagan Library, WHORM Subject File CO 165 325593.

21. L. M. Thomas, EPA administrator, letter to G. Keyworth, 26 July 1985, and attached Keyworth memo to Robert McFarlane, national security advisor, 18 Sept. 1985, Ronald Reagan Library, WHORM Subject File, IT097 342839.

22. Von Hippel, "Arms control physics," 40. See also Levi, "US and USSR scientists."

23. S. Singer, manuscript titled "Nuclear winter and nuclear freeze," dated 10 June 1984, Ronald Reagan Library, WH Staff File, Keyworth, box 23, folder NW#4.

24. L. Gouré, testimony, in hearings, 12 Sept. 1984, 71.

25. Gerald Boyd, "Reagan says US will keep abiding by '79 arms pact," *New York Times*, 11 June 1985.

26. L. Gouré, "'Nuclear winter' in Soviet mirrors," *Strategic Review* 13 (summer 1985), 22–38, esp. 34. This paper appears to have been taken from a DNA-sponsored report by Gouré ("Soviet exploitation of the 'nuclear winter' hypothesis," DNA-TR-84-373, dated 5 June 1985) written under contract with Science Applications International Corporation. For coverage of a slightly later period, see Gouré, "An update of Soviet research on and exploration of 'nuclear winter,' 1984–1986," DNA-TR-86-404, dated 16 Sept. 1986.

27. Shenfield, "Nuclear winter and the USSR," quote on 197.

28. Schneider, interview by Badash, 13 Feb. 1985.

29. B. Martin, "Nuclear winter: Science and politics," *Science and Public Policy* 15 (Oct. 1988), 321–334, on 326.

30. For a willful and/or ignorant misinterpretation of some American views, see A. Krivopalov, "Answer to falsifiers," *Izvestiya*, 12 Dec. 1986, and a draft of a letter to the editor by George Rathjens, Stephen Schneider, and Starley Thompson dated 20 Mar. 1987. Both documents were provided by Professor Rathjens.

31. Von Hippel, interview by Badash, 8 Feb. 1993.

32. A. Ginsburg, G. Golitsyn, and A. Vasiliev, "Global consequences of a nuclear war: A review of recent Soviet studies," in *World Armaments and Disarmament: SIPRI Yearbook 1985* (Taylor and Francis, 1985).

33. M. May, letter to A. Hecht, 24 May 1984, and attached paper titled "Uncertainties in the generation and evolution of the atmospheric smoke burden," Ronald Reagan Library, WH Staff File, Keyworth, box 23, folder NW#1.

34. E. Teller, "Defensive weapons development" [letter to editor], *Science* 223 (20 Jan. 1984), 236.

35. Velikhov, *The Night After*, 9.

36. J. Hamblin, *Oceanographers and the Cold War: Disciples of Marine Science* (University of Washington Press, 2005).

37. Shenfield, "Nuclear winter and the USSR," 198.

38. G. Stenchikov, "Climatic consequences of nuclear war," in Velikhov, *The Night After*. See also Gouré, "An update."

39. D. Dickson, "Shakeup continues at Soviet Academy," *Science* 242 (11 Nov. 1988), 862.

40. G. Golitsyn and A. Ginsburg, "Possible climatic consequences of nuclear war and some natural analogs: Scientific investigation" (Soviet Scientists' Committee for the Defense of Peace Against Nuclear Threat, 1984). For another survey, see A. Ginsburg, *Planet Earth in the "Post-Nuclear" Age* (Nauka, 1988).

41. A. Gromyko et al., "Global consequences of nuclear war and the developing countries" (Soviet Scientists' Committee for the Defense of Peace Against Nuclear Threat, 1984), quote on 5.

42. The English translation is M. Budyko, G. Golitsyn, and Y. Izreal, *Global Climatic Catastrophes* (Springer-Verlag, 1988). For a brief survey of Russian research, see N. Moiseyev, "The ecological imperative," *Kommunist*, no. 12 (Aug. 1986) (English translation issued as Lawrence Livermore National Laboratory report UCRL-Trans-12141).

43. Budyko et al., *Global Climatic Catastrophes*, 81.

44. A. Ginsburg [also Ginzburg], "Some atmospheric and climatic effects of nuclear war," *Ambio* 18 (1989), 384–390.

45. "Excerpts from Gorbachev's speech on A-test moratorium," *New York Times*, 19 Aug. 1986.

46. R. Smith, "No trace of Soviet researcher," *Science* 229 (20 Sept. 1985), 1246; A. Revkin, "Missing: The curious case of Vladimir Alexandrov," *Science Digest* 94 (July 1986), 32–43; V. Rich, "Aleksandrov still not found," *Nature* 316 (8 Aug. 1985), 479; T. Beardsley, "Soviet missing person," *Nature* 317 (19 Sept. 1985), 191. For the view that the CIA or MI-6 was involved in the disappearance, because Washington militarists could not allow proof that NW was real, see I. Andronov, "Where is Vladimir Aleksandrov?" *Literaturnaya Gazeta*, no. 30 (23 July 1986) (English translation: Lawrence Livermore National Laboratory report UCRL-Trans-12103). For a summary of Aleksandrov's contributions to NW

and his disappearance, see Sagan and Turco, *Path*, 135–142. For a fictional account of Aleksandrov's disappearance, see T. Deary, *The Nuclear Winter Man (Classified)* (Houghton Mifflin, 1997).

47. V. Rich, "Scheme for world laboratory," *Nature* 317 (5 Sept. 1985), 7.

48. V. Rich, "Soviet researcher's part hyped," *Nature* 319 (16 Jan. 1986), 165.

Chapter 16

1. At least two novels for young readers appeared. See S. Curley, "Nuclear novels ask 'what if?' and get scary answers," *Orlando Sentinel*, 26 Jan. 1986.

2. S. Singer, "Nuclear winter and nuclear strategy," typescript dated 7 June 1984, p. 5, attached to Singer, letter to Edward Teller, 26 July 1984, Ronald Reagan Library, WH Staff File, Keyworth, box 23, folder NW#1.

3. Ibid., 7–11, quote on 8.

4. S. Singer, "Nuclear winter and nuclear freeze," *Disarmament* 7 (autumn 1984), 63–72, on 72.

5. Singer, "Nuclear winter and nuclear strategy," 7–11.

6. M. May, comments in panel on "Nuclear winter," California Workshop on American Foreign and Defense Policy, University of California, Berkeley, 3 Oct. 1984.

7. Singer, "Nuclear winter and nuclear strategy," 12–14.

8. Ibid., 14–15.

9. P. Romero, "Nuclear winter: Implications for US and Soviet nuclear strategy," Rand Graduate Institute report P-7009-RGI, Dec. 1984, quote on 3. See also D. Drew et al., *Nuclear Winter and National Security: Implications for Future Policy* (Air University Press, 1986).

10. Romero, "Nuclear winter," quote on 14.

11. Ibid.

12. J. Gertler, "Some policy implications of nuclear winter," Rand Corporation publication P-7045, Jan. 1985, quote on 7.

13. Ibid..

14. G. Quester, *The Future of Nuclear Deterrence* (Heath, 1986), 134–137, quote on 137.

15. Ibid., 138–142.

16. K. Payne and C. Gray, "Nuclear policy and the defensive transition," *Foreign Affairs* 62 (spring 1984), 820–842, quotes on 840–841.

17. C. Sagan, testimony, in US Congress, House of Representatives, Committee on Science and Technology, Subcommittee on Natural Resources, Agriculture Research, and Environment, and Committee

on Interior and Insular Affairs, Subcommittee on Energy and the Environment, *Nuclear Winter*, joint hearing, 99th Congress, 1st Session, 14 Mar. 1985, 23–24.

18. R. Turco, public lecture at UCLA, 11 Feb. 1991.

19. C. Gray, written testimony, in hearing, 14 Mar. 1985, 278–303, quotes on 288, 289, 290. See also C. Gray, "The nuclear winter thesis and US strategic policy," *Washington Quarterly* 8 (summer 1985), 85–96.

20. F. Hoeber and R. Squire, "The 'nuclear winter' hypothesis: Some policy implications," *Strategic Review* 13 (summer 1985), 39–46, esp. 41.

21. Ibid., 41.

22. M. May, "Nuclear winter: Strategic significance," *Issues in Science and Technology* 1 (winter 1985), 118–120, quote on 118.

23. Ibid..

24. A. Gore Jr., "Nuclear winter: Strategic significance," *Issues in Science and Technology* 1 (winter 1985), 120–123, quote on 122.

25. G. Rathjens and R. Siegel, "Nuclear winter: Strategic significance," *Issues in Science and Technology* 1 (winter 1985), 123–128, quote on 127.

26. T. Postol, "Nuclear winter: Strategic significance," *Issues in Science and Technology* 1 (winter 1985), 128–131.

27. J. Stone, written and oral testimony, in hearing, 14 Mar. 1985, 71–80, 150. For another centrist statement, published a year later, see J. Nye, "Nuclear winter and policy choices," *Survival* 28 (Mar.-Apr. 1986), 119–127.

28. A. Lynch, *Political and Military Implications of the "Nuclear Winter" Theory* (Institute for East-West Security Studies, 1987), 10–13.

29. A. Wohlstetter, "Between an unfree world and none: Increasing our choices," *Foreign Affairs* 63 (summer 1985), 962–994, quote on 962.

30. Ibid., 964–967, quotes on 964.

31. Ibid., 968–972, quotes on 971 and 972.

32. Ibid., 972–980, quote on 980.

33. Ibid., 980–994, quote on 990.

34. D. Horowitz and R. Lieber, "Nuclear winter and the future of deterrence," *Washington Quarterly* 8 (summer 1985), 59–70, quote on 59.

35. Ibid., 60–61, quotes on 60.

36. Ibid., 62–64.

37. Ibid., 64–69.

38. E. Cornish, "Mankind likely to survive nuclear war," *Los Angeles Times*, 9 Aug. 1985. For a popular survey of ways the Earth might end that does not mention NW, see Antony Milne, *Doomsday: The Science of Catastrophic Events* (Praeger, 2000).

39. P. Grier, "Is proving the terror of global nuclear war a waste of time?" *Christian Science Monitor*, 20 Nov. 1986.

40. S. Schneider, "Nuclear winter: Its discovery and implications," *1985 Britannica Book of the Year*, 27–33, on 32–33.

41. C. Sagan, testimony, in hearing, 14 Mar. 1985, 21, 25.

42. C. Sagan, "Fire and ice: Nuclear winter, part 2," quoted from radio show titled *Prescription for Survival*, Pacifica Radio Archive, 1986.

Chapter 17

1. J. Gertler, "Some policy implications of nuclear winter," Rand Corporation publication P-7045, Jan. 1985, quote on 17.

2. M. Altfeld and S. Cimbala, "Targeting for nuclear winter: A speculative essay," *Parameters, Journal of the US Army War College* 15 (autumn 1985), 8–15, quote on 8.

3. J. Nye, "Nuclear winter and policy choices," *Survival* 28 (Mar.-Apr. 1986), 119–127, on 122.

4. M. May, quoted in Powers, "Nuclear winter and nuclear strategy," on 63. For Theodore Postol's views on the value (none) of a treaty to ban targeting of cities, see his written reply to questions, in US Congress, House of Representatives, Committee on Science and Technology, Subcommittee on Natural Resources, Agriculture Research and Environment, *The Climatic, Biological, and Strategic Effects of Nuclear War*, hearings, 98th Congress, 2nd Session, 12 Sept. 1984, 210. For Leon Gouré's views, see hearings, 12 Sept. 1984, 199–200.

5. T. Postol, "Strategic confusion—with or without nuclear winter," *Bulletin of the Atomic Scientists* 41 (Feb. 1985), 14–17; Postol, "Nuclear winter: Strategic significance," *Issues in Science and Technology* 1 (winter 1985), 128–131; W. Broad, "US weighs risk that atom war could bring fatal nuclear winter," *New York Times*, 5 Aug. 1984; R. Smith, "DoD says 'nuclear winter' bolsters its plans," *Science* 227 (15 Mar. 1985), 1320.

6. Sagan, letter to Badash, 8 Sept. 1986.

7. Carrier, interview by Badash, 11 Feb. 1993.

8. A. Latter and E. Martinelli, "SDI: Defense or retaliation?" R&D Associates, 1985, quote on 5.

9. C. Herzenberg, "Nuclear winter and the Strategic Defense Initiative," *Physics and Society* 15 (Jan. 1986), 2–5; Herzenberg. "SDI—Weapons of mass destruction?" [paper delivered at annual meeting of the American Association for the Advancement of Science, Chicago, 1987]; T. Trowbridge, "Threat of laser winter from the Strategic Defense Initiative," Red Mesa Research, 1986. See also R. Scheer, " 'Star

Wars' lasers held able to incinerate cities," *Los Angeles Times*, 12 Jan. 1986; "Out of the frying pan" [editorial], *Los Angeles Times*, 14 Jan. 1986. Whether or not defense contractors consciously tried to avoid this hazard of directed-energy beams, R&D in following decades focused on kinetic energy (impact) concepts. The Soviets were highly critical of SDI, in large part because of its offensive potential. For this argument, see P. Westwick, " 'Space-strike weapons' and the Soviet response to SDI," *Diplomatic History* 32 (Nov. 2008), 955–979.

10. J. Gerstenzang, "Report warns Pentagon of perils of a nuclear winter," *Los Angeles Times*, 4 Sept. 1985; anon., "Civil defense doubts raised," *Washington Post*, 5 Sept. 1985.

11. William Cohen, quoting from Palomar Report, in US Congress, Senate, Committee on Armed Services, *Nuclear Winter and Its Implications*, hearings, 99th Congress, 1st Session, 2–3 Oct. 1985, 126.

12. E. Teller, "Civil defense is crucial," *New York Times*, 3 Jan. 1984; Matthew Wills, letter to editor, *New York Times*, 12 Jan. 1984.

13. P. Mitchell, remarks, in US Congress, Joint Economics Committee, Subcommittee on International Trade, Finance, and Security Economics, *The Consequences of Nuclear War*, hearings, 98th Congress, 2nd Session, 11–12 July 1984, 121.

14. R. Smith, "Nuclear winter attracts additional scrutiny," *Science* 225 (6 July 1984), 30–32, quote on 32.

15. Carrier, *The Effects on the Atmosphere*, 2.

16. R. Turco and C. Sagan, "Fire and ice: Nuclear winter, part 2," quoted from radio show titled *Prescription for Survival*, Pacifica Radio Archive, 1986.

17. A. Broyles and C. Chester, "Civil defense and the nuclear winter," presented at 1984 conference in Erice and published in W. Newman and S. Stipcich, eds., *International Seminar on Nuclear War, 4th Session* (World Scientific, 1992).

18. H. Maccabee, "Nuclear winter: How much do we really know?" *Reason* 17 (May 1985), 26–35, quotes on 26, 28.

19. Sagan, hearings, 11–12 July 1984, 76–77.

20. Rathjens, interview by Badash, 11 Feb. 1993.

21. C. Martin, letter to editor, *Washington Post*, 24 Dec. 1983, replying to E. Goodman's column, *Washington Post*, 10 Dec. 1983.

22. L. Gouré, written reply following testimony, in hearings, 12 Sept. 1984, 195–196; Gouré, "Mitigation of nuclear war impacts on agricultural production," in W. Newman and S. Stipcich, eds., *International Seminar on Nuclear War, 5th Session* (World Scientific, 1992).

23. L. Gouré, "An update of Soviet research on and exploration of 'nuclear winter,' 1984–1986," Defense Nuclear Agency report DNA-TR-86–404, 16 Sept. 1986, 39.

24. Gerstenzang, "Report warns Pentagon."

25. For a technical survey of the status of NW ca. 1986 and the repercussions for civil defense, see B. Levi, "Civil defense implications of nuclear winter," in J. Dowling and E. Harrell, eds., *Civil Defense: A Choice of Disasters* (American Institute of Physics, 1987).

26. J. Bennett, "Nuclear deterrence is itself vulnerable," *Christianity and Crisis* 44 (13 Aug. 1984), 296–301, quotes on 300.

27. D. Forrest, letter to editor, *New York Times*, 12 Aug. 1984.

28. B. Sparks, "The scandal of nuclear winter," *National Review* 37 (15 Nov. 1985), 28–38, quotes on 28.

29. R. Turco, B. Toon, and T. Ackerman, letter to editor, *National Review* 38 (31 Jan. 1986), 4, 10.

30. R. Whitten, letter to editor, *National Review* 38 (31 Jan. 1986), 10.

31. R. Seitz, letter to editor, *National Review* 38 (31 Jan. 1986), 14.

32. S. Singer, letter to editor, *National Review* 38 (31 Jan. 1986), 14. See also letter by A. Robock, *National Review* 38 (14 Feb. 1986), 6, another letter by R. Seitz, 38 (28 Feb. 1986), 10, and replies by Sparks, 38 (31 Jan. 1986), 15, 69, and 38 (14 Feb. 1986), 6, 10.

33. See, e.g., Turco et al., letter to editor. For some comments on professionalism and exclusion, see M. Curry, "Beyond nuclear winter: On the limitations of science in political debate," *Antipode* 18 (Dec. 1986), 244–267, esp. 260–261.

34. R. Seitz made this point at a Heritage Foundation symposium on 21 May 1985, as reported by Brad Sparks ("The scandal of nuclear winter," 32–33). See also the discussion in chapter 11 of this volume and A. Ehrlich, "Nuclear winter," *Bulletin of the Atomic Scientists* 40 (Apr. 1984), 1s-16s. The quoted passage is from 4s of Ehrlich's paper.

35. R. Seitz, "More on nuclear winter," *Nature* 315 (23 May 1985), 272.

36. R. Seitz, "Siberian fire as 'nuclear winter' guide," *Nature* 323 (11 Sept. 1986), 16–17.

37. Notes from meeting on 25–27 Feb. 1986 taken by L. Badash. For Turco's comment, in the official notes of the meeting, see R. Turco, "Summary of the DNA Global Effects Meeting," dated 25 Mar. 1986, and sent to participants, p. 26.

38. A. Ginsburg [also Ginzburg], "Some atmospheric and climatic effects of nuclear war," *Ambio* 18 (1989), 384–390, on 387.

39. R. Seitz, "In from the cold: 'Nuclear winter' melts down," *National Interest*, no. 5 (fall 1986), 3–17.

40. S. Schneider, "Nuclear autumn," *Wall Street Journal*, 25 Nov. 1986. See also letters by Glenn Helton and by Richard Raymond, *Wall Street Journal*, 18 Nov. 1986.

41. Sagan, letter to Badash, 23 Dec. 1986, with enclosure, dated 24 Nov. 1986, consisting of original version of TTAPS's letter to *Wall Street Journal*, responding to Seitz, edited and printed on 12 Dec. 1986.

42. R. Turco et al., "Nuclear winter remains a chilling prospect," *Wall Street Journal*, 12 Dec. 1986.

43. R. Seitz, "Apocalypse never," *Wall Street Journal*, 29 Jan. 1987.

44. E. Marshall, "Nuclear winter debate heats up," *Science* 235 (16 Jan. 1987), 271–273.

45. B. Bohor and R. Seitz, "Cuban K/T catastrophe," *Nature* 344 (12 Apr. 1990), 593; E. Marshall, "GE's cool diamonds prompt warm words," *Science* 250 (5 Oct. 1990), 25–26; T. Maugh II, "Their blue jade heaven is found," *Los Angeles Times*, 27 May 2002.

46. For a sociological analysis of the interplay of science and politics in the NW debate, see B. Martin, "Nuclear winter: Science and politics," *Science and Public Policy* 15 (Oct. 1988), 321–334.

Chapter 18

1. P. Shabecoff, "Conservationists urge policy shifts," *New York Times*, 26 June 1985. On Sagan's award, see *SANE World* 24 (Jan. 1985), 1. On Crutzen's award, see *Discover* 6 (Feb. 1985), 6.

2. K. Hendrix, "Beyond War: Movement takes disarming approach to world tensions," *Los Angeles Times*, 15 Sept. 1985. On the disappearance of nuclear activists, see P. Boyer, "Arms race as sitcom plot," *Bulletin of the Atomic Scientists* 45 (June 1989), 6–8.

3. L. Thomas, "A new hope in the nuclear age," *UNESCO Courier* 38 (May 1985), 24–25, quotes on 24.

4. D. Hafemeister, "History of the Forum on Physics and Society," *Physics and Society* 28 (Jan. 1999), 3–5.

5. D. Fisher, *Fire and Ice: The Greenhouse Effect, Ozone Depletion, and Nuclear Winter* (Harper and Row, 1990); Sagan and Turco, *Path*. For a positive review of the book by Sagan and Turco, see Len Ackland, "Chilly scenes of nuclear winter," *New York Times*, 6 Jan. 1991; for a sarcastically negative review, see J. Queenan, "Apocalypse again," *Wall Street Journal*, 3 Jan. 1991.

6. A. Druyan, "Does science need to be popularized?" in Y. Terzian and E. Bilson, eds., *Carl Sagan's Universe* (Cambridge University Press, 1997), 163–169, esp. 166.

7. G. Kauffman and L. Kauffman, "Atmospheric chemistry comes of age," *Today's Chemist at Work* 5 (Nov. 1996), 52–58, quote on 53.

8. S. Gould, "Continuity," *Natural History* 93 (Apr. 1984), 4, 6, 10.

9. A. Geyer, "The nativity and nuclear winter," *Christian Century* 101 (19–26 Dec. 1984), 1199–1200.

10. Toon, interview by Badash and Kirtman, 6 Mar. 1985.

11. The text of the appeal appears in "Mrs Gandhi joins appeal for nuclear disarmament by six world leaders," *India News* (Information Service, Embassy of India, Washington), 23 (28 May 1984), 1. See also "Leaders of 6 nations urge nuclear freeze, arms cuts," *Los Angeles Times*, 23 May 1984.

12. "Delhi Declaration," issued 28 Jan. 1985, available from the Embassy of India, Washington. See also R. Tempest, "India summit calls for ban on space weapons," *Los Angeles Times*, 29 Jan. 1985.

13. Powers, "Nuclear winter and nuclear strategy," quote on 64.

14. S. Singer, "Nuclear winter and nuclear freeze," *Disarmament* 7 (autumn 1984), 63–72, quote on 72.

15. B. Gwertzman, "New Zealander wants to avoid fight with US," *New York Times*, 16 July 1984; Gwertzman, "US is rebuffed on visit by ship to New Zealand," *New York Times*, 5 Feb. 1985; C. Mohr, "New Zealand rebuff: A baffling furor," *New York Times*, 7 Feb. 1985; P. Reynolds, "Popular responses to the New Zealand government's nuclear weapons policy: 1984–1986," *Politics: Journal of the Australasian Political Studies Association* 22 (May 1987), 60–66.

16. R. Lindsey, "US, in talks with Australia, bars defense of New Zealand," *New York Times*, 12 Aug. 1986. See also Dora Alves, *Anti-Nuclear Attitudes in New Zealand and Australia* (Government Printing Office/National Defense University Press, 1985); M. Pugh, *The ANZUS Crisis, Nuclear Visiting, and Deterrence* (Cambridge University Press, 1989); F. Donini, *ANZUS in Revision: Changing Defense Features of Australia and New Zealand in the Mid-1980s* (Air University Press, 1991).

17. Statement by the Honourable David Lange, Prime Minister of New Zealand, on 25 September 1984, to the UN General Assembly. A copy is preserved in the Ronald Reagan Library, WH Office File, European and Soviet Affairs Directorate, National Security Council, box 91037, folder Nuclear Winter.

18. Ibid.

19. K. Dewes and R. Green, *Aotearoa/New Zealand at the World Court* (Raven, 1999), 7, 15, 17–19; "The queen down under" [editorial], *Wall Street Journal*, 28 Feb. 1986.

20. Council of the New Zealand Ecological Society, a "Statement of Concern" titled "The environmental consequences to New Zealand of nuclear warfare in the Northern Hemisphere" (New Zealand Ecological Society, 5 Dec. 1964). See also Alves, *Anti-Nuclear Attitudes*, 36–38.

21. E. Bollard et al., *The Threat of Nuclear War: A New Zealand Perspective* (Royal Society of New Zealand, 1985), 48–49.

22. W. Green, T. Cairns, and J. Wright, *New Zealand After Nuclear War* (New Zealand Planning Council, 1987). For a summary of the report, see Wren Green, "New Zealand after nuclear war," *Environment* 30 (June 1988), 28. For the report's methodology, see Karen Cronin and W. Green, "The New Zealand nuclear impacts study," *Ambio* 18 (1989), 407–410. See also W. Green, "Nuclear war impacts on non-combatant societies: An important research task," *Ambio* 18 (1989), 402–406.

23. Peace and Justice Forum, Wellington Labour Regional Council, "Alternatives to ANZUS: A paper for discussion," unpublished document in National Library of New Zealand, undated but probably 1983, especially 9–10. See also Alves, *Anti-Nuclear Attitudes*, 29–36.

24. L. Arnold, *Britain and the H-Bomb* (Palgrave, 2001), 96–98, 154.

25. Peace and Justice Forum, "Alternatives to ANZUS," 13.

26. J. Falk, *Taking Australia Off the Map* (William Heinemann Australia, 1983), 116–118; D. Ball, *A Suitable Piece of Real Estate: American Installations in Australia* (Hale and Iremonger, 1980).

27. L. Arnold, *A Very Special Relationship: British Atomic Weapons Trials in Australia* (HMSO, 1987).

28. Ball, *A Suitable Piece of Real Estate*.

29. L. Wittner, *Resisting the Bomb: A History of the World Nuclear Disarmament Movement, 1954–1970* (Stanford University Press, 1997), 25–26, 76–78.

30. G. Brown, "Detection of nuclear weapons and the US non-disclosure policy," working paper 107, Strategic and Defence Studies Centre, Australian National University, Nov. 1986, 1–4; Alves, *Anti-Nuclear Attitudes*, 41–45; Falk, *Taking Australia Off the Map*, 122, 158–162.

31. Ball, *A Suitable Piece of Real Estate*, 17. For further context about nuclear issues in Australia, see Alice Cawte, *Atomic Australia, 1944–1990* (University of New South Wales Press, 1992); Roy MacLeod, "The atom comes to Australia: Reflections on the Australian nuclear programme, 1953 and 1993," *History and Technology* 11 (1994), 299–315; MacLeod, "Resistance to nuclear technology: Optimists, opportunists, and opposition in Australian nuclear history," in M. Bauer, ed., *Resistance to New Technology: Nuclear Power, Information Technology, and Biotechnology* (Cambridge University Press, 1995); J. Hymans, "Isotopes and identity: Australia and the nuclear weapons option, 1949–1999," *Nonproliferation Review* 7 (spring 2000), 1–23.

32. I. Galbally, P. Crutzen, and H. Rodhe, "Some changes in the atmosphere over Australia that may occur due to a nuclear war," in M. Denborough, ed., *Australia and Nuclear War* (Croom Helm Australia, 1983).

33. A. Pittock, review of P. Ehrlich, *The Cold and the Dark* in *Climatic Change* 7 (June 1985), 253–255, quote on 254.

34. A. Pittock, "The atmospheric effects of nuclear war," in Denborough, ed., *Australia and Nuclear War*.

35. A. Pittock, "Poor outlook for tropical weather," *Nature* 315 (20 June 1985), 634. See also Pittock, "Rapid developments on nuclear winter," *Search* 17 (Jan.-Feb. 1986), 23–24. For a popular survey, see R. Beckmann, "Nuclear winter down under," *Ecos* 49 (spring 1986), 3–8.

36. A. Pittock, *Beyond Darkness: Nuclear Winter in Australia and New Zealand* (Macmillan, 1987), 133, 166–168, 170–171, 178, 188, 202, quote on 132. See also Pittock's juxtaposition of NW and global warming in "Climatic catastrophes: The international implications of the greenhouse effect and nuclear winter," working paper 20, Peace Research Centre, Australian National University, 1987.

37. Department of Foreign Affairs, "Uranium, the joint facilities, disarmament, and peace" (Commonwealth Government Printer, 1984), quotes on 11, 16–17. The policies stated in 1984 did not change two years later, in another position paper, although the phrase "early nuclear extinction" had to suffice for a gesture to NW. See Department of Foreign Affairs, "Australia and disarmament: Steps in the right direction" (Australian Government Publishing Service, 1986).

38. P. Keable, "Sold for a brass razoo?" in J. Wober, ed., *Television and Nuclear Power: Making the Public Mind* (Ablex, 1992), on 240.

39. Ye Du Zhang, interview by L. Badash, 7 Sept. 1994. For an example of British interest, see N. Myers, "Nuclear war: Potential biospheric impacts in Britain," *Ambio* 18 (1989), 449–453.

40. "Dead dinosaurs, live politics" [editorial], *New York Times*, 2 Nov. 1985.

41. H. London, "The new prophets of doom," *USA Today*, Sept. 1984. [This article, from the newspaper's microfilmed edition, bears only the month and year.]

42. Singer, "Nuclear winter and nuclear freeze," quote on 65.

43. G. Rathjens, comments in panel on "Nuclear winter," California Workshop on American Foreign and Defense Policy, University of California, Berkeley, 3 Oct. 1984.

44. G. Rochlin, comments in panel on 3 Oct. 1984.

45. F. Dyson, *Infinite in All Directions* (Harper and Row, 1988), 259.

46. J. Holdren, comments in panel on 3 Oct. 1984; G. Rathjens, letter to L. Grinspoon, 3 June 1986; Rathjens, letter to J. Galbraith, 2 Jan. 1987. Copies of these letters were provided by Professor Rathjens. Others warned of overstating the consequences of nuclear war; see, e.g., E. Zuckerman, "The end-of-the-world scenarios," *New York Times*, 25 Nov. 1984.

47. G. Rathjens, comments in panel on 3 Oct. 1984.

48. C. Sagan, *Cosmos* (Random House, 1980), 320–331.

49. Rathjens, interview by Badash, 11 Feb. 1993; Rathjens, letter to L. Grinspoon, 3 June 1986; Rathjens, letter to J. Galbraith, 2 Jan. 1987. Copies of these letters were provided by Professor Rathjens.

50. Rathjens, interview by Badash, 11 Feb. 1993. The quoted phrase is from Rathjens, comments in panel on 3 Oct. 1984.

51. Dyson, *Infinite in All Directions*, 259–260. This book is the published version of the Gifford Lectures, delivered at Aberdeen, Scotland, in 1985.

52. C. Sagan, "On minimizing the consequences of nuclear war," *Nature* 317 (10 Oct. 1985), 485–488.

53. E. Teller, "Widespread after-effects of nuclear war," *Nature* 310 (23 Aug. 1984), 621–624, quote on 624.

54. Sagan, "On minimizing the consequences," 488.

55. E. Teller, "Climatic change with nuclear war," *Nature* 318 (14 Nov. 1985), 99.

56. Ben Franklin, "Cool Republicans," *Washington Spectator* 24 (15 Sept. 1998), 4.

57. Of course there may have been an occasional exception, but the lack of widespread activity is noticeable. For confirmation that one organization deliberately edged around NW, see R. Bland, letter to L. Badash, 28 Dec. 1989.

58. Toon, interview by Badash and Kirtman, 6 Mar. 1985.

59. E. Yoder Jr., "Good Lord, deliver us," *Los Angeles Times*, 31 Dec. 1985.

Chapter 19

1. Informal comments by several scientists, recorded by L. Badash at conference on NW sponsored by DNA, Santa Barbara, 12 Feb. 1985.

2. R. Turco, "Summary of the DNA Global Effects Meeting, NASA Ames Research Center, February [25–27], 1986," dated 25 Mar. 1986, and sent to participants, p. 8. See also many of the papers, overheads, or abstracts from the meeting in *Technical Papers Presented at the Defense Nuclear Agency Global Effects Review* (Kaman Tempo, 1986).

3. L. Badash, notes of several lectures at DNA conference, 25–27 Feb. 1986; "Abstracts of talks for Defense Nuclear Agency program technical review held at NASA Ames Research Center, Moffett Field, Calif, Feb 25–27, 1986."

4. T. Beardsley, "Nuclear winter: Has winter become fall?" *Nature* 320 (13 Mar. 1986), 103.

5. A. Broyles, "The uncertainties in nuclear winter predictions," Lawrence Livermore National Laboratory preprint (UCRL-94060, Jan. 1986) of paper prepared for forum on "Nuclear Winter: Strategic and Diplomatic Implications," Virginia Polytechnic Institute.

6. J. Knox, "Personal reflections on the diplomatic and policy implications of the environmental consequences of nuclear war," Lawrence Livermore National Laboratory preprint (UCRL-94059, Jan. 1986) of paper prepared for forum on "Nuclear Winter: Strategic and Diplomatic Implications," Virginia Polytechnic Institute.

7. G. Betourne, "Position paper" and G. Waxmonsky, "US-USSR environmental agreement: Potential for nuclear winter dialogue," distributed before the conference at Virginia Polytechnic Institute by its organizer (Morton Nadler) to all attendees, with cover letter and packet of briefing papers, 5 Feb 1986.

8. "Towards a mild nuclear winter?" [editorial], *Nature* 323 (11 Sept. 1986), 95–96; G. Golitsyn, "New developments from the USSR," *Environment* 28 (Oct. 1986), 5, 44.

9. D. Simonett et al., "Estimation of the magnitude and spatial distribution of combustible materials in urban areas: A case study of the San Jose area, California," *Fire and Materials* 12 (1988), 95–108. See also the papers, overheads, or abstracts from the meeting in *Technical Papers Presented at the Defense Nuclear Agency Global Effects Review—7–9 April 1987* (Kaman Tempo, 1987), vol. 1, pp. 2, 6, 34; H. Veregin, "Error modeling and macro-risk assessment for spatial data: The case of the nuclear winter base term," a summary of his dissertation, presented at the IGCC Fellows Conference, fall 1989.

10. *Defense Nuclear Agency Global Effects Review*, vol. 1, pp. 51, 105, 121, 127, 247, 248, 264, 286, quotes on iii.

11. For a concise survey of the literature, with commentary on the value of some publications, see D. Diermendjian, "'Nuclear winter': A brief review and comments on some recent literature," report P-7233, Rand Corporation, 1988. For a technical survey of climatic effects, see M. MacCracken, "The environmental effects of nuclear war," in D. Schroeer and D. Hafemeister, eds., *Nuclear Arms Technologies in the 1990s* (American Institute of Physics, 1988).

12. Pittock, *Environmental Consequences of Nuclear War*, volume 1, xxxviii–xl; SCOPE ENUWAR Committee, "Environmental consequences of nuclear war: An update. Severe global-scale effects of nuclear war reaffirmed," *Environment* 29 (May 1987), 4–5, 45; R. Small, "Atmospheric smoke loading from a nuclear attack on the United States," *Ambio* 18 (1989), 377–383; S. Ghan, M. MacCracken, and J. Walton, "Climatic response to large atmospheric smoke injections: Sensitivity studies with a tropospheric general circulation model," *Journal of Geophysical Research* 93 (20 July 1988), 8315–8337. See also F. Warner, "Severe global effects of nuclear war," *Disarmament* 10 (summer 1987), 63–71; Warner, "The environmental effects of nuclear war," *Environment* 30 (June 1988), 2–7.

13. G. Golitsyn and M. MacCracken, "Possible climatic consequences of a major nuclear war," World Climate Research Programme report 142 (World Meteorological Organization, 1987), 11. For another detailed survey, see S. Schneider and S. Thompson, "Simulating the climatic effects of nuclear war," *Nature* 333 (19 May 1988), 221–227. See also A. Berger, "Nuclear winter, or nuclear fall?" *Eos* 67 (12 Aug. 1986), 617–621.

14. R. Malone, L. Auer, G. Glatzmaier, M. Wood, and O. Toon, "Influence of solar heating and prescription scavenging on the simulated lifetime of post-nuclear war smoke," *Science* 230 (18 Oct. 1985), 317–319; Malone, Auer, Glatzmaier, Wood, and Toon, "Nuclear winter: Three-dimensional simulations including interactive transport, scavenging, and solar heating of smoke," *Journal of Geophysical Research* 91 (20 Jan. 1986), 1039–1053; Pittock, *Environmental Consequences*, volume 1, xl–xli; R. Turco and G. Golitsyn, "Global effects of nuclear war," *Environment*, 30 (June 1988), 8–16. See also R. Vupputuri, "The effect of ozone photochemistry on stratospheric and surface temperature changes due to large atmospheric injections of smoke and NOx by a large-scale nuclear war," *Atmospheric Environment* 20 (1986), 665–680.

15. C. Covey, "Protracted climatic effects of massive smoke injections into the atmosphere," *Nature* 325 (19 Feb. 1987), 701–703.

16. S. Thompson, V. Ramaswamy, and C. Covey, "Atmospheric effects of nuclear war aerosols in general circulation model simulations: Influence of smoke optical properties," *Journal of Geophysical Research* 92 (20 Sept. 1987), 10,942–10,960; Ghan et al., "Climatic response," 8315.

17. B. Golding, P. Goldsmith, N. Machin, and A. Slingo, "Importance of local mesoscale factors in any assessment of nuclear winter," *Nature* 319 (23 Jan. 1986), 301–303; S. Schneider, S. Thompson, and C. Covey, "The mesoscale effects of nuclear winter," *Nature* 320 (10 Apr. 1986), 491–492, quote on 491.

18. C. Molenkamp, "Simulation of coastal flow fields when the incident solar radiation is obscured," Lawrence Livermore National Laboratory preprint (UCRL-94994, Dec. 1986).

19. Golitsyn and MacCracken, "Climatic response," 12–19; A. Pittock, "Climatic catastrophes: The international implications of the greenhouse effect and nuclear winter," working paper 20, Peace Research Centre, Australian National University, July 1987, 14–15; Pittock et al., "Climatic effects of smoke and dust produced from nuclear conflagrations" and Ackerman et al., "Persistent effects of residual smoke layers," both in P. Hobbs and M. McCormick, eds., *Aerosols and Climate* (A. Deepak, 1988). See also Secretary-General, *Study on the Climatic and Other Global Effects of Nuclear War*, report A/43/351 (United Nations, 1989), 21.

20. S. Singer, "Re-analysis of the nuclear winter phenomenon," *Meteorology and Atmospheric Physics* 38 (1988), 228–239; G. Maranto, "The infrared herring of nuclear summer," *Discover* 8 (May 1987), 8–9. See also Singer, "Nuclear winter or nuclear summer?" in S. Singer, ed., *Global Climate Change: Human and Natural Influences* (Paragon House, 1989).

21. R. Turco et al., "Nuclear winter: Global consequences of multiple nuclear explosions," *Science* 222 (23 Dec. 1983), 1283–1292; Turco et al., "Climate and smoke: An appraisal of nuclear winter," *Science* 247 (12 Jan. 1990), 166–176. For a reporter's view emphasizing how wrong (not how correct) the NW idea was, see M. Browne, "Nuclear winter theorists pull back," *New York Times*, 23 Jan. 1990. For a letter to the editor replying to Browne, see C. Sagan and R. Turco, "Don't relax about nuclear winter just yet," *New York Times*, 5 Mar. 1990. For another technical review, see Turco et al., "Nuclear winter: Physics and physical mechanisms," *Annual Review of Earth and Planetary Sciences* 19 (1991), 383–422.

22. P. Crutzen, I. Galbally, and C. Brühl, "Atmospheric effects from post-nuclear fires," *Climatic Change* 6 (1984), 323–364; J. Penner, "Uncertainties in the smoke source term for 'nuclear winter' studies," *Nature* 324 (20 Nov. 1986), 222–226; R. Turco et al., "Climate and smoke: An appraisal of nuclear winter," paper presented at SCOPE workshop in Bangkok, 9–13 Feb. 1987, cited by Pittock, *Environmental Consequences*, volume 1, xxxii; R. Small, B. Bush, and M. Dore, "Initial smoke distribution for nuclear winter calculations," *Aerosol Science and Technology* 10 (1989), 37–50; Golitsyn and MacCracken, "Possible climatic consequences," 3–6. See also B. Bush and R. Small, "A note on the ignition of vegetation by nuclear weapons," *Combustion Science and Technology* 52 (1987), 25–38; Bush and Small, "Nuclear winter source-term studies: Volume II—The classification of US cities," DNA-TR-86–220-V2 report (Pacific-Sierra Research Corporation, 1987).

23. W. Einfeld, B. Mokler, B. Zak, and D. Morrison, "A characterization of smoke particles from small, medium and large-scale hydrocarbon pool fires," in M. Pilat and E. Davis, eds., *Aerosols 87*, abstracts of the American Association for Aerosol Research, annual meeting, 14–17 Sept. 1987, Seattle, cited by Pittock, *Environmental Consequence*, volume 1, xxxii, 48–49; Small et al., "Initial smoke distribution"; I. Petryanov-Sokolov, A. Sutugin, and A. Andronova, "Possible influence of mass fires on composition and optical properties of the atmosphere," paper presented at SCOPE workshop in Moscow, 1988, cited by Pittock, *Environmental Consequences*, volume 1, xxxiii; G. Golitsyn, "New developments from the USSR," *Environment* 28 (Oct. 1986), 5, 44; R. Small, "Some notes on counterforce attacks, urban fires, and uncertainties in nuclear winter theories," distributed before conference at Virginia Polytechnic Institute by its organizer (Morton Nadler) to all forum members, with cover letter and packet of briefing papers, 5 Feb 1986.

24. J. Penner and C. Molenkamp, "Predicting the consequences of nuclear war: Precipitation scavenging of smoke," *Aerosol Science and Technology* 10 (1989), 51–62; Secretary-General, *Study on the Climatic and Other Global Effects*, 4, 18; J. Penner and W. Porch, "Coagulation in smoke plumes after a nuclear war," *Atmospheric Environment*, 21 (1987), 957–969. See also Golitsyn and MacCracken, "Possible climatic consequences," 7–10; L. Edwards and J. Penner, "Potential nucleation scavenging of smoke particles over large fires: A parametric study," in Hobbs and McCormick, eds., *Aerosols and Climate*.

25. Pittock, *Environmental Consequences*, volume 1, xxxiii–xxxvi; Secretary-General, *Study on the Climatic and Other Global Effects*, 4; Jenny Nelson, "Fractality of sooty smoke: Implications for the severity of

nuclear winter," *Nature* 339 (22 June 1989), 611–613; Shawna Vogel, "Up in smoke," *Discover* 10 (Nov. 1989), 26. Schneider is quoted in W. Booth, "Soot study puts new chill into 'nuclear winter,'" *Washington Post*, 22 June 1989.

26. Pittock, *Environmental Consequences*, volume 1, xxxv–xxxviii; A. Robock, "Enhancement of surface cooling due to forest fire smoke," *Science* 242 (11 Nov. 1988), 911–913; L. Stammer, "N. California fires boost nuclear winter theory," *Los Angeles Times*, 11 Nov. 1988; Turco and Golitsyn, "Global effects"; C. Covey, "Environmental studies of nuclear war: A recent synthesis and future prospects—An editorial/review essay," *Climatic Change* 10 (Feb. 1987), 1–10, on 3. See also K. Heikes, L. Ransohoff, and R. Small, "Early smoke plume and cloud formation by large area fires," DNA-TR-87–176 report (Pacific-Sierra Research Corporation, 1987).

27. Golitsyn and MacCracken, "Possible climatic consequences," 5–7.

28. Anon., "A safe test for nuclear winter," *Newsweek*, 7 Apr. 1986, 7; A. Revkin, "Theory to stand test of fire, smoke," *Los Angeles Times*, 3 Sept. 1986; Revkin, "1,000-acre forest fire to burn in the name of science," *Los Angeles Times*, 3 Dec. 1986; Revkin, "Scientific burn of brush ends when copter crashes at site," *Los Angeles Times*, 4 Dec. 1986; J. Mathews, "To build a fire, just for the research of it," *Washington Post*, 4 Dec. 1986; Revkin, "Delayed test blaze finally touched off," *Los Angeles Times*, 13 Dec. 1986; J. Cummings, "Brush set afire to test nuclear war aftermath," *New York Times*, 13 Dec. 1986.

29. L. Stammer, "'Nuclear winter' theory put to test in burn near L.A.," *Los Angeles Times*, 23 June 1987; anon., "Trying to gauge nuclear effects," *New York Times*, 6 Sept. 1987; anon., "Fires in West aiding study of nuclear war," *New York Times*, 20 Oct. 1987.

30. G. Carrier, "Nuclear winter, current understanding," *Proceedings of the American Philosophical Society* 134 (June 1990), 83–89, quote on 89.

31. T. Ackerman and W. Cropper, "Scaling global climate projections to local biological assessments," *Environment* 30 (June 1988), 31–34; M. Harwell and T. Hutchinson, *Environmental Consequences of Nuclear War*, volume 2: *Ecological and Agricultural Effects*, second edition (Wiley, 1989), xxxx–xlvii; Harwell and Christine Harwell, "Updating the 'nuclear winter' debate," *Bulletin of the Atomic Scientists* 43 (Oct. 1987), 42–44.

32. M. Harwell and A. Freeman, "The biological consequences of nuclear war: Initiating national case studies," *Environment* 30 (June 1988), 25–30, quotes on 26; Harwell and Hutchinson, *Environmental Consequences*, volume 2, final quote on xxxiii.

33. S. McNaughton, R. Ruess, and M. Coughenour, "Ecological consequences of nuclear war," *Nature* 321 (29 May 1986), 483–487, quote on 487.

34. Harwell and Freeman, "The biological consequences," first quote on 27; Harwell and Hutchinson, *Environmental Consequences*, volume 2, quotes on l.

35. Committee on Interagency Radiation Research and Policy Coordination, *Review of SCOPE 28 Report on Environmental Consequences of Nuclear War*, volume 2: *Ecological and Agricultural Effects* (Office of Science and Technology Policy, 1988), quote on xiv.

36. No records were located in the Ronald Reagan Library. Freedom of Information Act requests to the Department of Agriculture and to the Office of Science and Technology Policy turned up no relevant documents. No articles were found in the *New York Times*, the *Washington Post*, or *Science*. For the only places where the CIRRPC report was noted, see Harwell and Hutchinson, *Environmental Consequences*, volume 2, xxxviii–xxxix; Sagan and Turco, *Path*, 77–78.

Chapter 20

1. General Accounting Office, "Nuclear winter: Uncertainties surround the long-term effects of nuclear war," GAO/NSIAD-86-62 (Mar. 1986). No stories on this report were found in the *Washington Post*, the *New York Times*, or the *Wall Street Journal*. The AP account by Tim Ahern was published in the *Lexington* [Kentucky] *Herald-Leader*, 30 Mar. 1986, the *San Diego Tribune*, 29 Mar. 1986, and the *Philadelphia Daily News*, 29 Mar. 1986. See also anon., "Nuclear winter status report," *Science News* 129 (19 Apr. 1986), 249.

2. S. Begley, "A milder nuclear winter: A new Pentagon report finds the danger more remote—but still real," *Newsweek* 107 (31 Mar. 1986), 65.

3. Anon., "Technical issues update," undated and without cover or letterhead, but with covering letter from William H. Taft IV, deputy secretary of defense, to Barry Goldwater, chair, Senate Committee on Armed Services, 9 May 1986.

4. Anon., "Scientists question Pentagon report," *Nuclear Winter* [newsletter of Center on the Consequences of Nuclear War], spring-summer 1986, 1, 3.

5. G. Wilson, "Pentagon reform bill sweeps through Senate," *Washington Post*, 8 May 1986.

6. Anon., "Immediate criticism greets DoD nuclear winter report," *Nuclear Winter* [newsletter of Center on the Consequences of Nuclear War], spring-summer 1986, 1, 4; R. Smith, "DoD declines to consider impact of nuclear winter," *Science* 232 (30 May 1986), 1088–1089; anon., "DoD makes little comment on nuclear winter policy," *Environment* 28 (June 1986), 21.

7. A search of the printed index to the *Congressional Record* failed to locate any comments on the 1986 DoD report.

8. Anon., "Pentagon report: Nuclear winter of discontent," *Washington Post*, 14 May 1986.

9. Computer searches of the *New York Times*, *Wall Street Journal*, *Los Angeles Times*, and America's Newspapers databases found no stories.

10. The Defense Authorization Act for FY 1987 and the Secretary of Defense's reply are reproduced in A. Robock, "Policy implications of nuclear winter and ideas for solutions," *Ambio* 18 (1989), 360–366, on 364 and 365. The DoD's "reports" for 1987 and 1988 thus seem to have been a page or so of disclaimers that anything new was worth reporting. Computer searches for these years in the newspapers and database mentioned above were unsuccessful, and a request for the reports to the Pentagon's public information office went unanswered.

11. S. Schneider, letter to F. Press, 15 May 1986. A copy of this letter was provided by Professor Schneider.

12. G. White, letter to S. Schneider, 29 May 1986. A copy of this letter was provided by Professor Schneider.

13. S. Thompson, "Global interactive transport simulations of nuclear war smoke," *Nature* 317 (5 Sept. 1985), 35–39.

14. A. Pittock, "Climatic catastrophes: The international implications of the greenhouse effect and nuclear winter," working paper 20, Peace Research Centre, Australian National University, 1987; Pittock, letter and enclosure to S. Schneider, 1 Nov. 1986 (a copy of this letter was provided by Professor Schneider).

15. S. Thompson and S. Schneider, "Nuclear winter reappraised," *Foreign Affairs* 64 (summer 1986), 981–1005, on 981–982.

16. R. Ebisch, "The fall of civilization," *Boulder* [Colorado] *Camera*, 23 May 1986.

17. Thompson and Schneider, "Nuclear winter reappraised," quote on 983.

18. Ibid., quotes on 988.

19. Ibid., quote on 991.

20. For a popular summary of the SCOPE report, see L. Dotto, *Planet Earth in Jeopardy: Environmental Consequences of Nuclear War* (Wiley, 1986), 3, 18–19.

21. Thompson and Schneider, "Nuclear winter reappraised," quote on 998.

22. On "cold and dark" views, see "Nuclear thaw" [editorial], *National Review* 42 (19 Feb. 1990), 18; S. Sinberg, "Springtime for nuclear winter: No need to duck and cover; just let a smile be your bomb shelter," *Omni* 14 (Apr. 1992), 98.

23. "Nuclear autumn" [editorial], *Detroit News*, 30 June 1986. Images of pointy-headed scientists who were out of touch with reality or who pursued sinister political goals were not uncommon, with Sagan often depicted. See "Nuclear thaw," *National Review*; Sinberg, "Springtime for nuclear winter." See also S. Schneider and S. Thompson, "Thanks News, but we disagree" [letter to editor], *Detroit News* (26 Aug. 1986); J. Gleick, "Less drastic theory emerges on freezing after a nuclear war," *New York Times*, 22 June 1986; "Towards a mild nuclear winter?" [editorial], *Nature* 323 (11 Sept. 1986), 95–96.

24. "The nuclear winter debate" [letters to editor by C. Sagan, R. Turco, and G. Rathjens and R. Siegel, with reply by S. Thompson and S. Schneider], *Foreign Affairs* 65 (fall 1986), 163–178. For a summary, see "Nuclear autumn" [Science and the Citizen column], *Scientific American* 255 (Sept. 1986), 66.

25. A. Pittock, letter to S. Thompson, 15 May 1986, and S. Schneider's reply, 3 June 1986; Schneider, letter to Sen. Albert Gore Jr., 4 June 1986; Schneider, letter to Sagan, 4 June 1986, and Sagan's reply, 20 June 1986; Sagan, letter to Schneider and Thompson, 27 Aug. 1986, and Schneider's reply, 23 Sept. 1986; Pittock, letter to Schneider, 2 Sept. 1986, and Schneider's reply, 16 Sept. 1986; Schneider, letter

to T. Malone, 15 Sept. 1986; Schneider, letter to "Dear Colleagues," 20 Mar. 1987 (the quote is from this letter). Copies of these letters were provided by Professor Schneider.

26. E. Marshall, "The little chill," *New Republic* 196 (16 Feb. 1987), 4.

27. W. Kahrl, "Can war-ready environmentalists deal with Wilson?" *Los Angeles Times*, 9 Dec. 1990.

28. A search of the Roper database found no questions on NW.

29. F. Schwarz, "How probable is nuclear war?" *Newsletter of the Christian Anti-Communist Crusade* 26 (15 Jan. 1986).

30. R. Lifton, quoted in *CTA Reports* 6 (May 1986), 3.

31. R. Ehrlich, "We should not overstate the effects of nuclear war," *International Journal on World Peace* 3 (July-Sept. 1986), 31–43, quote on 42. See also S. Singer, "Comment," *International Journal on World Peace* 3 (July-Sept. 1986), 43–46.

32. D. Drew et al., *Nuclear Winter and National Security: Implications for Future Policy* (Air University Press, 1986), quote on 1. See also F. Reule, *Nuclear Winter: Asymmetrical Problems and Unilateral Solutions* (Air University Press, 1986).

33. E. Marshall, "Nuclear winter debate heats up," *Science* 235 (16 Jan. 1987), 271–273, quotes on 271. In a letter to the editor (*Science* 235, 20 Feb. 1987, 832), Seitz disclaimed saying there was a conspiracy of media and policy analysts (consumers) accepting NW; in rebuttal, Eliot Marshall quoted Seitz in what sounds like conspiracy theory concerning those who originated and supported NW. Rathjens's comparison with Lysenkoism is historically inaccurate, for Lysenko's discredited views on genetics were backed by the power of the Soviet state; the TTAPS conclusions bore no official imprimatur. See also R. Turco et al., "Nuclear winter revisited," *Amicus Journal* 9 (winter 1987), 4–6.

34. J. Gleick, "Science and politics: 'Nuclear winter' clash," *New York Times*, 17 Feb. 1987.

35. C. Covey, "Nuclear winter debate" [letter to editor], *Science* 235 (20 Feb. 1987), 831.

36. H. Lewis, *Technological Risk* (Norton, 1990), 280–289, quotes on 288–289.

37. B. Heinrich, "Nuclear winter debate" [letter to editor], *Science* 235 (20 Feb. 1987), 831. See other letters on p. 832.

38. See, e.g., A. Geyer, "Nuclear winter and the call for disarmament," *Christian Century* 104 (12–19 Aug. 1987), 677–678.

39. R. Turco, "Severe environmental effects of nuclear war confirmed," Nuclear winter press briefing, Room 458, Russell Senate Office Building, Washington, 28 May 1987.

40. R. Turco, "Synthesis of global fallout hazards in a nuclear war," *Ambio* 18 (1989), 391–394.

41. J. Maddox, "What happened to nuclear winter?" *Nature* 333 (19 May 1988), 203.

42. A. Rosemarin, "Nuclear war and the environment: The urgent need for new policies," *Ambio* 18 (1989), 357; P. Crutzen, "Confirmation of the consequences of nuclear war," *Ambio* 18 (1989), 359.

43. Robock, "Policy implications," 360.

44. A. Pittock, "The environmental impact of nuclear war: Policy implications," *Ambio* 18 (1989), 367–371, quotes on 367.

45. R. Turco and C. Sagan, "Policy implications of nuclear winter," *Ambio* 18 (1989), 372–376.

46. Sagan and Turco, *Path*, 275–294.

47. T. Wicker, "Smoke over Kuwait," *New York Times*, 3 Apr. 1991; J. Horgan, "US gags discussion of war's environmental effects," *Scientific American* 264 (May 1991), 24; M. Simons, "British study disputes lengthy climatic role for Kuwait oil fires," *New York Times*, 16 Apr. 1991; M. Hoffman, "Taking stock of Saddam's fiery legacy in Kuwait," *Science*, 253 (30 Aug. 1991), 971; D. Johnson et al., "Airborne observations of the physical and chemical characteristics of the Kuwait oil smoke plume," *Nature*, 353 (17 Oct. 1991), 617–621; C. Sagan, "Kuwait fires and nuclear winter" [letter to editor], *Science* 254 (6 Dec. 1991), 1434; Carl Zimmer, "Ecowar," *Discover* 13 (Jan. 1992), 37–39; P. Hobbs and L. Radke, "Airborne studies of the smoke from the Kuwait oil fires," *Science* 256 (15 May 1992), 987–991; C. Sagan and R. Turco, "Nuclear winter in the post-Cold War era," *Journal of Peace Research* 30 (Nov. 1993), 369–373, esp. 370; R. Turco, "Carl Sagan and nuclear winter," in Terzian and Bilson, eds., *Carl Sagan's Universe*; E. Scigliano, "Scorched-earth tactics ultimately burn all of us," *Los Angeles Times*, 15 Sept. 2002.

48. M. Wald, "No global threat seen from oil fires," *New York Times*, 25 June 1991; T. Wicker, "Kuwait still burns," *New York Times*, 26 July 1991.

Chapter 21

1. A. Revkin, "Hard facts about nuclear winter," *Science Digest* 93 (Mar. 1985), 62–68, 77, 81, 83, quote on 64.

2. S. Schneider, "Nuclear winter: Its discovery and implications," *1985 Britannica Book of the Year*, 27–33, quote on 27.

3. See, e.g., S. Philander, "El Niño Southern Oscillation phenomena," *Nature* 302 (24 Mar. 1983), 295–301.

4. For claims that NW proponents were motivated by their liberal politics, see S. Rosenfeld, "Nuclear winter: The sun peeks through," *Washington Post*, 26 Jan. 1990; N. Wade, "Lessons of nuclear winter," *New York Times*, 5 Feb. 1990.

5. Turco, interview by Badash and Kirtman, 20 Feb. 1985; Toon and Ackerman, interviews by Badash and Kirtman, 6 Mar. 1985.

6. Turco, interview by Badash and Kirtman, 20 Feb. 1985; Toon and Ackerman, interviews by Badash and Kirtman, 6 Mar. 1985; A. Robock, "New models confirm nuclear winter," *Bulletin of the Atomic Scientists* 45 (Sept. 1989), 32–35, on 35; Sagan and Turco, *Path*, 465–466.

7. For an argument that both science and the nuclear arms race are riddled with male symbolism, see B. Easlea, *Fathering the Unthinkable: Masculinity, Scientists and the Nuclear Arms Race* (Pluto, 1983).

8. W. Lanouette, *Genius in the Shadows: A Biography of Leo Szilard, the Man Behind the Bomb* (Scribner, 1992), 181.

9. See, e.g., R. Hewlett and O. Anderson, *The New World, 1939–1946: Volume I of a History of the United States Atomic Energy Commission* (Pennsylvania State University Press, 1962); L. Badash, *Scientists and the Development of Nuclear Weapons: From Fission to the Limited Test Ban Treaty, 1939–1963* (Humanities Press, 1995); E. Mesthene, "Can only scientists make government science policy?" *Science* 145 (17 July 1964), 237–240.

10. See, e.g., A. Smith, *A Peril and a Hope: The Scientists' Movement in America, 1945–47* (University of Chicago Press, 1965); P. Michelmore, *The Swift Years: The Robert Oppenheimer Story* (Dodd, Mead, 1969); K. Bird and M. Sherwin, *American Prometheus: The Triumph and Tragedy of J. Robert Oppenheimer* (Knopf, 2005).

11. See, e.g., D. Price, *Government and Science: Their Dynamic Relations in American Democracy* (New York University Press, 1954); Price, *The Scientific Estate* (Harvard University Press, 1965); J. Stine, "A history of science policy in the United States, 1940–1985," report prepared for the US Congress, House of Representatives, Committee on Science and Technology, Task Force on Science Policy, 99th Congress, 2nd Session, Sept. 1986.

12. J. Monod, *Chance and Necessity* (Knopf, 1971), 176.

13. F. Dyson, *Disturbing the Universe* (Harper and Row, 1979), 5–6.

14. R. Paddock, "Alcohol, cancer linked by governor's science panel," *Los Angeles Times*, 23 Apr. 1988.

15. D. Yankelovich and J. Doble, "The public mood: Nuclear weapons and the USSR," *Foreign Affairs* 64 (fall 1984), 33–46, quote on 34.

16. See, e.g., Russell W. Peterson's account of his interview with some members of the *New York Times* editorial board in mid 1985 in *Rebel with a Conscience* (University of Delaware Press, 1999), 398.

17. J. Hersey, *Hiroshima* (Knopf, 1946); P. Sharp, "From yellow peril to Japanese wasteland: John Hersey's 'Hiroshima,'" *Twentieth Century Literature* 46 (winter 2000), 434–452; J. Wober, ed., *Television and Nuclear Power: Making the Public Mind* (Ablex, 1992).

18. J. Isaacs (president of Council for a Livable World), "Anatomy of a victory: Clinton decides against national missile defense," sent to his email list, 5 Sept. 2000.

19. For a penetrating study of the SDI debate, see P. Westwick, "'Space-strike weapons' and the Soviet response to SDI," *Diplomatic History* 32 (Nov. 2008), 955–979.

20. For a survey of reasons the Cold War ended, see J. Tirman, "How we ended the Cold War," *The Nation*, 1 Nov. 1999.

21. Pollack, interview by Badash and Kirtman, 6 Mar. 1985.

22. See B. Smith and J. Stine, "Technical advice for Congress: Past trends and present obstacles," in M. Morgan and J. Peha, eds., *Science and Technology Advice for Congress* (Resources for the Future Press, 2003).

23. P. Boyer, *By the Bomb's Early Light: American Thought and Culture at the Dawn of the Atomic Age* (Pantheon, 1985), 166–167.

24. C. Weinberger, quoted in T. Weiner, "Military accused of lies over arms," *New York Times*, 28 June 1993.

25. G. Rathjens, testimony, in US Congress, House of Representatives, Committee on Science and Technology, Subcommittee on Natural Resources, Agriculture Research, and Environment, and Committee on Interior and Insular Affairs, Subcommittee on Energy and the Environment, *Nuclear Winter*, joint hearing, 99th Congress, 1st Session, 14 Mar. 1985, 155.

Epilogue

1. *Defense Monitor* 22: 10 (1993).

2. See, e.g., L. Wittner, "Reagan and nuclear disarmament: How the Nuclear Freeze movement forced Reagan to make progress on arms control," *Boston Review* 25 (Apr.-May 2000), 4–6; V. Zubok, "Gorbachev's nuclear learning: How the Soviet leader became a nuclear abolitionist," *Boston Review* 25 (Apr.-May 2000), 7–12; R. Forsberg, "Eliminating the danger: What can we do to prevent a nuclear catastrophe?" *Boston Review* 25 (Apr.-May 2000), 16–19; Ambassador Linton F. Brook, letter to L. Badash, 28 May 2007.

3. R. Norris and H. Kristensen, "Global nuclear stockpiles, 1945–2002," *Bulletin of the Atomic Scientists* 58 (2002), 103–104; O. Toon, R. Turco, A. Robock, C. Bardeen, L. Oman, and G. Stenchikov, "Atmospheric effects and societal consequences of regional scale nuclear conflicts and acts of individual nuclear terrorism," *Atmospheric Chemistry and Physics Discussions* 6 (22 Nov. 2006), 11745–11816, esp. fig. 1 on 11805; Toon, email to Badash, 28 Dec. 2006.

4. A. Robock, L. Oman, G. Stenchikov, O. Toon, C. Bardeen, and R. Turco, "Climatic consequences of regional nuclear conflicts," *Atmospheric Chemistry and Physics Discussions* 6 (22 Nov. 2006), 11817–11843.

Index

Von Hippel, Frank, 59, 95, 126, 148–150, 223, 249, 264

W. Alton Jones Foundation, 58, 119, 208
Wagner, Richard, 99, 111, 125, 131, 132, 165, 192, 234, 288
Wall Street Journal, 91, 142, 153, 154, 166, 250, 251, 289, 312
Walton, John, 182, 183, 276
Warheads. *See* Nuclear weapons: arsenals
Warner, Frederick, 207, 213
Warner, John, 121, 129, 170
Warnke, Paul, 131
Warsaw Pact, 199, 230, 237, 272, 274
Washington Post, 80, 88–91, 105, 126, 202, 246, 289
Washington University, St. Louis, 202
Watt, James, 5
Waxmonsky, Gary, 273
Weapons. *See* Conventional weapons; Directed-energy weapons; Nuclear weapons
Weart, Spencer, 49
Weather, 9, 14, 16, 20, 23–26, 34, 49, 53, 109, 140, 146, 152, 153, 181, 191, 195, 209, 235, 246, 247, 250, 257, 277, 278, 282, 308, 309
Weinberger, Caspar, 4, 94, 131, 163–169, 180, 184, 217, 220–222, 287, 288, 296, 311, 317
Weisskopf, Victor, 59, 87, 103, 265
Westing, Arthur, 214
White, Gilbert, 99, 120, 215, 289
Whitten, R. C., 27, 28, 55, 248
Wicker, Tom, 93, 197, 202
Williamson, David, 169, 170
Wilson, Edward, 80
Wilson, Pete, 170
Wilson, Robert, 85
Wirth, Timothy, 128, 129, 162, 165–168, 173, 289
Wohlstetter, Albert, 122, 236–238
Wolbach, Wendy, 192
Wood, Michael, 184
Wood, Rob, 89
Woods Hole Marine Biological Laboratory, 59, 64

Woodwell, George, 64, 99
World After Nuclear War. *See* Meetings: Washington (1983)
World Climate Programme, 277
World Health Organization (WHO), 101, 207, 211, 237, 266
World War I, 86, 205, 207, 260
World War II, 6, 7, 21, 29, 30, 64, 72, 77, 94, 102, 207, 223, 237, 248, 258, 294, 303, 304, 309
World Wildlife Fund, 59
Worldwide Effects of Nuclear War (1976), 49
Worst-case analysis, 7, 60, 61, 76, 95, 101, 107, 110, 132, 138, 143, 147, 154, 189, 197, 222, 249, 251, 262, 264, 285, 291, 311, 313

Ye, Du Zhang, 263
Yoder, Edwin, 267

Zraket, Charles, 125, 245
Zuckerman, Solly, 255

Transformations: Studies in the History of Science and Technology
Jed Z. Buchwald, general editor

Dolores L. Augustine, *Red Prometheus: Engineering and Dictatorship in East Germany, 1945–1990*

Lawrence Badash, *A Nuclear Winter's Tale: Science and Politics in the 1980s*

Mordechai Feingold, ed., *Jesuit Science and the Republic of Letters*

Larrie D. Ferreiro, *Ships and Science: The Birth of Naval Architecture in the Scientific Revolution, 1600–1800*

Sander Gliboff, *H. G. Bronn, Ernst Haeckel, and the Origins of German Darwinism: A Study in Translation and Transformation*

Kristine Harper, *Weather by the Numbers: The Genesis of Modern Meteorology*

Sungook Hong, *Wireless: From Marconi's Black-Box to the Audion*

Jeff Horn, *The Path Not Taken: French Industrialization in the Age of Revolution, 1750–1830*

Myles W. Jackson, *Harmonious Triads: Physicists, Musicians, and Instrument Makers in Nineteenth-Century Germany*

Myles W. Jackson, *Spectrum of Belief: Joseph von Fraunhofer and the Craft of Precision Optics*

Mi Gyung Kim, *Affinity, That Elusive Dream: A Genealogy of the Chemical Revolution*

Ursula Klein and Wolfgang Lefèvre, *Materials in Eighteenth-Century Science: A Historical Ontology*

John Krige, *American Hegemony and the Postwar Reconstruction of Science in Europe*

Janis Langins, *Conserving the Enlightenment: French Military Engineering from Vauban to the Revolution*

Wolfgang Lefèvre, ed., *Picturing Machines 1400–1700*

Staffan Müller-Wille and Hans-Jörg Rheinberger, eds., *Heredity Produced: At the Crossroads of Biology, Politics, and Culture, 1500–1870*

William R. Newman and Anthony Grafton, eds., *Secrets of Nature: Astrology and Alchemy in Early Modern Europe*

Gianna Pomata and Nancy G. Siraisi, eds., *Historia: Empiricism and Erudition in Early Modern Europe*

Alan J. Rocke, *Nationalizing Science: Adolphe Wurtz and the Battle for French Chemistry*

George Saliba, *Islamic Science and the Making of the European Renaissance*

Nicolás Wey Gómez, *The Tropics of Empire: Why Columbus Sailed South to the Indies*